Friendship

Critical Histories of Subjectivity and Culture

Editors: Barbara Caine, Monash University, and Glenda Sluga, University of Sydney

This series highlights the relationship between understandings of subjectivity, identity, culture and broader historical change. It seeks to foster historical studies which situate subjectivity in social, political and cultural contexts. Some of these studies interrogate and elucidate broad historical themes and periods, and cultural and social change, by analysing discourses about personal identity and subjectivity, others focus on lifestories and representations of the self.

The series has no chronological or geographical limitations, although preference will be given to comparative work and to studies which approach their questions in a broad transnational framework. As the emphasis on subjectivity suggests, questions about gender and sexuality, and national or ethnic identity are central issues in all volumes. Detailed studies also offer a sense of the broad context of historical change: for example, questions of national identity are discussed within transnational and imperial frameworks.

The emphasis on "critical" histories is indicative of our interest in studies with a theoretical and historiographical edge, especially those that open up new historical approaches and problematize standard ways of dealing with subjectivity and culture.

Published:

Histories of Sexuality
Antiquity to Sexual Revolution
Stephen Garton

Memory and Utopia
The Primacy of Intersubjectivity
Luisa Passerini

Forthcoming:

Remembering Dispossession
Aboriginals, Colonization and History
Maria Nugent

Friendship
A History

Edited by
Barbara Caine

Routledge
Taylor & Francis Group
LONDON AND NEW YORK

First published 2009 by Equinox, an imprint of Acumen

Published 2014 by Routledge
2 Park Square, Milton Park, Abingdon, Oxon OX14 4RN
711 Third Avenue, New York, NY 10017, USA

Routledge is an imprint of the Taylor & Francis Group, an informa business

Notices
Practitioners and researchers must always rely on their own experience
and knowledge in evaluating and using any information, methods,
compounds, or experiments described herein. In using such information
or methods they should be mindful of their own safety and the safety of
others, including parties for whom they have a professional responsibility.

To the fullest extent of the law, neither the Publisher nor the authors,
contributors, or editors, assume any liability for any injury and/or damage
to persons or property as a matter of products liability, negligence or
otherwise, or from any use or operation of any methods, products,
instructions, or ideas contained in the material herein.

British Library Cataloguing-in-Publication Data

A catalogue record for this book is available from the British Library.

ISBN-13   978 184553 196 6   (hardback)
          978 184553 197 3   (paperback)

Library of Congress Cataloging-in-Publication Data

Friendship : a history / edited by Barbara Caine.
    p. cm. — (Critical histories of subjectivity and culture)
  Includes bibliographical references and index.
  ISBN 978-1-84553-196-6 (hb) — ISBN 978-1-84553-197-3 (pbk.) 1. Friendship—
History. I. Caine, Barbara.
  BF575.F66F725 2008
  302.3'409—dc22

                              2008007702

Typeset by S.J.I. Services, New Delhi

CONTENTS

INTRODUCTION

No one can underestimate the importance attributed to friendship in contemporary society. It is seen as an indication of social integration and a requirement of both physical and mental health as well as a source of happiness. It is a relationship subject to constant representation, discussion and analysis in newspapers and magazines and in contemporary film and television programs, as the popular series simply called *Friends* attests. As is so often the case, the current popular interest in friendship has an academic counterpart in the immense amount of research which has been done recently into the meaning and nature of friendship in different societies, and in earlier stages of our own. Scholars working in many different disciplines including sociology, psychology and anthropology as well as literature, history and philosophy have all turned their attention to questions about friendship. Most of this research has sought to explore the many different ways in which friendship was described, understood, organized and experienced in different societies and cultures, and to analyse its meaning, role and importance in a range of different contemporary societies and cultures and in the past.

Friendship: A History seeks to build on and to extend this research by looking at the history of friendship in the West over the past 2500 years – from the days of Classical Athens to the present day. This lengthy period enables us to show the long-standing importance accorded to friendship as a relationship fundamental both to social and individual wellbeing. It also allows us to explore both the continuities and changes in how people have understood the meaning, nature and position of friendship in terms of other social, sexual and familial relationships. All of these concepts have been the subject of extensive discussion across this period, as indeed have ideas about which groups of people can or should enter into or be involved in friendships.

It is hard to say whether it is the continuities or the changes in ideas about friendship that have been most marked in the West across this period. There is no question about the importance of the continuities. Indeed, one of the things that was most striking for us all in researching this book was the great influence of some of the ideas on friendship of prominent classical Greek and Latin philosophers, particularly Aristotle and Cicero, until the eighteenth, and in some cases well into the nineteenth century. In the world of Classical Athens, which provides our starting point, friendship was a complex issue and the subject of keen interest to many philosophers concerned to explore its social importance, its moral underpinnings and its ethical demands. The Greek term *philia*, which is usually translated as "friendship," covered a much wider range of relationships than we would usually characterize as friendships today. Members of one's family and business associates, those we in the modern era might call "loved ones" or "acquaintances" rather than friends, could be described as *philoi*, as well as those with whom one had a form of close personal companionship. Aristotle provided a taxonomy that enabled people to classify different kinds of friendships amongst the *philoi*, paying particular attention to three major types of friendship: advantage-friendship, pleasure-friendship and virtue-friendship. For him, as for most other classical writers, it was virtue-friendship that, while probably the rarest form of friendship, was also the most valuable. The rarity of this form of friendship was emphasized by ancient Greek philosophers, most of whom thought that this ideal relationship could only obtain between morally virtuous people. Three centuries later, Cicero, while accepting the view that friendship could only really exist amongst virtuous people, extolled rather more fulsomely the importance of friendship in individual lives, the nature of the personal and social bonds that it involved and some of the questions and problems that friendship might have to face.

The value accorded to classical literature and thought in the West ensured that the philosophical texts on friendship produced by the classical Greek and Roman philosophers continued to be influential for many centuries. The works of Aristotle and Cicero were translated into many different European languages as well as being studied in the original. In the Renaissance, for example, it could be taken for granted that educated young men would know by heart many passages from Cicero's *De amicitia* extolling the incomparable value of friendship and stressing the way that friendship required complete harmony in tastes, pursuits and sentiments. These ideas continued to hold sway amongst members of the educated elites in much of Europe in the eighteenth and nineteenth centuries.

Classical ideas on friendship were not the only ones in evidence over this long period and neither did they go entirely unchallenged. These ideas of the importance of civic friendships, about the services and support that friends might be expected to provide for one another and about the connection between friendship and a moral life continued but were augmented, and in some cases questioned or even replaced, in later centuries by new approaches and concerns. Religious beliefs, especially Christianity, brought a rather different set of values into the discussion of friendship and from at least the twelfth century onwards, vernacular ideas and popular customs also brought different ways of thinking about sociability and about close interpersonal relationships. New ways of thinking about friendship were articulated within Christian communities in the medieval period, in which close relationships amongst friends were supported by a new understanding of love as something spiritual and transcendent and fully embodied in Christ. This new ideal of Christian friendship, based on a shared belief in and love of Christ, sometimes added a new emotional element to friendship. It also brought new tensions as close personal friendships could be seen as threatening to Christians, who were supposedly focused on a transcendent idea rather than on personal affections or needs. In a similar way, in the course of the fifteenth and sixteenth centuries, while Cicero and his ideal of an elite and learned circle of friends remained extremely influential, there was a whole range of different approaches to friendship evident in vernacular culture and in intimate correspondence. Moreover, while classical ideas may have remained very important, there were marked changes in the ways in which the classical tradition itself was understood. Thus, while earlier periods were perhaps more interested in the moral connotations and significance of friendship, or in the forms of mutual assistance that friendship offered, in the later part of the nineteenth century extensive attention was focused on the extent to which friendships between men might challenge rather than support social norms by including erotic or sexual relationships rather than being asexual or chaste.

In each of the periods dealt with in the book, we trace both the continuation of classical ideas and the new issues that came to the fore, sometimes as a consequence of wider social, economic and political change, sometimes in connection with intellectual developments and new ideas. Urbanization and the establishment of increasingly large urban communities have had a particularly important impact on the changing patterns of friendship. But so too have new intellectual preoccupations such as the emphasis on scepticism and rationality in the nineteenth century, that brought with it a questioning of earlier ideals of Christian friendship. In the course of the Enlightenment, as in the medieval period, there was a tension connected with the new ideas – expressed in terms of the conflict between the duty of universal benevolence and the pull of particular relationships. Imperialism too raised new questions, stressing for some the extent to which friendship was possible only with those who shared common ethnic, religious and cultural roots. For others it brought to the fore questions about the possibility of friendship across racial and imperial boundaries.

For much of the period we cover, one major underlying assumption of the classical idea of friendship remained dominant: that friendship was possible only between men. This was emphatically the case in the classical world. Since many, but not all, philosophers additionally supposed that only *men* could be virtuous, they also thought that true friendship was distinctively masculine. By the nineteenth and twentieth centuries, this idea had undergone an almost complete reversal so that, not only were women seen as capable of friendship, but often their friendships were thought of as more sincere, more meaningful and more significant than those of men. We trace here the ways in which over many centuries the exclusive ideal of masculine friendship was challenged: by women in religious communities in the medieval and Renaissance periods; by individual authors and aristocratic women who established and wrote about friendship in the fifteenth and sixteenth centuries; and by philosophers and novelists fascinated by the possibilities and potential of women's friendship in the nineteenth century. By the nineteenth century, women had themselves entered into this discussion in large numbers, as novelists, essayists and, indeed, in political campaigns for women's rights, many of which depended on and gave voice to the importance of female friendship.

In the course of the nineteenth century, and increasingly in the twentieth, the classical ideal of male friendship was rejected and challenged by popular cultures that took for granted the idea that female friendships provided the underlying structures for communities and offered support to individuals.

One point that will be immediately evident is that this study rejects any idea that there is now or that there was a "golden age" of friendship at any particular time in the past, or that there is any particular set of ideas about friendship that are somehow truer or more valuable than others. What is evident is rather the extent to which it was a relationship that could encompass great variation and also one which – while often seen as particularly valuable, rewarding and important – almost always involved negotiation between conflicting ethical, social or familial demands. The demands and the conflicts that surrounded friendship changed over time, as indeed did the kinds of relationship that were given the label of friendship. Like any social relationship, friendship was articulated and developed within a particular social context and one of the things we have sought to do here is to show how different economic, social and political frameworks affected friendships, made them more or less possible or imposed particular kinds of demands on them. In many cases, the friendships that we have explored occurred in urban settings with established public institutions or with the possibilities of frequent contact between those living in a domestic world. But the form of these urban communities in turn allowed for and encouraged, or sometimes made more difficult, particular kinds of friendship. The intimate friendships enjoyed by many members of the middle class in the nineteenth century, and which were often conducted within the home, for example, required a level of domestic comfort and affluence that was not available to most members of the working class. Working men and women tended rather to establish the very different kinds of relationships that were made possible with people whom one met and saw at work, or in a pub, café or friendly society.

Friendship, of course, is not an easy relationship to define – and we have not sought to find or to develop a single or particular definition to apply to the past. We have attempted rather to find and to understand how the terminology and language of friendship was used by different social groups in different periods and how the language of friendship itself developed and changed over time. One of the difficult questions that we have had to deal with constantly, both in terms of the language of friendship and in terms of how it is understood as a relationship, centres on the extent to which one includes within this broad category marriage and sexual relationships, including those involving both same-sex and opposite-sex couples or groups. This is the more difficult because, as we have already seen, the Greek term that is used for friendship includes many of these relationships. Moreover, as several writers have pointed out, there are often erotic overtones or currents even in relationships that are not explicitly or primarily sexual ones. We have attempted to focus primarily on non-erotic friendships of the kind that have long been regarded as important civic and intellectual relationships as well as social and emotional ones, and that usually existed alongside marital or other sexual relationships. An erotic element may have been present in many of these relationships but it was not usually the most significant aspect of the relationship. Rather than concentrating on the sexual and the erotic, we have looked at the question of where and how the borders between friendship and other kinds of relationship are articulated or emerge. These "other" relationships include both instrumental relationships and intimate familial or sexual ones. We trace some of the shifting borders between these different kinds of relationships and the changes evident in the ways in which these boundaries have been thought about and described.

The field that this book covers is potentially enormous. It would have been possible to write a lengthy book about each of the periods to which we have devoted a chapter. As our primary concern has been to explore the continuities and changes in ideas about and practices of friendship over time, we have not been able to cover every period exhaustively. Rather, we have tried to focus on some key themes among our sources in order to show what we see as significant patterns of both continuity and change. These themes include discussion of the moral nature and significance of friendship and of questions about where, how and with whom friendships could be made. The question of civic friendship, and of the ways in which friendship has been seen to contribute to or provide the foundation for good government has been a theme of considerable importance – often serving to illustrate why so many discussions of friendship focus entirely on the men who were the dominant group within the public world. Following on from this, we have looked closely at questions about gender, at the ways in which masculinity is both assumed and defined in some forms of friendship, at the differences in the ways in which masculine and feminine friendships have been seen and understood. We have also looked the question of when and how it was deemed possible for there to be friendships between men and women, either within marriage or outside it. Just as gender is often important in thinking about friendship, so too are questions about family. We have looked at the changing ways in which familial relationships were understood in relation to friendships and at the ways in which they overlapped at some periods, in contrast to a more modern notion that tends to differentiate between familial relationships and friendship. In all of this, we have sought to elucidate the frameworks within which friendship was understood and discussed. In addition, we have tried to explore some of the practices of friendship and the changing ways in which friends might address, treat or think about each other, both in the public sphere and in the confines of the domestic and private world

The continuities and changes evident in the history that we trace reflect not only social and intellectual changes, but also some of the differences in the nature of our source materials. We have tended throughout to make extensive use of published sources, as these offer a very clear indication of the kinds of ideas that were not only articulated but also in circulation at particular times. But the form of these sources has changed and these changes in themselves reflect changing concerns and preoccupations in regard to friendship. There were a number of philosophical texts on friendship produced in the classical world, many of which serve to demonstrate how important a relationship it was and how it figured in broader discussions of ethics. These philosophical texts continued to be republished over many centuries, but were added to by others reflecting new concerns. Thus we explore the manuals on letter-writing that became prominent in the medieval and Renaissance periods and the other literary texts that tend to focus on the emotional content, rather than the moral basis, of friendship: drama, poetry, essays and particularly fiction, which became one of the dominant sources for discussions of friendship in the eighteenth and nineteenth centuries. Other sources have been important and added very different insights into the experience of friendship and its meaning in different social contexts. Law court records have been used to provide information about the importance of friendship in the lives of the poor in the eighteenth and nineteenth centuries. Periodicals and journals became increasingly prominent in the nineteenth century, as indeed did the new literature on the social sciences, especially with the development of sociology with its interest in the place of friendships in an industrializing world. In the twentieth century, these sources have been augmented by the evidence available from other media: from cinema, television and recorded popular music. In addition to published sources, we have used other material, including letters and diaries, which offer more insight into the actual experience of friendship for particular individuals than published texts.

The necessary emphasis on published works and our interest in ideas about friendship means that this is in many ways an intellectual history. We have included many discussions of actual friendships and, especially in the later chapters, have explored the ways in which friendship is understood and experienced amongst many social groups, including the working class and the poor. There still remains a very considerable emphasis on the ways in which friendship has been described and discussed amongst intellectuals and writers. We have been interested here to trace the changing framework in which friendship has been discussed, and have traced the move from the moral concerns of the classical world, through the religious and social concerns of the medieval one to the concern with psychological questions and concerns about the meaning of intimacy in the nineteenth and twentieth centuries.

Chapter 1

THE CLASSICAL IDEALS OF FRIENDSHIP

Dirk Baltzly and Nick Eliopoulos

Ancient Greek philosophical writings on friendship cast a long shadow in Western culture. The year 1508 saw the publication of Erasmus' distillation of the wisdom of the ancient Greeks and Romans in his *Adages*.[1] The very first adage Erasmus provides is a philosophical pronouncement on friendship: "friends hold all things in common" – a saying attributed to Pythagoras. Erasmus notes:

> [A]nyone who deeply and diligently considers that remark of Pythagoras ... will certainly find the whole of human happiness included in this brief saying. What other purpose has Plato in so many volumes except to urge a community of living, and the factor which creates it, namely friendship?

In a further expansion of this circle of like-minded friends, Erasmus goes on to suggest that the Pythagorean communitarianism is nothing less than a foreshadowing of the community of life and property that Christ taught.

In 1644 the young Isaac Newton began a new notebook of reflections during his studies at Cambridge.[2] At the top of the first page he wrote, "*Amicus Plato, amicus Aristoteles, magis amica veritas.*" The slogan, invoked by those enamoured of the new science, alludes to a remark in Aristotle's *Nicomachean Ethics* in which he somewhat reluctantly criticizes Plato's theory of Forms. Aristotle notes that since "philosophy" means love of wisdom, philosophers must criticize the mistaken views even of friends "for while both are dear, piety requires us to honour truth above our friends (*NE* 1096a15–17, our trans.)."

These two first lines, written over a millennium after the deaths of Pythagoras, Plato and Aristotle, show us something about the longevity of Greek philosophical reflections on friendship. Friendship is one of the most pervasive themes in the writing that have come down from the ancient Greeks. Friendship often drives the plot in Greek epic poetry (for example, Achilles and Patroclus) and in tragedy (for example, Euripides' *Philoctetes*). Greek oratory involves appeals to friendship, and writers such as Hesiod and Theognis were full of advice about the importance of friendship. But what had the greater historical impact were the facts that the Greek philosophers of the Classical and Hellenistic periods took up friendship as a *philosophical topic* and that their various theories of the nature of friendship were normative – indicating clearly what friendship *should* be like and the role it *should* play in the political life of their communities. These ancient Greek ideals of friendship dominate self-reflective writing on the topic of friendship until the eighteenth century. As a consequence, this chapter will concentrate less on the practices of friendship in the ancient world or the literary depiction of friendships and more on the normative ideals of friendship offered by the philosophers.

One thing to note at the outset is that the Greek word translated as friendship – *philia* – takes in a much wider range of relationships than those described by the word "friendship" in contemporary English. Indeed, as we will see throughout this book, the use of "friendship" or related terms to refer exclusively to close companion friends is a relatively recent innovation. *Philia* for the ancient Greeks takes in family members and people we would describe as acquaintances, not friends. So philosophical theories of *philia* cover much more ground than one might initially expect.

Though *philia* encompasses many relationships, our evidence from the ancient Greek philosophers looks at it from fewer viewpoints than one might like. As with nearly every other document from antiquity, the theorizing about friendship takes place entirely in a masculine voice. Sometimes the male philosophers of ancient Greece did discuss cross-gender friendship, but we know of no writings on the topic of friendship from female philosophers. (The works attributed to women of the Pythagorean School are forgeries of a later era whose authorship must remain uncertain.) We must recognize that these philosophical discussions of friendship are situated against the backdrop of very different social and political structures. (We will discuss in more detail the contrast between the relatively independent Greek city-states of the Classical period and the kingdoms that dominated the landscape after the death of Alexander the Great.) However different these political settings were from one another, they were even more different from our modern view of the liberal state. This is especially true when we consider the question of the state's purpose. The Greek philosophers were nearly unanimous that the state exists in order to make the citizens *better men* and – to the extent that this was thought possible – to make the women in it better women. This is true not only of city-states like Sparta, but of the democratic city-state of Athens that we tend to think of as more akin to our modern way of thinking about such matters. We need to factor in this difference if we are to understand what ancient Greek philosophy has to say to us.

This notion of "better men" (or women) brings out another point of contrast with much of modern liberalism. Greek philosophers felt free to provide normative theories of what friendship *should* be like because their shared ethical framework was *eudaimonistic*. *Eudaimonia* is the ancient Greek word most frequently translated as "happiness" but it is more accurately translated as "human flourishing" or "wellbeing." Though this sounds somewhat less natural, it has the advantage of cancelling the implication that *eudaimonia* is some sort of transient state of subjective contentment. *Eudaimonia* is more than this, and reflects the way that the point of living, for the Greeks, was not merely to be content, but to live well and thus to achieve repute and lasting fame.

Aristotle defined *eudaimonia* as a life in which one's activity manifests *aretê* – a term often translated as "virtue" but perhaps better captured by "excellence." Virtues or excellences are those qualities that make a thing a good thing of its kind. As such, they are not confined to human beings. One can speak of the virtues of a good racehorse and mean the qualities that make it good at winning races. Human virtues, then, will be those qualities – in particular, deep-seated character traits – that make a man good at "performing the human function," that is, fulfilling human nature.

Virtue or excellence is intimately connected to flourishing. A person who possesses the virtues and acts from them acts well. It is an analytic truth for the Greeks that to act *kat' aretên* (in conformity with virtue) is to act finely, nobly, beautifully and well. (Terms like "finely," "nobly" and "well" are all shades of meaning taken by the adjective *kalon*.) Surely the person who thus acts finely, nobly, beautifully and well – and does so consistently – achieves *at least an important part* of living well. (Whether there is more to happiness than living in conformity with virtue was a matter of disagreement among the philosophers.) Given the connection between flourishing and living well, most philosophers agreed that virtue was at least a necessary condition for flourishing.

Finally, it is important to note that the happiness of a person, and the place of excellences in securing it, are matters for public consumption, as well as inner satisfaction. Dover notes the pervasive tendency for Greek writers to say things like "I wanted to be seen to be just" where we might simply say, "I wanted to be just." It is not, he thinks, that *only* the appearance matters. Rather, "goodness divorced from a reputation for goodness was of little interest" to the Greeks of the fifth to fourth centuries BCE.[3] This is because actions that embody virtue ought to be recognized by the members of one's community and should translate into good reputation and fame.

These related notions of wellbeing and virtue thus provide the background against which the ancient Greeks considered the importance of friendship. Friendship is able to form a substantial piece in the puzzle of how one lives a good life because the extension of the term *philia* is far wider than that of the English word "friendship." Thus reasoning about the importance of *philia* in a good life involves a great deal more than our consideration of the place of what we call "companion friendship" in a happy life. Moreover, what holds the various relations subsumed under *philia* together is the principle that one should seek to benefit friends and harm enemies. This is *the* overarching principle that governs all *philia* relationships. We find it in Hesiod: "be friends with those who are friendly" (i.e. those who are disposed to do you a good turn), and in Pindar: "Let me be a friend to my friend; but I will be an enemy to my enemy, and pounce on him like a wolf, treading every crooked path." It is not confined to poetic texts, but appears as a basic axiom of moral action in Lysias' forensic defence of a soldier: "I considered it ordained [*tetachthai*] that one should harm one's enemies and serve one's friends." Most famously, Plato turns the saying of Simonides "to render to each that which is his due" into a commonsense definition of justice articulated by Polemarchus – "justice is benefiting one's friends and harming one's enemies."[4]

As a result of this principle, it seems that a Greek's world was divided into three camps: those inside one's circle of friends, those outside and those who were neither one's friend's nor one's enemies.

As even those in this last group were seen as potential friends or potential enemies,[5] the distinction between friends and enemies is nearly exhaustive in practice. But we should remember that, though friendships were seen as having instrumental utility, the value of friendship was not exhausted by this aspect. Mary Blundell notes that some writers (for example, Democritus, Demosthenes, Aristotle) warned that we ought not to have friends solely for the sake of benefit.[6] Instead, we ought to form friendships that provide the best kind of good – that which is good in itself *as well as* good in terms of its consequences.

Naturally, these relations of friendship and enmity between individuals within the city-state itself present a challenge to collective action. In response to this tension a notion of "civic friendship" – characterized as "like-mindedness" or *homonoia* – emerged as a political commonplace.[7] Friendship thus has a political dimension as well.

We are now in a good position to understand why the ancient Greeks approached friendship as a worthy subject of normative theorizing. All our actions aim at achieving a *eudaimon* life. This is a matter not merely of subjective contentment but of objective human flourishing. Virtues or excellences are the qualities – whatever qualities they might turn out to be – that enable us to achieve human flourishing. They do this by enabling us to perform fine and noble actions. Friends are required (on pain of doing what is ignoble and shameful) to assist their friends in achieving goals. So, the variety of *philia* relations thus provide both *objects* (that is, my friends) upon whom I can bestow benefits (thus performing fine and noble actions) and also *assistance* in the achievement of my ends. In order to understand how to live well and achieve wellbeing, we should reflect upon the nature of friendship and what this relationship ought to be like.

If what we have said so far is right, then it provides a matrix for thinking about the various ancient Greek ideals of friendship. There are *various* ancient Greek ideals of friendship because, though all the philosophers who attempt to theorize about it may accept the framework sketched in the last paragraph, they understand slightly different things by them. Aristotle and Epicurus would agree, for example, that all our actions aim at *eudaimonia* but they would disagree sharply about what *eudaimonia* is. Accordingly, they arrive at different conceptions of what friendship is ideally like.

We will now survey the range and variety of social relations that fall under the term *philia* in the Classical period – that is, the period of the fifth to fourth centuries BCE. We will also consider in somewhat more detail the common assumption that one should help one's friends and harm one's enemies. We will then look at the similarities and differences between competing theoretical ideals of friendship, primarily derived from the writings of Greek philosophers in the Classical period. The most influential of these writers was Aristotle and we will give his account of friendship the fullest treatment before considering both the practice and the theory of friendship in the Hellenistic and Imperial periods (third to first centuries BCE). We will conclude with a brief examination of the Pythagorean tradition of friendship and its role in the Neoplatonist philosophy of late antiquity – that is, up to the closure of Plato's Academy by the Christians in 529 CE.

Varieties of *Philia* Relations

Guest-friendship

Among the plurality of relations that fall under *philia*, perhaps the least familiar to us is that of guest-friendship or *xenia*. This is a conception of friendship rooted in Homeric times and exemplified in the exchange between Diomedes and Glaucus in *Iliad* VI. About to do battle, they discover that the one's father entertained the other's father while the latter was a traveller. The institution of guest-friendship was a reciprocal relationship of benefit between host and traveller. One who provided hospitality could have the expectation of reciprocity, not merely for himself, but for his descendants. This relationship of guest-friendship is sanctioned by Zeus who is its particular protector. It typically involves not only hospitality, but also the exchange of gifts. Thus it is that Diomedes and Glaucus not only elect not to fight one another, but they exchange armour. Failure to observe the strictures that govern guest-friendship, both on the part of the host and on the part of the guest, could lead to disaster. The Trojans are doomed to lose the war with the Acheans because Zeus is against them, and arguably Menelaus is right to say that he is against them because of Paris' actions with respect to his host's wife.[8]

From these Homeric origins, the institution of guest-friendship endures into the Classical period – despite the availability of paid accommodation. The reciprocal relations of hospitality between families were sometimes passed down through generations and guest-friends sometimes found that their hosts could assist them in a variety of ways. For example, a guest-friend in Delphi could secure an audience with the Pythia in a more timely fashion than the visitor could without such local assistance.[9]

It is important to note that ancient Greek political leaders used the institution of *xenia* as a way of entering relations with their non-Greek counterparts, thereby establishing a friendship between their respective states. Overall, such relations were a failure. Non-Greeks failed to understand the institution of *xenia*, its egalitarian nature and its duties and commitments.[10]

Collaborators in Common Projects

It is easy to see how the relation of *xenia* could become relatively formalized because of the benefits that derive from it, both for individuals and for groups in which its strictures are observed. Other forms of friendship directly linked to mutual benefit include the friendship of fellow travellers, soldiers engaged in a common cause, business associates, people who belong to social clubs, or those who cooperate in the maintenance of a religious site.[11] (The friendships of political clubs deserve a treatment all of their own.) We might prefer to speak of people who stand in these relations as *acquaintances* rather than friends. Ancient Greek does not mark such a distinction – at least linguistically: all are *philoi*. Aristotle is presumably responsive to common sense when he remarks that these relations of friendship have their origins in association and the degree of friendship is proportional to the extent of the association.[12] In his taxonomy of forms of friendship, Aristotle categorizes these as friendships of utility. Though not as long-lasting as the other categories of friendship – friendship for the sake of mutual enjoyment or friendship grounded in mutual virtue – friendships for utility are still friendships.

The fact of mutual advantage is the glue that holds together this disparate collection of friendship relations. The ancient Greeks not only characterized people who cooperate in mutually beneficial ways over a period of time as friends, they also supposed that the conferring of benefits on another meant that the pair should now be described as friends. This comes across clearly in Pericles' funeral oration in Thucydides:

> Again we [Athenians] are opposite to most men in matters of virtue: we win our friends by doing them favours, rather than by accepting favours from them. A person who does a good turn is a more faithful friend: his goodwill toward the recipient preserves his feeling that he should do more; but the friendship of the person

> who has to return a good deed is dull and flat, because he knows
> that he will merely be paying a debt – rather than doing a favour
> – when he shows his virtue in return.[13]

Correspondingly, to act to another person's detriment makes you his enemy. Dover notes the following two examples. In Aristophanes' *Frogs*, the character of Dionysius is hesitant to cast a vote for either Aeschylus or Euripides to win in a contest. Both are *philoi* to him, and voting for one over the other will make him an enemy. In the more serious context of a trial, an adulterer becomes an enemy to his former lover when he breaks off the affair. In so acting to her disadvantage, he has inflicted what she regards as a wrong or injustice and this is sufficient for him now to become an enemy.[14]

What these reflections show is that the help friends/harm enemies principle is not one that governs actions toward different groups whose identity is antecedently fixed. People sometimes come to count as friends – people *you should help* – precisely because *they have helped you*, or because you have already helped them. Similarly, people can come to count as enemies to whom you owe ill will by what they have done to you – or indeed, by what they have done to your friends or ancestors. Relations of enmity, like relations of guest-friendship, can be inherited.[15]

Kinsmen

The issue of mutual aid raises the question of kinship and friendship. Those persons who stand in kinship relations are regularly described by the adjective *philoi*. We could say, then, that they are "friends" or, perhaps more modestly, that they are "dear to one another."[16] This, of course, marks the ancient category of friends as different from the modern one. We moderns *may be* friends with our parents but we are not friends merely by virtue of the fact that they are our parents and we are their children. We should not suppose that ancient Greek family life was so much better than our own, that all Greek children regarded their parents as we moderns regard the people we call friends. Rather, the fact that the same term was used across these relationships suggests that the core notion of *philia* is that of duties of mutual assistance. Doubtless many *philia* relationships were warm and affectionate, as many of our friendly relations are. But what marks them out as *philia* relations is not the feeling, but rather the idea that these are people one is obliged to help.

Even in the fifth and fourth centuries BCE, there were people who regarded this assimilation of family to friends as undesirable. The objection was not on the ground that friends ought to be those with whom one shares an essential emotional intimacy. Demosthenes writes: "Men are not our friends and our foes by natural generation; they are made such by their own actions." Demosthenes is thus objecting that family members should not automatically be characterized as friends, for they may not have done what is essential for friends – benefiting one another. Francisco Gonzales has argued that Socrates and his followers also sought to undermine the notion of kinship-*philia*.[17]

These are the exceptions that prove the rule. If the ancient Greeks did not themselves take kinship and friendship to be one in kind, then these dissenting voices would be hard to explain. The typical Greek use of *philos* and *philia* tends to elide the differences between what we moderns call friendship and other relations, such as kinship and relations of mutual benefit. Because all the relations that fall under *philia* are governed by the imperative to help friends (dear ones) and harm enemies (hateful people), the ancient Greeks tended to regard companion-friendship, kinship, club membership and so on as positions along a continuum.

Politics and Friendship

We know that for the Greeks the giving and receiving of services or favours (*charites*) was important for the maintenance of *philia* relationships.[18] But the place of friendship in the mutual project of politics deserves special consideration, for it is in this context that we find a particular form in which political friendship is manifested, the *hetaireia* or political club. One could not practice politics "without friends and trusted followers."[19] This has been taken by most scholars to be an accurate description of ancient Greek political reality. (The best evidence for this comes from Athens and the following discussion is restricted to that city.)

In the democratic city-state of Athens in the fifth century BCE, political power was centred in groups of friends (*philoi*).[20] These friendship groups were of various types: the *oikeia* or immediate family, the *genos* or kinship group, the *kedeia* or marriage alliance, the *hetaireia* or political club.[21] Since members of these groups were *philoi*, they were bound to each other by the principle of helping friends and harming enemies.[22] Thus a man who needed support in the law courts, the assembly, or the council would seek the help of his *oikeioi*, *gennaitai*, *kedestes* (in-laws) or *hetairoi*.[23] These were his *philoi*. They were bound to support him, and he was bound to repay them in appropriate ways for this support.

How widespread were these friendship groups? It seems that they played a role only in the lives of the rich and well-established citizens. It was they, and not citizens from lower segments of Athenian society, who participated in the political life of the city by means of the intimate and personal *philia* bonds of the friendship group.[24] Such groups, it seems, were elitist. What of the poorer citizens? Did friendship play a part in their political lives? Yes, but in a somewhat different way.

In the late sixth century BCE, Cleisthenes sought power by making the people or the masses his friends *(ton dêmon prosetairizetai)*.[25] Cleisthenes' successful technique was imitated by politicians such as Pericles and Cleon. They appealed directly to the people for support, and did so using the language of friendship, claiming to be the friends of the people.[26] It is important to note that, upon entering public life, Pericles and Cleon withdrew from their personal friendships. It seems that the point of such withdrawal was to give the appearance of impartiality and thus strengthen the claim of friendship with the people.[27]

Thus, alongside the elitist friendship groups there existed another type of political friendship in fifth-century Athens, one that bound the politician not to individual *philoi*, but to the *dêmos*.[28] This second type of friendship involved "winning the good will [that is, political support] of the common run of citizens by timely acts of generosity [festivals, parks, public sacrifices, acts of philanthropy] and by sustained affability of manner. This was the politics of largess."[29]

The Peloponnesian war (431–404 BCE) introduced changes to both of these forms of political friendship. One of the effects of the war on Athenian politics was to make status, wealth and good marriage unnecessary for a successful political career. New Athenian politicians of the fourth century "did not belong to the established friendship networks of the wealthy and great families."[30] Accordingly the *philia* ties of *oikeioi*, *gennaitai*, *kedestes* and *hetairoi* (at least in the fifth-century sense) had little place in the politics of fourth-century Athens. There were still friendship groups but they were much more fragmented and subject to shifting allegiances.[31]

Politicians of the fourth century apparently also continued to try to cultivate "friendship with the people."[32] But they were not as successful, perhaps because Athens' depleted wealth meant that they were less able to engage in the politics of largesse as successfully as Pericles and Cleon had.

The Peloponnesian war brought to the Greek world not only inter-city strife, but strife of the worst sort – intra-city strife or civil war (*stasis*). The situation on Corcyra, as described by Thucydides, was typical, as pro-Athenian (democratic) and pro-Spartan (oligarchic) factions brutalized each other:

> There was death in every shape and form ... people went to every extreme and beyond it. There were fathers who killed their sons; men were dragged from the temples or butchered on the very altars; some were actually walled up in the temple of Dionysus and died there ... Later, of course, practically the whole Hellenic world was convulsed, with rival parties in each state – democratic leaders trying to bring in the Athenians, and oligarchs trying to bring in the Spartans ... So civil wars broke out in city after city.[33]

These civil wars did not cease with the end of the Peloponnesian War, but continued well into the fourth century.[34] M. M. Austin writes: "It is no accident that it was precisely at the end of the fifth century that *homonoia* – concord – between citizens emerged as a political slogan ... to become a much used catchword of internal and external Greek politics in the fourth century."[35] Xenophon, Demosthenes, Tacticus, Lysias, Isocrates, Plato, and Aristotle all lauded such concord among citizens. What does this have to do with friendship? Aristotle tells us that, among the Greeks, concord or *homonoia* "is said to be" specifically *political* friendship, that is, friendship among fellow citizens. Such *homonoia* consists in agreement about constitutional fundamentals: for example, who should rule and be ruled.[36] Using Aristotle as our guide, we can say that the demand by orators and philosophers that fellow citizens live in *homonoia* was a demand that fellow citizens become friends of a particular sort. Some[37] went even further and urged *homonoia*/friendship not only at the intra-city level, but also at the pan-Hellenic level. The demand for *homonoia* continued in the Hellenistic period, both at the level of political theory where the Stoics sometimes identified civic friendship with *homonoia*, and sometimes made *homonoia* the basis of friendship,[38] and at the level of political practice, where "the Macedonian kings persistently urged keeping the common peace, receiving back exiles and forsaking revolution."[39]

Conclusion

The most salient difference between modern friendship and Greek *philia* is the extent of the latter relation. Though the ancient Greeks themselves could, and doubtless did, draw differentiations within the range of relationships encompassed under *philia* and its cognates, the fact that they brought them under a common genus is revealing. What ties this multitude of relations together is that they are unified under the action-guiding principle: "help friends and harm enemies." The application of this truism in particular cases was undoubtedly complicated, for friendship relations may overlap and intersect in ways that make it difficult to see how you can honour all your obligations. Nor are the obligations themselves all that clear: the asymmetries of power and relations of hierarchy in many friendships make it impractical to insist that equivalent benefit is owed by each party to the friendship. Even so, there was no apparent discomfort with the fact that there is an "economy of friendship." These friendships were, and were seen to be, relations of mutual benefit. But they were, in addition to this, clearly regarded as goods in themselves. This may seem odd to us moderns since we tend to regard things as exclusively divided into ends we value in themselves and mere *means* that we value *only* insofar as they help us to achieve our ends. But the Greek philosophers who attempted to theorize about the value of things operated with a tri-partition: things that are good as a means to other good things as well as being valuable in themselves; things like idle enjoyments that are valued only for themselves; and things like medical care that are valued only in as much as they contribute to health. Friendship belongs to the first and most valuable class of things.

Philosophical Ideals of Friendship in the Classical Period

Socrates (469–399 BCE), Plato (429–347 BCE) and Aristotle (384–322) are the philosophers of the *polis* or Greek city-state. Plato and Aristotle wrote about the ideal form that this political unit should take. Socrates' conversations are directed to the wellbeing of the *individuals* with whom he is speaking, and so are not as directly political, yet they have Athens as their essential backdrop. Faced with the choice between escape to another city-state and death, Socrates preferred death because he supposed that what he regarded as philosophy could not be carried on in a place that did not have Athenian law and custom. This presupposition about the superiority of the city-state to other political arrangements is one that is shared by the three philosophers, and a point of difference with the later philosophers of the Hellenistic period and of the Roman Empire.

The evidence we possess for the philosophical views of the three authors is problematic – though for different reasons in each case. Socrates himself wrote nothing. We are dependent upon the way in which other philosophers chose to depict him in order to make any guesses about his philosophy. It seems that the Socratic dialogue became an established genre in the years after Socrates' death. We have full examples from only two authors: Plato and Xenophon (c. 430–c. 354 BCE). Their depictions of Socrates differ in various ways and it is not easy to know how much the genre of the Socratic dialogue demanded fidelity to the actual thought of Socrates. The early dialogues of Plato and Xenophon's *Memorabilia* contain several sustained discussions of the nature of friendship and its value. Of particular importance are the Platonic *Lysis* and *Alcibiades* I,[40] as well as Xenophon's *Mem.* II.6.

Plato makes use of other characters in his dialogues apart from Socrates – particularly in those dialogues written later in his life. Yet Plato himself makes no appearance. Nor does Plato ever provide a "user's manual" for the dialogue form. We are hard-pressed to know how much of what one of Plato's lead characters – whether it be Socrates, Timaeus or the Stranger from Elea – says should be taken to indicate Plato's view on any subject. In our attempt to isolate a Platonic contribution to ancient ideals of friendship, we shall concentrate on the *Republic, Laws, Symposium* and *Phaedrus*.

Aristotle's writings provide a different interpretive challenge. Mercifully, those that we possess are written as treatises, so there is not the gap between author and character that there is in Plato's dialogues. But while we do have all the works that Plato wrote, we possess only a fraction of the works of Aristotle. All manuscripts trace back to the edition of Aristotle's works prepared by Andronicus of Rhodes in the first century BCE. We have no idea what editorial principles Andronicus used and the works in the surviving Aristotelian corpus are written in prose that is terse and dense. (This style, together with some references to diagrams and other things that suggest a lecture setting, has led to the speculation that these were Aristotle's notes.) The main source for Aristotle's views on friendship are books 8 and 9 of his

Nicomachean Ethics and – at least relative to a work like the *Metaphysics* – this is relatively easy to comprehend.

We have very little evidence concerning the dissemination of these philosophical texts during their authors' lifetimes or in the couple of centuries after their deaths. Certainly Athenians could have stopped off in the public spaces occupied by Plato's Academy or Aristotle's Lyceum to see what was going on.[41] Yet the means by which one might acquire a copy of a Platonic dialogue are not clear. Things are even less clear in the case of Aristotle's "in-house" or esoteric works. (Like Plato, Aristotle also wrote dialogues – the exoteric works – that survive only in fragmentary form.) Some scholars have been sceptical about the extent to which Aristotle's works were known even to philosophers in the period after his death, right down to the edition of Andronicus.[42] This conclusion has not been generally accepted and it seems clear to most that subsequent *philosophers* knew the content of these works. Yet this tells us little about what the Greek in the street knew about philosophical writings on friendship. It is perhaps best not to assume that Socrates, Plato and Aristotle had an enormous impact on the practice of friendship in the Classical period. Rather, their works contain their reflections on those practices and the ideals to which they supposed friendship should aspire. Their importance for the history of friendship arguably comes later. Classical and later Hellenistic ideals of friendship provide the intellectual backdrop that dominated self-conscious thinking and writing about friendship down to the eighteenth century.

Socratic Self-sufficiency

Two ideas that seem potentially at odds with one another emerge from Plato and Xenophon's Socratic dialogues. The first is that friendship is grounded in utility or usefulness. The second is that only those who are morally virtuous can be friends.

In the *Lysis*, Socrates is shown in conversation with two teenagers, Lysis and Menexenus. The scene is one that combines erotic undertones with peculiarly Socratic education, so thoughtful readers will be attuned to a gap between what Socrates says and what one might suppose he (or Plato) believes. He puts the following line of reasoning to young Lysis: happiness consists in doing whatever you desire. Even though you are his son, your father forbids you to do some things that you would like to do, while at the same time he permits his household slaves to do these very things (for example, to drive the racing chariots). Those things that you are permitted to do are just those things in which you have understanding or knowledge. So, a person is trusted and empowered to do those things in respect of which he has knowledge. The knowledgeable person is thus able to derive benefit from what he possesses and also benefits others. Socrates then links this potential to benefit others to the possibility of friendship:

> Well therefore will we be friends (*philoi*) with anyone in respect of those matters in which we are of no benefit (*anôpheleis*) to them? Or will we be endeared (*philêsei*) to anyone [in these matters]? Surely not, said Lysis. So now, you see, your father does not cherish you, nor does anyone cherish anyone else, so far as one is useless. Apparently not, he said. Then if you can become wise, my boy, everybody will be your friend, every one will be akin (*oikeion*) to you, since you will be useful and good. If not, no one at all – not your father, nor your mother, nor your kinfolk – will be your friends.[43]

Socrates does not say so explicitly, but Lysis ought to apply this reasoning to the case of his own mother and father. They should be his *philoi* just to the extent that they are capable of benefiting him. And if wisdom is a necessary condition for deriving benefit from anything – another common Socratic theme – Lysis should count his family as friends just to the extent that they are wise. If friendship should be based on wisdom rather than on blood relations, then the ideal friendships will be those among people who are wise, or who are at least seeking after wisdom.

The most influential writer on Socrates of the twentieth century, Gregory Vlastos, drew the inference from Plato's *Lysis* that Socratic friendship is defective in relation to Aristotle's conception of friendship. Aristotle insists that we wish our friend's good *for his own sake*. Of course, Aristotle also insists that we will find the best friendships inevitably beneficial to ourselves as well.[44] Vlastos, however, thought that the Socratic notion of friendship cannot account for the fact that we cherish our friends as persons – not merely insofar as they are productive of benefit. We can also see from this passage that his line of reasoning would seem to undercut the idea that family members are *philoi* merely by the fact of blood relation. If utility forms the foundation of friendship, and if genuine utility presupposes wisdom, then there can only really be friendship among the wise.

The second striking feature of Socrates' conversations on friendship may be thought to counterbalance this seemingly distasteful focus on the utility of friends. In both Plato's early dialogues and in Xenophon, Socrates insists that *only morally virtuous people can be friends*. This comes across clearly when Socrates examines the Homeric adage that "like is friend to like."[45] But this cannot be so, since wicked people are alike, but are incapable of friendship with one another. The wicked commit injustices and those who commit injustice make enemies, not friends. Indeed, the wicked person is not even *like himself*, since he is so unsteady and capricious. If likeness is the basis of friendship, the wicked man is not even his own friend, let alone anyone else's. Xenophon's *Memorabilia* pursues the same theme.[46]

Socrates' remarks on the subject of friendship probably strike us moderns as odd (at least) – and perhaps slightly repugnant as well. The two claims considered here seem inhumanly cold and primly moralistic in turn. They would have struck his contemporaries the same way. But Socrates thinks that his job is not to represent, or rather re-present, the wisdom of common sense. It is rather to build a logically consistent and irrefutable set of beliefs from what he takes to be ordinary people's inconsistent musings on matters moral. With respect to the connection between friendship and benefit, the key insight is that benefit depends on knowledge or wisdom. Socrates is *philo-sophos* – a lover of wisdom – first and foremost. Such *philanthrôpeia* or love of humanity as he is capable of is only love of people insofar as they are sources of wisdom, or as touchstone against which to test his own modest claims to knowledge.

The overriding value of knowledge in Socrates' ethics sheds light on his insistence that only the morally good can be friends. Socrates rejects part of the "help friends/harm enemies" principle that governs ancient Greek friendship because he rejects retaliation. To harm another is to perform an injustice, even if it is in return for a harm unjustly done.[47] We have an overriding reason to avoid injustice because we have an overriding reason to seek knowledge, and Socrates equates moral virtues, such as justice, with knowledge. But if the overriding value of knowledge forbids us from retaliating, it nonetheless casts the original injustices perpetrated against us in a new light. My enemies may take my property or my life but they cannot make me foolish or a morally wicked man – only *I* can inflict this greatest of harms upon myself. This restriction on the extent to which my enemies can harm me is matched by a corresponding restriction on the extent to which I can help my friends. If I lack the knowledge of good and evil with which Socrates equates moral virtue, then I am prevented from bestowing upon my friends the greatest of blessings.

If we really care for one another as friends, then we should make common cause in the search for wisdom and subordinate all our other efforts to this end. Few of the partners with whom Plato or Xenophon show Socrates in conversation with are worthy of this form of friendship. They get distracted or discouraged. They care about appearing foolish in the admission of their ignorance. None are worthy friends for Socrates. Socrates does not chide them or belittle them for dropping out of the race for the greatest prize of all. But neither does he slow down or stop in order to encourage them to keep running. So in the end he is a man alone, but equally a man untroubled by this fact within his solitary self-sufficiency.

The ancient Greek philosophers' writings on happiness play out a dialectic between competing values of self-sufficiency (*autarcheia*) and relatedness to community. The latter value is often represented concretely by the place of friendship in the good life. Along the spectrum of views, Socratic ethics gives pride of place to self-sufficiency. There is a correspondingly austere sense of friendship – an austerity that we will encounter again in Stoicism.

Platonic Politics, erôs *and* philia

Plato's middle and late period dialogues reflect on the political role of friendship in ways that the Socratic dialogues do not. Moreover, they explore the notion of *erôs* or erotic love in the context of Plato's metaphysics of immortal, incorporeal souls and abstract paradigmatic forms. Whatever Plato's own intentions, these reflections on *erôs* were subsequently taken to present an ideal of friendship.

Let us turn first to the political dimensions of Plato's discussions of friendship. In the *Laws*, Plato gives us advice on how to keep our friends:

> As for friends and comrades, one will make them favourably disposed in the intermingling of life if one thinks more highly than they do of the worth and importance of their services to oneself, and assigns to one's own favours to friends less value than that assigned by the friends and comrades themselves.[48]

As we have mentioned the giving and receiving of services or favours (*charites*) was important for the maintenance of *philia* relationships. It is clear that Plato agrees. But what is the source of *philia* for Plato? To answer this question we need to turn to Plato's distinction (again in the *Laws*) between genuine and spurious friendship. The latter is a relationship "between opposites." Such friendship "is terrible and savage, and is seldom mutual among us." An example of such friendship is "the needy in its relationship to the wealthy." In contrast, genuine friendship is "gentle and mutual throughout life" and binds parties in a relationship of "harmonious assent." Genuine friends commune "in peace and with good will." For genuine friendship is a relationship between "equals" and "similars in point of virtue."[49]

What does Plato mean by "equals"? Since Plato presents us with the relationship between the needy and wealthy as an example of spurious friendship, it seems plausible to say that by "equals" Plato means equality in social status. Why does genuine friendship require that parties be equal in status? Plato is convinced that wealth and poverty cultivate "insolence," "injustice" "jealousies" and "ill-will." Thus, rich and poor spend all their time "plotting against each other."[50]

Since Plato thinks that genuine friendship requires equal status, we could perhaps attribute to him the view that genuine friendship occurs between members of the same class, that is, between those who are poor and between those who are rich. But this form of likeness is not enough. Like Socrates, Plato suggests that friendship also requires virtue but Plato thinks that neither the rich nor the poor tend to be particularly virtuous.[51] Since rich and poor typically lack the virtue that friendship requires, it follows that friendship among the rich is unlikely, as is friendship between the poor. According to Plato, then, only one group of social equals is capable of true friendship – namely those who are situated between poverty and wealth. We must not forget that, to be friends, members of this group also require likeness in virtue. Let us take a closer look at the sort of virtue that Plato thinks is necessary for genuine friendship.

One of the virtues that parties must share in order to be genuine friends is the virtue of moderation or *sôphrosunê*. This term is often translated as "temperance" or "self-control." It is connected with being measured in one's appetites and actions and with steering clear of excess. That friendship demands likeness in moderation for Plato comes out where he endorses the "ancient saying: 'like is dear to like, *if it is measured*.'"[52] Plato adds: "Things that lack measure are dear neither to one another nor to things that possess measure." Plato says the same thing in the *Gorgias*. Here Plato has Socrates tell us that "one man is a friend to another most of all when, as wise men of old say, like is friend to like." Plato also has Socrates tell us that "[a man] should not allow his appetites to be intemperate ... For no other man would be a friend to such a man."[53] If we put the two passages together, then we get the idea that genuine friendship requires likeness in moderation.

But why does genuine friendship require that parties be alike with respect to the virtue of moderation? At one point we are told that the intemperate man cannot restrain his desires. He wants more than his fair share,[54] a vice called *pleonexia* and one that is opposed to justice or *dikê*. In other words, the intemperate man cannot abide by the demands of justice. This is why genuine friendship requires the virtue of moderation. Hence, friendship for Plato requires the virtue of justice in addition to the virtue of moderation. Plato tells us that "the ancient pronouncement is true that 'equality produces friendship.'" By "equality" Plato means geometrical or proportionate equality; and such equality is identified with justice.[55]

For Plato, then, virtue (or character) is the source and basis of personal friendship. Seemingly for Plato, Smith is a friend to Blogs *qua* virtuous person. It is a short step from this to suppose that it is Blogs' character that Smith values as much, or more, than Blogs himself. This has led one scholar to make the following complaint:

> Friendships formed in the Platonic manner ultimately have character rather than the individual's possession of it as their basis. Hence if one loses a friend, it does not matter much as long as the desired character traits are still possessed by many.[56]

The same complaint has been raised about Aristotle.

Let us turn from Plato's discussion of the politics of friendship to the connections between *philia* and erotic love. Plato's *Symposium* and *Phaedrus* discuss erotic love between a man and a teenage boy. Both works suggest, or simply presuppose, that this is the highest form of erotic love. The power of these dialogues owes more to the striking images of the lovers than to any clear and compelling line of argument. Images also provide much more latitude for interpretation and thus adaptation by subsequent thinkers. We will concentrate on the *Phaedrus* since the connections between *erôs* and *philia* are more prominent in it than in the *Symposium*. Famously, Plato argued for the immortality of the soul and asserts that this immortal soul is reincarnated in various types of bodies, depending upon the character of its previous life.[57] The soul also exists in a disembodied state at some points in its career and it turns out that this fact is relevant to *erôs* and *philia*.

The *Phaedrus* introduces the famous image of the soul as a charioteer driving two winged horses, one good and noble, the other badly
behaved.[58] In the soul's initial disembodied state it soared with the
gods to the highest vault of heaven where it looked outside the universe at the Forms. The Forms correspond to properties such as justice, goodness, beauty and so on. They are eternal abstract objects
grasped by the mind alone and paradigms that are deficiently imitated by the visible or tangible things that homonymously bear their
names. The value possessed by the visible imitations of Beauty Itself
or Justice Itself is eclipsed by their abstract paradigms. Hence in the
Phaedrus, human souls prior to embodiment are said to be nourished
by the mental vision of these Forms as the gods are on ambrosia.[59]

Our troubles begin when our badly behaved horse gets out of control and prevents us from feeding on this vision. Malnourished, the
soul loses its wings and descends into a body. In our embodied condition, we forget much that we knew in our previous existence. The
idea that what we call learning is actually the recollection of knowledge attained in a previous life is one explored in other dialogues.[60]
In the *Phaedrus* it is given a new twist. The recollection of the Form of
Beauty is especially easily aroused. When the lover who is worthy
sees in the beloved a reflection of the Form of Beauty, the charioteer
and the good horse are inclined to treat him with a kind of religious
awe. The visual flow of beauty through the eyes stimulates the regrowth of the soul's wings, with an attendant itching and discomfort
that drives the lover to a kind of madness. This process of regrowth
is *erôs*.

The optimal situation is one in which this manic love is transformed
into *philia*. The bad-natured horse in the pair is all for approaching
the boy and proposing the pleasures of sex.[61] But the charioteer and
the other horse should discipline him until he too comes to regard the
beloved with a mixture of associated fear and religious awe.[62] It is
only at this point in the narrative that the boy's attitudes and desires
enter the picture. Since he receives all care and service from the lover,
he comes to regard him as a friend. Indeed, the *Phaedrus* insists that it
is a cosmic law that "an evil person is never a friend to another evil
person, nor does the good ever fail to be friendly to the good."[63]
Moreover, the beloved's own beauty, reflected in the eyes of his lover,
will stimulate the growth of his own wings. Hence he too comes to be
in love, for *erôs* is just the condition of regrowing one's wings. Yet he

does not know this, and regards it instead as *philia*.[64] In this confused state, he will offer sexual intimacy to the lover.

> [W]hen they lie together, he would not refuse his lover any favour, if he asked it; but the other horse and the charioteer oppose all this with modesty and reason. If now the better elements of the mind, which lead to a well ordered life and to philosophy, prevail, they live a life of happiness and harmony here on earth, self-controlled and orderly, holding in subjection that which causes evil in the soul and giving freedom to that which makes for virtue; and when this life is ended they are light and winged, for they have conquered in one of the three truly Olympic contests.[65]

It is tempting to see in this a deep ambivalence about a specifically homosexual form of sexual intercourse but this may be unwarranted. A recurring theme in Plato's dialogues is the control of all forms of desire – and specifically of sexual desire – by reason. In any case, even if the lover and beloved are not up to the job of controlling sexual desire, they too wind up as friends.

> If however they live a life less noble and without philosophy, but yet ruled by the love of honour, probably, when they have been drinking, or in some other moment of carelessness, the two unruly horses, taking the souls off their guard, will bring them together and seize upon and accomplish that which is by the many accounted blissful; and when this has once been done, they continue the practice, but infrequently, since what they are doing is not approved by the whole mind. So these two pass through life as friends, though not such friends as the others.[66]

It would seem then that the friends that we moderns would also call lovers are not so much friends as those we would not call lovers. Paradoxically, the friends that we would not call lovers are more truly lovers than those in relation to whom we would not use this term.

The relationship between *erôs* and *philia* in the *Phaedrus* is complex – to say the least. The boy mistakenly supposes that he is merely a friend to the older man, yet he is actually in love since his wings are sprouting. The lover seeks to make his beloved a friend, not a lover. If they are lovers, in our sense of the word, then even then they are friends. In any event, their relationship –whether we regard it as *erôs* or *philia* – is distinctly superior to the heterosexual form of love, since this inevitably involves the body and "eagerness to make babies."[67]

When later readers encounter this text – already confusing in its own right – and they wish to remove from their beloved Plato the stain of the "unspeakable vice of the Greeks" there is ample room for manoeuvre. Plato's text is so rich in meaning that it is easy to find what one likes in it. But the most obvious themes involve the idea that masculine *erôs* or *philia* is superior to that which men may have with women; the notion that love and friendship have a spiritual dimension of mutual improvement toward a god-like state; and that the best interpersonal friendships involve a degree of intimacy that verges on the sexual.

Aristotle

Aristotle is full of praise for friendship, telling us that *eudaimonia* requires friendship, that friendship is a source of great pleasure, and that no one would choose to live without friends, even if he had all other goods.[68] But what does Aristotle mean by friendship?

Aristotle identifies three things that people pursue as objects of love: the useful (or advantageous), the pleasant, and the good (or virtuous). It is one of these qualities that we find lovable in another. On the basis of these three objects of love Aristotle distinguishes three major types of friendship: advantage-friendship, pleasure-friendship and virtue-friendship.[69]

Advantage-friendship arises when we enter a relationship with another because we find him to be useful or advantageous to us. We love him as something useful. This is friendship for the sake of one's own advantage. Pleasure-friendship arises when we enter a relationship with another because of the pleasure he gives us. We love the other as something pleasant. This is friendship for the sake of one's own pleasure.[70] Here we should note that Aristotle considers pleasure-friendships to be better than advantage-friendships. Advantage-friendships are more easily dissolved than pleasure-friendships, and unlike those who are friends for the sake of pleasure, those who are friends for the sake of advantage rarely take pleasure in each other's company.[71]

Virtue-friendship is the best form of friendship, Aristotle called it *teleia philia* (complete or perfect friendship). Such friendship arises when we love another as someone who is good or virtuous.[72] This third type of friendship is possible only between the good, unlike friendships for the sake of pleasure and utility, which are possible between bad people. While virtue friendship is both pleasant and advantageous for its participants, it has neither pleasure nor advantage as its object. Rather it is for the sake of the goodness of the other:

"Complete friendship is the friendship of good people similar in virtue; for they wish goods in the same way to each other insofar as they are good, and they are good in their own right."[73]

Because virtue-friendship is possible only between the good it is rare and restricted to a few, unlike the other types of friendship:

> No one can have complete friendship for many people, just as no one can have erotic passion for many at the same time for [complete friendship, like erotic passion] is like an excess, and an excess is naturally directed at a single individual. And just as it is difficult for many people to please the same person intensely at the same time, it is also difficult, presumably, for many to be good. [To find out whether someone is really good], one must both have experience of him and be on familiar terms with him, which is extremely difficult. If however the friendship is for utility or pleasure it is possible for many to please; for there are many people of the right sort, and the services take little time.[74]

Aristotle points to other differences between virtue-friendship, on the one hand, and pleasure- and advantage-friendships, on the other. Unlike the other types of friendship, virtue-friendship is "enduring and immune to slander." Further, virtue friends help each other avoid error. They spend time with each other, make the same choices, and share each other's joys and sorrow. This latter characteristic of perfect friendship indicates that, for Aristotle, such friendship is an intimate and affective relationship. This is also suggested when Aristotle speaks of the virtue friend as "another himself."[75]

While pleasure-, advantage- and virtue-friendships differ from each other in important ways, they do share a common core: all are relationships involving *goodwill* (wishing the other good) that is *reciprocated* and *recognized*.[76] It is in virtue of this common core that the three types of friendship are in fact friendships but we should note that only in the case of virtue-friendship does one wish good for the other for the sake of the other. In advantage- and pleasure-friendships, one wishes good for the other for one's own sake.[77] Yet this does not preclude virtue friendships being advantageous to oneself. Indeed, since the friend is, in this case, "another self," I care for my own good in caring for the other's good:

> And in loving a friend men love what is good for themselves; for the good man in becoming a friend becomes a good to his friend. Each, then, both loves what is good for himself, and makes an equal return in goodwill and pleasantness; for friendship is said to

be equality, and both these are found most in the friendship of the good.[78]

Since pleasure-, advantage- and virtue-friendships involve reciprocity they are friendships between equals in some sense.[79] But Aristotle notes that not all friendships are between equals in every sense. Some friendships are between people of unequal status. His main examples of such friendships are those within the household, between father and son, husband and wife, mother and child, brother and brother. In these friendships, "loving accords with the comparative worth of the friends" and the one who is better, more beneficial or in some other way superior (father, husband, mother, dominant brother) "must be loved more than he loves."[80] Family friendships can involve pleasure, utility and virtue. Friendship between parent and child includes pleasure and utility. So can the friendship between husband and wife. Aristotle adds that if husband and wife are decent then their friendship may be one of virtue.[81] It seems that friendship between parent and child can also be based on decency (and therefore virtue), as can friendship between brothers.[82]

Aristotle's explicit remarks here seem to be potentially at odds with other, apparently inescapable, inferences from equally explicit claims. Virtue in the fullest sense presupposes practical wisdom or *phronêsis*.[83] Yet in the *Politics*, Aristotle claims that in women the capacity for rational decision-making is not as authoritative as it is in men.[84] Since it is distinctive of the person who possesses practical wisdom to deliberate well, this appears to preclude women possessing it and so possessing full virtue. And this would seem to preclude them from virtue friendships, unless Aristotle supposes that virtue-friendships is still possible between persons who have different kinds of virtue. The *Politics* also claims that the virtues of courage, justice and self-control are different in men and women. The virtues of children are also different.[85] It is difficult to see, then, how Aristotle can suppose that man and wife, or parents and children, can be in virtue-friendships. Some interpreters have sought to credit Aristotle with a sort of crypto-feminist viewpoint on the basis of such apparently inconsistent remarks. He is signalling to the sufficiently careful reader that he does not share his contemporaries' views on women.[86] We think that it is far more likely that, as Richard Mulgan has argued, Aristotle's remarks on women are inconsistent because they are few and ill-considered.[87] This would be unsurprising if Aristotle thought that there was nothing very interesting, philosophically, about women and their role in Greek society.

Earlier we noted Aristotle's view that virtue-friendship is more enduring than both pleasure-friendship and advantage-friendship, for both pleasure and advantage are temporary features of any relationship. Thus it is permissible to dissolve an advantage-friendship or a pleasure-friendship when it ceases to be advantageous or pleasant.[88] But is it ever permissible for virtue-friends to dissolve their friendship? It is, Aristotle says, if one of the parties goes bad.[89] But the virtuous party must be careful here, Aristotle adds. He must make sure that his friend has become "incurably vicious."

> If someone can be set right, we should try harder to rescue his character than his property, insofar as character is both better and more proper to friendship. Still, the friend who dissolves the friendship seems to be doing nothing absurd. For he was not the friend of a person of this sort; hence, if the friend has altered, and he cannot save him, he leaves him.[90]

Aristotle thinks that this same idea holds true in family friendships: "[I]t presumably seems that no one would ever withdraw from a son, except from one who was far gone in vice."[91]

What Aristotle has to say about the dissolution of virtue-friendships is perfectly consistent with his view that such friendships are based on virtue. Yet scholars have wondered about the adequacy of Aristotle's perfect friendship, arguing that, since it is not founded on personal uniqueness or particularity, it makes friends replaceable. We noted above in our discussion of Socratic friendship Vlastos' claim that it is directed not at the person, but at the *qualities* of the person. Aristotle's view is subtly different. We value our friends – that is, we wish them good for their own sake – but we value them *because of* their qualities. Hence even the highest form of friendship is conditional on the friend retaining the character that forms the basis of the friendship. This does seem to have the consequence that a virtue-friend "far gone in vice" could and should be replaced in one's affections with another without loss.

Aristotle's account of friendship is also perhaps mildly less normative than that of Socrates or Plato. He at least concedes that there is a relationship that we can call friendship that obtains between people with less than sterling moral character but he still insists that the highest and best form of friendship requires the best moral character. His ideals of friendship also concede ground to the popular "economy of friendship" – even the highest friendship is a source of utility, although this is not the *basis* of the best friendships. Aristotle's ethics concede more to the commonsense belief that human happiness is vulnerable and in need of friendship. The virtuous man is the most self-sufficient of all men, but even he needs friends – as well as a modicum of health, wealth and external advantages[92] – in order to enjoy complete happiness. Aristotle's moral philosophy in general, and his account of friendship in particular, stands at some distance from the austere self-sufficiency of Socratic friendship.

Greek *philia* in the Hellenistic Period: Philosophical Ideals and Reality

Socrates, Plato and Aristotle are the philosophical giants of the Classical period (500–323 BCE). The opening point of the Hellenistic era (323–331 BCE) marks a transition in Greek politics from an era in which the city-state was the centre of power to one in which Alexander's empire was divided into large swaths – the Macedonian, Selucid and Ptolemaic empires – ruled by kings. The end point marks the fall of the last of these three empires to the Roman general, Octavian. Roman political domination of Greece and Macedon proper, however, came earlier in a series of wars in 214–205, 200–196, and 171–168 BCE. These changes, as well as the integration of Greek culture and learning into the burgeoning Roman empire, had implications at least for the political forms of friendship, as well as for philosophical *theorizing* about friendship and the good life. In what follows we will not confine ourselves strictly to this time period, though we will concentrate on sources written in Greek.

The Practice of Friendship in the Hellenistic Period

As noted, the political context of the Hellenistic period is very different from the age of the city-state. Though Greek culture was now disseminated around the eastern part of the Mediterranean thanks to the conquests of Alexander, the political unit of the Greek city-state or *polis* was eclipsed by the various kingdoms into which Alexander's empire was divided. This changes the context for discussions of civic friendship or *philia politikē*. So let us begin this section with *philia* in the political realm, specifically within the Hellenistic courts, where the king's trusted courtiers were given the official title of "Friends." Frank Walbank observes that in all Hellenistic courts

> the king was surrounded by his Friends (*philoi*) whom he appointed
> to a position close to his own person, where they enjoyed an

intimate relationship profitable to both parties, and he often re-
warded them with gifts of land which established them among the
propertied class, whose support was vital to the security of his
rule.[93]

This contrasts rather sharply with the friendships within political clubs
of the fifth and fourth centuries BCE discussed earlier. In those friendship groups, there was at least a notional equality among members,
even if real differences of wealth, reputation and influence meant that
they were not in fact equals. The institution of kingship changes this
considerably.

But this is not the only way in which friendship features in the
political world of Hellenistic Greece. A quick look through the documents collected by Stanley Burstein shows that the terms "friend,"
"friends" and "friendship" were used frequently in the treaties and
decrees of the time. Here friendship, which is sometimes associated
with the term "alliance," usually involves the promise to respect territorial integrity and the promise to provide military assistance in times
of need.[94] These same documents reveal more interesting information about the role and nature of friendship in the political world of
the Hellenistic Greeks. For example, King Ptolemaios II tells the
Militians that he will "repay" their "friendship" "by conferring benefits" upon them (c. 262 BCE).[95] In a political echo of ancestral guest-
friendship, Attalos II provides money for the education of the children
of Delphi because he is "an ancestral friend" of the city (160/159 BCE).[96]
The rise of Rome's power later in the Hellenistic period shows how
these political friendships could cross cultural boundaries too. For
example, Ptolemaios VIII Euergetes II declares (155 BCE):

> If anything happens to me, in accordance with human destiny,
> before successors are left [by me] for my kingdom, I bequeath to
> the Romans the kingdom belonging to me, for who from the be-
> ginning friendship and alliance have been preserved by me with
> all sincerity.[97]

This friendship between Greek rulers and the Romans was not an
isolated example. We frequently find the term "friendship" used in
official documents to describe relations between Romans and Greeks.
Here friendship usually involves Greeks granting the Romans power
of control over their city. In return, the Greek city was permitted to
govern itself according to its own laws.[98] Such friendship with the
Romans was beneficial to the Greeks in other ways. For example,

because of their "friendship" with the Romans, the Ephesians are promised "the establishment of theatrical and [gymnastic] games coming
every fourth year" (98/97 or 94/93 BCE).[99] And because the people of
Plarasa-Aphrodisias were "good friends of the people of Rome,"
Q. Oppius promises "both in public and in private ... to do for you
whatever I can and for your public affairs to be of service and always
of some good to be the author (for you)" (85/84 BCE).[100] Further, as a
result of their service to Rome, three Greek naval captains are

> entered on the roll of friends, [and are] ... permitted to set up on
> the Capitolium a bronze tablet of friendship and to perform a
> sacrifice there, and that gifts to them, according to official proce-
> dure, and lodging and board be contracted for and sent by the
> urban quaestor ... and if concerning their own affairs they desire to
> send envoys to the senate or to come themselves, permission is to
> be granted to them, their children, and their descendents to come
> as envoys or to send them (78 BCE).[101]

The benefits of Roman friendship explain why, in 112/111 BCE, the
people of the Greek city of Epidauros erected a statue in honour of
their fellow citizen Archelochos, son of Aristophantes. For it was as a
result of his efforts that "friendship and alliance with the Romans were
concluded for the city of Epidauros."[102] Such benefits also explain
Plutarch's advice to Greek statesmen:

> [N]ot only should the statesman show himself and his native state
> blameless towards our rulers [the Romans], but he should also
> have always a friend among the men of high station who have the
> greatest power as a firm bulwark, so to speak, of his administration;
> for the Romans themselves are most eager to promote the political
> interests of their friends.[103]

(We shall say more about political friendship in Roman Greece later
when we return to Plutarch.)

At this point we need to turn to personal friendship as it was actually practised and experienced by Greeks of the Hellenistic and
Roman periods. Here we have more source material to draw on than
for the Classical period. While the political uses of *philia*-discourse
may have shifted with the new political forms of the Hellenistic period, there is much continuity when it comes to personal friendship
and relations among blood relatives.

One source for information about such friendship are the documents preserved on papyrus. Katherine Evans has examined these

documents for information about how the terms "friend" and "friend-ship" were used in real-life situations. She has discovered that it was common for a man to act as a proxy for his friend in business and official matters, and that a man would look after his friend's family while he was away. Also friends often performed services for each other, especially "the borrowing, lending, collecting, and transport-ing of money." Finally, Evans notes that women refer to men as friends in a number of documents.[104]

It is possible to assemble further evidence to add to Evans' find-ings. These show that other features of friendship from the Classical period endure. In a letter to the priests at Tebetunis, Poseidonios mentions "the hereditary friendship which you have towards me from old" (99 BCE). Poseidonios adds, "so, whatever you should need, in-struct me and I will gladly oblige."[105] This shows that inherited rela-tions of friendship are still recognized and continue to form the basis of an obligation to act. In a fragmented letter (2 BCE), the author tells the recipient "you must assist him [Damas] because of our friendship"[106] indicating that the governing axiom of *philia* – "help friends" – is still common wisdom and that there is a personal "economy of friend-ship" parallel to the political one. In another letter, a penitent prodi-gal son asks his mother to forgive him. He writes: "it is just to pardon friends who stumble" (second century CE),[107] indicating that the vocabulary of *philia* still extends to familial relationships.

The evidence from these letters agrees with the contemporary his-torians of the period. That the "help friends/harm enemies" principle still governs the *philia* relation is clearly illustrated by the historian Polybius (c. 200–118 BCE). He notes that – while a good man should love his friends and his country, and hate in common with his friends their enemies – the historian must ignore this common convention. As a historian he may rather unnaturally be required to speak well of his enemies and criticize his friends.[108] As we noted, political clubs ceased to have the same significance that they had in the Classical period. But this does not mean that similar civic associations passed beyond the language of friendship. Polybius comments on how far things were gone in Boeotia in 192 BCE. Some men who died childless did not will their estates to their closest relatives, as had been the practice in times past, but instead left their money to their friendship groups for travel and dining. Even men with families left large por-tions of their estates to their dining clubs. So popular and well-resourced were such clubs, Polybius tells us, that many Boeotians had more dinner dates than there were days in the month![109]

In addition to letters, we can perhaps also find information about personal friendship as it was actually practised and experienced by the Hellenistic and Roman Greeks from the poetry of the time. Several of these poems portray personal friendship as an intimate and emotional attachment. For example, Theocritus (c. 308–240 BCE) wrote *Idyll* 28 to accompany a gift to a married female friend, Theugenis. Theocritus ends the poem: "For seeing this [gift] someone will say, 'indeed great affection exists in a small gift; and all that comes from friends is precious.'" Whatever doubts philosophers might voice about the possibility of *philia* between men and women, Theocritus seems genuine in his affection for his married friend.

Kallimachos (c. 300–240 BCE) laments the death of his friend in the following moving poem:

> Someone spoke of your death, Herakleitos. It brought me
> to tears, and I remembered how often together
> we ran the sun down with talk ... somewhere
> you've long been dust, my Halikarnassian friend.[110]

Perhaps Kallimachos also regrets that his friend is no longer in a position to benefit him, but the source of his grief is the absence of their talk together – the simple pleasure of companionship.

Finally, a poem by Palladas (fourth century CE) reveals not only the intimacy of personal friendship (as displayed in the last line of the poem), but also the link between letter-writing and personal friendship for the Greeks:

> Nature, loving the duties of friendship, invented
> instruments by which absent friends can converse,
> pens, paper, ink, handwriting, tokens of the heart
> that mourns afar.[111]

The link between friendship and letter-writing can also be found in the epistolary novel *Chion of Heraclea* (first century CE; author unknown). Letter 9 is addressed to Chion's friend, Bion. Chion complains that Bion has not written to him. He tells Bion that he should "write often as one remembering [their] friendship to another remembering it also." Commenting on this passage, Patricia A. Rosenmeyer writes:

> The letter is perceived, as in the epistolary theorists, as a sign
> of friendship [e.g., Cicero *Ep. ad Fam.* 2.1 ; Seneca *Ep. Mor.* 40].

The bond forged while together must be sustained while apart, and ignoring a friend by not writing implies a low opinion of friendship.[112]

Philosophical Ideals of Friendship

It is dangerous to make broad generalizations about the philosophy of different eras and to suppose that there is any particularly tight connection between the circumstances of philosophical composition and the content of philosophical reflection. None the less, some patterns seem to emerge from the philosophical writings of the Hellenistic period. First, while the political thought of Plato and Aristotle assumes the backdrop of the city-state as a given, the philosophers of the Hellenistic period look to either bigger or smaller notions of community. On the one hand, the Cynics and Stoics envision a community of all rational beings and coin the term *kosmopolitês* or "citizen of the world."[113] On the other hand, Epicurus encouraged his followers to avoid political engagement with the wider affairs of the world and to retreat within Epicurean communities. Second, the philosophical schools of the Hellenistic period address themselves to a wider audience. Plato imagined that there were few people who could engage in philosophy and Aristotle was similarly elitist about the matter. There is no point in anyone hearing the lectures on ethics unless he has been raised properly as a gentleman to appreciate what is fine and noble. By contrast, Epicurus insisted that philosophy could be of benefit to every person.[114] Finally, the philosophers of the Hellenistic period are much more explicit about the soteriological (salvationist) character of philosophy. Philosophy is the pathway to salvation – an escape from the unhappiness that will otherwise befall a person. Moreover, this salvation is both personal and unconditional. The philosopher can be happy or *eudaimonos* even while being cooked alive in the bull of Phalaris.

It is easy to overstate the extent to which the uncertain character of the times influenced the content of Hellenistic philosophy. Zeller's magisterial 1883 *Grundriss der Geschichte der Griechischen Philosophie* put it this way:

> [T]he Greek motherland, robbed of its independence and political activity, became an object of contention for foreigners and the scene of strife ... Under these circumstances it was natural that the desire and power of a free and purely scientific view of the world should disappear; that practical problems should come to the fore

and philosophy should find its chief value in providing a refuge
from the miseries of life.[115]

Zeller's remarks evince his view that the Stoics and Epicureans were
merely an unfortunate interlude between the glories of Plato and
Aristotle and philosophy's rebirth in Plotinus. Even if we reject Zeller's
judgment of the value of Hellenistic philosophy, we must recognize
that there has been a subtle shift. The philosophical ideals of friendship articulated by the Stoics and the Epicureans are, respectively,
more austere and more limited than the ideals of friendship that we
find in the Classical period.

The Stoics

The Stoic school of philosophy takes its name from the customary
meeting-place of the companions and students of Zeno of Citium (344–
262 BCE) – the painted porch or stoa in Athens. The essential outlines
of Zeno's philosophy were little modified by his successors, Cleanthes
(d. 232 BCE) and Chrysippus (d. 206 BCE), though they were significantly
refined and strengthened especially by Chrysippus. Our evidence for
the Stoic school in the next two centuries is more fragmentary. Stoics
of this period include Poseidonius and Panaeteus (discussed in Chapter 2 with Cicero's treatise, "On Friendship"). We have an abundance
of writings from Romans who adopted Stoicism, including Seneca
(4 BCE–65 CE), who wrote in Latin, as well as Epictetus (c. 55–135 CE)
and Marcus Aurelius (121–180 CE), who wrote in Greek.

In order to appreciate the radical nature of the Stoic ideal of friendship, it is necessary to say a few things about their moral philosophy.
Here there are two really salient facts. First, the Stoics embraced whole-
heartedly one thesis that is often assigned to Socrates: that moral virtue is both necessary and sufficient for wellbeing or *eudaimonia*. Though
it is natural and rational for humans to *prefer* health to sickness, or
material sufficiency to grinding poverty, these things are strictly indifferent to the question of whether a person is *eudaimonos* or not. These
"preferred indifferents," as the Stoics called them, are merely the raw
material for virtuous living. We are happy only if we pursue these
indifferents virtuously. It is the *virtuous pursuit* of goals such as health,
wealth and security that matters – not their actual achievement. Since
the Stoics equate moral virtues such as justice, self-control and courage with rational understanding or *epistêmê*, our happiness depends
solely upon the perfection or full realization of our rational nature.

The Stoics were also strict causal determinists. All events come about in accordance with the law of nature, which they identified with divine presence that interpenetrates all things and brings about all things in a single, supremely rational narrative. This story is so good that the gods play it again and again. The cosmos is subject to periodic episodes in which all things are consumed in the fire that is Zeus. From the conflagration, the cycle begins again and plays itself out exactly as it did before. In this doctrine of eternal recurrence, the next cycle will include someone indistinguishable from you who will read this very page in the same circumstances in which you now find yourself. Whatever your future holds, you may be certain that it is an essential part in the maximally rational and best narrative for a world history. The wise, and thus fully rational, person positively welcomes all aspects of his role in this narrative. His wellbeing or *eudaimonia* depends not on what happens to him, but on how he plays the part that has been assigned to him. So he never wants anything unless he is fated to have it. Likewise, he never resents anything, for it was always fated to befall him. As Epictetus said:

> Men are not troubled by things but rather by the [mistaken] beliefs that they form about things. Death, for instance, is not something [objectively] terrible, else it would have appeared so to Socrates [who was wise enough to know what was objectively terrible]. Rather, the terror consists in the belief that death is terrible.[116]

This claim about what terror consists in takes us on to a second distinctive thesis of Stoic moral philosophy – their view about the *pathê*. A *pathos* is literally something that one undergoes – what happens to you. It is contrasted with *praxis*, or what one does. It is from this origin that we get the rather old-fashioned term that includes emotions – "the passions." The Stoic catalogue of passions includes many of the things that we call emotions, as well as some things that we might not. They include anger, fear, jealousy, pity and envy, but they also include intense sexual urges, confusion, annoyance and pleasure or delight (*hêdonê*). All these states share two important properties according to the Stoics. First, they are all judgments of a certain sort. Second, they are *mistaken* judgments: the person in whom reason is fully developed makes no mistakes, and hence suffers none of these passions. The fully wise person is thus *a-pathetikos*, but this does not mean that he is apathetic in the modern English sense. It simply means that in all aspects of life, he is the actor, not the patient. Indeed, the wise Stoic was strongly motivated – indeed, he was *only motivated* – to do that which justice, courage, wisdom and self-restraint demanded. Confronted with government corruption, he will denounce it fearlessly. That is, he will not merely master the fear of retribution and do what his conscience and reason tell him is right, he will not experience any fear to master. To feel fear would be to mistakenly believe that something other than one's own moral integrity and rationality matters to one's happiness – for instance, one's life or the lives of one's family. But this is simply false.

What becomes of friendship within a moral philosophy like this? The Stoics claimed that *real* friendship is actually *only* possible between such emotionless Stoic sages.[117] Moreover, this friendship is selfless and knows no boundaries. It is "a certain sort of community that pertains to *all things* that bear on life in which one treats one's friend as you would yourself."[118] It is possible only among sages because only they are of like mind (*homonoia*) about all these matters that bear on life.[119] It is also possible between such sages and the gods, who are equal in virtue to these extraordinary human beings.[120]

We can see that this will necessarily be a very austere ideal of friendship. The Stoics do not locate the basis of friendship in any human need. While other forms of association – affection for relatives and what the world calls "friendship" – arise naturally in us because we have not yet perfected our rational natures, when we become all that we can be, real friendship fills no gap in our lives. This is not to say that friends do not benefit the Stoic sage. In fact, the Stoics insist that every other wise person, whether known to him or not, benefits any particular sage in everything that he does.[121] Our sources do not explain the nature of this benefit, but it is not too difficult to speculate. The Stoic wise person unreservedly strives after only one thing: virtue and virtuous action. Because virtue is the perfection of our rational capacity, in another sense the wise person seeks only to be rational and to make the world around him conform to the normative dictates of reason. The god who orders the world so that it is intelligible to rational beings does this. The other Stoic sages who make their actions, and the human world in which they live, proceed rationally do the same. In a sense, all Stoic sages are "brothers in the Lord" – that is, in the all-pervasive reason of Zeus.[122] As such, their austere form of friendship with one another – a bond that consists simply in their total dedication to an ethical goal – can form a model for other people who share a similar overriding commitment to such a goal. It may be the austerity of comrades working for the revolution, or of brothers in Christ who seek the triumph of God's kingdom. The core of the friendship is not warm feelings of affection, but like-mindedness or *homonoia* – commitment to the cause.

In spite of the fact that it holds up an ideal that seems unachievable, the Stoic theory of friendship hovered in the background of the most influential of ancient works on friendship, Cicero's *De amicitia*. Like the Stoics, Cicero defines friendship in terms of complete like-mindedness (but Latin *concordia* rather than Greek *homonoia*) about all things. Like the Stoics, he insists that virtue produces friendship and sustains it and that friendship is not possible without it. Yet in his practical Roman manner, Cicero stresses that he means "virtue" in its ordinary sense – not in the high-flown sense of some philosophers – and he includes among the class of the virtuous those who are commonly regarded as such.[123] Arguably, Cicero's ideal of friendship is "stoicism lite."

Stoic ideas of political, as opposed to personal, friendship may have left their mark on Cicero as well. The founder of Stoicism, Zeno of Citium, wrote a work entitled the *Republic* – perhaps in opposition to Plato's work of the same name. The reports that we have of this now lost work make it difficult to determine with certainty just what was contained in it. One report that became well known, even if misleading, is that the Stoics agreed with Alexander the Great's ambition of establishing a world state.

> The Republic of Zeno which is the object of such amazement ... is aimed at this one main point – that we should not dwell in city-states or our own particular neighbourhoods, each one delineated by its own particular laws and norms, but rather we should think of all people as our fellow-citizens and neighbours, and there should be a single way of life and order (*kosmos*), just like herd-animals feeding together nourished by a common law (*nomos koinos*).[124]

It is difficult to square this apparent cosmopolitanism with another report that Zeno restricted the citizenship of his *Republic* to sages.

> Again, they criticise Zeno for setting up a city-state that has only the wise as friends, family members, and free people, so that it turns out that for the Stoics parents and children are enemies because they are not wise.[125]

While there have been various attempts to generate a consistent account of Zeno's political thought, it is the subsequent influence of the idea of such a world state that is important here.

In Zeno's cosmic city the herd of humanity is nurtured by a *common law*. This common law is the Stoic notion of correct reason, which is one and the same with Nature or the immanent presence of Zeus in everything. In *de Legibus*, Cicero identifies the origin of justice in this natural law, defining it in Stoic terms. We all fall under the rule of this law and, as such, there is a community that includes every human being. Now, if all people were fully rational, we would all live in accordance with this natural law. But while the mere fact that something is forbidden by natural law prevents those who are good and rational from doing it, things are otherwise with the wicked and irrational.[126] What is to be done about those who are wicked and irrational within our universal community? We surmise that Cicero thought that our fellow world citizens need to be brought to the light of reason by force if necessary. And what better, more noble force than that of Rome?

The sections of book 3 of Cicero's *Republic* subsequent to 3.33 are very fragmentary, but it appears as if this is building up to a justification of Rome's empire ("our people by defending their allies have gained dominion over the whole world").[127] Augustine's *De Civitate Dei* seems to be a discussion of this very section of Cicero's text and Augustine characterizes Cicero's argument in these terms: "this situation [Rome's dominion] is just, on the ground that servitude is in the interest of such men as the provincials, and that it is established for their benefit."[128] Because Rome acts in the interests of all those people who fall within its dominion, it is actually more accurately called a protectorate of the world than an empire.[129] The ground for this generous attitude of benevolence toward the peoples that Rome now rules is one and the same as the basis of friendship. In *De amicitia*, Cicero observes that the basis of the highest and most proper form of friendship is likeness in virtue. It is wholly natural for those who are good to be attracted to those who are good, and this is the font or source of friendship. But the general run of humanity is good. Hence the Romans, through their virtue, "are concerned to protect the universal community (*populos universos*) and to plan the optimum measures for their well-being."[130]

The question of a Stoic source for Cicero's justification of empire is a matter of dispute.[131] But it is entirely possible that some Roman intellectuals such as Cicero might have sought to justify Rome's empire on the basis of a Stoic account of political friendship. It is, of course, easy to be cynical about such justifications and to regard them as mere rationalizations – whether it be Roman *imperium* or the USA's recent friendly attempts to bring democracy to the Middle East. Some persons perhaps do sincerely believe that friendship for others may demand that we invade them. Right or wrong, this is a conception of friendship that has a long pedigree.

Epicureans and Other Hedonists

Apart from Stoicism, the other most significant philosophical school of thought in the Hellenistic period was Epicureanism. Epicurus was born on the island of Samos in 341 BCE to parents who were Athenian citizens. He learned philosophy from a teacher influenced by Democritus' ideas, and the philosophy that Epicurus later developed is akin to materialist Democritean atomism in many ways. After teaching on Lesbos and at Lampsacus, he moved to the city of philosophers, Athens, in 307. He purchased a plot of land and formed a community of like-minded friends called the Garden. Epicurus' ideas on friendship and the practices of friendship within the Garden present us with philosophical ideals of friendship between men and women – an idea that is not encountered in the overwhelmingly masculinist writings of other Greek philosophers. It is no coincidence that this is so, since the central plank of Epicurean moral philosophy was hedonism – the claim that pleasure is the sole good – and pleasure has a distinctly feminine association in ancient Greek thought.

To appreciate the context for the various hedonistic moral philosophies of the Hellenistic period, it is necessary to note a certain ancient Greek prejudice against pleasure. It was commonly thought to have a weakening and feminizing effect. Self-controlled men are able to resist the siren call of pleasures, while women are not.[132] While few would deny that pleasure is *a* good thing, it was a good thing thought to need careful watching, lest it undermine one's virtue, strength and rationality. Epicurus' specific form of hedonism was preceded by other variations on this theme whose philosophical fortunes well illustrate the problematic character of friendship.

The various anecdotes about Aristippus the Elder neatly illustrate the problems around hedonism and friendship – specifically cross-gender friendships. Aristippus was a wealthy bon vivant and companion of Socrates. Part of his fame in antiquity arises from his open association with courtesans (*hetairai*).[133] In this context, he seems to have attempted to challenge the idea that pleasure – and particularly sexual pleasure – is debilitating: "I *have* Laïs (a well-known and beautiful *hetaira* from Corinth) but I am not *had by* her: it is better to conquer pleasure than to abstain from it, but to do so without being used."[134] Aristippus' attitudes toward the offspring of these disciplined campaigns in gratification were equally challenging. In one anecdote he brutally denies paternity. In another, he responds to the claim that he has exposed one of his children with the rejoinder that we spit out phlegm, though it too is of our own making, since it is useless.[135]

Whether Aristippus' lifestyle was underwritten by a coherent philosophy is open to question. But attempts were made in the latter fourth and early third century BCE to provide one. The philosophers who undertook this project are known collectively as the Cyrenaics and they included Aristippus' grandson, Aristippus the Younger. The Cyrenaic school was distinctive in rejecting the idea that *eudaimonia* should be identified with the goal toward which all our efforts should be directed. This condition, you will recall, is not one of momentary enjoyment or satisfaction, but one of lifelong flourishing. The interesting philosophical question is, "What is it specifically?" The Cyrenaics answered that it was the sum total of individual pleasant episodes across a lifetime. But trying to plan so as to maximize one's lifetime pleasure is too much work. So instead they advocated the pursuit of the goal or *telos* that they identified with particular pleasures easily at hand. Why should we take such a seemingly irrational attitude toward our long-term enjoyment of pleasure? The Cyrenaics seem to have been ethically "short-sighted" because they were similarly epistemologically short-sighted: we don't really *know* anything apart from the way that things feel now, so we should make the most of the moment.

It is hard to know where friendship fits in this picture. One line of thought – probably that of Aristippus the Younger – was that we make friends for the sake of utility. Another Cyrenaic, Hegesias, argued that there simply was no such thing as gratitude, friendship or beneficence, since we do not choose to do things like this for their own sake, but only with an eye to our own utility.[136] The Cyrenaic philosopher Anniceris initially appears to cut the Gordian knot another way: by accounting something valuable other than pleasure. But, of course, if you are a hedonist that is just giving the game away, philosophically speaking.

Unsurprisingly, the Cyrenaic school did not last long. It faded from view in the internal disagreements of Aristippus, Hegesias, Anniceris and Theodorus. But its existence provided an important impetus for other hedonists to refine their views so as to avoid the unpalatable conclusions of the Cyrenaics. One way to see the philosophy of Epicurus is to think of it as substantially altering the Cyrenaics' notion of what pleasure consists in. For the Cyrenaics, pleasure is the *process* in which we get what we *want*. Epicurus posited that this sort of kinetic or process pleasure is subordinated to an even greater good: the *state* in which we *have* all that we really need. What do we really need? Certainly not all the things that we sometimes foolishly want. This is the basis for Epicurus' rejection of the voluptuary character of Cyrenaic hedonism:

> For it is not drinking bouts and continuous partying and enjoying boys and women, or consuming fish or the other dainties of an extravagant table, which produce the pleasant life, but sober calculation which searches out the reasons for every choice and act of avoidance and drives out the opinions which are the source of the greatest turmoil for men's souls.[137]

All we really need is the tranquillity that results from freedom from bodily pain (*aponia*) and freedom from mental distress (*ataraxia*). Freedom from bodily pain is easily enough understood. But Epicurus means something quite deep by freedom from mental disturbance or ataraxia. This condition arises when all that disturbs us has been expunged permanently. This requires us to rid ourselves of the fear of death, as well as fear of divine punishment. It also requires that we really learn and fully internalize the truth that "more is not better" and that "what is necessary is easy to find." This is the Epicurean *tetrapharmakon* or "four-fold cure." It turns out that we get psychologically cured with a little help from our friends.

Friendship plays a crucial role in securing freedom from pain and anxiety, according to Epicurus. This is so along a variety of dimensions. First, friendship provides us with the sort of security that can prevent physical pains associated with hunger and lack of shelter. Equally important, however, is the confidence that we may have of such support, for this reduces mental anxiety. But perhaps most important is the relationship between philosophy and friendship.

It is philosophy that will cure us of the groundless fears that prevent us from achieving *ataraxia*. But *philosophizing* and coming *to really absorb* the truth is a pursuit that we undertake among friends. After all, it is one thing to rehearse the arguments until one can quote them.[138] But it is quite another to make them second nature so that they banish fears, like the fear of death, that disturb our tranquillity.[139]

Philosophical therapy – the internalization of philosophical truth – requires "frank speech" (*parrhêsia*) and this, in turn, presupposes friendship. The fragmentary remains of *On Frank Criticism* by the Epicurean Philodemus (c. 110–35 BCE) are explicit about the therapeutic role of candour. But unlike the relation between therapist and patient in our day, Philodemus regards this as a relation among friends.[140]

The Garden of Epicurus was such a community of friends, as were other Epicurean communities such as that at the villa of the papyri in Herculaneum.[141] The evidence is difficult but a consensus is emerging that the friendly relations – particularly between men and women within Epicurean communities – may have been very different from those in the surrounding social context. We should indeed think of them as deliberately separated from their surrounding cities. Epicurus advised a withdrawal from public life to the extent that this was possible. The maxim "live unknown" was entirely counter-cultural for both the Greeks and the Romans who regarded the space of public life as the place where one found a real man.[142] This deliberate abandonment marked out Epicureans for abuse as "girly men."[143] Critics of Epicureanism claimed the presence of several *hetairai* among the first generation of Epicureans. While Diogenes Laertius treated this as a slander, he thinks the obvious intent is to show that the male Epicureans in the Garden kept these loose women around as their sexual playthings. But the slander might have gone deeper, and this is revealed by some of those who engage in it. In Cicero's *On the Nature of the Gods*, the sceptic's spokesman, Cotta, dismisses the Epicurean views of Leontion, calling her "a little prostitute" (*meretricula*) who nonetheless writes fine Attic prose. It is presumably the fact that she is writing philosophy *at all* that leads him to add: "such was the permissiveness (*licentiae*) that prevailed in Epicurus' household."[144] Not only did Epicureans retreat from the public, masculine space of political life – in the privacy of their communities they permitted women to write philosophy!

Evidence such as Leonteon's compositions led Jane Snyder to a very optimistic assessment of class and gender relations in Epicurean communities.

> The members of the Garden included not only full Athenian citizens like Epicurus himself but also several women and slaves, who, within the context of Athenian society at large, enjoyed few legal rights or privileges. Within the enclosure of the Garden, however, all members of the group – male and female, slave and free

– were entitled to the benefits and responsibilities of the Epicurean school.[145]

Snyder connects this real-life practice with a theoretical view in which neither wealth nor fame matters with respect to the achievement of tranquillity. Indeed, one might add that Epicureanism regards great wealth or repute as positive dangers to the realization of their negative hedonic ideal.

The writings of Epicurus and other Epicureans were not preserved and studied by subsequent Christian culture in Europe, so the Epicurean ideals of friendship are not as obvious in the discourse of friendship as those of, say, Aristotle. Indeed, it might be thought that a specifically Christian culture would be least influenced by Epicureanism among all the Greek schools of philosophy. After all, the Epicureans utterly deny the possibility of an afterlife, as well as the existence of a personal god who exercises divine providence. And for this they came in for abuse in a text that eventually made its way into the canonical New Testament (Acts 17:32). But, in fact, there are striking parallels between early Christian communities and the community of the Epicurean Garden. First, both were communities that deliberately set themselves apart from the wider Greco-Roman culture. Both were dismissive of the "high culture" of the Greek tradition.[146] In each case the members of the community sought salvation through the imitation[147] of someone whom they regarded as both a man and a divinity – or perhaps in the case of the Epicureans a man who had been divinized.[148] Members of the community utilized the technique of frank speech among friends in order to help one another in emulation of their chosen sage.[149] And in general, Christians adopted many of the techniques of Epicurean therapeutic philosophy, though they gave them quite different content.[150] One final parallel is worth noting. In each case the question of whether women enjoyed a very different version of cross-gender friendship is a matter of current scholarly dispute.[151] The ideal of a community of friends built around the goal of achieving mental or spiritual health and committed to benefiting one another in their progress toward a kind of counter-cultural conception of salvation is one that occurs again and again in Western intellectual life. It is Epicurean, even if it does not have Epicurus' name attached to it.

Plutarch on Friendship

We close out the Hellenistic era with a brief survey of the advice on *philia* found in the philosophical works of Plutarch of Chaeronia (45–120 CE). Plutarch offers us several things that we do not find in the literary remains of other philosophers. First, he considers friendship between husbands and wives in a fairly positive light. He also reflects on familial *philia* and, in particular, friendship between brothers. Here too, Plutarch gives the priority to familial relations over acquired companion friendships, and this sets him at odds with many earlier philosophers. In addition, he deals with some problems about friendship that were felt keenly in later writers. Is there a trade-off between the *number* of friends that one may have and the *quality* of the friendships? Even more importantly, how does one discern the difference between a friend and one who simply flatters you in order to curry favour?

In considering these questions, Plutarch feels free to draw on a number of different philosophical traditions, though he is himself a Platonist of sorts. As a result, he is interesting in the context of antiquity for his synthetic efforts. There is also the question of Plutarch's subsequent influence. He is not now regarded by philosophers as the original Platonist thinker that, for example, Plotinus was. But the judgment of earlier centuries may have been quite different.

Few ancient authors, save perhaps Cicero, garnered as much attention and admiration as representatives of the glories of Classical learning. What secured Plutarch this fame was not his philosophical essays, but rather his biographical works. We have forty-four "Parallel Lives" that compare the lives and moral characters of famous Greeks and Romans. These essays did not merely aim to record the important events in the lives of, say, Cicero and Demosthenes – though doubtless telling the stories of famous men was sufficient to attract the attention of many readers. Rather, Plutarch used these *Lives* as the basis for reflection on how one ought to live and on the importance of up-bringing in determining the sorts of characters men have. Needless to say, friendship figures frequently in the *Lives*. While Plutarch's *Lives* dominated in translations into Latin and other modern languages in the fourteenth–fifteenth centuries, his moral essays or *Moralia* were edited by Erasmus in 1509. Erasmus also translated a number of these essays, including a version of Plutarch's essay on friends and flatterers that he dedicated to Henry VIII in 1513. The influence of Plutarch's thoughts on friendship is, we think, a topic that would repay more careful study. The following summary only touches the high points.

Echoing the Xenophontic Socrates, Plutarch condemns "the fashion nowadays, by which many get the name friend by drinking a single glass together, or by playing ball or gambling together, or by spending a night under the same roof, and so pick up a friendship from inn, gymnasium, or market-place."[152] Friendship is morally serious business and Plutarch warns that we ought not to become friends with such "chance acquaintances." Rather, we should adopt people as friends "only after spending a long time passing judgment upon them." But what is it about a person that we ought to judge before we can make him a friend? The answer can be derived from Plutarch's characterization of true friendship: "True friendship seeks after three things above all else: virtue as a good thing, intimacy as a pleasant thing, and usefulness as a necessary thing."[153] Thus, before accepting a man as a friend we must judge that he is virtuous, and useful, and that intimacy with him is possible.

Intimacy, for Plutarch, is important because (as the above quote suggests) intimacy brings pleasure. And Plutarch emphasizes the pleasure of friendship: "friendship is the most pleasant thing in the world ... nothing else gives greater delight."[154] But, while pleasure is an important part of friendship, it is not the "final aim" (*telos*) of friendship. Thus, friendships are not always pleasant. It is the flatterer who always aims at pleasure, not the friend. For a friend's task is to emend a friend's ways when necessary, preserving or restoring his moral health. Like a physician, then, at times one will have to hurt a friend. But "one ought to hurt a friend only to help him; and ought not by hurting him to kill the friendship, but to use the stinging word as a medicine which restores and preserves [moral] health in that to which it is applied." Thus "the friend, by doing always what he ought to do, is often times agreeable and often times disagreeable." Notice that in the above quote it is by means of "the stinging word of medicine" that one achieves his end of emending a friend's ways. But not just any words can act as medicine. The words must be frank. This is why Plutarch tells us that "frankness of speech ... is the language of friendship."[155]

It is because a friend's task is to restore and to preserve a friend's moral health that Plutarch makes friendship seek after virtue. For it is only a virtuous man who can recognize when a friend's moral health is in danger and knows what must be done to rescue the friend. In addition, this task is the main way in which friendship is useful for Plutarch. Thus, Plutarch calls virtue the most important part of true friendship. But friends are useful for other reasons. They provide "refuge and protection." They help each other "in their counsels, their public life, their ambitions ... their dispensing of hospitality." Further, one will "join [a friend] ... on a voyage to foreign parts ... help him in defending a suit ... sit with him as judge ... help him in managing his buying and selling ... help him to celebrate his wedding ... mourn with him at a funeral." Friendship involves sharing in a friend's "anxieties, preoccupations, and troubles."[156]

Plutarch stresses that services provided by a friend must be repaid. This is why Plutarch thinks that "*mutual* acts of kindness" hold friendships together.[157] It is also the reason that Plutarch says that we should be friends "only with those who are qualified to keep up the same participation, that is to say, those who are able, in a like manner, to love and participate."[158] This is one more thing, then, that one must look for when judging whether or not to make another a friend.

It is clear that friendship is hard work according to Plutarch – which is one reason that Plutarch thinks that *poluphilia* or having many friends is impossible. Plutarch knows that friendship has its lighter moments: "[T]here are times when friends enjoy together jest and food and wine, and indeed even mirth and nonsense." But, while Plutarch welcomes these lighter moments, he calls them "a sort of spice for the noble and serious" side of friendship.[159]

One of the consequences of friendship is enmity, "for enmities follow upon close friendships, inasmuch as it is impossible for a friend not to share his friend's wrongs or disrepute or disfavour." Another consequence of friendship is complete likeness: "friendships seek to effect a thorough-going likeness in characters, feelings, language, pursuits, and dispositions."[160] This is not the same as imitation: "I have no use for a friend that shifts about just as I do and nods assent just as I do (for my shadow better performs that function)." Imitation is characteristic of the flatterer. It is he who changes his likes and dislikes in order to endear himself to the object of his flattery. Thus "the flatterer is nowhere constant." By contrast, "the true friend is neither an imitator of everything, nor ready to commend everything, but only the best things."[161] It is by commending the best things that our friend preserves and restores our moral health.[162]

We began this section by noting that for Plutarch friendship has its origin in judgment. But we need to add that for Plutarch the friendships that depend on judgment are inferior to "that first friendship which Nature has implanted in children towards parents and in brothers towards brothers." All other, non-familial, friendships "are in reality shadows and imitations and images" of this "first friendship."[163] So, while "we must not grow to love those not of our blood and then judge them, but judge them first and love them later,"[164] this is not so in the case of those of our blood (in other words, family). Here, *philia* ought not to depend on judgment, but rather on the "principle of love" (*archê tês philias*) that has been implanted by nature.[165]

The fact that familial *philia* is natural does not mean that for Plutarch this *philia* automatically and inevitably springs up between members of a family. That this is so is clear from Plutarch's detailed discussion of one form of familial *philia*, namely that between brothers. *On Brotherly Love* is filled with advice on what brothers should do in order to ensure that *philia* is created and preserved between them. Such advice is necessary because "brotherly love is as rare in our day as brotherly hatred was among the men of old ... all men today, when they encounter brothers who are good to each other, wonder at them."[166]

While Plutarch makes friendship between brothers the focus of his attention – perhaps because "through the concord of brothers family and household are sound and flourish"[167] and if the household were sound then the state would be sound[168] – we should not leave the topic of familial *philia* without noting what Plutarch has to say about marital *philia*:

> No greater pleasure comes from others, no more continuous services are due to others; no other friendship possesses so notable and enviable an element of esteem as when "a man and woman dwell in their house together, united in mind."[169]

This *philia* between husband and wife, Plutarch tells us, is the result of sex, for sex

> is like a joint participation in some great holy ritual (*hierôn megalôn koinônêmata*). The pleasure itself is not important. It is the respect and grace and contentment with each other and the confidence that springs from this [that produces marital *philia*].[170]

This friendship between husband and wife for Plutarch does not seem to be one between equals, and it is possible that this fact reflects the way in which the Greeks and Romans took the sexual roles of men and women to be indicative of relations of subordination. Plutarch says that it is always "the husband's leadership and preferences" that dominate in a marriage and "a wife ought not to make friends of her own, but enjoy her husband's friends in common with him," for the things of friends were held in common.[171]

We have already noted Plutarch's advice in *Precepts of Statecraft* to Greek politicians living under Roman rule that they should be friends of the Romans. But it was not only the Romans with whom the Greek politician had to deal. He also had to deal with the inhabitants of his own city. In *Precepts of Statecraft* Plutarch gives politicians advice on this topic. In this context, the subject of friendship arises once more.

"Friends," Plutarch says, "are the living and thinking tools of the statesman."[172] (Note that Aristotle describes slaves in just the same manner – they are automated tools.)[173] Thus a politician should not, like Cleon, renounce all his friendships. Rather, he should surround himself with friends "who will aid him and share his enthusiasm for what is noble." To do this the politician must "choose friends whose convictions are like his own," namely, virtuous and noble. Plutarch adds that it is perfectly permissible for a politician to do favours for his friends. This does not mean that he should grant "base and absurd requests" that outrage the general public. But there are "favours [a politician can grant his friends] which arouse no ill-will, such as aiding a friend to gain office, putting into his hands some honourable administrative function or some friendly foreign mission." A politician can also help a friend to acquire money without offending the public: "Hand over to one friend a case at law which will bring in a good fee as advocate in a just cause, to another introduce a rich man who needs legal oversight and protection, and help another to get some profitable contract or lease."[174] It would seem that then, as now, one can give political mates a position as ambassador to Ruritania or a lucrative consultancy.

Given his views on these political friendships, it is small wonder that Plutarch thought that friendships among family members were primary and natural. Plutarch stands out among the ancient Greek philosophers whom we have considered thus far as something rather like an exponent of "family values." His attitudes toward women are – relative to his time and place – somewhat enlightened. (Plutarch is also the author of a short essay, *The Brave Deeds of Women*, as well as essays arguing for the rationality of animals and the moral wrongness of eating meat.)[175] If it is less clear what philosophical ideal of the good life his views on friendship are meant to promote, perhaps that is because his idea of happiness is as much a laundry list as our own.

Pythagorean and Neoplatonist Friendship

We now turn to a discussion of Pythagorean views on friendship. Notionally, this takes us back in time, since Pythagoras (c. mid-sixth century BCE) lived before Socrates, Plato and Aristotle. However, the actual Pythagoras and the community of friends around him are less important for the history of Western thought than the body of literature that was composed much later and attributed to him and his fellows. This includes not only the Pythagorean forgeries of the Hellenistic period but also the works on Pythagoras and Pythagoreanism by Neoplatonists such as Porphyry (c. 232–304 CE) and Iamblichus (c. 242–347 CE).[176] These Neoplatonist writers sought to portray Platonism as in agreement with their understanding of Pythagoreanism, as well as with their understanding of religious and magical traditions in Orphism[177] and the Chaldean Oracles. The result was an attempt to synthesize the great works of ancient Greek culture into an integrated philosophical and religious system. The high point of this synthetic enterprise is the work of Proclus (411–85 CE), who was the brightest among the last heads of Plato's Academy before the school was closed in 529 by the Christians, who regarded it as a hotbed of paganism.

What is important for our purposes is the notion of friendship based around initiation into this system, as well as the notion of friendship with the gods that results from a correct understanding of the truths of genuinely divine messengers like Plato, Pythagoras and Orpheus.

Pythagoreanism, and subsequently Neoplatonism, finds deep cosmological and moral significance in mathematical facts. This tendency is well illustrated in the definition of friendship attributed to Pythagoras by Iamblichus and its connection with "friendly numbers." Two numbers are friends to one another when each is the sum of the proper divisors of the other. Thus 220 and 284 are friends to one another since the proper divisors of 220 are 1, 2, 4, 5, 10, 11, 20, 22, 44, 55 and 110. These numbers sum to 284. Similarly, the proper divisors of 284 (1, 2, 4, 71 and 142) sum to 220.[178] This mathematical fact was supposed to vindicate Pythagoras' response to the question, "What is a friend?" – "Another me."[179] Since it is customary to call the factors of a number its "parts," there is a certain sense in which 220 is another way of *being* 284, and vice versa.

Of course, you need to know some mathematics to get the point! Much of the wisdom of Pythagoreanism is similarly encoded in gnomic sayings, called *akousmata* ("things heard") or *symbola* (symbols or passwords). It is said that the content of these sayings in the initial

Pythagorean communities of the sixth and fifth centuries BCE were kept secret. Various admonitions purporting to be of Pythagorean origin find their way into Aristotle, so the secret was not too long in getting out. The *interpretation* of these symbols, however, was another matter.

The Pythagoreans proposed that there was a specific form of friendship – Pythagorean friendship – shared among those who understood the deep content of this philosophical tradition.

> It is said that even when they did not know one another, the Pythagoreans tried to do friendly deeds on behalf of those they had never seen before, whenever they received a *sure sign* that they shared the same doctrines.[180]

Iamblichus illustrates the extent of this Pythagorean friendship based on shared knowledge with the following story: a Pythagorean fell ill on a journey and took refuge in an inn along the road. The keeper of the inn took pity on him and gave him all that he needed, though the Pythagorean could not pay. Feeling that his end was near, the Pythagorean wrote a *symbolon* on a tablet and told the innkeeper that in the event of his death he was to hang the tablet by the road. Much later another Pythagorean travelling the road saw the *symbolon*, and upon recognizing it, made enquiries about how it came to be there. The innkeeper received what was owed many times over. The story illustrates the familiar principle that one should help friends. But here the friendship is based *solely on membership in a group defined by a shared, esoteric knowledge.*

This is an elitist ideal of friendship that actually includes the already elitist friendship of the virtuous to the virtuous.[181] The comprehension of Pythagorean teachings is supposed to travel hand in hand with moral virtue. The Neoplatonists, who assimilated much of the Pythagorean way of life into their philosophy, supposed that there are a variety of levels of moral virtue. The most basic are those virtues that permit us to treat our fellows well.[182] The highest forms of virtue enable us to become like gods. This is the goal of living, according to the Neoplatonists – to return to the divine from which all souls descend. Since it is proverbial that "like is friend to like," the person who transforms his character and intellect to resemble the gods is a friend to the gods.[183]

In the Neoplatonic and neo-Pythagorean synthesis, the activity of making oneself like, and thus united to, the gods was not purely by study or meditation. Iamblichus argued that *theurgy* played an important role in reuniting the soul of the philosopher with the divine. Theurgy was a form of worship that combined esoteric knowledge, some of it mathematical in character, with ritual magic. Its object was not that of ordinary magic – control of the weather or of one's lover or whatever – but rather the specific goal of uniting the practitioner with various divinities. The period of Constantine's reign (306–337 CE) was one in which there was a deep fear of the black arts, and correspondingly severe laws for sorcery. Christian authorities were probably not overly sensitive to distinctions between normal magic and theurgy. This meant that the display of "sure signs of shared doctrine" that might initiate friendships among Neoplatonists was much more delicate. This may be illustrated by the events that initiated the lifelong friendship between Syrianus and Proclus.

When Proclus came to Athens to study at the Academy, he was met by a fellow countryman from Lycia at the port – a paradigmatic example of *philia* among people based on their common origin. His friend took him to his initial meeting with Syrianus, who was then head of the Academy. As Proclus talked with Syrianus and his companion Lachares, the sun set and the moon appeared for the first time in its new cycle. Syrianus wanted to send the young men away in order that he and Lachares might worship the lunar goddess by themselves. But when Proclus saw the moon he took off his sandals in front of these strangers and greeted the god.[184] Both were struck by Proclus' *parrhêsia* – his frankness of speech and action – in doing so. Proclus' willingness to openly display his pagan piety contrasts with their initial desire to rid themselves of the stranger so that they might worship in private. This devotion to the gods, plus Proclus' native philosophical talent, so endeared him to Syrianus that they became the closest *philoi* – so close that he lived in Syrianus' house, calling him "father." Upon his death, Proclus was buried in the same tomb as his "father" Syrianus on the hill of Lycabettus.

Proclus' ideas on metaphysics, esoteric knowledge, love and friendship, and the ascent of the soul back to the divine had a dramatic impact on subsequent Christian mysticism, though not under Proclus' own name. First, a thinly veiled version of Proclus' philosophy was presented as the work of Dionysius the Aeropagite – the philosopher whom Paul converts in Acts 17. This attribution was widely accepted up through the late medieval period. The most influential translator and interpreter of ancient Platonism to the Italian Renaissance, Marsilio

Ficino (1433–1499), read Plato's works with Proclus' commentaries at his side.

Pythagorean and Neoplatonic traditions concerning friendship thus present us with an ancient Greek ideal of this relationship that has considerable significance for the world to come. It is universal in the sense that it is grounded in shared, esoteric teaching rather than in membership in a particular *polis* or other social setting. The display of the proper signs indicating that one shares in the esoteric teaching becomes a means of securing the benefits of friendship. These are features that still characterize friendship groups today – the secret hand-shake, the Rosacrucian symbol, whatever it might be.

Conclusion

The philosophers of ancient Greece left to subsequent European high culture a variety of ideals of friendship. These ideals govern not only what we moderns would call companion friendship, but also relations with blood relatives, fellow citizens and even God. They are ideals in the sense that they are explicitly normative: they say what friendships should be like, what they should be based on and who may genuinely be friends. These ideals are not plucked from thin air. Rather, they depend on competing philosophical theories about the nature of men and women, society and even the nature of the divine. These philo-sophical theories run the gamut from a picture of human beings as pleasure-seeking, material and mortal congeries of atoms (the Epicu-reans) to the picture of humanity as fallen souls temporarily and unfortunately lodged in bodies, hungering for a return to their native star above (the Neoplatonists). Each of these philosophical self-conceptions has been attractive to different people at different times, and they have carried along with them associated ideals of friendship.

The Greek philosophical ideals of friendship are ideal in another way too: they do not concede much to human frailty and they do not let concerns about practical implementation stand in the way of a consistent and intellectually attractive theory. As we shall see in sub-sequent chapters, much of the intellectual discussion of friendship that follows is dominated by the desire to harvest from Greek philosophy a conception of friendship that works – one that is an appropriate conception of friendship for the weak, fallible and self-interested people that we actually are most of the time.

We have situated this philosophical discourse on friendship in two different political contexts – the city-states of the Classical period and the Hellenistic kingdoms. The most important Roman philosophical voice on friendship speaks from a political context that is an odd mix of these two. Marcus Tullius Cicero (106–43 BCE) saw the official demise of the Roman Republic, the death of Julius Caesar and the beginnings of the wars that gave Rome its succession of emperors. Even though the Roman Republic was no city-state but rather a mighty empire like the Hellenistic kingdoms, it was nonetheless one with the vestigial form of a limited democracy. Cicero was a man who was well versed in Greek philosophical writings but also a Roman with practical Roman sensibilities. It is his little essay on friendship, *Laelius de Amicitia*, that dominated learned Latinate discussions of friendship in Western Europe. In this treatise, Cicero begins the task of making the Stoic ideals of friendship more down to earth. But Cicero was not only a theorist of the distinctively political form of friendship that existed among men of the late Roman Republic, he was an active participant as well, as his collection of letters to his friends (*Epistulae ad familiares*) makes clear. Cicero's treatise and the rediscovery of his letters by Petrarch in the early fourteenth century provide the thematic boundaries for our next chapters.

Notes

1. Kathy Eden, "'Between Friends All Is Common': The Erasmian Adage and Tradition," *Journal of the History of Ideas* 59.3 (1998), pp. 405–19.

2. Henry Guerlac, "Amicus Plato and Other Friends," *Journal of the History of Ideas* 39.4 (1978), pp. 627–33.

3. K. Dover, *Greek Popular Morality in the Time of Plato and Aristotle* (Oxford: Oxford University Press, 1974), p. 226.

4. Hesiod, *Works and Days* (trans. H. G. Evelyn-White; Loeb Classical Library; Cambridge, MA: Harvard University Press, 1936), p. 353; Pindar, Pythian II.83–85, in *Odes* (trans. J. Sandys; Loeb Classical Library; Cambridge, MA: Harvard University Press, 1937); Lysias, "For the Soldier" §20, *Orations* (trans. W. R. M. Lamb; Loeb Classical Library; Cambridge, MA: Harvard University Press, 1930); Plato, *Republic* 332a–b (*Rep.*), in *Complete Works* (ed. J. Cooper; Indianapolis: Hackett Publishing, 1997).

5. Lynnette Mitchell, *Greeks Bearing Gifts: The Public Use of Private Relationships in the Greek World, 435–323 BC* (Cambridge: Cambridge University Press, 1997), p. 15.

6. Mary Whitlock Blundell adds: "This may be one of the points on which the moralizing ideal diverges furthest from ordinary practice." *Helping Friends and*

Harming Enemies: A Study in Sophocles and Greek Ethics (Cambridge: Cambridge University Press, 1989), p. 35. As an illustration of Blundell's point consider the following from a distinctly non-moralizing, forensic context: "I therefore willingly resign your friendship, since, by Heaven, I cannot see what penalty I shall suffer by not associating with you; for neither did my association with you bring me benefit" (Lysias, Accusation of Calumny against Fellow-Members of a Society §18 in *Orations*).

7. Aristotle, *Ethica Nicomachea* 1167b2–3, *Nichomachean Ethics: Translated with Introduction, Notes and Glossary* (trans. T. Irwin; Indianapolis: Hackett Publishing, 2nd edn, 1999), hereafter *NE*.

8. Homer, *Iliad* 13.625.

9. Naturally guest-friendships could evolve to become more like what we would call companion-friendships, and the Greeks were well able to note these transitions: "Thrasyllus, the father of the testor, had inherited nothing from his parents; but having become the guest-friend of Polemaenetus, the soothsayer, he became so intimate (*oikeiôs*) with him that Polemaenetus at his death left to him his books on divination and gave him a portion of the property which is now in question" (Isocrates, "Aegineticus" §5, in *Orations* [trans. George Norlin; 3 vols; Loeb Classical Library; Cambridge, MA: Harvard University Press, 1928–45]).

10. See Mitchell, *Greeks Bearing Gifts*, esp. pp. 131–33. According to Plato, friendship between Greeks and barbarians was impossible. The two are "by nature enemies" (*Rep.* 470c). For Plato, barbarians were fit for nothing but slavery. However, there is evidence that Athenian citizens entered into relations of friendship with their slaves. See Lin Foxhall, "The Politics of Affection: Emotional Attachments in Athenian Society," in Paul Cartledge, Paul Millett and Sitta von Reden (eds), *Kosmos: Essays in Order, Conflict and Community in Classical Athens* (Cambridge: Cambridge University Press, 1998), pp. 52–67 at p. 62. This, Foxhall notes, suggests a "disjunction" between the ideal and reality.

11. Cf. Aristotle, *NE*, 1160a9, ff.

12. Aristotle, *NE*, 1159b30.

13. Thucydides, II. 40.4, in *Thucydides on Justice, Power and Human Naure – Selections from the History of Peloponnesian War* (trans. Paul Woodruff; Indianapolis: Hackett Publishing, 1993).

14. Dover, *Greek Popular Morality*, p. 181; Lysias, "On the Murder of Eratosthenes" §15–16 in *Orations*.

15. Lysias, "Against Diogeiton" §22, in *Orations*.

16. David Konstan, "Greek Friendship," *American Journal of Philology* 117 (1906), pp. 71–94, has argued that the ancient Greeks did distinguish linguistically between loving relationships and friendships. The adjective *philos* can modify an object or person and may then be read passively as "dear so and so" or "beloved uncle." (It can also be read actively as in *philo-sophos* – loving wisdom.) The adjective is related to the noun *philein* – to love – and the abstract term *philia* is derived, in turn, from the adjective. Finally, the adjective with a definite article

can be translated as the noun: *oi philoi* – the friends; *ho philos* – the friend. It can also appear without the definite article: *philoi* – friends. Konstan argues that Greek usage typically singled out the relationship we moderns call companion friendship with the use of the definite article, so the Greeks did not really see kinship and companion-friendship as relationships on a continuum and even had a linguistic means of conveniently distinguishing between them.

This is not the place to take up such a complex issue, but we are not convinced by Konstan's case. For the opposing view that the Greeks did regard kinship relations as on a par with other friendly relations see Blundell, *Helping Friends and Harming Enemies*, pp. 39–43, 46 and Mitchell, *Greeks Bearing Gifts*, pp. 10–11.

17. Demosthenes, "Against Aristocrates" §56, in *Meidias, Androtion, Aristocreates, Timocrates, Aristogeiton*, vol. 3 of *Demosthenes* (trans. J. H. Vince *et al.*; 7 vols; Loeb Classical Library; Cambridge, MA: Harvard University Press, 1926–49); Francisco Gonzales, "Socrates on Loving One's Own: A Traditional Conception of ΦΙΛΙΑ Radically Transformed," *Classical Philology* 95 (2000), pp. 379–98.

18. Mitchell, *Greeks Bearing Gifts*, pp. 18–21.

19. Plato, *Seventh Epistle* 325c–d.

20. Lynette G. Mitchell, "New for Old: Friendship Networks in Athenian Politics," *Greece & Rome* 43 (1996), pp. 10–21 at p. 11. Also W. Robert Connor, *The New Politicians of Fifth-Century Athens* (Princeton: Princeton University Press, 1971), p. 41: "Political groups in fifth century Athens were largely groups of *philoi*."

21. Connor, *New Politicians*, pp. 9–29.

22. This principle was active, not only in daily life, but in political life too. See Connor, *New Politicians*, pp. 41–43.

23. One could help a friend in litigation by appearing as a witness or an advocate on his behalf, by suppressing evidence, by bribing officials. See George Miller Calhoun, *Athenian Clubs in Politics and Litigation* (New York: Burt Franklin, 1970, rpt), pp. 40–96. In the political realm, "[friends] could supply a claque and the support needed to form a majority [in the Assembly]. They could heckle other speakers and sometimes provide a politician with a spokesman in the Council (the *boulē*) when he himself was not a member ... Furthermore, a friend who was a politician could help a citizen gain office, put into his hands an administrative or military task that would bring him repute, [or] arrange some ambassadorial junket ... The pattern is familiar enough today and was no less common in antiquity (Connor, *New Politicians*, p. 36.) Calhoun (*Athenian Clubs*, pp. 107–11) notes a further way that friends could be useful in the political realm – namely, by assassinating political opponents.

24. Connor, *New Politicians*, p. 77: "It is not likely that the most poor people were fully included in the system of friendship ties which ... constituted the basic pattern of Athenian politics." See also pp. 11–12, 29, 88, 134. Connor notes that the poor citizens of Athens "constituted a group outside the centers of real power" (p. 88). Their "influence ... was disproportionately small" (p. 89) and it is very

likely that they "look[ed] upon existing friendship groups with some suspicion" (p. 88).

25. Herodotus 5.66, *Histories* (trans. A. D. Godley; 4 vols; Loeb Classical Library; Cambridge, MA: Harvard University Press, 1921–25). Connor, *New Politicians*, pp. 90–91.

26. Connor, *New Politicians*, pp. 87–136.

27. Plutarch, *Pericles* 7.5, and *Moralia* 806F, in Plutarch of Chaeronia, *Moralia* (trans. F. C. Babbit *et al.*; 16 vols; Loeb Classical Library; Cambridge, MA: Harvard University Press, 1927–76); Connor, *New Politicians*, pp. 91–94, 119–22.

28. Connor, *New Politicians*, p. 135 tells us that the two types of political friendship "represent systems of politics that actually existed and competed over a long period of time."

29. Connor, *New Politicians*, p. 91; see also pp. 19–22. Mitchell (*Greeks Bearing Gifts*, p. 42) calls the same practice "patronage" and adds: "In Greece patronage belongs to the repertoire of *philia* relationships" (p. 42, n. 6). Connor, by contrast, denies the existence of patronage in Greece: *New Politicians*, p. 18

30. Mitchell, "New for Old," p. 15.

31. Mitchell, "New for Old," pp. 16–19.

32. Cf. Isocrates, "On the Peace" §121, in *Orations*.

33. Thucydides, *History of the Peloponnesian War* III 81–82 (trans. Rex Warner; Harmondsworth and New York: Penguin, 1954), trans. after Rex Warner with slight emendations.

34. M. M. Austin, "Economy and Society," in D. M. Lewis, J. Boardman, S. Hornblower, M. Ostwald (eds), *The Cambridge Ancient History*, vol. VI, *The Fourth Century* (Cambridge: Cambridge University Press, 2nd edn, 1994), pp. 527–64, at pp. 530–31. G. E. M. de Ste Croix, *Class Struggle in the Ancient World* (Ithaca: Cornell University Press, 1981), p. 296: "The most sanguinary of the many fourth-century outbreaks of *stasis* was the *skytalismos* at Argos in 370, when 1200–1500 of the upper class were said to have been massacred by the *demos*."

35. Austin, "Economy and Society," p. 530.

36. Aristotle, *NE* 1167b2, 1167a22–b16.

37. Plato, *Rep.* 469b–471c; Isocrates, *Antidosis* §77, "Panathenaicus" §13, in *Orations*; *Gorgias* (Philostratus, *Lives of the Sophists* §493 [trans. W. C. Wright; Loeb Classical Library; Cambridge, MA: Harvard University Press, 1921]).

38. Andrew Erskine, *The Hellenistic Stoa: Political Thought and Action* (Ithaca: Cornell University Press, 1990), p. 59.

39. William C. West, "Hellenic Homonoia and the New Decree from Plataea," *Greek, Roman, and Byzantine Studies* 18 (1977), pp. 307–19 at p. 317.

40. It is a live question among scholars whether *Alcibiades* I is genuinely a work of Plato's. However, it is thought to be so by the Neoplatonists and thus has formed part of the Platonic canon from very early on. Since our concern is with the reception of various Classical ideals of friendship, the question of the dialogue's

authorship is not crucial: it is enough that it has long been taken to be a work of Plato and a source for what Socrates thinks.

41. The nature of these "schools" has been the subject of debate. For Plato's Academy the most recent work is John Dillon, *The Heirs of Plato* (Oxford: Oxford University Press, 2003). For Aristotle's Lyceum, see J. Lynch, *The School of Aristotle* (Berkeley, CA: University of California Press, 1972).

42. One story from antiquity – found in Strabo, *Geography* 13.1.54 (trans. H. L. Jones; 8 vols; Loeb Classical Library; Cambridge, MA: Harvard University Press, 1930–37) – says that on his death, Theophrastus inherited "Aristotle's books." They then passed to Theophrastus' nephew, Neleus, who hid the works in a cave in Scepsis in present-day Turkey. They were discovered two centuries later, greatly decayed. They were taken to Athens and then on to Rome where the peripatetic philosopher Andronicus prepared an edition.

43. Plato, *Lysis* 210c–d in *Complete Works*.

44. *NE* 1166a2–3; *NE* 1157b33–36: "Moreover, in loving their friend they love what is good for themselves; for when a good person becomes a friend he becomes good for his friend. Each of them loves what is good for him, and repays in equal measure the wish and pleasantness of his friend."

45. *Lysis* 214b–d.

46. Xenophon, *Memorabilia* II.6.19–20 (trans. E. C. Marchant; Loeb Classical Library; Cambridge, MA: Harvard University Press, 1923).

47. *Crito* 49b–e.

48. *Laws* (trans. with notes and an interpretative essay Thomas Pangle; Chicago: University of Chicago Press, 1979), 729d.

49. *Laws* 837b; 837a; 837b; 837e; 640b; 837a.

50. *Laws* 679b–c; *Rep.* 551d.

51. *The Laws* 679b; 919b–c (trans. Pangle), cf. *Rep.* 421e–422a. *Laws* 919b–c, sums up Plato's reasons very pithily: poverty and wealth corrupt the soul in different ways. Poverty, on account of the pain it brings, makes people shameless in their striving to overcome it. Wealth, by contrast, leaves the soul corrupted by licentiousness and softness.

52. *Laws* 716c.

53. *Gorgias* 510b; 507e.

54. *Gorgias* 508a.

55. *Laws* 757a; 757c1–8. The relevant idea of equality is conveyed through statements of proportion, e.g. 2:4 :: 6:12. Though the number 6 is larger than the number 2, it represents the same part or proportion of 4 as 6 is of 12. Juxtaposed to a political context, a proportional assignment of benefits would give a greater amount to those who deserve it than those who are less deserving. Such an assignment may none the less preserve proportional equality. For an account of the political and ethical dimensions of various kinds of proportionality, see Hayden Ausland, "The Mathematics of Justice," in H. Tarrant and D. Baltzly (eds), *Reading Plato in Antiquity* (London: Duckworth, 2006), pp. 107–23.

56. Julius Moravcsik, "The Perils of Friendship and Conceptions of the Self," in J. Dancy, J. Moravcsik, and C. W. W. Taylor (eds), *Human Agency: Language, Duty, and Value* (Stanford: Stanford University Press), pp. 132–51, at p. 135.

57. *Phaedo* 81d, ff, in *Complete Works*; *Phaedrus* 248d ff (trans. H. N. Fowler; Loeb Classical Library; Cambridge, MA: Harvard University Press, 1914); *Rep.* 620a; *Timaeus* 41e ff, in *Complete Works*.

58. *Phaedrus* 246a.

59. *Phaedrus* 247e.

60. *Meno* 82b–85b, in *Complete Works*; *Phaedo* 72e–77a.

61. *Phaedrus* 254a.

62. *Phaedrus* 254e.

63. *Phaedrus* 255b.

64. *Phaedrus* 255e

65. *Phaedrus* 256a–b.

66. *Phaedrus* 256b-c.

67. *Phaedrus* 250e, cf. *Symposium* 208e.

68. *NE* 1169b–1170b; e.g., *NE* 115713–24; *NE* 1158a1–10; *NE* 1155a5–6.

69. *NE* 1155b17–1156a10.

70. *NE* 1156a10–1156a19.

71. *NE* 1162b; *NE* 1156a27.

72. *NE* 1156b7–12.

73. *NE* 1157b1–5; *NE* 1156b14–17; *NE* 1156b7–9.

74. *NE* 1158a10–17. A parallel passage in Aristotle's *Eudemian Ethics* (*EE*), in *The Complete Works of Aristotle* (ed. J. Barnes; 2 vols; Princeton, NJ: Princeton University Press, 1984), forms – in a rather perverse way – the basis of Derrida's book, *The Politics of Friendship* (trans. G. Collins; London and New York: Verso, 1997). Derrida's work is in many ways an extended meditation on a saying attributed to Aristotle by Montaigne: "O friends, there is no friend." Montaigne derives his authority for this attribution from Diogenes Laertius – or so he supposed. But a quick look at a modern edition of Diogenes Laertius reveals not that, but rather this: "to the person for whom there are [many] friends there is no [one, true] friend" (V.21, cf. Aristotle, *EE* 1245b20). The edition of Diogenes Laertius edited by Issaac Casaubon in 1616 "corrected" a dative to a vocative form, which gives the reading "O friends, etc." The correction is unnecessary and wrong. The text makes perfectly good sense as it stands. Giorgio Agemben (*Contremps* 5, 2004) asserts that he wrote to Derrida to point out this philological oddity and to suggest that it would be a mistake to base a reading of Aristotle on friendship around such a misattribution. Derrida did not see fit to acknowledge this, perhaps, as Agemben suggests because he – like Nietzsche – needed the incorrect manuscript reading to generate an internal tension in Aristotle's thought on friendship.

75. *NE* 1158b9; 1159b6–7; *NE* 1166a6–8; *NE* 1166a31–32.

76. *NE* 1155b28–1156a6.

77. *NE* 1156b7–12; *NE* 1156a9–19.

78. *NE* 1157b31–1158a2.

79. *NE* 1158b1–5.

80. *NE* 1158b27, 1158b25.

81. *NE* 1162a7–9; *NE* 1162a24–25; *NE* 1162b25–26.

82. *NE* 1158b21–23; *NE* 1162a9–11.

83. *NE* 1144b30.

84. *Politics (Pol.)* 1260a11 in *Complete Works*, ed. Barnes.

85. *Pol.* 1260a20–33.

86. See, e.g., H. L. Levy, "Does Aristotle Exclude Women from Politics?" *Review of Politics* 52 (1990), pp. 397–416.

87. Richard Mulgan, "Aristotle and the Political Role of Women," *History of Political Thought* 15 (1994), pp. 179–202.

88. *NE* 1165b1–8.

89. *NE* 1165b13–17.

90. *NE* 1165b17–23.

91. *NE* 1163b22–23.

92. *NE* 1099a31–b9.

93. Frank Walbank, "Monarchies and Monarchic Ideals," in F. W. Walbank, A. E. Astin, M. W. Fredriksen and R. M. Ogilvie (eds), *The Cambridge Ancient History*, vol. VII (Part 1) (Cambridge: Cambridge University Press, 1984, 2nd edn), pp. 62–100, at p. 68. Walbank goes on to note (p. 70) that, as a result of Greco-Macedonian prejudice, Egyptians, Syrians, Persians and other non-Hellenes were excluded from becoming a King's Friend. For more on this type of Hellenistic political friendship, see Gabriel Herman, "The 'Friends' of Early Hellenistic Rulers: Servants or Officials?" *Talanta* 12/13 (1980–81), pp. 103–49.

94. For example, see the following documents in Stanley M. Burstein (ed. and trans.), *The Hellenistic Age from the Battle of Ipsos to the Death of Kleopatra VII* (Cambridge: Cambridge University Press, 1985): "Treaty between Antiochos I or II and Lysimacheia" (281/early 260s BCE), p. 29; "Decree of the Aitolian League recognizing the inviolability of Magnesia on the Maeander" (207/206 BCE), p. 40; "Treaty ending a war between Miletos and Magnesia on the Maeander" (about 196 BCE), pp. 48–50; "Treaty between King Pharnakes I of Pontus and the city of Chersonesos" (155 BCE), p. 101.

95. Burstein, *The Hellenistic Age*, "Letter of Ptolemaios II to Miletos," pp. 120–21.

96. Burstein, *The Hellenistic Age*, "Delphi honors Attalos II for establishing an educational endowment," p. 113.

97. Burstein, *The Hellenistic Age*, "Testament of Ptolemaios VIII Euergetes II, leaving his kingdom of Cyrene to the Romans," p. 135.

98. See, e.g., "Letter of L. Cornelius Scipio and his Brother to Herakleia in Karia (190BC)," in Robert K. Sherk (ed. and trans.), *Rome and the Greek East to the Death of Augustus* (Cambridge: Cambridge University Press, 1984), p. 13. While

the term friendship does not occur in this letter, it is full of language associated with friendship.

99. Sherk, *Rome and the Greek East*, "Letter of Q. Maciuss Scaevola to Ephesus," p. 68.

100. Sherk, *Rome and the Greek East*, "Letter of Q. Oppius to Plarasa-Aphrodisias after the war against Mithridates," pp. 71–72.

101. Sherk, *Rome and the Greek East*, "Decree of the Senate concerning three Greek naval captains," pp. 81–82.

102. Sherk, *Rome and the Greek East*, "Epidauros honors one of its prominent citizens," p. 55.

103. Plutarch, *Precepts of Statecraft*, 814C, in *Moralia*.

104. Katherine Evans, "Friendship in Greek Documentary Papyri and Inscriptions: A Survey," in John T. Fitzgerald (ed.), *Greco-Roman Perspectives on Friendship* (Atlanta, GA: Scholars Press, 1997), pp. 181–202, at pp. 189–90, 194, 198.

105. John L. White, *Light from Ancient Letters* (Philadelphia: Fortress Press, 1986), p. 89.

106. White, *Light from Ancient Letters*, p. 110.

107. White, *Light from Ancient Letters*, p. 181.

108. Polybius, *The Histories* 1.14.4–5 (trans. W. R. Paton; 6 vols; Loeb Classical Library; Cambridge, MA: Harvard University Press, 1922–27).

109. Polybius, *The Histories* 20.6.5–7.

110. Peter Jay (ed.), *The Greek Anthology* (Harmondsworth: Penguin Classics, 1982), p. 93.

111. *The Greek Anthology*, 9. 401 (trans. W. R Paton; Loeb Classical Library; Cambridge, MA: Harvard University Press, 1998).

112. Patricia A. Rosenmeyer, "The Epistolary Novel," in J. R. Morgan and Richard Stoneman (eds), *Greek Fiction: The Greek Novel in Context* (London and New York: Routledge, 1994), pp. 146–65, at p. 156.

113. Diogenes Laertius, *Lives of Eminent Philosophers*, 6.63 (trans. R. Hicks; 2 vols; Loeb Classical Library; Cambridge, MA: Harvard University Press, 1925).

114. Cf. Plato, *Rep.* 496a–b; Aristotle, *EN* 1095b3–10; Epicurus, *Ep. Men.* 122 in Diogenes Laertius, *Lives*, book 10.

115. Eduard Zeller, *Outlines of the History of Greek Philosophy* (trans. Palmer; London: Thoemmes Press, 1955), p. 207. Compare Léon Robin, *Greek Thought and the Origins of the Scientific Spirit* (*La pensée greque et les origines de l'esprit scientifique*) (trans. M. R. Dobie; New York: Russell and Russell, 1967), p. 313: "The political and social circumstances which immediately preceded and followed the death of Alexander had intensely aggravated urgent needs to which philosophy had to supply new answers. In the great centralised state of which he was now a subject, the citizen of the old small city asked himself what attitude he should take up; he felt lost. Then he turned upon himself, considered his inner salvation, asked to be told what was the object of life, to be given an ideal in pursuing which he would find his lost liberty, with a view to his own happiness.

The ideal would be different in every school, but it would always be the ideal of the Wise Man, who belongs to no age or country."

116. Epictetus, *Manual* 5 (trans. W. A. Oldfather; Loeb Classical Library; Cambridge, MA: Harvard University Press, 1925–28).

117. This is the view ascribed to them in Diogenes Laertius VII. 124 = SVF 3.631, *Stoicorum Veterum Fragmenta*, ed. H. von Arnim, 4 vols (Stuttgart: Teubner, 1903–24). However, other sources credit them with forms of friendship that are not so exclusive, cf. Clement of Alexandria, *Stromateis* 2.483 (Potts) = SVF 3.723. The explanation for this apparent disagreement is probably the fact that friendship is spoken of in a variety of ways. These ways are catalogued in Stobaeus *Eclog.* II. 94.26 (Wachsmuth) = SVF 3.98. The friendship that can obtain only between the virtuous is probably the third of these, and friendship in the strictest sense.

118. Diogenes Laertius, *Lives* VII. 124

119. Stobaeus, *Eclog.* II 108,5 (Wachsmuth) = SVF 3.630: "The Stoics accept that there can only be friendship among the wise, since among them alone is there likeness of mind regarding the matters of life, since likeness of mind is the certain knowledge of the common good. For true friendship – not that which is falsely called friendship – cannot exist without faith (*pistis*) and security. But in the case of those who are lacking in virtue and worth, there is lack of faith and insecurity, and so they do not have friendship but different ties and attachments come to be between them adventitiously through their opinions and from necessity."

120. When one sage so much as extended a finger in a rational – and thus virtuous – way, every sage around the globe was benefited. Plutarch, *On Common Notions* 1076A = SVF 3.246.

121. Plutarch, *On Common Notions* 1068F = SVF 3.627, cf. Stobaeus, *Eclog.* II 101, 21 = SVF 3.626

122. This is meant literally. The Stoics regard god as an immanent – not transcendent – source of order in the world. God is, in fact, a material breath or *pneuma* that interpenetrates all things. *Pneuma* comes in gradations of tension ranging from mere tenor (the sort of god-stuff that interpenetrated inanimate objects), to soul (the god-stuff that animates living beings) to rationality (god-stuff at its highest degree of tension). God's providence consists not in making the world free of pain or suffering, but simply in making it such that rational creatures are able, through the perfection of their reason, to see that pain and suffering simply do not matter to their wellbeing. See D. Baltzly, "Stoic Pantheism," *Sophia* 34 (2003), pp. 3–33.

123. Cicero, *Amic.* 6.

124. Plutarch, *On the fortune of Alexander the Great* 329A-B = SVF 1.262.

125. Diogenes Laertius, *Lives* 7.33.

126. Cicero, *De Re Publica* (*Rep.*) 3.33 (trans. C. W. Keyes; Loeb Classical Library; Cambridge, MA: Harvard University Press, 1928); Cicero, *De Legibus*

(trans. C. W. Keyes; Loeb Classical Library; Cambridge, MA: Harvard University Press, 1928).

127. Cicero, *De Re Publica* 3.35.

128. Augustine, *City of God* 19.21 (trans. H. Bettenson; London: Penguin, 1972).

129. Cicero, *De Officiis* 2.27 (trans. W. Miller; Loeb Classical Library; Cambridge, MA: Harvard University Press, 1913.

130. Cicero, *Laelius: De amicitia* 50 (trans. W. A. Falconer; Loeb Classical Library; Cambridge, MA: Harvard University Press, 1948).

131. The case for a direct Stoic influence was put by W. Capelle, "Griechische Ethik und römischer Imperialismus," *Klio* 25 (1932). Capelle, however, was relying on the picture of a very innovative Panaetius and Posidonius found in A. Schmekel's *Die Philosophie der mittleren Stoa in ihrem geschichtlichen Zusammenhänge* (Hildesheim: Weidmann, 1892). M. van Straaten's much more conservative estimate of the evidence concerning Panaetius (*Panétius, sa vie ses écrits et sa doctrine avec une édition des fragments* [Amsterdam: H. J. Paris, 1946]) discouraged such speculation about the way in which the middle Stoa altered the teaching of the early Stoa. Jean-Louis Ferrary, *Philhellénisme et impérialisme: aspects idéologiques de la conquête romaine du monde hellénistique, de la seconde guerre de Macédoine à la guerre contre Mithridate* (Rome: École française, 1988) urges reasons for agnosticism about the influence of Greek philosophical thought on Roman ideology. Capelle's case is taken up again by J. Barlow, "The Moral and Political Philosophy of the Middle Stoa in its Historical Context" (MA thesis, Monash University 2001).

132. Cf. Anaxandrides, a comic poet of the fourth century BCE: "To make oneself the slave of pleasure – this is what randy women do, not men," Theodorus Kock (ed.), *Comicorum Atticorum Fragmenta*, Leipzig, 1880, vol. 2, fr. 60.

133. Greek sources recognize a class distinction between a woman who was a *hetaira* and one who is a *porné* that perhaps approximates the English language distinction between courtesan and whore. The former were sometimes influential, well-educated women such as Aspaius, the "companion" of Pericles.

133. Diogenes Laertius, *Lives* 2.75.

135. Diogenes Laertius, *Lives* 2.81.

136. Diogenes Laertius, *Lives* 2.93. Hegesias' pessimistic view of friendship is of a piece with his pessimistic view of life. On the whole, life presents more opportunities for suffering than enjoyment. Hence happiness – perhaps understood as a preponderance of pleasure over pain across a lifetime – is certainly impossible. So effective was Hegesias in communicating this message that he was given the nickname "the death persuader." Cicero tells us that King Ptolemy forbade him from lecturing on the theme that death removes us from bad things rather than taking away good things. Too many members of his audience committed suicide afterwards! *Tusculan Disputations* 1.83 (trans. J. E. King; Loeb Classical Library; Cambridge, MA: Harvard University Press, 1927).

137. Diogenes Laertius, *Lives* 10.132, trans. B. Inwood and L. Gerson, *Hellentistic Philosophy* (Indianapolis: Hackett, 2nd edn).

138. Epicurus advocated, *Lives* 10.36, that philosophical recruits should memorize the key sayings.

139. Epicurus was adamant that philosophy was to be judged by its therapeutic success: "Empty is the argument by which no human illness is cured, for just as there is no benefit in medicine if it does not drive out the illnesses of the body, so too there is no benefit in philosophy if it does not drive out the illnesses of the soul," Porphyry, *Letter to Marcella* 31 = 221 Usener. Cf. Cicero's complaint on the terse and inefficacious quality of Stoic philosophical arguments in *On Goals*, 4.7.

140. Cf. Martha Nussbaum, *The Therapy of Desire* (Princeton, NJ: Princeton University Press, 1994), pp. 134–37.

141. Cf. Marcello Gigante, *Philodemus in Italy: The Books from Herculaneum* (trans. Dirk Obbink; Ann Arbor, MI: University of Michigan Press, 1995).

1402. The Platonist polemicist, Plutarch of Chaeronia, dedicated a whole work to attacking the Epicureans on this point (*Is "Live Unknown" a Wise Precept?* – frequently referred to by its Latin title, *An recte dictum sit latenter esse vivendum*).

143. Pamela Gordon argues that it was not only the abandonment of the political sphere, but also the rejection of high culture "*paideia*" that earned Epicurus the rebuke of *kinaidologos* from the Stoic Epictetus: "Remembering the Garden: The Trouble with Women in the School of Epicurus," in J. Fitzgerald, D. Obbink and G. Holland (eds), *Philodemus and the New Testament World* (Leiden: E. J. Brill, 2004), p. 227.

144. Cicero, *On the Nature of Gods* 1.93 (trans. H. Rackham; Loeb Classical Library; Cambridge, MA: Harvard University Press, 1931).

145. Jane McIntosh Snyder, *The Woman and the Lyre: Women Writers in Classical Greece and Rome* (Carbondale: Southern Illinois University Press, 1989), pp. 101–102.

146. Compare *Vatican Sayings* 45; Diogenes Laertius 10.6 (Usener 163) and Athenaeus, *Deipnosophists* 13, 588ab (Usener 117) with Paul's views wisdom of the world (1 Cor. 1:18 ss).

147. To be sure, Paul in particular regards discipleship as more than an (inevitably doomed) *imitatio Christi*. But in the documents of the early Church, Paul's emphasis on Christ as emancipator through God's grace is not universally shared. See, e.g., Ignatius of Antioch, who urges his community to "imitate Jesus as He imitated the Father" (*Philad.* 7:2) or to live "not in the human way, but in Jesus Christ's way" (*Trall.* 2:1), *Epistulae inerpolatae et epistulae suppositiciae* (ed. F. Funk and F. Diekamp; Laup: Tubingen, 1913).

148. On the emulation of Epicurus, see Lucretius' proem to book III, lines 4–6. For his divinization, cf. the proem to book V, where he is greater than Hercules. There is ample evidence that Epicureans possessed images of Epicurus – rings, cups, etc. We reject the hypothesis of Frischer, *The Sculpted*

Word (Berkeley, CA: University of California Press, 1982) that these were fetishes, thinking it much more likely that they served to remind the initiate to conduct himself in the same tranquil manner as the sage whose calm visage is constantly present to him.

149. Cf. B. Fiore, sj, "The Pastoral Epistles in the light of Philodemus' 'On Frank Criticism.'" in Fitzgerald, Obbink and Holland (eds), *Philodemus and the New Testament World*.

150. See, e.g., Richard Sorabji's treatment of the way in which various "spiritual exercises" of the Stoics and Epicureans were adapted by Evagrius of Pontus in *Emotion and Peace of Mind* (Oxford: Oxford University Press, 2000) or Tim Gaden, "Looking to God for Healing: A Rereading of the *Second Letter of Clement* in the Light of Hellenistic Psychagogy," *Pacifica* 15 (2002), pp. 154–73.

151. Cf. R. Kraemer, *Her Share of the Blessings* (Oxford: Oxford University Press, 1992), ch. 10.

152. *On Having Many Friends* 94A; *De amicorum multitudine*, Plutarch, *Moralia*.

153. 94E; 94F; 94B.

154. *How to Tell a Flatterer* 51B, *Quomodo adulator ab amico internoscatur*, Plutarch, *Moralia*.

155. 54D–55A; 55C–D; 55A; 51C. As noted above, frankness of speech is an important feature of Epicurean therapeutic friendships. But they are not unique among Hellenistic philosophers in this regard: Cf. Diogenes the Cynic: "Other dogs bite their enemies, I my friends – so that I may save them," Stob. 3. 13. 44, collected in G. Giannantoni, *Socratis et Socraticorum Reliquiae* (4 vols; Naples: Bibliopolis, 1990); Maximus of Tyre, *The Philosophical Orations* 14. 5 (trans. M. B. Trapp; Oxford: Clarendon Press, 1997); Themistius, *The Private Orations of Themistius* 22. 277 (trans. Robert J. Penella; Berkeley, CA: University of California Press, 2000); and the New Testament. It seems that the link between frankness and friendship can also be found in Isocrates. See David Konstan, *Friendship in the Classical World* (Cambridge: Cambridge University Press, 1997), pp. 93–95.

156. Plutarch, *On Having Many Friends* 94C–95E.

157. Plutarch, *On Having Many Friends* 95A; emphasis added.

158. Plutarch, *On Having Many Friends* 96D.

159. Plutarch, *How to Tell a Flatterer* 54F.

160. Plutarch, *On Having Many Friends* 96A–B; 97A.

161. Plutarch, *How to Tell a Flatterer* 53B; 50A–B; 52F–53C; 53A; 53C.

162. Others who deal in detail with the question of how to distinguish a flatterer from a friend were Maximus of Tyre (*Orations* 14) and Themistius (*Orations* 22. 276 ff.).

163. Plutarch, *De fraterno amore* [*On Brotherly Love*] 479C–D, in *Moralia*.

164. This is a piece of advice that Plutarch takes from Theophrastus.

165. *De fraterno amore* 482B.

166. *De fraterno amore* 478C.

167. *De fraterno amore* 479A.

168. *Political Advice* 824D–825F, in *Moralia.*

169. Plutarch, *Amatorius [On Love]* 769F, in *Moralia.*

170. Plutarch, *Amatorius [On Love]* 769A, in *Moralia.*

171. Plutarch, *Coniugalia praecepta [Advice to Bride and Groom]* 139D, 140D, in *Moralia.*

172. *Precepts of Statecraft* 807D.

173. Aritstotle, *Politics* 1253b28, in *Complete Works.*

174. Plutarch, *Precepts of Statecraft* 806F; 807C; 808D; 808B; 809A.

175. Plutarch, *Mulierum virtutes, Moralia* (Virtues of Women); *Bruta animalia ratione uti, sive Gyrllus* (Beasts are Rational or Gryllus) and *De essu carnium orationes* (On the Eating of Flesh), all in *Moralia.*

176. On the incorporation of elements of Pythagoreanism into Neoplatonism, see D. J. O'Meara, *Pythagoras Revived: Mathematics and Philosophy in Late Antiquity* (Oxford: Oxford University Press, 1989), p. 260.

177. Like Pythagoreanism, Orphism has both pre-Platonic origins – origins that are similarly shrouded in mystery – as well as substantial post-Platonic additions. The Orphic poems may include elements as early as fifth century BCE. However, the bulk of the Orphic material stems from the period after the death of Aristotle. The Neoplatonists draw heavily on what is now called the "Rhapsodic Theogony." Thus it is unsurprising that they can find resonances of Platonism and Pythagoreanism in these "ancient" Orphic works. Cf. M. L. West, *The Orphic Poems* (Oxford: Oxford University Press, 1983).

178. These friendly numbers were the only ones known in antiquity, and this doubtless added much to the mystical significance that this fact was supposed to hold for friendship. A second pair was not discovered until 1636 when Fermat did so. Descartes added a third pair in 1638.

179. Iamblichus, *Commentary on Nicomachus of Gerasa's Introduction to Arithmethic* (ed. H. Pistelli; Leipzig: Teubner, 1894), §35.

180. Iamblichus, *VP* 33.237. Translations from Iamblichus, *De Vita Pythagorica,* are by John Dillon and Jackson Hershbell, *Iamblichus: On the Pythagorean Way of Life* (Atlanta, GA: Scholars Press, 1991).

181. This is so at least for the highest form of friendship, which obtains only among those who manifest the highest gradation of intellectual virtue. To be fair, Pythagoras also teaches "friendship of all for all": of the divine to the human; of doctrine to doctrine; of soul to body; of the body to itself; of man to "certain irrational animals"; and "of human beings [anthropôn] with each other" (Iamblichus, *De Vita Pythagorica,* 229).

182. Iamblichus argues that "our fellows" included even animals and other parts of nature. This kinship is based on the fact that the entire cosmos is a single, living being animated by a World Soul. The Pythagorean injunction to abstain from eating meat is based on this kinship among all living beings. His interpretation of the Pythagorean symbolon "plant mallows" in your garden stresses the interconnectedness of all visible nature. The mallow plant moves with the sun.

This shows how all things in the visible realm are connected by links of sympathy and kinship.

183. Iamblichus, *De Vita Pythagorica* 33.229, in Dillon and Hershbell, *Iamblichus*.

184. This could be interpreted as an act of worship toward Athena. However, it is equally possible that the goddess in question is Artemis and/or Hecate, both of whom are associated with the moon. If the latter interpretation is correct, then the action is doubly bold. Hecate is associated with the theurgy and magic. Even if Proclus' worship were directed instead to the "tamer" Athena, it is still reasonably bold. An imperial decree in 391 CE notionally prohibited all pagan cults and closed their temples, though the enforcement of this law – like the enforcement of marijuana laws in our own times – depended a bit on how far the local authorities wanted to push matters.

Chapter 2

CICERO ON FRIENDSHIP

Constant J. Mews

Few writers have exercised such an enduring influence on Western thinking about friendship as Marcus Tullius Cicero (106–43 BCE). As a student of philosophy, fluent in reading Greek, Cicero was profoundly familiar with many of the debates about friendship that had occupied thinkers from the time of Plato and Aristotle in the fourth century to the age of the great Hellenistic schools of philosophy active in his own age. Yet he was also actively involved in public life, and acutely aware of the yawning divide that could separate friendship as a noble ideal from the tawdry realities of friendship in everyday life. What makes his contribution to the Western tradition so important is that he is both a theorist and a practitioner of friendship, whose writings have been studied and imitated by generations of students throughout the medieval and Renaissance periods, and, indeed, well into the modern age. In particular, his philosophical dialogue *Laelius de amicitia* (*Laelius on friendship*), written under the shadow of the political crisis of the late Roman Republic, describes an ideal of friendship as he imagined it might have been practised by the great political figures – all male – of an age that he feared was now slipping away.[1] Cicero has also left us a vast body of letters addressed to friends, many to Atticus but also to a wider circle of intimates (*familiares*), that testify to the complex set of ideals and social norms evoked by *amicitia* in the Roman world.[2] No comparable body of correspondence survives in Latin from classical antiquity. Directly or indirectly, these ideals and norms had a powerful effect in shaping conceptions of friendship in the

Western tradition, at least until the nineteenth century. While Cicero would not be the only influence on European ideals of friendship, his contribution deserves attention, if only because the model of friendship that he presented would provide an unconscious point of departure for so much subsequent thinking about friendship as an ideal.

Cicero admired the achievement of the many Greek philosophers who had reflected on the principles behind *philia*, recognizing that it constituted the basis of political life in the *polis*. Yet Cicero was living at a time when the ideal of the city-state had receded into the remote past. Traditionally independent city-states, such as Athens and Syracuse, were now having to come to terms with the political and military dominance of just one city, that of Rome, over much of the Mediterranean world. Cicero's writings provide an extraordinarily vivid insight into the tensions provoked by the political crisis that was transforming the late Roman Republic in the last century of its existence, and would eventually cost him his life. Inevitably, ideals of friendship were put under strain, as political life became increasingly dependent on the favour of an ambitious political elite.[3]

Born into a well-to-do equestrian family of ancient Rome, Cicero pursued a career as a lawyer and orator, actively engaged in the political life of the Republic. Not being connected to the small circle of aristocratic families that traditionally governed ancient Rome, Cicero used his skill in the law as the vehicle for his political ambition. In the senatorial world in which he moved, political loyalties were shaped by ties of *amicitia* that did more than connect social equals. They involved ties of loyalty between old, powerful families and those dependent on their patronage, and effectively became an instrument for political promotion and self-interest.

In one of his earliest writings, the *De inventione rhetorica* (a manual on rhetorical argument that would become a staple of the educational curriculum throughout the Middle Ages and Renaissance), Cicero defined friendship as "a good will towards anyone for the benefit of the one he loves, reciprocated in equal measure."[4] Cicero took for granted Aristotelian ideals that true virtue and true friendship go hand in hand, and that a true friend was another self. He shared Aristotle's sense that true friendship was an exceedingly rare commodity, found only a few times in history. Cicero was aware of older currents of Stoic thinking about friendship, such as the argument of Zeno (335–263 BCE) that *philia* should form the basis of the world-state, but he had more sympathy for the thinking of Panaetius of Rhodes (c. 185–109 BCE).[5]

Panaetius shifted away from the ideal of the detached sage to that of the good man, committed to the ideal of perfect detachment (*apatheia*). He recognized that not all good men were necessarily friends, and held that friendship is a form of exclusive affection between individuals who are alike not just in virtue but also in character.[6] While Cicero was attracted by the more personal dimension of friendship that Panaetius promoted, he still viewed friendship as a masculine ideal.

In his *Epistulae ad familiares*, he included a number of letters to Terentia, whom he eulogized as his "most loyal and excellent wife" and on whose private wealth he was always reliant.[7] A letter written as he was about to go into a period of political exile betrays more concern about her role as mother of his daughter, Tulliola, than as an individual in her own right:

> But what is to become of my Tulliola? You at home must take care of that – I have nothing to suggest. But assuredly, however matters turn out, the poor little girl's marriage and good name must be a primary consideration. Then there is my son. What will he do? I hope that *he* will always be with me, my darling child.

Cicero is concerned with Terentia's welfare, but never addresses her as a friend, only as one who has supported his career: "How you have fared I do not know – whether you still have something left, or, as I fear have been stripped of all ... For the rest, dearest Terentia, bear up with all the dignity you can muster. It has been a good life, a great career."[8] Most of his letters to her are brief and concern practical matters, rather than celebrate friendship. It does not cause surprise that they would eventually divorce, very likely because of differences of opinion about money.

The overwhelming majority of these "Letters to Friends" (more accurately, "to intimates") are addressed to male friends. For Cicero, friendship involved obligations of reciprocity within a political world that might not necessarily reflect personal feeling. In that same letter to Terentia, written at a time of political duress, he commented of a political friend with whom he stayed in Brindisi that "he refused to be deterred by the penalties of a wicked law from carrying out the established duties of hospitality and friendship." Yet Cicero also had a few intimate male friends on whom he did not hesitate to lavish lengthy letters. The most important of these friends was Atticus, his wealthy friend, business partner, and patron, to whom Cicero could frequently vent his feelings about politics, not least because Atticus always remained apart from public life. In his letters to Atticus, Cicero could reflect on the continuous tension between friendship as a political necessity and friendship as a way of releasing himself from those constraints. In one letter, written while travelling, he apologizes for his brevity:

> Until I get settled somewhere, you must not expect my letters to be long or always in my own hand, but when I have the leisure I shall guarantee both ... Knowing my curiosity about politics to be quite as keen as your own, I hope you will tell me everything, what is going on and what is to come. You can't do me a greater kindness, or rather only one, the greatest of all, and that is to dispatch my commissions, above all that "domesticity" which you know lies nearest my heart. Here then is a letter fully of hurry and dust.[9]

There were other male friends too, to whom Cicero waxes eloquent in expression of feeling, although often because he was asking some favour in return. To C. Memmius, he recalls: "I love Pomponius Atticus like a second brother. Nothing is more precious and delightful to me than to have him as a friend. Nobody is less of a busybody, less inclined to importune, but I have never known him request anything of me so pressingly as this."[10] Extravagant expressions of friendship often concealed a request for help.

Friendship was seen as a precious commodity, inextricably bound up with expectations of mutual assistance. To Appius Pulcher, Cicero protests:

> But I want you to believe that I am not only your friend, but your very good friend. Naturally I shall do all I can in a practical way to enable you to decide that this is really so. As for yourself, if your object is not to appear bound to work for my interests while I am away as heartily as I worked for yours, why, I hereby relieve you of that preoccupation.

This is not to say that Cicero is not genuine in his expressions of affection. In a letter to his secretary, Tiro, a freed slave on whom he was dependent for recording so much of his literary activity, he is outspoken in his feeling:

> I read your letter with varying feelings. The first page upset me badly, the second brought me round a little. So now, if not before, I am clear that until your health is quite restored you should not venture upon travel either by land or water. I shall see you soon

> enough if I see you thoroughly strong again ... Take my word for
> it, dear Tiro, that nobody cares for me who does not care for you.
> Your recovery is most important to you and me, but many others
> are concerned about it.

Cicero needed Tiro to be his secretary as much as his friend.[11]

Towards the end of his life, political pressures drove Cicero towards an increasingly critical view of the political establishment. He remained committed to applying philosophical ideals to the service of the Republic, but he saw these ideals as under threat as three powerful military generals (Pompey, Julius Caesar and Crassus) competed for dominance. Cicero was forced into exile. In the civil war that followed the death of Crassus in 49 BCE, and the crowning of Julius Caesar as emperor in 48 BCE, he was sympathetic to moves to restore republican values. Fearful that his friendship with Brutus would lead him to be accused of complicity in the plot against Caesar, Cicero wanted to go into exile to Athens after Caesar's assassination but was persuaded to return to Rome, where he delivered his *Philippics* against the emerging leader, Mark Antony. These were the circumstances in which Cicero composed his reflections on friendship in the *De amicitia*, presented as a philosophical dialogue between a great Roman of the previous century, Gaius Laelius Sapiens, and his friends. Cicero used the figure of Laelius, a close friend of Scipio Africanus the younger, to project those ideas and values that he saw as in decline in his own day. Cicero was acutely aware of the self-seeking reciprocity and sheer pragmatism underpinning the practice of Roman *amicitia* that would provide subsequent centuries, certainly down to the Renaissance, with a vivid description of a practice that he saw as at odds with the selfless ideals of true friendship:

> Most people are not prepared in their daily lives to accept that
> anything can be good unless it is a source of profit. They choose
> their best friends as they choose their cattle, lavishing the greatest
> affection where they hope for the most lucrative results. But if this
> is what they are going to do, they will miss the finest and most
> natural sort of friendship; I mean the sort which is desirable for its
> own sake and for itself. Such people deprive themselves of the
> opportunity to experience for themselves how powerful, how won-
> derful and how all-embracing this kind of relationship can be.[12]

Political life during the late Republic had been defined above all by the concept of *amicitia*, a sharing of values between members of the senatorial political class.[13] Cicero was one of those who saw Julius

Caesar as betraying those values, forcing friendship to move from a relationship between relative equals to a more structured and hierarchical relationship between client and patron.[14] By recalling the friendship of Laelius for Scipio Africanus, another idealized figure in Cicero's memory, he emphasizes that the essence of friendship lies in a harmony of ethical values, above all a commitment to virtue: "Both in our public and private lives he and I shared all the same interests. Our tastes and aims and views were identical and that is where the essence of a friendship must always lie."[15] Framing these ideals as those of public figures, Cicero engages in a critique of political friendships in which virtue, honesty and truth had given way to flattery and self-interest.

Cicero draws on a Stoic sense that friendship is itself a consequence of an inherent desire for connection in the natural world.

> The bonds which nature has established to link one member of
> the human race with another are innumerable; but friendship not
> only surpasses them all but is something so choice and selective
> that its manifestations are normally restricted to two persons and
> two persons only – or at most extremely few.

He is openly critical of those who argue that pleasure is the highest good, arguing that friendship and moral goodness must go together.[16]

While he observes that all sorts of people can be friends, he advances the example of Scipio and Laelius as an exemplary model of friendship:

> We need friendship all the time, just as much as we need the
> proverbial prime necessities of life, fire and water. I am not speak-
> ing of ordinary commonplace friendships, delightful and valuable
> though they can be. What I have in mind instead is the authentic,
> truly admirable sort of relationship, the sort that was embodied in
> those rare pairs of famous friends.

The examples that he cites of wrong behaviour, like that of the Gracchi, are those of political demagogues. If friendship was about self-interest, he observes, it would be used more by women and the poor, than wealthy and powerful men.[17]

Unlike traditional Stoics, Cicero does consider friendship to be a special bond, deeper than purely conventional political ties. True friendship is born of a natural desire, he argues, imitating nature:

> Birds and fishes and the beasts of the field, tame and wild, every
> living being loves itself. The feeling is inborn in every creature. The

urge that impels them to do so bears some resemblance to human love ... For they too love themselves; and they too search for a partner whose personality they can unite so utterly with their own that the two are almost transformed into one.[18]

Yet his goal is moral, to urge an ideal of friendship in both public and private life. He has Laelius speak of his friendship with Scipio: "One of its features was the total harmony between us on matters of state. Another aspect was the advice he was always prepared to give me about all my private affairs." The friendship Cicero advocates is political, between men, and is based on moral virtue: "No one can be a friend unless he is a good man. But next to goodness itself, I entreat you to regard friendship as the finest thing in the world."[19]

The sort of friendships that Cicero idealized in his *De amicitia* contrasted sharply with the abuse of *amicitia* that he decried in many of his orations, in which he castigated the use of political friendship for self-interest. The moralism that Cicero generated in his writings about friendship was itself a reaction to the way the upper echelons of Roman society used such relationships to promote their own interests. There were undoubtedly many other types of friendship in Roman society than described to us by Cicero from within his own social circle. We are much less well informed about friendships between women, whether at elite or more popular levels of society, or indeed between working people in general within the Roman world. By virtue of the fact that Cicero was such a master of prose style, his letters and treatises commanded wider attention than those of most of his contemporaries. His voice was remembered long after the names of most of his friends had receded from the public mind. For good or ill, he provided generations of students with an ideal of friendship that could never be easily realized, but served to provoke admiration as a goal to which they should aspire.

Notes

1. Numerous editions and translations have been made of Cicero's *Laelius* (often known simply as the *De amicitia*). There is a critical edition of the Latin text by Karl Simbeck (Leipzig: Teubner, 1961; reprinted Stuttgart: Teubner, 1971), a Latin–English version in Cicero, *Laelius, on Friendship and the Dream of Scipio* (ed. and trans. J. G. F. Powell; Warminster: Aris & Phillips, 1990), and a new Latin edition by J. G. F. Powell, *De re publica; De legibus; Cato maior de senectute; Laelius de amicitia* (Oxford: Oxford University Press, 2006). Michael Grant provides a translation in Cicero, *The Good Life* (Harmondsworth, UK: Penguin,

1971), pp. 175–227. An excerpt, translated by Frank Copley, is given within *Other Selves: Philosophers on Friendship* (ed. Michael Pakaluk; Indianapolis: Hackett Publishing, 1991).

2. Cicero, *Letters to Atticus* (ed. and trans. D. R. Shackleton Bailey; 7 vols; Cambridge: Cambridge University Press, 1965–70); *Epistulae ad familiares* (ed. D. R. Shackleton Bailey; 2 vols; Cambridge: Cambridge University Press, 1977), updated as *Letters to Friends* (3 vols; Cambridge, MA: Harvard University Press, 2001). Shackleton Bailey provides an anthology of letters from both collections in *Cicero: Selected Letters* (Harmondsworth, UK: Penguin, 1982).

3. On ideals of friendship in ancient Rome, there is much of value in John T. Fitzgerald (ed.), *Greco-Roman Perspectives on Friendship* (Atlanta, GA; Scholars Press, 1997), pp. 59–76; David Konstan, *Friendship in the Classical World* (Cambridge: Cambridge University Press, 1997); P. A. Brunt, "Amicitia in the Late Roman Republic," *Proceedings of the Cambridge Philological Society* 191 (1965), pp. 1–20.

4. Cicero, *De inventione rhetorica* 2.55.150.

5. Horst Hutter, *Politics as Friendship: The Origins of Classical Notions of Politics in the Theory and Practice of Friendship* (Waterloo, ON; Wilfrid Laurier University Press, 1978), pp. 126–27.

6. Hutter, *Politics as Friendship*, pp. 128–31.

7. *Epistulae ad familiares*, ed. Shackleton Bailey, nos 6–9, 119, 144–45, 155, 159–73, 1:37–44, 220–21, 244–46, 260–61, 264–70.

8. Cicero, *Selected Letters*, no. 7, p. 61.

9. Cicero, *Selected Letters*, no. 46, p. 119.

10. Cicero, *Selected Letters*, no. 45, p. 118.

11. Cicero, *Selected Letters*, no. 49, p. 125; no. 57, pp. 136–37.

12. *De amicitia* 21, 79–80 (Grant, *The Good Life*, p. 216).

13. P. A. Brunt, *The Fall of the Roman Republic and Related Essays* (Oxford: Oxford University Press, 1988).

14. David Konstan offers lucid, if relatively brief comments on the relationship between friendship and political allegiance in *Friendship in the Classical World*, pp. 124–35.

15. *De amicitia* 4, 14 (Grant, *The Good Life*, p. 184).

16. *De amicitia* 5, 20 and 6, 20 (Grant, *The Good Life*, p. 187 for both).

17. *De amicitia* 6, 22 and 13, 46 (Grant, *The Good Life*, pp. 188, 201).

18. *De amicitia* 21, 78 (Grant, *The Good Life*, p. 216).

19. *De amicitia* 27, 101 (Grant, *The Good Life*, p. 227).

Chapter 3

THE LATIN WEST

Constant J. Mews and Neville Chiavaroli

Friendship has always remained a treasured ideal in the Latin West, from the time that Greek thought was first absorbed by Latin writers in the age of the late Roman Republic to the Renaissance, when a renewed interest in classical antiquity asserted itself throughout Western Europe. In truth, classical traditions of friendship never completely disappeared in those centuries that scholars came to identify as "medieval." Yet there were also profound shifts in the understanding of friendship, provoked not least by the encounter between the elitism of classical culture and the universalizing ambitions of the Christian religion. Above all, we see – at least in the context of formal religious life – an apparent tendency to subordinate the ideal of friendship to that of union with God in the life to come. At the risk of great simplification, this chapter will explore how the dominant ideals of friendship evolved in the world of ancient Rome and Latin Europe (that of the Byzantine world deserves a study of its own) and were defined in overwhelmingly male terms, both in the public and private spheres.

While we cannot doubt that friendships existed between women throughout this period, it is only occasionally that they come to public attention. The issue of male–female friendship was even more fraught, as women became idealized as objects of love rather than as equal partners in a relationship. Women did sometimes engage in friendships with men but often in circumscribed ways if they were to avoid the perception that they were subverting the established order of society. In the medieval, as in the Roman world, our knowledge of friendship is largely confined to particular sectors of society, overwhelmingly to male elite. Many more languages than Latin were spoken in that vast region of Europe that has come to be known as the Latin West, stretching from Spain to Poland. Undoubtedly, many of the artefacts from the ancient and medieval world, preserved in modern museums, once reflected treasured friendships in the eyes of their original owners. Most of these friendships are now mute to us. This chapter offers no more than an introduction to a few moments in the history of friendship, articulated mostly through the medium of Latin, across a period of some fifteen centuries.

Although there have been some excellent studies of particular friendships within Roman antiquity and within the Middle Ages, there have been few attempts at any form of global synthesis. Friendship within a monastic milieu has been well studied by Brian McGuire.[1] There has been a growth of interest in friendship circles within eleventh- and twelfth-century Europe.[2] The task of spanning such a long period, in which there were so many distinct moments of change, is not an easy one. To give order to our overview of such a vast time period, we can consider three main phases: the late Roman Republic and the Empire; late antiquity and the early Middle Ages, up to the eleventh century; and finally, the high Middle Ages, between the twelfth and fourteenth centuries, when writing about friendship was influenced by the increasingly urbanized and competitive character of medieval Europe.

The Sources for a History of Friendship in the Latin West

The cult of friendship was an important theme in the literature of the late Roman Republic, as well as during the Roman Empire, when power became increasingly centralized in particular families that vied with each other for control of the *imperium*.[3] Our major sources for the history of friendship in the Roman world are theoretical treatises like Cicero's *De amicitia* as well as letter collections, such as those of Cicero and Pliny. The letters of Seneca to Lucilius in effect constitute a continuous ethical treatise, often commenting on the principles of friendship.[4] Their influence in shaping moralistic ideals of friendship in both the medieval and Renaissance periods cannot be underestimated. These philosophical ideals were very different, however, from the norms that defined friendship in practice in Roman society. We should not ignore the rich vein of commentary on the complexities of friendship in practice offered by Roman comedy and satire. The plays of Plautus frequently take as their theme the fragile nature of social relationships, focusing more on the difficulty of maintaining mutual advantage than the lofty idealism of the philosophers.[5]

Probably the most important witness to the many ways in which friendships were negotiated and maintained through the ancient and the medieval world, indeed well into the early modern period, was the letter. Very few missives survive from either the ancient or medieval world in their original form. Occasionally, fragments of papyrus letters, unearthed from the Egyptian desert, give us precious insight into the realities of friendship in one particular province of the Roman Empire – whether relating to a deal between business partners or perhaps expressing longing for some friend or family member to return.[6] The chance preservation of an intimate letter to a Roman official suggests that women in the Greco-Roman world were more literate than the canon of surviving classical texts might lead us to think.[7] From the opposite end of the Empire, letters written by Roman soldiers from their base at Hadrian's Wall provide a rare glimpse into the practicalities of relationships normally obliterated from the historical record. Such chance survivals of original letters remind us that most of the vast corpus of letters written between friends in the medieval as much as the ancient world has otherwise disappeared from sight.[8] For the most part, the letters that have come down to us are those that a letter writer, or perhaps a personal secretary, thought fit to preserve for posterity for purposes of educational, instruction or spiritual edification.[9] From the age of late antiquity, the letters sent by great masters of prose style, such as Cicero, were preserved in registers of letters that could be used as models of style and thus of instruction as to how a letter should be written. After a renewal of interest in the fourth and fifth centuries CE, the art of letter writing enjoyed a resurgence in the Carolingian period, among a small educated elite, with a more broadly based revival in the twelfth century. While it used to be thought that the art of prose composition (the *ars dictaminis*) was a totally new development in the educational curriculum of twelfth-century Europe, it is emerging that the art of learning to write letters, and thus of maintaining friendships through the written word, has a continuous history, perhaps going back to the age of Cicero himself.[10]

Ideals of friendship were inevitably transformed within a Christian context. Writing about friendship tended to become absorbed into a

larger body of writing about asceticism and the religious life. We must
rely largely on letters exchanged between Christian ascetics, teachers
and administrators, for an understanding of ideals of friendship during the fourth and fifth centuries. Within the Latin West, Augustine
and Jerome would become two of the most widely read exponents of
the art of Christian friendship, at least among an educated elite. In the
eleventh and twelfth centuries, their letters would help stimulate letter writing and thus ideals of friendship within monastic and clerical
circles.

While much can be learned about the values of friendship within a
warrior society from vernacular literature in the Middle Ages, we have
to turn to a select group of treatises written in Latin during the twelfth
century to discover how friendship was theorized.[11] In the twelfth century two important treatises about friendship were written, one by a
Cistercian monk, Aelred of Rievaulx, the other by a secular cleric,
Peter of Blois.[12] Only with the development of an urban culture in the
thirteenth century, particularly in northern Italy, do we begin to discern themes of friendship in a consciously non-aristocratic environment, recorded above all by teachers of prose composition, like
Boncompagno da Signa, author of major manuals of letter writing
and a treatise of his own on friendship, providing his own response to
the arguments raised by Cicero. Albertano of Brescia is another such
teacher, whose reflections on friendship have never been accorded
the full attention they deserve.[13] In the less hierarchical, indeed more
fractious, environment of the city-state, there would be many more
ways in which friendships could be articulated, whether in the worlds
of business, religion, or of politics.

Love and Friendship in the Roman World

As has already been seen in the discussion of Cicero, Roman ideals of
amicitia were profoundly masculine in orientation, and closely influenced by the strictly male code of public life in Roman society. As an
ideal, *amicitia* operated at the level of reason, very differently from
amor or passionate desire, a relationship frequently perceived as irrational in nature, into which an otherwise rational person might "fall."
Under Augustus, there was a notable flowering of poetry about relationships between men and women, celebrated perhaps most brilliantly by Ovid in his *Amores* but also satirized mercilessly by him in
his *Art of Loving*.[14] Ovid is a precious witness to the practice that he

reports of men and women writing love letters and verses to each other. Yet while he advises women as to how best to lure men, he always considered *amor* as an affair of the heart, operating at a very different level from that of friendship, a rational relationship. Ovid makes fun of love letters written by women in his *Amores* while, in his *Cures for Love*, he mockingly warns that once a relationship was over, a woman's love letters were best destroyed.[15] By *amor*, Ovid was referring not to passion of the heart in Stendhal's sense of *amour-passion* but to sexual seduction, usually outside of marriage. As Paul Veyne has argued, Roman love poetry differed radically from that developed in the medieval period, because passion was not conceived of ethically "as an experience or as a relationship with the loved object but in relation to the subject who underwent it."[16]

Ovid was not simply a satirist of love. In his *Tristia*,[17] written in exile, he recalls how he and his stepdaughter Perilla used to read their poetry aloud to each other, proclaiming that she would be surpassed only by Sappho, "the lesbian singer" whom Ovid held in high esteem. In the *Heroides* Ovid invents poems written by mythic women to their lovers (Penelope to Ulysses, Dido to Aeneas) as well as poetic exchanges between a man and a woman (Paris to Helen, Helen to Paris etc.), yet never invokes the concept of *amicitia* to describe these relationships. Within the Roman world, friendship was reserved for relationships between members of the same sex. Ovid was unusual in writing as much as he did about the interaction of women with men.

By the time of the despotism of Nero, there was little place for literature reflecting on the complexities of relationships between men and women. Ovidian poetry was viewed as potentially frivolous by serious-minded moralists. The letters of Seneca to Lucilius offer a more autarchic conception of friendship than any of Cicero's writing. For Seneca, friendship is not so much an end in itself as a means to a virtuous life, and a state of equanimity over and beyond the vicissitudes of this world. *Amicitia* is thus a more impersonal association of wise men, all of whom reflect on the divine *logos* that orders creation. Seneca's letters are an endless source of aphorism about surviving hypocrisy and false pride but they do not celebrate friendship in itself. They present friendship as a relationship in which individuals can pursue moral excellence and transcend the pettiness of pursuing worldly success. In a society in which the only way to survive was through friendship with an emperor who thought (or needed to think) he had been chosen by the gods, it was not possible for friendship to be imagined as having a political role, as had been the case for Cicero. Particularly from the twelfth century on, Seneca's letters to Lucilius provided a rich source of stoic ethical ideals that could easily be integrated into a Christian framework, well into the early modern period.

The Christian Revolution

From the earliest decades of the movement, Christianity offered a radically different set of ideals from those that prevailed in the political structures of the Roman Empire. While Jewish scripture did offer some famous examples of friendship, such as that between David and Jonathan, the earliest documents of the Christian movement, the letters of St Paul, offer an ideal not of *philia* (or as the Romans would say, *amicitia*), but of *agape*, defined in Christian usage as a selfless love that did not define itself in terms of a social elite.[18] Whereas Cicero had held up as a consciously elitist ideal the mutual friendship of great men of the Roman Republic, St Paul offered a very different ideal of *agape*, an ideal of universal love perceived to have been embodied in the person of Jesus, the Christ or anointed of God. Paul's letters often included a personal dimension that reveal his affection for particular women and men involved in spreading the Christian message (e.g. Romans 16:12-16), but he addresses them not as friends, but as saints, working for a common cause. All the authentic letters of Paul are addressed to communities rather than to individuals. The early Christian communities inherited values about friendship similar to those of the ancient philosophical schools. The statement in Acts 2:42, that the early Christians were of one heart and soul, and did not claim private ownership but held all things in common, consciously picks up on a traditional Hellenistic saying about friendship as creating a single heart and soul.[19] Within Christian rhetoric, however, it was more important to share in the community of those called to follow Christ than to be described as friend. Only in the farewell discourse of Jesus as reported by John 15:12-15, are friendship and love fully brought together:

> No one has greater love than this, to lay down one's life for one's friends. You are my friends if you do what I command you. I do not call you servants any longer, because the servant does not know what the master is doing; but I have called you friends,

because I have made known to you everything that I have heard
from my father.

Christianity provided a new paradigm for classical ideals of friendship, by presenting it as embodied in the relationship between Jesus
and his disciples. The novelty of its teaching is highlighted by the fact
that the terms chosen by Latin Christians to translate *agape*, namely
dilectio and *caritas*, had not been used in this way within classical Latin
literature (indeed *dilectio*, or personal, selfless love, had not previously existed as a term). Christians used *caritas* and *dilectio* to identify
an ideal that they perceived as higher and more universal than that of
amicitia as celebrated by ancient philosophers.

In its struggle with gnostic sects during the second and third centuries, orthodox Christianity became suspicious of the small group of
friends around a spiritual teacher when they threatened to break away
from the universality of the Church. Yet opportunities for Christian
friendship did develop after the official recognition given to Christianity by Constantine in 313 CE. At the same time as educated pagans, like Libanius (313–394) in Antioch and Symmachus (345–405)
in Rome, continued to preserve traditional values of friendship through
the medium of letters and speeches, Christians such as Basil the Great
and his friend Gregory Nazianzus, started to redefine classical ideals
of friendship within the framework of the new religion.[20] The commitment of these educated Christians to the ascetic movement provided an opportunity for women to share in friendship circles in a
way that had not been possible in traditional Roman society. In the
Greek East, John Chrysostom corresponded extensively with his
patron and supporter, the aristocratic Olympias (whose letters have
unfortunately not been preserved). The Greek Church Fathers laid
the foundation for a new understanding of friendship within a
Christian context.

By the fourth century, these ideals were also starting to develop in
Latin Christian circles. An intellectually well-informed author composed an imaginative exchange of letters between Seneca and St Paul
that would become popular in some circles in the twelfth century. It
highlights common ground between the Stoic pagan and a Hellenized
Jew in letters shaped by Stoicism as well as by Christocentric religious
thought.[21] For both, commitment to ideals of virtue had greater value
than individual friendships within this world. As a model of prose
style, however, few authors would be as dominant in the Latin West
as Jerome (c. 347–420), a classically trained scholar who became

absorbed by the Hebrew scriptures, which he spent much of his life translating and expounding afresh for his fellow Christians (who had hitherto been reliant only on the Septuagint version). Jerome shared these translations and commentaries, as well as a large number of letters, with a circle of friends who shared similar ascetic ideals. Whereas Cicero had addressed his letters to a political elite within the Roman republic, Jerome shared his correspondence mostly with fellow ascetics who had renounced the world, not sparing what he considered to be the worldly abuses creeping into a Church that was beginning to profit from imperial patronage. Jerome's epistolary circle included some very wealthy Roman women, such as Paula and Marcella, Eustochium and Blesilla, who did much to support his studies in the Holy Land. Paradoxically, however, the correspondence of these women was not preserved in the registers of letters preserved by Jerome's admirers.

These circles of educated Christians effectively forged a new ideal of friendship in the fourth century, based around an often highly allegorized reading of the Scriptures. The letters of Paulinus of Nola were never widely disseminated but they celebrate a cult of friendship within a privileged circle, sometimes not unlike that of Cicero four centuries earlier. With the writing of Augustine, however, we find perhaps the most sophisticated reflection on friendship within a larger understanding of the ideal of divine love. Augustine (354–430) had been fully trained in rhetoric and Latin literature before he turned to Christianity. In his *Confessions*, we find eloquent testimony to his attachment to the ideal of friendship, but now always transposed to a reflection of *caritas*, which he understands as a transcendent love binding Christ to God the Father and thus Christians to each other. His lament over the death of a friend in the *Confessions* is both an elegy and a theological reflection on the difficulty of true friendship:

> He was not then such a friend to me as he was to become later, though even at the later time of which I speak our union fell short of true friendship, because friendship is genuine only when you bind fast together people who cleave to you through the charity poured abroad in our hearts by the Holy Spirit who is given to us. I did love him very tenderly, though, and similarity of outlook lent warmth to our relationship; for I had lured him from the true faith, which he had held in a thoroughly immature way and without conviction, to the superstitious and baneful fables which my mother deplored in me.[22]

Augustine writes acutely about the delight of friendship: "There were other joys to be found in their company which still more powerfully captivated my mind – the charms of talking and laughing together and kindly giving way to each other's wishes, reading elegantly written books together, sharing jokes and delighting to honour one another."[23] But his message is always that such friendship is transient compared with true love for God. Augustine speaks of love as a movement of the soul to love what is good for the sake of God. Under the influence of St Paul (whose Christological focus he internalized with an intensity perhaps greater than that of any other Church Father), Augustine eulogized *caritas*, a more abstract, selfless love, defining it as:

> a movement of the soul to enjoy God for God's sake, and to love oneself and one's neighbour for the sake of God. Its opposite was lust, a movement of the soul to love oneself and one's neighbour, for their sake, not for God.[24]

Augustine's sense that all things, even friendship, were for the sake of God was very different from the ideal of Cicero that true friendship was offered for the sake of the other person, not for any material benefit. Augustine had little time for the worldliness of political life, even under nominally Christian rulers. He considered it better to be a friend of God than of the emperor. While Augustine privately relished friendship, he was always aware that his discourse had as much a public role in the service of the Church as for giving pleasure to a select group of readers. In the Christian dispensation, friendship was no longer an end in itself.

The Early Medieval Period

Between the fifth and the late eleventh centuries in the Latin West, literary ideals of friendship were inevitably overshadowed by the values of monasticism. Byzantium continued as a quintessentially urban culture, under the authority of the Holy Roman Emperor, and preserved a degree of continuity with Greek philosophical culture, albeit under a Christian framework. On the other hand, the Latin West experienced a period of political fragmentation, with a brief but significant respite in the ninth century during the time of Charlemagne and his immediate successors. During these six centuries, the most successful political structure was not that of the empire or the papacy, but the monastery. The Rule of Benedict established a working constitution for a stable, all-male community, under the authority of an abbot elected in theory by his monks. There was no place for special friend-ship in the monastery, which Benedict defined in his famous phrase as a *schola caritatis*, a school for love. There should be no secrets in a closed community. Although the vow of stability taken by a monk provided a degree of permanence within religious life, monks could be sent all over Europe as missionaries. In the early sixth century, the vast letter collection of Gregory the Great provides magnificent testi-mony to how letter writing could help establish a network of personal relationships between himself as bishop of Rome and a far-flung net-work of bishops, abbots and senior clerics. By invoking ideals of friend-ship with the saints, above all with himself as guardian of the See of Peter, Gregory sought to create an image of spiritual and ecclesiastical unity across a politically fragmented world.

In the ninth century, Charlemagne succeeded in imposing a short-lived measure of political unity across France, Germany and northern Italy. He promoted the interests of an educated monastic elite, charged with finding and copying the manuscripts of Roman antiquity (includ-ing the letters of Cicero). Intellectuals like Lupus of Ferrières and Raban Maur attempted to recreate ideals of literary friendship within this monastic elite, absorbing elements of Ciceronian *amicitia* within a framework provided by the letter writers of classical antiquity. Be-cause such a small percentage of Carolingian society was literate in the sense of being able to write, we know little about how ties of friendship impacted on the much larger, non-monastic sector of soci-ety. Their bonds of friendship, expressed in personal terms, should not disguise the dominant understanding of *amicitia* found in the period. Letters written by political figures, or rather their monastic secretaries, leave no doubt that *amicitia* remained what it had been in the Roman world, a political tie, with the subtle difference that it was often a tie, not between equals, but of an inferior who had pledged allegiance, freely given, to his superior. As Gerd Althoff has demon-strated, such ties of friendship, freely given and invoking mutual sup-port, effectively created a framework for political structures in the early medieval period.[25] As in the Roman world, friendship was as much political and private. If one was not in a relationship of *amicitia*, then one was an *inimicus* – very literally a non-friend. In such an environ-ment, there was little space for an amity or friendship different from the political ties by which any individual defined his or her identity.

The Re-emergence of Personal Friendship in the Twelfth Century

By the mid-eleventh century, a network of Christian kingdoms began to consolidate their authority across Europe, all professing at least nominal loyalty to the papacy and the Latin rite. In Germany and northern Italy, the consolidation of the power of the German king, who claimed the title of Holy Roman Emperor, led to a confrontation with the papacy that would take over a hundred years to resolve. Political stability and a new economic prosperity (provoked in significant part by Christian military conquests in Spain, Sicily and the Holy Land) encouraged a subtle transformation in ideals of *amicitia*, taking it beyond a purely political function to a more personal role, of expressing individual identity.

Signs of this shift in the way friendship was celebrated can first be glimpsed in the late eleventh and early twelfth century, both in southern Germany and in the Loire valley. Within a German context, examples of expressive friendship, rich in erotic intensity, survive in isolated letters (some between women, as well as between a man and a woman) from Tegernsee, and in a poetic exchange between a teacher and certain female students in Regensburg.[26] There is a more consciously literary aspect to the various *Carmina* that a Benedictine abbot from the Loire valley, Baudri of Bourgueil (1045–1130), exchanged with a wide range of friends, clerical, monastic, and lay, including some educated women, nuns of the abbey of Le Ronceray, Angers. The model for Baudri was not the letters of Cicero, but the poetic epistles of Ovid, so often concerned with celebrating values of true love (*amor*) between men and women. While we know very little about Baudri's own life, it seems that he felt a degree of kinship with Ovid, whom he interpreted in a new way.[27] Ovid had often been spoken about by moralistic Church fathers as a preacher of immorality, because of his satires on Roman society. Baudri understood Ovid in a more serious light as the poet who describes *amor* as a force of divine origin. Inevitably there is a tension between his celebration of mythic lovers and the more general *caritas* invoked in the New Testament. Not all Baudri's poems talk about love. They may celebrate small exchanges or achievements of an individual, or are epitaphs sent when someone has died. Although the collection of his *Carmina* includes only one poem by a correspondent of his, a remarkable woman by the name of Constance, it seems clear that Baudri's poems record only one side of a widespread practice in the late eleventh and early

twelfth century of educated monks, clerics, and nuns exchanging poetic compositions with each other. These poems served to create a
friendship circle that rested on common reverence not just for Ovid
but for a rethinking of religious values, driven by concerns for authen-
ticity and a distaste for hypocrisy as well as a love of classical literature. While monks such as St Anselm (1033–1109) developed the art
of writing spiritual letters to monastic friends, often outspoken in their
warmth and intimacy, other monks and clerics (of which Baudri was
simply the most gifted) drew on secular themes to develop a more
personal style of friendship than had been known in previous generations. The practice of using increasingly elaborate greetings to introduce letters highlights a more personal cult of friendship before manuals
of letter-writing sought to codify such practices.[28]

The most celebrated reader of Baudri's verse may have been the
young Heloise (c. 1094–1164), brought up in the abbey of Argenteuil
before she moved to Paris to lodge in the house of her uncle, a canon
of Notre Dame. The story of her relationship with Peter Abelard (1079–
1142) is well known from his account in an autobiographical letter,
known as the *Historia calamitatum*, in which he relates his love affair
with this gifted young student as the episode which brought his early
career as a brilliant teacher of logic to a crisis. The way he tells the
account of his meeting with her, some seventeen years earlier, is
shaped by a desire to emphasize that he had been driven only by lust:

> Knowing the girl's knowledge and love of letters I thought she
> would be all the more ready to consent, and that even when
> separated we could enjoy each other's presence by exchange of
> written messages in which we could speak more openly than in
> person and so need never lack the pleasures of conversation.[29]

In his narrative, Abelard dwells little on this early exchange of messages and the evident friendship he had enjoyed with the young
Heloise. He focuses more on the opportunity for sexual misconduct
afforded by his gaining accommodation in her uncle's house and the
crisis that followed their liaison being discovered and her becoming
pregnant. He sees that early relationship as a mistake on his part that
merited the punishment that ensued. A secret marriage to an unwill-
ing Heloise failed to assuage her uncle, who had him castrated, pro-
voking both of them to enter religious life, while the child was looked
after by his sister, back in his home region on the borders of Brittany.
Abelard tells the story of this early relationship to drive home a moral
point: from the most difficult circumstances, a positive end might come.

In this case, it was the story of how they eventually succeeded in founding a new religious community, dedicated to the Paraclete or Holy Spirit, under the direction of Heloise. Abelard may well have addressed his account to a fictional male friend as a device by which he could communicate to Heloise his own vision of the past, and the nature of the relationship which he thought he could legitimately maintain with her, modelled no longer on the writings of Ovid, but on the letters of Jerome to his ascetic disciples.

The letters that Heloise wrote in response to Abelard's account have rightly been celebrated by readers for their eloquent passion ever since they were first reported by Jean de Meun within his *Romance of the Rose*, written in the 1260s. She skilfully transforms a letter addressed to her spiritual father into a declaration of love, modelled on one of the great heroine's letters composed by Ovid. She took particular exception to the way Abelard had summarized her arguments against marriage: "The name of wife may seem more sacred or more binding, but sweeter for me will always be the name of friend (*amica*), or if you will permit me that of concubine or whore."[30] Although *amica* has often been translated here as mistress, Heloise is consciously evoking ideals of Ciceronian friendship, as much as the love celebrated by Ovid:

> You kept silent about most of my arguments for preferring love to wedlock and freedom to chains. God is my witness, that if Augustus, Emperor of the whole world, thought fit to honour me with marriage and conferred all the earth on me to possess for ever, it would be dearer and more honourable to me to be called not his Empress, but your whore.[31]

The dramatic tension in the epistolary dialogue that follows is created by the contrast between Abelard's insisting that they should maintain a spiritual distance from their early fornication, and Heloise's insistence that her intentions towards Abelard had always been pure, and that she could not feel true remorse for her past behaviour or banish the memories of past pleasure: "I should be groaning over the sins I have committed, but I can only sigh for what I have lost."[32] There is also, however, a practical dimension to their relationship. She wants Abelard to resume the correspondence she had once enjoyed with him in the past, but now within the context of religious life. This leads her to reflect on the need of her community for some authority by which they can live, in particular for an account of religious women in the past and a Rule for the Paraclete, documents that Abelard proceeds to supply. Her greeting to him in her third letter, in which she puts these requests, is still uniquely personal, "To him who is hers specially, she who is his singularly."[33] She was recalling the different ways in which they had addressed each other in the past.

While the epistolary relationship between Abelard and Heloise was in many ways an unusual one, it crystallizes a tension increasingly evident in the twelfth century between traditionally masculine ideals of friendship, from which sexuality and physical intimacy were excluded, and a growing fascination with ideals of love and personal interiority. These tensions are also very evident in the remarkable *Epistolae duorum amantium*, a fifteenth-century copy of an exchange between a celebrated teacher and his student, very close indeed to Abelard and Heloise, at the time of their affair.[34] (For example, he calls her singular or unique, while she calls him special, a term that a dialectician would understand as belonging to a species.) These letters indicate a shared fascination for combining Ciceronian ideals about true friendship with Ovidian reflections on love. There are subtle differences between the teacher and the student in this relationship. While he is fully expert in Ovidian conventions on professions of love, she is more philosophically interested in defining the obligations imposed by *amor*, perceived as true friendship. In letter 24, in response to a question she was asking him about the nature of *amor*, he adapts Cicero's definition that in true friendship *caritas* exists only between two people (precisely the one passage of the *De amicitia* included by Abelard in his *Sic et Non*) to the terminology of dialectic, by claiming that *amor* is a universal thing that exists between themselves alone. Her response in letter 25 rejects the notion that love fully exists between them, but rather picks up on the deeper theme of Cicero, that true friendship seeks only the other person, not any personal advantage. This recurring theme in the young woman's letters is given more mature definition by Heloise in her response, many years later, to the *Historia calamitatum*. After a particularly eloquent discourse from her on the nature of true love and friendship, her teacher expresses awe at her capacity: "You seem not to have read Tully, but to have given those precepts to Tully himself! ... Your talent, your command of language, beyond your years and sex, is now beginning to extend itself into manly strength."[35] His comments about this young woman's capacity to transcend her sex betray the lingering influence of a classical understanding of friendship – that it was fundamentally masculine in character.

It was much easier in the twelfth century for celibate men to express intimacy, even ardour, in their relationships with other men than with women. There are a few remarkable treatises from the late eleventh and early twelfth century, addressed to women in religious life, such as the *Liber confortatorius* written by Goscelin of St Bertin to his beloved Eve, a recluse, who had abandoned her abbey at Wilton (and Goscelin himself) for a hermit called Roger, who lived in the Loire valley.[36] Emotional intensity could easily develop within the framework of women's religious communities, in which monks were engaged as pastors and spiritual guides. By 1139 official prohibitions were imposed on women living outside any rule other than that of Benedict, Augustine or Basil, as well as on religious women singing in the same choir as men. While this did not stop the development of close friendships between spiritual directors and the women in their charge, such friendships were viewed with suspicion by many within authority. In the thirteenth century, the Franciscan and Dominican orders provided a degree of legitimacy to such friendships, although only within the strictest of controls, if they were not to attract suspicion of fomenting dangerous heresy.

The widely copied letter collections of St Anselm (1033–1108) and Bernard of Clairvaux (1090–1153) enable us to see how Ciceronian ideals of *amicitia* could be integrated into a Christian and indeed specifically monastic milieu. Brian McGuire has written extensively on monastic friendship in the twelfth century, an enthusiasm that finds its apotheosis in the writing of an English Cistercian monk, Aelred of Rievaulx (1110–1167).[37] St Anselm, and even more Bernard of Clairvaux, had waxed eloquent about their enthusiasm for personal friends within the monastic life, in language that can easily be perceived as homoerotic. For Bernard, the erotic imagery of the Song of Songs provided a rich medium through which to explore his enthusiasm for love for God as emerging out of love of self and neighbour. A generation later, Aelred of Rievaulx extended these themes in a treatise on spiritual friendship (*De amicitia spiritali*) that openly raises the question that Bernard never fully confronts: how do we reconcile Cicero's celebration of ideal friendship, as distinct from the selfish friendships of the world, with the more general Christian ideal of love for neighbour and for God? Aelred never abandons the Augustinian vision that the goal of the Christian and monastic life is that of the sublime *caritas* in the world to come. Nonetheless, he selects from Cicero's *De amicitia* elements to support a very un-Ciceronian notion that through friendship with Jesus, we come to know the love of God. The official *Life of Aelred* presents him as an extraordinarily intense and affectionate abbot, unusual in the way he was not ashamed to identify his close friends.[38] Yet if we look at most monastic literature, we see that personal friendships are viewed with suspicion. While there is no doubt that friendships continued, it was often not possible to publicly acknowledge their reality within the constraints of a single-sex community.

By the mid-twelfth century, reforming ideals within monasticism were beginning to fade. Ideals of friendship started to be articulated more visibly within the correspondence of secular clerics like John of Salisbury (c. 1115–1180), again a great enthusiast for Cicero.[39] Whereas Aelred selects elements of Cicero's *De amicitia* to develop his religious themes, John of Salisbury has a much deeper understanding of the statesman of the Roman Republic. This was in large part because John, a diplomat who spent most of his life in the service of archbishops of Canterbury, lived out the same tension as Cicero of commitment to the ethics of public life while being engaged in politics. Privately, he was fascinated by the ideal of the philosophic life and despaired of the short-term pragmatism and hypocrisy that defined political relationships. When he wrote to Thomas à Becket, murdered at the behest of Henry II in 1170, he uses rhetoric of friendship, but always in a cautious way, quite differently from the way that he would address Peter of Celle, a Benedictine abbot with whom John felt a much deeper unanimity of mind. It was only when sharing thoughts with a fellow scholar that John fully expounds what he sees to be the richness of the Ciceronian tradition in reflecting on friendship as an end in itself.

By the late twelfth century, another secular cleric, Peter of Blois (1130/35–1211/12), composed a treatise "About Christian Friendship and about the Love of God and Neighbour" (*De amicitia christiana et de dilectione dei et proximi*), in part inspired by Aelred of Rievaulx but directed to a much wider audience than the monastery.[40] He imitates Aelred in incorporating Ciceronian notions into an Augustinian perspective on friendship but goes much further in trying to systematize principles of how one could combine love of one's neighbour in general with love of God. Whereas Aelred was a monk, reflecting on the delights of friendship within the cloister, Peter of Blois created a less personal synthesis of instruction about all manner of relationships that might develop in society, at least between members of the same sex.

His concern is not just with Christian friendship but with love (both *caritas* and *dilectio*) of God and of neighbour. While Peter's treatise is traditionally seen as dependent on that of Aelred, its focus is much broader in that it seeks to relate Ciceronian ideals within a Christian framework, Augustinian in its fundamental principles. Although Peter praises *amicitia*, his driving theme is the supremacy of *caritas*, an ideal that Cicero would not have understood. Peter of Blois forged a synthesis of pagan and Christian thought that would remain widely popular in the thirteenth and fourteenth centuries precisely because it gave legitimacy to celebrating *amicitia*, while not questioning obligations of love imposed on all Christians. The fact that this treatise circulated under the name of Cassiodorus, rather than as a composition of Peter of Blois, only added to the authority it enjoyed as a theory of Christian friendship.

Friendship in the Thirteenth Century

The thirteenth century was a period of increasing mobility, both geographic and economic, in Europe, especially in the urban culture of Northern Italy, and it has been observed that "friendship flourishes in a period of meritocratic social mobility."[41] Perhaps in such a climate earlier idealistic views seemed less than adequate as guides to friendship in the real world, and indeed the Ciceronian view, while seldom directly challenged, is rivalled by other sources of thinking on the matter. Increasingly, writers on the topic seem to be more concerned with the practical aspects of friendships than on philosophic ideals.

Around 1238, for example, the northern Italian judge and lawyer, Albertano of Brescia, composed a book of advice for one of his sons, a work whose title would seem to echo that of Peter of Blois: *On love and affection for God, for neighbours, and for other things, and on the way of life.*[42] In the section devoted to relations with one's *proximi*, literally "neighbours" but used by Albertano in the broader sense of one's "fellow man," Albertano considers the nature of friendship and offers advice as to how it may be preserved.

Albertano starts from the traditional premise that love is the basis of friendship. But Albertano has in mind primarily the kind of Christian social love, or *caritas*, described by writers such as Augustine, a universal form of love: "you should love all fellow men, generally and universally." From this form of love emerges friendship, a process which Albertano tries to explain through a physical metaphor.

Drawing on a reference which he appears to have believed was written by Seneca, Albertano writes: "Love arises in the manner of a crystal: it coagulates or congeals, and in so doing, it becomes devotion and turns into friendship" – in short, Albertano suggests, love "crystallizes" as friendship.

Such a transformation of love into friendship, according to Albertano, relies on four main activities between friends: faithfulness, sharing meals together, conversation, and through good mutual "services." Years earlier, Peter of Blois had suggested that friendship was demonstrated by faithfulness, intention, discretion and patience.[43] This difference suggests a subtle shift in the conceptualization of friendship from a relationship of virtue to a more pragmatic concern, although the connection with virtue, through the continuing importance of faithfulness, remains.

True friendship, however, now seems to lie quintessentially in the exchange of services. "Friendship is acquired and maintained and preserved through the giving and receiving of mutual services," Albertano declares early in his discussion, marshalling a host of classical authors in support, each selected to emphasize the reciprocality of friendship: "if a friend has often given to you, it is fitting that you give back to him" (Publilius Syrus); "one who never does any favours has no right to ask for them" (again Publilius Syrus); and "nothing is more odious than the shame of dishonouring a favour" (Seneca). Nor is it enough simply to return the favour: quoting Seneca again, Albertano declares that one should repay a favour more willingly than it was received. It should also be done spontaneously and without expectation of return, otherwise it is negotiation, not friendship (Seneca again). But Albertano could also be more pragmatic about this too: "But if you are unable to repay favours with deeds, at least pay them back through the acknowledgment of the favour." And again Seneca provides the voice of authority: "sometimes acknowledgment itself is the repayment." These latter sentiments, as we shall see, suggest the possibility of friendship between unequals.

Cicero seems no longer to be the principal voice of authority of friendship. While he is still quoted by Albertano, it is less often than writers in the Senecan tradition. And while Cicero noted only in passing that there were certain people with whom one should avoid friendships, Albertano devotes the latter part of his treatment of friendship to detailing such types. The list reads rather like the treatises, very popular in the Middle Ages, on the virtues and the vices: one should avoid friendships with the foolish or unwise, the greedy or lustful, the haughty or wicked, the loquacious or talkative or ridiculous, the man who is prone to anger, and anyone about whose character one has doubts. In short, Albertano warns, "the uncertain friendship of all bad men should be completely avoided, for it is through friendship and continuing familiarity with such people that good character is corrupted."

Such condemnation of false friendship had been a regular element in Western discussions of the topic: Aelred had spoken disapprovingly of the "carnal" and "worldly" friendships of those outside the community of Christ; John Cassian[44] had noted the pragmatic circumstances giving rise to many friendships which eventually proved to be fragile and temporary; and of course Cicero had shown little interest in the "insubstantial" friendships of the common people. The inherent failings of such friendships seemed obvious and, equally as obvious, it seemed that they in no way undermined the merits of true friendship. It seems to have occurred to no one that such friendships might actually be the norm and that the philosophers were simply pursuing a literary ideal rather than a social reality.

The exception to this was a teacher of rhetoric at Bologna and professional letter-writer, Boncompagno da Signa, who in his work titled *The Book on Friendship*, written in the early years of the thirteenth century, challenged the idealistic view of friendship that had dominated medieval thought for so many centuries by focusing and exploring the inherent selfishness of friendship.[45] By casting the work as an interior dialogue between his own Body and Soul, with Reason as the mediator, Boncompagno is able to contrast this idealistic view (articulated by the Soul) with a more pragmatic, indeed pessimistic, view of everyday friendships as perceived by his Body. Displaying an obvious love of classification, Boncompagno has his Body identify twenty-six different types of friends, only four of whom are truly worthy of the name "friend." Of these, the "true friends" are those he labels "the friend for friendship's sake," the faithful friend, the equal friend, and the substantial (*realis*) friend. The remaining types of friends are variations of the "false friend," and are characterized in such detail as to offer us a vivid portrait of how many, or indeed most if we are to trust Boncompagno, friendships would have played out in medieval society.

An example is the type of friend whom Boncompagno called the "vocal" friend. Such a "friend" sees his friend who has just returned from a long trip, and with a big smile welcomes him, saying: "My friend, you've been away so long! Thanks be to God who has brought you back home. I heard that things went well for you, which makes me very happy." Yet through all this the vocal friend will scarcely lift his bottom off the chair. The vocal friend will enthusiastically offer someone use of his house – but only once he knows the person already has somewhere to stay. And if his friend has not yet found a place to stay, the vocal friend will say: "I'm sure you can stay at Titus' house very comfortably," or "Find somewhere to stay, then let me know if there is anything I can do for you; for I am busy with various matters and can't come with you right now."[46] In other words, says Boncompagno, using a strikingly modern metaphor, the vocal friend is "full of hot air," and he is the opposite of the "real" or "substantial" friend, who backs up his words with deeds.

Then there is the conditional friend, who regards friendship as a negotiation or a matter of quid pro quo; the backstabbing friend, who says nice things in front of his friend but slanders him behind his back; the fickle friend, who is full of enthusiasm at first, but quickly loses interest; the fair-weather friend, who quickly disappears in times of need; or the calculating friend, who banks on getting back more than he gives; all types which we might easily recognize today. Other categories reveal the particular concerns of another time and place: the imaginary friend, who pursues certain friendships under the illusion of some hoped-for benefit which never eventuates; the friend who has been deprived of his senses, who is so spell-bound or captivated by a woman that he loses all judgment and sense; the inflated friend, who is driven only by the pursuit of fame; the vitreous or brittle friend, who is driven by envy; the steely or adamantine friend who is motivated by avarice; the friend who is only a friend because of a common enemy, and on Boncompagno goes, describing in total twenty-two different types of false friends. Doubtless he could easily have extended the list, for it is clear from this point of view that false friends are infinite in number, true friends are few and rare.

The common element among the false friendships is that they are based on self-interest: whether money, reputation, personal convenience, the very kind of friendship which the ancient philosophers had dismissed as not even worthy of the name. Against this background, Boncompagno's treatise is an extraordinary break with tradition: not only in focusing on such inferior examples of friendship but even treating such relations *as friendship* – false, untrustworthy, yet representative of actual friendships in the world around him. Or so it seems for the major part of the work. In the end, Boncompagno still tries to make the case for true friendship. Reason, in his role as final arbiter, argues that two kinds of friendship should be distinguished: "heavenly friendship," which is true and eternal and originates from the "true and living God," and "earthly friendship," which is only the semblance of friendship and the preserve of the devil. Only equal, faithful and substantial friendship can rightly be considered heavenly; the remainder are "earthly" and therefore illusory. The terms may be different but the connection to Aelred's "spiritual" and Peter of Blois' "Christian friendship" is obvious. This is why, Reason continues, Boncompagno's Body and Soul have been at odds: the Body has been condemning earthly friendship, while the Soul has been defending heavenly friendship. The treatise then ends on a cautiously optimistic note through the persona of Reason: revere heavenly friendships and the people of your own circle,[47] with heartfelt prayers and through useful services, placing your hope in the supernal friend, because the friendship of the inhabitants of this world is always subject to frailty. As an attempt to reconcile the genuine paradox of friendship – the sublime nature of a few true friendships and the self-interested nature of most "real" friendships – this conclusion seems, in the end, rather tame, and ultimately not too different from the Ciceronian, or its Christianized version, view after all.[48] It is as though Boncompagno, faced with the conclusion that the very concept of friendship is hopelessly idealistic and ultimately deceptive, loses his nerve and retreats to a more conventional and reassuring notion of divine friendship. Yet, Boncompagno's treatise also seems to capture the mood of a society grappling with that age-old question, how to recognize a true friend.

Friendship in the Letter-writing Manuals

It is probably no coincidence that both Peter of Blois and Boncompagno were great letter-writers, professionals in the genre, whose letters were read as models of style at every level of clerical and lay society. Such letters were much more relevant to this audience than the personal letters of Cicero. They also provided a model of how new social relationships could be negotiated, whether with a friend or with a senior churchman. The popularity of letter collections throughout the thirteenth century testifies to the way in which letters could provide guidance not just on how to conduct official business, but on how friends could, or perhaps should, relate to one another. With the increasing importance of the letter came also the need for instruction, not only in Latin grammar, the "universal" language of the literate and educated, but also in the protocols of writing to people of different rank, order and relationship. This task of codifying, and often too of composing on behalf of correspondents, fell to the professional writers, or *dictatores* (from the Latin word "to draft" or "compose"). The manuals of these writers, who included in their number renowned men of the status of Pier della Vigna (Frederick II's protonotary) and Albert of Morra (later Pope Gregory VIII), professional letter-writers such as Peter of Blois, Boncompagno and his fellow Bolognese Guido Fava, as well as countless anonymous writers, survive in hundreds of manuscript copies in libraries across Europe.

Such letter collections offer us a precious picture of the day-to-day practices and rituals of friendship in later medieval society, and of the language of everyday friendship. They also give a sense of the concerns that people had about friendships, such as: what can one expect from a friend? How does one establish a friendship? With whom could one be friends? Finally, as codifications of social practice, the manuals tell us how friendship was conceived, articulated and conducted in medieval society; in short, they offer us a view of friendship in the medieval period from a thoroughly practical, and largely secular perspective.

Friendship seems to have occupied such an important place in medieval letter collections for several reasons. First, it was generally held that the letter owed its genesis, at least in part, to the particular needs of friends to conceal their secrets. Secondly, the letter was central to the quintessentially medieval act of *petitioning*, that is, the asking of a favour or material benefit from one in a position to assist. Accordingly, sample letters of petition make up a large part of the letter-writing manuals. Finally, it is clear from many of the commonplaces about friendship in the Middle Ages that the preservation of friendships over long distances was a perennial and key concern. The letter, naturally, was seen as a crucial way of overcoming this problem, and a number of maxims and proverbs on this issue exist: "The frequent exchange of letters between friends gives great solace to one who is absent," and "Companions separated by distance, not in soul but only in body, should still visit each other by exchanging letters," to mention a couple.[49] In a very real sense, then, and not just as a result of the vagaries of preservation of historical documents, the letter in the thirteenth century represented the genre of friendship *par excellence.*[50]

In these practically oriented manuals, friendship is seldom discussed in theoretical terms, but rather tends to be exemplified through model letters. Scattered in large numbers throughout the manuals, the relevant letters are normally signalled by rubrics of varying explicitness, such as "From a friend to a friend," "From a friend seeking advice from a friend," "A letter of commendation on behalf of a friend," "A letter of consolation to a friend" or "A friend commends his exiled son to a friend, with a response in which the friend's son is willingly received." According to medieval letter-writing protocol, the salutation, or greeting, was of crucial importance, if one was to render the recipient suitably benevolent and, thus, compliant. Hence many of the models simply offered a list of appropriate ways to address different kinds of friends. The *inimicus*, the "non-friend," on the other hand, was denied a salutation altogether. The terms and principles used in the letter manuals in connection with friendship prove to be consistent across time and location in the Latin West, and thus offer us the possibility of better understanding the conception of friendship underlying its conventional language.

The Language of Friendship

The manuals reveal that two ideas dominated the way friendship was spoken of in the Middle Ages. The first of these conceptualizes friendship as a kind of "bond" or "tie": the terms *vinculum* ("tie," "band" or "chain") and *nodus* ("knot") were the most frequently used words to express this idea; occasionally we find the term *nexus* ("entwining"). These terms were obviously used figuratively, as they are in modern English where their literal meanings have all but disappeared in the context of friendship. In Latin texts on friendship, however, the literal meaning would not have been far away in the medieval mind, especially when strengthened, as they frequently were, by one of the many Latin verbs referring to the act of binding (such as *iungor, copulor, concathenor* or *constringor*). This language seemed to remind medieval writers that while friendship could be a particularly close and strong relationship, it could also be severed, either intentionally or by circumstance. Accordingly, the employment of this imagery is often accompanied by a concern or desire for preservation or strengthening of the bond, frequently in the salutation part of the letter.[51]

Notwithstanding the physical nature of this image, the use of terms for "bond" could also be used to emphasize the affective nature of the bond. The bond is very often spoken of as a bond of love (*vinculum amoris*) or affection (*vinculum dilectionis*), when it is not explicitly called a bond of friendship (*vinculum amicitie*).

A different, though equally common, way of expressing friendship was through the concept of a kind of "pledge" or "agreement." This idea is almost always conveyed by the term *fedus* (*foedus* in classical Latin) or its related form *confederatio*, literally meaning a "pact," "alliance" or "contract." The phrase *fedus amicitie* is very common in all types of medieval texts; occasionally the word *pactus* is also used for the same idea. This language seems to conceptualize friendship as more of a deliberate arrangement rather than as an affective tie. At times it could sound frankly strategic.

The term *fedus,* in particular, would also have carried with it the connotation of service and obligation, reminiscent of the relationship between lord and vassal under the feudal system. While *amicitia* would have been clearly distinguished in nature from the feudal relationship, nevertheless the two concepts shared a common manifestation contained in the idea of service, as is well attested by the models. The letter manuals are full of promises of and requests for such services between friends. Such services commonly involved money or material goods or "intercessions" through the use of one's influence or connections, such as a letter of recommendation or, better, a position or benefice. Frequently, such requests for services are explicitly justified by an appeal to the "laws" of friendship, emphasizing perhaps the contractual conception of friendship. This offers linguistic support to Adalberto's view of friendship, with its emphasis on mutual services.

Medieval commonplaces about friendship confirm this impression. Sentiments such as "The rule of reason demands that, between friends, one should condescend to the entreaties of the other," or "Friendship is strengthened whenever favourable service is rendered to the seeker," are regularly found in the letter manuals, cited to affirm the legitimacy of this expectation of help or service from a friend. In Boncompagno's main compilation of model letters, he offered an example of this sentiment in practice under the title of "General letter for those who seek assistance from others":

> Every time I am afflicted with some necessity or trouble, I turn to
> you, without hesitation, as one of those friends I have found to be

special in all manner of events, with the certain hope that you will
attend to my entreaties efficaciously.[52]

Leclercq sums up this notion neatly: "A friend [in medieval society] is
essentially someone from whom you can ask something. Friendship
assigns the right to insist, and entails, between equals, the obligation
of mutual service."[53]

Naturally, the idealists argued that such expectations were beneath
true friendship. One of Aelred's interlocutors had noted sceptically
that "some people believe that they satisfy the demands of friendship
if they repay a friend in turn for every benefit or favour rendered by
the friend."[54] Bene of Florence, a contemporary of Boncompagno,
includes in his list of proverbs the following caution: "The pleasing
sweetness of favours does not preserve the bond of friendship."[55] But
such doubts were outweighed by the reality of the language attached
to friendship. Among the most common Latin words used to express
the manifestations of friendship were *servitia, obsequia, beneficia, grata,
blanditia* and *suffragia*, and all represented the notion of favours, services, or benefits that one might legitimately expect to receive, and in
turn be expected to provide, in the name of friendship. Words such as
servitia and *obsequia*, in particular, were formerly indicative of the feudal relationship, and indeed there can sometimes appear to be considerable overlap between friendship and feudal allegiance. Marc
Bloch, the historian of feudalism, has written that in the Middle Ages
the feudal relationship of vassalage and the ancient tie of kinship were
two "equally binding ties" that took precedence over all others.[56]
Where those partaking of the feudal relationship made explicit "pacts
of protection and obedience," friends seem to have made tacit pacts
of mutual service and legitimate expectation. The obligations accepted
as part of the feudal bond, according to Bloch, were generally called
servitia, adding, "Not so long before, the word would have horrified a
free man."[57] Far from horrifying the late medieval mind, the word
servitia, and its associated terms, in the context of friendship, would
have sounded very reassuring, as the legitimate expectation of some
benefit or advantage.

This connection between friendship and feudalism also hints at the
flexibility of the term *amicus* in medieval society. In a very broad
sense, the word "friend" could cover a wide range of relationships. In
the feudal era, it was common to refer to one's family as "friends,"
with the qualification "friends by blood" apparently needing to be
used only rarely.[58] A similar breadth occurs in late medieval society,

where the term could conceivably cover kin, neighbours, fellow townsfolk, associates, and even the wider members of one's household (*domestici*) – in other words, all those one might expect to turn to for support or as allies.

Friendship between Unequals

Whereas early Western ideas of friendship emphasized the importance of equality of friends,[59] medieval Europe was willing to accept that friendship could exist between unequals. In fact, there seems to have been a strong belief that the very act of entering into a friendship *made* people equal, traces of which can be seen in Cicero ("It is very important in friendship to treat inferiors as equals") and in Aelred ("You should not neglect to make your friend your equal, if you really wish to be a friend. For those who do not maintain equality do not rightly cultivate friendship").[60] Nevertheless, some ambivalence remained, and many writers felt the need to justify the practice. Brunetto Latini, a late thirteenth-century Italian scholar best known as the teacher and friend of the great Italian poet Dante Alighieri, spoke of such friendships not only as permissible but mutually beneficial:

> the great should give profit to the small [that is, the lower ranks], and the small should give honour and reverence to the great, and this should be done according to what is suitable for each, for it is in this way that friendship is preserved.[61]

But the most elaborate and eloquent defence of friendship between unequals is contained in a letter that has come down to us in the name of Dante Alighieri himself writing to Can Grande, Lord of Verona, evidently his superior in rank:

> I am not afraid, in taking on the name of friend, as some perchance may object, that I will incur the guilt of presumption, since unequals are not less bound by the sacred bonds of friendship than are equals. Indeed, if one is willing to look at pleasurable and useful friendships, most frequently it will be obvious to him that they join persons of pre-eminence to their inferiors. And if the understanding turns to true, disinterested friendship, will it not show that frequently men of obscure fortune, outstanding in honesty, were friends of most illustrious princes? Why not? Since not even friendship between God and man is impeded by the disparity! But if to anyone that which is asserted seems now to be improper, let him hear the Holy Spirit offering certain men the sharing of his

love. For in *Wisdom* one reads concerning wisdom: "For she is an infinite treasure to men; which they that use, become the friends of God." But the inexperience of the common people has judgment without discrimination; and just as the sun is thought to be the size of a foot, thus concerning customs they are deceived in vain credulity. For us, however, to whom it is given to know the best that is in us, it is not proper to follow the tracks of the herd, but rather we ought to confront their errors. For, being lacking in intellect and reason, though endowed as it were by divine freedom, they are restricted by no custom. It is not strange, since they are not directed by law, but rather the law by them. It is clear then, as I said above, namely, that I am your servant and friend, is in no way presumptuous.[62]

Regardless of whether or not Dante was the author of this remarkable document (there is some debate over this issue), the text captures perfectly the medieval concern with status, and its implications for friendship. In such skilled hands, friendship is easily endowed with the force of a great social "equalizer."

Yet, however "equal" such friendships might be in theory, in practice social convention still dictated that superiors were to be acknowledged and addressed as such, and this inevitably gave rise to some uncertainty and tension. The letter-writing manuals claimed to offer specific examples exactly for such circumstances. "Should the recipient be a superior friend," Guido Fava writes, "one should write in the following terms":

"To his beloved lord and friend"; or "To his special friend P., as though to a lord, shining with honourable character"; or "To I., distinguished by great wisdom; greetings, and all that can be of love and service"; or "greetings and may our friendship continue unharmed for all time."[63]

In phrases such as these, with the combination of terms such as "friend" and "lord" and expressions of love and service, the traditional appeal to friendship is mixed with echoes of the old feudal relationships. And yet the expression "lord and friend" – or its opposite "servant and friend," as found in the Letter to Can Grande – manages to both confirm the paradoxical nature of the relationship while somehow resolving it, offering a subtle and neat way of paying due respect without sacrificing the equality represented by true friendship. Most revealing perhaps is the following excerpt from an early fourteenth-century letter-writing manual (after a series of model salutations):

> Such a friendly manner of speaking is possible for a king to a king,
> soldier to soldier, judge to judge, doctor to doctor, cleric to cleric,
> and from anyone to someone who is his equal, and even from a
> superior to an inferior, if he so wishes. However, an inferior should
> not speak to a superior in such a friendly manner, *however much*
> *they may be bound by friendship*, but in a way befitting his own
> status.[64]

This is a remarkably explicit acknowledgment of the tension inherent
in "unequal friendships": such friendships were evidently possible,
but the norms and expectations of a different social relationship, the
protocol accompanying interactions between people of different ranks,
apparently determined how those friendships played out in public.

Another way of negotiating the competing demands of friendship
and social protocol was possible through the use of the second person
plural pronoun *vos*, in place of the standard singular pronoun *tu*, as a
marker of the social superiority of the addressee. The availability of a
formal pronoun (which English has had to do without ever since the
originally plural pronoun *you* subsumed the function of *thou* as the
standard pronoun for singular usage several hundred years ago) enabled medieval correspondents, and speakers, to dutifully observe
the social hierarchy and at the same time to appeal, with a sense of
legitimacy and rightful expectation, to the language and convention
of friendship. In due course through the thirteenth century, this usage, to judge from the letter manuals, would become so common that
the use of the formal pronoun seems to have become standard even
between friends of equal status, almost to the point of becoming
meaningless. (Boncompagno scoffs that he had even heard it being
used between barbers and publicans.) But to the end of the medieval
period, at least, it remained a very useful way of recognizing, justifying, and helping to resolve the paradoxical nature of the unequal
friendship.

Aristotle Rediscovered

By the mid-thirteenth century, the primacy of the Ciceronian view of
friendship was challenged even further when a new source of inspiration for reflecting on friendship became available: Aristotle's
Nichomachean Ethics, translated into Latin in the late twelfth century
by Burgundio of Pisa. One of its most lucid exponents was Thomas
Aquinas (1225–1274), who drew extensively on Aristotle's discussion

of friendship within a very different context from that of the Italian *dictatores*, that of theology. Aquinas was determined to draw on the *Ethics* to show how Aristotelian thought might relate to that of Christian tradition. As part of his commentary on Peter Lombard's Sentences, he explains how Aristotle's discussion of friendship can be situated within a Christian contest.[65] Thus he regularly cites the authority of "the philosopher" to support his understanding that all friendship has virtue as a foundation, and that friendship always delights in conversation and the company of the other. He even acknowledges that friendship can exist between a man and wife as something natural, and containing what is "honest, useful and delightful." He is aware that Aristotle had described different kinds of friendship, and that not all may approach the ideal of friendship that does not seek any other reward, thus approaching *caritas* most fully.[66] Aquinas comes back to these themes in his final attempt at a grand synthesis of philosophy and theology, his *Summa theologia*, begun in the 1260s but never completed. In it,[67] he lays out his theme that the goal of the law of charity is to make friendship between men as well as between man and God. Reflecting on the relationship between *amicitia* and *caritas*, he concludes that *caritas* is "a kind of friendship of man to God."[68] Unlike ordinary friendship, the friendship of charity extends even to enemies, whom we love for the sake of God. In linking friendship and charity in this way, Thomas achieves a synthesis that Augustine had always shied away from, relating a classical ideal of *amicitia* to the Christian goal of *caritas*. Thomas recognizes that there can be different kinds of friendship, whether political or personal, but his major concern is to show what Aristotle does not talk about, that all true friendship depends on *caritas*, and that its foundation must be God as the principle of happiness.[69] Just as the philosopher had explained that it was the particular gift of friends to seek to live together, thus Christ promises to be present in his Church.[70] Whereas Augustine had contrasted friendship with the love of God, Aquinas creates a theology based around a celebration of friendship. His interest in friendship is, however, primarily theological rather than concerned with its implementation in practice.

Friendship in Vernacular Literature

While ideals of comradeship had frequently been evoked in the literature of romance in the twelfth and thirteenth centuries, the classical ideal of friendship was first disseminated in a vernacular context by Brunetto Latini in his *Livres dou Tresor*. A Florentine who spent much time in the court of Alphonso X of Castille and then in France (including Paris) during the 1260s, Latini presented a vast synthesis of classical learning in the French tongue, including a significant section on friendship culled from Cicero and Seneca, mostly, as with Albertano, through the medium of twelfth-century Latin compilations of classical learning, like the *Moralium dogma philosophorum*. While he endeavoured to cover most of the curriculum, Latini's particular interest was in ethical questions, such as those covered by Aristotle, Cicero and Seneca. Being the master whom Dante would draw from (though paradoxically also consign to hell), Latini provides a fascinating link between the world of the Parisian schools and the self-confident urban societies of northern Italy.

Rather than friendship, however, it was love (*amor*) that was attracting heated debate among those concerned with literature. Jean de Meun's continuation to the *Romance of the Rose*, initiated by Guillaume de Loris, brought the issue of the passion felt by a male lover for his female beloved, imagined as a rose, ripe for conquest, diverted attention away from friendship between men, such as Cicero had written about. Jean de Meun reports that he made a translation into French of Aelred's *De spiritali amicitia*, but no copy of this has survived. Jean de Meun was interested in the letters of Abelard and Heloise (which he also translated), but failed to grasp the Ciceronian values of friendship that inspired Heloise. In the *Romance of the Rose*, Heloise became the lover of Abelard, who would stop at nothing in protesting her love, rather than a woman who shared Cicero's conception that true love did not seek any reward.

In a world in which great attention was attached to the subtleties of social hierarchy, whether in the clerical and courtly circles of France and England or in the competitive environment of the city-states of northern Italy, the bond of friendship between equals was accorded a privileged and indeed sacred status. Chronicles and romances alike acknowledge the power and symbolic value of the "pact of friendship" (*foedus amicitiae*), often sealed with a kiss. This might be a formal bond between two kings, such as Richard the Lionheart and Philip Augustus, or it could simply be a sacred pact between two men of similar social status and concerns.[71] Such ideals were celebrated in vernacular literature throughout the medieval period. In great epics such as the *Song of Roland*, composed probably in the eleventh century but perhaps on the basis of older traditions, the friendship of Roland and Oliver is presented as between great warriors, without any distraction from women. In romances like *Ami and Amile*, first known through a Latin verse composition by Raoul Tortaire, an eleventh-century monk of Fleury, but expanded in a host of vernacular languages between the twelfth and fourteenth centuries, friendship becomes more complex.[72] Ami and Amile (or Amis and Amiloun) were identical in every way, though born to different parents, but fall into a tragic situation after Amile has been seduced into sleeping with Belissaunt, daughter of Charlemagne. Ami, married to the shrewish Lubias, agrees to take Amile's place in a mortal combat with the evil Hardret, Charlemagne's seneschal. The ensuing drama celebrates not the unsatisfactory relationships with women in which they are involved, but the willingness of Ami to save the life of Amile, and of Amile to save that of Amis by being prepared to kill his own children (echoing the biblical story of Abraham and Isaac). Here, as in so much medieval romance literature, friendship is portrayed as a quintessentially masculine bond, very different from the perilous nature of love for a woman.

The sacred character of "the pact of friendship" was not simply a literary ideal, conveyed through romances. In medieval churches it was not uncommon for two male friends to be buried together, reflecting a desire to perpetuate that bond of friendship into eternity, with as much seriousness as a husband and wife might be buried together. Picking up themes of a sacred commitment in same-sex friendship initially explored by John Boswell, Alan Bray situates tombs like that of John Bloxham and John Whytton from the late fourteenth century in Merton College, Oxford, within a much longer tradition that he traces back to Aelred of Rievaulx but that would flourish in the sixteenth and seventeenth centuries. The practice of being buried together would even be continued into the late nineteenth century, as exemplified in the desire of John Henry Newman (1801–1890) to be buried in the same tomb as his close friend, Father Ambrose St John, who had died in 1875.[73] This great admirer of medieval Christian Europe himself believed that friendship should last beyond death.

Conclusion

Friendship in the medieval period, as in classical antiquity, was always delicately poised between awareness of a relationship that might be mutually advantageous within society and a sense of an ideal relationship between equals, freely chosen and accorded special status. Cicero had lamented the gulf between friendships that were self-seeking and those that were genuinely selfless in his treatise *De amicitia*, setting up ideals that would frequently be championed in the medieval and early modern period. Yet Ciceronian ideals would be powerfully modified in late antiquity by being adapted to Christian values, in which friendship served to provide not a forum for political engagement in the service of the state but a preparation for eternity within the framework of the Church. A classical emphasis on celebrating friendship had to coexist with Christian teaching about the priority of universal love, embodied in the figure of Jesus.

A renewed enthusiasm for Ciceronian teaching about friendship in the late eleventh and twelfth centuries made an impact both within and outside monastic circles. The friendship of Abelard and Heloise offers a particularly bold example of how ideals of *amicitia* could seek to cross the boundaries of gender. Such attempts remained exceptions to the norm, which tended much more to celebrate friendship within a same-sex relationship. Within both monastic and vernacular literature, masculine norms prevailed. While Aelred of Rievaulx developed an emotionally intense ideal of friendship within a monastic context, Peter of Blois extended similar ideals to a wider clerical audience. In thirteenth-century Italy, the epistolary manuals of Boncompagno, Guido Fava and other *dictatores* provide precious insight into the vitality and variety of the bonds of friendship that could be found in the context of the self-confident Italian communes of the thirteenth century. They provided guidance to the negotiation of friendship between men, paralleling the instruction given by romance epics in the vernacular tongues of Europe. Yet the very popularity of these epistolary manuals would also be the cause of their undoing. While they provided a step-by-step guide to the way friendships and alliances might be entered into, they could easily drift away from the literary elegance that had shaped some of the most eloquent literary relationships of the twelfth century, such as that of Abelard and Heloise, or of John of Salisbury and his circle of both clerical and monastic friends.

A major transformation in the study of letter-writing would take place in 1345, when Petrarch (1304–1374) discovered a manuscript in the cathedral library of Verona that contained several hundred letters written by Cicero to a small circle of friends. During the thirteenth century, scholarly enthusiasm for Latin translations of Aristotelian writings had the effect of displacing the wave of interest in Cicero's *De amicitia* that had attracted such attention in the twelfth century. Individual copies could be found of many of Cicero's prolific writings, in well-stocked medieval libraries. Yet it was due in no small part to Petrarch's discovery of a collection of Cicero's letters that attention would return once again to Ciceronian ideals. Petrarch had not come across this particular set of letters before. He seized on them as providing an image of the "real" Cicero, not a statesman or orator, but someone with whom he could be on intimate terms. Inspired by these letters to compile his own collection of personal letters addressed to friends, Petrarch addressed one of them to Cicero himself, to whom he writes as if he were a long-lost friend:

> Francesco sends his greetings to his Cicero. After a lengthy and extensive search for your letters, I found them where I least expected, and I then read them with great eagerness. I listened to you speak on many subjects, complain about many things, waver in your opinions, O Marcus Tullius, and I who had long known the kind of preceptor that you were for others now at last recognize who you were for yourself.[74]

Petrarch shared his excitement at discovering how Cicero used letters to maintain a circle of close friends, by addressing similar letters to his own circle of like-minded friends in fourteenth-century Europe. Petrarch's claim that he had recovered "the real Cicero" would be of enormous influence in shaping subsequent perception that he was responsible, through this discovery, of initiating a renaissance of classical culture, after centuries of neglect. Petrarch modelled his *Epistulae ad familiares* on those of Cicero. He was able to draw from Cicero a philosophical vision subtly different from previous generations because he did not seek to fuse their understanding of friendship with that of Augustine, as previous theorists had done.[75] Petrarch was more at home in the elite environment of princely courts, whether of cardinals or of great noble families, such as the Visconti, than in the turbulent world of the Italian city-state. The sort of friendships that he sought to cultivate with the great and powerful was very different from those which Cicero had delighted in cultivating during the last decades of the Roman Republic. Nonetheless, Cicero's letters provided both Petrarch and his many admirers with a template by which to build up friendships with like-minded, scholarly friends.

In many ways, the coming of the Black Death in 1347–1348 heralded the beginning of the end of an old order in which Latin had been the accepted way for centuries of establishing and maintaining friendships within an educate elite. In the towns and cities of Italy, friendships outside that scholarly milieu would become articulated in the Italian language, most eloquently for example, in the letters of Catherine of Siena (1347–1388). The use of the vernacular would become more normal in France by the end of the fourteenth century, as the letters of Christine de Pizan (1364–c. 1430) critical of the misogyny implicit within Jean de Meun's *Romance of the Rose*, would illustrate. Within England, the expansion of literacy outside a clerical elite would only become fully established by the mid-fifteenth century, as the letters exchanged by members of the Paston family would attest. The value of friendship had been celebrated across the centuries within the Latin language. By the mid-fourteenth century, the cultural monopoly once enjoyed by Latin was no longer assured. Petrarch's enthusiasm for the letters of Cicero and the values of friendship to which he was attached, would now have to be translated into a vernacular context. The way in which friends could communicate with each other was set to change.

Notes

1. Brian Patrick McGuire, *Friendship and Community: The Monastic Experience 350–1250* (Kalamazoo, MI: Cistercian Publications, 1988).

2. For an excellent overview of the transmission of Ciceronian ideals in the medieval period see James McEvoy, "The Theory of Friendship in the Latin Middle Ages: Hermeneutics, Contextualization and the Transmission and Reception of Ancient Texts and Ideas, from c. AD 350 to c. 1500," in Julian Haseldine (ed.), *Friendship in Medieval Europe* (Stroud, UK: Sutton, 1999), pp. 3–36. This volume contains many valuable contributions to the theme, not least by Julian Haseldine himself.

3. On ideals of friendship in the ancient Rome, there is much of value in John T. Fitzgerald (ed.), *Greco-Roman Perspectives on Friendship* (Atlanta, GA: Scholars Press, 1997), pp. 59–76, David Konstan, *Friendship in the Classical World* (Cambridge: Cambridge University Press, 1997) and P. A. Brunt, "Amicitia in the Late Roman Republic," *Proceedings of the Cambridge Philological Society* 191 (1965), pp. 1–20.

4. Seneca, *Ad Lucilium epistulae morales* (ed. and trans. Richard M. Gummere; London: Heinemann, 1917–25); *Letters from a Stoic: Epistulae morales ad Lucilium* (trans. Robin Campbell; Harmondsworth: Penguin, 1969).

5. Paul J. Burton, "*Amicitia* in Plautus: A Study of Roman Friendship Processes," *American Journal of Philology* 125 (2004), pp. 209–43.

6. Translations of a number of such letters are included within the study of Stanley K. Stowers, *Letter Writing in Greco-Roman Antiquity* (Philadelphia: The Westminster Press, 1986), especially pp. 72–74, 97–99, 145–47, 156–59.

7. A letter survives from Taus to her lover, Apollonius, a married man and civil governor in Egypt in the second century CE, *Select Papyri* 1, ed. A. S. Hunt and C. C. Edgar (Loeb Classical Library; London: Heinemann, 1949), no. 115, 1:309–31.

8. Mary Garrison, "'Send More Socks': On Mentality and the Preservation Context of Medieval Letters," in *New Approaches to Medieval Communication* (ed. Marco Mostert; Turnhout: Brepols, 1999), pp. 66–99.

9. A useful brief synthesis on letters, although unfortunately only up to the twelfth century, is that of Giles Constable, *Letters and Letter-Collections*, Typologie des sources du moyen âge (Turnhout: Brepols, 1976).

10. William D. Patt, "The Early 'ars dictaminis' as Response to a Changing Society," *Viator* 9 (1978), pp. 133–55, and more fully Carol Dana Lanham, "Freshman Composition in the Early Middle Ages: Epistolography and Rhetoric before the Ars Dictaminis," *Viator* 23 (1992), pp. 115–34.

11. Numerous editions and translations survive of Cicero's *Laelius* (often known as *De amicitia*). There is a critical edition of the Latin text by Karl Simbek (Leipzig: Teubner, 1917; reprinted Stuttgart: Teubner, 1971). Michael Grant provides a translation in Cicero, *The Good Life* (Harmondsworth: Penguin, 1971), pp. 175–227. An excerpt, trans. Frank Copley, is given within *Other Selves: Philosophers on Friendship* (ed. Michael Pakaluk; Indianapolis: Hackett Publishing, 1991).

12. Aelred, *De spiritali amicitia* (ed. A. Hoste; Corpus Christianorum Continuatio Mediaeualis, 1; Turnhout: Brepols, 1971), pp. 287–350; *Aelred of Rievaulx's Spiritual Friendship* (trans. Mark F. Williams; London: Associated University Presses, 1994). There is no English translation of Peter of Blois, *De amicitia christiana* (ed. M.-M. Davy; *Un traité de l'amour du XIIe siècle. Pierre de Blois* [Paris: De Boccard, 1932]).

13. On the treatises of Boncompagno and Albertano, see pp. 93–95 below.

14. Ovid, *Ars amatoria* 2.281–86.

15. *Amores* 1.11.19–28; *Remedium amoris* 717–20.

16. Paul Veyne, *Roman Erotic Elegy: Love, Poetry and the West* (trans. David Pellauer; Chicago: University of Chicago Press, 1988), pp. 83, 188.

17. 3.7.53–54.

18. On Christian terminology of love, see Bernard V. Brady, *Christian Love* (Washington, DC: Georgetown University Press, 2003), pp. 52–54.

19. McEvoy, "The Theory of Friendship," p. 7.

20. See, e.g., Libanius, *Autobiography and Selected Letters* (ed. and trans. A. F. Norman; 2 vols; Cambridge, MA: Harvard University Press, 1992); Symmachus, *Lettres* (ed. and trans. Jean Pierre Callu; Paris: Belles lettres, 1972–1982).

21. *Epistolae Senecae ad Paulum et Pauli ad Senecam* (ed. C. W. Barlow; Horn: American Academy in Rome, 1938).

22. *Conf.* 4.7.

23. *Conf.* 4.8.

24. *De doctrina christiana* 3. 10.

25. Gerd Althoff, "Friendship and Political Order," in Haseldine (ed.), *Friendship*, pp. 91–105 and *Family, Friends and Followers: Political and Social Bonds in Early Medieval Europe* (trans. Christopher Carroll; Cambridge: Cambridge University Press, 2004).

26. These texts have been edited and translated by Peter Dronke, *Medieval Latin and the Rise of the European Love Lyric* (2 vols; Oxford: Oxford University Press, 1968), II, pp. 422–27, 472–82.

27. On this theme, see Gerald Bond, "'Iocus amoris': The Poetry of Baudri of Bourgueil, and the Formation of the Ovidian Subculture," *Traditio* 42 (1986), pp. 143–93.

28. See Carol Dana Lanham, *Salutatio Formulas in Latin Letters to 1200: Syntax, Style, and Theory* (Eugene, OR: Wipf & Stock, 2004 [1974]).

29. *The Letters of Abelard and Heloise* (trans. B. Radice; London: Penguin, 1974), p. 66.

30. *Letters of Abelard and Heloise*, p. 113.

31. *Letters of Abelard and Heloise*, p. 114.

32. *Letters of Abelard and Heloise*, p. 133.

33. Mistranslated in *Letters of Abelard and Heloise*, p. 159.

34. Constant J. Mews, *The Lost Love Letters of Heloise and Abelard: Perceptions of Dialogue in Twelfth-Century France* (New York: Palgrave, 1999), a volume that includes a translation by Chiavaroli and Mews of the love letters in question.

35. Letters 49, 50.

36. For translations and commentary on Goscelin's treatise, see Stephanie Hollis (ed.), *Writing the Wilton Women: Goscelin's Legend of Edith and Liber confortatorius* (Turnhout: Brepols, 2004).

37. *Aelred of Rievaulx's Spiritual Friendship* (trans. Mark F. Williams); see also Brian Patrick McGuire, *Friendship and Community*, pp. 296–338 and *Brother and Lover: Aelred of Rievaulx* (New York: Crossroad, 1994).

38. Walter Daniel, *The Life of Ailred of Rievaulx* (trans. F. M. Powicke; London: Thomas Nelson, 1950).

39. For an excellent introduction to John's writing and thought, see Cary J. Nederman, *John of Salisbury*. (Tempe, AZ: Arizona Center for Medieval and Renaissance Studies, 2005).

40. Pierre de Blois, *Un traité de l'amour du XIIe siècle* (ed. M.-M. Davy; Paris: De Boccard, 1932).

41. Margaret Mullet, "Friendship in Byzantium: Genre, Topos and Network," in Haseldine, *Friendship*, pp. 166–84 at p. 166.

42. In the original Latin, *De amore et dilectione Dei et proximi et aliarum rerum et de forma vitae*. Edition by Sharon Hiltz Romino, Bibliotheca Augustana website, http://www.hs-augsburg/Chronologia/Lspost13/Albertanus/alb_amo0.html, accessed 8 February 2009. There is no published English translation of the work. All citations are from Book II, preamble Chapter 1, except where indicated. Translations are ours.

43. *Pierre de Blois*, ed. Davy, p. 176.

44. Conference 16.

45. Edited by Sarina Nathan, in *Amicitia di Maestro Boncompagno da Signa* (Miscellanea di Letteratura del Medio Evo, III; Rome: Società Filologica Romana, 1909). There is as yet no full English translation of the work. The article by Michael Dunne, "Good Friends or Bad Friends? The *Amicitia* of Boncompagno da Signa," published in *Amor amicitiae: On the Love that is Friendship: Essays in Medieval Thought and beyond in Honor of the Rev. Professor James McEvoy* (ed. Thomas A. F. Kelly and Philipp W. Rosemann; Leuven: Peeters, 2004), pp. 147–66, offers a brief overview of the work with translated extracts.

46. Nathan, *Amicitia* XIX. All translations of texts in this chapter are ours, unless otherwise indicated.

47. *aula:* a key term originally meaning a hall or court, but also used to signify the people one associated with in those places.

48. cf *De Amicitia*: "the fact remains that the two things which most commonly prove men to be unreliable and weak are these: if, when they are prospering, they drop their friends, or if when their friends are in trouble, they desert them. And so, when anyone in either of these circumstances has shown himself a man of conviction, reliable, and loyal, we are bound to adjudge him one of a very rare species of men – *a species virtually divine*" (trans. Frank Copley; our italics).

49. Guido Fava, *Exordia*, edited by Giuseppe Vecchi, in "Il proverbio nella pratica letteraria dei dettatori della scuola di Bologna," *Studi mediolatini e volgari* II (1954), pp. 283–302.

50. A point recognized by Jean Leclercq over sixty years ago in his article "L'amitié dans les letters au moyen âge" in the *Revue du moyen âge latin* 1 (1945), pp. 391–410. However, the contents of many of the major letter-writing manuals of the medieval period were far less known at the time of his writing.

51. For example, "Greetings, and whatever customarily restores a bond about to break" ("Master Godfrey," in Vincenzo Licitra, "La *Summa de arte dictandi* di Maestro Goffredo," in *Studi medievali*, 3rd series, 1966 (VII), pp. 865–913 at p. 889.

52. *Boncompagnus*, 5.7.3. Edited by Steven M. Wight, published on http://dobc.unipv.it/scrineum/wight, also accessible via the Bibliotheca Augustana website, http://www.fh-augsburg.de/~harsch/augustana, accessed 1 October 2007.

53. Leclercq, "*L'amitié dans les lettres au moyen âge*," p. 404.

54. Aelred, *De spiritali amicitia*, p. 31; *Aelred of Rievaulx's Spiritual Friendship* (trans. Williams), p. 49.

55. Edited by Gian Carlo Alessio, in *Bene Florentini Candelabrum* (Thesaurus Mundi: Bibliotheca scriptorum latinorum mediae et recentioris aetatis, 23; Padua: Antenore, 1983).

56. Marc Bloch, *Feudal Society* (trans. L. A. Manyon; London: Routledge & Kegan Paul, 1961), p. 149.

57. Bloch, *Feudal Society*, p. 150

58. Bloch, *Feudal Society*, p. 124.

59. McEvoy, "The Theory of Friendship," p. 35.

60. *De amicitia*, 69; *De spiritali amicitia*, pp. 96–97; *Aelred of Rievaulx's Spiritual Friendship* (trans. Williams), p. 97.

61. *Tresor* II.44.17; trans. Paul Barrette and Spurgeon Baldwin, in *Brunetto Latini, The Book of the Treasure* (Garland Library of Medieval Literature, 90; New York: Garland, 1993).

62. Based on the translation of James Marchand, published on http://www.english.udel.edu.dean/cangrand.html, accessed 2 January 2007.

63. Guido Fava, *Summa Dictaminis*, XXVI, ed. Augusto Gaudenzi, in *Il Propugnatore*, III (1890) 1, pp. 287–338.

64. Bichilino da Spello, *Pomerium rethorice*, II.xi.5, under the rubric "On salutations between friends and associates." Edited by Vincenzo Licitra, *Il* Pomerium Rethorice *di Bichilino da Spello* (Spello: Centro Italiano di Studi sull'Alto Medioevo, 1992), p. 33 (our italics).

65. *In III Sent.* D. 27, q.2; Bernard V. Brady summarizes Thomas's teaching on the relationship between friendship and love in *Christian Love*, pp. 164–79. There is suggestive comparison of his ideas on love and friendship with those of Islamic thinkers in David B. Burrell, *Friendship and Ways to Truth* (Notre-Dame, IN: Notre Dame Press, 2000), pp. 67–86. Janice Schulz explores his ethical teaching in "Love of Friendship and the Perfection of Finite Persons," in *Medieval Masters: Essays in Memory of Msgr. E. A. Synan* (ed. R. E. Houser; Houston: University of St Thomas, 1999), pp. 209–32.

66. d. 27, q.2; *In IV Sent.* D. 31 q.1.1.2; *In III Sent.* D. 29, q.1.4–6.

67. Aquinas, *Summa theologia* 2–1.99.1–2.

68. Aquinas, *Summa theologia* 2–2.23.1, 5; 24.2; 25.3.

69. Aquinas, *Summa theologia* II.2, q. 26.2.

70. Aquinas, *Summa theologia* III, q. 75.1.

71. C. Stephen Jaeger opens his study of the ideal of love with this particularly well-recorded example, observing the fallacy of identifying it as homosexual, in *Ennobling Love* (Philadelphia: University of Pennsylvania Press, 1999), pp. 7–12.

72. Raoul Tortaire. *Ami and Amile* (trans. Samuel Danon and Samuel N. Rosenberg; York, South Carolina: French Literature Publications Company, 1981).

73. Alan Bray, *The Friend* (Chicago: University of Chicago Press, 2003), esp. pp. 78–139, 289–306. Bray draws on the earlier work of John Boswell, *Same-sex Unions in Premodern Europe* (New York: Villiard Books, 1994).

74. Petrarch, *Epistulae ad familiares* 24.3.

75. Claude Lafleur, *Pétrarque et l'amitié* (Paris: Vrin, 2001), pp. 85–86.

Chapter 4

RENAISSANCE FRIENDSHIPS: TRADITIONAL TRUTHS, NEW AND DISSENTING VOICES

Carolyn James and Bill Kent

Two Images of Renaissance Friendship

Two images, one documentary and English, the other visual and Italian, give us at once some idea of the rich variety and vitality of the lived friendships experienced in European societies between the late thirteenth and early seventeenth centuries; and of the ubiquity of late medieval and Renaissance discourses on friendship that informed, and were in turn shaped by, those everyday experiences and exchanges. Both examples afford us, too, the knowledge that Renaissance people, like their medieval counterparts, continued to be absorbed by classical concepts of friendship while nuancing and adapting (sometimes abandoning) them according to changing circumstances, audiences, experiences and ideas.

Our first example takes us to England. Early in 1460, William Worcester, a connection of the Paston family, wrote thanking an unnamed friend for his kindly letter. "A very frende at nede," he began – quoting, whether consciously or not, the title of a popular English poem in praise of friendship written by John Lydgate – "experience will schewe be deede, as wele as be autorité of Aristotle in the *Etiques* that he made of maralité; also by the famous Reamayn Tullius [Cicero] in his litell booke *de Amicicia*; thangyng you for olde contynued frendschip stidffastely grounded ..."[1] Worcester had read Cicero's *On Friendship* in the original language, as numerous people had done before him and countless others were to do after. The Roman author was to remain, with Aristotle whom the Englishman also mentions, the most cited classical theorist on friendship in the Renaissance period. Cicero's authority on the subject had been further reinforced by Petrarch's mid fourteenth-century discovery of his superb familiar letters. These, with the Italian writer's own eloquent Latin epistles to friends in emulation, served as models for humanist scholars such as Desiderius Erasmus, who by the sixteenth century had created a cult of friendship widely embraced by Europe's social and political elites. One object of this chapter is to trace the course of this high Latinate tradition of the discussion of classical friendship, which, as we have seen, had its origins in twelfth-century clerical circles and was still flourishing in the curricula of grammar schools and universities into the twentieth century. It is this learned Latinate tradition that the content of Worcester's letter illustrates.

The form of Worcester's letter – in English – hints, however, at another current. There was a strong vernacular strand in the history of friendship to which Worcester's friendly letter also belongs. If this more popular tradition inevitably began with thirteenth-century discussions of friendship in French and Italian based upon the standard ancient authorities, and the obvious Christian sources, it had a long and vigorous life of its own touching many more people, women as well as men, than the humanist writers were able, or cared, to reach. The very act of writing vernacular letters to friends found its beginnings in a late medieval Italian urban environment sympathetic to the popularization and utilization of those twin classical preoccupations: letter-writing and the practice of friendship.

The confluence of these two traditions is nicely illustrated in the person of Worcester. Two centuries after the Italians had begun the process, and in a very different society, Worcester was himself active in disseminating Ciceronian ideas in his native tongue. At some time in the 1470s, he borrowed from the Pastons what must have been a manuscript version of John Tiptoft's English translation of *De amicitia* made by that nobleman during his Italian travels in Italy a decade or so before. No doubt Worcester wanted to consult Tiptoft's very competent translation by way of preparation for his own English version of Cicero's treatise on old age. Both translations were very soon to be published by William Caxton, who in his edition of 1481 praised Tiptoft's *Tully of Friendship* because it "treateth so wel of frendship and amyte."[2] Contemporaries agreed. The translation was already in circulation by the 1470s in manuscript and had reached not-very-bookish Norfolk gentry such as the Pastons (who talked about friendship in their celebrated correspondence); the Newberry Library copy has many Latin annotations in a contemporary hand. By the close of the next century, Caxton's printed edition had made Cicero's reflections widely available to the vast majority of Elizabethans who could not read the Latin text.

Figure 1. Jacopo Carrucci, known as Pontormo, *Double Portrait of Two Friends*, Palazzo Cini Gallery, Venice.

Our second example tells much the same tale. In another medium, painting, and in the very different milieu of urban Italy, a more self-conscious sixteenth-century devotion to the Ciceronian ideal of special and virtuous friendship between men found perfect expression. In a portrait of two friends painted by Pontormo in the 1520s (Fig. 1), the men, whose soberly dressed bodies are virtually indistinguishable one from the other, display almost ostentatiously to the viewer a letter on which is clearly legible in a cursive script a passage from the *De amicitia*: "all other objects of desire are each, for the most part, adapted to a single end ... but friendship embraces innumerable ends; turn where you will it is ever at your side; no barrier shuts it out; it is never untimely and never in the way." The passage immediately following in Cicero's text is not given but any Renaissance reader of *On Friend-ship*, or one of the many popular digests of ancient wisdom available, would have known it by heart: "he who looks upon a true friend, looks, as it were, upon a sort of image of himself." The double portrait also celebrates friendship in another, quite intricate and contemporary, way. The painter was almost certainly a close friend of his two subjects who, like the protagonists of Cicero's treatise, were themselves very likely brothers-in-law joined in amity. No more than Worcester's letter is this striking painting the artefact of an elite or learned friendship. The Ciceronian epistle is written in Italian, and the two men are evidently members of the well-to-do artisan class, as was, of course, the famous portraitist.[3]

Nothing makes clearer the wide and almost popular diffusion of classical ideas of friendship in the sixteenth century – in England and northern Europe as well as in Italy – than this fashion for double portraits, this obsession with letter-writing. Another such Italian portrait, a very recently rediscovered painting by Filippino Lippi, depicts himself and perhaps the most satisfied patron of his art: the merchant Piero del Pugliese. As it happens, a contemporary once condemned Piero by saying in a letter to a friend that he was a "man who's more for himself than for friends."[4] This judgment was at odds with Lippi's commemoration of their close working and personal relationship, his assertion in this painting that a talented artist such as himself – belonging to an artisan class still almost universally regarded as inferior – might be the equal of a rich Florentine citizen. Behind the two friends, to the viewer's right, there is an open book. The text is illegible, but surely it must be Cicero's *De amicitia*, which is displayed in at least one other northern Italian friendship portrait of the period. In paintings such as these, the high humanist cult of friendship and an older Italian popular and vernacular preoccupation with this perennial theme, find common ground.

New Evidence, Changing Contexts and Questions of Definition

The period 1300–1600 saw not only the flourishing of new and old ideas about friendship, but an explosion in the forms of evidence available to historians enquiring into friendship.

It will already be evident that new and old ideas about friendship, as well as friendships themselves of almost every variety imaginable, flourished in the European centuries with which this chapter deals. The twelfth and thirteenth centuries perhaps produced more formal treatises on the subject but in those that followed the words "friend" and "friendship" and cognate expressions are to be found again and again in an increasing volume of documents in a number of genres, some of them new, as literacy in both Latin and the vernaculars spread among lay people, government became more sophisticated and personal and private archives came into existence. First in Italy and other parts of Europe's "urban belt," then elsewhere, there emerged new and expanding groups of "free literates," as Armando Petrucci has called them: men (and some women) who could read and write in their own vernaculars and did so not for professional purposes, as did clerics and teachers, merchants, notaries and bureaucrats, but for personal and family reasons.[5] Letters and private and family diaries written by lay people proliferate in this period, as do commonplace books and translations and digests of the classics. These new genres of evidence make it clear that words denoting friendship were on almost everyone's lips and, if the concept and practices of friendship inherited from the classical authorities were almost exclusively masculine, as time passed more and more women, both religious and lay, came to participate in the Renaissance discourses of friendship. In part as a result of certain Christian impulses, these expanded, too, to include notions of close personal intimacy between women, chaste friendship between women and men and even the desirability and attainability of marital amity. What little we can know about understandings of friendship among the non-literate classes – still the vast majority of the population – suggests that they too spoke the language of everyday and Christian, if not Ciceronian, friendship.

The richer vein of evidence about friendship needs to be mined carefully. Friendship was in the air but it would be exaggerated to claim that this was an "age of friendship." These centuries already struggle under the weight of too many competing epithets – age of cultural "renaissance," age of "discovery," age of "transition" between the late medieval and early modern eras, and so on – without our adding another. Whatever we choose to call these centuries, they did not witness a "flight from friendship," as one scholar of the spiritual friendships enjoyed in twelfth-century clerical and monastic circles has argued.[6] Rather, the debate widened among a growing number of protagonists, while continuing to include these older ideas of exclusive spiritual friendship in Christ. Nor was the city of Florence merely a nest of "conspiracies ... not friendships," to quote John Tiptoft's teacher in Italy, the Veronese humanist Guarino Guarini. He has convinced a modern scholar that his is a proper description of the society of this famous city.[7] Yet even allowing for the fact that the Veronese had some bad encounters with the arrogant and faction-ridden Florentine literati, friendship in its several manifestations – personal, sexual and civic, utilitarian and idealistic – was discussed there with familiar intensity. The archives of Florence have yielded up some of our choicest evidence concerning Renaissance friendship.

Between about 1300 and 1600, women and men talked about, and more importantly experienced, an expanding menu of friendships that must have served to comfort, support and inspire them in this period of war and political division, which began with a dramatic demographic decline, as plagues and famines violently punctuated almost every decade, and ended with radical religious upheaval and transformation. The political and other divisions of the age left their mark on the discourse about friendship by bringing its opposite, enmity, to the centre of the conversation. It was an age of "anxiety" indeed, as William Bouwsma dubbed it,[8] during which contemporaries realized that good friends were essential while knowing very well, in the words of an Italian diarist, that "one enemy can injure you more than four friends can help."[9] Contemporaries talked a good deal about enemies because friends mattered to them so much; a non-friend was more likely than not to be a potential enemy. "Love and serve your friends (amis), hate and harm your enemies," as the fourteenth-century French writer on chivalry, Geoffroi de Charny, forthrightly put it in words any ancient Greek would have approved.[10] Florentine citizens in the next century were on the whole more urbane, although few went so far as Leon Battista Alberti who, in the 1440s in his treatise on friendship, deplored in an almost Socratic spirit feelings of enmity, especially towards former friends. "Sell to your neighbours and enemies at a lower price," one moralist advised, "since more often than not you conquer an enemy by serving rather than stabbing him."[11]

One Florentine chronicler of the Quattrocento, Francesco Giovanni, noted down for his descendants in his *Remuneratorio,* or *Book of Reckoning*, the names of his particular friends and also those of enemies who had injured him; not in a vengeful spirit, he explained, but to vindicate his own behaviour.[12] He was not alone in doing so, for how to decide if an associate was a true friend, not an enemy in disguise, much preoccupied Renaissance people. Bouwsma has a point when he emphasizes that the calculated "self-fashioning" in which Renaissance people engaged made the task almost impossible.[13] Plutarch had discussed the theme long before; it was to become increasingly pressing as the sixteenth century went on. And, besides, friendship could so quickly turn into enmity, as Dora del Bene made clear to her husband, whom she suspected of sexual infidelity, in an eloquent letter of May 1381. Signing herself "Thy enemy Dora," she went on cryptically to observe that "it seems to me that it's very dangerous to be your friend, since all your friends are dying off."[14]

It is even possible that friendship in its several senses was becoming more important to Renaissance Europeans than it had been to their ancestors. From the mid fourteenth century onwards, the majority of people – Petrarch most famously – had witnessed the sudden and agonising deaths of many of their closest friends and family as the mortality rate went as high as 50% in some urban centres. "Where are our sweet friends now?" Petrarch lamented; "Where are the beloved faces ... We should make new friends, but where or with whom, when the human race is nearly extinct." Whole households and lineages crumpled and in some cases were destroyed, communities large and small were broken and demoralized, and scandalized chroniclers remarked upon how familial and other intimate social relations snapped in an atmosphere of self-preservation. After the first plague outbreaks, however, people adapted more quickly than has been traditionally understood.[15] One creative response to this sense of social dislocation, resorted to in southern France, was to reconstitute the shattered fraternal households in which people had been accustomed to live by creating artificial brotherhoods whose members were not blood relatives. Another may have been to reach out to friends with a new intensity, as Petrarch indeed did with concentrated energy and flair. It is telling that there began to emerge about this time the sentiment that friends were in certain circumstances to be relied upon more than kinsmen. To be sure, one meaning of "friend" remained "kinsman" in several European vernaculars, as continued to be the case for centuries in England; the two words, often yoked as well to "neighbour," were used almost as synonyms, as in the Italian formulation "*parenti, amici e vicini*" to be found in Boccaccio and hundreds of later texts, and pregnant with meaning for contemporaries.

However, even the mid fifteenth-century Florentine Matteo Palmieri, for all his good Aristotelian sense that friendship, like other social bonds, grew naturally from family affections, thought that in a political context, at least, friends might be preferable to kin; he was not the only Italian contemporary to think so.[16] Ben Jonson, too, over a century later and in a very different milieu, agreed about the primacy of friendship over family. His compatriot, the diarist and clergyman Ralph Joscelin, put personal friends before kin in his prayers, while still referring to his relations-in-law as "friends" in the traditional way, and was firmly of the opinion that friends should be selected with the greatest care. Of one man who "desireth my friendship," Joscelin wrote that "freinds (sic) are not hastily to bee chosen."[17] Friendship, indeed, might be employed in this new and active spirit to bolster, or create, family relationships. "Whereas before there existed between us the best of friendships (*hottima amicizia*)," one Florentine gentleman wrote to another, "now (with this marriage) we can add a further bond."[18] Good friends inserted themselves into the heart of the family. Another family diarist, Cristoforo Rinieri, left for his descendants and posterity one of the most eloquent Renaissance descriptions of a "very close friend (*amicissimo mio*)," one drawn from life as much as from classical sources. The notary ser Angelo da Terranuova was, Rinieri wrote in his private commonplace book in early 1507:

> a most generous gentleman and as true and tried a friend as one could find; in whom I've invested a good deal, not because I expect profit, for he's not well-off, but on account of his kind nature: and I beg and command whosoever shall come after me to oblige to the utmost him and his descendants.[19]

There was something at once personal and affectionate about at least some of the friendships mentioned so far, and at the same time often something "instrumental" and "utilitarian," as scholars of the subject put it. The classical authors, of course, and Cicero above all, sought to distinguish clearly between these two sorts of friendship. True amity could only exist between two individuals, or within a small group, of like-minded and virtuous men; friendly relations contracted for the sake of profit, advantage or even pleasure were what the Roman referred to as "common" or "frivolous," "friendships of the ordinary kind." To remove mutual love from friendship, Cicero memorably wrote, is to "take from friendship's chain its loveliest link,"[20] a point some Renaissance moralists, Montaigne included, continued to insist upon. Aristotle, too, had long before given virtuous and selfless friendship top marks, as it were. But the Athenian, viewing friendship as part of humankind's inborn social impulse as he did, also acknowledged that other sorts of close and amiable relationships were friendships of a kind, even the bond between wife and husband.[21]

As many late medieval and Renaissance writers followed Aristotle's more practical discussion of the theme as shared Cicero's more exclusive vision or, rather, many writers blended these classical traditions and therefore blurred the distinctions they made. Brunetto Latini, for example, writing in French for an international audience in the 1260s, believed with Aristotle that friendship is of three types, for "*bien, profit et delit*" –good, profit and pleasure – and agreed that the first was the superior.[22] His treatment of the subject in *Li Livres dou Tresor*, however, in effect acknowledges that friendships can and do have mixed motivations and uses. Latini conveyed this more usable sense of friendship's role in people's lives autobiographically in the Preface to his other major work, *La Rettorica,* a commentary on Cicero's rhetorical ideas. Recounting in the third person how he found himself in exile in France on account of factional struggles in Florence, Latini describes meeting there "a friend from his own city and party, very rich, gentlemanly and extremely wise, who very much honoured and helped me," whereupon he resolved to write the present book "for love of him." There was an exchange of favours here, and a shared partisan loyalty, as well as the proper Ciceronian insistence that friendship is, as Latini explains in one of his glosses, "not for gain or only for advantage but for the sake of steady virtue."[23]

After all, as Cicero himself had written in the treatise upon which Latini was commenting, while some men believed friendship existed for utility and others for its own sake, "others again ... value it on both counts."[24] If they agree about little else, the scholars from several disciplines who write about friendship and friendly patron–client ties concur that in everyday usage and intercourse the semantic and emotional fields encompassed by the word and its cognates remained broad and inclusive from antiquity until at least the early modern period. "The range of *amicitia* is vast," writes Peter Brunt of the use of that word in Cicero's time.[25] It retained its "expandable" register up and down the social scale in sixteenth-century France, according to Natalie Davis, where people spoke of "relations and friends (*parents et amis*)" in one breath and a husband could describe himself as his wife's "faithful husband and assured friend (*vostre fidele mary et amy asseuré*)."[26] In what follows we too will argue that *pace* Cicero it is usually misleading to seek to distinguish too clearly between "real" and "instrumental" friendships, not least when discussing those patron–client relationships, to be found everywhere in pre-modern societies, that might at first glance appear to have been quintessentially "friendships" contracted only for profit.

This is not for a moment to deny that the rhetoric of friendship was frequently employed by Renaissance people in situations where mere self-advancement or self-protection was at stake. Lord Lisle was urged by his man of business John Husee in August 1537 to "send some loving letter unto Mr Wriothesley ... The truth is, the man standeth in place where he may please and displease. It shall therefore be good to entertain him amongst the number of your friends." "Having some friend (*l'amico*) there would be helpful," the Italian merchant Salvestro del Cica had written a century before in a letter concerning some fragile negotiations with the tax officials. The very compulsion to invoke that rhetoric in such mundane circumstances suggests, however, how powerful and pervasive contemporary discourses of friendship could be. And the better one knows the context of even many "utilitarian" exchanges, the more likely friendships of a more durable and profound kind reveal themselves at work in some way or another. Husee, for example, who once wrote that he was "wholly to your lordship bounden during life," was by any standards the English nobleman's friend, and explicitly acknowledged as such by Lisle; the merchant del Cica's correspondent was Bartolomeo Cederni, his childhood friend with whom he remained intimate for decades.[27]

Moreover, a persistent tradition attacked the invocation and use of friendship merely for the purpose of advancing one's own prospects. Clerical and lay writers criticized the gift-giving culture that pervaded the patron–client relationships of the time, not least in Florence, where they were ubiquitous. How wrong it is, wrote the layman Feo Belcari in the mid fifteenth century, to attain political office "by means of simony or gifts, through ... connections by marriage and friendships (*amicizie*), or through other illicit means."[28] As for the category of "friend" described by the English of John Husee's day as "back" or "privy friends" – "fee'd men" or "espials" of whom Francis Bacon was to write that they "inquire the secrets of the house [to which they belong] and bear tales of them to others" – they were at once in demand and roundly condemned.[29]

Amity and friendly social intercourse in a variety of senses mattered very much, perhaps increasingly, to many Europeans, we might conclude, while it goes without saying that numerous "friendly" exchanges we encounter in the documents were less than altruistic. For the practice and theory of friendship drew upon and sought to activate classical and Christian traditions of ideal *amicitia* and *caritas* (charity) – distinct in themselves but still intertwined – which, if almost always too lofty for any human being to live up to, still provided the indispensable stuff of contemporary discourse and life. The most practical and pedestrian social and political arrangements were as likely as not to be touched by these ideas, as one telling example will illustrate. A highly secret and solemn political pact of mutual support sworn by a group of Florentine citizens in 1449 in order to bolster the dominant Medici regime in that city may at first sight appear to be nothing more than a temporary – and, it must be stressed, illegal – union of political, indeed, partisan convenience. Yet this *intelligenza,* as these pacts were called – and they were commonplace in Italian urban politics – invoked the traditional language of brotherhood, neighbourliness and friendship that had been used as a rallying cry by the republican communes themselves since at least the twelfth century. This swearing of oaths of unity, which usually bound descendants as well, was not taken lightly. The Florentines pledged "*caritativa fraternità et perfecta amicitia*" (brotherly love and perfect friendship), one for the other. The second phrase was Cicero's, repeated by Brunetto Latini, as at least one or two of the signatories might have known, and conjured up the living, pagan tradition of ideal masculine friendship; the first, instead, spoke the language of Christian charity, of love for one's neighbours, used by preachers in their sermons and central to the ethos of the religious confraternities in which lay people such as these men took an active part.[30] As for the partisan attachment to the Medici regime the pact expressed, some contemporaries and the Medici family itself were adamant that it was based upon an ideal of shared political friendship entered into with a kind of reverence for the sake of the city. Cosimo de' Medici's had been a "holy government," one partisan had written around 1470, and so it followed that it was "sinful," according to an early sixteenth-century apologist, to oppose Medici regimes politically.[31]

Despite the linguistic, geographic and political diversity of Western Europe, and the intense localism nurtured within its hamlets, villages, towns and regions, Christian injunctions to love one's neighbours were heard, if not heeded, everywhere, and classical conceptions of friendship, usually somewhat watered down, were available for consumption by the literate, who in urbanized areas were growing dramatically in number. If the *De amicitia* was read more widely, and perhaps better, more instinctively, understood, in this "urban belt" – north western continental Europe, the Rhineland, southern Germany and Switzerland, parts of southern France and the Iberian peninsula, north and central Italy – still it was translated into the vernacular and prized in monarchical northern France and England in the fifteenth century. During the next, it became available in printed translations in languages such as Czech, Portuguese and Polish in still other Western European societies that remained overwhelmingly agrarian in economic terms and post-feudal in political arrangements.[32]

Late medieval and Renaissance Europe, in all its diversity, did not inherit several separate streams of thought about friendship so much as a broad river of ideas and practices, within which individual currents and eddies may be discerned. For the sake of analysis so far, and in what follows, one can distinguish between, say, clerical and lay currents, between high humanist and vernacular traditions, between urban and chivalric values, but never for long and not with convincing rigour. The case of Erasmus of Rotterdam makes the point. He, a great classical scholar, knew and loved Cicero's ideas about virtuous friendship at first hand, and put them at the heart of his whole humanist enterprise and of his mission to make ancient wisdom relevant to early sixteenth-century Europe at large. Yet as a young Augustinian monk he had experienced and celebrated intense friendships in a monastic milieu that owed everything to the twelfth-century tradition of clerical *amicitia,* itself inspired directly by a thorough knowledge of Cicero's treatise, and to St Augustine's much earlier emphasis on spiritual amity among good Christians.[33]

The Vernacular Strand of Friendship in Cities and Post-feudal Societies

Petrarch and the later Italian and northern European humanists, such as Erasmus who revered him, did not begin, although they were to make more refined, the Renaissance romance with friendship, which had firm medieval foundations not only in monastic and chivalric circles but in the emergent urban civilization of north and central Italy. The teachers or *dictatores* of letter-writing, the *ars dictaminis,* made the composition of letters to friends, and friendship itself, central themes of their art and of the model letter-books they produced. As Jean Leclercq pointed out over half a century ago, and Giles Constable has more recently underlined, the rise of the *ars dictaminis* and the flowering of conceptions of friendship went hand in hand.[34] One of the early thirteenth-century *dictatores,* Boncompagno da Signa, himself wrote a work on friendship, as we have seen. Brunetto Latini belonged to the next generation of notaries cum *dictatores* with a passion for friendship, to which he devoted several chapters in *Li Livres dou Tresor* that duly put the ideas of his principal authorities, Aristotle and Cicero, into a contemporary urban context. Friendship was at once "one of the virtues of God and of man" and "very necessary for the life of man." In a short Italian poem on the theme, "Il Favolello," Brunetto borrowed as heavily from Boncompagno himself by redeploying the older rhetorician's charming taxonomy of fair-weather and false friends: "friends of glass," "friends of iron," and so on. A "friend in deed (*amico del fatto*)" was inevitably the most desirable friend of all.[35]

Letter-writing manuals kept buoyant and relevant these thirteenth-century ideas about friendship in a way that historians have still to explore in detail. Between 1472 and 1500 alone, no fewer than 90 such manuals were printed. One of them, the *Formulario de Epistole*, a vernacular work by Cristoforo Landino first published in Bologna in 1485 and dedicated to Ercole d'Este, the Duke of Ferrara, had a quite astonishing sixteenth-century fortune when one considers that it was really a very traditional hands-on manual offering model letters to "an older friend," advice on how "to enter into a friendship with a prominent man," and so on. Landino protested in the Preface to his book that many "citizens and gentlemen" had long urged him to compose what another contemporary declared to be "a fine and useful little work." It is the epistolary practice of amity, not theories about friendship, that the *Formulario* teaches, although there is one solemn editorial admission that "I always take due note of the importance of the bond of friendship." Over 30 editions of Landino's unremarkable work, the very authorship of which became confused at one stage, were published after 1485.[36]

For several centuries men, and a few women, began to learn to write letters in the vernacular from such manuals. Who read which manuals, and how and when and with whom, are largely unanswered questions that beg to be systematically studied. We know how merchants were taught to write business letters, and bureaucrats official correspondence, but how ordinary people learned to compose the often eloquent personal, family and patronage letters they have left in their tens of thousands in Italian archives is not yet evident. What is clear is that these letter-writers somehow imbibed not only the ethos but the several languages of friendship – the "pure" Ciceronian discourse, the idiom of patron–client intercourse, and so on – whether from their teachers and these manuals, or picked up from some sort of urban or family osmosis, requires further analysis. As it happens, we do know something of the epistolary education of Margherita Datini, the wife of Iris Origo's "Merchant of Prato," Francesco Datini, in the late fourteenth century. As an act of friendship extended to his friend's wife, the notary Lapo Mazzei taught Margherita, then in her mid 30s, to read and tutored her in the art of composing a letter. To demonstrate her new mastery of the letter of recommendation – an essential vehicle for winning and keeping friends in Renaissance Europe – Margherita wrote to her teacher using the conventional masculine forms, which, however, she adapted to the purposes of her own gender. This was a very daring thing to do in a society where the rules of decorum made it almost impossible for a woman to write a friendly letter to someone other than her husband or a relative, even if the manuals had supplied the vocabulary with which to do so. "This familiarity is pleasing to me," Margherita assured her friend, "(and) you should treat me as if I were your younger sister since I love you as an elder brother. I don't believe there exists a person to whom I am more attached and, I can tell you, you are never out of my thoughts."[37]

In other cases we can only speculate on the relationship between how people were taught and what they wrote. When English sources use the phrase "speciall frendes,"[38] does this reflect its existence as a category of recipient (the *specialis amicus*) in the language of the *ars dictaminis*? We cannot be sure. Almost certainly, those moderately well-educated Italians who in their correspondence write sentences such as these – "we are never together without talking of you, which is a true sign of friendship" (the last phrase in Latin), or "it seems to me it is the duty of friends (*officio dell'amico*) to visit each other with letters when apart"[39] – had learned such sub-classical allusions from grammar masters. What is one to make, however, of the provenance of the phrase "put me in the number of your friends," which is commonly found in bread-and-butter letters seeking political patronage, especially in Italian correspondence but also in the Lisle collection in Tudor England. A formula by this time, by whatever means it had entered the language of patron–client relationships in the Renaissance period, it had behind it an ancient lineage. Horace, the "poet of friendship" himself as he has been described, used the phrase of his intimacy with Maecenas, who invited him to be "*in amicorum numero.*" The reference is very likely to the more-or-less clearly defined group of clients, followers and friends whose duty it was to visit the house of their Roman patron each morning to give the *salutatio.*[40]

The vernacular legacy of Latini and his successors to discussions about, and to the very practice of, friendship extended beyond letter-writing and phrase-making. Upon Latini's death in 1294, the chronicler Giovanni Villani had (over)praised his mastery of philosophy and rhetoric, which as "secretary of our commonwealth" (head of the Florentine chancery) he had used for the good of the community. Although a "worldly man," Villani continues – Latini's reputation as a sodomist almost certainly compelled Dante to consign his former teacher to hell in the *Divine Comedy* – Brunetto was "the beginner and master in refining the Florentines and in teaching them how to speak well, and how to guide and rule our republic according to policy."[41] The chronicler was not to know that Brunetto Latini would go on to become the teacher of half of Europe; Dante may have sensed that this might turn out to be the case, as he allowed his mentor to recommend "my *Treasure* ... in which I live still, and ask for nothing more" to posterity in the pages of his great poem.[42] This really quite practical guide to ancient wisdom, distilled from his authorities by a scholarly man of action who knew about politics at first hand, enjoyed a remarkable popularity and longevity. Some 80 manuscripts of the French original survive, and 30 of the Italian translation, which was also printed in Treviso in 1474, just over 200 years after Brunetto composed or rather compiled it. Around 17 manuscripts exist in Iberian languages, including Catalan.[43]

The book perhaps appealed most to urban dwellers, above all to the citizens of autonomous or semi-independent city-states. In an age of burgeoning monarchical and princely pretensions, if not always power, Latini had declared with astonishing boldness that of the three varieties of contemporary government – monarchical, oligarchic/baronial and communal – this last, the self-governing republican city-state, was the best.[44] In his own particular urban context, similar in some respects to those ancient Athenian and Roman city-state civilizations from which classical doctrines of friendship had emerged, Latini's Aristotelian sense that the *polis* – the *comune* in contemporary parlance – depended for its survival on what modern critics call "civic friendship" had a particular and timely resonance. This theme, which Brunetto and the *dictatores* did so much to bring to the attention of citizens struggling to maintain just republican government in a princely age, remained important into the fifteenth century. In his vernacular *On Civil Society,* Matteo Palmieri developed faithfully Aristotle's argument that friendships are "so necessary and so convenient (*comodo*) to existence that without them no one would willingly choose to go on living." "Friendship," in brief, "is the mainstay of cities, without which not only a city but not even a small group (*compagnia*) can endure" because amity among citizens ensures the civic unity and concord so desirable and yet so hard to attain in the faction-torn urban societies of the day.[45] The contention that a city's fabric was held together by "friendships, marriages and kinship networks" was repeated a little later in the century by the Roman humanist Bartolomeo Platina, whose audience was more an aristocratic than a civic one, and by the Sienese political theorist Francesco Patrizi. Citizens of some northern European towns thought the same. Renaissance Nuremburgers swore an oath to maintain the "faith and friendship binding each man to his neighbour." In a very different monarchical context towards the end of the sixteenth century, Jean Bodin still maintained that friendship was a basic building block of every sort of political society.[46]

The very partisan attachments that threatened civic unity in the one-party regimes of quasi-republican Bologna and Florence in the fifteenth century themselves assumed the respectable mantle of "civic friendship." "By nature we in this city (Bologna) are given to obliging (*servire*) friends so that they may oblige us when the occasion arises," the aristocratic Malvezzi brothers, prominent members of the dominant Bentivoglio faction, wrote in a letter of December 1467 to Piero de' Medici, himself leader of the Florentine regime.[47] Piero was even more bluntly reminded of the tit-for-tat mentality of factional politics by a leading partisan of his own family, Dietisalvi Neroni (with whom in fact he was soon dramatically to fall out): "friendship (*amicitia*) is useful and necessary in all things, and above all in politics (*negli stati*), as you well know."[48] The point was put more acceptably, dressed up in a way Palmieri, who was a Medici supporter if not a henchman, would have approved, by Piero de' Medici himself when he declared in a public oration in 1461 that "all citizens are brothers" and should act accordingly.[49] It had been Piero, in company with the humanist Alberti (very soon afterwards to write perhaps the most original Quattrocento treatise on friendship), who in October 1441 had sponsored a celebrated civic contest in the Florentine cathedral during which poets competed to write the best verses in Tuscan on the theme of "what is true friendship" (*de vera amicitia*).[50] The tone of the offerings was high minded, their inspiration impeccably classical and Christian.

The same language was moreover used without self-conciousness by partisan citizens when they spoke of the bonds that united them to their fellows and leaders. For not a few Medici *amici*, "friends" as they explicitly called themselves, the Medici party or faction was nothing other than an extended family, "the union of friends inside and without the city," in Filippo Arnolfi's words in 1465, "the friendship (*amicizia*) that is this city."[51] The Medici themselves, and their more idealistic followers, would have looked on the bright side of Sallust's aphorism that "between good men, friendship exists, between bad, faction." Their enemies, one of whom said that Medicean Florence was "a paradise inhabited by devils," decidedly would have concentrated on the Roman historian's second phrase.[52]

The urban and civic overtones of Latini's *Tresor* and the traditions of friendship promulgated by the *ars dictaminis* must have fallen upon less receptive ears outside Europe's "urban belt." Vernacular letter-writing in French and English, even in a very practical way, did not begin to flourish in England until the end of the fourteenth century.[53] That country's grand collections of family correspondence, the reading of which made Virginia Woolf feel that early English history was coming alive for her for the first time, belong to the two centuries following. There was, nevertheless, a culture (if not cult) of friendship in existence among the landed families of post- feudal France and England; one expressed more clearly in actions than in words. This reticent culture bears more than a passing family resemblance to the more articulate world of political friendships and alliances to be found in urban Europe, for all the differences existing between the two milieux. For in the general conditions of demographic crisis and rapid political and social change that obtained throughout Europe in this period, the "affinities" and "alliances" of northern landed gentlemen, of which more in a moment, served the same political and psychological ends, *mutatis mutandis*, as the factional friendships endemic to Italian and other city cultures; both drew their inspiration from traditional, lived, notions of familial and neighbourly solidarity as much as from classical and Christian sources. In the name of these older values, rural affinities and urban factions offered their adherents in the new prevailing circumstances a precious sense of group togetherness and the tangible leadership of a man or family they knew and respected, even revered.[54]

One should not, even so, underestimate the possible impact of the vernacular classicizing tradition on northern European conceptions of friendship. The *De amicitia*, for example, was translated into French by Laurent Premierfait as early as the second decade of the fifteenth century, and into Spanish about the same time. It was Premierfait's earnest intention to use "such clear and ordinary language that moderately lettered men will understand me completely and quickly."[55] Tiptoft's English version was circulating in manuscript among country gentlemen by the 1470s, as we have seen, and was very soon after in print. Its ready availability in the next century would have contributed to one Elizabethan Englishman's conviction that to be "marvelously friended" was an excellent thing. Reading Cicero, too, would have sanctioned those inseparable friendships between two men described in contemporary English documents and imaginative literature that were a source of moral concern as well as approbation. For the "shadow" of sodomy "was never far from the flower-strewn world of Elizabethan friendship," in Alan Bray's words. The scholar Roger Ascham encouraged his "deare frende" and "bedfellow," John Whitney, to learn Latin by undertaking a double translation of the *De amicitia* "out of Latin into English, and out of English into Latin agayne." Of another, fictional, intimacy of this kind, during which two friends ate, drank, danced and read together, at times sharing the same bed, John Lyly wrote that the companions "could not refrain the company of the other one minute ... All things went in common between them, which all men accounted commendable."[56]

What distinguishes the later medieval friendships among landed gentlemen in northern Europe from the social and political bonds of the feudal ages proper is above all that they appear to have been more egalitarian and personal, even when there existed obvious differences in rank and authority between the parties. With the gradual disappearance of liege homage and of the hierarchical structures and mentalities of classic feudalism, there occurred a freeing up of personal and social ties that gave "friendship," variously defined, space to manoeuvre and grow. Perhaps Cicero's manly and egalitarian definition, born of late republican Roman politics, supplied what this post-feudal society needed. The brotherly devotion of one knight to another, described most deliciously in the late medieval literature of chivalry but also to be found in rather stodgier archival documents, was a special friendship of this kind, "sweeter than woman's love," or so it was said.[57] The creation of a brotherhood-in-arms was a solemn act sealed by an oath or exchange of documents (even, it might be, by the fraternal mingling of blood); in one literary version of this pledge, one protagonist swears that "I will be the friend of your friend and the enemy of your enemy."[58] More prosaic – but somehow more reassuring, at least for the modern reader – were the words of Thomas, Duke of Clarence, who in an actual contract of 1412 promised "to be a true and good kinsman, brother, companion at arms and friend (*amy*)" to Charles d'Orléans.[59] Two Scottish earls pledged at the end of that century that they should be "tender, kind and loyal" to each other as paternal kinsmen are.[60] These contractual friendships, almost invariably made between social equals, were personal but meant to last. In England two brothers-in-arms might be buried side by side in the same tomb; Alan Bray has teased out the social, religious and psychological meanings of this long-lived and remarkable tradition. The companies and fraternities of knights, and the still larger chivalric orders, that were so prominent a feature of late medieval European society, were an extension of this deeply felt personal bond between two aristocratic companions-at-arms.

In the less rarefied air of everyday military cooperation and social intercourse between members of the landed aristocracy and gentry in England and France, there developed other close ties, not dissimilar from the brotherhoods in arms in some respects, that contemporaries themselves at times called friendships, as well as by other names. In England, magnates increasingly "retained" supporters for military and other purposes by means of formal contracts or "indentures," which provided for the payment of a sum of money to these retainers in exchange for their services and loyalty (this payment replacing the granting of a fief or fief-rente in return for homage that had character-ized the tie between lord and vassal). The indenture constituted a legal agreement, each party keeping a copy, both of which had been originally drawn up on the same parchment and sealed interchange-ably. These paid followers constituted a "retinue" or "affinity," or, as the French put it, an *alliance*. It used to be thought that these post-feudal arrangements, apparently merely mercenary and inherently unstable, were as much a cause as a symptom of the political disor-ders and lawlessness of fifteenth-century English and French society; that they represented a falling away from the solider values of classi-cal feudalism. Recent scholarship concerning this so-called "bastard feudalism" has insisted, however, that the formation of these new sorts of relationships between members of the aristocracy and gentry, which anyway can be seen to be as much a logical development of feudal and other traditional social relationships as a wilful distortion of them, was a creative and often beneficial response to the vicissitudes of this period of recurrent plague and the Hundred Years War.[61]

In uncertain times, gentlemen in the country above all sought "good lordship," in the contemporary English phrase, and found it in the affinities, retinues and alliances they joined, often – it must be empha-sized – for long periods or for life. As large and as formidable as a few of these might be – the affinity of John of Gaunt, the grandest in late fourteenth-century England, included a household or *familia* of 115 men, 170 indentured retainers and an even larger number of an-nual pensioners – they were nevertheless neither monolithic nor sub-ject to strict internal discipline. Such a retinue, it has been said, was as much a "network of clientage and patronage" as anything else.[62] These groupings accordingly employed the rhetoric of friendship and kin-ship to express the bond created between lord and follower, who in some cases were of similar social status, although not so consistently and forcefully as did the adherents of urban factions in Italy. A French contract of *alliance* of 1413 talks of "*amor et amistance*"; in another the two parties contract to establish "a good, firm, loving and loyal friend-ship, league and confederation to last all the days of our lives."[63] Re-tainers owed fealty to their "patrons," as one English scholar describes such magnates,[64] but did not perform homage. Companions or allies of their lord, not his vassals, they offered counsel and good fellowship as well as military co-operation. In return, a patron promised to be, in the words of several English indentures of the fifteenth century, a "good and tender lord" who guaranteed "faithful, true heart, love and kind cosinage."[65] There was a complementarity in these post-feudal arrangements, often a longstanding intimacy that permits us to speak of them, to paraphrase Aristotle, as friendships of a kind.

Even so, it must have irked some country gentry to have to pay deference, in however friendly a way, to magnates whose interests scarcely coincided with their own; as John Paston I once wrote "I have not usid to meddel wyth lordis materis meche forther than me nedeth."[66] It has been suggested indeed that the Pastons and their connections in Norfolk actively sought to avoid the vertical ties of dependence at least implicit in magnate affinities, choosing to reach out horizontally, as it were, to find their friends and confidants among the circles of kin and neighbours that constituted their county community. The world of the Pastons was a local one of "kynnysmen and frendys," in which ideal and utilitarian concepts and practices of friendship merged comfortably enough together.[67] "[M]ake your frynds to take your part, as frynds shold doe," Sir Robert Plumpton was urged when fighting a lawsuit in 1500.[68] It is perhaps not surprising after all that the country gentleman John Paston II owned an early copy of the first English translation of Cicero's *De amicitia*. If many of his contemporaries sought good lordship from an amiable patron, he preferred to seek out true friends among his peers.

The Humanist Cult of Friendship after Petrarch

This strong and broad vernacular tradition of friendship pre-dated the learned, Latinate, "rediscovery" of *amicitia* by Petrarch (1304–74), and for well over a century it coexisted and, inevitably, overlapped with the high humanist fascination with the theme that flowed from the Italian scholar's authoritative example. It has very recently been demonstrated that it was the Latin authors, Cicero above all in the *De amicitia* and in his newly discovered familiar letters, who shaped Petrarch's unsystematic but deeply felt ideas about friendship, which he consistently put into admirable practice within his own large group of epistolary friends. He concluded a Latin letter written in old age to Philippe de Cabassole by saying "Farewell, dear friend, and rest assured that, after the pleasure which comes from God and virtue ... for me the most important is the possession of true and honest friendships."[69] But, as we have seen, this idea was already a commonplace in late medieval Europe, where it competed, while at times merging, with more practical definitions of friendship. Latin readers of the *De amicitia*, which enjoyed popularity throughout the medieval period as a school text, had firsthand access to it, while vernacular readers found competent summaries in books such as Latini's *Tresor* and later had available translations of the work itself.

Petrarch did not bequeath to the Renaissance a new, more personal conception of "private friendship" or "companion friendship," as it has been variously called. He did, however, decisively re-emphasize that strand within the classical and medieval traditions, and for a new, humanist, audience: the Italian and European elites that embraced what P. O. Kristeller described as a "cult of friendship," which became "a standard topos" of learned correspondence and discourse.[70] It is intriguing that the Renaissance as a cultural movement produced few systematic treatises on this theme that preoccupied it. It is as if Petrarch's ideas themselves served instead as a source of inspiration, while his enthusiastic and quite single-minded taking up of Cicero's contribution in the *De amicitia* made that work *the* Renaissance treatise on friendship. The Latin text in manuscript and then print was much in demand throughout the Renaissance; well-off Florentine households in the fifteenth century might own a copy; the Jesuit schools used it as a text in the next.[71]

Letters to friends and about friendship, self-conscious collections of letters to commemorate oneself and one's friendships, these, if not treatises, are to be found everywhere in the period – as one would expect, given the ancient models that they sought to emulate. The so-called Roman Academy of the late fifteenth century produced one such collection of sample letters in both Latin and Italian; Donato Giannotti in the next brought together his Latin epistles recreating a lifetime of friendships.[72] John Donne, who once said that friendship was his second religion, believed, as he said to Sir Henry Wotton, that "more than kisses, letters mingle Soules, for thus friends absent speake."[73] Erasmus of Rotterdam loved this ubiquitous enabling fiction, as John Najemy has described it, this Greek conceit – that letters are "a conversation between two absent friends" – which launched a thousand letter collections. Montaigne confessed toward the end of the sixteenth century that he owned no fewer than a hundred Italian letter-books.[74]

Desiderius Erasmus (c. 1466–1536), himself a mighty writer and receiver of Latin letters with a European-wide network of correspondents, also wrote a major letter-writing manual in Latin. His doing so underlined further his commitment to the positive cult of friendship that exchanges of eloquent epistles fuelled.[75] In early letters written at the monastery at Steyn, he had assured a monastic friend that "there is nothing on earth more pleasant or sweeter than loving and being loved"; "My mind is such," he declared to the same man, "that I think nothing can rank higher than friendship in this life, nothing should be desired more ardently, nothing should be treasured more jealously."[76] Later, in his widely circulated *Adages,* friendship emerges as a reigning theme of the whole Erasmian enterprise. A subsequent edition begins with the celebrated dictum "*amicorum communia omnia* (between friends all is common)," and repeats the Ciceronian "laws of friendship" to the effect that "friendship is equality: a friend is another self," and so on. There is as well in the *Adages* a Christian insistence on the possibility of one's being "united in friendship with Christ, glued to Him by the same binding force that holds Him fast to the Father."[77]

The Dutch humanist acknowledged with a gift of paintings his friendship with Sir Thomas More, with whom he shared a consuming desire to persuade other New Testament scholars to return to the original Greek if they were to savour afresh the pure springs of Christian doctrine. More's *Utopia,* it has persuasively been suggested, can be read as an oblique treatise on friendship. In May 1517 Erasmus and his colleague Pieter Gillis commissioned for More a diptych consisting of portraits of themselves depicted working away in their studies and surrounded by learned theological and classical texts – one of them may have been the *Utopia* itself – from the Antwerp portrait painter Quentin Massys (Figs 2, 3). Gillis holds a letter addressed to him in More's hand, a moving acknowledgement – apparently without precedent – of their friendship and fellowship.[78] The exchange of ancient coins and medals, still comparatively cheap yet prized by the humanists for the classical images and inscriptions they preserved, became perhaps the most common token of learned friendship throughout sixteenth-century Europe. Erasmus, inevitably, attracted such gifts, as when the Bishop of Olmutz presented him with four gold coins of the "good emperors" (one can hardly imagine Erasmus wanting images of the bad ones!), as "a paltry pledge of my regard for you."[79]

Aristocratic women in the Italian courts cultivated friendship by sending portraits of themselves as gifts. After Isabella d'Este left her native Ferrara to marry the Marquis of Mantua, Francesco Gonzaga,

Figure 2. Quentin Massys, *Portrait of Erasmus of Rotterdam*, Galleria Nazionale d'Arte Antica in Palazzo Barberini, Rome, inv. 1529, Archivio Fotografico Soprintendenza Speciale per il Patrimonio Storico, Artistico ed Etnoantropologico e per il Polo Museale della città di Roma.

she wrote frequently to her family and friends at the Ferrarese court. One of her mother's ladies-in-waiting with whom she maintained close ties reported in a letter of 10 April 1495 that she had the portrait that Isabella had sent to her propped up before her as she wrote.[80] In 1497

Figure 3. Quentin Massys, *Portrait of Pieter Gillis*, Koninklijk Museum voor Schone Kunsten, Antwerp, c. Lukas – Art in Flanders VZW.

Isabella distributed a fine classicizing portrait medal by the artist Gian Cristoforo Romano to her most favoured friends and clients. How such gifts were used is suggested by a letter from Margherita Cantelmo, an intimate member of Isabella's circle, who wrote from Milan in 1505 that she had taken a portrait of Isabella with her and that since she was ill it was a particular source of comfort:

> I don't know whether I am dead or alive. I do know that being deprived of the presence of Your Ladyship, gives me little hope of recovery. I will try to regain my health with the help of your dear portrait [and] I pray Your Ladyship to help me by sending your usual delicacies without which it seems to me I cannot get better.[81]

Her friend's portrait served in effect as an ex-voto. That women also occasionally recorded their friendships in paintings is suggested by the depiction of Isabella d'Este and a woman who is almost certainly Margherita Cantelmo as the donors in an altar piece of about 1514 by Francesco Bonsignori. It records their devotion to the Blessed Osanna Andreasi, a holy Mantuan nun renowned for her power to heal the sick, who had died in 1505. It also represented the successful collaboration by these two friends to have this local saint beatified and given a splendid tomb.[82]

There were other manifestations of this gift culture of humanist friendship. At some point in the first part of the fifteenth century, the Venetian Leonardo Giustinian apparently began to inscribe in his books the phrase "*et amicorum*," to make it clear that his friends and other men of letters might share his library, and that he and his books belonged to the commonwealth of letters. Variations of this amiable formula, in Greek as well as Latin, became common in Italy as the century passed (Lorenzo de' Medici used it), and widespread in Europe in the next, only petering out around 1600.[83] In precisely this period and milieu, a new literary genre appeared. Some 1500 examples of the *liber amicorum* – the "book of friends" – survive, including a few compiled by women who were at this time beginning to enter into, and participate in, the discourses of friendship. A traveller would invite friends, or prominent persons encountered on the way, to write something of their choice in this special "friends' book."

This last expression of the Renaissance cult of amity, correctly described by one scholar as the "stylization of friendship,"[84] has something distinctly artificial not to say precious about it, which cannot be said of the earnest and thoughtful Petrarchan and Erasmian musings on the same theme that gave birth to it. Even within the humanist camp, however, and rather earlier, there had been one very learned student of the classics, Leon Battista Alberti (1404–1472), who politely made it clear in his short treatise on friendship that he found overreliance on the venerable classical teachings unhelpful in the hurly-burly of Italian civic and commercial life, a theme to become dominant by the end of the sixteenth century. In this dialogue, Alberti has members of his famous lineage debate the question of what true friendship is, and from the start the discussion is more subversive than some critics acknowledge. The occasion of this family conversation is the arrival of an old domestic servant bearing a gift of fruit. This uneducated man, identified only by the (slightly comical, perhaps rustic) name Buto, mixes with his Alberti betters in an intimate way that is clearly meant to convey that he and his aristocratic companions are friends, although true friendship between a retainer and his employers was unimaginable to the classical authors, with the exception of Seneca. When the discussion is joined, Buto actually scoffs at the (unstated Ciceronian) position that friendship is "the union of two persons so that they become one" by joking about the experience of his own unhappy marriage.

While the standard Aristotelian as well as Ciceronian ideas are duly and respectfully canvassed by the speakers, on several occasions the down-to-earth Adovardo Alberti, who may or may not speak for Leon Battista himself but is certainly allowed to express an opinion that must have been abroad at the time, signals his dissatisfaction with the received lore. "No ancient writer," he argues, "has ever been able to give me" a definition of friendship that accommodates "the actual ways and habits of men" in a world where "everything ... is profoundly unsure." If he seems more comfortable with traditional teaching as the debate continues, still Adovardo convinces his kinsman Lionardo that there is "a better hope of learning the art of friendship in living conversation than in books." Written in Italian in the very early 1440s, Alberti's work belongs more to the vernacular, popular, tradition of practical discussion of this great theme than to the Latinate current established by Petrarch of which it is an implicit critique. It anticipates, too, radical late sixteenth-century reflections on the subject. Alberti's subversive contribution, tacked on as it was to form the fourth book of his treatise on the family (only the third section of which became widely known and cited), went unnoticed and was unable to provide a salutary corrective to the high-minded classicizing discussion of friendship that became so fashionable in the sixteenth century before new developments and ideas began to undermine it.[85]

Changing Christian Concepts of Charity and Friendship

Alberti's treatment of friendship was quite secular in tone, it has been remarked, and was and remained quite unusual in being so. Otherwise, only Petrarch, surprisingly enough, concentrated almost solely on the Latin pagan tradition, good Augustinian though he may have been in other respects. From the start, writers on friendship mixed Christian with classical ideas and allusions. Friendship for that faithful Aristotelian and Ciceronian Brunetto Latini in the 1260s had been "one of the virtues of God and of man." That his audience instantly would have understood this proposition is clear from a late thirteenth-century Florentine compilation of extracts, drawn from biblical and patristic as well as classical sources, offering moral guidance in both Latin and Tuscan on a range of subjects. Prepared by a Dominican friar for a prominent citizen, Geri Spini, this very typical late medieval *florilegium* devotes a whole chapter to *amistà*, which is described as "very useful and a blessing." While Christian friendship in this compilation is a personal virtue, the atmosphere it breathes is the social and civic one of Dante's city.[86] An older Christian tradition that rather emphasized more exclusive spiritual friendships – the *amicitia Christiana, amicitia spiritualis*, and *amicitia Dei* of twelfth-century monastic and clerical circles – continued vigorously into the later period, as in Jean Serra's *De contemplacione amicicie* of the mid fifteenth century. Such works drew essentially on the same sources; above all St Augustine and the authority of scripture, to which later fifteenth-century writers added massive Neoplatonic reinforcements. Augustine himself and several other early Christian writers on the theme of friendship of course owed a direct debt to Cicero's treatise, so helping to create the broad river of classical and Christian ideas on the theme that then flowed through the medieval and Renaissance periods. Just as Petrarch had wanted him to be, Cicero became a Christian *avant la lettre*, at least when it came to discussions on friendship. What is "friendship or companionship," according to a very popular vernacular late fifteenth-century compilation of moral reflections, the *Flowers of Virtue*? It is "wanting permissible and honest things from one another, just as Cicero tells us in his book *On Friendship*."[87]

Among the religious the cultivation of an intense spiritual friendship between two persons, or within a small group, in order to find friendship with God Himself had a particular and obvious attraction. Notions of spiritual friendship found a natural home among the

Italian Augustinians in the fifteenth century; for one Italian Benedictine a man of faith was simply "a friend of the Lord."[88] In northern Europe, self-conscious and intense friendships flourished both among reforming Catholics such as Erasmus, who described oneness with God as being in accordance with Cicero's "laws of friendship," and in some German circles of Protestant theologians. Spiritual friendship might even include the chaste love of a woman and a man. It was the practice in certain observant German convents – carefully monitored by the abbess to be sure – for some nuns to cultivate spiritual friendships with men, with whom they might exchange intimate letters and whose portraits they might be allowed to keep in their cells. This conventual cult of friendship existed in an atmosphere that also encouraged nuns from different establishments and even orders to regard each other with tender feelings. One convent sent another the gift of a pious book as "a sign of our eternal friendship and love for you, and yours for us, in constant faithfulness to God."[89]

At this very time, however, a chill wind blew from Tuscany upon these emerging spiritual friendships between women and men, and women and women. The priest Marsilio Ficino (1433–99), the most learned Neoplatonist of the fifteenth century, took up the theme of spiritual friendship with gusto in the Latin letters he sent to his male friends. These were really small treatises on various moral and philosophical themes inspired by Marsilio's Platonic, Aristotelian, Augustinian and Thomist sources. According to Ficino, friendships contracted for any other purpose than to unite two men in love of God "are nothing but acts of plunder." His beloved Platonic philosophers, he pointed out, defined friendship "as the permanent union of the lives of two men," as a form of love, and "there cannot be the two friends on their own, but there must always be three, the two men and God; God, or in other words Jupiter, the patron of hospitality, protector of friendship, and sustainer of human life."[90] "Esteem everyone, choose and love only one, and confide in God alone," Ficino wrote on another occasion.[91] For his Platonizing follower in the next generation, Francesco Cattani da Diacceto, spiritual friendship existed so that two friends might together contemplate "the bottomless sea of divine beauty."[92]

If Ficino's perception of Platonic love and masculine friendship enjoyed wide acceptance in Italy and abroad, and among educated laypeople as well as in clerical circles, still the laity had long had at its disposal, and made increasing use of, the more inclusive idea of spiritual friendship. The English mystic Richard Rolle (d. 1349) had believed that true friendship might exist between chaste laywomen and laymen, defining it very sympathetically as "mutual enjoyment and pleasant friendship and helpful conversation. And if this friendship is founded in God's grace, and is wholly his, related and directed to him, it can then be called a holy friendship and it is very rewarding."[93] Giulia Gonzaga and Piero Carnesecchi practised an intimate and dangerous friendship of this kind in the mid sixteenth century, when they belonged to a proto-Protestant religious circle that was indeed to fall foul of the ecclesiastical authorities. "Friendship is a wonderful thing," Piero wrote on one occasion in 1559 to his noble patron and confidant (in the third person, for safety's sake), "particularly when it is born from honest causes and grows and is confirmed with the years and with judgment, and to the end is founded in God."[94] The secret letters of friendship and spiritual comfort he shared with Giulia Gonzaga became Piero Carnesecchi's death warrant in the hands of the Inquisition.

A number of early Christian writers had preferred to use the word *caritas,* rather than *amicitia,* of Christian friendship. There was indeed a certain tension, even conflict, between the emotions each word described. *Caritas,* "charity" or "affection," was the love all Christians owed to their neighbours, indeed, all humankind, as distinct from the intense and focused intimacy invoked by the word *amicitia,* whether used of a secular friendship between two men or of an exclusive spiritual relationship from which God was inseparable, such as Gonzaga and Carnesecchi had known. As John Bossy explained a generation ago, this more religiously and socially unifying impulse was at the heart of late medieval spirituality as experienced by most laypeople.[95] It manifested itself in many ways. One was the institution of godparenthood, by which natural parents chose acquaintances – often neighbours and friends, dozens of them in some cases – to share the spiritual upbringing of their children, an obligation that was taken seriously. The choice of godparents by both rich and poor frequently crossed lines of social class and gender.[96] The granting of interest-free loans, and other financial concessions made to friends, were traditional Christian practices that even the hard-nosed Florentines observed in the name of neighbourly *caritas.* Cristoforo Rinieri, a good friend to have judging by the many references to active friendship throughout his diary, prayed God that he might come to no harm after agreeing to stand surety for Andrea Carnesecchi for a large sum, "since I've asked no security of the said Andrea other than his word (*persona sua*), because being his friend I wanted to do what friendship (*l'amicitia*) demanded."[97]

Charity found its most long-lasting and effective expression, perhaps, in the lay confraternities to which a remarkable number of men, women and children belonged throughout the period, until the distaste of Luther and other reformers for this very sociable manifestation of late medieval Catholicism weakened their influence. Perhaps a quarter to a third of the adult male population in Renaissance Italy at some time joined one or more of these religious companies, which were heavily but not exclusively concentrated in urban areas. There were literally thousands in early modern Spain, both in villages and towns. These lay companies, with their elaborate statutes, top-heavy hierarchies of elected officials and regular round of festivities, were so much part of the social fabric as to invite not only Protestant disapproval but the satiric wit of Niccolò Machiavelli himself. One of his funniest and least-known pieces is a parody of the solemn and portentous regulations of a typical company. Should one of its women members be declared by two witnesses to be too beautiful, under Machiavelli's regime she was obliged to display a carefully specified portion of her bare leg by way of testing the proposition; a man similarly accused had to confess whether or not "he had a handkerchief stuffed down the front of his breeches, or something similar."[98]

That Machiavelli's religiosity was complicated is well known. Many, perhaps most, of his contemporaries would not have laughed at the joke. At their best, the confraternities inculcated in their members a profound sense of the Christian importance of fraternal and sororial solidarity, which they expressed in very useful ways by offering what were in effect social services to their brethren: charity for the poor, visits to the bedside of the sick, attendance at funerals, help to the dependants of the bereaved. Their aim was above all to foster communal harmony, to bring the peace of God to communities that craved it. In late medieval societies that were often "agonistic," as a distinguished scholar of confraternal institutions has put it, these companies enabled laypeople who found it difficult to distinguish a friend from an enemy to work through their fears, to be assured that the shared ritual life of the confraternity would very likely help convert a potential Judas into one's brother.[99] It is a striking thing about the confraternities that many of them were not socially or otherwise exclusive. Rather, by recruiting men (and some women) from different

social classes and occupations, and from diverse parts of a city or lo-
cality, they made more achievable their aim of bringing spiritual, and
with it social, integration to a community. In a sermon preached to a
youth confraternity on Holy Thursday 1476 in Florence, Giovanni
Nesi praised the virtue of humility by which "the rich man befriends
the poor man, the great befriends the lowly, the powerful befriends
the powerless, and the lord befriends his servant ... let each (as is
the precept of the Lord) not love his neighbor less than he loves
himself."[100]

This injunction to love one's neighbour, in the sense of extending
charity towards her or him, is a commonplace of confraternal religiosity. "Charity makes man love God above all things and his neighbour
as himself," the fourteenth-century Dominican Iacopo Passavanti had
said.[101] Neighbourliness itself becomes almost an aspect of religious
belief and practice; a form of friendship, we would say. For the French-
man Jean Bouchet two centuries later it was a variety of "familiar
affection" that united "a street, a parish, a town, a burg, a village, a
community."[102] A Florentine grocer accused of sodomy with a younger
friend, and required by the authorities to explain his actions, put a
gloss on the meaning of confraternal neighbourliness that may surprise some modern readers. His words underline, however, that the
homoerotic love which was at times identical with friendship was also,
in Michael Rocke's words, "often only a single thread of a weblike
network of social relations." "This he did out of great love and brotherhood," the scribe quotes the older man as saying, "because they are
in a confraternity together, and he did as good neighbours do."[103]
The point was taken to its logical, and as it turned out fatal, conclusion by the late sixteenth-century Friullian miller Domenico Scandella,
one of whose principal heresies was to declare that "I say that it is a
greater teaching to love one's neighbour than to love God": by which
he meant, he explained to his incredulous inquisitors, that he believed that a poor neighbour *was* God.[104]

Confraternal literature talked almost exclusively about "charity"
and "brotherhood" rather than "friendship" but there is a strong case
to be made that this sociable Christian love was perhaps the most
universally accepted late medieval and Renaissance vernacular understanding of what friendship was. Just occasionally, a contemporary
witness helps us out here. "Friendship and charity should be one and
the same thing" (*amicizia e caritate sieno una propria cosa*), one of the
participants in Alberti's poetic contest to define true friendship stated

explicitly in 1441, adding that Jesus was present in any such friendship. Another man, Feo Belcari, once sent a collection of his religious
poems to the Marchioness of Mantua in the hope that this would be
the "beginning of a spiritual friendship."[105] The statutes of a Castilian
confraternity early in the next century confirm that its members should
not only be brothers in Christ but friends. No "enemy" of any confrere
might be accepted into the company until "they become friends, because it is not right that among brothers who are to live in concord
there be hostility and discord."[106] Luther dismissed late medieval lay
confraternities as sites of swinish gluttony and drunkenness. If he had
a point – consider, say, the ludic excesses of the aristocratic company
of the Immaculate Conception in Rouen, which in 1546 marked the
occasion of its annual sacred poetry contest by serving a festive meal
of 32 appetizers, 43 main courses and 40 desserts[107] – Luther's judgment, shaped by his own new sense of how humankind should relate
to God, was still uncharitable in overlooking the potent force most
confraternities had sought to be in encouraging among the laity social
cohesion and Christian love and friendship for one's neighbour.

Beyond the Pale of Renaissance Friendship?

Buoncompagno da Signa and other writers had acknowledged that
one could have "greater" and "lesser" friends; many of the friendships
described so far were in some sense cross-class. There were, however,
limits to how far and to whom neighbourly love and amity might be
extended. Almost without exception, Renaissance people agreed that
the domestic slaves – eastern Europeans, Tartars and, increasingly,
Africans – at the beck and call of even some quite modest households
could neither become their friends nor be befriended. Very unusu-
ally for his time, Seneca had been able to envisage that a Roman
patrician's household slaves might also be his "humble friends (*humiles
amici*)," but for Petrarch, rich in friends and eloquent on friendship,
they were nothing other than the "domestic enemy."[108] This was especially true of the black African slaves appearing in growing numbers
in southern Europe from the mid fifteenth century onwards as a consequence of Portuguese and Spanish maritime expansion. Burdened
with racial stereotypes that seem depressingly modern, not even free
birth or emancipation enabled more than a handful of these unfortunates to become part of societies that so valued friendship, despite the
relatively benign attitude to them adopted by many ecclesiastical

authorities. One such man was Juan Latino, professor of Latin at the University of Granada in the mid sixteenth century; another was his contemporary, the Portuguese writer of sacred plays, Alfonso Alvares.[109]

Renaissance discourses of patron–client friendship did embrace the possibility of close ties of mutual obligation, even affection, between people of very different social status; at least in Italy, where the abundant documentation allows one to begin to discuss in some detail a theme about which there is, however, a good deal of scholarly disagreement. Certainly, in letters of recommendation Florentine patricians routinely described very humble clients – usually people without surnames – as the "friends" of themselves and families, at times showing knowledge of and liking for these people they also sometimes called their "creatures"; Meo di Guerriere was "very much my friend (*amicho*), and a respectable peasant," Piero Tornaquinci assured the gentleman from whom he sought a favour on this client's behalf.[110] Well-to-do Venetian women, too, numbered among their "friends" their poorer female acquaintances and dependants in the tightly knit neighbourhood enclaves of that city of islands.[111] What terminology those obscure people so favoured employed in referring to their benefactors is not at all clear – the word friendship surely did not slip so easily from their tongues when addressing social superiors – but there is nevertheless firm evidence that at least some of these cross-class relationships could be important to both parties, and long lived. This was especially the case with trusted domestic servants and wet-nurses; one is reminded of Leon Battista Alberti's evocation of the friendship between the ex-retainer Buto and the Alberti lineage.

Humble people in town and country needed the help and protection a powerful benefactor might afford them, in everything from avoiding imprisonment to marrying off their daughters as decently as possible. The urban patrician or landowner, in his or her turn, gained status and reputation from the possession of a (preferably large) following of *amici* among the lower classes, above all in the countryside where tough peasant friends were ready to provide more practical aid. As the aristocratic Guglielmo Capponi informed a friend in 1495, one Biagio di Giovanni was "our very intimate friend (*amico nostro familiarissimo*) ... just the man to stand guard over some strategic place."[112] The Medici ascendancy in Renaissance Florence depended in part on the successful mobilization of armed rustic retinues raised not only from among their tenants but throughout the countryside at large. In these intensely class-conscious and increasingly hierarchical

Renaissance societies, the powerful and well-to-do might despise and fear the lower orders en masse, while befriending individuals and families from among their ample numbers.

Women and Men Debate Friendship

We have to wait until the late fifteenth century before women begin to voice their own views of friendship. This had a good deal to do with their greater literacy and the ready access to classical and vernacular texts which printing had made less expensive and more widely available, so enhancing the possibilities for self-education. The emergence of literary salons, particularly in the Veneto region of Italy, also gave crucial support to a small number of female writers, as did the patronage of aristocratic women in both Italy and France. Although women poets and writers of literary dialogues or letter collections were mostly valued as curiosities by their male patrons, some important female authors took advantage of the new opportunities to disseminate their work. One of the first references to friendship in a female-authored text, which demonstrated a thorough knowledge of classical ideas on the subject, is in a letter by a well-educated daughter of a magistrate from Brescia, Laura Cereta (1469–1499). Her letter to Santa Pelegrina, one of a collection of 82 Latin letters written by Cereta in about 1487, was prompted by an attempt to repair a quarrel and by Pelegrina's long epistolary silence.[113] Cereta suggested that friendship was a delicate plant that needs regular sustenance if it was not to wither and die.

> Thus, though the seed of mutual love that was sown between us had already grown strong from a deep root of honor, it suddenly died, as if sucked dry in ground without water: it was as though this seed were stubborn enough to flee by itself from both nature and humankind.[114]

In her view, and here Cereta demonstrated her familiarity with Cicero, friendship could not be nourished by gifts and flattery but rather by profound empathy and truthful communication.

Cereta maintained a number of intellectual friendships with women and men and saw those who committed themselves to learning as a community bound together by common values and interests. Friendship was no easy matter, however, in a society where, in her view, too many women conformed to misogynist stereotypes by their exaggerated obsession with adornment and luxury; as for most men, they

treated women as if they were children or even pet dogs. In a letter to
a male adversary which displays her mastery of humanist invective,
Cereta defended women's right to education but revealed the personal costs of her own life choices.

> I have been too much burned, and my injured mind has accumu-
> lated too much passion, for tormenting itself with the defending of
> our sex, my mind sighs, conscious of its obligation. For all things –
> those deeply rooted inside us as well as those outside us – are
> being laid at the door of our sex.[115]

Not surprisingly, discussions of friendship in early modern texts written by, or on behalf of, women are often embedded within genres
associated with their defence. The "woman question" or *querelle des
femmes*, to which Christine de Pizan had famously contributed in the
early fifteenth century, gathered momentum in Italy later in that century. This was at least partly a result of the challenge to conventional
norms posed by the visible presence of educated and powerful women
in the northern Italian courts and the southern kingdom of Naples.
Princely regimes required the active help of female as well as male
family members to ensure the stability and efficiency of states that had
only fragile claims to political and legal legitimacy. The
significant cultural and political influence of some Italian aristocratic
women stimulated both virulent attacks from conservatives and de-
fences by humanists who described their alliances with elite women
as intellectual and platonic friendships. Bartolommeo Goggio, a
Ferrarese notary and court official, wrote a work in 1487 for the Duch-
ess of Ferrara, Eleonora d'Aragona, which he called *De laudibus
mulierum* (*In Praise of Women*), that set out to dismantle the traditional
philosophical basis for male superiority. He referred explicitly at the
beginning of the text to his alliance with women, acknowledging "the
virtues of women and the friendship that joined me to them."[116]

That women wanted access to the discourse about friendship, and
realized that greater equality with men was necessary before men and
women could truly be friends, is suggested by yet another example
from northern Italy. Agostino Strozzi, an Augustinian canon, wrote
for his cousin, Margherita Cantelmo, whom we have already met, not
only a *Defensio mulierum* (*Defence of Women*) of 1501 which asserted
the equality of female and male natures, but also an Italian translation of his Latin tract on friendship.[117] His intention was, he stated in
the Preface to this little-known but interesting work, to give Margherita
an entrée to ideas that he knew engaged her. Given his cousin's close

friendship with the Marchioness of Mantua, Isabella d'Este, it is likely that Strozzi's work was also appreciated by her and the other aristocratic women connected to the courts of Milan, Mantua and Ferrara.

The idea that marriage was a social institution in urgent need of reform began to emerge in this princely environment, perhaps because the disparity in age and education between spouses was less marked than in the Italian Renaissance republics, where mature men married teenage brides who were often barely literate. Isabella d'Este, for example, was only eight years younger than her husband and if in the early letters to his wife Francesco Gonzaga treated Isabella as if she were a promising but inexperienced apprentice, there was also a clear acknowledgment of Isabella's intelligence and political contribution. The language of marital and princely hierarchy was still firmly in place in their marital correspondence. There was, nonetheless, a marked preference by Francesco to negotiate with his wife rather than to command her, as husbands were entitled and indeed expected to do, that suggested that friendship had flowered in a relationship contracted for dynastic and strategic purposes.[118] Mario Equicola, who was to become Isabella d'Este's secretary, commended himself to her by arguing in his *De mulieribus* (*Concerning Women*) of 1502 that marriage was the crucial instrument of female oppression. His conception of marriage as a collaborative partnership of equals was designed to win female approval, but was not taken up by later, less radical, defenders of women.[119] However, Equicola's argument that marriage should not be the battlefield so often portrayed in misogynist tracts but a companionable partnership welded by mutual respect and love became a more frequent theme and gained its most prestigious advocate in Erasmus.[120]

In an English adaptation of one of Erasmus's colloquies on marriage, the *Conjugium* of 1523, Edmund Tilney reveals some of the contradictions within mid sixteenth-century ideologies of marriage. In *The Flower of Friendship*, first published in 1568 and dedicated to Queen Elizabeth, Tilney praises marriage (although, he tactfully adds, "setting virginitie aside, as the purest estate") because it "containeth the felicity of man's life, the *Flower of Friendship*, the preservation of Realmes, the glorie of Princes, and that which is most of all, it causeth immortalitie."[121] On the one hand, Tilney acknowledged "that equalitie is principally to be considered in this matrimonial amitie, as well of yeares, as of the gifts of nature, and fortune. For equalness herein, maketh friendlynesse."[122] On the other, the text subtly endorsed the idea that women should willingly and lovingly submit to the authority of their husbands so as not to threaten social norms.[123]

Female commentators on the possibility of friendship between the sexes, either within or outside marriage, were more sceptical, although there is evidence that they too were exercised by this theme in the mid sixteenth century. Marguerite, Queen of Navarre and the sister of Francis I of France (1492–1549), commissioned from Bonaventure des Périers a French translation of Plato's dialogue on friendship, *Lysis*, as part of what has been called her "veritable 'Plato project'"; another member of her circle, Antoine Héroët, composed a work entitled *The Perfect Friend*. Discussions of Ciceronian friendship among Marguerite's friends went so far as to canvass the idea that it might form the basis of an idyllic marriage. In her posthumous *Heptameron*, however, a collection of stories modelled on Boccaccio's *Decameron*, relationships between the sexes and marriage in particular are shown in a pessimistic light. Beneath the rhetoric of courtly love, men were revealed in many of the tales to be sexual predators who were willing to ruin the reputations of their beloveds for the sake of conquest. Masculine and female honour had nothing in common, and a major theme of the tales was an implicit criticism of a masculine culture that assumed that rape was the punishment for self-assertive women, or the solution should a socially inferior man desire a well-born lady. In this selfish and cynical climate the trust and generosity required for friendship were shown to be rare commodities and Marguerite's male protagonists in particular "are not up to the demands of the relationship."[124]

It is idle to speculate, as a few scholars have not been able to resist doing, whether or not the very young Marie de Gournay (1565–1645) and Montaigne attempted the risky enterprise of an intense sexual friendship in the old man's last years. What is certain is that Marie became his "*fille d'alliance*" (adoptive daughter), before his death in 1592, after which she devoted much of her abundant energy to the cause of keeping his reputation alive. Whatever Montaigne felt privately about their friendship, Marie wrote of it in the Preface to her *The Promenade of Monsieur de Montaigne* that "the good will that allies us ... surpasses that of real fathers and children – the first and closest of all the natural ties." In a bold conclusion, de Gournay enrolled his and her "name among those renowned for friendship" by quoting this same line from Etienne de La Boétie's Latin description of his own supposedly inimitable intimacy with Montaigne.[125]

At precisely this time, Moderata Fonte (1555–1592) suggested that the cause of female–male friendship was a lost one. In her *The Worth of Women*, a literary dialogue written in 1592 and published posthumously around 1600, the speakers were all women. They found common ground in the belief that:

> many men see the world in a blinkered way, and are so firmly convinced by the unwarrantable fallacy that they are created women's superiors, and so incapable of seeing past this lie, that they believe themselves fully justified in treating women as tyrannically and brutally as they like.

In the course of a mini-dialogue on friendship, Fonte's female speaker asserted that "women make friends with other women more easily than is the case with men, and their friendships are more lasting," an "extremely distinctive" viewpoint within Renaissance friendship literature as the modern editor of the text, Virginia Cox, dryly remarks.[126] Fonte's playful but still revolutionary intent is underlined by the fact that the whole tone of the discussion was explicitly Ciceronian – "true friendship, true affinity, is the cause of all good" – but it is made clear that it is only women who can achieve this higher state of being. Intimate friendships between men are very rare "because men's innate malignity stands in the way."[127]

From a totally different perspective, Montaigne in effect agreed that his male contemporaries were incapable of friendship: "among men of today you see no trace of it in practice," the essayist wrote in *Of Friendship*. His own "unspotted friendship" with de La Boétie, as John Florio beautifully translated Montaigne's description for an Elizabethan audience, was a rare migratory bird that came along only every three centuries or so.[128] On his deathbed de La Boétie, at least as reported by his friend, agreed absolutely that "the practice of [virtuous friendship] has for so long been driven from among us by our vices that there remain of it only a few old traces in the memory of antiquity."[129] If modern men were hardly capable of friendship, women were simply not constitutionally up to it, according to Montaigne. Indeed it was as if he set out in his famous essay to rebut most if not all of the usual definitions of friendship, ancient and modern. Sexual love was "an impetuous and fickle" if seductive folly; "that other, licentious, Greek love" was indecorous (because not between equals) and broke the moral code. Montaigne wrote in a letter to his own wife in 1570 that he had "none more intimate than you" but his verdict in the *Essais* on the possibility of married friendship was less sanguine, although almost regretful: "there supervene a thousand foreign tangles to unravel, enough to break the thread and trouble the course of a lively affection."[130]

On the face of it, Montaigne is here being a good Stoic, dismissing from the canon of true *amicitia* the majority of emotional attachments and other "acquaintanceships and familiarities formed by some chance or convenience" that people ordinarily call friendships. More profoundly, however, he is on the point of departing from this ancient tradition, from these "few old traces in the memory of antiquity" as his soul mate had expressed it. Without knowing it, the two Frenchmen were agreeing with Leon Battista Alberti's much earlier judgment about the inadequacy of canonical understandings. For his feelings for de La Boétie were so intense, Montaigne admitted, as to make all the ancient descriptions of true friendship seem "weak." Theirs was a spiritual union, by which "our souls mingle and blend with each other," he added in an observation that owes a good deal to the then fashionable ideas of Neoplatonism. Montaigne and his older friend loved each other "because it was he, because it was I." Montaigne's universe was one in which even friendship between men could not exist, save in his own exceptional circumstance. In effect he was saying, a modern critic has observed, that a man's best friend could and had to be himself. "O my friends, there is no friend," Montaigne had also written, quoting an apparently paradoxical Greek proverb that Jacques Derrida was to make much of in his own discussion of friendship.[131]

John Florio's English translation of the *Essais* in 1603 made Montaigne's ideas accessible to the generation of Francis Bacon. The English statesman's own *Essays* had appeared in 1597 but on the subject of friendship, at least, he traversed a different line of country while arriving at a similar, but much more pessimistic, destination. Friendship was precious to Bacon for the very reason that "the world is but a wilderness" without it. The true friend remained one's alter ego, though Cicero was not cited by name, and Bacon's "fruits" of friendship were more or less those of the Roman author: the sharing of one's deepest emotions with another, the exchange of wise council, mutual aid. There was, however, a decidedly utilitarian air about this reference to "fruits" that is alien to Cicero. Moreover Bacon gave no impression that he agreed with Aristotle that friendship found its proper context in a political community, to whose wellbeing it was essential. His world was indeed a "wilderness," as he was to experience at first hand in his last years when imprisoned in the Tower for corruption and subject to accusations of sodomy with a young servant.[132] In the conclusion of "Of Followers and Friends," Bacon may have left us his final, bleak, account of friendship. "There is little friendship in the world, and least of all between equals, which was wont to be magnified." With Cicero and Aristotle as it were summarily disposed of, Bacon went on to give a pragmatic nod of approval to amiable relations between superiors and inferiors – what we have called patron–client ties – when it should happen that "their fortunes may comprehend the one the other."[133]

In the heartland of the Renaissance cult of friendship, Italy, several male writers were similarly dismantling portions of its superstructure, and even probing at its foundations. Sperone Speroni (1500–1588) and Torquato Tasso (1544–1595) both wrote short vernacular treatises on the theme that began abruptly with the ticklish problem of how to distinguish true friendship from its base twin, flattery or adulation. This dilemma had preoccupied Plutarch, whom Tasso cited copiously, and was hardly unknown to earlier Renaissance writers. No previous Renaissance treatment of the theme plunged straight into the issue; it was evidently becoming more pressing in the elaborate courtly culture of the northern Italian princely states of the sixteenth century. If Tasso's longer discussion asserted the optimistic view that true friendship could triumph over its slippery rival, Speroni's fragment was not at all so sanguine. Friendship and adulation were not the same thing, Speroni had Socrates insist, only then to allow him to concede that "these days ... true friends are few" because it is man's innate nature to be malicious.[134] Stefano Guazzo (1530–1593) went much further in his *La Civil Conversazione* of 1574. "But these days," he had one of his protagonists in the dialogue ask, "where are these true friends?" Aristotle of course, might have said that friendship could only be extended to one person, this speaker goes on to say, at once adding: "I don't know if you have found your perfect friend (*perfetto amico*), but I certainly haven't found mine, with whom I can enjoy that stark, simple and open freedom you are alluding to." The hierarchical society in which Guazzo moved was inhabited not by friends but (at best) by "well-disposed persons" (*benivoli*), and they could easily be alienated. His spokesman complained that if one did decide to extend the brotherly hand of friendship even to a social equal, he was very likely to rebuff you by calling you "Lord" and addressing you in the formal mode, after which even his benevolence was lost. The implication was clearly that Ciceronian friendship was impossible between men (precisely as Moderata Fonte was coolly observing at the time), and Guazzo's protagonist ended the discussion on a suitably grim, indeed sordid, note. With regard to friendship, it was better to follow the example of the fly, "who sticks around humans and eats our food, but doesn't however want to become familiar with us."[135]

Renaissance Friendship in Crisis?

Just as the end of the Cold War hardly witnessed "the end of history," friendships true or otherwise were not dead because some men of Bacon's generation more or less said they were. People, inevitably, went on talking about and being friends. Men and (more) women continued reading Cicero on friendship, and perhaps went away convinced. Indeed, several articulate women decisively entered the discussion, using the traditional ideas and vocabulary, in which some of their male counterparts were losing faith, to talk about and idealize their own friendships and those of their sex. In several early seventeenth-century images, *amicitia* is portrayed as a handsome woman. The French writer Pierre de Bourdeille wrote openly about love-making between women, *donna con donna* as the phrase went. Shakespeare's plays illustrate his immersion, it has been pointed out, in a rich culture of friendship; *Henry IV* has been described as "a friendship play."[136] Amity between women and men, and in several senses, was now permanently on the agenda, and the early modern period saw the growth of still other expressions of and variations on the theme of friendship; not least in Nicolas Poussin's paintings, inspired by Montaigne's essay on the subject. There was, however, clearly a crisis in the understanding of long-received ideas about the subject towards the close of the sixteenth century (not least in Shakespeare's England), and not only because women writers had helped change the terms of the discussion by the very fact of entering it. Male writers seem to be saying that "perfect friendship" as the ancients had defined it could not work in the modern, and in many ways extremely unsatisfactory, world they experienced. If, according to Alberti, "everything ... [was] profoundly unsure," even in the relatively stable civic environment of mid fifteenth-century Italy, then sixteenth-century Tudor England was a "wilderness," or so Bacon believed. There "friendship taketh small place when money faileth," observed Lord Lisle's gentleman-factotum John Husee: "it is hard trusting this wily world."[137]

It is hardly surprising that notions of friendship born in small city-states two thousand years before, and much later nurtured above all in late medieval urban republics, should become problematical in late sixteenth-century Europe. Montaigne and Bacon, Speroni and Guazzo, struggled with, only to ignore or largely discard, canonical teachings on friendship that must have seemed more and more irrelevant; at the very least, they adopted positions closer to Senecan Stoicism, born of late Roman despotism, than to earlier and more optimistic formulations. They were not alone in questioning the absolute authority of classical authors as an infallible guide to contemporary life. Much earlier in the century, Francesco Guicciardini had pointed out more generally that "they deceive themselves, who cite the Romans at every turn," as if that long-vanished world were identical to one's own.[138] Ideas of civic friendship, for example, made increasingly less sense in the powerful and centralizing principalities and monarchies of the early modern period. The independent city-states that had kept the conception alive had largely lost their independence; Florence itself, from Latini's time onwards a power house of civic *amicizia,* had become a small principality under the autocratic rule of a Medici duke. Philosophical discussion of this Aristotelian conception of political friendship dropped away at this time, as modern scholars wishing to revive interest in it have pointed out.[139] Moreover, many of these principalities were engaged in violent sectarian and political conflict, both within their own borders and with each other. Traditional conceptions of Christian community and friendship, of fraternal and familial neighbourliness, were as much the causes as the victims of these sectarian battles, as theologians and political powers tried to deal with competing understandings of an individual's relationship with God and the Church's with the state. The secularization of the idea of friendship, to become a central theme in the next chapter, now began to emerge, and fraternal friendship was to gain a fresh lease of life in predominately secular forms.

As for the intense and perfect friendship between two men, Bacon grasped that its very habitat – the smallish urban centre – was facing extinction, and with it that increasingly rare and precious bird itself: "because in a great town friends are scattered so that there is not that fellowship, for the most part, which is in less neighbourhoods." In the context of discussing how many friends a man might have, Aristotle had written that a "city" of 100,000 people could not be a *polis* in his sense. If the very numerous pre-Black Death Florentines of Latini's time might have begged to differ, Bacon in effect picked up the point. Writing as he did at a time of expanding population, after several centuries of demographic crisis, and of increased urbanization and migration to the towns and cities, the Englishman bemoaned the difficulty of making and maintaining friendships in large towns, and the sad result when one could not; "for a crowd is not company, and faces are but a gallery of pictures, and talk but a tinkling cymbal, where there is no love."[140]

The princely courts of Europe's ancient regime, also in their way intimate and face-to-face mini-societies, had very definitely not replaced the now overcrowded piazza and anonymous city square as the fruitful breeding ground for friendships. If one contemporary, Cesare Ripa, did suggest that the High Renaissance court was the ideal setting for "conversations and friendships," the majority view was that its hierarchical and artificial structures and labyrinthine internal politics made courtly society rather a "coming together of malignant foxes," as Tommaso Garzoni put it.[141] The court in England was, rather, a bear pit. The false friend was depicted in English images as a savage bear which fell upon a prostrate victim; beware "the friendly foe with his double face," as the courtier-poet Thomas Wyatt had said.[142] Such persons "fashion themselves to nothing more than how to become speculative into another," wrote one contemporary theorist of friendship, "to the end to know how to work him, or wind him, or govern him; but this procedeth from a heart that is double and cloven; and not entire and ingenuous."[143] Survival at court demanded not the gift of friendship but volpine cunning and mastery of the very arts of flattery and dissimulation that were the mortal enemies of true friendship. Despite the pessimism of some male contemporaries, however, it was above all the idea of personal, more or less voluntary, friendship that survived into the modern era, although it was to assume shapes and forms, and inhabit worlds, that would have been inconceivable to Cicero, not to mention Petrarch.

Notes

1. N. Davis (ed.), *Paston Letters and Papers of the Fifteenth Century* (2 vols; Oxford: Oxford University Press, 2004), II, p. 203. Standard histories of the period usually fail to mention friendship at all. There is, however, a brief discussion

in G. Duby (ed.), *A History of Private Life: Revelations of the Medieval World* (Cambridge, MA: Harvard University Press, 1988), pp. 163–68, 240–45, and a more substantial contribution in R. Chartier (ed.), *A History of Private Life: Passions of the Renaissance* (Cambridge, MA: Harvard University Press,1989), pp. 5–6, 148–51, 447–91. See too the work of the British Academy Network, "Medieval Friendship Networks," http://www.univie.ac.at/amicitia, accessed 1 October 2007. An excellent very recent work of synthesis is A. Bray, *The Friend* (Chicago: Chicago University Press, 2003). Unless otherwise indicated, translations are our own.

2. Quoted in R. J. Mitchell, *John Tiptoft (1427–1470)* (London: Longmans, Green, 1938), p. 174. See too Davis, *Paston Letters*, I, pp. lxix–xxii, 516–18; D. Gray, "Some Pre-Elizabethan Examples of an Elizabethan Art," in E. Chaney and P. Mack (eds), *England and the Continental Renaissance: Essays in Honour of J. B. Trapp* (Woodbridge, Suffolk: Boydell Press,1990), pp. 23–36; L. Shannon, *Sovereign Amity: Figures of Friendship in Shakespearian Contexts* (Chicago: University of Chicago Press, 2002), pp. 25–26.

3. Cicero, *De amicitia* vi, 22, vii, 23; C. B. Strehlke (ed.), *Pontormo, Bronzino, and the Medici* (Philadelphia: Philadelphia Museum of Art, 2004), pp. 17–19, 64–66.

4. Quoted in J. Burke, *Changing Patrons: Social Identity and the Visual Arts in Renaissance Florence* (University Park, PA: Pennsylvania State University Press, 2004), p. 91, who also discusses the painting (ch. 4). On the friendship portrait, see P. Burke, "Humanism and Friendship in Sixteenth-Century Europe," in J. Haseldine (ed.), *Friendship in Medieval Europe* (Stroud, UK: Sutton, 1999), pp. 262–74 at pp. 268–69; J. Anderson, "*Bittersweet Love*: Giorgione's Portraits of Masculine Friendship," in D. R. Marshall (ed.), *The Italians in Australia: Studies in Renaissance and Baroque Art* (Florence and Melbourne: Centro Di and the Ian Potter Museum of Art, University of Melbourne, 2004), pp. 87–94. For England, see Bray, *The Friend*, p. 75.

5. A. Petrucci, *Writers and Readers in Medieval Italy* (trans. C. M. Radding; New Haven, CT, and London: Yale University Press, 1995), p. 179.

6. B. P. McGuire, *Friendship and Community: The Monastic Experience, 350–1250* (Kalamazoo, MI: Cistercian Publications, 1988), pp. 413–18.

7. R. Sabbadini, *Guariniana*, ed. M. Sancipriano (Turin: Bottega d'Erasmo, 1964), p. 18; A. Field, *The Origins of the Platonic Academy of Florence* (Princeton, NJ: Princeton University Press, 1988), p. 201. R. C. Trexler, *Public Life in Renaissance Florence* (New York: Academic Press, 1980), ch. 4 and *passim*, brilliantly paved the way for later discussions of Florentine friendship.

8. W. J. Bouwsma, *A Usable Past: Essays in European Cultural History* (Berkeley, CA: University of California Press, 1990), ch. 6.

9. *Giovanni Rucellai ed il suo Zibaldone, I, "Il Zibaldone Quaresimale"* (ed. A. Perosa; London: Warburg Institute, University of London, 1960), p. 9.

10. R. W. Kaeuper and E. Kennedy, *The Book of Chivalry of Geoffroi de Charny* (Philadelphia: University of Pennsylvania Press, 1996), pp. 128–29.

11. Quoted in K. Olive, "Creation, Imitation, Fabrication: Renaissance Self-Fashioning in the Codex Rustici" (3 vols; PhD thesis, University of Sydney, 2004), I, p. 211; L. B. Alberti, *The Family in Renaissance Florence* (trans. R. N. Watkins; Columbia, South Carolina: University of South Carolina, 1969), Book 4.

12. B. V. Wilson, "A Florentine Chronicler of the Fifteenth Century: Francesco di Tommaso Giovanni and his Ricordanze" (MA thesis, Monash University, 1980), pp. 212–15.

13. Bouwsma, *A Usable Past*, p. 169.

14. G. Passerini, "Dora Guidalotti del Bene: Le Lettere (1381–1392)," *Letteratura Italiana Antica* 4 (2003), pp. 101–59 at pp. 117, 149, 153.

15. S. K. Cohn, "The Black Death: End of a Paradigm," *American Historical Review* 107 (2002), pp. 703–38. For Petrarch, see J. Aberth (ed.), *The Black Death: The Great Mortality of 1348–1350* (New York: Palgrave Macmillan, 2005), pp. 71–74.

16. M. Palmieri, *Vita Civile* (ed. G. Belloni; Florence: Sansoni, 1982), p. 162; K. J. P. Lowe, "Towards an Understanding of Goro Gheri's Views on *amicizia* in Early Sixteenth-Century Florence," in P. Denley and C. Elam (eds), *Florence and Italy: Renaissance Studies in Honour of Nicolai Rubinstein* (London: Westfield College, 1988), pp. 91–105 at p. 97.

17. Cited in A. MacFarlane, *The Family Life of Ralph Joscelin* (Cambridge: Cambridge University Press, 1970), pp. 150, 155, 157; R. Finkelstein, "Ben Jonson's Ciceronian Rhetoric of Friendship," *Journal of Medieval and Renaissance Studies* 16.1 (1986), pp. 103–24.

18. Letter by Francesco Caccini to Lorenzo Strozzi, 9 May 1450: Archivio di Stato, Florence (henceforth ASF), Acquisti e Doni, 140, insert 8, fol. 93.

19. ASF, Conventi Soppressi, 95, 220, fol. 4v.

20. Cicero, *De amicitia* xiv, 51; xxi, 76–77; xxvi, 100, and *passim*.

21. Aristotle, *Nichomachean Ethics* VIII, 12.

22. *Li Livres dou Tresor* (ed. S. Baldwin and P. Barrette; Tempe, AZ: Arizona Center for Medieval and Renaissance Studies, 2003), p. 187.

23. *La Rettorica* (ed. F. Maggini; Florence: Galletti e Cocci, 1915), pp. 6, 10–11.

24. *De Inventione*, ii, 167, cited by P. A. Brunt, "*Amicitia* in the Late Roman Republic," *Proceedings of the Cambridge Philological Society* 191, n.s. 11 (1965), pp. 1–20 at p. 3.

25. Brunt, "*Amicitia*," p. 20. See too P. Lowell Bowditch, *Horace and the Gift Economy of Patronage* (Berkeley, CA: University of California Press, 2001), pp. 15–16,19 n36,165 n9; R. Saller, "Patronage and Friendship in Early Imperial Rome: Drawing the Distinction," in A. Wallace-Hadrill (ed.), *Patronage in Ancient Society* (London and New York: Routledge, 1989), pp. 49–62; S. N. Eisenstadt and L. Roniger (eds), *Patrons, Clients and Friends* (Cambridge: Cambridge University Press, 1984).

26. N. Zemon Davis, *The Gift in Sixteenth-Century France* (Madison: University of Wisconsin Press, 2000), pp. 19–20.

27. For Husee and Lisle, see *The Lisle Letters: An Abridgement* (ed. M. St Clare Byrne; London: Folio Press, 1983), pp. 18–20, 138, 294. Del Cica's letter is in ASF, Corporazioni religiose soppresse sotto il governo francese, 78, 314, fol. 256r, 5 March 1447, modern style; for his friendship with Cederni, and the ethical dimensions of patron–client friendships, see F. W. Kent and G. Corti, *Bartolommeo Cederni and his Friends* (Florence: Olschki, 1991).

28. Feo Belcari, *Lettere* (ed. D. Moreni; Florence: Magheri, 1825), p. 24.

29. St Clair Byrne, *Lisle Letters*, pp. xiii, xix; Francis Bacon, "Of Followers and Friends," *Essays Civil and Moral* (London: Cassell & Company, 1895), pp. 154–55.

30. A. Sapori, "Cosimo Medici e un 'patto giurato' a Firenze nel 1449," in *Eventail de l'histoire vivante –Hommage à Lucien Febvre* (2 vols; Paris: A. Colin, 1953), II, pp. 115–32.

31. Lowe, "Towards an Understanding," pp. 91–105; F. W. Kent, "'Lorenzo ... amico degli uomini da bene,'" in G. C. Garfagnini (ed.), *Lorenzo il Magnifico e il suo Mondo* (Florence: Olschki, 1994), pp. 43–60, esp. pp. 56–58.

32. R. R. Bolgar, *The Classical Heritage and its Beneficiaries* (Cambridge: Cambridge University Press 1958), pp. 526–28; Burke, "Humanism and Friendship," p. 265. For the "urban belt," see P. Blickle (ed.), *Resistance, Representation, and Community* (Oxford: Oxford University Press, 1997), part V.

33. R. J. Schoeck, *Erasmus of Europe: The Making of a Humanist, 1467–1500* (Edinburgh: Edinburgh University Press, 1990).

34. J. Leclercq, "L'amitié dans les lettres au moyen âge," *Revue du moyen âge latin* 1 (1945), pp. 391–410; G. Constable, *Letters and Letter Collections* (Turnhout: Brepols, 1976). For the *dictatores* and letter-writing, see R. G. Witt, *Italian Humanism and Medieval Rhetoric* (Aldershot: Ashgate, 2001).

35. Brunetto Latini, *Il Tesoretto: Il Favoletto*, ed. F. Mazzoni (Alpignano: A. Tallone, 1967); *Tresor*, ed. Baldwin and Barrette, p. 186.

36. We refer to the edition published in Bologna in 1487, and to its *Proemio* in Cristoforo Landino, *Scritti Critici e Teorici* (ed. R. Cardini; 2 vols; Rome: Bulzoni, 1974), I, pp. 175–82. See too N. Longo, "De Epistola condenda: L'arte di 'componer lettere' nel Cinquecento," in A. Quondam (ed.), *"Le Carte Messaggiere"* (Rome: Bulzoni, 1981), pp. 177–201, esp. pp. 182–84, and A. Quondam's "Dal 'Formulario' al 'Formulario': Cento anni di 'Libri di Lettere,'" in Quondam (ed.), *"Le Carte Messaggiere,"* pp. 13–156, esp. pp. 75–80.

37. Cited and discussed by C. James, "A Woman's Path to Literacy: The Letters of Margherita Datini (1384–1410)," in M. Cassidy Welch and P. Sherlock (eds), *Practices of Gender in Late Medieval and Early Modern Europe* (Turnhout: Brepols, 2008), pp. 43–56; I. Origo, *The Merchant of Prato* (New York: J. Cape, 1957).

38. See, for example, J. Murray, "Kinship and Friendship: The Perception of Family by Clergy and Laity in Late Medieval London," *Albion* 20.3 (1988), pp. 369–85 at p. 375.

39. The first quotation of 1488 is cited by Kent and Corti, *Bartolommeo Cederni*, p. 44; the second is in ASF, Corporazioni religiose soppresse sotto il governo francese, 78, 317, fol. 26n, 12 November 1489.

40. N. Horsfall, *Poets and Patrons: Maecenas, Horace and the "Georgics," once more* (Sydney: School of History, Philosophy and Politics, Macquarie University, 1981), p. 5; Bowditch, *Horace*, p. 23; R. S. Kilpatrick, *The Poetry of Friendship: Horace, Epistles I* (Edmonton, Alberta: University of Alberta Press, 1986).

41. *Villani's Chronicle* (trans. R. E. Selfe and ed. P. H. Wicksteed; London: Constable, 1906), pp. 312–13.

42. *La Divina Commedia: Inferno*, xv, 119–20.

43. *Tresor*, ed. Baldwin and Barrette, p. xiv; J. Bolton Holloway, *Brunetto Latini: An Analytic Bibliography* (London: Grant & Cutler, 1986). One of the Catalan versions is *Llibre del Tresor*, ed. C. J. Wittlin (Barcelona: Editorial Barcino, 1971). There is a modern English translation: *The Book of the Treasure* (trans. P. Barrette and S. Baldwin; New York and London: Garland, 1993).

44. *Tresor*, ed. Baldwin and Barrette, p. 188.

45. Palmieri, *Vita Civile*, ed. Belloni, pp. 161–62.

46. Bartolomeo Platina, *De optima cive* (ed. F. Battaglia; Bologna: N. Zanichelli, 1944), pp. 270–71; A. Black, *Guilds and Civil Society in European Political Thought from the Twelfth Century to the Present* (London and New York: Methuen, 1984), pp. 57, 97, 129–31.

47. Cited in I. Robertson, *Tyranny under the Mantle of St. Peter: Pope Paul II and Bologna* (Turnhout: Brepols, 2002), p. 59.

48. Cited by A. Molho, "Cosimo de' Medici: Pater Patriae or Padrino?" *Stanford Italian Review* I (1979), pp. 5–33 at p. 33 n66.

49. Cited in Field, *Origins of the Platonic Academy*, p. 49.

50. *De vera amicitia: I testi del primo Certame coronario*, ed. L. Bertolini (Modena: Panini, 1993), p. 516.

51. Letter to Piero de' Medici, 12 September 1465: ASF, Archivio Mediceo avanti il Principato, XVII, 459.

52. Brunt, "*Amicitia*," p. 1, quotes Sallust; see too F. W. Kent, "'Un paradiso habitato da diavoli': Ties of Loyalty and Patronage in the Society of Medicean Florence," in A. Benvenuti, *et al.* (eds), *Le Radici Cristiani di Firenze* (Florence: Alinea, 1994), pp. 183–210. For Medici conceptions of *amicizia*, see above all D. Kent, *The Rise of the Medici* (Oxford: Clarendon Press, 1978), part 1 (vi).

53. J. Taylor, "Letters and Letter Collections in England, 1300–1420," *Nottingham Medieval Studies* 24 (1980), pp. 57–70.

54. This argument requires further development but is outlined in F. W. Kent, "Patronage," in P. F. Grendler (ed.), *Encyclopedia of the Renaissance* (New York: Charles Scribner's Sons, 1999), IV, pp. 422–24.

55. Published by R. Hyatte, *The Arts of Friendship: The Idealization of Friendship in Medieval and Early Renaissance Literature* (Leiden: E. J. Brill, 1994), p. 211.

56. Roger Ascham, *The Scholemaster*, ed. J. E. B. Mayor (London: 1863, reprinted New York: AMS Press, 1967), pp. 96–97, and J. Goldberg, *Sodometries: Renaissance Texts, Modern Sexualities* (Stanford: Stanford University Press, 1992), p. 79. The other quotations are in A. Bray, "Homosexuality and the Signs of Male Friendship in Elizabethan England," *History Workshop Journal* 29 (1990), pp. 1–19 at pp. 3, 6–7, 16. See too L. Hutson, *The Usurer's Daughter: Male Friendship and Fictions of Women in Sixteenth-Century England* (London and New York: Routledge, 1994); Shannon, *Sovereign Amity*, pp. 23–24 and *passim*: Bray, *The Friend, passim.*

57. Hyatte, *Arts of Friendship*, ch. 3.

58. For the quotation, and generally, see M. Keen, "Brotherhood in Arms," *History* 47 (1962), pp. 1–17 at p. 6.

59. Published by P. S. Lewis, *Essays in Later Medieval French History* (London and Ronceverte: Macmillan, 1985), p. 60.

60. Cited by J. Powis, *Aristocracy* (Oxford: B. Blackwell, 1984), p. 52.

61. On this last theme, see G. Holmes, *The Estates of the Higher Nobility in Fourteenth-Century England* (Cambridge: Cambridge University Press, 1957); C. Carpenter, "The Beauchamp Affinity: A Study of Bastard Feudalism at Work," *English Historical Review* 95 (1980), pp. 514–32; and the various works cited in the notes immediately following. See Bray, *The Friend*, for double-burials among the English into the early modern period.

62. S. Walker, *The Lancastrian Affinity, 1361–1399* (Oxford: Clarendon Press, 1990), pp. 3, 17 and *passim*.

63. Published by Lewis, *Essays*, pp. 63, 67.

64. J. M. W. Bean, *From Lord to Patron: Lordship in Late Medieval England* (Manchester: Manchester University Press, 1989).

65. Published by W. H. Durham, *Lord Hastings' Indentured Retainers 1461–1483* (New Haven, CT: Connecticut Academy of Arts and Sciences, 1955), pp. 41, 123, 128, 133.

66. Cited by Walker, *Lancastrian Affinity*, pp. 208–209.

67. P. Maddern, "'Best Trusted Friends': Concepts and Practices of Friendship among Fifteenth-Century Norfolk Gentry," in N. Rogers (ed.), *England in the Fifteenth Century* (Stamford: P. Watkins, 1994), pp. 100–17.

68. Cited by J. S. Bellamy, *Bastard Feudalism and the Law* (London: Routledge, 1989), p. 59.

69. For the quotation, and generally, see C. Lafleur, *Pétrarque et l'amitié* (Paris and Quebec: Presses de l'Université Laval, 2001), pp. 86, 196, and *passim*.

70. P. O. Kristeller, *Studies in Renaissance Thought and Letters* (Rome: Edizioni di Storia e Letteratura, 1985), II, pp. 358, 486.

71. C. Bec, *Les livres des Florentins (1413–1608)* (Florence: Olschki, 1984), pp. 150, 160, 166, 179, 196; Bolgar, *Classical Heritage*, p. 357. Hyatte, *Arts of Friendship*, lists the late medieval treatments of friendship at pp. 203–208.

72. W. Bracke, *"Fare La Epistola" nella Roma del Quattrocento* (Rome: Associazione Roma nel Rinascimento, 1992); *Donato Gianotti and his Epistolae* (ed. R. Starn; Geneva: Droz, 1968).

73. Cited by C. Guillén, "Notes toward the Study of the Renaissance Letter," in B. Kiefer Lewalski (ed.), *Renaissance Genres: Essays in Theory, History, and Interpretation* (Cambridge, MA: Harvard University Press, 1986), pp. 70–101 at p. 79.

74. J. M. Najemy, *Between Friends* (Princeton, NJ: Princeton University Press, 1993), p. 47. Ch. 1, "Renaissance Epistolarity," is a splendid treatment of the theme.

75. The *De conscribendis epistolis* of Erasmus is translated by C. Fantazzi in *Collected Works* (ed. J. K. Sowards; Toronto, Buffalo and London: University of Toronto Press, 1985), XXV, pp. 1–254; see too "A Formula for the Composition of Letters," pp. 255–67.

76. Both passages cited by Schoeck, *Erasmus of Europe*, pp. 21–22, 141.

77. For the quotation, and in general, see K. Eden, "'Between Friends All Is Common': The Erasmian Adage and Tradition," *Journal of the History of Ideas* 59.3 (1998), pp. 405–19 at pp. 409, 413; "From the Cradle: Erasmus on Intimacy in Renaissance Letters," *Erasmus of Rotterdam Society Yearbook* 21 (2001), pp. 30–43; *Friends Hold All Things in Common* (New Haven, CT, and London: Yale University Press, 2001).

78. For the portrait, see J. B. Trapp, *Erasmus, Colet and More: The Early Tudor Humanists and their Books* (London: British Library, 1991), pp. 64–73. D. Wootton, "Friendship Portrayed: A New Account of Utopia," *History Workshop Journal* 45 (1998), pp. 29–47, discusses *Utopia* as a friendship treatise.

79. For the quotation, and generally, see J. Cunnally, "Ancient Coins as Gifts and Tokens of Friendship during the Renaissance," *Journal of the History of Collections* 6.2 (1994), pp. 129–43 at p. 132.

80. S. Hickson, "Female Patronage and the Language of Art in the Circle of Isabella d'Este in Mantua (c.1470–1560)" (PhD thesis, Queens University, Kingston Ontario, 2003), p. 132.

81. Hickson, "Female Patronage," Appendix II, 4, p. 332.

82. Hickson, "Female Patronage," ch. 2.

83. G. D. Hobson, "'Et Amicorum,'" *The Library*, 5th series, 4 (1949), pp. 87–99.

84. Burke, "Humanism and Friendship," p. 269.

85. Alberti, *Family in Renaissance Florence*, Book 4, pp. 247, 265–66, 279. For the context and other analyses, see A. Grafton, *Leon Battista Alberti: Master Builder of the Italian Renaissance* (London: Allen Lane, 2000), ch. 5; Hyatte, *Arts of Friendship*, pp. 172–94; U. Langer, *Perfect Friendship* (Geneva: Droz, 1994), ch. 6.

86. Fra Bartolommeo da San Concordio, *Ammaestramenti degli Antichi* (ed. V. Nannucci; Florence: Ricordi e Compagno, 1840), pp. 301–17; for Latini, see n35, above.

87. E. Beltran (ed.), *Humanistes francais du milieu de xve siècle* (Geneva: Droz, 1989), pp. 27–55; *The Florentine Fior di Virtu of 1491* (trans. N. Fersin; Washington, DC: Library of Congress, 1953), pp. 9–11. On this general theme, see the preceding chapter and the work cited in n92 below.

88. Cited by B. Collett, *Italian Benedictine Scholars and the Reformation* (Oxford: Clarendon Press, 1985), p. 43. See too M. J. Gill, *Augustine in the Italian Renaissance* (Cambridge: Cambridge University Press, 2005), pp. 14–15, 23, 26–27, 100.

89. Cited in A. Winston-Allen, *Convent Chronicles* (University Park, PA: Pennsylvania State University Press, 2005), p. 173; see too pp. 46–47.

90. *The Letters of Marsilio Ficino* (no ed; 4 vols; London: Shepheard-Walwyn, 1975–1988); the quotations are from III, p. 67, and I, pp. 96–97, respectively.

91. For the quotation, and in general, see A. Canavero Tarabochia, "L'amicizia nell'epistolario di Marsilio Ficino," *Rivista di Filosofia Neo-Scolastica* 67 (1975), pp. 422–31 at p. 428.

92. "Panegyric on Love," in J. Kraye (ed.), *Cambridge Translations of Renaissance Philosophical Texts*. Vol. I, *Moral Philosophy* (Cambridge: Cambridge University Press, 1997), pp. 156–65 at p. 163.

93. Cited by McGuire, *Friendship and Community*, p. 411.

94. Cited by C. Russell, *Giulia Gonzaga and the Religious Controversies of Sixteenth-Century Italy* (Turnhout: Brepols, 2006), p. 138.

95. J. Bossy, *Christianity in the West, 1400–1700* (Oxford: Oxford University Press, 1985), and his "Blood and Baptism: Kinship, Community and Christianity in Western Europe from the Fourteenth to the Seventeenth Centuries," in *Studies in Church History* (Oxford: Oxford University Press, 1973), X, pp. 129–43; see now Bray, *The Friend, passim*. For the relationship between classical and Christian conceptions of friendship, see R. W. Southern, *Medieval Humanism and Other Studies* (Oxford: Basil Blackwell,1970), pp. 34–35; McGuire, *Friendship and Community*, pp. xxv–xxix; Hyatte, *Arts of Friendship*, ch. 1; Haseldine, *Friendship in Medieval Europe, passim*; D. Konstan, *Friendship in the Classical World* (Cambridge: Cambridge University Press, 1997), pp. 156–73; L. Pizzolato, *L'idea d'amicizia nel mondo antico classico e cristiano* (Turin: Einaudi, 1993).

96. Bossy, *Christianity*, pp. 15–19, 117. For detailed case-studies, see C. Klapisch-Zuber, *La maison et le nom* (Paris: Éditions de l'École des Hautes Études en Sciences Sociales, 1990), chs 5, 6.

97. ASF, Conventi Soppressi, 95, 220, fol. 17r. See Bossy, *Christianity,* pp. 61, 76–78.

98. Niccolò Machiavelli, *Tutte le Opere* (ed. M. Martelli; Florence: Sansoni, 1971), pp. 930–32. For confraternities, see C. F. Black, *Italian Confraternities in the Sixteenth Century* (Cambridge: Cambridge University Press, 1989); W. Callahan,

"Confraternities and Brotherhoods in Spain, 1500–1800," *Confraternitas* 12 (2001), pp. 17–25; G. Rosser, *Medieval Westminster, 1200–1540* (Oxford: Clarendon Press, 1989), pp. 281–93; D. Reid, "Measuring the Impact of Brotherhood ... ," *Confraternitas* 14 (2003), pp. 3–12; and the works cited in the notes immediately following, below.

99. R. F. E. Weissman, *Ritual Brotherhood in Renaissance Florence* (New York and London: Academic Press, 1982), p. 27 and *passim*.

100. Cited in Weissman, *Ritual Brotherhood*, p. 102.

101. Cited by J. Henderson, *Piety and Charity in Late Medieval Florence* (Oxford: Clarendon Press, 1994), p. 19.

102. Cited by Zemon Davis, *The Gift*, p. 20.

103. Cited by M. Rocke, *Forbidden Friendships: Homosexuality and Male Culture in Renaissance Florence* (New York and Oxford: Oxford University Press, 1996), pp. 148, 182 and ch. 5.

104. Published in A. Del Col, *Domenico Scandella known as Menocchio: His Trials before the Inquisition (1583–1599)* (trans. John and Ann Tedeschi; Tempe, AZ: Medieval and Renaissance Texts and Studies, 1997), p. 36; see too pp. li, lxx, lxxx, 75, 77.

105. *De vera amicitia*, ed. Bertolini, p. 447; N. Newbiggin, *Feste D'Oltrarno: Plays in Churches in Fifteenth Century Florence* (2 vols; Florence: Olschki, 1997), II, pp. 252–53.

106. M. Flynn, "Rituals of Solidarity in Castilian Confraternities," *Renaissance and Reformation, Renaissance et Réforme* 25 (1989), pp. 53–68 at p. 63. For the practical difficulties of maintaining confraternal solidarity, however, see J. Fisk Rondeau, "Homosociability and Civic (Dis)order in Late Medieval Italian Confraternities," in N. Terpstra (ed.), *The Politics of Ritual Kinship: Confraternities and Social Order in Early Modern Italy* (Cambridge: Cambridge University Press, 2000), pp. 30–47.

107. D. Reid, "Moderate Devotion, Mediocre Poetry and Magnificent Food: The Confraternity of the Immaculate Conception of Rouen," *Confraternitas* 7 (1996), pp. 3–10.

108. Seneca, *Seventeen Letters* (ed. and trans. C. D. N. Costa; Warminster, Wiltshire: Aris & Phillips, 1988), pp. 28–35; I. Origo, "The Domestic Enemy: The Eastern Slaves in Tuscany in the Fourteenth and Fifteenth Centuries," *Speculum* 30 (1955), pp. 321–66.

109. T. F. Earle and K. J. P. Lowe (eds), *Black Africans in Renaissance Europe* (Cambridge: Cambridge University Press, 2005), chs 15, 16 and *passim*.

110. Cited in F. W. Kent, "'Be rather loved than feared': Class Relations in Quattrocento Florence," in W. J. Connell (ed.), *Society and Individual in Renaissance Florence* (Berkeley, CA: University of California Press, 2002), pp. 13–50 at p. 35.

111. D. Romano, *Patricians and Popolani: The Social Foundations of the Venetian Renaissance State* (Baltimore, MD: Johns Hopkins University Press, 1987), ch. 6.

112. For the quotation, and generally, see Kent, "'Be rather loved than feared,'" p. 35 and *passim*.

113. Laura Cereta, *Collected Letters of a Renaissance Feminist* (ed. and trans. D. Robin; Chicago: Chicago University Press, 1997).

114. Cereta, *Collected Letters*, pp. 136–38

115. Cereta, *Collected Letters*, p. 80.

116. Bartolomeo Goggio, *De laudibus mulierum*, f. 2v, as cited in S. Kolsky, *The Ghost of Boccaccio, Writings on Famous Women in Renaissance Italy* (Turnhout: Brepols, 2005), p. 176

117. Agostino Strozzi, *De amicitia* (Venice: Biblioteca Marciana), Codici italiani, Classe II, 106. See C. James and F. W. Kent, "Margherita Cantelmo and Agostino Strozzi: Friendship's Gifts and a Portrait Medal by Costantino da Ferrara," forthcoming in I *Tatti Studies*, 12 (2008).

118. C. James, "Friendship and Dynastic Marriage in Renaissance Italy," *Literature and History 17* (2008), pp. 4–18.

119. Mario Equicola, *De mulieribus* (ed. G. Lucchesini and P. Totaro; Pisa and Rome: Istituti Editoriali e Poligrafici Internazionali, 2004), pp. 44–46.

120. E. Telle, "Érasme et les Mariages Dynastiques." *Bibliothèque d'Humanisme et Renaissance* 12 (1950), pp. 7–13.

121. Edmund Tilney (ed.), *The Flower of Friendship: A Renaissance Dialogue Contesting Marriage* (Ithaca, NY: Cornell University Press, 1992), p. 105.

122. Tilney (ed.), *The Flower of Friendship*, p. 108.

123. Tilney (ed.), *The Flower of Friendship*, p. 135.

124. Langer, *Perfect Friendship*, p. 117 and ch. 4; Marguerite de Navarre, *The Heptameron* (trans. P. A. Chilton; Harmondsworth, UK: Penguin, 1984). See too P. F. and R. C. Cholakian, *Marguerite de Navarre* (New York: Columbia University Press, 2005), pp. 204–205, 319 n31.

125. Marie de Gournay, "The Promenade of Monsieur de Montaigne," in R. Hillman and C. Quesnel (ed. and trans.), *Apology for the Woman Writing* (Chicago: Chicago University Press, 2002), pp. 29, 32; M. Fogel, *Marie de Gournay* (Paris: Fayard, 2004), pp. 47–48, 312.

126. Moderata Fonte, *The Worth of Women* (ed. and trans. V. Cox; Chicago: Chicago University Press, 1997), p. 123 n4.

127. Fonte, *The Worth of Women*, pp. 123, 128, 259, and *Il Merito delle Donne* (ed. A. Chemello; Mirano and Venice: Eidos, 1988), pp. 75–79.

128. "Of Friendship," in *The Complete Works of Montaigne* (trans. D. M. Frame; London: Hamish Hamilton, 1958), pp. 135–44 at p. 136; Florio's translation of 1603 can be found in "Renaissance Editions," http:www.uoregon.edu/~rbeer/montaigne/lxxvii.htm, accessed 1 October 2007.

129. *Complete Works of Montaigne*, trans. Frame, p. 1050.

130. *Complete Works of Montaigne*, trans. Frame, pp. 137–38, 1065–66.

131. For Montaigne's words see *Complete Works of Montaigne*, trans. Frame, pp. 135–44, and J. Derrida, "The Politics of Friendship," *Journal of Philosophy* 85 (1988), pp. 632–44. The critic cited is L. Smith-Pangle, *Aristotle and the Philosophy of Friendship* (Cambridge: Cambridge University Press, 2003), pp. 72–78 at p. 74.

132. "Of Friendship," in Bacon, *Essays*, pp. 87–94; A. Bray, *Homosexuality in Renaissance England* (London: Gay Men's Press, 1982), p. 49.

133. "Of Followers and Friends," in Bacon, *Essays*, pp. 154–56. See D. Wootton's subtle analysis in "Francis Bacon: Your Flexible Friend," in J. H. Elliott and L. W. B. Brocklisse (eds), *The World of the Favourite* (New Haven, CT, and London: Yale University Press, 1999), pp. 184–204.

134. Sperone Speroni, "Dialogo della Amicizia," in *Opere* (ed. M. Pozzi; 5 vols; Rome: Vecchiarelli, 1988), II, pp. 368–74 at p. 369; Torquato Tasso, "Il Manso overo de l'amicizia," in *Dialoghi* (ed. G. Baffetti; 2 vols; Milan: Rizzoli, 1998), II, pp. 900–55. See too *L'Arte della conversazione nelle corti del Rinascimento* (ed. F. Calitti; Rome: Istituto Poligrafico e Zecca dello Stato, 2003), pp. 187–89.

135. Stefano Guazzo, *La civil conversazione* (ed. A. Quondam; 2 vols; Modena: Panini, 1993), I, p. 118; II, pp. 235–36.

136. Shannon, *Sovereign Amity*, p. 165, and ch. 5: see too pp. 34–35 and figs 2 and 3 for friendship portrayed as a woman. For *donna con donna*, see L. Faderman, *Surpassing the Love of Men: Romantic Friendship and Love between Women from the Renaissance to the Present* (New York: Morrow, 1981), ch.1, and P. Simons, "Lesbian (In)Visibility in Italian Renaissance Culture: Diana and Other Cases of *donna con donna*," *Journal of Homosexuality* 27 (1994), pp. 81–122.

137. Alberti, *Family in Renaissance Florence*, p. 266; St Claire Byrne, *Lisle Letters*, pp. 138, 142. In general, see Wootton, "Francis Bacon," pp. 184–204. For Poussin, see E. Cropper and C. Dempsey, *Nicolas Poussin: Friendship and the Love of Painting* (Princeton, NJ: Princeton University Press, 1996).

138. Francesco Guicciardini, *Ricordi* (ed. V. De Caprio; Rome: Salerno Editrice, 1990), p. 89.

139. S. A. Schwarzenbach, "On Civic Friendship," *Ethics* 107 (1996), pp. 97–128; Smith-Pangle, *Aristotle*, p. 3.

140. Bacon, *Essays*, p. 87; Aristotle, *Nicomachean Ethics* IX, 10.

141. Both quotations are in *L'Arte della Conversazione*, ed. Calitti, pp. 206–207.

142. Shannon, *Sovereign Amity*, pp. 207–209, 223–24.

143. Cited in Wootton, "Francis Bacon," p. 191.

Chapter 5

FROM CHRISTIAN FRIENDSHIP TO SECULAR SENTIMENTALITY: ENLIGHTENMENT RE-EVALUATIONS

David Garrioch

The seventeenth and eighteenth centuries brought significant shifts in the way people thought and talked about friendship, and to some extent in the ways they experienced it. As in earlier periods, the political, economic and social context strongly shaped trends even in such an apparently personal relationship as friendship. The late sixteenth century had seen bitter civil wars over religion across Europe, after the Reformation, and sectarian tensions remained high through the seventeenth century. Many historians have linked these religious wars to the development of new structures of government, strong monarchies that little by little brought the great aristocratic families under their control and that in some cases also challenged the power of the Church. Many of the city republics of Italy, Germany and the Low Countries were taken over by princely dynasties, while increasingly powerful monarchies developed in Sweden, Spain, central Europe and England, then in France and later Prussia, dominating Europe both economically and militarily.

The courts of these rulers became the new focus of political and cultural life, initially restricted to a very small aristocratic elite. The new monarchies, building on Renaissance models, understood the symbolic power of cultural and scientific patronage, founding scientific academies and actively encouraging the arts. This had unanticipated consequences. Building on the work of humanists and scientists of the preceding period, seventeenth- and eighteenth-century scholars – particularly those associated with the so-called "scientific Revolution" and with the cultural and intellectual movement known as the Enlightenment – developed new approaches to knowledge and questioned many of the assumptions that underlay earlier ideas about society. In particular, some of the Christian principles that had been taken for granted by Protestants and Catholics alike now began to be challenged. If the seventeenth century remained a deeply religious age, one marked by war, food shortages, epidemics and hardship for much of the population, by the mid eighteenth century death rates were falling in Western Europe and there was a growing optimism about the capacity of human beings to fashion their own destiny. The ability of the churches to dictate forms of behaviour and ways of thinking was slowly eroded, challenged both by state power and by social change.

This was also a period when European society was transformed by merchant capitalism. The discovery of the New World and the subsequent growth of the Spanish and Portuguese empires, then of English and French colonies in North America, the West Indies, around the African coast and in India, led to a huge expansion in trade. This in turn promoted urban growth, particularly along the Atlantic seaboard, creating new markets and increasing the numbers, wealth and influence of merchants. New financial institutions such as stock exchanges and joint stock companies sprang up all over Europe, encouraged by governments that were well aware of the importance of economic growth in maintaining their power. By the early eighteenth century, Amsterdam, London and Paris had become centres of consumer industries, and manufacturing was expanding to meet growing demand from aristocrats, merchant elites and a newly prosperous "middling sort" in cities and towns across Europe. Literacy rates rose, especially in the cities, where by the late eighteenth century artisans, shopkeepers and domestic servants were often able to read books and newspapers as well as broadsheets and pamphlets.

These social and economic changes accompanied extraordinary shifts in the political domain. By the eighteenth century the growth of state power was producing "administrative monarchies," increasingly bureaucratic forms of government that slowly replaced personal forms of rule. These expanding administrations left ever-increasing numbers of records that give us access to the lives and words of wider sections of the population. At the same time, growing numbers of men and women began to feel that government was not solely the domain of a small circle of ruling dynasties and courtiers but that the views and interests of the wider educated population should be taken into account. Newspapers, books and pamphlets appeared in unprecedented numbers, while coffee houses, clubs, salons, literary and scientific societies and freemasons' lodges provided new forums for discussion of issues of all kinds. In this changed political and social climate, new ideas flourished.

All of these developments had a direct impact on thinking about friendship. While most of the examples in this chapter will be drawn from Britain and France, the trends described were widespread in Europe and to varying degrees in the developing European colonies of the New World. There were significant challenges to the assumptions about female and male nature that underlay inherited notions of what friendships should be. The secularization of many forms of social interaction led to a reduced emphasis on the religious elements underpinning relationships. Family life and ideas about the family were changing and the growth of new forms of literature, notably novels and autobiographies, provided fertile ways for an ever-expanding reading public to explore new ways of thinking about friendship. Letter-writing manuals and treatises continued to be produced but people increasingly took their models from novels. Changes in public life had an impact on thinking about political friendship. The forms of patronage that were so central to political life – indeed to every sphere of life – in the smaller polities of the fifteenth and sixteenth centuries were now challenged as the development of wider cultural markets began to make it possible for scientists and writers to make a living without direct dependence on aristocrats or even princes. Key figures of the Enlightenment used models of ideal friendship to critique both the society and the forms of government of their day. And towards the end of the eighteenth century, dramatic new challenges rocked European society. The influence of the American and French revolutions brought a revival of notions of political friendship, but within a context that gave them new meanings.

Yet these changes were not easy and they did not happen overnight. Some of the core values of the Enlightenment – philanthropy, cosmopolitanism and humanitarianism – sat uneasily alongside older but still powerful ideas about loyalty, about family ties, and about personal and group identity. How could one be a true philanthropist, a friend to all humanity, while retaining a primary loyalty to kin and lineage, to the local community, even to one's king or – as new ideas of the nation developed – to one's country? What was the relationship between private friendships and one's duty to all human beings? The gradual secularization of many areas of life, too, opened up tensions between religious and secular conceptions of friendship. Did one's primary loyalties belong, as the churches had long taught, with one's co-religionists or even with other Christians? And in an age when the prestige of the ancients remained enormous, reinforced by the study of the classics among ever-wider sections of the population, how could Aristotle and Cicero's pre-Christian notions of friendship be reconciled with those of the Church fathers or, for that matter, with everyday, commonsense understandings of friendship?[1] While educated people continued to read Cicero and Aristotle, and writers on friendship still regarded the works of the ancients with veneration, they read them in new ways.

Ideal Friendship: Philosophical Approaches and Moral Advice

Philosophical discussions are found in treatises, pamphlets and sermons, in advice literature and letters, but also embedded in fictional works. Few writers developed original arguments about friendship, most preferring to cite universally recognized authorities, generally Scripture, Cicero or Aristotle. This was partly because male education during the seventeenth and eighteenth centuries placed a heavy emphasis on reading and imitating Latin and, to a lesser extent, Greek authors: there were some 29 editions of Cicero's *De amicitia* published in Latin in Britain during the seventeenth century and as many again in the eighteenth. In France, Cicero was the most studied author in the colleges of higher education throughout the period, including his writing on friendship.[2] It is hardly surprising that so many authors drew on these sources and used examples drawn from classical history or mythology to illustrate the virtues and duties of friendship.

Most writers recognized that there were different kinds of friendship, both in theory and in practice. Drawing on a tradition coming from Aristotle, they distinguished friendships based on need or self-interest, those founded on the pleasure taken in each other's company, and those based on virtue, usually interpreted as mutual respect and concern. But they invariably focused on "true" friendship, which they saw as the purest human relationship. For the mid seventeenth-century writer Jeremy Taylor, whose *Measures and Offices of Friendship* of 1657 continued to be read for the next century, it "is the greatest bond in the world," "a union of souls," "the allay of our sorrowes, the ease of our passions, the discharge of our oppressions, the sanctuary to our calamities, the counsellour of our doubts, the clarity of our minds."[3] In 1764 Voltaire defined it more succinctly in his *Philosophical Dictionary* as "the marriage of the soul." A little later Marie-Charlotte Thiroux d'Arronville evoked "a sentiment in which our senses have no part. Our soul alone is touched by it," thus distinguishing the highest form of friendship from emotional or utilitarian considerations. For John Locke in the 1690s, as for David Hume half a century later, one of the virtues of friendship was that service to a friend was provided without thought to any gain.[4] It was a disinterested and spiritual relationship.

There were a few dissenting voices. The article on "Amitié" (Friendship) in the *Encyclopédie* (1751) was quite lukewarm, suggesting that the need for friendship pointed to the basic inadequacy of individual human beings and devoting most of its discussion to what could and did go wrong in friendships. La Rochefoucauld asserted in 1665 that there was no such thing as a totally disinterested friendship and a century later the materialist philosopher Claude Adrien Helvétius agreed, citing human desire for pleasure, money, intrigue, wit or for support in unhappiness. But this was very much a minority opinion. Denis Diderot replied to Helvétius in a satirical short story that showed, he wrote in the postface, "that in general there can only be sound friendships between men who have nothing. For then a man is the whole fortune of his friend." Most authors agreed with the French moralist Louis-Silvestre de Sacy that true friendship, as opposed to lesser relationships that people sometimes erroneously confused with it, was based on mutual esteem, combined with "the inclination of the Heart." It was, wrote Adam Ferguson in 1792, "mutual conviction of unalterable worth, entire affection, and unlimited confidence."[5]

For most eighteenth-century writers this meant that real friendship between people of significantly different ranks was not possible. Those in positions of authority attracted flattery and could never truly confide in an inferior. De Sacy was prepared to admit the possibility of unequal friendships, which had the advantage that there was no rivalry involved, but they depended on the superior party being prepared to stoop and the inferior one maintaining an air of servility in public. But he nevertheless felt that "Friendship is more common amongst those who are on a Level." Most authors, though, were un-compromising. The *Encyclopédie* affirmed that equality was necessary between friends. Kant agreed: "The relation of a patron, as benefactor, to his protegé, as a beneficiary obliged to be grateful, may indeed be a relation of mutual love, but not of friendship; for the respect due from each to the other is not equal." This marked quite a shift in thinking from two centuries earlier when Francis Bacon had observed that "there is little friendship in the world, and least of all between equals ... that that is, is between superior and inferior," for they were mutually dependent.[6]

There was much discussion, too, of the duties of friendship. True friends, all writers agreed, love, support and defend each other. "What is *Friendship* when compleat?" asks Ephelia in a poem by Anne Finch. Her friend Ardelia replies:

> 'Tis to share all Joy and Grief;
> 'Tis to lend all due Relief
> From the Tongue, the Heart, the Hand;
> 'Tis to mortgage House and Land;
> For a Friend be sold a Slave;
> 'Tis to die upon a Grave,
> If a Friend therein do lie.[7]

Perfect friendship depended, insisted many authors, on intimacy and openness, on what Antoine Thomas described in 1772 as "the sweet confidences that friendship bestows and receives." All barriers and pretence were dropped, so that friends knew each other's innermost thoughts. As Samuel Johnson put it, more prosaically, "Many men ... would wish to have an intimate friend, with whom they might compare minds, and cherish private virtues." This meant, of course, that they knew each other's faults, and much ink was consumed in discussion of whether such knowledge might undermine friendship, on whether friends should be blind to each other's flaws (as the *Dictionnaire de Trévoux* believed), overlook them or, on the contrary, try to correct them. Some writers agreed with Aristotle or with Plutarch that they had a responsibility to correct and improve each other: "there is no such Instructor and Tutor, as a Friend," affirmed the seventeenth-century cleric Simon Patrick. But while friends should be honest with each other, any reproach should be made lovingly and in ways that enabled them to preserve their self-respect. Thus, said de Sacy, it should always be expressed in private, never publicly. Friends should only correct each other, suggested Charles Duclos in the 1750s, if such honesty is necessary for the welfare of the friend. Immanuel Kant agreed that friendship involves "the complete confidence of two persons in disclosing to one another their secret thoughts and feelings," but only "so far as such disclosure is compatible with mutual respect."[8]

Another key question for most writers on friendship was how to distinguish it from other relationships, particularly family ones. Could parents and children truly be friends and was the rapport between brothers or sisters necessarily one of friendship? Unlike many literary works most treatises concluded, like Taylor in the 1650s, that parent–child relations were unequal and asymmetrical "and therefore another kind of friendship than we meane in our inquiry." "Fraternity," he continued, "is the opportunity and the preliminary dispositions to friendship, and no more." Although the closeness of family ties could lead to friendship they were not of the same nature. "As for Trust and Confidence," opined Simon Patrick, "neither Kindred, nor alliance to great Persons, nor Riches, nor any Thing else can so much assure it, as generous Friendship."[9]

The major debates on friendship, however, arose from other issues. The question of exclusivity was a significant one. Most authors imagined friendship as exclusive and therefore, in its purest form, involving only two people. For Kant it was "an association of two persons through equal and mutual love and respect." "The most perfect friendship," agreed Dupuy de La Chapelle, "is a sweet, tender and constant union between two people." More generally, early modern writers thought of friendship as operating within an emotional economy in which there was only so much goodwill to go round, in much the same way that economists of the time believed that wealth was limited and could only be redistributed, not expanded. "We have only a given part of sensibility," wrote Charles Duclos in 1751: "[therefore] those who love the public good ... have many connections and few friends." Writers conventionally used economic terminology to refer to human relationships: "What men call friendship," wrote La Rochefoucauld, "is ... but a commerce where self-interest always finds something to gain."[10]

This idea of friendship as limited and exclusive led religious writers to grapple with the concern, raised by Augustine, that human friendship might distract from and compete with that of God. They generally resolved this by reinterpreting Aristotle's idea of the highest form of friendship. Virtue was indeed the basis of true friendship, suggested François de Sales in 1609

> but if your mutual and reciprocal communication be founded on
> charity, on devotion, on Christian perfection, O God! how pre-
> cious will your friendship be! It will be excellent because it comes
> from God ... All other friendships ... are but shadows in compari-
> son with this.

Seventy years later Nicolas Malebranche too constructed a model of
"Christian friendship" in which a faithful man loved God through his
friend and with no desire for reward other than from the Almighty.
Jean-François Senault (1641) agreed that the basis for real friendship
must be Christian piety but he held out hope that even pagans and
thieves could be saved because while they might disregard the laws of
society they did recognize friendship.[11]

Yet many moralists worried that exclusive friendships between individuals might compete with the Christian obligation to love all humanity. Jeremy Taylor resolved this by arguing that human friendships,
while imperfect, were reflections of divine ones, a form of charity,
and that Christians had a responsibility to form as many friendships as
possible. Pierre Nicole, starting from the same premise that Christians
should love all men equally, suggested that while for practical reasons
the obligations of friendship did not extend to everyone in the world,
they should operate "as soon as one enters into intercourse with someone by forming a particular connection." A hundred years later Samuel
Johnson raised the same issue:

> All friendship is preferring the interest of a friend, to the neglect, or
> perhaps, against the interest of others; so that an old Greek said,
> "He that has friends, has no friend." Now Christianity recommends
> universal benevolence, to consider all men as our brethren; which
> is contrary to the virtue of friendship, as described by the ancient
> philosophers.[12]

A related question, as for many earlier authors, concerned the limits
of friendship and the moral dilemmas that might arise when friendship conflicted with other loyalties and responsibilities. This could
occur, for instance, when the interests of a friend and those of one's
family diverged. Taylor warned sternly that duty to parents and to
children is "such a duty which no other friendship can annul: because
their mutual duty is bound upon them by religion long before any
other friendships can be contracted." He also insisted that friendship
could not justify committing a crime, however much danger one's
friend might be in. "No friendship can excuse a sin." Thus it was not

permissible to rebel against one's prince or country in support of a friend, or to commit perjury, which was an offence against God. Fifty years later de Sacy agreed that one's duties to the Creator, to the state and to one's family came ahead of obligations to a friend. Nor was it acceptable to break an oath, even in order to save a friend's life, because to do so would lead to social chaos. At the very end of the eighteenth century Kant and Benjamin Constant debated the same question, though in a secular context: was it morally justifiable to lie to protect a friend from harm? Both men mounted their arguments in terms of the duty one has to other human beings and to society.[13]

Further debates centred on what qualities were required for true friendship. As in earlier periods, from the ancient world onwards, there was near universal agreement that only virtuous (religious writers added "Christian") people could become friends because friendship depended on selflessness, mutual trust and confidence. "Vicious or blockish persons," wrote de Sacy, were not capable of friendship because of the corruption of their minds. For Voltaire, "evil people have only accomplices; sensualists have companions in debauchery; those who pursue self-interest have associates; intriguers gather the factious around them; ordinary, idle men have associations; princes have courtiers; only virtuous men have friends." Adam Smith agreed: the best friendships, arising from:

> an involuntary feeling that the persons to whom we attach ourselves are the natural and proper objects of esteem and approbation; can exist only among men of virtue. Truly secure and permanent friendship ... is shared only by the virtuous.

Many authors, like Aubry in 1776, enumerated those character flaws that rendered most people unsuitable: avarice, ambition, apathy, a suspicious nature, a penchant for gambling, even genius. An anonymous moralist of 1796 pointed out that "the sour, cold, unimpassioned tempers of some" would never attract friends: "their manners, their looks, their expressions, and actions, are disagreeable and forbidding." For Dupuy de La Chapelle, true friendship depended on "the pleasure that arises from the conformity of character, of honour and of good manners, cultivated by self-respect that is perfectly directed and rectified by reason."[14]

Most writers agreed that this excluded much of the population. Madame de Lambert spoke for many when she stated that "Persons of distinction are more anxious to amass riches than to acquire friends."

But it was equally difficult for the plebs. De Sacy felt that "Persons of the Meanest Parts are not wholly incapable of the Ties of Friendship," since it "consists more in the Goodness of Manners, and in Affection, than in an Extensive Knowledge and Comprehension of Things." But such plebeian friendships were most unusual. Most writers were more dismissive. As Thiroux d'Arronville suggested, the common people had only prejudices and were guided by passion and must therefore be unable to experience the noble feelings upon which friendship rested. It was not their fault, she added. The conditions of life for the bulk of the people harden their hearts and make only utilitarian relationships possible. She also suggested that merchants are too unimaginative and calculate everything in monetary terms; that worldly people are content with superficialities; and that in the final analysis only People of Letters, especially those of mature years, can experience true friendship because they are reflective, rarely jealous and form relationships for pleasure, not through ambition or flattery.[15] This is one of the central features of many discussions: writers tend to define their terms in ways that exclude people different from themselves.

Nowhere is this clearer than in debates over whether women could experience true friendship. The classical and biblical models were primarily male and although fiction, as we shall see, was full of female friendships, many theorists seriously doubted that women could really experience such relationships. This was partly because of the opposition commonly made between love, which male writers associated with women, and friendship, identified as essentially masculine. Thus La Rochefoucauld commented that "most women are little touched by friendship, because it is bland when one has tasted love." Such assumptions remained widespread: for example, permeating adaptations of the correspondence of Abélard and Héloïse that were widely popular in both France and England throughout the eighteenth century. The argument was also used that friendship was above all rational and therefore quintessentially male. Jean-Jacques Rousseau spoke for many when he argued in *Émile* (1762) that women were both coquettish and domineering and therefore unable to sustain either the equality or the devotion to the other that was necessary. Mary Wollstonecraft agreed with Rousseau that women were less able to experience reason than men and therefore less capable of friendship, but she saw this as a question of education and not as a result of women's essential nature. Because women were made into sexual objects and taught that their role was to please men, they could not maintain "the tender confidence and sincere respect of friendship" either with men or with other women, whom they were educated to regard as rivals. Her German contemporary Carl Friedrich Pockels made the same point: women competed for men's love and were therefore unable to form true friendships. Yet many theorists believed true friendships to be possible between women. Jeremy Taylor did, and so did his seventeenth-century French contemporary Jean-François Senault who, after discussing various classical examples, affirmed that "the soul has no sex, and ... in the body of a woman one may find the mind of a man." Hester Chapone, like many others in the eighteenth century, did not doubt women's capacity for friendship.[16]

Equally contested was the question of whether true friendship between the sexes was possible. For Thiroux d'Arronville, as for most moralists, it was dangerous because it easily turned into love, and for men carried the additional disadvantage that "it narrows the circle of their ideas by the habit they contract of occupying themselves only with the small things that fill the lives of women." Throughout this period it was a commonplace that love – synonymous with passion – was incompatible with friendship because friendship depended on reason. Love, wrote Mary Wollstonecraft, was based on "chance and sensation" and not on "choice and reason," whereas friendship was "founded on principle, and cemented by time ... In a great degree, love and friendship cannot subsist in the same bosom." Since the dominant view, among both men and women, was that men were rational and women more guided by their emotions, this made true friendship between the sexes difficult. Such thinking reflected both the extreme inequality between the sexes in everyday life and the fact that friendships between men and women were liable to be interpreted in sexual terms.[17]

Nevertheless, a long tradition of writing on friendship maintained, on the contrary, that female–male friendship was possible, particularly within marriage. In the mid seventeenth century Jeremy Taylor, writing in response to the poet Katherine Phillips, believed that marriage "is the Queen of friendships, in which there is a communication of all that can be communicated by friendship: and ... made sacred by vowes and love, by bodies and souls, by interest and custome, by religion and by lawes." Many eighteenth-century authors agreed. David Hume suggested that "Nature has implanted in all living creatures an affection between the sexes, which ... is not merely confined to the satisfaction of the bodily appetite, but begets a friendship and mutual sympathy, which runs through the whole tenor of their lives." The more radical writers drew out the full implications of combining the ideas that the ideal marriage was a friendship, and that friendship required equality. Thus the Scottish philosopher Francis Hutcheson declared marriage to be "a state of equal partnership or friendship" and condemned laws and customs that gave the husband unjust power over his wife.[18]

Outside marriage, friendship between men and women was generally believed to be more difficult, although Charles Sorel, writing in 1663, spoke of "the honest affection between two people of different sex, which makes them glad to see each other and to converse, and to do each other service whenever they have the opportunity." In the same period Madeleine de Scudéry argued for a model of "tender friendship" between women and men that was chaste and respectful yet intimate. Madame de Lambert, in 1736, felt that friendship between men and women was delicate but possible. It required virtue and restraint, but was more agreeable than friendship between people of the same sex. A popular compromise was to identify male and female friendships as equally possible but different in nature, corresponding to the different characteristics of the two sexes. Antoine Thomas, who believed women were above all governed by feeling, thought this made women better at providing emotional support. Male friendships, being based more on mutual interest and on rationality, might be nobler and more constant but were also harsher. "For great occasions one should wish for a male friend, but for the happiness of everyday life, the friendship of a woman."[19]

By the late eighteenth century, however, some writers were prepared to blur the distinction between love and friendship. The French economist Dupont de Nemours argued that the physical pleasure involved in love was the only difference and that even this was not a necessary distinction. Friendship, he suggested, had its "desires, caresses, tears, smiles, a beating of the heart, a sensuality, delicate worries and even jealousy, that rather bitter seasoning of which just a touch is perhaps a necessary part of all human attachments."[20]

Fictional Representations

Fiction provided a safe way for authors and readers to explore relationships and to experiment with the implications of forms of behaviour that were not acceptable in real life or that most of the educated public was simply unlikely to encounter. Many novels, poems and plays were vehicles for expressing particular moral views and can therefore be set alongside advice literature and even philosophy. Yet while fiction often offered cautionary tales, it also presented situations that advice literature did not deal with, particularly those of individual and social corruption where taboos were breached. In particular, the development of the novel as a new and immensely popular literary form encouraged new explorations of friendship, largely replacing letter collections as models of how to behave (and how not to) – though significantly, many early novels took the form of exchanges of letters between the characters. They were not entirely free in their depictions of friendship, of course. Classical models exerted a powerful effect, and the extremely moralistic social and religious conventions of early modern societies limited the plot and even dictated the types of characters: thus in the late seventeenth and early eighteenth centuries the protagonists were primarily nobles. Yet increasingly novels introduced bourgeois characters, particularly with the hugely popular work of Samuel Richardson. This too expanded the range of possible situations as well as the appeal of the genre.

Throughout the period, friendship was a key literary theme. The tension between it and other bonds was one of the dramatic elements of Pierre Corneille's *Horace* (1640), which set love of homeland against duty to friends and kin, the former emerging victorious. A string of novels and plays, from Madeleine de Scudéry's *Clélie: histoire romaine* (1654-58) to the work of Pierre Marivaux in the early eighteenth century, explored the boundaries between love and friendship. The advice and activities of false friends and true drove the action of novels like Sarah Fielding's *The Adventures of David Simple, Containing an Account of his Travels through the Cities of London and Westminster in Search of a Real Friend* (1744). Its naive hero experiences a wide variety of betrayals and their consequences before eventually finding the true friendship of the title in the arms of a virtuous wife. Friendship networks also structure the plot of Eliza Haywood's *The History of Miss Betsy Thoughtless* (1751), whose heroine's poor choice of friends gets her into all kinds of strife. Fortunately she is saved by her true friends. In Samuel Richardson's *Clarissa* (1747–1748), on the other hand, the main character is betrayed by her friends and dies in shame and misery. Carlo Goldoni's play *Il Vero amico* (1751) and Gotthold Lessing's *Damon* (1747) centred on the anguish of friends who fell in love with the same woman. Audiences devoured the moral dilemmas and sentimental trials of these characters, apparently drawing vicarious satisfaction from the most improbable situations.

The way fictional friends are portrayed reveals clearly what authors meant when they used the term. Friends are those who have one's honour and welfare at heart. They provide sound advice, moral support and material assistance if necessary. In English literature (though not in French) family relationships were deemed to be a form of friendship and kin are often described as "natural friends," people with mutual interests and unavoidable responsibilities to each other. *Clarissa* is the story of what happens to a young woman of gentle birth whose "natural friends" – her parents, brother and sister, her uncle and aunt – fail her. A second meaning of friendship found in literary sources is simply goodwill or benevolence. Mr Burnet, in Madame Riccoboni's *History of Miss Jenny* (1764), obtained for the heroine "the protection and the friendship" of Lady Lindsay, whom she did not yet know.[21]

Another kind of fictional friend is closer to the modern sense of someone who is chosen voluntarily and in a relationship of mutual affection. They can be business associates, relatives or social acquaintances and are usually of similar rank. After the middle of the eighteenth century this usage increasingly supplants the others and where kin do become friends it is because they share both blood and affection. In accordance with the extraordinary sentimentality of much late eighteenth- and early nineteenth-century writing, Germaine de Staël's *Corinne* (1807) portrays a man's relationship with his father as a near-perfect form of friendship.

> How unhappy are orphans! ... How, in effect, can one ever replace that affection that is born with us, that mutual intelligence and sympathy of blood, that friendship prepared by heaven between a child and his father? One can still love, but giving one's whole soul is a form of happiness one will never find again.[22]

In fiction, successful friendships can exist between men, between women or between the sexes. But friends must be trustworthy and their relationship depends – like that between Betsy Thoughtless and Lady Loveit – on "a great parity of sentiment and principle." Chosen friendships are normally disinterested, though in some cases individuals can be united by mutual interests. Thus a husband or wife, as in *David Simple* or *Betsy Thoughtless*, can be true friends. A patron can also be described in terms of friendship, though often more ambiguously: Lord **** is a man of superior rank and after Betsy

Thoughtless rebuffs his attempts to seduce her she is rebuked by her husband who "feared her idle resentment had lost him all his interest with the best of friends." Occasionally servants and employers become friends, although the relationship tends to work more to the benefit of the latter. This is the case in Madame Riccoboni's novel *Histoire de Miss Jenny* (1764), where the heroine is deeply attached to her servant. The two share many vicissitudes and the servant protects her mistress on many occasions before finally dying while telling Miss Jenny not to be sad because she is losing but "a useless friend." "O Lidy," cries her mistress, "my sister, my companion, my friend."[23]

Perhaps because novels were thought of as having a largely female audience, and undoubtedly because many were written by women, they frequently explored female friendships. Eliza Haywood's heroines often had close women friends. In *The Surprize* (1724) the heroine, Alinda, rejects a suitor who had jilted her friend (and cousin) Euphemia: "Never Woman gave a greater Proof of her Friendship to Another," commented the author. In Haywood's *The British Recluse* (1723), the story ends with the two main women characters deciding to live together, "happy in the real Friendship of each other." The French writer Françoise de Graffigny was more cautious in her bestselling novel *Peruvian Letters* (1747), suggesting that women were less likely to become close friends than men. Samuel Richardson too had one of his characters declare that "Friendship, generally speaking ... is too fervent a flame for female minds to manage ... Like other extremes, it is hardly ever durable."[24] Nevertheless, after Richardson's depiction of Clarissa Harlowe and Anna Howe, then Jean-Jacques Rousseau's description of the intimate relationship between Julie and Claire in *La Nouvelle Héloïse* (1761), such doubts were largely dispelled and their characters provided a model for subsequent literary and even real-life friendships between women. Despite Rousseau's insistence on women's "natural" role as helpmeets to men, Julie and Claire offered a potentially subversive example since they were stronger characters than the male ones in the novel and their relationship was in competition with that between Julie and her lover Saint-Preux. Mary Wollstonecraft subsequently provided another subversive model in her final and unfinished work, *Maria or the Wrongs of Women* (1798). Through the figure of Jemima, the warden in an insane asylum and a woman who has known extreme poverty, want and degradation, Wollstonecraft points to the ways in which women's subordination and their economic dependence on men for survival destroys any sense of solidarity or friendship between them. At the same time, however, once understood, this facet of women's oppression can be transcended. In the relationship that develops between Jemima and Maria, a woman who has been incarcerated in the asylum by a brutal and dishonest husband, the story suggests that women can offer each other a kind of devotion and selfless love that is unknown to men. The gothic setting provided by the mental asylum from which Maria escapes with Jemima's help also provides the background for one of the first close cross-class relationships – outside the mistress–servant one – to appear in fiction.

While the language of seventeenth-century fiction was in general restrained, even prudish, by the mid eighteenth century images of friendship between women had become emotional and sentimental. In Elizabeth Carter's poem "To Miss Lynch" (1744) friendship is described as "the brightest Passion of the human Breast."[25] The relationship between Clarissa Harlowe and Anna Howe is intense and spiritual: "I must, I will love you; and love you for ever"; "I love you, as never woman loved another"; "We had but one heart, but one soul, between us; and now my better half is torn from me." In *La Nouvelle Héloïse* the relationship between Julie and her cousin and intimate friend Claire is presented in similar terms: "My sweet friend, my saviour, my guardian angel?" cries Julie. Historians also refer to a veritable "cult of friendship" in late eighteenth-century German literature, which Kant was reacting against in his writing on the subject and which he dismissed as "the hobby horse of those who write romances."[26]

In the second half of the eighteenth century, furthermore, the language of fictional friendships between women is often eroticized. In Marmontel's short story "The Two Unfortunates" the two heroines exchange confidences about their misfortunes and sufferings in love and end in each other's arms. Rousseau's heroine Julie tells Claire "When I hug your daughter, I feel it is you I am pressing against my breast." Eliza Fenwick's novel *Secresy* (1795) tells of the romantic friendship between Sibella and Caroline: "You pressed my hand as it held yours ... I stood still, unknowing whether to fall at your feet or to clasp you in my arms." Clarissa was somewhat affrighted at Anna's "flaming Love"; after the heroine's death Anna kissed her lips, her forehead, "and sighed as if her heart would break." Such depictions have been interpreted by some authors as explorations of lesbian emotions, yet the plots almost always temper them by a highly conventional return to heterosexual relationships. Later in the eighteenth century, as awareness of lesbianism began to make authors and readers anxious about overtly eroticized depictions, the language generally became more restrained.[27]

Many novels explore the tension between women's friendship and marriage. It is the theme of Eliza Haywood's novel *The Surprize* (1724). In Richardson's *Clarissa* the heroine and Anna denounce matrimony as destructive of friendship, while for the heroine of Hannah Foster's *The Coquette* (1797) marriage is "a very selfish state" in which "the tenderest ties between friends are weakened, or dissolved."[28] In *La Nouvelle Héloïse* it is the friendship between the cousins Julie and Claire that interferes with their heterosexual relationships: "Your inseparable cousin never leaves you," complains the hero. Women's friendships occasionally emerge as superior to marriage, as in Katherine Phillips' poems in the mid seventeenth century or Sophie von La Roche's *Geschichte des Fräuleins von Sternheim* (1771). "A lover is not worth a friend," declares Madame de Riccoboni in her novel *The History of the Marquis de Cressy* (1758). Richardson's Clarissa similarly declares, "How much more binding and tender are the Ties of pure Friendship and the Union of Like minds, than the Ties of Nature!" while in Mary Wollstonecraft's *Mary* (1787) the heroine finds in female friendship a respite from the sufferings of marriage.[29]

Friendships between men did not present either the same problems or the same attraction for novelists or dramatists. Schiller planned to write a play centred on the loving friendship of two Maltese knights, which would surpass that of women, but he never got round to it.[30] Richardson and Rousseau were among the very few writers to explore male friendship in depth. In *Clarissa* the relationship between Lovelace and Belford is developed and complex, yet ultimately it is competitive and unsatisfactory, hardly a model for male readers. The depiction of the friendship between Saint-Preux and the English lord Edouard in Rousseau's *Nouvelle Héloïse* is more sentimental, the two men supporting each other physically and emotionally throughout the story. In most novels and plays, however, male relationships described as "friendships" are not explored in depth and are often little more than drinking partnerships. This lack of interest in male friendships was no doubt in part, as David Robinson suggests, because the vulnerability and openness required for "true" friendship ran counter to eighteenth-century notions of the "manly" hero. It may also have been because married men, unlike women, were not expected to give up other relationships and devote themselves to their families, so the possibilities for dramatic tension were reduced. And perhaps readers were simply less interested in male than in female virtue: Richardson's later exploration of male sensibility in *Sir Charles Grandison* (1753–1754) was far less successful than his earlier works *Pamela* and *Clarissa*. At the very end of the eighteenth century Goethe's depiction of youthful homoerotic friendship in his "Letters from Switzerland" (1796), with appropriate classical references to Adonis and Narcissus, opened a new area of fictional experimentation, but the early nineteenth-century reaction against homosexuality soon put an end to such exploration.[31] Overall, the shortage of successful fictional friendships between men allowed a shift towards the idea that friendship, in its sentimental late eighteenth-century form, was essentially female.

Friendship between men and women was even more problematical for fiction writers. There is an ambiguity about some texts that results from the widespread seventeenth-century literary convention – evident in Pierre Corneille's plays – of using the word "friendship" as a synonym for love. The fact that this was possible points to the overlap between the two terms and to the common assumption that platonic friendship between the sexes was difficult. Some authors nevertheless felt that it was perfectly possible, though requiring delicate management. Madeleine de Scudéry, in *Clélie* (1654–1660) had evoked the image of a "tender friendship" between the sexes, based on mutual respect and liking and on "an exchange of hearts and of secrets." She developed this in her later non-fiction writing. Her novels also explored the notion that such friendship, while it might be independent of sexual love, was not only compatible with such love but necessary in a durable relationship. "For a love to last, a woman must be the friend and the mistress of her lover."[32] This was unusual, most authors preferring – perhaps because it made for better plots – to present heterosexual friendships as unstable, generally tipping over into passion. And passion – sexual love – was almost universally deemed to be incompatible with friendship because it was based on animal instinct whereas friendship depended on reason. It also enlivened the story to portray characters wrestling with conflicting emotions.

By the early nineteenth century, notions of romantic love had made it easier to imagine relationships between men and women that combined passionate love and friendship. Germaine de Staël's *Corinne* (1807) traces the growing affection between Corinne and Oswald, made possible by the purity of their souls and by their presence in Rome where the nobility of the ancients guided them. Here too the fictional form allows the exploration of strong emotions, although the novel always uses the term "friendship" to describe their increasingly intimate relationship.

Most fiction was openly moralizing. "Friendships begun in childhood," states Mr Trueworth in Haywood's *History of Miss Betsy Thoughtless*, "ought to be continued or broke off, according as the parties persevere in innocence, or degenerate into vice and infamy." Only the virtuous deserve to be considered as friends, a philosophy entirely consistent, as we have seen, with the views of Aristotle and Cicero. In marriage, too, honour was vital: "There is more true felicity in the sincere and tender friendship of one man of honour, than in all the flattering pretensions of a thousand coxcombs," advises Lady Trusty in *Betsy Thoughtless*. Friendship was purer than "love," a base passion "which always triumphs in vulgar souls, suffering domination by *friendship* only among people who are in essence reasonable and virtuous."[33] Friendship strengthened over time, writers assured their readers, whereas love was capricious and lost its intensity with age. "Happy are those women" declares the narrator in Germaine de Staël's *Corinne* (1807), "whom the sacred bond of marriage has led gently from love to friendship, without a single cruel moment tearing apart their lives."[34]

Thus the novel fulfilled something of the role of the modern soap opera, providing examples of situations that readers might not themselves encounter. Yet while eighteenth-century writers transparently offered ample advice, either directly through the authorial voice or more commonly through the provision of wise characters, the novel gave readers considerable autonomy. Richardson's *Clarissa* was discussed earnestly by Susanna Highmore and her female friends, who appreciated some aspects of his portrayal of women but objected to others. Some of them corresponded with him on the subject and he made use of their letters in a later novel. Here we can see fiction enabling readers to work through emotional, ethical and social issues, and this was undoubtedly a major reason for its popularity. But the example also illustrates the way that these discussions in turn influenced literary creation.[35]

Fictional and philosophical treatments of friendship, then, were in broad agreement about its character yet differed in some significant ways. They had in common a focus on ideal types, an opposition between friendship and love/passion, a desire to link friendship with sociability, virtue, and reason, and an increasing discomfort with religious justifications of friendship. Both types of literature were written for educated audiences and saw real friendship as confined to their own class. Both, furthermore, were increasingly sceptical about the possibility of real friendships between people of significantly different rank, rejecting older ideas of patron–client relations as perfectly acceptable and even superior forms of friendship. We can also see the development of Romanticism reflected in both types of literature, which placed increasing emphasis on the sentimental aspects of perfect friendship, imagined as a union of two kindred souls. Yet many philosophers and moralists also condemned the extreme sentimentality of fictional depictions and wished to insist on the rational basis of friendship. They more often dealt with male friendship and were keenly interested in the tensions between the loyalties of friendship and duties to kin, to one's fellow Christians or to humanity as a whole. Thus whereas English works of fiction often described family members as "natural friends," philosophers were more inclined to see a conflict between kinship and friendship. Another difference, of course, is that while often giving illustrations from classical history or mythology, treatises and moral essays spoke in more abstract terms. Fiction, on the other hand, explored issues through the travails of individual characters. It was far more concerned with female friendships, both with other women and with men, and with the relationship between love and friendship.

Neither fiction nor philosophical treatments was an entirely accurate reflection of the reality of seventeenth- or eighteenth-century friendships. In everyday life friendship was on the whole more utilitarian and more likely to overlap with kinship and other ties. Both normative and everyday uses of the terminology of friendship, though, were evolving as social conditions changed.

Everyday Usage

Few historians have focused on the way people in the past used the terminology of friendship in their daily lives, tending instead to refer to literature and philosophy or simply to treat friendship as a universal human relationship. Yet if we look at the way people actually employed the terminology of friendship and the way they interacted with people whom they described as their friends, we find a complex relationship between everyday usage and the ideas expressed in philosophical and literary texts. There were also social and geographical differences that are sometimes clearly explicable but in other cases intriguing. I will focus primarily on examples from eighteenth-century England and France to illustrate both common features and cultural differences. Different types of sources, furthermore, give us access to different uses and meanings.

Naomi Tadmor has used diaries (especially that of a rural shopkeeper, Thomas Turner), and a range of other sources to identify how the term "friend" was used and imagined in eighteenth-century England. She examines the kinds of people who were described as "friends" and explores the nature of these relationships. Using her analysis as a framework we can identify a number of types of people who were termed "friends." First, as in fiction, there were family members. The shopkeeper Thomas Turner commented in his diary on the complaints that his "friends" – mainly his mother and brothers – made about his marriage, and he referred individually to his father, his mother, his brothers, and various cousins and other relatives as "friends." The same usage occurs in a variety of other sources: people said of someone that they were "come of good friends," meaning of good family; and sometimes a distinction was made between "natural friends," meaning kin, and other friends. For Mrs Delany in the later eighteenth century, "no friends can be so truly depended upon as relations": kinship was thus a subset of friendship. Legal sources also referred to next of kin as "next friend." William Wright, in *The Complete Tradesman* (1787) wrote of the "friends" of apprentices, the family members who put up the money. A variety of material thus confirms that this usage, found in English fictional sources, was common in a range of contexts and social groups.[36]

A second common use of friendship terminology was to describe people with whom one had other kinds of close ties, those of business, sport, visiting and socializing, and usually more than one of these. There was in these cases almost always some type of mutual dependence, generally an exchange of services – shared business interests, borrowing money, renting or hiring – which formed the basis for social interaction and for the development of close, sometimes affectionate relationships. The most fascinating one, in Thomas Turner's case, is his friendship with a number of excise officers. Spirits being one of the most commonly smuggled goods, these men had an indirect connection with his trade and sometimes negotiated for him to sell confiscated liquor, on occasion even drinking it with him! "Friends" of this type, as described in Turner's diary, were almost always men of similar education and standing, if not necessarily of similar wealth, and they were both useful contacts and individuals whose company Turner clearly enjoyed. These relationships fall somewhere between the utilitarian friendships often dismissed by moralists and the pleasurable friendships that formed another category in philosophical works. Here too Turner's usage is corroborated in other sources. James Boswell, for instance, extolled the friendliness of Lord Mountstuart and admired the way that Adam Smith combined learned discourse with "friendship": in both cases what he liked was their lack of formality, what he called "manly ease."[37] The nuances were different in the world of letters, but there was a similar enjoyment of the company of men who were pleasant and might be useful.

A third everyday use of "friend," in Thomas Turner's diary, was to describe patron–client relationships. In an age when patronage remained the key to promotion, in almost any social or occupational context, those in positions of power were expected to look after their supporters, whether it was in appointing a bishop, a clerk, or a servant. Turner referred to his own patrons as friends, but also to himself as friend to a former servant and to one of the parish paupers, both of whom he looked after in various ways. It is worth noting that the former servant was a woman, to whom he was a friend but whom he did not describe as his friend. This might have been a risk to his reputation and to hers[38] but above all there was an unbridgeable social difference. This type of relationship involved benevolence and protection but not the equality that mutual friendship implied. The same usage is found in other domains. Authors, for example, dedicated works to potential patrons, as did Francis Hutcheson who reminded the Bishop of Elphin that "my excellent Father ... was formerly honoured with a place in your friendship." At a more modest level, the black African slave Ukawsaw Gronniosaw used the word "friend" to describe various protectors and benefactors. They included the owners who eventually bequeathed him freedom in their wills, and an American pastor and his wife and five sons, whom Gronniosaw termed "my dear and valued friends." The pastor had converted him to Christianity, given him schooling and treated him well.[39]

These different uses of "friend" were not mutually exclusive. Patronage was particularly extended to relatives: Robert Walpole, the leading government minister from 1721 to 1742, "frankly owned that while he was in employment, he had endeavoured to serve his friends and relations; than which, in his opinion, nothing was more reasonable, or more just." The social elites often moved in quite narrow circles and were related to those with whom they also socialized and had political and economic ties. In the late seventeenth century Sir Richard Wynn had a wide acquaintanceship but had an inner circle of male friends, primarily composed of cousins of the same generation who lived in the same county and with whom he hunted and caroused.[40]

An interesting variant on these connections, though, was what we might call "political friendship," which could be wider and which unlike patronage was very much reciprocal. Edward Gibbon wrote that the reason for going into Parliament was "to employ the weight and consideration it gives in the service of one's friends."[41] What this might mean is clear from the diary of Thomas Turner, who despite his humble rank was a "friend" to the Duke of Newcastle, as were many of his fellow tradesmen in the area. There was clearly, in this case, no necessary personal connection, but rather a mutually profitable political alliance whose responsibilities were described in the terminology of friendship. Friendship of this kind, however, applied only to males.

Other sources permit us to add to Tadmor's analysis. The evidence of epitaphs points to a long English tradition of close same-sex friendships. Alan Bray has found examples going back to the fourteenth century where men were buried in the same grave. From the early seventeenth century, female burials of the same sort become common, and while older examples seem to refer to "brotherhood" or "love," eighteenth-century versions often bear inscriptions such as "Fidissimum Amicorum Par" (the most faithful of friends) and describing their "close Union and Friendship." It is likely that other examples exist in other European countries, since Jean-Baptiste Dubreuil and Jean Pechméja were buried together in 1785 under a similar inscription.[42] These tombs indicate the existence, at least among those who could afford such monuments, of a conception of close personal friendship very similar to certain literary and philosophical ideals.

Other, older uses survived. Diplomatic parlance had long referred to "friendships" between different countries and this continued to be used in peace treaties and in works such as an anonymous pamphlet of 1712 that celebrated *The ancient amity restor'd: or, France the best friend. Containing an historical account of the fair and friendly dealings of the French towards the English.* A similar notion underlay the instructions given to colonists in Carolina in 1676, to "observe the rules of strict justice, friendship and amity with the neighbour Indians." It would be "very agreeable to our design," Lord Shaftesbury had written three years earlier, "to get and continue the friendship and assistance of the Indians."[43] It was to be a purely instrumental relationship, with little evidence of reciprocity. This was not to say, however, that cross-cultural or cross-racial friendship was inconceivable. On the contrary, Enlightenment cosmopolitanism celebrated international brotherhood between noble-minded individuals of different backgrounds. And real-life examples do exist. The former slave Olaudah Equiano, taken to England in 1757 and eventually freed, wrote an autobiography that was much used by the anti-slavery movement. In it he described his friendship with the white American Richard Baker, with whom he "became inseparable."

> Although this dear youth had many slaves of his own, yet he and I have gone through many sufferings together on shipboard; and have many nights lain in each other's bosoms, when in great distress. Thus such a friendship was cemented between us, as we cherished till his death ... I lost at once a kind interpreter, an agreeable companion, and a faithful friend ... being not ashamed to notice, to associate with, and to be the friend and instructor of one who was ignorant, a stranger, and a slave!

Also in a New World context, the French nobleman Hector St John de Crèvecoeur, who lived for some years as a farmer in North America, wrote of one group of Indians who were "particular friends" to "Mr P.R.," another white farmer.[44]

We are fortunate, for the eighteenth century, to have sources that give us access to the way the terminology of friendship was used on a day-to-day basis among a variety of other social groups. The majority of the defendants and witnesses who appeared in trial proceedings from the Old Bailey courts in London were working people living in or near London, while most of the victims and prosecutors were somewhat better off. Yet both groups overwhelmingly used the term "friend" in the second sense identified above, to refer to people who were not relatives but who cared about and looked after each other. A man would take care of a friend who was drunk, ensuring that he got home safely. He would help him when in trouble, borrowing money to get him out of the debtors' prison; would buy things on his behalf, lend him what he needed, give him gifts and undertake "other offices of Kindness."[45]

We do need to be cautious here, because some of those who testified before the courts adjusted their language to suit the occasion.

They used what they felt to be more formal terminology and "friend" may have sounded more dignified than "mate" or "comrade," terms widely used among working men and that may have been more common. There is nonetheless a broad consistency in the language used by victims, by witnesses and by the accused, and in a variety of different contexts. This seems to suggest that it was how many of them actually spoke. In general they described the relationship as one of mutual confidence. Friends would not betray each other and even thieves could feel safe at a friend's lodging: an accomplice to a burglary reportedly assured the culprit "that he was a trusty Friend, and would never betray him."[46] References to male friends being named as executors, as godfathers to people's children, or being consulted about a marriage, also indicate a relationship of confidence. Furthermore, the language used to describe the behaviour of friends is sometimes similar to that of literary sources. People often referred in the court records to two men as "intimate friends," and to the "love" between them. There are also references to friends – both male and female – embracing each other.

These are the most common uses of the term, but there were others. Prisoners sometimes told the court that they had no friends, meaning they had no one who could vouch for them: no patron or employer, no relatives, no neighbours of sufficient respectability. "I have no friend at all," said Ann Felton, a charwoman. John Butler's sole defence was denial: "What they say is quite entirely wrong. I know nothing about them. I have not a friend within two hundred miles." "I am going to make a friend to bail her," said William Horsford, though he admitted having "but a small acquaintance with the woman."[47] In practice, those who did vouch for people indicted were often neighbours.

In other cases a "friend" seems to be simply a workmate or colleague. An excise officer, for example, referred to the man with whom he was on patrol as "my friend." A journeyman coachmaker similarly described as "my friend" a man whom he worked with.[48] There were also examples where a "friend" was apparently simply a casual acquaintance, like Benjamin Moore and "another young fellow," whom he later described as "my friend," who were robbed by two prostitutes in a tavern. A more unusual usage was that of a Mrs Priddle, who took a liking to the daughter of an innkeeper in Burford. She proposed to her to accompany her to London as a kind of helpmeet: "her told me, her should be very glad to have a young woman to run up and down stairs for her as a friend." She was not a servant, explained

Harris, though she occasionally made the beds. But she never cleaned, and she dined with the family and not with the servants.[49]

A further everyday usage is simply to indicate a degree of benevolence, even where there was no previous relationship. Benjamin Mac Mahone, a house painter accused of stealing from Lord Delaware's residence in 1749, confessed and requested "Pray my Lord Delaware, be so far my friend, as to let me be transported." "Friend" could also be used as a form of address between strangers, generally in a potentially tense situation. William George, suspected of stealing a silver tankard in the hope of receiving a reward for its return, recalled "this gentleman comes and says, friend, I understand you have got a pewter tankard about you. Yes, says I, I have bought one today; says he, my friend, it looks as though you had a design to make an exchange with me. I am no such man, says I."[50]

If we look at the kinds of people referred to as "friends" in the court records we find they are primarily of the same sex. Female friends, for example, looked after each other in sickness and could be trusted with each other's valuables. Yet there are also a number of cases where men and women referred to each other as friends. A man who confessed to stealing several silver spoons from a tavern asked (according to the victim) "a Woman whom he call'd his Friend" to retrieve them from the goldsmith to whom he had sold them. Mary Smith claimed to have been "a good Friend" to the man who now accused her of stealing a riding hood. She had stayed at his house on the occasion in question. Half a century later, Ann Carter supposedly described Thomas Pixley as "the greatest friend she ever had in the world," since he had stood bail for her, helped find her lodgings and paid her rent.[51] Only same-sex friends, however, were described as taking pleasure in each other's company: "the Prisoner and the Deceas'd were very intimate dear Friends," reported a witness, "never happy out of one another's Company."[52]

Examples of references to family members as friends do occur in the Old Bailey record, but they are rare. In 1679 a soldier described his kinsman as "the best friend he ever had in the world." In 1775 Mr James Adair, Esquire, recommended a Mrs Rudd to Mr William Adair, "a near Relation and intimate friend of his." On some occasions, on the other hand, "Relations" are opposed to "friends": Mrs Shepherd "always complained of her Relations, who she said had been very rude and uncivil," but her friend Mrs Flood had looked after her. There are also occasional references to patrons as friends. "The late

Duke of Rutland was my principal friend," claimed John Hetherington in 1790, no doubt hoping to avoid conviction by citing his military service. A similar use of the term was made in a fraudulent letter written to a member of parliament, supposedly by a gentleman fallen on hard times, "petitioning you to be my friend; as it will be doing me a great piece of service, and yourself no diskindness."[53] But this usage too is infrequent in the court proceedings.

French was in many ways similar to English in the everyday use of friendship terms, but with some significant variations. The French words for friend and for friendship (*ami, amitié*) were used in almost exactly the same way to describe a range of supportive relationships that involved and implied mutual affection and regard, trust and long acquaintanceship. People in eighteenth-century Paris, both male and female, spoke of "friends" as people they turned to when in need: after a husband's suicide, the wife of a mercer turned for emotional support to her "friend," an older woman who sold fruit in her street; a butter-merchant asked his "friend," a plasterer, to stay at his place after the death of his wife.[54] Occasionally friends of the same sex shared accommodation and this was one of the only circumstances where young women could live away from parents or an employer. Friends lent things to each other, gave advice, collected and paid debts for each other. They ate and drank together and saw each other frequently. Very often these friendships overlapped with neighbourhood and occupational ties, and occasionally with a common provincial origin, although the use of phrases like "neighbour and friend" and "fellow-countryman and friend" suggests that these other relationships did not automatically imply friendship.

Friendship could link people of very different ages: for example the 22-year-old waiter in a wineshop asked his "friend," a 40-year-old fruiterer who lived opposite, to help him find the person who had robbed him. It is possible that this was a protective rapport of some kind, the older man looking after the younger one. A 17-year-old woman who sold fruit in one of the markets was described as "one of the friends" of a mercer's wife, aged 35, and went to support her when her husband committed suicide.[55]

The same terminology of "intimate friendship" is used in both Paris and London. However, as in the English capital, the Parisian use of "friendship" to refer to a close, affective and trusting relationship occurs almost exclusively between people of the same sex. The main exceptions were when male friends protected women: for example, when a noblewoman, beaten by her husband, sought refuge with a priest, their "mutual friend." It is conspicuous that this usage appears only among more affluent people, no doubt because the presence of servants attenuated suspicions of sexual liaison. The other exception is marriage, where friendship was clearly, for "the middling sort" and for respectable artisans and shopkeepers, the ideal. When people wanted to present their marriage relationship as a good one they would say it was based on "esteem and friendship." Courtship could be described in similar terms: the wife of a master tailor explained that after the death of her first husband "he was not slow to display sentiments of friendship and attachment to her and to propose marriage."[56]

Among people of middling and higher status references to "friends" occur in the context of dinner parties, visits to the country, of seeking protection (in instances of domestic violence), and (in bankruptcy suits) of giving sage but unheeded advice. The evidence of wills, among the same social groups, stresses the emotional connection. If there was no family member available to act as executor, it was very common to ask someone to fulfil this task as a "last mark of friendship." In such cases the friend was often left a gift of sentimental rather than purely monetary value, such as a ring or a portrait. There are also very clear indications of mutual affection, as in Marguerite Doucet's bequest of all her belongings to Marie Henault "for the good friendship she bears her and in recognition of the great good and immense service she has given the testatrix during her illnesses and notably since she fell into paralysis." They had lived together for six years.[57] In these cases the friendship was almost always between people of roughly equal rank and was less likely than among working people to include neighbours. It could also more readily cross gender boundaries.

The use of "friend" to mean a political ally was also common among the French nobility in the early seventeenth century, as Jean-Marie Constant has shown. After the death of Louis XIII Cardinal Mazarin "took steps to obtain the friendship of those that [the Queen] had always considered faithful to her. He began with M. de Marsillac ... and requested his friendship in the most polite and most urgent terms one can imagine." In 1617, again at a moment of political crisis, another nobleman promised to support the King and "I offered him not only my person but that of my brothers and of fifty of my friends whom I could in a short time bring to him."[58] It is not clear to what extent friendship, in this context, also implied an affective connection, but it was clearly one of the relationships that structured political life among the French nobility, along with lineage and religious affiliation.

It was closely linked to patronage and involved both men and women, as the Comte de Montrésor indicated when he spoke with disapprobation of the way that the Queen's former favourite, Madame de Chevreuse, had been abandoned "by all those whom she had obliged and who had been connected by friendship and by interest with her." In seventeenth-century France, as in England and its colonies, the language of friendship was routinely used to refer both to patrons and to supporters. "I entered not only into his friendship," wrote Charles de Grimaldi of his patron, "but I had his entire confidence, and as his generosity led him to obtain favours for his friends, it is certain that he always did me every kind of good office." As Sharon Kettering has shown, such "friends" could be kin, they could be co-religionists, or they could operate within a regional, military or inherited patron–client network. If this was a departure from classical ideals of friendship, it was nevertheless a voluntary engagement which did involve reciprocity and on some occasions a degree of intimacy.[59]

This meaning of "friend" does not seem to have survived into the eighteenth century but friendship as patronage did. Among the examples given in the 1694 dictionary of the French Academy were "the Prince honours me with his friendship" and "he had much friendship for his servants." Although these were omitted from mid eighteenth-century editions of the dictionary the usage was still around in 1792, when a father writing to the director of the Gobelins manufactory in Paris, seeking a position for his son, hoped to obtain the "amitié" of this personage. In relationships between people of very different rank it was the person of higher rank who was a friend to the other, rather than the reverse. In other contexts the friendship of patronage shaded into benevolence or mere kindness, for instance when the widow of a court official wrote to the police to say that blood ties, friendship and good examples would be more likely to encourage her niece to mend her ways than imprisonment.[60]

In everyday language, as in London, there were also more casual usages. In testimony to the police eighteenth-century Parisians would describe two men who came to drink in a wineshop together as "friends," even when they didn't know anything about the relationship. Sometimes the term is used almost as a synonym for "acquaintance," particularly where men went drinking together. These "friendships" were always same-sex and seem to be exclusively plebeian.

Such examples seem to suggest that literary uses of friendship terminology were quite conservative and that in the larger cities everyday usage was closer to that of today. Friends there were less often kin or patrons, but were overwhelmingly those with whom people associated by choice, whom they trusted and relied upon, whom they might know through work, family connections, chance encounters or (less often) as neighbours.

Examination of everyday uses of the terminology of friendship also reinforces two important conclusions about early modern conceptions of friendship that Naomi Tadmor draws in relation to England. First, while in philosophical treatises or in some cases literary sources "true" friendship was often seen to exclude material considerations or any thought of what one might gain materially from the relationship, in everyday usage this was not so. The rural shopkeeper Thomas Turner had "friends" who were both relatives and commercial partners; others with whom he had both business contracts and close social and emotional ties. The reasons for this are clear enough. Seventeenth- and eighteenth-century Europe remained a society in which economic survival was a daily preoccupation for most of the population and in which an economic slump, a harvest failure, an exceptionally cold winter or the sudden death of a wage-earner could spell disaster. Even the middling sort, who might own some property and have economic reserves, enjoyed only relative security. In trade there were limited mechanisms for enforcing contracts between strangers and heavy reliance on credit made rich and poor alike very vulnerable if someone who owed them money suddenly went bankrupt. For this reason detailed knowledge of one's business partners was highly desirable, hence a marked preference to borrow from family members rather than strangers and to enter into partnerships with siblings, cousins and other close relatives. Europe remained, on the whole, a face-to-face society in which people were felt to have obligations only to their kin and to those in their immediate vicinity. It is hardly surprising therefore that friendships overlapped significantly with these other relationships or that they were important elements in economic survival and not simply a form of sociability. Even in the largest cities, in London and Paris, most of the inhabitants found their friends among kin, neighbours, professional colleagues and workmates, and among those of the same provincial origin or language group. In everyday life, of course, friendships were found at all levels of society, even if they were rarely of the ideal type favoured by philosophers.

Secondly, while seventeenth- and eighteenth-century friendship was usually between people of similar rank, interests and age, as novels and philosophical discussions suggested it should be, in practice there were certain important ways in which it crossed these boundaries. Patron–client connections were a central part of the way early modern society worked, once again an aspect of a largely face-to-face society in which one could rely only on those one knew and with whom one was bound by mutual obligation. Socially unequal relationships were obviously very different from those between people of the same status who shared an intimate friendship, but in everyday life the same term was used to describe both. In so far as it crossed boundaries in these ways, as Tadmor points out, friendship was central to social cohesion.

A further difference between literary and everyday uses of friendship terminology relates to gender. Men and women could be friends if they were related and perhaps if they were married, but outside these contexts friendship across gender lines was highly suspect, however much some novelists and moralists might argue for it. It was permissible where an older family "friend" looked after the interests of a woman whose parents and siblings were dead. It could also safely occur where the friendship was with a married couple. The late seventeenth-century clergyman Ralph Josselin and his wife had close friendships with other couples but also with Mary Church, with whom they often dined and who assisted Mrs Josselin in childbirth.[61] Female-male friendships were also possible in certain kinds of patronage relationships – looking after a former servant, for instance – but needed to be very circumspect. Here too the nature of friendship reflects the structures of European society. Gender distinctions and the separate roles of men and women were a crucial aspect of social order. They were of vital concern in a world in which family was central to the survival for the poor and to the status of the rich and in which any suspicion about paternity endangered both the lineage and male honour and power. Women, and particularly single women, were surrounded with taboos that deliberately isolated them from men.

There are, however, some significant differences between English and French uses of the terminology of friendship, and these are worth exploring. Most conspicuously, in French *ami* was rarely used to mean kin, as it routinely did in England. This is true both of everyday language and of legal terminology. Witnesses at weddings were divided into relatives and "friends," and so were those present at the official meetings called to choose guardians for young children after the death of one or both of their parents. In France, kin – like neighbours or workmates – *could* be friends, but were not necessarily so, although there are a few examples where the usage is ambiguous. In 1715, for example, two Parisian merchants left a small sum of money to their nephew, "as a sign of the friendship they have for him." But as the gift was conditional on his agreeing to look after their mother in her old age it was hardly philanthropic and the terminology appears to be simply conventional, implying no real sense of mutual responsibility.[62] This observation from everyday contexts is reinforced by the evidence of Abel Boyer's bilingual dictionary (1729). The definition of the French term *ami* makes no mention of kin, whereas that of the English word "friend" gives "relations" as one of the core meanings. In 1771 the *Dictionnaire de Trévoux* defined friendship as a matter of choice and explicitly excluded family ties.

There were other apparent differences too. In eighteenth-century French a "friend," in the masculine form, could also refer to the lover of a married woman. This was consistent with the reluctance to talk about friendship between men and women in any context where ambiguity could arise. The phrase *mon ami* was also frequently used in French as a condescending term of address by superiors speaking to inferiors: it would have been disrespectful the other way round. It is possible that this was found in England but we have not come across any examples.

Finally, in France one does not find the same concept of political friendship as in England. While in the seventeenth century the term was used of the political alliances among the great French nobles, by the eighteenth this usage had largely disappeared. The political system was of course entirely different from the English one, and although patronage was equally important in France, the powerful did not have to rely on the political mobilization of the middling sort as they did in England. In 1751 Charles Duclos, in his widely read *Considérations sur les moeurs*, could assert that powerful men had few friends, because "ambition and business occupy them too much to leave room in their hearts for friendship."[63] Friendship and public life were almost mutually exclusive.

This absence of friendship metaphors in French politics is consistent with the absence of references to kin as "friends." In both countries kinship terms were used to describe and shape relationships of political loyalty: hence the King was the "father" of the nation. When the American rebels took the name of "sons of Liberty," they were metaphorically rejecting their filial duty to the King. But in France, friendship was not a kinship term, so it was not so readily applied to relationships of political patronage. It was perhaps this that freed the terminology of friendship for use in claims to equality, as we shall see.

Changing Meanings and Uses of Friendship

Ideas and images of friendship were not static. Because friendship was so central to the way people thought about social relationships, shifts in usage and meaning reflect significant social and political changes. One of the most important developments, already alluded to, was the growing sentimentality of friendship from the middle of the eighteenth century. This is apparent not only in fiction but in everyday expressions of friendship. The will of a wealthy Parisian widow, written in 1781, left to each of her friends a seal bearing an engraving of "a symbol of friendship" and the caption "she was true to her." In her letters, Queen Marie-Antoinette addressed the Princesse de Lamballe, for whom she had "conceived a real friendship" (according to her mentor Mercy-Argenteau), as "my dear heart." In similar vein and at the same time, Fanny Burney could write of "sweet Mrs Delany, whom I love most tenderly." In the early 1800s Germaine de Staël's letters to Juliette Récamier also spoke the language of love: "My angel, at the end of your letter say to me: *I love you*. The emotion I will feel at these words will make me believe that I am holding you to my heart."[64]

Not only were representations of friendship extraordinarily sentimental but in letters just as in novels were frequently eroticized, at least in educated circles. Elizabeth Carter wrote of Catherine Talbot that she is "absolutely my passion; I think of her all day, dream of her all night, and one way or another introduce her into every subject I talk of." Luise Gottsched used "love" and "friendship" synonymously in her letters to Dorothea Runckel, to whom she dedicated her "most fiery embrace" and pledged "love eternal."[65] Women sent each other locks of hair, exchanged lockets with miniature portraits of each other that they kissed. Male friends used similar rhetorical gestures, which can be found much earlier: "A Friend may sometimes proceed to acknowledge Affection, by the very same Degrees by which a Lover declares his Passion," wrote John Dennis in 1693. "I shall be imperfect without the communication of such friends as you; you are to me like a limb lost, and buried in another country; tho' we seem quite divided, every accident makes me feel you were once a part of me," wrote Alexander Pope to Jonathan Swift in 1734. "Believe no man now living loves you better, I believe no man ever did," he had written two years earlier. There are also many examples of references to what appear to be physical desire. "I dream of you still," Pope told Lord Bathurst in 1735 (he was 47), "and you are the object of my Dotings; like an old Woman that loves the man that had her Maidenhead ... 'tis the serious Wish of my heart, to be lovd as much as you can, and protected by You." A few years earlier Lord Hervey confided to Stephen Fox that "I have often thought, if any very idle body had curiosity enough to intercept and examine my letters, they would certainly conclude they came rather from a mistress than a friend." Raymond Stephanson suggests that this kind of verbal cross-gender play that was fairly common in the seventeenth and early eighteenth centuries, at least in literary circles, was to disappear later, as male effeminacy became associated with homosexuality. But the language of love remained. Samuel Johnson included male friendship under "Love" in his *Dictionary*, and even treatises on friendship were not immune from the cult of sensibility of the late eighteenth century. In letters, like those from Marin Guillaume Doin to Pierre Gaspard Chaumette in the late 1780s, "friendship" and "love" were almost interchangeable ("the sincerest of friends would take the place of the most tender of lovers"), while in 1801 Heinrich von Kleist mourned his estranged friend Brokes:

> who fills the whole of my heart ... He has left me ... – and with him I lost the *only* person in the populous capital who was my *friend*, the only one whom I truly honoured and loved, the only one for whom, in Berlin, I could have heart and feelings, the only one for whom I had opened the whole of my heart and who knew every one of its, and even its most secret, folds.[66]

Some of these may have been lesbian or homosexual relationships, but others were not. The point is that these were perfectly acceptable forms of speech and behaviour between heterosexual friends. Strangely, although people felt more comfortable talking about marriage in terms of friendship rather than of love, the great emphasis placed on affection and trust between friends of the same sex made it quite possible to use the language of love in this context.

It seems indisputable that the use of intensely emotional language to describe friendship spread to a wider range of social groups at the same time as the reading public expanded and as more and more Europeans felt themselves to belong to the Enlightenment world. Was this a case of literary representations influencing actual behaviour? It is likely that models of sentimental friendship were disseminated by novels and through new kinds of "intimate" literature – personal letters, journals, autobiographies – that were published in ever-growing numbers across the century. (The letters of Elizabeth Carter and Catherine Talbot, with their emotional and eroticized language, were published in 1809.) Helvétius was in no doubt of the influence of literature: "In friendship, as in love, people often create novels: they search for the hero everywhere; they believe they have found him; they seize on the first comer, they love him for as long as they know little of him and are curious to know more."[67]

Fictional or not, published work provided models of behaviour that we see people adopting, consciously or unconsciously, and that legitimized emotional outpourings which in the twentieth century became confined to lovers. Sophie Cottin found in Rousseau's portrayal of the friendship between Julie and Claire in *La Nouvelle Héloïse* a parallel for her own relationship with her cousin Julie Vénès. Sentimentality, once established as a norm, became almost a social necessity, so that when Louisa Stuart read Henry Mackenzie's novel *The Man of Feeling* (1771) she was "secretly afraid lest she should not cry enough to gain the credit of proper sensibility." Boswell too was "uneasy that I do not feel enough ... in the keen manner that others say they do."[68]

The extreme sentimentality surrounding friendship met a variety of social needs. Some have seen it as linked to the rise of the middle class, though it was not confined to that social group. Yet it was potentially subversive. Like other forms of moral superiority it was certainly used by men and women of letters, who found themselves on the fringes of "polite" society, to make claims to social acceptance. It was part of a shift of emphasis from blood and breeding, formerly the key sources of social distinction, to refinement: a man of feeling did not necessarily have distinguished ancestors but he was worthy of consideration nonetheless. Readers of novels who were of relatively humble rank might identify with the behaviour of the characters and feel themselves morally equal, or even superior, to their betters. If, as Madame de Lambert wrote in her "Advice to her Son," "all the duties of civility (*honnêteté*) are contained in the duties of perfect friendship," then why should that be confined to an elite defined by birth?[69]

Pressure to conform to models of sensibility was partly fashion, and no doubt a way for a younger generation to mark itself off. But it was also an element in a late eighteenth-century campaign to reform men and create a new masculinity. As many of the examples already given have illustrated, in the early modern imagination friendship was closely associated with models of manliness. It could be linked to male companionship based on military life, drinking and ribaldry, but classical models could also be invoked in support of new models of masculine sensibility that were sometimes directed, as Philip Carter has suggested, against the courtier, who was deemed incapable of sympathy for anyone else.[70] It could therefore become part of a court–country struggle. But it might also, as in Henry Fielding's *Tom Jones* (1749), be directed against the boorish country squire, becoming a defence of a quintessentially urban elite culture (whether the hero lived in the city or the country). More broadly, the insistence on sensibility and on virtue, which generally turn out to be qualities possessed exclusively by the propertied classes, was important in the consolidation of an educated elite, distinguishing them from the masses and legitimizing, in their own eyes, their wealth and leisure.

Yet "enlightened" male friendship could serve many ends, as Frederick the Great showed when he built a Temple of Friendship near his palace in Potsdam, adorned with portraits of fabled ancient Greek and Roman (male) friends. Built in memory of his sister, but inspired by a poem of Voltaire, Frederick was consolidating his claim to the laurels of enlightened ruler, putting on display his respect for the classics but simultaneously positioning himself as heir to their virtues. In another domain altogether, the qualities associated with eighteenth-century male friendship could be used to distinguish civilized Europeans, in their own eyes, from the uncivilized natives of other parts of the world. This was the implication of Adam Smith's assertion that "a savage ... whatever the nature of his distress, expects no sympathy from those about him" – any sentiment, according to Smith, even love, was regarded as weakness. Hume too believed that "Asiatic manners are as destructive to friendship as to love" because polygamy made men jealous of each other.[71]

The new models of female friendship too served a range of purposes. As the quality of female friendship became more widely depicted and started to challenge older male models, it began to be used by some women writers, as we have seen, to mount a claim to moral equality with men, even to superiority. "Men rarely know the exquisiteness of friendship," wrote Luise Adelgunde Gottsched to Dorothea Henriette von Runckel. This could justify women's demands to enter fields from which they were partly or fully excluded. Modesty, wrote Madame de Lambert to her daughter, was not a woman's sole virtue: "A woman of quality (*une honnête femme*) possesses the virtues of men: friendship, probity, fidelity in the fulfillment of her duties," such as authorship. The inclusion of such qualities allowed literary women like Madame de Lambert to lay claim to full participation in the semi-public world of early eighteenth-century noble sociability. As Anne Vincent-Buffault points out, this kind of female participation depended on the celebration of friendship between men and women and not exclusively among women.[72]

In other contexts, the elevation of same-sex friendship to something akin to or even superior to heterosexual love could legitimize lesbian or homosexual relationships. It might also justify resistance to marriage, which many eighteenth-century women characterized as the "tomb of friendship." "People when they marry," wrote Elizabeth Carter, "are dead and buried to all former attachments." Given the loss of autonomy that women experienced within marriage or indeed within the limited alternatives – living with family or in a convent – the possibility of sharing life with a female friend was an attractive and in some cases a socially acceptable alternative. There were also individual instances where the convergence between the language of friendship and that of love allowed people to disguise a romantic attachment, as in the relationship between Catherine Talbot and George Berkeley. In deference to her family's wishes she refused his marriage proposal, but the two retained a lifelong attachment that Berkeley's wife recognized as unconsummated love.[73]

Friendship was also widely employed in social criticism. Thiroux d'Arronville repeated commonplaces of the period when she attacked arranged marriages that made it difficult for couples to become true friends and paternal discipline that instilled fear in children rather than the friendship they should feel for their parents. She went on to condemn "the Great": "the emptiness of their greatness, with which they are inebriated, fills their soul, and leaves no place for friendship." For the same reasons Madame de Lambert believed that there was little hope of finding true friends at the royal court.[74]

In a similar vein, arguments about friendship were employed in debates over luxury and more broadly over the growing commercialization of urban society. In his deeply conventional 1784 novel *Télèphe*, the French novelist Jean Pechméja portrayed "Ephesus" as a selfishly commercial place where friendship was impossible. The influence of Rousseau is clear in a story where true friendship flourished only in rural settings and primarily between men who were able to divest themselves of the irrational passions associated with women. On the other side of the same argument were Adam Smith and other Scottish moral economists, who argued that only in a commercial society of the kind they advocated, and that they believed was emerging, was true friendship possible. For Smith, the development of markets, which were impersonal and based on self-interest, promoted the appearance of another, qualitatively different sphere of life in which a superior form of friendship could be cultivated. Whereas in the past those whom people thought of as "friends" were in fact kin, patrons, or people whom they needed to get on with, in modern eighteenth-century commercial society it became possible to form voluntary friendships based on "a natural sympathy" between "men of virtue." Here the idealization of friendship was harnessed in support of a particular brand of economic and social theory.[75]

Some Enlightenment commentaries moved beyond social criticism and linked a perceived decline in the quality of friendship to forms of government, again an idea taken from Aristotle who observed that "there is little of friendship in tyrannies but more in democracies." Certain types of government, Kant implied, made it dangerous for people to reveal their inner thoughts and hence made them cautious about forming real friendships. Helvétius used the same argument in a savage critique of both government and public morality. "In the present form of our government," wrote Helvétius:

> individuals are not united by any common interest. In order to make one's fortune one has less need of friends than of protectors ... luxury, and what is called "sociability" (*l'esprit de société*) has left countless people with no need of friendship ... There is no longer any friendship.[76]

Here Helvétius was drawing on an ancient tradition that saw in friendship the basis of civil society. He linked it to absolute monarchy, but to our eyes it was more a result of the development of larger states in which close ties between patrician equals were no longer a satisfactory basis for government.

Lurking behind Helvétius' critique was perhaps an awareness of the extent to which, in the mid to late eighteenth century, friendship had become associated with the private sphere. Patronage as friendship was in retreat; men in public life were felt to have responsibilities that made friendships difficult for them. The ideal that many people attempted to realize was now that of the intimate friend, a very personal and exclusive relationship that was a very long way from the Ciceronian ideal of virtuous friendship as the basis for political life. Furthermore, sentimental friendship was something women – by convention emotional beings – were felt to excel at, and this feminization of ideal friendship accentuated its association with the private domain where middle- and upper-class women were expected to spend their lives. Whereas in the past there had been debate about whether women were capable of true friendship, by the mid to late eighteenth century close female relationships had become the model for literary friendships and increasingly for real-life ones.

While there is much debate among historians over the implications of shifts in gender roles in the second half of the eighteenth century, these new ideas of friendship may have had an impact on family life. There is fairly widespread agreement among family historians that the parent–child relationship was becoming less authoritarian in the later eighteenth century, at least in relation to matters such as arranged marriages. There was also an increasingly widespread model of marriage, at least among educated Europeans, in which husband and wife enjoyed a more sentimental and perhaps even a more equal relationship. It is possible that the language of friendship facilitated such a shift, allowing some women to renegotiate aspects of marriage or to make new claims. If friendship was indeed becoming more sentimental and more equal, then a description of parents and children or of marriage partners as "friends" could make the relationships subtly different.

Yet perhaps in reaction against the "privatization" of friendship, the second half of the eighteenth century also witnessed a revival of notions of civic friendship in the context of an expanding press and of new institutions of sociability and philanthropy – what Jürgen Habermas described as a new "bourgeois public sphere." It was, as Habermas suggested, a domain in which private individuals met, physically or metaphorically, to discuss public affairs. Thus many pamphlets written by people with no public office or role, right across Europe but particularly in England and France, took up issues of public interest. Authors increasingly proclaimed themselves to be "a friend to society" and "a friend to the publick." In France one of the first to use this terminology was the Marquis de Mirabeau in his best-selling work of political economy, *L'Ami des hommes* (1756). It was taken up again in the name of the key group in the French anti-slavery campaign of the 1780s, the Society of the Friends of the Blacks (Société des Amis des Noirs). Here the semantic fields of friendship, public and private virtue, philanthropy and sociability all merged.

The Enlightenment emphasis on sociability brought together personal and civic friendship in a new way. In a secular version of Taylor's universal Christian friendship, the *abbé* Pluquet maintained that "friendship, in uniting men more or less according to the degree of their similarities, tends to produce a constant harmony in the moral order, universal concord and an equal well-being for all men."[77] This was very much the spirit of the "friendly societies" that provided mutual aid or insurance and that first appeared in England in the late seventeenth century and proliferated both there and in America in the eighteenth. This terminology may have grown out of the language of religious groups like the Quakers and other Dissenters: the Quakers' epithet, "the Society of Friends," dates from the late 1600s. Like political friendship it was a metaphorical usage, but one that nevertheless implied mutual interest, support, and solidarity and that attempted to put rhetoric into practice through meetings and local discussion.

But the most widespread manifestation of the new form of public friendship was freemasonry. By the late eighteenth century friendship had become central to masonic vocabulary. Whereas Paris lodges of the 1760s were largely named after saints, in the 1770s and 1780s we find lodges named "Les Vrais Amis" (The True Friends) or "la Réunion des Amis Intimes" (The Meeting of Intimate Friends). Such references associated friendship not only with sociability but also with philanthropy and with fraternity, since the freemasons referred to each other as "brothers" and philanthropy (along with sociability) was one of the key functions of the lodges. Although in practice quite hierarchical, freemasonry spoke the language of equality: its members were brothers and friends. This led to some critics condemning the lodges as "republican" institutions.[78]

These usages prefigure those of the 1790s, when the terminology shifted again. As the French Revolution progressed, in both Britain and France friendship took on powerful overtones both of political equality and of patriotism in the names of clubs such as "Les Amis de la Constitution" (The Friends of the Constitution, the original name of the Jacobin Club) or "Les Amis de l'Egalité" (The Friends of Equality); and in Britain, the "Friends of Universal Peace and Liberty" of 1791 or the Irish "Friends of the Constitution, Liberty and Peace." In April 1792 a number of British Opposition politicians formed "The Friends of the People," whose central aim was "a more equal representation of the people in Parliament." The nation-building dimension of their work was clear in their identification with "the people in its amplest, and most harmonious sense, distinguished in their order, but united and inseparable in their mutual interests and relations as constituting A PEOPLE."[79] There were soon branches all around Britain. The Parisian club named the Conferation of the Friends of Truth (Confédération des Amis de la Vérité) took this further still, since it was the first club to admit women. All these uses drew on the association of "friend" with trustworthiness and benevolence, but added a very classical notion of public virtue. This link was clearer in the name of one of the Paris sections, which for a time was called "Les Amis de la Patrie" (Friends of the Fatherland), a nomenclature that was ambiguously national and civic. And of course the title of Jean-Paul Marat's infamous newspaper *L'Ami du peuple* (Friend of the People) was drawing on the same set of meanings.

Yet these uses created a new tension between public and private friendships. Marisa Linton has demonstrated the French revolutionaries' idealization of revolutionary friendship as the basis for a new Rome, yet also their intense suspicion of private friendships that might be exclusive and conspiratorial. In 1794, as the revolutionary leadership increasingly insisted on the idea of a regenerated France as a "Republic of Virtue," Saint-Just drew on the old idea that only virtuous men could be friends in order to elaborate a view of citizenship based on friendship. He suggested that

> every man of the age of twenty-one will declare in the temple who his friends are. This declaration must be renewed every year ... Those who have remained friends all their lives will be buried in the same tomb ... If a man commits a crime, his friends will be banished. He who says he does not believe in friendship, or who has no friends, will be banished.

Underpinning this was the idea that those without friends were devoid of virtue and therefore could not be true citizens. These were notions derived from Cicero, but in a late eighteenth-century context the French revolutionaries were merging public and private by conflating "fraternity" and "friendship." When they abandoned the formal *vous*, even between people who did not know each other, and replaced it with *tu*, the term used between close friends, they were attempting to transfer the virtues of personal friendship into public life. Yet at the same time they viewed personal friendship with great suspicion. It might conflict with public duty, leading to favouritism or even to conspiracy. One of the key accusations against the Jacobins' rivals, the Girondins, was that they were friends to traitors like General Dumouriez. The irony of these conflicting attitudes to friendship became clear when Robespierre, in a speech in March 1794, listed the various revolutionary leaders who had been his friends and whom he had abandoned when their treason became clear. Although he was distinguishing between true and false friends, the reality of revolutionary politics meant that personal friendship could not be the basis of public virtue after all.[80]

It is important that these new uses of friendship terminology were all secular ones. This too reflects a major shift across the period of the Enlightenment. In the seventeenth century there was a religious nuance to the term "friend," particularly where it was associated with brotherhood, with sociability, and with charity. This is evident not only in the name of the Society of Friends but also in the many religious confraternities of Catholic Europe. The members of the Confraternity of Notre Dame de la Carole, for instance, were instructed to treat each other with "respect and friendship." And when a group of neighbours on one of the Paris bridges formed a "Christian association" to erect a stand for the Blessed Sacrament each year they too stressed their intention to create closer bonds of friendship. The English preacher Matthew Audley made the same point when he suggested that a perfect friendship between two souls, modelled on that between David and Jonathan, was "too high for common Life." "But there is another Degree of Friendship productive also of very good Effects," he went on, "namely, when several Persons form themselves into a Brotherhood." In the second half of the eighteenth century, as we have seen, these associations were increasingly supplanted by secular bodies as clubs replaced confraternities and humanistic philanthropy replaced religiously inspired charity. In April 1785 the educated Parisian public flocked to see the new play by Passot de Saint-Aime, *Le triomphe de la bienfaisance ou l'ami de l'humanité* (The triumph of philanthropy or the friend of humanity).[81]

In philosophical discussions too the idea of friendship was secular-
ized. In the seventeenth or early eighteenth centuries most writers saw
God's love for humankind as the model of true friendship. Those like
Jeremy Taylor and Pierre Nicole had stressed friendship as a Christian obligation. But by the late eighteenth century even Christian apolo-
gists generally tried to combine theological and humanistic arguments.
The anonymous author of *Moral Essays* stressed that friendship was
sanctioned by reason, and began with purely secular arguments, only
at the end holding up Jesus' relationship with St John as a model and
friendship as a Christian duty.[82] The stress on Jesus as friend was to
become far more common in the nineteenth century. But most Enlightenment writers discussed friendship exclusively in terms of secular morality and rationality, stressing an individual's duty to society,
and of the benefits of friendship to humanity rather than obligations
to God and to fellow Christians.

Friendship and the language of friendship played a central role in
the way people thought about social relationships in seventeenth- and
eighteenth-century Europe. As Naomi Tadmor observes in the case
of the English middling sort and elites, what unites most eighteenth-
century uses of the language of friendship is that it described a range
of relationships that implied "sympathy, loyalty, mutual interest, and
many reciprocal exchanges and 'services,'" as well as moral expectations: honesty and virtue.[83] Political friendship too implied loyalty,
steadfastness, sympathy and mutual interest. The terminology and
behaviour of friendship was thus a way of making claims on people in
a wide variety of contexts. It was not simply a descriptive term for a
fixed relationship, but a powerful way of negotiating one's place in a
complex society. This applied both to individuals and to groups. From
the late seventeenth century on, there was a shift towards a notion of
collective friendship that implied secular as well as spiritual equality
and that was expressed in the appearance of "friendly societies." When
these new nuances were extended into politics, the metaphor facilitated a growing claim among members of the middling sort to be
heard and to participate.

In France, while the political uses of friendship terminology had
disappeared by the mid eighteenth century, there too friendship became a metaphor for particular kinds of public or semi-public relationships based on philanthropy and virtue. If freemasonry was not
overtly political, the anti-slavery movement was, and during the French
Revolution there were very clear if diffuse links between the

metaphorical uses of friendship and claims of equality and popular participation and sovereignty. In both England and France, if in different ways, we find changes in society and in politics bringing about extensions in the way that the terminology of friendship was used, and hence shifts in meaning. At the same time, we can observe the terminology of friendship being used in new ways to effect changes in relationships in both the public and the private sphere. In neither is it a clear-cut case either of language shaping behaviour or of the reverse, but rather a dialectical relationship between the two that was extremely powerful.

Notes

1. Naomi Tadmor, *Family and Friends in 18th-Century England: Household, Kinship, and Patronage* (Cambridge: Cambridge University Press, 2001), pp. 237–39.

2. British Library English Short Title Catalogue; Lawrence Brockliss, *French Higher Education in the Seventeenth and Eighteenth Centuries: A Cultural History* (Oxford and New York: Oxford University Press, 1987), pp. 111–13, 135–36.

3. Jeremy Taylor, *Measures and Offices of Friendship* (London: R. Royston, 1657), pp. 27, 64.

4. Marie-Charlotte Thiroux d'Arronville, *De l'amitié* (1761), published as *Les Oeuvres morales de Monsieur Diderot* (Franckfort, 1770), p. 7; John Marshall, *John Locke: Resistance, Religion and Responsibility* (Cambridge: Cambridge University Press, 1994), p. 186; Hume, *A Treatise of Human Nature* [1749] (ed. L. A. Selby-Bigge; Oxford: Clarendon Press, 1888), p. 521.

5. François, duc de la Rochefoucauld, *Maximes, suivies des Réflections diverses* (Paris: Garnier, 1967), p. 304 (no. XCIV); Helvétius, *De l'esprit* (Paris: Durand, 1758), p. 350; Diderot, *Les Deux Amis de Bourbonne* (1773), quoted in Anne Vincent-Buffault, *De l'exercice de l'amitié: Pour une histoire des pratiques amicales aux XVIIIe et XIXe siècles* (Paris: Seuil, 1995), p. 106; Louis-Silvestre de Sacy, *A Discourse of Friendship* [1703] (London: 1707), pp. 12, 47; Ferguson, *Principles of Moral and Political Science* (1792), quoted in Allan Silver, "Friendship in Commercial Society: Eighteenth-Century Social Theory and Modern Sociology," *American Journal of Sociology* 95 (1996), pp. 1474–504 at p. 1486.

6. De Sacy, *Discourse*, p. 42; *Encylopédie*, art. "Amitié"; H. J. Paton, "Kant on Friendship," in Neera Kapur Badhwar (ed.), *Friendship: A Philosophical Reader* (Ithaca, NY: Cornell University Press, 1993), pp. 133–54 at p. 153; Francis Bacon, "Of Followers and Friends," in *The Essays* (Harmondsworth, UK: Penguin, 1985), p. 206.

7. Anne Kingsmill Finch, "Friendship between Ephelia and Ardelia," in *Miscellany Poems on Several Occasions* (London: J[ohn]. B[arber]. and B. Tooke, 1713), p. 253.

8. Antoine Léonard Thomas, *Essai sur le caractère, les moeurs et l'esprit des femmes dans les différents siècles* (Paris: Moutard, 1772), p. 101; James Boswell, *Life of Johnson* (ed. R. W. Chapman; Oxford: Oxford University Press, rev. edn, 1970), p. 1020. *Dictionnaire de Trévoux* (Paris: Libraires associés, new edn, 1771), art. "Ami"; Simon Patrick, *Advice to a Friend* (London: printed for R. Royston, 4th edn, 1681), p. 167; De Sacy, *Discourse*, p. 79; Charles Duclos, *Considérations sur les moeurs de ce siècle* (Amsterdam, 1751), p. 57; Paton, "Kant on Friendship," p. 142.

9. Taylor, *The Measures and Offices of Friendship*, pp. 69, 77. Patrick, *Advice to a Friend*, p. 167.

10. Paton, "Kant on Friendship," p. 150; Dupuy de La Chapelle, *Réflections sur l'amitié* (Paris: Langlois, 1729), p. 68, quoted in Vincent-Buffault, *De l'exercice de l'amitié*, p. 88; Duclos, *Considérations*, p. 341; La Rochefoucauld, *Maximes*, p. 26 (1678 edn, no. 83).

11. François de Sales, *Introduction to the Devout Life* (trans. Allan Ross; London: Burns Oates & Washbourne, 1950 [1608]), p. 161; Nicolas Malebranche, *Treatise on Ethics* (trans. Craig Walton; Dordrecht, Kluwer, 1993 [1684]), pp. 218–19; Jean-François Senault, *De l'usage des passions* (Paris: Fayard, 1987 [1641]), pp. 180–81.

12. Taylor, *Measures and Offices*, pp. 8–11; Pierre Nicole, *Essais de morale contenus en divers traittez sur plusieurs devoirs importants* (3 vols; Paris: G. Desprez, 1701), III, pp. 326–27; Boswell, *Life of Johnson*, p. 946.

13. Taylor, *Measures and Offices*, pp. 60–62, 69; De Sacy, *Discourse*, pp. 107–16; Peter Fenves, "Politics of Friendship – Once Again," *Eighteenth-Century Studies* 32:2 (1998–99), pp. 133–55 at pp. 132–34.

14. De Sacy, *Discourse*, p. 23; Voltaire, *Dictionnaire philosophique*, art. "Amitié"; Adam Smith, *The Theory of Moral Sentiments* (ed. Raphael and Macfie; Oxford: Clarendon Press, 1976 [1759]), pp. 224–25; Aubry, *L'Ami philosophique et politique*, cited in Vincent-Buffault, *De l'exercice de l'amitié*, pp. 80–81; A. M., *Moral Essays, Chiefly Collected from Different Authors* (2 vols; Liverpool, 1796), I, p. 191; de La Chapelle, *Réflections sur l'amitié*, p. 68, quoted in Vincent-Buffault, *De l'exercice de l'amitié*, p. 88.

15. Anne Thérèse de Marguenat de Courcelles, Marquise de Lambert, *Essays on Friendship and Old-age, by the Marchioness de Lambert* (London: J. Dodsley, 1780 [1736]), p. 62; de Sacy, *Discourse*, p. 23; Thiroux d'Arronville, *De l'amitié*, pp. 100–102.

16. La Rochefoucauld, *Maximes*, p. 101 (no. 440); Wollstonecraft, *A Vindication of the Rights of Woman* (1792) (ed. Miriam Brody Kramnick; Harmondsworth, UK: Penguin, 1975), pp. 167–68, 312. Susanne T. Kord, "Eternal Love or Sentimental Discourse? Gender Dissonance and Women's Passionate 'Friendships,'" in Alice A. Kuzniar (ed.), *Outing Goethe and his Age* (Stanford, Stanford University Press, 1996), pp. 228–49 at p. 231; Taylor, *Measures and Offices*, pp. 100–105;

Senault, *De l'usage des passions*, p. 183; Hester Chapone, *Letters on the Improvement of the Mind, Addressed to a Young Lady* (2 vols; London: J. Walter, 1773).

17. Thiroux d'Arronville, *De l'amitié*, p. 69; Wollstonecraft, *Vindication*, pp. 113, 167.

18. Taylor, *Measures and Offices*, pp. 83–84; David Hume, "Of the Rise and Progress of the Arts and Sciences," in *Essays*, I, p. 117; Francis Hutcheson, *System of Moral Philosophy* (2 vols; London: A. Millar & T. Longman, 1755), II, p. 163.

19. Sorel, *Discours* (1663), quoted in Chantal Morlet-Chantalat, *La Clélie de Mademoiselle de Scudéry* (Paris: Champion, 1994), p. 333; Lambert, *Essays*, p. 86; Thomas, *Essai*, p. 105.

20. *Philosophie de l'univers* (1792), quoted in Vincent-Buffault, *De l'exercice de l'amitié*, p. 96.

21. Riccoboni, *Histoire de Miss Jenny* (4 vols; Paris: Brocas & Humblot, 1764), II, p. 54.

22. Germaine de Staël, *Corinne, ou l'Italie* (3 vols; Paris: INALF, 1961), I, p. 43.

23. *History of Miss Betsy Thoughtless* (London and New York: Pandora, 1986), pp. 525, 517; *Miss Jenny*, III, p. 82.

24. *The Surprize* (London: J. Roberts, 1724), p. 24; Janet M. Todd, *Women's Friendship in Literature* (New York: Columbia University Press, 1980), pp. 309–10, 312; Samuel Richardson, *Clarissa, or the History of a Young Lady* (ed. Angus Ross; Harmondsworth, UK: Penguin, 1985 [1747–48]), p. 1449.

25. "To Miss Lynch: Occasioned by an Ode Written by Mrs. Philips," in *Poems on Several Occasions* (1744) in Robert Demaria Jr (ed.), *British Literature 1640–1789: An Anthology* (Oxford: Blackwell, 1996), p. 987.

26. Jean-Jacques Rousseau, *La nouvelle Héloïse, ou Lettres de deux amans, habitans d'une petite ville au pied des Alpes* (Londres [Paris: Cazin], 1781), Part I, Letter XXIX; Richardson, *Clarissa*, pp. 514, 40, 502; Paton, "Kant on Friendship," p. 151.

27. Rousseau, *La nouvelle Héloïse*, Part IV, Letter I; Susan Sniader Lanser, "Befriending the Body: Female Intimacies as Class Acts," *Eighteenth-Century Studies* 32 (1998–99), pp. 179–98 at pp. 186–88; Todd, *Women's Friendship*, pp. 55, 320–27.

28. Lanser, "Befriending the Body," p. 189.

29. Rousseau, *La nouvelle Héloïse*, Part I, Letter VIII; Barbara Becker-Cantarino, "Friendship," in *Encyclopedia of the Enlightenment* (ed. Alan Charles Kors; 4 vols; Oxford: Oxford University Press, 2003), II, 91–96 (pp. 93–94). Todd, *Women's Friendship*, pp. 357, 58, 192–226.

30. Alice A. Kuzniar, "Introduction," *Outing Goethe*, pp. 15–16.

31. David Robinson, "Unravelling the 'Cord which Ties Good Men to Good Men': Male Friendship in Richardson's Novels," in Margaret Anne Doody and Peter Sabor (eds), *Samuel Richardson. Tercentenary Essays* (Cambridge: Cambridge University Press, 1989), pp. 167–87; Robert D. Tobin, "In and Against Nature:

Goethe on Homosexuality and Heterotextuality," in Kuzniar, *Outing Goethe*, pp. 94–110 at pp. 104–105.

32. Morlet-Chantalat, *La Clélie de Mademoiselle de Scudéry*, p. 276.

33. *History of Miss Betsy*, pp. 203, 179; Abbé Girard, *Synonymes françois, leurs différentes significations, et le choix qu"il en faut faire pour parler avec justesse* (Paris: d'Houry, new edn, 1780), 1: 42.

34. Germaine de Staël, *Corinne* (1807), II, p. 186.

35. Sylvia Harcstark Myers, *The Bluestocking Circle: Women, Friendship, and the Life of the Mind in Eighteenth-Century England* (Oxford: Clarendon Press, 1990), pp. 70, 140–48.

36. Tadmor, *Family and Friends*, pp. 130–31, 175–92; Delany, quoted in Randolph Trumbach, *The Rise of the Egalitarian Family* (New York: Academic Press, 1978), p. 65; Wright quoted in Harold Perkin, *The Origins of Modern English Society, 1780–1880* (London: Routledge and Kegan Paul, 1969), p. 46.

37. Tadmor, *Family and Friends*, 198–208. Philip Carter, *Men and the Emergence of Polite Society, Britain 1660–1800* (London: Longman, 2001), p. 188.

38. Tadmor, *Family and Friends*, pp. 209–11.

39. Hutcheson, *System of Moral Philosophy*, dedication; *A Narrative of the Most Remarkable Particulars in the Life of James Albert Ukawsaw Gronniosaw, an African Prince, Written by Himself*, [*c.* 1770], extract in Adam Potkay and Sandra Burr (eds), *Black Atlantic Writers of the Eighteenth Century* (London: Macmillan, 1995), p. 41. See also pp. 44, 45, 50.

40. Walpole quoted in Perkin, *Origins of Modern English Society*, p. 45. Katharine W. Swett, "'The Account between Us': Honor, Reciprocity and Companionship in Male Friendship in the Later Seventeenth Century," *Albion* 31 (1999), pp. 1–30.

41. Gibbon quoted in Perkin, *Origins of Modern English Society*, p. 45.

42. Alan Bray, "A Traditional Rite for Blessing Friendship," in Katherine O'Donnell and Michael O'Rourke (eds), *Love, Sex, Intimacy, and Friendship between Men, 1550–1800* (Houndmills: Palgrave Macmillan, 2003), pp. 87–98; Jeffrey Merrick, "Male Friendship in Prerevolutionary France," *GLQ: A Journal of Lesbian and Gay Studies* 10.3 (2004), pp. 407–32 at p. 417.

43. *The ancient amity restor'd: or, France the best friend. Containing an historical account of the fair and friendly dealings of the French towards the English* (London: A. Baldwin, 1712); quoted in Barbara Arneil, *John Locke and America: The Defence of English Colonialism* (Oxford: Clarendon Press, 1996), pp. 126–27.

44. *The Interesting Narrative of the Life of Olaudah Equiano, or Gustavus Vassa, the African. Written by Himself* [1789], extract in Potkay and Burr (eds), *Black Atlantic Writers*, p. 193; Hector St John de Crèvecoeur, *Letters from an American Farmer* (London: J. M. Dent, 1912), p. 79.

45. "Old Bailey Proceedings Online," http://www.oldbaileyonline.org, 28 December 2004: 13 October 1703, trial of Ann Finch (t17031013-5); 27 February 1712, Alice Farendon and Katherine Johnson (t17120227-18); 6 September 1710,

Anne Goodwin (t17100906-50); 8 April 1719, Thomas Lander (t17190408-20); 26 May 1680, a waterman (t16800526-2).

46. "Old Bailey Proceedings Online," 14 January 1702, Richard Morris, Benjamin Jones, Francis Turnley, Francis Turnley, Thomas Wagstaffe, John Hodges (t17020114-34).

47. "Old Bailey Proceedings Online," 5 April 1769, Ann Felton (t17690405-25); 10 May 1769, John Butler (t17690510-19); 6 December 1769, William Horsford (t17691206-34).

48. "Old Bailey Proceedings Online," 5 April 1749, Dominick White and William Horner (t17490405-12); 22 February 1749, Archibald Blare, Richard Morton, Abraham Clark (t17490222-51).

49. "Old Bailey Proceedings Online," 26 April 1775, Mary Pollard and Margaret Berry (t17750426-42); 18 February 1775, William Priddle (t17750218-1).

50. "Old Bailey Proceedings Online," 9 December 1749, Benjamin Mac Mahone (t17491209-2); 13 January 1749, William George (t17490113-26).

51. "Old Bailey Proceedings Online," 13 January 1716, Edward Smith (t17160113-3); 14 January 1715, Mary Smith (t17150114-33); 12 July 1775, Thomas Pixley and Richard Rees (t17750712-48).

52. "Old Bailey Proceedings Online," 6 September 1716, Thomas Hardwick (t17160906-18).

53. "Old Bailey Proceedings Online," 27 August 1679 (t16790827-6); 31 May 1775, Robert Perreau (t17750531-1); 7 December 1715, Elizabeth Flood (t17151207-14); 8 December 1790, John Hetherington (t17901208-4); 17 July 1759, Samual Scrimshaw and John Ross (t17590717-1).

54. Archives nationales, Paris (hereafter AN), Y15100, 11 November 1788; Y11239, 14 March and 8 November 1752.

55. Y15350, 1 March 1752; Y15100, 1 November 1788.

56. Y15099, 16 March 1788; AN Minutier central (MC) XVIII 886, 23 November 1789; Y13290, 27 March 1788.

57. AN, Minutier central, XVII 665, 14 February 1731; Archives de Paris, DC6 252, fol. 95 (13 December 1770); AN Y62, fol. 341 (4 October 1788); Y11239, 5 August 1752; quotation from Archives de Paris DC6 212, fol. 227 (15 April 1713).

58. *Mémoires de La Châtre contenant la fin du règne de Louis XIII et le commencement de celui de Louis XIV*, quoted in Jean-Marie Constant, "L'amitié, moteur de la mobilisation politique dans la noblesse du premier XVIIe siècle," *XVIIe siècle* 51 (1999), pp. 593–608 at p. 595.

59. Constant, "L'amitié," pp. 597, 607; Sharon Kettering, "Friendship and Clientage in Early Modern France," *French History* 6 (1992), pp. 139–58; quotation p. 139 n2. See also Laura Gowing, "The Politics of Women's Friendship in Early Modern England," in Laura Gowing, Michael Hunter, Miri Rubin (eds), *Love, Friendship and Faith in Europe, 1300-1800* (Houndmills: Palgrave Macmillan, 2005), pp. 131-49.

60. *Dictionnaire de l'Académie française* (1694); O1 2052B, Belle to Audran, 8 September 1792; Bibliothèque de l'Arsenal, MS 11037, fol. 2 (1731).

61. Alan Macfarlane, *The Family Life of Ralph Josselin, a Seventeenth-century Clergyman: An Essay in Historical Anthropology* (Cambridge: Cambridge University Press, 1970), pp. 150–51.

62. MC VII 209, 21 October 1715.

63. Charles Duclos, *Considérations sur les moeurs* (1751), p. 159.

64. Archives de Paris DC6 275, fol. 43 (10 June 1781); Marie-Antoinette quoted in Christine Roulston, "Separating the Inseparables: Female Friendship and its Discontents in Eighteenth-century France," *Eighteenth-Century Studies 32.2* (1998-1999), pp. 215-31 at p. 225; Burney quoted in Myers, *The Bluestocking Circle*, p. 259; de Staël, quoted in Maurice Levaillant, *The Passionate Exiles* (Freeport, New York: 1958 [Paris: 1956]), p. 184.

65. Carter, quoted in Lanser, "Befriending the Body," p. 183. Gottched, quoted in Kord, "Eternal Love," p. 238.

66. Raymond Stephanson, "'Epicoene Friendship': Understanding Male Friendship in the Early Eighteenth Century, with Some Speculations about Pope," *The Eighteenth Century* 38 (1997), pp. 151–70 at p. 155; Merrick, "Male Friendship," pp. 418–23; Kleist quoted in Thomas Schestag, "Friend ... Brockes: Heinrich von Kleist in Letters," *Eighteenth-Century Studies* 32 (1998–99), pp. 261–77 at pp. 264–65.

67. *De l'esprit*, p. 351.

68. Roulston, "Separating the Inseparables," p. 219; Stuart, quoted in Colin Campbell, "Understanding Traditional and Modern Patterns of Consumption in Eighteenth-century England: A Character-action Approach," in John Brewer and Roy Porter (eds), *Consumption and the World of Goods* (London and New York: Routledge, 1993), pp. 40–57 at p. 49; Boswell (1769), quoted in Carter, *Men and the Emergence of Polite Society*, p. 191.

69. Anne-Thérèse de Marguenat de Courcelles, Marquise de Lambert, *Avis à son fils* (London: A. Dulau, 1799 [1726]), pp. 31–32.

70. Carter, *Men and the Emergence of Polite Society*, pp. 27–32, 100–11, 124–28.

71. Smith, *Theory of Moral Sentiments*, p. 205. David Hume, "Of Polygamy and Divorce" (1742), in *Essays and Treatises on Several Subjects* (2 vols; London: J. Jones, new edn, 1822), I, p. 172.

72. Gottsched quoted in Kord, "Eternal Love," p. 238; Anne-Thérèse de Marguenat de Courcelles, Marquise de Lambert, *Avis d'une mère à sa fille* (London: A. Dulau, 1799 [1728]), pp. 16–17; Vincent-Buffault, *De l'exercice de l'amitié*, p. 92.

73. Lanser, "Befriending the Body," p. 189; Myers, *The Bluestocking Circle*, pp. 216–20.

74. Thiroux d'Arronville, *De l'amitié*, pp. 22–23, 59, 88. Anne-Thérèse de Marguenat de Courcelles, *Avis d'une mère à son fils*, p. 22.

75. Merrick, "Male Friendship"; Silver, "Friendship in Commercial Society."

76. Aristotle quoted in Mark Vernon, *The Philosophy of Friendship* (London: Palgrave Macmillan, 2005), p. 93; Fenves, "Politics of Friendship," p. 138; Helvétius, *De l'Esprit*, p. 356.

77. Pluquet, *De la sociabilité* (Yverdon, 1770 [1767]), p. 147, quoted in Vincent-Buffault, *De l'exercice de l'amitié*, p. 86.

78. Bibliothèque nationale, Fonds maçonnique; Margaret C. Jacob, "Polite worlds of Enlightenment," in Martin Fitzpatrick, Peter Jones, Christa Knellwolf and Iain McCalman (eds), *The Enlightenment World* (London and New York: Routledge, 2004), pp. 272–87 at pp. 277–85; see Kenneth Loiselle, "'Nouveaux mais vrais amis': La franc-maçonnerie et les rites de l'amitié au dix-huitième siècle," *Dix-huitième siècle* 39 (2007), pp. 303–18.

79. Iain Hampsher-Monk, "Civic Humanism and Parliamentary Reform: The Case of the Society of the Friends of the People," *Journal of British Studies* 18.2 (1978), pp. 70–89 at pp. 77, 82; Thomas Paine, *Address and declaration of the friends of universal peace and liberty held ... August 20th, 1791* (n.p., n.d. [1793?]); *The proceedings of the Association of the Friends of the Constitution, Liberty and Peace, held at the King's Arms Tavern ... Dublin, December 21, 1792* ([London] Russel-Court, Drury-Lane: T. Browne, 1793.

80. Marisa Linton, "Fatal Friendships: The Politics of Jacobin Friendship, 1793–1794," *French Historical Studies* 31.1 (2008), pp. 51–76. I am grateful to Marisa for her comments on the present chapter. Louis de Saint-Just, *Œuvres choisies* (Paris: Gallimard, 1968), p. 344.

81. Abbé Migne, *Nouvelle encyclopédie théologique*. Vol. 50, *Dictionnaire des confréries et des corporations d'arts et métiers* (Paris: J-P. Migne, 1854), col. 565; MC CVIII 332, 10 April 1718. Matthew Audley, *A Sermon Preach'd at St Paul's, Deptford, Kent, on June 23d, 1739* (London: John Carter, 1739), pp. 11–12; Catherine Duprat, *Le temps des philanthropes* (Paris: Editions du C.T.H.S., 1993), p. 41.

82. A. M., *Moral Essays*, pp. 199–202.

83. Tadmor, *Family and Friends*, pp. 212, 205.

Chapter 6

TAKING UP THE PEN: WOMEN AND THE WRITING OF FRIENDSHIP

Barbara Caine

There is no author who has been as significant in articulating and developing ideas about friendship as Cicero, and no modern text that can compare to his *De amicitia* in its influence on the ways in which friendship was understood and written about over the following centuries. On the contrary, few modern philosophical works even consider friendship and none has come to be seen as indispensable to anyone currently engaged in writing about it. Friendship was certainly discussed in sermons, letters and essays in the late eighteenth century, but increasingly towards the century's end and throughout the nineteenth century, it is to fiction rather than to philosophy that one needs to turn to find extended discussions of friendship.

The discussion of friendship that appeared in fiction at this time was in many ways very different from that which had continued from classical times until the eighteenth century. One of the most significant of these differences was evident in the central place of women, both as the subjects whose friendship featured in fiction and increasingly also as the authors who wrote about it. Indeed, the now quite widely discussed rise of the woman novelist and of the "woman of letters" in the course of the eighteenth and early nineteenth centuries can also be seen as heralding the move of women into a predominant place in writing about friendship.[1] Many of the women writers who published novels in this period have now been entirely forgotten but a small number retain a significant place in the literary canon. Jane

Austen is the most important of these writers and she serves well to demonstrate the importance of friendship, especially female friendship, as a theme for women novelists.

Austen occupies an important place in the history of women's writing generally and especially in terms of the ways in which women novelists depicted the lives of other women. It was she, Virginia Woolf argues in her classic essay, "A Room of One's Own," who first established a distinctive way for women to write by developing a female sentence that served better than did the hearty male one to delineate both the domestic world in which women lived and their feelings and ideas.[2] Moreover, Woolf insists, it was not until Austen that the daily lives of women came to be incorporated into fiction in any significant way. Almost a century later, Woolf was herself greatly to expand discussion of the complex nature of women's friendships in both the real world and in fiction.

The way in which Austen's novels focus on the daily lives of women, dealing in detail with the many hours each day that women lived in the company of other women rather than of men, gave the question of women's relationships with each other a quite new kind of prominence. Prior to that, as noted in the previous chapter, women had been written about largely by men and primarily in terms of their sexual relationships with men. Jane Austen pointed out the false depiction of women in literature in one of her own novels, *Persuasion*, in which the heroine, Anne Elliot, protests against the authority accorded the many literary depictions of men's fidelity and women's fickleness. When her male opponent insists that he has hardly "ever opened a book in my life which had not something to say upon woman's inconstancy. Songs and proverbs, all talk of woman's fickleness," she responds by insisting that all this literature was written by men. "Men have had every advantage of us in telling their own story. Education has been theirs in so much higher a degree; the pen has been in their hands. I will not allow books to prove anything."[3] And in this particular novel, Austen uses Anne Elliot herself to demonstrate the exceptional capacity of women to be faithful – while ostensibly suggesting also that fidelity is not a universal female characteristic, or specifically a virtue of either sex but is rather a quality evident in sensitive, intelligent and honourable people of both sexes.

As this discussion in *Persuasion* suggests, heterosexual relationships and particularly courtship and marriage are central themes in Austen's novels. But these very courtships are often the subjects of discussion amongst women who take a very close interest in every aspect of the lives of their friends. Indeed, in her reading of *Emma*, Ruth Perry insists that, while the marriage plot provides the novel's frame, much of the action calls attention to the ways in which compulsory hetero-sexuality disrupts the relationships between women.[4] *Emma* involves several female friendships: an ideal and deeply pleasurable one be-tween Emma and her former governess, a problematic one between Emma and Harriet, the young woman of unknown parentage whom she somewhat unwisely befriends, and the friendship that should de-velop, but never does, between Emma and the impoverished but in-telligent, educated and well-born Jane Fairfax. It is the imperative to marry, Perry argues, that destroys these relationships – an imperative to which in her own life Austen did not subscribe – and which she questions even while accepting its dominance in the construction of her novels.

As Perry argues, the importance of women's relationships with each other depicted in *Emma*, and the sense that they are threatened and interrupted by marriage, reflects their central importance in Austen's own life. Although there is a story of a possible suitor, Austen seems to have sought little emotional sustenance or companionship beyond that which she found with her beloved sister and domestic compan-ion, Cassandra, and with some of her nieces. Her surviving letters to these women point not only to the deep and frequently expressed affection that underlay these relationships but also the range of issues that were discussed and the immense pleasure that these women de-rived from their frequent communication with each other. This sense of pleasure is made most clear in her letters to her niece, Fanny Knight. After a number of letters dealing with Fanny's uncertainty as to how to choose between two possible suitors, Austen was unable to contain her amusement. "You are inimitable, irresistible. You are the delight of my life," she wrote early in 1817, in a letter that seems to provide some evidence for her dislike of the imperative to marry.

> Such letters, such entertaining letters as you have lately sent! Such a description of your queer little heart! Such a lovely display of what imagination does. You are worth your weight in gold, or even in the new silver coinage. I cannot express to you what I have felt in reading your history of yourself – how full of pity and concern, and admiration and amusement, I have been! You are the paragon of all that is silly and sensible, commonplace and eccentric, sad and lively, provoking and interesting ... It is very,

very gratifying to me to know you so intimately you can hardly
think what a pleasure it is to me to have such thorough pictures of
your heart. Oh what a loss it will be when you are married! You
are too agreeable in your single state – too agreeable as a niece. I
shall hate you when your delicious play of mind is all settled
down in conjugal and maternal affections.[5]

Although never depicting a cross-generational family friendship of
the kind she enjoyed with her niece in her novels, Austen certainly
explored some of the different kinds of relationships that were possible within families, extending from the very close friendship of Jane
and Elizabeth Bennet through to the very cool and distant sisterly
relationships evident in *Persuasion*, in which the family fails entirely to
provide companionship and women's outside friendships are the ones
that matter. Austen captures the move in the nature of friendship that
would take place in the next two centuries as family and friends evolved
into separate categories.

Indeed, in her treatment of these different kinds of friendship both
within and outside the family, Austen provides, albeit in an informal
way, a kind of taxonomy of friendship, which includes marital friendship and friendship within families, friendship between equals, and
friendship across boundaries of age, of sex and of social class. Although Austen's lightness of touch means that she does not engage in
heavy moralizing, nonetheless, in her plots, her comments and her
irony, she makes clear that some forms of friendship are entirely beneficial to the parties concerned and ought to be widely approved,
while others are not. There is little but commendation for friendships
between women who are similar in age and equal in status, such as
Elizabeth Bennet and Charlotte Lucas in *Pride and Prejudice*. But questions certainly arise when it comes to friendships that develop across
barriers of age or particularly of class.

The question of cross-generational friendships, which had been
important in her own life in relation to her nieces, was one that Austen
explored in a couple of her novels. She did not establish any absolute
pattern, looking rather at different forms that this kind of friendship
might take. There are two very different examples of close friendships
between younger and older women in *Emma* and *Persuasion*. In *Emma*,
the significant cross-generational friendship is that between Emma
herself and Mrs Weston, the woman who had been Emma's governess and companion prior to her own marriage. Mrs Weston is very
affectionate and gentle, always intensely interested in Emma's life,

but intelligent and perceptive as well. She is able to see Emma's failings and seeks, although not always successfully, to offer her wise counsel. By contrast, the cross-generational friendship in *Persuasion* points rather to the ways in which the advice of an older woman almost wrecks the life of her younger friend. Lady Russell, although devoted to her young friend Anne Elliot, is manifestly less intelligent than Anne and quite unable to see what Anne really wants and needs. Indeed, while she is the only one closely connected to Anne's family circle who loves or cares for her, her advice to Anne is always based on narrow prejudices of her own, and is thus completely lacking in insight or wisdom. It is her insistence that made the eighteen-year-old Anne break off her engagement to Captain Wentworth. Lady Russell was quite unable to see either his talents or the strength of the attachment between the young couple. She regarded him simply as a man of undistinguished parentage and unknown prospects and as not good enough to marry Anne. In a similar way, she was completely taken in by Anne's unscrupulous Elliot cousin, seeing him as a desirable husband for Anne – until his duplicity was made absolutely manifest. It is a sign of Anne's own wisdom and maturity that, while well aware of the failings of her friend, she remains sympathetic to her and continues always to value her loyalty and devotion.

If friendship across age barriers is acceptable in Austen's world, friendship across class barriers is not. Unlike her contemporary Mary Wollstonecraft, Jane Austen does not support the idea that cross-class friendships between women are either truly possible or desirable. The close friendship that Emma forms with the young Harriet Taylor is frowned upon from the start by Emma's future husband, Mr Knightly. He sees it as extremely unwise because Emma, by bringing Harriet into her own social world, sets up expectations that cannot be realized. However pretty and engaging Harriet might be, no man of birth and wealth would be prepared to marry a woman of unknown parentage. At the same time, involvement in Emma's world (and Emma's own views) serves to separate Harriet from the class to which she belongs – and from the young man who wishes to marry her. Emma herself comes to see the wisdom of Mr Knightly's views when Harriet expresses a belief that Knightly himself is in love with her – and the women's relationship comes pretty swiftly to an end. Both Emma's wealth and status and her power of personality come into play in Austen's critique of this relationship, and the power imbalance between the two women prevents either from gaining any benefit from it.

The friendship that is set up as the one that Emma should pursue, offering her as it does the closest approximation to a friendship of equality, is that with Jane Fairfax. But this never comes to anything. Perry argues that it is impossible for Emma to engage in a friendship with equals, in view of the lack of equality evident everywhere else, including in the marriage she will eventually make with Knightly. But Austen does explore the question of an equal friendship between women in other novels, and with particular clarity in *Pride and Prejudice*. In this novel too, there is a clear contrast drawn between different kinds of friendship, and most particularly between the kind of close friendship that it is possible to establish between siblings and that with someone outside the family. Elizabeth Bennet has both: Charlotte Lucas is described as her "intimate friend"; in addition she is very close to her beloved older sister Jane. The relationship between Elizabeth and Charlotte is particularly interesting as she is very different from Elizabeth in her outlook and views, but quite as determined in the strength with which she holds them. Their friendship is placed under considerable strain when Charlotte accepts the proposal of Mr Collins, whom Elizabeth has absolutely rejected. Charlotte does so out of a prudential calculation. "I am not romantic, you know," she says to Elizabeth in explaining her decision, "I never was. I ask only a comfortable home; and considering Mr. Collins's character, connection, and situation in life, I am convinced that my chance of happiness with him is as fair as most people can boast on entering the marriage state."[6] Elizabeth is shocked by this, having never quite believed that, despite Charlotte's earlier comments on marriage, she would decide to do what to Elizabeth is sacrificing every finer feeling to material advantage. But Charlotte follows her own perceived self-interest and accepts the inevitable nature of her marriage, and she and Elizabeth manage to maintain their friendship and the occasional enjoyment of each other's company even after Charlotte's marriage. There is no reference to their friendship, however, after Elizabeth's marriage to Mr Darcy – and it does seem clear that Elizabeth would do her best to shield her husband from "the parading and obsequious civility"[7] of Mr Collins that he had had to endure when their engagement was known. Although Austen's treatment is not quite as extensive as in *Emma*, one does have here too a very clear picture of the ways in which marriage interferes with the friendships of women.

As we will see in Chapter 7, the question of women's friendship continued to be a significant theme in nineteenth-century women's novels, not only in Britain in the work particularly of Charlotte Brontë and Elizabeth Gaskell, but also in the United States in the novels of Louisa M. Alcott. But increasingly one can see more widely not only an acceptance of the idea that women are capable of friendship but even more a suggestion that they have greater capacities for friendship than men. The idea of women's friendship as providing a particularly close bond underlay the emergence of women's organised philanthropic and feminist activity in the nineteenth century and it was often celebrated by the women engaged in this activity. Thus in the mid-nineteenth century, when the increasing number of unmarried women in Britain was becoming the source of much discussion, the feminist writer and activist Frances Cobbe argued that, in view of the violence that it sometimes entailed, marriage was not always the most desirable state for women – and that women's friendships provided an alternative. If every woman had a sister or a woman friend with whom she could share her life, there would not need to be any pity for "that large class commonly called 'old maids.'" If a woman had no sister,

> She has yet inherited the blessed power of a woman to make true friendships, such as not one man's heart in a hundred can ever imagine; and while he smiles scornfully at the idea of friendship meaning anything beyond acquaintance at a club or the intimacy of a barrack, she enjoys one of the purest pleasures and the most unselfish of all affections.[8]

Cobbe's linking of the close ties of sisters to those between same-sex friends serves well to illustrate both the growing importance of intimacy in nineteenth-century ideas of friendship and the ways in which idealized familial bonds, especially those of sisters and brothers, provided a framework for thinking about both friendship and community.

Notes

1. See Norma Clarke, *The Rise and Fall of the Woman of Letters* (London: Pimlico, 2004) and Jane Spencer, *The Rise of the Woman Novelist: From Aphra Behn to Jane Austen* (Oxford: Blackwell, 1986).

2. Virginia Woolf, *A Room of One's Own* [1928] (Harmondsworth, UK: Penguin, 1945), p. 65.

3. Jane Austen, *Persuasion* (Oxford: Oxford University Press, 1971 [1817]), p. 221.

4. Ruth Perry, "Interrupted friendships in Jane Austen's *Emma*," *Tulsa Studies in Literature* 5.2 (1986), pp. 185–202 at p. 196.

5. Jane Austen to Fanny Knight, 20 February 1817, in *Jane Austen's Letters,* collected and ed. Deirdre Le Faye (Oxford: Oxford University Press, 1985), p. 328.

6. Jane Austen, *Pride and Prejudice* (Harmondsworth, UK: Penguin Books, 2001 [1813]), p. 140

7. Austen, *Pride and Prejudice*, p. 182.

8. Frances Power Cobbe, "Celibacy v. Marriage: Old Maids, their Sorrows and Pleasures," *Fraser's Magazine* 65 (1865), pp. 228–35.

Chapter 7

CLASS, SEX, AND FRIENDSHIP: THE LONG NINETEENTH CENTURY

Marc Brodie and Barbara Caine

Introduction

There is no sharp and sudden break between the eighteenth and the nineteenth centuries in ideas about or discussions of friendship. On the contrary, the continuing importance of many of the ideas about sexual difference, separate spheres and family life which had been so important in the Enlightenment, and of the stress on the place of sentiment and emotion in the arts, literature and general outlook associated with Romanticism, ensured that there were marked continuities at least until World War I. Some of these developments seem to have become more widely diffused. Thus, for example, a number of recent historians have written about the importance of intimate same-sex friendships between both men and women in the nineteenth century in a range of countries, including Germany, Britain, Russia and the United States. There was also a strong sense of the overlap between family and friends in the value accorded close and intimate familial bonds, evident not only in the ideal of companionate marriages, but also in close sibling ties which were often seen as providing lifelong forms of companionship and support. The ties of sisters were of particular interest to some English women novelists, but fraternal bonds and those between brothers and sisters were of great moment too.

This continuity is evident also in the terminology used to describe friendship. The term "friend" continued to be used as it had been in the eighteenth century to describe those with whom one had close ties

based on shared interests or activities and also those on whom one
might depend in difficult circumstances. It was also used in relation to
family – and in ways that often made it impossible to differentiate
between friends and kin. In situations in which a person looked to
their "friends" to support them in times of financial, moral or legal
need, for example, they could be looking either for family support, or
for support from people with whom they had social but no familial
ties. The language of family, and especially of brotherhood or sisterhood, was often used to designate the strength and intimacy of particularly close friendships.

The absence of a sudden break does not mean that there were no
new developments. On the contrary, several things came to the fore
in the nineteenth century that had not been evident in quite the same
way before. Some of these were closely connected to industrialization
and urbanization and the significant social and political changes that
accompanied them. Urbanization usually involved considerable personal and social upheaval, and the break-up of traditional rural communities. But the large modern cities of the nineteenth century also
offered new facilities for sociability. Cafés, for example, were not new
to Paris, but the significant increase in their number, especially in the
second half of the nineteenth century, brought what Scott Haine has
described as a new form of "café friendship," evident amongst both
working class and bourgeoisie.[1] In a similar way, the large depart-
ment stores that were noticeable in Paris, London and many other
European cities from the 1870s onwards, sometimes had dining and
discussion rooms in which middle-class women were encouraged to
meet, attend lectures and spend considerable amounts of time.

From the late eighteenth century onwards, men in many European
and American cities had been involved in a range of political associations, debating societies, dining clubs, chambers of commerce, learned
societies, and art associations. This practice continued and was augmented in the nineteenth century, with the emergence of new political beliefs and new ideals of citizenship. In the eyes of some historians,
these developments had a negative impact on friendship. George
Mosse, for example, argues that friendship between men declined in
Germany in the nineteenth century – overwhelmed by the demands
of nationalism. In his view, the eighteenth-century idea of friendship
"which came to symbolise the autonomy of personal relationships ...
as part of a highly self-conscious cult based upon the free interplay of
personalities and the acceptance of individual differences" was

incompatible with the all-encompassing claims of modern nationalism that denied the possibility of difference and demanded that personal relationships be subsumed into a devotion to some greater good.[2]

Others suggest that politics itself both encouraged and depended
on particular forms of sociability and in some ways encouraged the
development of friendship. Here we can also see an increasingly important role for women within the elite friendship networks which
organized the political patronage that made advancement possible.
Aristocratic women were, as they had been in the late eighteenth century, often central points within "social politics," as mutual friends
and conduits of information and influence between individuals or
groupings,[3] and the role of the "political hostess" was important in
the formation both of governments and of parties. While there was
clearly much that was instrumental in these social relationships, the
political world also included very close personal friendships. In the
1880s a close friendship had developed between Herbert Asquith and
Robert Haldane as young barristers in London, and they were soon
joined in their closeness by Lord Edward Grey. Later, as parliamen-
tarians, this led to many private discussions of which positions of power
each could claim, and after previously attempting to use his influence
to have Haldane appointed as Lord Chancellor, Asquith enacted this
himself after becoming Prime Minister in 1908. Haldane wrote to him
that:

> More than six years ago you fought a hard fight for your old friend
> over this great office and now you have bestowed it on him. My
> feeling I will not try to express. You know how deep it is. My
> mind goes back to the past, to the days when we travelled together
> to the Law Courts from John Street, Hampstead, days which I am
> not likely to forget and are very present to me now.[4]

Friendship and politics were closely entwined.

Friendship was important in terms of international as well as national politics, and at all levels of political and social engagement, not
just that of the social and political elite. The concept of an international friendship amongst workers that cut across national boundaries
was of course fundamental to the emerging socialist movement in this
period. Other writers also point to the centrality of friendship in the
development of many of the activist groups of the time – nationalist,
radical, socialist or feminist. These associations also spread into new
social groups with the formation of a range of new working-class bodies, including trade unions, co-operative guilds and societies and the

"friendly societies" that provided mutual aid and insurance. By the mid nineteenth century, as middle-class women in Germany, Russia and France as well as in Britain and the United States became increasingly involved in educational, philanthropic, social and political activities, they too found associations in which they could meet regularly with other women. Indeed, by the second half of the century, as the British feminist Frances Cobbe proclaimed, the principal of association for women was coming to be generally recognized.

The advent of new associations for women was accompanied by the entry of their voices into the discussion of friendship and its meaning. In Britain and the United States, in particular, the literary discussion about the nature, meaning, and limitations of women's friendships, which had been of so much interest to male French and British novelists and philosophers in the course of the eighteenth century, came in the nineteenth to be dominated by the voices of women. In both of these countries, as generally in Europe, there were still some who argued that sexual rivalry made friendship between women impossible – or that, if possible, it was only a prelude to the more significant form of friendship that women would experience in marriage. But there was an ever-growing number of others who stressed the lifelong importance of the affection, loyalty and support that women could offer each other.

Questions about the possibilities, the meanings and the problems involved in friendship and social intimacy for the working class also gained importance at this time. The work of social investigators, new organizations and movements and greater working-class articulacy brought forward previously unheard voices. The bodies known as "friendly societies," which had emerged in the eighteenth century, vaguely mirroring some of the social position and functions of the medieval guilds, became, in Britain at least, the largest independent working-class organizations of the period. With membership numbers three to four times that of the organized trade unions, these societies had five and a half million participants by the end of the century. Notably, the leaders of these organizations did not simply think of their "friendly" nature in terms of financial support and mutual assistance amongst members but were often drawn to discuss the philosophical basis of their objectives – and the true meaning of friendship. With a leadership generally drawn from the highest levels of the working class, and often overlapping with those in the popular "mutual improvement" movements of education, these discussions often drew upon classical and high literary thought. While these friendly societies were a largely British development, they had a counterpart in a range of political and other organizations and movements that emerged across Europe in the second half of the nineteenth century. It is interesting to note more generally the increasing use of the term "friend" by many of those seeking to provide philanthropic aid or social protection to those deemed less fortunate – and the ways in which this usage of the term replaced an earlier use of "friend" to describe patron–client relationships.

This philanthropic use of the language of friendship is evident also in missionary and anti-slavery rhetoric across the nineteenth century, as several different groups in Europe and the United States sought to assist and "befriend" slaves and heathens in an endeavour both to improve their immediate circumstances and to ensure their eternal salvation. The growing importance of empire and the involvement of a range of different groups of people within it also brought to the fore in some new ways questions about the intimate nature of imperial relationships and cross-racial friendship more generally.

Sources

Friendship continued to be discussed in sermons, in etiquette and conduct manuals and most particularly in periodical essays across the nineteenth century. It was in periodicals, for example, that the English debates concerning the relative merits of male versus female friendships were carried out in the course of the 1870s. *The Saturday Review*, which was renowned for its hostility to women's rights and indeed for its misogyny, set off the debate with two articles respectively entitled "Friendship" and "The Exclusiveness of Women," both of which questioned the possibilities of friendship amongst women in view of their shallowness, competitiveness and untrustworthiness. At best, friendships between women were seen as a preparation or rehearsal for the "serious business of relationship with men," or as something possible only amongst unmarried women tending towards middle age and even then, only between women of markedly different temperaments so that one was able to lead and protect the other.[5] These articles sparked off a spirited debate that was carried both in the pages of the feminist *Victoria* magazine (which was written, edited and published entirely by women), and in a number of other prominent journals. Women were the major contributors to the debate – and upheld both sides of the argument. The feminist writer Frances Cobbe rejected the claims of the *Saturday Review* entirely, arguing that single women often lived in the greatest of peace and harmony because they inherited the blessed power "to make true and tender friendships, such as not one man's heart in a hundred can even imagine."[6] But other women, particularly Eliza Lynn Linton and Dinah Mulock Craig, accepted the *Saturday Review's* depiction and suggested that friendships between women were impossible and indeed dangerous – unless they were rehearsals for marriage.[7]

Periodicals offered not only debates about contemporary questions but also discussions of the ways in which earlier ideas and texts on friendship were read and reviewed. Lengthy reviews of new editions of the works of Aristotle, Cicero and Bacon, for example, show how they were seen and understood by a variety of different groups within society. These included working-class as well as middle-class ones. Thus, for example, Francis Bacon's ideas on friendship were discussed at considerable length in 1859 in the journal of the largest British friendly society, the Manchester Unity of Oddfellows, which had the motto *Amicitia, Amor, et Veritas*. It quoted admiringly his description of a "true friend" being one "to whom you may impart griefs, joys, fears, hopes, suspicions, counsels, and whatsoever lieth upon the heart to oppress it, in a kind of civil shrift or confession."[8] The aspect of Bacon's theory most applauded was that the intimacy and counsel of friendship could result in the personal improvement of those in the relationship:

> as his wits and understanding do clarify and break up in the communicating and discoursing with another: he tosseth his thoughts more easily; he marshalleth them more orderly; he seeth how they look when turned into words; finally, he waxeth wiser than himself.

This was the "best preservative to keep the mind in health," and also avoid "gross errors and extreme absurdities."

But while there were many essays on friendship, some of which dealt with earlier philosophical works, there were few nineteenth-century philosophers who considered the question of friendship. The most prominent work to do so, G. E. Moore's *Principia Ethica,* was published in 1903 – and serves very much as a work demarcating the transition between the long nineteenth century and the short twentieth. In his final chapter titled "The Ideal," Moore suggested that the most valuable things that can be known or imagined are "certain states of consciousness, which may be roughly described as the pleasures of human intercourse and the enjoyment of beautiful objects."[9] What is perhaps most interesting here is the extent to which, while seeking to establish both the value and the nature of the human affection that he praised so highly, Moore found it necessary to equivocate over the relative importance of "the appreciation of mental qualities," on the one hand, and "an appreciation of the appropriate *corporeal* expression of the mental qualities" on the other. Friendship was clearly the issue – but the border between intellectual friendship and something rather more complex in emotional and sexual terms was for him, as for so many others at the turn of the twentieth century, a hard one to establish.

Fiction and poetry continued to be sources for nineteenth-century ideas on friendship, although the coverage varied somewhat from one country to another. In Britain in particular, there was an extensive literature on this subject – with the continuing rise of the woman novelist perhaps producing a situation in which more attention was paid to women's friendships than to those of men. But the interest in and adulation of friendship in British and American literature is not echoed around Europe. In Russia, for example, despite the importance of friendship within the literary and radical intelligentsia, it is rather the tensions and problems in friendship that are evident – whether resulting from sexual rivalry and jealousy as in *Eugene Onegin*, from the impotence of friends to intervene in personal tragedy, as in *Oblomov,* or from the impact of the generational struggles that characterized the intelligentsia on friendships, as in *Father and Sons*. In France too, despite the occasional celebration of friendship, such as that in *The Three Musketeers*, there is rather more literature on the disillusionment of friendship than on its significance. With growing working-class literacy, cheaper short fiction and magazines also grew in importance as representations of ideas and ideals of friendship to the poorer in society. In these it is often the limitations or boundaries to intimate friendship that are most clearly expressed.

More than in earlier periods it is possible to chart the developments of friendship and their place in many different lives through the vast wealth of both published and unpublished personal writings available in libraries, archives and family collections. The immense expansion in autobiographical writing that followed the publication of Rousseau's *Confessions* continued unabated across the century, extending beyond the limited world of literary men to include many women, workers of all kinds and even freed slaves. There are also substantial collections of diaries and personal correspondence, some of which have been used in important articles seeking to delineate the precise nature of friendship in particular countries. These personal writings illustrate the ways in which friendship was discussed and in which it was thought about in private moments – and in periods of reflection. At the end of each year, Beatrice Webb, for example, listed all her friends – and examined carefully the state of their relationships. For the later part of the period, important oral history collections have been gathered from those who remembered their childhood or young adulthood before the Great War. Although unavoidably distorted by modern understandings and terminology, these memories do give us a previously unavailable window into the relationships of ordinary people. In a similar way, the letters and diaries of members of the Bloomsbury group contain an almost continuous discussion of particular friendships and of the importance of intimacy within social relations. The comments illustrate the growing importance of psychology and the emerging interest in psychoanalysis as different members of the group explored both the importance of their friends in terms of their own emotional states and the psychological states of their friends.

Friendship in Literature and Literary Friendships

The nineteenth century was the first period in which, particularly in Britain and in the United States, the literary discussion of women's friendship was both more extensive and more important than that of men. Not only was it the case that women were deemed by many to be more capable of true friendship than were men, but as Nancy Armstrong has recently argued, it was also often women who were the key figures in important new kinds of friendship that developed across class and sometimes racial boundaries and were thus significant in the establishment and maintenance of social harmony. As we have seen, particularly in regard to Mary Wollstonecraft, the importance of women's friendship was an important element in feminist discourse at least from the 1790s.

Some recent critics have argued that, despite the appeal of Wollstonecraft to contemporary feminists, in the nineteenth century it was the approach that Rousseau took in *Julie, ou la Nouvelle Héloïse* in which female friendship could be accommodated comfortably within a heterosexual romance – rather than the subversive one of Wollstonecraft – that held sway. [10] Tessa Coslett, for example, insists that, "the coming together of two women is often essential to the resolution of the plot, figuring as a necessary stage in the heroine's maturation and readiness for the marriage that conventionally closes the action" – rather than being suggested as an alternative form of relationship. [11]

In England, the depiction of women's friendship continued across the nineteenth century, expanding in some ways, in accordance with the issues that came to the fore in the ongoing "woman question." As discussion about the merits and problems of marriage for women, of the growing numbers of single women, and about the need for education and occupations for middle-class women emerged, so one begins to see the treatment of these issues alongside new kinds of relationships and communities for women in fiction. The sociability of schools and the kinds of friendship possible between pupils or between mistresses and pupils is integral both to Charlotte Brontë's *Jane Eyre* and to her *Villette*. In a more explicit way, in *Shirley*, Brontë depicts a fierce debate on the merits and problems of marriage between the close friends, Shirley and Caroline Helstone – before each succumbs to the appropriate suitor. The social problem novels of the 1840s dealt with other aspects of women's friendship. For example, Elizabeth Gaskell's *North and South* includes an affectionate and trusting friendship between the southern middle-class Margaret Hale and the northern textile worker Higgins, which serves greatly to reduce community tension and to demonstrate the importance of recognition of humanity across marked social divides.

The depiction of women's friendships in these novels has few of the erotic overtones evident in some of the eighteenth-century novels on women's friendship discussed in Chapter 5. On the contrary, these novels may, as Ruth Perry suggests, take as themes friendships that are spoilt or interrupted by marriage, but they never suggest that female friendship is superior to or might interfere with marriage. This is not to suggest that the idea of erotic relationships between women was absent in the nineteenth century. On the contrary, it remained a source of both fascination and concern, both in literature and in life. One particular nineteenth-century form that it took centred on the relationship between an older woman and a young girl – and the possibility that an ostensibly maternal relationship might hide quite other feelings. This issue was rarely dealt with in women's writing.

Rather, as Martha Vicinus points out, it was dealt with by men, early in the century, in Coleridge's poem Christabel (1816) and slightly later in Sheridan LeFanu's novel, *Carmilla* (1827) both of which deal with the threat posed to prepubescent girls by female strangers who come into their homes, evoke their desire and destroy their familial relationships.[12]

The prominence of women's friendships in fiction and indeed of women authors that is so marked a feature of nineteenth-century Britain is not evident in other European countries or in the United States. There are few depictions of women's friendship in the fiction of nineteenth-century Russia, Germany or even France. The interest in women's friendship shown by Madame de Staël was not followed through by her successors in France. On the contrary, George Sand accepted and replicated in her novels a sense that sexual competition between women was such as to make friendship impossible. This was not always because women distrusted each other, but rather, as in *Indiana,* because male fickleness and lack of understanding or honour meant that women were faced with the need to sacrifice themselves for their friends. For Sand herself, it was the freedom to have both sexual relationships outside marriage and close and caring non-sexual friendships with men that mattered rather more than friendships with women. This was a reflection not only of her personal inclinations but also of the centrality of relationships with men both in her political views and in her particular concerns about the nature of women's oppression.

There was slightly more discussion of male friendships in Europe. Indeed, the close friendship that underlies Alexandre Dumas' *Three Musketeers* probably remains the best-known nineteenth-century depiction of friendship. The setting of the novel in the seventeenth century, in the reign of Louis XIII, allows for a sense of chivalry along with the swashbuckling action. The friendship of Athos, Porthos, Aramis and D'Artagnan combines an enthusiasm for derring-do with a tender and quite sentimental affection.

> The friendship which united these four men, and the want they felt of seeing one another three or four times a day, whether for duelling, business, or pleasure, caused them to be continually running after one another like shadows; and the Inseparables were constantly to be met with seeking one another, from the Luxembourg to the Place St Sulpice, or from the Rue du Vieux-Colombier to the Luxembourg.[13]

This relationship followed a pattern that was not uncommon in some nineteenth-century military friendships in both its intensity and its duration. It was essentially a relationship of early adulthood that came to an end completely the minute that each of these young men ceased to be a Musketeer.

The closeness and the consistent mutual support depicted by Dumas in this novel makes an interesting contrast to the much more problematic male friendship depicted by Gustave Flaubert in *A Sentimental Education* or by Turgenev in *Fathers and Sons*, although, in these novels too, the friendship between young men is a key theme.

A very different model of male friendship is evident in some of the English novels that consider this theme – not least because of the importance of their familial setting. Anthony Trollope, for example, depicts several different kinds of male friendship in both his Barchester series and in his political novels, but these friendships usually sit very comfortably alongside marriage, and both professional and family life. Friends made at college prove indispensable to Archdeacon Grantly in his battle against the forces of Evangelicalism which threaten to reduce his power and to challenge his way of life, for example, but his friends are entertained by his wife – and the closest of them marries his sister-in-law, Eleanor Bold, simultaneously strengthening a friendship and solving a family problem. Trollope shows clearly the importance of male friendships, the pleasures they offer, and the ways in which they are linked with other institutions, including the Church, political parties, the national press and sport, especially racing. But despite its immense value, this particular form of male friendship is under threat as the privileged social world on which it depended is increasingly challenged. Richard Dellamora argues that Trollope's novel *The Prime Minister*, written shortly after the 1867 *Reform Act* enfranchised some members of the working class, depicts a world in which the ideal of a government of friends is no longer possible. The emergence of Jews into political prominence, the demands of women for political power, and the presence of people without a sound financial standing in the political world, called the social framework that had surrounded politics into question and makes the life of Trollope's Duke of Omnian one of increasing social isolation.[14] The necessary qualities for friendship here are not so much moral as religious and racial – or rather, in Trollope's view, they go together. A gentleman could only make a friend of another member of this same group –

and friendship in this world is unthinkable across the boundaries of class and race.

For Thomas Arnold at Rugby, school friendships were a powerful vehicle in the maturation of boys, in containing their potentially subversive energies and in directing their religious and spiritual lives. Arnold encouraged close friendships between masters and boys as well as between older and younger boys. "God knows," he wrote, "that many a lesson, which might come in vain from older lips is heeded when coming from the lips of a familiar friend; He knows that the mind's and soul's growth never expanded so healthfully as in the society of equals."[15] Boys at Rugby took up these exhortations, writing glowingly about school friendships and extolling the virtues of friendship in the Rugby magazine. This highly idealized image both of Rugby and of the close male friendships formed there was widely publicized in biographies of Arnold and even more in Thomas Hughes' very popular and ostensibly autobiographical novel *Tom Brown's Schooldays*. In this work, Hughes offered a detailed discussion of how friendships were made, challenged and sustained in public schools, stressing always how essential such friendships were not only for comfort, but also for survival.[16] Those who were unable to make friends had no place at school – while those who made them often had friends for life. Other novelists took these issues up as well and extended them. For example, Thackeray's *Vanity Fair* took a friendship made at school into a later stage of life, looking rather at how it weathered and survived maturity and adulthood, especially when it brought one friend a growing knowledge and understanding of the character defects in the other.

While Arnold and his disciples stressed the moral component of schoolboy friendship, for many parents of public-school boys pragmatic concerns were more evident. Parents spending considerable amounts of money sending their sons to school were concerned to ensure that they made the most of their opportunities there – and this included making the kinds of friends who would stand them in good stead in their later business and professional lives. The private correspondence between parents and sons in many upper middle-class families makes it clear that schoolboys were expected to report as regularly on their desirable friends and invitations to visit prominent family homes as they were on their place in class. In some ways, this was recognition of the importance of friends to those seeking to establish themselves in business or in professional and political life.

Male friendship clearly had its instrumental side, but the growing emphasis on the importance of sentiment and feeling in women's friendships in the nineteenth century was also evident in relation to men. It is, moreover, a male friendship, that of Alfred Tennyson and Arthur Hallam, that produced the best-known and most intense nineteenth-century work on friendship, Tennyson's poem "In Memoriam." The intensity of Tennyson's love for Hallam, his pleasure at Hallam's engagement to his own sister Emily, combined with the story of Tennyson's own long engagement, broken at one point but resumed and leading to marriage after the poem was completed, has led to a great deal of discussion about the nature of Tennyson's sexual and emotional life. Both the friendship between Tennyson and Hallam and this poem, which was written in some measure as an attempt by Tennyson to assuage his intense grief over Hallam's death, have attracted considerable comment in recent years from those interested in nineteenth-century sexual and erotic relationships. That discussion and the complexity of the poem are useful here in pointing, on the one hand, to the impossibility one faces in establishing an absolute border between erotic relationships and other forms of friendship in the nineteenth century, in relation to men as well as women, but on the other, to what often strikes a modern reader as excessive statements of affection and desire between friends who would never have dreamed of engaging in any form of sexual intimacy. Expressions of eternal love, or of a desire to kiss and caress the face of a friend, are the commonplace expressions of many same-sex Victorian friendships in which both friends were deeply engaged in heterosexual relationships. These expressions of love and devotion thus make clear a new focus on the emotional content of friendship and other relationships in the nineteenth century. This point is made clear by Tennyson himself – in the ways in which he acknowledges the importance of romantic love and the intensity of parental love in his poem. While stressing the devastating nature of his own loss, "In Memoriam" does not suggest that he is alone in this grief. His emphasis is rather on the way in which the loss of a close friend is as great a loss as is that to a parent of a child or to a woman of her lover.

> O what to her shall be the end?
> And what to me remains of good
> To her, perpetual maidenhood,
> And unto me no second friend.[17]

The discussion of friendship in fiction was not confined to same-sex relationships. On the contrary, there was also considerable discussion of friendship in heterosexual relationships of different kinds. The most significant of these was companionate marriage. This was a form of relationship strongly extolled by Jane Austen very early in the century and increasingly prominent by the 1860s and 1870s. In some very well-known works, such as Louisa M. Alcott's *Little Women* and *Good Wives,* companionate marriage is set up not only as a goal but also as something that has to be learned and worked for, requiring women to relinquish romantic dreams, to take responsibility for their household – and to understand the needs of their husbands to become their closest friends.

A very different kind of heterosexual relationship is depicted in some of the Russian novels of the 1860s, particularly those associated with the *nihilist* movement of those years. These members of the radical intelligentsia were strongly opposed to the sexual double standard – and felt an obligation both to atone for it in some measure and to enable women to enjoy some of the freedoms previously known to men. Thus in his programmatic novel, *What Is To Be Done*, Nikolai Chernashevsky depicts a situation in which an educated young man befriends the sister of a boy he is employed to tutor. He seeks not only to educate her, but to enable her to escape the confines of her restrictive home by marrying her. The marriage is a fictitious one, however, and he does not presume to demand his own sexual rights – leaving his wife free to pursue other relationships. This extreme form of male self-sacrifice was the subject of much mirth in Russia, but it does illustrate the extent to which heterosexual friendship was an issue of significance within the intelligentsia at this time. The novels of Turgenev, particularly *A Nest of Gentlefolk*, serve also to show the ways in which friendships between men and women underlay much of the radical movement.

While the importance and the value of friendship was often depicted in serious nineteenth-century fiction, so too were its limits. As we have seen, questions about the borders and boundaries of friendship and about the dangers of attempting to cross or transgress class boundaries were raised by women writers in the late eighteenth and early nineteenth centuries. In the mid and late nineteenth century, these questions were raised also in terms of religious and racial differences. Charlotte Brontë's depiction of Bertha Mason – the half-caste West Indian woman whom Rochester is tricked into marrying and whose limited understanding and unrestrained sensual appetites make her an impossible wife and ultimately turn her into the savage mad-woman who threatens not only Rochester's peace of mind but his life – has been much discussed in terms of its orientalism and its racist and imperial assumptions. But it is worth stressing here the contrast that Brontë draws between the friendship in marriage that was possible between Rochester and Jane Eyre – and the impossibility of such a friendship across any form of colour bar.

In a general way, English fiction in the nineteenth century stressed and re-enforced the impossibility of friendship across either racial or religious boundaries. Dickens and George Eliot joined Trollope to make this point in the course of the 1880s, albeit in different ways. Dickens, in *Little Dorrit,* made a similar point to that which Trollope had made in *The Way We Live Now*, pointing to the dishonesty and unscrupulousness of Jewish speculators who brought ruin to all who trusted them. Eliot made the point in a rather different way in *Daniel Deronda*. In this novel, what appears to be the possibility of close friend-ship between a Jew and a non-Jew, evident in the friendship between Sir Hugo and Deronda, or Deronda and Mordechai, is ultimately undermined when Deronda discovers his own Jewish origin – and thus the underlying reason for his attraction to Mordechai. The self-hatred and anxiety of being Jewish evinced by Mirah serves further to show both how Jews were seen – and how impassable a barrier this particular religious difference was.

In a similar way, although some individuals found in friendship a way to question imperial values and to assert new social possibilities, the fiction of empire rarely offered such a vision. On the contrary, the best-known novel to explore this question, E. M. Forster's *A Passage to India*, shows in immense detail precisely how imperial values and assumptions make it impossible for there to be friendship between Indians and their English rulers. Although the book was published in 1924, Forster's experience of India was a prewar one, when the atti-tudes and mindset of the nineteenth century still endured. At the start of the novel, a group of Indians discuss the question of whether or not it is possible to be friends with an Englishman. One contends that it may be possible in England – but not in India: once there even a person who might have had cordial relations with Indians back home rapidly comes under the antagonism towards them evinced by the white community. The whole novel is an illustration of this process and its tragic consequence for anyone who attempts to question or to cross the absolute distance deemed appropriate between the races in Anglo-India.

In discussing questions of friendship, it is necessary to look at the popular fiction and the periodicals designed for working-class readers as well as at their middle-class counterparts. The reading of fiction by the poorer working class was not always approved of by the middle-class missionaries and philanthropists who made their way into the homes of the poor. The report of a visit to a "Mrs F." made by a biblewoman on the Isle of Dogs in London in 1892 makes this clear. Mrs F.'s "home, herself, and her children, were wretchedly dirty. I often saw fragments of novelettes on the floor ... She tried to defend herself by saying she had learned many things from them she had not known before."[18] The biblewoman was clearly not convinced – but the reading habits she deplored were widespread. As Sally Mitchell notes, the standard Victorian novel "was written by, and for, and largely about the 60,000 or so families who could afford a guinea for a year's library subscription or a shilling a month to buy a new book as it came out in parts or in a magazine." Nonetheless, penny or halfpenny novelettes or the serials in cheap magazines were the main form of reading material for the English working class. Most popular of all amongst working-class women for much of the later part of the century in Britain were the *London Journal* and the *Family Herald*, which typically included "an instalment of an adventurous serial ... a piece of short fiction or a true-life adventure, and a page of answers to correspondents on personal, legal, and medical problems." In the middle of the century the magazines' combined weekly sales were around three-quarters of a million (in contrast, Dickens' serialized novels sold perhaps an eighth of this number). The magazines, says Mitchell, "must have reached nearly one person in three amongst the literate population" but had a particular readership, at least later in the century, amongst "servants, shop girls and the wives of unskilled labourers." Similar magazines and readership appeared, for example, in the United States, with the *Family Story Paper* and *Girls of Today*.

Friendship was considerably less prominent as a theme in these magazines and in their fiction than was the case in their middle-class counterparts. The centrepiece of most stories in the magazines was romantic love and the idealization of family life as the ultimate feminine goal. In a similar way, the family was the focus of the practical advice in such journals. They were in stark contrast to ideas of improvement through the clarification of the "wits and understandings" of the individual mind and the avoidance of "gross errors and extreme absurdities" through the essential counsel of a friend, as in Bacon's philosophy approved by the friendly society leaders. The direct message given in this literature for working-class women, as the advice column in the *London Journal* instructed in 1849, was to: "Turn your attention to matrimony ... nothing rationalizes the mind quicker than the marriage; and we recommend it as a certain cure for those little follies which, somehow or other, manage to creep into the wilful heads of our young women."[19] Self-improvement came through marriage and family only, and perhaps an avoidance of the "follies" of young intimacy.

This conclusion is not at all surprising in light of Mitchell's description of the true themes of the most popular romantic fiction of the nineteenth century:

> A high proportion of the tales in the *Family Herald* are romantic. Wedding bells provide the suitable ending. But despite the sentiment and the sentimentality there is a note – sometimes overt, more often an undercurrent – of antiromanticism and feminine individualism. Some of the most sentimental tales serve to counteract the ethos that woman is properly a creature of the emotions. Woman's goal is marriage, which provides her with station, role, duties, and economic security; anything – including emotion – that interferes with the goal is counterproductive; and it is woman's responsibility to provide for her own happiness.[20]

The intimacy of friendship, as with other "romantic" ideals could "interfere" with the goals of success or survival. Ultimately, the family and its preservation are the key.

The emphasis on family ensured that the older usage of "friend" to apply to members of family or kin was evident everywhere in the popular magazines, particularly in the short fiction and adventure stories. For example, the short story "Mistress Molly's Moonstone," which appeared in the *Family Herald* in June 1897, has a scene in which the heroine Molly finds herself alone and in dire straits: "'But,' she said almost in despair, 'I have nowhere to go! The only friend I have is an aunt, my mother's sister ... ' 'I felt so friendless, so alone, except for you, cousin!'"

Although Dickens was quite popular amongst the working class by the end of the century, for much of this period it was the adventure story, such as short or serialized versions of W. H. Ainsworth's *Jack Sheppard* or G. W. M. Reynolds' *Mysteries of London*, that were most widely read by the male working class. Like the female fiction read by the working class, these stories generally use the term "friend" in an older way, to refer to a patron or to family. If there was a depiction of close friendship, it was much more likely to be between members of the upper classes (or at least undiscovered rightful heirs) than amongst members of the working class. Working-class heroes were not expected to display the kind of emotion for another person on which close friendships depended – their emotion was directed rather towards beloved and needed animals. Louis James' summary of two major events in H. D. Miles' bestselling cheap version of the Dick Turpin story, published in 1839, makes this very clear. "Turpin kills his friend Tom King by mistake, and shows his manly self-control by not flinching a muscle. When, however, his horse Black Bess dies, he collapses in tears. The love of Turpin and Bess formed the basis of all Turpin stories."[21] James notes this was a common theme across the extremely popular stories of the period – such as *Jack Sheppard* – which romanticized some criminals for a working-class readership. In Ainsworth's *Rokewood*, also after the same scene of the death of Turpin's horse in a chase, the hero exclaims in his heartbreak: "But Bess – I cannot leave her." His pursuer then arrives: "'Poor Black Bess!' said Major Mowbray, wistfully regarding the body of the mare, as it lay stretched at his feet ... 'In thee, Dick Turpin has lost his best friend.'"

There are engaging similarities here with Henry Mayhew's telling of a London costermonger's real story of the sadness of a fellow trader on the death of the donkey:

> He was very fond of his donkey and kind to it, and the donkey
> was very fond of him. He thought he wouldn't leave the poor
> creature ... so he dropped all notion of doing business, and with
> help got the poor dead thing into his cart; its head lolloping over
> the end of the cart, and its poor eyes staring at nothing. He thought
> he'd drag it home and bury it somewheres. It wasn't for the value
> he dragged it, for what's a dead donkey worth? There was a few
> persons about him, and they was all quiet and seemed sorry for
> the poor fellow and for his donkey.[22]

While the working animal may have fostered such emotions, the idea of domestic dogs or cats being in any sense even close companions was rare amongst the working class in this period. One of Mayhew's informants did note that "It's the pet dogs as is our best friends,"[23] but this was a dog-collar seller simply thinking of the growing middle-class habit of pet ownership as being his own best commercial "friend," another common working-class usage of our word that we will see again below. However, middle-class attachment to domestic animals, and the ascent of these pets towards what later became their relatively common inclusion within the status of "friend,"[24] did begin to make an impact in various forms of higher-class literature.

Ivan Kreilkamp argues that Britain in the nineteenth century became "pre-eminently associated with long novels and beloved pet animals, two cultural forms which, I argue, developed not just in parallel but in tandem ... the history of English domestic fiction is deeply bound up with that of the domestic animal." He gives as an example of this the "animalistic" aspects of *Wuthering Heights*. Emily Brontë was greatly influenced in its writing, Kreilkamp says, by what her sister's biographer, Elizabeth Gaskell, reported in 1857 as Emily's lack of "regard to any human creature; all her love was reserved for animals," and that the pet-human relationship between Emily and her dog, Keeper, were as "with friends." Kreilkamp emphasizes the literary influence by noting that like "Heathcliff, Keeper is both and alternately 'friend' and 'brute.'"[25] The usage of the language of friends for animals continued to grow in this period, in works such as those of the anti-vivisectionist campaigner, Frances Cobbe's *The Friend of Man and His Friends, the Poets* (1889), a collection of celebrations of dogs in verse, which includes the chapter: "Dogs as Friends and Comforters." In France, the canine pet was eulogized as "that friend of the last hour," or on elaborate memorial stones, as the "faithful and sole companion of my otherwise rootless and desolate life."[26]

The sense of the close connection and friendship between man and working beast, particularly in popular fiction, was not confined to Dick Turpin or to Britain. Jochen Schulte-Sasse mentions the "erotic" nature of the relationship between horse and hero in most of the similarly structured Wild West adventures popular in the United States and Germany late in this period. But he also importantly notes the centrality in such popular literature of the underlying human "solidarity" and a sense of "brotherhood of all,"[27] a characteristic to be further considered below. In fact the most common relationships of all, apart from the romantic, in the male hero story are those with the mates or "pals" who appear only when they are needed to rescue the hero – or for some other collective pursuit.

It is interesting to note that in the cheap fiction read by women, the relationships that seem perhaps to be closest to modern ideal friendship are cross-class relationships. But these also show it is

working-class women who are the sensible ones, not to be "swept away"
by emotion. In such material, as Kate Flint notes:

> If there was to be a working-class heroine with whom the reader
> might identify herself ... she must, in some way or another, possess
> particular, innate qualities. [The *Spectator* noted in 1863] "servants
> – ladies' maids especially – must be on terms of familiarity with
> their mistresses, the depositaries of their most dangerous secrets,
> and the chief sharers of their confidence ... it is not an unusual
> thing to find the lady of title in these stories consulting her maid as
> to her future husband."[28]

As an example, Jane, the maid in *Lady Ashley's Secret* (1889), a cheap
work in a popular novelette series, "tries to advise her mistress to send
away Harold Tremaine, a house-guest whom we already know is an
adventurer."[29] Flint refers specifically to this as "counsel" offered by
the working-class companion – the core perhaps to friendship.

Love, Ritual and the World of Friendship

In an extremely influential article that served to establish some new
directions in the study of women's history in the mid 1970s, Caroll
Smith-Rosenberg pointed to the immense importance of women friends
to each other in nineteenth-century America, and to the ways in which
women turned to and were supported by their women friends through
all the major episodes in their lives – especially marriage, childbirth,
illness and bereavement. The separation of the sexes in Victorian
life, and the distance of men from the rituals of domesticity, Smith-
Rosenberg argued, meant that women provided emotional sustenance
for each other in times of particular stress that their menfolk were
absolutely unable to offer. Tracing the ways in which friendships were
described and articulated through private correspondence, Smith-
Rosenberg stressed the acceptance of women's close friendships within
marriage and the extent to which many women both confided in and
offered physical affection and comfort to each other.[30]

Smith-Rosenberg's was the first of many studies of nineteenth-
century British and American women seeking to trace the importance
of their same-sex friendships both in their personal and in their public
lives. Particular attention has been paid to the importance of close
friendships with other women to women writers. As Pauline Nestor
has shown, female friendships and communities are dealt with very
clearly in some women's novels – especially those of Elizabeth Gaskell

and Charlotte Brontë, for example – both of whom were connected in different ways to other women writers and valued the friendship and the support that this form of community and the new female literary subculture offered.[31] The importance of close friendships to many feminist pioneers has also been explored, often in order to stress the ways that these friendships sustained them through the arduous years of their campaigns. The American feminist leaders Elizabeth Cady Stanton and Susan B. Anthony are perhaps the best known but, as Philippa Levine and others have shown, there were many other close networks of friends who made up the women's movements in both Britain and the United States in addition to the trans-Atlantic feminist circles that have been explored by Sandra Holton.[32] But many other networks of women have also been explored, including those involved in campaigns for the abolition of slavery or for sanitary reform or who worked together to support political parties at parliamentary elections. Some of these networks were international – like the group of British and American women who lived and worked in Italy in the mid nineteenth century. This latter group in particular, consisting as it did of some women who were clearly engaged in sexual relationships with each other as well as others who were not, illustrates one of the issues that has been of great interest to historians – and was of increasing concern to contemporaries especially in the later part of the nineteenth century: the question of precisely what was involved in women's friendships and the extent to which they involved sexual partnerships rather than being simply platonic. Smith-Rosenberg argued that it was necessary to see relationships along a continuum that extended from heterosexual to homosexual ones, but to accept that there was widespread acceptance in the mid nineteenth century of open and sometimes intense expressions of love and affection between women which were not seen as in any way either erotic or morally and sexually questionable.

There were, however, as Martha Vicinus has recently shown, many different forms of erotic friendships amongst nineteenth-century women, some of whom made a determined effort to live together as couples, regardless of the disapproval of family and friends, as was the case with the ladies of Llangollen.[33] Many others were recognized as intimate friends who shared their lives and homes and were accepted by the society in which they lived. There were other forms of erotic friendship too, some involving older women (often married) who loved and cared for younger ones – sometimes in the midst of

their own families, and others involving young women whose devotion to same-sex friends made them look askance at offers of marriage. Some anxiety about the intimacy of women's friendships was
expressed across the century, particularly in terms of its potential to
upset patriarchal and heterosexual norms by preventing girls from
marrying. This anxiety reached a peak at the end of the nineteenth
century with the naming of lesbianism – and the growing sense of
same-sex relationships between women as pathological and "morbid."
The question of how widespread such relationships were is impossible to answer – and is often puzzling because of the expressions of
intense love and deep devotion that were common amongst women
friends for whom close friendships with women were not thought of
as alternatives to heterosexual relationships and indeed coexisted easily
with passionate and loving marriages.

While Smith-Rosenberg and several other feminist historians stressed
that these intense friendships were a particular facet of women's lives,
a number of historians have argued recently that intense same-sex
friendships were quite as important in the lives of men. Picking up
very directly on Smith-Rosenberg's arguments, Anthony Rotundo
suggests that intimate and romantic friendships were evident in the
lives of many middle-class youths across the nineteenth century. Such
friendships, he insists, were important at the particular stage in life
between boyhood and adulthood when late adolescents were beginning to deal with the separation from family and the demands they
would face as adults. In this stage, lasting roughly between 18 and the
mid 20s, many young men felt a need both for the experience and the
expression of close intimacy with a male friend. Sometimes, as with
women, it involved the sharing of beds as well as declarations of love.
This was clearly the case, for example, in the friendship of Wyck
Vanderhoof and James Blake, two young engineers who were deeply
attached to each other. Vanderhoof recorded their last night together,
before the two went their separate ways to follow employment, in his
diary.

> We retired early, but long was the time before our eyes were
> closed in slumber, for this was the last night that we will be to-
> gether for the present, and our hearts were full of that true friend-
> ship which could not find utterance in words, we laid our heads
> upon each other's bosoms and wept, it may be unmanly to weep,
> but I care not, the spirit was touched.[34]

Unlike the women studied by Smith-Rosenberg, young men tended to give up these romantic friendships on marriage, Rotundo points out. The fact that they were often accompanied by a kind of marital language indicated, not that the friendships were sexual but rather that they were a kind of functional equivalent of marriage emotionally – and could not be sustained once marriage had occurred. Many of the men in Rotundo's sample made vows to continue their friendships through marriage, but none maintained the intensity or closeness of this pre-married phase.

This form of intense male friendship has been studied also in relation to nineteenth-century Russia where it seems to have a clearer philosophical foundation than it did in the United States, to have lasted longer and to have been more closely connected with a range of political ideas and beliefs. The best-known description of such a friendship is that provided by Alexander Herzen in his autobiography, *My Past and Thought,* concerning his friendship with Nick Ogarev. The two met when Herzen was 21 and were immediately attracted to each other. Like many other serious young members of the Russian gentry in the 1830s, they were devoted to Schiller – and their shared love of his poetry both cemented their friendship and gave it its particular cast as a close and tender relationship that encompassed every aspect of their lives. They became inseparable, but their friendship also involved a dedication of themselves to humanity and to a struggle against the repressive Russian regime. On one particular day, says Herzen, the two young men went up to the Sparrow Hills outside Moscow and there, "we stood leaning against each other and, suddenly embracing, vowed in sight of all Moscow to sacrifice ourselves to the struggle we had chosen." Their lives after this remained intertwined in complex ways through arrest and imprisonment in Russia, exile abroad – and through the very complex marriages that each man made. It never lost its centrality in their lives. "İ do not know," Herzen wrote later,

> Why the memories of first love are given such precedence over the memories of youthful friendship. The fragrance of first love lies in the act that it forgets the difference of the sexes, that it is passionate friendship. On the other hand, friendship between the young has all the ardour of love and all its character, the same delicate fear of touching on its feeling with a word, the same mistrust of self and absolute devotion, the same agony at separation, and the same jealous desire for exclusive affection.[35]

Despite its particular form and manifestation, this friendship was far from unique. On the contrary, argues Rebecca Friedman, close and often romantic friendship was "part and parcel of growing into manhood" in nineteenth-century Russia, particularly for university students. These friendships were formed against a backdrop of Romanticism and many of them drew, as did that of Herzen and Ogarev, on the ideas of Schiller, who was extremely influential throughout the century. In many cases, close friends were drawn into the family, something facilitated by the large and flexible family forms that obtained in Russia, as Ogarev was into the Herzen family. These close friendships became an integral part, and in the view of some historians, one of the defining characteristics of the radical Russian intelligentsia.[36]

Friedman argues that the interpretations of these same-sex friendships within Russia is narrow and limited by the absence of any clear ways of thinking about same-sex sexual relationships – or of interrogating the close friendships that one has evidence for in terms that might illuminate these questions. In Britain there has been a little more investigation into questions about the border between same-sex friendship and erotic or sexual relationships. Some historians argue that this issue only became important towards the end of the century and that, prior to that, the lack of any clear terminology for or idea about homosexuality meant that it did not necessarily enter into the picture of close same-sex friendships. But this view is not universally accepted. Thus, as Richard Dellamora has recently argued, even the idea of civic friendship was infected with sexual anxiety in Britain as the classical dream that a just society would be one governed by friends continued to be espoused by the Victorians, but much prominent nineteenth-century fiction indicates that even before the end of the nineteenth century, the ideal of male friendship and fraternity was troubled in a number of new ways, especially by "anxieties about the possible conversion of intimacy into sexual anarchy."[37]

Friedman sees Romantic poetry and radical political beliefs as providing the framework for a particularly Russian version of friendship; Stefan-Ludwig Hoffman finds a distinctive framework for German male friendship, one that also stressed ritual and particular forms of social commitment, in Masonic societies. In the second half of the nineteenth century, he argues, Masonic lodges combined an emphasis on the need to promote civility which appealed to many members of the middle class, with the provision of a secret space away from family and home in which close male bonds could be developed and formed. They provided a form of male civic religion surrounded by complex and satisfying rituals that allowed for equality amongst insiders, but complete exclusion of others. Although the form taken was very different from that amongst Russian radicals, for members of Masonic lodges, close and loving friendship also involved higher purpose and a sense of the "brotherhood of humanity."[38]

It is interesting to note here that, while close male friendships have been explored in a number of different countries in the nineteenth century, the discussion of female friendship seems to have been confined largely to Britain and the United States. Women were certainly involved in much of the activity of the nineteenth-century Russian radical movement, and they were engaged in a number of different enterprises and presumably different kinds of relationships. But even when research has been done into their activities – for example the establishment of collectives and cooperatives in the 1860s, designed to enable working women to obtain better pay and conditions and involving both working women and daughters of the gentry – no analysis has been done of the relationships between the women involved.[39]

Just as the treatment of fictional friendship involves heterosexual as well as same-sex ones, so too questions about marital and other friendships between men and women is evident in correspondence and personal writing and has been the subject of interest from historians. In the past few years, there has been a marked re-evaluation of Victorian marriage: once seen as an absolutely patriarchal institution, enshrining the power of a man over every aspect of the life of his wife, many of those who have studied the marriages of prominent middle-class and upper middle-class men and women have stressed the importance of affection, mutual trust and respect and a sense of friendship evident in their lives. John Stuart Mill's protest against the power that marriage gave him over his wife, and his insistence on the mutual respect, dependence and support that would follow from an equal relationship between a husband and wife was revered by many feminists – and also described many Victorian marriages. It was clearly evident in the marriages of those prominent women – like Millicent Fawcett or Josephine Butler – whose husbands aided and supported their public lives and activities, even when they cost them dearly.

Friendship and Neighbourhood Reality

In the nineteenth century, as earlier, most discussion of friendship
was both undertaken by and focused on members of the middle and
upper-middle classes. Yet ideas of the personal and social benefits of
the ideal friendship were known and appealed to the upper reaches
of a working class taken with the growing contemporary doctrines of
independence and "self-improvement." Friendly society praise of
Bacon's ideas of the mutual advantages of true friendship was heard
earlier. Friendly society journals were often professionally edited by
literary men. But they were widely distributed and read at lodge meetings and by the most active of working-class members, who were, in
the main, of the better-off and more educated artisan class. These
members also wrote to the journals. In the Manchester Unity's South
Australian chapter's magazine, one wrote in 1844:

> Friendship, I think, may fairly be considered one of the greatest of
> all earthly blessings, and should be cherished by us as one of the
> first objects of our ambition. We feel pleasure in contemplating the
> sources whence friendship flows, the varied scenes in which it
> delights to exhibit itself, and the benign influence which it exer-
> cises. Virtuous friendship we ought at all times to cultivate, as a
> means of improving our minds by social communion, and of el-
> evating our thoughts above the gratification of mere sensual im-
> pulses.[40]

Later editions of the society's British journal continued this discussion. Coleridge, Addison, Cowper and Wordsworth as well as the
Bible were used to illustrate arguments all of which generally came
back to the issue of improvement. The man with a friend "better ac-
complishes his purposes, carries on his enterprises, or administers his
philanthropies ... enters into the fuller enjoyments of life."[41] An essayist in 1894 drew upon Robert Pollok's religious poem *Course of Time*
(1827), again to provide some echoes of the ideas expressed by Bacon
and other philosophers:

> Friends in my mirth, friends in my misery too,
> Friends given by God in mercy and in love;
> My counsellors, my comforters, and guides,
> My joy in grief, my second bliss in joy;
> Companions of my earnest desires; in doubt
> My oracles, my wings in high pursuit ...
> As birds of social feather helping each.[42]

Although formally apolitical, the ideals of such working-class organizations were not just of individual improvement but of making a better world, clearly an implication to be drawn also from this poem.
The person with a true friend to talk to him not only thus improves
himself through this contact – which, as Bacon argued, reading "good
books of morality" cannot do by itself – but gains, as the Manchester
Unity essayist quoted Keats: "the fellow-feeling which makes one won-
drously kind,"[43] Each member who practised the Society's aims of
"Friendship, Love and Truth," said the Oddfellows' journal editor
George Frederick Pardon, "makes the world so much better ... better
husbands, better fathers, and better members of society." The Aristotelian framework of the components of true friendship can be seen
throughout these discussions: of mutual enjoyment; of being of use to
each other, in that each friend would be improved; but also that they
should be committed to wider virtue. Across Europe, and elsewhere,
the idea amongst reformers that radical improvement in society could
be brought about not so much by political change as by the development of such personal relationships was one which grew in strength as
the century went on.

The "counsel" between friends which provided the key to Bacon's
model of friendship is in isolation of course a form of intimacy very
similar to the individualized apparently middle-class ideal, defined in
Stacey Oliker's description of the modern idea of friendship: "the sharing of one's inner life or mutual self-exploration – not simply familiarity and interdependence."[44] Yet although the advantages of such
relationships were promoted at the higher levels of working-class organizations, these were less clear for many of the less well-off. Instead
of intimacy leading to personal and social benefits, in their view it
could perhaps damage hopes for improvement.

The historical discussions of friendship that have taken place regarding the nineteenth-century working class have been dominated
by an imagery of close bonds between women in poor communities.
These were the links of reciprocal sharing or "survival networks," in
which families could often only struggle through because of the existence, as Ellen Ross puts it, of "ties of friendship and mutual aid" with
others in the area.[45] In Antwerp in the nineteenth century, Catharina
Lis finds that the working class:

> continued strenuously to maintain close relations with neighbours
> and friends to solve their problems ... poor people turned to their
> neighbours when they were ill; proletarian families shared their

food with hungry friends ... Antwerp samples show how essential
were the ties of kinship and friendship for this group.[46]

Alain Faure gives a similar general picture of working-class Paris.[47] As
John Burnett notes, British descriptions of this period tend to stress
"the sense of local community in working-class districts and the importance of an informal network of support composed of relatives, friends
and neighbours."[48] Yet the usage of the term "friends" by historians
here needs careful delineation.

As Elizabeth Roberts points out, in their own descriptions of their
relationships in English working-class communities in the late nineteenth and early twentieth centuries, "women talk of friendly, helpful
or good neighbours, but they rarely talk simply of friends."[49] This
seems to suggest that for these women simple familiarity and interdependence, as Oliker put it, were insufficient to make a "friend." The
concept of friendliness, which seems to cover this lesser form used in
regard to neighbours, is quite different from that of modern friendship, although Lis and other historians do not clearly make this
distinction.

In the 1880s, Beatrice Webb, who constantly analysed the intimacies, the pleasures and the pain involved in her own close relationships, reported that poorer male London workers made a point of
"not mixing up with anyone – women get thick together and then
there's always a row."[50] Getting "thick together" was something not to
be encouraged. Yet of course in middle-class terms, this could be another way of describing the ideal friendship. Similar comments were
made by many working-class men and women: "There's nothing wrong
in being sociable, but after that I've finished; it always leads to trouble.
Certainly not coming into your house."[51] Faure also suggests that in
Paris, while "mutual aid" was strong, true closeness was limited by an
"unspoken rule" not to meddle in each other's affairs.

Public, not private, sociability was the norm in the poorer urban
areas in which houses "were small, their furnishings sparse and their
comfort minimal," all of which "encouraged their women to spend
whatever time they could on the street."[52] Formal rituals of invited
intimacy were neither possible nor desired in these conditions. As
Roberts notes, instead of needing to make a special effort to "keep in
touch":

> you bumped into them in the street, or outside the local shops ... It
> was assumed that informal casual contacts would be frequent, as

indeed they usually were ... The working-class habit of public sociability, usually in the form of conversations in the street, was a
remnant, an echo, of a social custom which had once been widespread throughout all ranks of society.[53]

But London woman Grace Beales clearly described her childhood
perception of who could and could not be "friends," and the distinction between this and friendliness or similar solidarity. Mrs Beales
noted that:

> if a woman was ill – she had – things called neighbours, like I told
> you, they would come in and take the children away, they would
> attend to the woman – because everybody did it for everybody
> else. The spirit of comradeship in those days was marvellous.

She was then asked: "'Did your mother have any friends of her own
that used to come around?' 'No,' she replied, 'because she had two
sisters living just round the corner and that was – they were who she
made the friends you see.'"[54]

Neighbours were comrades, but not friends. Examples of wariness
towards, and the walling off of, individual intimacy outside the
family can be found throughout the sketchy evidence that exists of
nineteenth-century and early twentieth-century poorer neighbourhood
relationships. Robert Roberts notes the views of his neighbours in
his autobiographical work on the Edwardian "classic slum" in
Manchester:

> The burgeoning of goodwill between any pair of families on the
> same socio-economic level – [was] an activity, condemned by the
> respectable, known as "neighbouring." For weeks together one
> would notice the members of two households constantly in and
> out of each other's home, often bearing small gifts. This intimacy,
> watching cynics knew, was far too fervid to last. And sure enough,
> one Saturday night shrieks, screams, scuffles and breaking glass
> would herald the end of another lovely friendship. Confidences
> foolishly bestowed were now for bruiting loud on the common
> air, much to the neighbourhood's pleasure.[55]

Such closeness clearly had a perception of danger for the poor. One
could perhaps not afford to invest such resources, with the risk of
failure, into a single, ideal, friendship. Although a more rural example, Anna Bravo found similar circumstances and views in her study
of women in Piedmont in Italy, born between the 1880s and World
War I. Their memories of relationships in their community show that

while there also existed high levels of mutual aid and support, and of "solidarity" between families, this was "a wider solidarity to which other possibilities of relationships were subordinated ... It was a solidarity based on rigid and implicit rules, which did not give way to special friendship." The harsh conditions in the area meant that "closeness – and not only for women – was apparently undifferentiated, inspired by utility and necessity, and scarcely personalized." The concept here of "undifferentiated" or "scarcely personalized" closeness is an interesting one in terms of friendship – it is of course a collective "friendship," possibly a comradeship as described by Grace Beales. In regard to the terminology used by these women, it seems it was only during adolescence that females in Bravo's study could conceive hesitatingly that they had, as one put it, perhaps "I don't know, friends."[56]

Social investigator and journalist Henry Mayhew's massive *London Labour and the London Poor*, published first in 1851, provides an extensive sample of the voices of the urban poor, including how they used "friend." It is clear that the word for them had a similar vagueness and breadth of meaning to the eighteenth-century popular usage described in Chapter 5. The idea of the "friend" as supporter or patron is still obvious: "the master butcher lent me 10*s.* to start in the line. He was the best friend I ever had";

> A few women street-sellers, however, do attend the Sunday service of the Church of England. One lace-seller told me that she did so because it obliged Mrs. — , who was the best friend and customer she had, and who always looked from her pew in the gallery to see who were on the poor seats.

A related use can be seen in the assertion by the seller of printed sensational stories and tracts that "things hasn't been so good this last year as the year before. But the Pope, God bless him! He's been the best friend I've had since Rush [an executed murderer], but Rush licked his Holiness."[57] In this last sense best friend simply meant the cause of increased sales, as we saw earlier. Mayhew then interprets (in the brackets) a further common usage by a poor worker during an interview: "I lost my parents and friends (relatives) when I were young." But particularly interesting is the use of the term in this way in a statement by a homeless cabinet-maker:

> I had no friends (my brothers are both out of the country) and no home. I was sleeping about anywhere I could. I used to go and sit at the coffee-houses where I knew my mates were in the habit of

going, and they would give me a bit of something to eat, and
make a collection to pay for a bed for me. At last this even began
to fail me, my mates could do no more for me.[58]

Friends here referred to family, but not to "mates." These were mates
who gathered together at a particular eating-house, and would provide some support to the unfortunate companion. These distinctions
we will touch on again below. Although "friend" is used occasionally
by Mayhew's informants to mean a fairly transitory acquaintance, or
one with whom one travelled, it is in the majority of cases used by the
poor to mean either family or ally/supporter or patron.

Yet ideas of the ideal friend being one in whom one invested emotion and confided one's deepest thoughts were not unknown to the
poor of course. Mayhew recounts the description of a story sold and
told in the street by a street "patterer," which suggested a man might
have no "real friend in the world but his wife, to whom he can communicate his private thoughts, and in return receive consolation."[59]
The acceptance of a wife as the "real friend" is telling, while linking
the concept again predominantly to family.

In a more metaphysical sense the idea of the ideal friend can be
seen in the advice by the Bishop of Durham to a number of charitable
and religious workers involved with visits to the poor in London in
1909. The Bishop's address contained a message for these workers to
spread to those they visited. They should emphasize that "The Lord
becomes the Friend, to whom you could say what you could not to
any other, even the nearest and dearest; He knows all about you, and
yet *loves* you."[60] To those of the working class hearing this message,
the implication may have been that this was the ultimate, ideal, friendship. But for them it may have been also that Jesus was unusual in this
love, which existed *despite* his knowing all about you and your business – again very different to the dangers inherent in the "confidences
foolishly bestowed" upon and "intimacy too fervid to last" with mere
neighbours. Other biblewomen also wrote of how women would tell
of their love for the hymn: "I've found a Friend, Oh, such a Friend,"
emphasizing the point made by the Bishop of Durham.[61] In a sense,
this religious message emphasized an attitude that ideal friendship
was not of "their" real, small, world. Other texts, as we saw earlier, in
some ways did the same.

This sense that friendship was not an integral part of their world
was clearly articulated in the approach to daily life of many women.

Margaret Loane, one of the charitable visitors to the poor, wrote of attitudes in working-class areas of London

> "Not to let any one know your business," is at once a duty, a joy, a burden, an absorbing occupation, and a consolation. [But] It is often practiced more strictly with regard to near neighbours than with regard to educated visitors ... [to them] men and women alike will reveal many things which they fondly hope are not even dimly suspected by the ... neighbours[62]

Other nurses and similar visitors often commented upon precisely the same welcome and intimacy of conversation. The intimate cross-class friendship, or that with the outside visitor, was not feared, although the neighbourhood one may be. Some fear of local intimacy was the trouble it might cause though jealousies or gossip within the broader neighbourhood but some of the wariness concerned worries about the breaking of group bonds, by playing favourites in friendship and, by doing so, losing the breadth of support from the entire neighbourhood.

This ability to make friends with the poor certainly did not only apply to religious or health visitors, or even only to women, but also perhaps to even slightly more educated workers who had cause to come into the neighbourhood. Melanie Tebbutt quotes oral history again from women in the north of England remembering their child-hood, who said: "The insurance man called once a week, he was your mother's best friend ... The same was often true of the rent collector and the club man." Such a visitor, Tebbutt says, "whose own liveli-hood depended on not breaking the intimate confidences which were frequently shared with him, was allowed across the threshold in ways that neighbours frequently were not," again suggesting an acceptance of male–female friendships.[63]

An insurance society collector remembered that his subscribers "treated you as friends when you got to know them properly."[64] Rob-ert Roberts repeats this view almost exactly regarding such visitors: "somewhat better educated than his members, he was usually wel-comed in homes as a friend."[65] It was said to the 1872 British Parlia-mentary Select Committee on Friendly Societies that in Liverpool, the society collector "is considered more as one of their own family ... They apprise him and he advises them in all matters even of family disputes of all sorts."[66]

This, and particularly Grace Beales' comment earlier recognizing that her aunts were not already to be called her mother's friends, as in older usage, but were the "ones she made the friends," suggests the important change by the end of the century from the earlier use of the word "friend" implicitly to describe family to a newer meaning in which the term described one who was *like* family. This is a theme that is important in a number of other ways in the use of the word in this period. Importantly also, the evidence of their usage clearly shows that the term "friendly," as used in relation to neighbours generally, starts to replace the common use of "friend" to mean an ally or supporter.

Could All Be Friends?

As in other circumstances, in a poorer neighbourhood the key to a true friendship was its parallel to the kin relationship. This was not just a use of the term to refer to family, but a descriptive inclusion into the family. One poor woman in Bow, for example, said of a middle-class charitable visitor to her home in 1892, "I have cause to love her; she has been a good friend to me ... she has filled a gap in my life that I never expected would again be filled after my dear mother's death."[67] The concept of a "good friend" was described by Mrs Armstrong from Barrow as being in the "olden days" (late nineteenth and early twentieth centuries), closer to "sisterly love and more motherly love" than in more modern times.[68]

Cross-class friendships or intimacies of course had links to the "befriending" movements, which specifically sought to use friendship, and linked concepts of "sisterhood" or "brotherhood," as a way of reducing class conflict in this period. But these were only one aspect of the powerful stream in this period of ideas of improving the world through bringing people together in the "spirit of friendship."

We have been discussing more particularly the attitudes towards the idea of friendship amongst the poor, particularly poor women. For the better-off male worker, exposure to any deeply theoretical discussion of the nature of friendship was most likely to be through either the friendly society journal or a lecture at the lodge (if he attended). Again, the concept of friends within a "family" comes through. From the Manchester Unity comes the recommendation:

> Keeping in view the philanthropic principles by which we hail
> and style each other as brothers, regarding ourselves as one family,
> whose actions are founded on pure principles, that we may be
> social, steady, consistent, and humane. The duties of Oddfellowship

will always teach you to stretch out your hand to a brother in distress; to offer up your warmest petitions for his welfare; to assist him with your best counsel and advice, and to betray no confidence he may repose in you. "Golden Age of Harmony/Thou shalt from the Heaven descend/Earth shall rise and welcome thee/ Man to man be angel-friend" – Harris.[69]

The *angel-friends* were brothers to each other here.

Other influences were also clear in the friendly societies. This sermon at a Guernsey lodge by the local pastor was given prominence:

> [The Society] pledges you each one to personal religion; for without this you cannot cultivate the virtues of Friendship, Love and Truth. You must first feel in your own souls that God is your truest Friend; that He loves you; that He is your fast and faithful God, before you can entertain these same feelings towards your fellow-creatures ... Go wherever you may meet a fellow man; extend to him the hand of brotherhood and of fellowship; tell him that you are his friend and that you ask his friendship.[70]

In this way, peace and harmony were to be brought into the world.

Much the same message, and again, that of improvement, was given in the poem printed often in the South Australian *Odd Fellows Magazine*.

> Our laws are good, our precepts truly pure
> Hope is our beacon, our success is sure;
> Friendship we cherish, and our minds improve
> Truth is our motto, and our bond is love;
> Well may the *world* imagine we are odd
> We love our neighbour and we love our God.[71]

These ideas had much in common with other movements of the period designed to both spread friendship and change the world.

"Proletarians of all countries, unite, we shall never forget that the workmen of all countries are our friends and the despots of all countries our enemies." This declaration by delegates of the German Democratic Socialist Party in 1870, at the beginning of the Franco-Prussian War, sought to reject the national boundaries and conflicts that kept apart the workers of the world and to emphasize the common interests and natural friendship. Such concepts and rhetoric were central to the socialist movement, particularly in its Marxist form, as it developed through the century. The German workers claimed they were drawing here directly upon the language of the International

Working Men's Association (the "First International"), founded in 1864. Yet the appeal by Karl Marx in his inaugural address to the International was to "the bond of brotherhood which ought to exist between workers of different countries." The apparently easy substitution by the German delegates of "friendship" for "brotherhood" illustrates the vagueness in how the term was used in socialist thought throughout the century. The Democratic Socialists continued: "We are happy to grasp the fraternal hand stretched out to us by the workmen of France," and Marx wrote admiringly of the stand of the workers, adding that the "English working class stretch the hand of fellowship to the French and German working people." A collective relationship between workers is invoked here variously as friendship, fellowship, fraternalism or brotherhood, and these terms continue to have an interchangability in nearly all socialist language of the period, although friendship is perhaps the least used.

By the end of the nineteenth century the socialist intellectual "tradition," as Howe notes, had became one of concern with "changing institutions and power relationships."[72] Friendship, in its connection with socialism, also tended later to be drained of some meaning through its statist and propaganda usage such as in the "friendship organization" fronts by the USSR. Yet in the earliest period of socialist thought it meant more. There was a much clearer focus upon the type of society to be achieved, and particularly the personal relationships that would exist within it. John Wilson describes the common ultimate "end" of socialism (despite differences over the means of achievement) as the creation of "a society in which friendship was the dominant social value," meaning by this a universal willingness to act unselfishly and with the interests of others at heart, as if they were one's friends. These were the social characteristics variously thought of and described by socialists as brotherhood, fellowship or friendship in this period. There is clearly a vagueness, as Wilson admits, in applying friendship as a catch-all term for what was desired. But it is also clear that, for most, to call their ideal society a "society of friends" would have described it as well as any of the other words they commonly used.[73]

For Marxists, such a society and relationships could be achieved as a result of revolution and the transformation of economic structures. For other socialists in the nineteenth century, the adoption of friendship as a way of living was the way to change society. Christian socialism was one of the strands of ethical socialism which were important in both the middle and later years of the century in Britain, and which saw most hope for change in the direct establishment of friendly bonds between classes. Paul Daffyd Jones says of the Christian socialists that they did not see change occurring through political or legislative reform, but only through "'free, unreserved, honest' exchanges between different classes ... the group had a singular, and quite touching, confidence in the capacity of such conversations to cultivate a sense of 'brotherhood' and common purpose among Englishmen."[74] This meant friendship, as defined by one of the group's members (the author Charles Kingsley), in his description of a meeting with a man not of his class, while watching hummingbirds:

> "I turned to share the joy," as Wordsworth says, and next to me stood a huge, brawny coal-heaver, in his shovel hat, and white stockings and high-lows, gazing at the humming-birds as earnestly as myself. As I turned he turned, and I saw a bright manly face, with a broad, soot-grimed forehead, from under which a pair of keen flashing eyes gleamed wondering, smiling sympathy into mine. In that moment we felt ourselves friends. If we had been Frenchmen, we should, I suppose, have rushed into each others' arms and "fraternized" on the spot. As we were a pair of dumb, awkward Englishmen, we only gazed half a minute, staring into each other's eyes, with a delightful feeling of understanding each other ... I never felt more thoroughly than at that minute that all men were *brothers*; that fraternity and equality were not mere political doctrines, but blessed God! ordained facts.[75]

The leader of Christian Socialism, Frederick Maurice, was, as, Seth Koven notes, the "rehabilitator" of the idea of brotherhood in Victorian England. He constructed his ideals, says Koven, "out of the fact of the fatherhood of God, which, he insisted, necessarily implied the brotherhood of mankind," drawing perhaps upon the concepts of *caritas* discussed in earlier chapters.[76]

The Fellowship of the New Life, which took up the cause of ethical socialism in the 1880s, and which originally included many of the later founding members of the Fabian Society, took a similar line:

> Heaven is fellowship, and hell the absence of fellowship ... What we demand now, as the most vital principle of human deliverance, is Fellowship – the passion of kinship in relation to the loftiest and the lowliest concerns of our actual life here and now on earth, where we must find our heaven – or hell.[77]

Kinship – as in brotherhood or sisterhood – was used here to describe the desired relationship between all. In Europe and elsewhere what can be termed a "cult of fraternity" developed in the second half of the nineteenth century. As Koven says of Britain, there was a "proliferation" of clubs claiming some use of brotherly friendship, and

> what, for want of a more felicitous phrase, we might call "fraternalism" – was a mongrel ideology forged out of disparate elements. Brotherhood was conceptually unstable, riddled with tensions between inclusive universalism and its seemingly inescapable dependence upon various forms of exclusion. Not surprisingly, it also meant different things to different people. The rituals of comradeship among members of an Oxford literary society differed markedly from the "brotherly" practices of trade unionists. This did not, however, make it any less attractive to reformers in the 1880s and '90s. They eagerly embraced fraternal rhetoric as an alternative to the language of class division in establishing a wide array of social, educational, cultural, and religious institutions for the London poor, none more important than Oxford House and Toynbee Hall, the first university settlements in East London.[78]

The direct inclusion of friendship in the fraternal rhetoric can be seen no better than in the settlement movement. The aims of these urban missions were summarized in 1898 by Samuel Barnett, founder of Toynbee Hall: "Its classes, its social schemes, are not so true a test of its success as its effect in establishing friendship between man and man." The settlement had, he continued, "tended to mitigate class suspicion" because "individual friendships have been formed, along which currents of good feeling run from class to class ... because they are friends their eyes have been opened to see the good in their friend's friends."[79] This aim is what Carolyn Betensky calls the upper- and middle-class philanthropic "dream of a healing and problem-solving friendship across the classes."[80] However, these political and religious aims of friendship and doing-good, did cause Thomas Wright, a prolific contemporary writer on the lives of the poor, to comment:

> The working man is certainly a man of many friends and protectors – that is, if he believes the self-glorifying and interested assertions of a number of individuals who dub themselves "friends of the people," "the working man's friend," and so forth. But if the working man does not choose to take these assertions for granted, but, on the contrary, prefers to inquire how far they are true, and

what are the motives for making them, it is much to be feared that
he will often have occasion to exclaim, "save me from my friends!"[81]

Although not always with the same explicitly political motives, innumerable clubs, as mentioned earlier, sprang up across Europe and the
United States from the middle of the century that had at their heart
similar ideas. "'Moral improvement,' *Bildung, obrazovanie,* and
émulation," says Hoffman, "were the terms used in different countries
to express the political and moral objectives of sociability. Self-improvement, derived from social interaction, was intended to generate
and strengthen a belief in civic virtue and, more generally, humanity." Specifics were spelled out by the speaker at a gymnastics association meeting in Germany in 1865:

> Associations constitute a preparatory school for civic sense. They
> allow the most beautiful civic virtues to blossom: self-control, manly
> discipline and modesty, friendship and devotion. In sociability the
> narrowly drawn boundaries of society are blurred: men become
> men and begin to see others as men.[82]

The very male focus of such movements was of course common
throughout.

But what did friendship mean in this context, particularly for the
working class? It was used by many of the leaders of these movements
simply intertwined with ideas of kinship, brotherhood, or fellowship,
which made it, as Koven says, a "mongrel" of a concept. Yet in its
vagueness these connections also made friendship essentially "collective" in its usage, which in many ways suited a working-class understanding, as did the development of alternative words such as "brother"
to describe their relationship of solidarity. The formal discussion at
the higher levels of the friendly societies of friendship as intimacy and
with philosophical purpose did not necessarily relate to how the ordinary member felt about the benefits of society membership. Perhaps
they saw these instead, as Timothy Alborn suggests, on a more practical level: "As in any other club, membership in a friendly society
offered a young man friendship insurance, which included amongst
its benefits a familiar face at the pub or a good turnout at a member's
funeral."[83] This idea of friendship is an important one for the working
class, where the sites of sociability, at least for those of the same social
standing, did not generally extend into the home, and therefore
occurred in only group situations. Scott Haine, in his work on
nineteenth-century Paris, describes the similar situation of "the

pervasiveness of the concept of the café friend" particularly among the city's male working class. The "café friend" was one with whom one socialized at a venue away from home but with whom one only had a "casual closeness." One unemployed mason said he did not "know" those with whom he associated at the café, he only drank with them. Of a patron who had perhaps one hundred "parties" with others at the café, it was said: "he had hardly any comrades; he associated with habitués, I could not indicate to you anyone with whom he had intimate relations." Of another, it was said: "Yes, sir, I recognize that this is one of my friends, but I know him only as a café friend."[84]

Such "café friends" or, more particularly, "pub friends" are also seen in the English evidence. Grace Beales described where her parents met those with whom they socialized (but who were not as much "friends" as her mother's two sisters): "Well usual place, in the pub." Asked if they were ever invited into the home, she replied: "No. No."[85] A woman born in the 1890s remembers of her neighbours that while "My mother didn't mix up with them," as in the earlier meaning of getting "thick together," on "Monday they seemed to go out and have a drink together." They transferred any socializing or "casual closeness" to the public place of the pub. This concept of sociability, such as with Mayhew's informant having no "friends" but only "mates," has been theorized by Graham Allan who comments on working-class

> hesitancy about using the label "friendship" ... The term "mate" is often used in friendship talk but it is not altogether synonymous with "friend" ... Whereas "friend" celebrates a specific relationship over and above any specific contexts, the idea of "mate" is often linked more fully with a given context. Certainly, this is an important aspect in much working-class use of the term. Mates are, in other words, people who are seen in particular places, be these pubs, work, social clubs, or whatever, with interaction predominantly being restricted to that setting.[86]

These restrictions on relationships, what Ross McKibbin has described as the "wary mutuality" and "confinement of 'friendship' to kin," within working-class neighbourhoods continued long past the end of the century and even beyond World War I.[87]

Empire, Race and Friendship

The question of how to think about friendship across nineteenth-century racial and ethnic divisions and within the framework of imperialism is one that has recently become a matter of considerable interest. The subject of friendship is a recent addition to a growing body of scholarship concerned with imperial relationships, but which until now has tended to focus primarily on the issue of cross-racial sexual relationships and the anxieties about and regulation of inter-marriage and miscegenation in different colonial contexts. The meta-phorical use of the language of friendship has also featured in some post-colonial scholarship. Thus Catherine Hall has recently analysed the religious and imperial outlook that underlay the abolitionist ac-tivities of groups calling themselves the "Friends of the Negro" – and shown also how this form of friendship faltered in the face of the very difficult interpersonal relationships between white abolitionists and freed slaves that developed in Jamaica.[88] By contrast, analyses of ac-tual friendships within a colonial context have offered some new ways of thinking about imperial relationships. Thus while there is now broad agreement about the extent to which interracial sexual relationships embodied an exercise of imperial power over indigenous people (usu-ally women), in some recent analyses, same-sex friendships have been seen as allowing for or illustrating strong anti-colonial sentiments in both metropolitan and colonial locations.

There is no general agreement about the nature of imperial friend-ship. On the contrary, some historians dispute the very possibility of cross-racial friendships within empire. This point has been made strongly by feminist scholars exploring the place of women within the empire, many of whom have stressed the extent to which European feminists have endorsed the imperial values of their own societies and thus tended to infantilize other women and to deny them the possibil-ity of independence or adult status. This was the case even with women of exceptional intelligence seeking tertiary education in England. Antoinette Burton, for example, has stressed the absence of close friend-ship or any form of "sisterly solidarity" in the relationships developed by Panditai Ramabai, a Marathi educator and social reformer, who came to England in the 1880s seeking a medical education. Ramabai converted to Christianity while in England. But she was a strong and independent-minded woman – and her relationships with the religious women who had initially supported her could not withstand the strain when this independence became evident in her articulation of reli-gious doubts. On the contrary, it became clear that they had been driven far more by missionary zeal than by any more direct or per-sonal concern about her and her individual life and needs.[89]

A slightly different picture of friendship between Indians and British rulers, albeit one that ultimately also points to the difficulties and even impossibility of these relationships, is offered by Clive Dewey in his recent book, *Anglo-Indian Attitudes*.[90] Dewey suggests that the dominant attitudes of British rulers towards Indians since the first days of the Raj can be characterized in terms of two contrasting approaches: "uplift" and "friendship." "Uplift" essentially centred on the idea of British colonial rule as a civilizing mission that would "raise" Indians from what was seen as ignorance, poverty and heathenism into something more akin to European Christian society. It involved a strong sense both of distance and of hierarchy. "Friendship" entailed rather an idea that the most effective means by which the British could govern India was through the establishment of close personal relationships. Dewey suggests that there were pendulum swings from one to the other across the two centuries of British rule.[91] But his concern is particularly to explore the ways in which each of these approaches characterized the work and the beliefs of two senior civil servants, Frank Brayne and Sir Malcolm Darling, in the early twentieth century. Brayne was an Evangelical Christian with a strong sense of the importance of "uplift." By contrast, Darling believed that it was through friendship and understanding of Indian life and customs that British rule was possible. Darling began working as an Assistant Commissioner in the Punjab in 1904 and held many senior posts, including the vice chancellorship of Punjab University and the chairmanship of the Punjab Land Committee before he retired from India in 1940. He disliked the values, attitudes and way of life of most of his fellow countrymen in India – and was in turn ostracized because of his own sympathies for Indian nationalism. Darling was a close friend of E. M. Forster and both became friendly with a number of Indians, and particularly with Tukoji Rao Pur III, the young ruler of the small Maratha state of Dewas Senior. Dewey suggests that this was an intense and close friendship that extended to include the wives of both Darling and Tukoji and some of Darling's English friends who formed a circle around him. The friendship lasted for nearly 20 years – but it came to an unhappy end in the course of the 1930s. Darling finally realized that Tukoji was both able and prepared to deceive and lie to him – as he did to others. In Dewey's view, Darling's hope that racial harmony could be established through personal relations was wrecked through the difference evident between British and Indian ideas of friendship.

An Englishman's friends were the congenial companions of his
leisure hours. If they asked him for help, he had a host of
countervailing considerations to take into account: loyalty to the
institutions of which he was a member; respect for abstract moral
principles. Englishmen were "so damned impartial"; they hesitated
to promote a subordinate *because* he was a friend. Indians found
such scruples incomprehensible; a man had a sacred obligation to
help his friends to the best of his ability. The more incompetent
the subordinate, the more he needed help and the more meritori-
ous the assistance ... Friendship, in India, was an unconditional
alliance against all-comers.[92]

An entirely different approach to this question has been taken recently by Leela Gandhi.[93] Focusing her attention on London, Gandhi
looks at the ways in which a range of late nineteenth-century radicals
and socialists combined a strongly anti-imperial stance and a very clear
critique of imperialism with other forms of radical and unconventional
behaviour – including vegetarianism and homosexuality. In many
cases, Gandhi argues, socialists and sexual and social radicals went
out of their way to be hospitable and to extend a hand of friendship
to Indians visiting or living in London. Thus, she points out, Ma-
hatma Gandhi not only found acceptable and inexpensive food in a
London vegetarian restaurant called The Porridge Bowl, but he also
found there literature such as Henry Salt's *Plea for Vegetarianism*, which
he claimed made him a vegetarian (rather than the insistence of his
mother) – and gave him an entry point to the various vegetarian societies through which he made close friends. On his return to India,
Gandhi began to write a "Guide to London," in which he commended
the hospitality and friendliness of vegetarians to others who faced the
loneliness and alienation that he had experienced in his first days
there. The vegetarian movement, in Gandhi's view, offered not only
the possibility of personal friendliness, but also of political support.
Thus in 1894, he issued a public letter to Indians in London recom-
mending collaboration with vegetarians because "the vegetarian movement will aid India politically ... inasmuch as the English vegetarians
... more readily sympathise with the Indian aspirations (that is my personal experience)."[94]

   In her intensive exploration of the ways in which British radicals of
many different kinds became closely involved with Indian political
aspirations and established friendships with Indians, Leela Ghandi
also points to the attraction to some Westerners of Indian religious

beliefs and practices and to the role which some Westerners have played in the development of Indian religious thought. The important philosopher, nationalist and religious leader Sri Aurobinda had as one of his closest allies and collaborators a Paris bohemian of Egyptian Jewish origin, Mirra Alfassa. The two met in 1914 when Alfassa visited Pondicherry in India with her husband, Paul Richard. Alfassa and Sri Aurobinda felt an immediate affinity which led to a lifelong spiritual and practical collaboration: they produced a journal together and then worked together in the devotional Ashram community that Sri Aurobinda established in Pondicherry of which Mirra Alfassa was the Mother. Their spiritual affinity had as its counterpart a shared commitment also to Indian independence.[95]

The close connection between radical and oppositional political beliefs and the establishment of cross-racial and imperial friendships that underlies Leela Gandhi's study serves, as she points out, to raise fundamental questions about the ways in which friendship links with patriotism or with the making of national communities. It is not the Aristotelian idea of *philia* that is important here, she argues, but rather an alternative tradition of friendship harking back to Epicurean traditions that accorded an important place to an ethical ideal in which friendship was offered to strangers or foreigners. By the late nineteenth and early twentieth centuries, this ideal of friendship came quite explicitly into conflict with patriotism and loyalty to the state, and indeed sometimes became the basis of a direct critique of state authority. Thus the novelist E. M. Forster, who – in the early years of the twentieth century – was so heavily preoccupied with the question of whether and how it was possible for friendship to exist between Indians and the English, ultimately insisted that friendship was above loyalty to nation, state or political creed. In the years leading up to World War II, and at a time when he felt acutely disillusioned by the political values and behaviour of his contemporaries, Forster used the idea of friendship as a way to differentiate between real feeling and the kinds of unreal demands required by the modern state. "I hate the idea of causes," he wrote in his essay *Two Cheers for Democracy*:

> and if I had to choose between betraying my country and betraying my friend I hope I should have the guts to betray my country ... Love and loyalty to an individual can run counter to the claims of the State. When they do – down with the State say I, which means the State would down me.[96]

The Social Sciences and Friendship

While in earlier centuries, it was philosophy that provided the most significant general discussion of questions about the nature, meaning and significance of friendship, this ceased to be the case in the course of the nineteenth century. While literature might be seen to have taken this place in the first half of the century, towards its end it was the emerging social sciences that came to provide both the frameworks and the tools for analysing social relationships. The rapidity of economic and social change that had accompanied industrialization and urbanization brought to the fore not only new social forms, but also new questions about the nature of society and about how individuals interacted with each other and with the ever-changing external world. The social sciences were themselves partly a response to this rapid change. They were thus both a product of modernity and a series of new disciplines that attempted to define and explain what it was.

The question of friendship was sometimes implicit rather than explicit in much of the discussion of society produced within the social sciences, which tended to focus on broad questions about the nature of social ties and relationships rather than to interrogate specific forms of intimacy. Nonetheless, several social theorists made clear their sense of the impact of capitalism and of urbanization on the possibilities for or the difficulties involved in establishing friendships in the modern world. All of them were shaped by the analysis of capitalist modernity provided by Karl Marx. Within this broad framework, it is not Marx's analysis of class that is central, but rather his demonstration of the ways in which capitalism involved the destruction of folkways and tradition, the loss of agency in the face of economic imperatives, the illusion that unbounded growth makes everything possible when in reality the means of self-realization are being stripped away, and the change in the quality of life when "human" relations are subsumed by "economic" relations.

For the most part, the leading late nineteenth-century sociologists Weber, Ferdinand Tönnies and Emile Durkheim followed Marx in offering a very pessimistic reading of the possibility of friendship in the modern world. The socially fragmenting effects of rapid change in the course of which all existing relationships are swept away destroyed, in their view, the certainties on which friendly relations depended. On the whole, both Weber and Tönnies suggested that the possibilities for and importance of friendship declined with industrialization and urbanization. The social environments in which people lived were increasingly diverse and, as friendships are more likely to form between people who are similar to each other, these new environments would be less conducive to friendship formation. New forms of bureaucracy and organization that hired people because of their qualifications for specific jobs rather than as a result of their interpersonal connections also seemed to diminish the reach of friendship.

The possibilities of friendship within an urban environment were a matter of great interest and some dispute between social scientists. For Tönnies, the individualism of urban society, and the dominance of social relationships and collectives in which people were bound only by negotiation and calculation, destroyed the possibility of community and therefore of friendship. In opposition to Tönnies, Durkheim saw that there were possibilities for an alternative moral order to be fostered in the city. The division of labour, he argued, and the new forms of occupational association characteristic of modern industrialism would generate new integrating norms. The interdependence of occupational sectors in which each "specialist" element had to cooperate with others for the whole to prosper, just as the separate elements of an organism had to function together for it to survive, would bring with it new forms of association. But while Durkheim depicted a world in which there was more dependence upon society, and in which institutions and local areas and conditions could also provide a basis for friendship, his conception of anomie with its postulation of the erosion of integration between individuals posed another challenge to friendship.

While the possibilities of friendship within a new and modern society were being questioned by some social scientists, other questions were raised by the emergence of new forms of psychology and especially by psychoanalysis. Sigmund Freud is particularly significant here. This is despite the fact that Freud had little to say about friendship in any direct way. His main focus was on the family and its absolute centrality to the emergence and development of the individual. For Freud, the family was where the inevitable frustration of psychosexual rivalry with parents and to a lesser degree with siblings teaches us the limits of self, the nature of the forbidden and ultimately also the imperative of civilization. Having learned to live with others, Freud insists, we must accept that the price of civilization is always a degree of unhappiness: our deepest wishes cannot (must not) be satisfied lest the social order on which we depend be destroyed.

Preoccupied with the rivalries of primary relationships, Freud had little interest in friendship – it is mentioned only three times in his work. For him, ambition (for sexual possession, or to overthrow the patriarch) is always in tension with regard for others; friendship is a compromised and ambivalent relationship like any other, and as dependent on hypocrisy.[97] That his own theoretical breakthroughs emerged from passionate attachments to and communion with friends (for example, Wilhelm Fliess) and disciples (for example, Carl Jung) was evident. But his own ambivalence was strikingly expressed in his letters: on the one hand "nothing can take the place of a friend; it is a need which corresponds to something in me, perhaps something feminine," but on the other (after a rupture that was common in his friendships), "I no longer have any need to uncover my personality completely ... a part of homosexual libido has been withdrawn and made use of to enlarge my own ego."[98] On this reading, friendship is complex, ambivalent, marked by hypocrisy, instrumental in its purposes and an impediment to self-sufficiency. And yet, while Freud himself was ambivalent about friendship, psychoanalysis and the concern that it brought to probe the emotions and to explore the unconscious underlay a growing sense of the depth, importance and intimacy of friendship.

Intimacy, Sexuality and New Ideals of Friendship

It is more than a little ironic that, at the very time that social scientists of many different kinds were bemoaning the impossibility of friendship in the modern world, some of their contemporaries were insisting that it was the most important of all relationships and raising its value to new heights. E. M. Forster was one of these, and his insistence that friendship had an importance above any political or religious cause points not only to a very high evaluation of the significance of friendship, but also to new sense of it meaning. His understanding of friendship was not unique. On the contrary, he was reflecting here ideas that were quite widespread amongst a number of his friends and colleagues in the late nineteenth and early twentieth centuries and were articulated frequently by others who, like Forster, were associated with the Bloomsbury group.

Although often credited with playing a very significant role in the articulation of a number of different forms of modernism in literature, art and personal life, the Bloomsbury group is hard to define precisely, either in terms of its membership or its outlook. It was a loosely knit network of writers, artists and intellectuals bound together by shared interests and values and by close personal relationships. The nucleus of the group was a number of young men who had met and became close friends when they were students at Cambridge University in the 1890s, including Lytton Strachey, Leonard Woolf, Maynard Keynes, Thoby Stephen and Desmond MacCarthy. It gained its name when they had left Cambridge and several of them settled in Bloomsbury, following the lead of Thoby Stephen and his sisters, Vanessa and Virginia, who married respectively Clive Bell and Leonard Woolf, both members of the original Cambridge group.[99]

The new sense of friendship that was articulated within this group drew on a number of different strands, some emotional and others theoretical. The emotional element centred on the immense importance that all of these men attributed to their Cambridge years and to the friendships that they made there. All of them commented on their pleasure at experiencing for the first time a form of intellectual fellowship and close friendship that replaced the sense of isolation that all had felt in unsympathetic boarding schools and amidst families from whom they felt increasingly distant. Their sense of the importance of Cambridge friendships and of the close-knit intellectual community which they found there was augmented also by the inclusion of several of these men in one of the elite Cambridge discussion groups generally known as the Apostles, which brought them into close contact with an older generation of philosophers and intellectuals including Bertrand Russell and G. E. Moore. Close friendships had always been evident and highly valued amongst the Apostles. Indeed, as William Lubenow has argued, it was their friendships that sustained the critical intellectual approach that was the central feature of the group and that enabled them fearlessly and mercilessly to interrogate the values, beliefs and ideas of their society.[100] The Apostles had always stressed the importance of frank and honest discussion of any and every subject, extended within Bloomsbury to include emotional and sexual questions as well as aesthetic, political and more strictly philosophical ones. Recalling his Cambridge days, Leonard Woolf noted how, after a very few days of feeling lonely at Cambridge:

> everything changed and almost for the first time one felt that to be young was very heaven. The reason was simple. Suddenly I found to my astonishment that there were a number of people near and

> about me with whom I could enjoy the exciting and at the same
> time profound happiness of friendship.[101]

But there were particular features of these friendships that Woolf regarded as worthy of note. It was not simply the case that he had found
congenial people, but also that he had established a new kind of intellectual and emotional intimacy with them through the deep and detailed knowledge that he gained of their emotional lives and
psychological states. He and his closest friend, Lytton Strachey, developed a particular method:

> a kind of third degree psychological investigation applied to the
> souls of one's friends. Though it was a long time before we had
> any knowledge of Freud, it was a kind of compulsory psycho-
> analysis. It was intended to reveal to us, and incidentally to the
> victim, what he was really like; the theory was that by imparting to
> all concerned the deeper psychological truths, personal relation-
> ships would be much improved.[102]

If Freud, or at least an anticipation of Freud, provided one way of
characterizing this new approach to friendship, another was provided
by the philosopher to whom the group was most devoted, G. E. Moore.
In his *Principia Ethica,* published in 1903, but anticipated in some of
Moore's discussions at the Apostles, friendship of the kind most valued by these men is given a very special place. Moore argued that
aesthetic enjoyments and "the pleasures of human intercourse or of
personal affection" were the "ideal," in the sense of being the "great
unmixed goods." The personal affection that was so highly valued
involved an appreciation of mental qualities alongside an "appreciation of the appropriate *corporeal* expression of those qualities," and a
considerable capacity for reflection and contemplation.[103] Thus
Moore's writings seemed to accord the highest possible ethical value
to close personal friendship – and particularly of the kind experienced
by these young intellectuals.

The novelty of their approach to friendship was something of which
the Bloomsbury group was very conscious. Indeed, their ideas on friendship, and particularly their stress on the need for absolute honesty
and openness in all matters, including sexual questions and the most
intimate of feelings, served for many of them to define themselves
and their approach to life as "modern," in contrast to that of their
Victorian forebears. One of the signs of this new intimacy was the
introduction of first names in place of the older English custom of

referring to men only by their surnames and this rejection of an older form of address seemed to encourage the sharing not only of information about the most intimate of matters, but also of daily life. The new kind of friendship espoused by Bloomsbury involved an intimacy that sometimes included the sharing of homes and sexual partners, as well as their innermost thoughts. Rejection of conventional ideas of marriage was an important issue within Bloomsbury and a defining part of their sense of modernity. The homosexuality of many of those involved in Bloomsbury was also important here and a key aspect of Bloomsbury's sense of its own modernity was the open acceptance and discussion of homosexuality and homosexual relations, not only amongst men but also between men and women. But there were many heterosexual members as well and both the discussion and the demand for intimacy and for freedom encompassed all varieties of sexuality. The intimacy both desired and extolled by Bloomsbury raised rather complex questions about the meaning and nature of friendship, and especially about the borderlines between friendship and sexual love. Jealousy was not formally tolerated – although ultimately several close friendships were strained when close friends indulged their sexual passion for the same partner. But many of the friendships endured – and the letters, diaries and autobiographies of many of those involved in Bloomsbury testify to the endurance of these friendships and to the ongoing preoccupation that members of the group had with the lives, emotions and psychological states of their friends.

Bloomsbury may be the best-known group for whom close friendship provided a model for new forms of intimacy and of both domestic and social life that enabled people to avoid or escape the confines of Victorian homes and families, but it was not the only one. As Christine Stansell has shown recently, the bohemian world of Greenwich Village and its surrounds in the early nineteenth century also provided a new form of sociability that encompassed intense same-sex and opposite-sex relationships, which spilled easily over into sexual relationships and enabled people to see themselves as establishing a new kind of world.[104] More than its Bloomsbury counterpart, Greenwich Village encompassed people from many different countries, whose differences of language and origin became irrelevant in their shared social and political commitments and concern to bring a new world into being. This was a genuinely international group of friends and associates, in which native-born Americans mixed easily with an array of Polish, German, Russian and Italian émigrés without any sense of national hierarchy. Martha Vicinus makes a similar claim for the bohemian world of Paris at this time and all of these different examples point clearly to the importance of new forms of intimate and complex friendship at the dawn of the twentieth century.

We can talk about ideas of friendship in the nineteenth century in a different way to earlier periods partly because we simply have a far greater availability of sources about what people in this period, particularly ordinary people, thought about such personal matters. But important ideas and experiences of friendship of course changed during the century, particularly in regard to how women could experience friendship. The range of movements we have discussed that sought to improve society through either intra- or cross-class friendships represented one aspect of a growing unease with economic and social systems that led over time to a range of societal and political developments that changed how people related to their communities and so their experience and ideas of friendship. But these movements also in a less direct way perhaps presaged a future lessening of boundaries between elite and popular cultural understandings, and the growth of a more "modern," universal and homogenous concept and acceptance of what friendship could mean.

Notes

1. W. S. Haine, *The World of the Paris Café: Sociability among the French Working Class, 1789–1914* (Baltimore, MD: The John Hopkins University Press, 1996).

2. George L. Mosse, "Friendship and Nationhood: About the Promise and Failure of German Nationalism," *Journal of Contemporary History* 17 (1982), pp. 351–67.

3. K. D. Reynolds, *Aristocratic Women and Political Society in Victorian Britain* (Oxford: Clarendon Press, 1998), p. 153, and Elaine Chalus, "Elite Women, Social Politics, and the Political World of Late Eighteenth-Century England," *Historical Journal* 43.3 (2000).

4. William Verity, "Haldane and Asquith," *History Today* 18.7 (July 1968), p. 452.

5. Pauline Nestor, *Female Friendships and Communities: Charlotte Bronte, George Eliot, Elizabeth Gaskell* (Oxford: Clarendon Press, 1985), p. 12.

6. Barbara Caine, *Victorian Feminists* (Oxford: Oxford University Press, 1992), p. 137.

7. Nestor, *Female Friendships*, pp. 19–22.

8. G. F. Pardon, "Odd-Fellowship: Its Principles and Practice, Part V," *Quarterly Magazine of the Independent Order of Odd-Fellows, Manchester Unity* new series II (1859–1860), p. 325.

9. G. E. Moore, *Principia Ethica* (Cambridge: Cambridge University Press, 1966), p. 183.

10. Martha Vicinus, *Intimate Friends: Women Who Loved Women, 1778–1928* (Chicago: University of Chicago Press, 2004), p. xvii.

11. Tessa Coslett, *Woman to Woman: Female Friendship in Victorian Fiction* (Brighton: Harvester Press, 1988), p. 3.

12. Vicinus, *Intimate Friends*, p. xvii

13. Alexandre Dumas, *The Three Musketeers* (trans. William Barrow; London: Pan, 1968), p. 92.

14. Richard Dellamora, *Friendship's Bonds: Democracy and the Novel in Victorian England* (Philadelphia: University of Pennsylvania Press, 2004), p. 122.

15. Arnold, *Christian Life,* cited in William N. Weaver, "'A School-Boy's Story': Writing the Victorian Public Schoolboy Subject," *Victorian Studies* 46.3 (2004), pp. 455–87 at p. 456.

16. See also Arnold, *Christian Life,* cited in Weaver, "'A School-Boy's Story,'" p. 456.

17. Thomas Hughes, *Tom Brown's School Days* (London: Macmillan, 1979).

18. *Biblewomen and Nurses* 9 (1 February 1892), p. 35.

19. S. Mitchell, "The Forgotten Women of the Period: Penny Weekly Family Magazines of the 1840's and 1850's," in M. Vicinus (ed.), *A Widening Sphere: Changing Roles of Victorian Women* (Bloomington: Indiana University Press, 1977), pp. 31, 51, 276 fn3.

20. Mitchell, "The Forgotten Women of the Period," p. 46.

21. L. James, *Fiction for the Working Man 1830–1850* (Oxford: Oxford University Press, 1963), pp. 94, 157.

22. Henry Mayhew, *London Labour and the London Poor* (London: Griffin, Bohn & Company, 1851), I, p. 29.

23. Mayhew, *London Labour*, p. 358.

24. See P. O. Peretti, "Elderly–Animal Friendship Bonds," *Social Behavior and Personality* 18 (1990), pp. 151–56. Anna Sewell's *Black Beauty*, published in 1877, and perhaps the best-know example of animal-as-close-companion literature, would sell more than 20 million copies by the 1930s.

25. Ivan Kreilkamp, "Petted Things: *Wuthering Heights* and the Animal," *Yale Journal of Criticism* 18.1 (2005), pp. 87, 94, 100.

26. Kathleen Kete, *The Beast in the Boudoir: Petkeeping in Nineteenth-Century Paris* (Berkeley, CA: University of California Press, 1994), p. 35.

27. J. Schulte-Sasse, "Toward a 'Culture' for the Masses: The Socio-Psychological Function of Popular Literature in Germany and the U.S., 1880–1920," *New German Critique* 29 (Spring–Summer 1983), pp. 90, 92.

28. K. Flint, *The Woman Reader 1837–1914* (Oxford: Oxford University Press, 1993), pp. 163–64.

29. Flint, *The Woman Reader*, p. 166.

30. Carroll Smith-Rosenberg, "The Female World of Love and Ritual: Relations between Women in Nineteenth-Century America," *Signs* 1.1 (1975), pp. 1–29.

31. Nestor, *Female Friendships and Communities*.

32. Philippa Levine, *Victorian Feminism* (London: Hutchinson Education, 1971); Sandra Stanley Holton, *Suffrage Days: Stories from the Women's Suffrage Movement* (London: Routledge, 1996).

33. Vicinus, *Intimate Friends*.

34. Anthony E. Rotundo, "Romantic Friendship: Male Intimacy and Middle-Class Youth in the Northern United States, 1800–1900," *Journal of Social History* 23.1 (1989), pp. 1–25 at p. 5.

35. Alexander Herzen, *My Past and Thoughts: The Memoirs of Alexander Herzen* (London: Chatto & Windus, 1968), I , p. 71

36. Rebecca Friedman, "Romantic Friendship in the Nicholaevyan University," *Russian Review* 62 (April 2003), pp. 262–80.

37. Dellamora, *Friendship's Bonds*, p. 1.

38. Stefan-Ludwig Hoffman, "Democracy and Associations in the Long Nineteenth Century: Toward a Transnational Perspective," *Journal of Modern History* 75 (2003), pp. 269–99.

39. See, for example, Barbara Alpern Engel, *Mothers and Daughters: Women of the Intelligentsia in Nineteenth-Century Russia* (Cambridge: Cambridge University Press, 1983), pp. 78–80.

40. Letter to the editor by W. A. H. from Adelaide Lodge, *Oddfellows Magazine* (Adelaide) 1.4 (April 1844), p. 116.

41. H. Broughton, "The Social Aspect of the Manchester Unity," *Quarterly Magazine of the Independent Order of Odd-Fellows, Manchester Unity* new series XXV (1894), p. 146.

42. J. R. Jones, "The Social Aspect of Oddfellowship," *Quarterly Magazine of the Independent Order of Odd-Fellows, Manchester Unity* new series XXV (1894), p. 312.

43. J. R. Jones, "The Social Aspect of Oddfellowship," p. 314.

44. S. Oliker, "The Modernisation of Friendship: Individualism, Intimacy, and Gender in the Nineteenth Century," in R. G. Adams and G. Allan (eds), *Placing Friendship in Context* (Cambridge: Cambridge University Press, 1998), p. 18.

45. E. Ross, "Survival Networks: Women's Neighbourhood Sharing in London before World War One," *History Workshop* 15 (Spring 1983), p. 5.

46. C. Lis, *Social Change and the Labouring Poor: Antwerp, 1770–1860* (New Haven, CT: Yale University Press, 1986), pp. 158–59.

47. A. Faure, "Local Life in Working-Class Paris at the End of the Nineteenth Century," *Journal of Urban History* 32.5 (July 2006), p. 5.

48. J. Burnett, *Destiny Obscure: Autobiographies of Childhood, Education and the Family from the 1820s to the 1920s* (Harmondsworth, UK: Penguin, 1984), p. 227.

49. E. Roberts, *A Woman's Place: An Oral History of Working-Class Women 1890–1940* (Basil Blackwell, Oxford 1984), p. 188.

50. Beatrice Webb's MS Diary (Passfield Collection, British Library of Political and Economic Science), XI, p. 31, typescript 814.

51. Quoted in M. Tebbutt, *Women's Talk: A Social History of "Gossip" in Working-class Neighbourhoods, 1880–1960* (Aldershot: Scolar Press, 1995), p. 166.

52. Carl Chinn, *They Worked All their Lives: Women of the Urban Poor in England, 1880–1939* (Manchester: Manchester University Press, 1988), p. 115.

53. Roberts, *Woman's Place*, pp. 188–89.

54. Interview transcript of Mrs Grace Beales (int230), p. 35, oral history collection of P. Thompson and T. Lummis, *Family Life and Work Experience before 1918, 1870–1973* [computer file] 5th edn (Colchester, Essex: UK Data Archive [distributor], April 2005), SN: 2000.

55. R. Roberts, *The Classic Slum: Salford Life in the First Quarter of the Century* (Harmondsworth, UK: Penguin, 1973), p. 47.

56. A. Bravo, "Solidarity and Loneliness: Piedmontese Peasant Women at the Turn of the Century," *International Journal of Oral History* 3.2 (June 1982), pp. 79–80, 84.

57. Henry Mayhew, *London Labour and the London Poor* (London: 1851), I, pp. 162, 460, 224.

58. Mayhew, *London Labour*, I, p. 393; III, p. 231.

59. Mayhew, *London Labour*, I, p. 225.

60. *Biblewomen and Nurses* 26 (1909), p. 68

61. *Biblewomen and Nurses*, 1 February 1892, p. 37.

62. M. Loane, *Neighbours and Friends* (London: Edward Arnold, 1910), p. 260.

63. Tebbutt, *Women's Talk*, p. 69.

64. Quoted in M. Savage, *The Dynamics of Working Class Politics: The Labour Movement in Preston, 1880–1940* (Cambridge: Cambridge University Press, 1987), p. 130.

65. Roberts, *Classic Slum*, p. 65.

66. *Second Report of the Commissioners Appointed to Inquire into Friendly and Benefit Building Societies, Part II* (Parliamentary Papers, 1872), XXVI, p. 74.

67. *Biblewomen and Nurses* 9 (1 December 1892), p. 239

68. Roberts, *Woman's Place*, p. 191

69. Jones, "Social Aspect," p. 371.

70. *Quarterly Magazine of the Independent Order of Odd-Fellows, Manchester Unity* new series II (1859–60), pp. 264–65.

71. *Odd Fellows Magazine* (Adelaide) 1.2 (October 1843), p. 33.

72. Irving Howe, *A Handbook of Socialist Thought* (London: Victor Gollancz, 1972), p. 24.

73. John Wilson, "Towards a Society of Friends: Some Reflections on the Meaning of Democratic Socialism," *Canadian Journal of Political Science* 3.4 (December 1970).

74. P. D. Jones, "Jesus Christ and the Transformation of English Society: The 'Subversive Conservatism' of Frederick Denison Maurice," *Harvard Theological Review* 96.2 (2003), p. 212.

75. C. Kingsley, "The British Museum," *Politics*, No.11 (1 July 1848), p.185, quoted in Jones, "Jesus Christ," p. 213.

76. S. Koven, *Slumming: Sexual and Social Politics in Victorian London* (Princeton, NJ: Princeton University Press, 2004), p. 231.

77. W. J. Jupp, *The Religion of Nature and of Human Experience* (London, 1906), pp. 187, 179–80, quoted in K. Manton, "The Fellowship of the New Life: English Ethical Socialism Reconsidered," *History of Political Thought* 24.2 (Summer 2003), p. 296.

78. Koven, *Slumming*, pp. 235–36.

79. In W. Reason (ed.), *University and Social Settlements* (London: Methuen, 1898), pp. 20–22.

80. C. Betensky, "Philanthropy, Desire and the Politics of Friendship in *The Princess Casamassima*," *Henry James Review* 22.2 (2001), p. 156.

81. T. Wright, *Some Habits and Customs of the Working Classes* (London: Tinsley Brothers, 1867), p. 29.

82. Hoffman, "Democracy and Associations," pp. 284, 287.

83 T. Alborn, "Senses of Belonging: The Politics of Working-Class Insurance in Britain, 1880–1914," *Journal of Modern History* 73.3 (September 2001), p. 573.

84. Haine, *The World of the Paris Café*, pp. 167–69.

85. Interview transcript of Mrs Grace Beales, Thompson and Lummis, *Family Life*.

86. G. Allan, *Kinship and Friendship in Modern Britain* (Oxford: Oxford University Press, 1996), p. 88.

87. R. McKibbin, *Class and Cultures: England 1918–1951* (Oxford: Oxford University Press, 1998), pp. 181, 183.

88. Catherine Hall, *Civilising Subjects: Metropole and Colony in the English Imagination 1830–1868* (Cambridge: Polity Press, 2002).

89. Antoinette Burton, *At the Heart of the Empire: Indians and the Colonial Encounter in Late-Victorian Britain* (Berkeley, CA: University of California Press, 1997).

90. Clive Dewey, *Anglo-Indian Attitudes: The Mind of the Indian Civil Service* (London: Hambledon Press, 1993).

91. Dewey, *Anglo-Indian Attitudes*, pp. 14–15

92. Dewey, *Anglo-Indian Attitudes*, p. 196

93. Leela Gandhi, in her book *Affective Communities: Anticolonial Thought, Fin-de-Siècle radicalism and the Politics of Friendship* (Durham: Duke University Press, 2006).

94. Gandhi, *Affective Communities*, p. 73.

95. Gandhi, *Affective Communities*, pp. 116–20.

96. E. M. Forster, "What I Believe," in *Two Cheers for Democracy* (London: Edward Arnold, 1972), p. 66.

97. Graham Little, *Friendship: Being Ourselves with Others* (Melbourne: Text Publishing, 1993), p. 43.

98. Cited in Little, *Friendship*, 1993, pp. 44–45.

99. See Michael Holroyd, *Lytton Strachey* (London: Vintage, 1995); Quentin Bell, *Bloomsbury* (London: Weidenfeld & Nicolson, 1968); Peter Stansky, *On or about December 1910* (Cambridge, MA: Harvard University Press, 1996).

100. W. C. Lubenow, *The Cambridge Apostles, 1820–1914 Liberalism, Imagination, and Friendship in British Intellectual and Professional Life* (Cambridge: Cambridge University Press, 1998).

101. Leonard Woolf, *Sowing, An Autobiography of the Years 1880–1904* (London: Hogarth Press, 1960), p. 103.

102. Woolf, *Sowing*, p. 114.

103. Moore, *Principia Ethica*, p. 203. See also Paul Levy, *G. E. Moore and the Cambridge Apostles* (London: Weidenfeld & Nicolson, 1979).

104. Christine Stansell, *American Moderns: Bohemian New York and the Creation of a New Century* (New York: Henry Holt & Company, 2000).

Chapter 8

NEW WORLDS OF FRIENDSHIP: THE EARLY TWENTIETH CENTURY

Mark Peel

Introduction

In the first half of the twentieth century, a wider range of people came to regard a particular form of intimate and emotional friendship as a crucial component of a good life. More than family, kin or faith, friendship was the social glue of modernity. Friendship helped people to manage, endure and even enjoy dramatic transformations, strengthened the horizontal bonds of age and shared experience, and nourished those who lived beyond sanctioned boundaries. This was particularly true in the cities of the New World, where friendship helped millions of twentieth-century people become modern. Immigrants, travellers and the other more-or-less willing participants in a century of mass movement have relied upon the fact that friends – unlike family or kin – can be made and made again. Friends often opened up the best aspects of modernity, the new pleasures and possibilities of twentieth-century lives. They could also offer a kind of protection against the worst aspects of urban modernity, including the alienation and loneliness so often highlighted by social and cultural observers. To the extent that the twentieth century exposed more people to both the perils and possibilities of change, it also saw their growing reliance upon friendship, and not as some poor relation to community, neighbourhood and kinship, at least in Western societies. Instead, friends were those with whom changes could be experienced, anticipated, enjoyed and savoured.

From the United States, too, came a wider array of popular sources in which twentieth-century people could glimpse the possibilities of new lives – including relationships – that celebrated choice; to popular fiction and self-improving literature were added film, radio and the advice columns of magazines. What the city people of the New World took from their myriad origins and helped shape into a mass culture, Europeans incorporated, imitated and reshaped again. In other places and times, people might imitate or reject an American style but, in ways of living as much as global politics, the twentieth century was the American century.

Friendship was the conversation about who you had been, who you were and who you wanted to be. It was for the discussion of dilemmas and the rehearsal of new directions. Because you chose your friends, it also epitomized what was, for most people, a new degree of freedom to make their own way. What relatively few nineteenth-century people could enjoy became the realistic aspiration of many. Popular culture and popular conversation agreed on the growing significance of friends, and the importance of friendliness as a model for improving the relationships you had to have, such as those with family or neighbours. Cultural descriptions and prescriptions also focused on the links between friendship and successful selfhood: your friends, more than anyone, witnessed and assisted you develop a true sense of self. New forms of knowledge and leisure also shaped these understandings of friendship. More than philosophers and social scientists, advocates of friendship's instrumental virtues – such as Dale Carnegie – and the producers of mass entertainment moulded the idea and the expectations of friendship among twentieth-century people.

There was also a decisive shift in friendship's location, as those once presumed unfit for its responsibilities became its exemplars. If heterosexual men seemed to struggle with the demands of this more intense, emotional and self-exposing idea of friendliness, women and then homosexual men became its chief agents, advocates and public performers. The idea that women possessed a special capacity and desire for befriending – whether innate, socialized or perhaps even as an outcome of patriarchal oppression – was clearly important well before the twentieth century. As Stacey Oliker argued, and as earlier chapters have shown, women's increasing specialization in feeling, emotional communion, sentiment and disclosure was evident well before the turn of the century.[1] At its beginning, in 1907, one

American male writer had already declared that "in the emotional region, many women, but very few men, can form the highest kind of tie."[2] It was an interesting prophecy, for the twentieth century was the age of female friendship, or perhaps the age when friendship became female. As the boundaries between male intimacy, male friendship and homosexuality became ever more difficult to control, women focused more and more attention on the intimacy and enclosure of "true" friendship. Yet friendship among women – and among other outsiders, too – also changed its meanings and possibilities. From them came new or refreshed idealizations of inclusive friendship as a bulwark against oppression, as a crucial foundation for personal and collective liberation, and as a model for a better world. There were famous friendships of activism and mobilization, and there were congresses promoting the friendship of nations. And there were thousands of unrecorded intimacies, moments of connection and disclosure that just as surely changed the future.

Of course, some observers were less impressed. For them, the *fin de siècle* seemed to spell not just the end of those relationships that had nourished traditional societies – what Ferdinand Tönnies called *gemeinschaft* – but the emergence of new and potentially damaging forms of un-togetherness (or *gesellschaft*, in Tönnies' terms). The paradigms that dominated twentieth-century social thought – Tönnies' loss of community, Durkheim's erosion of meaning and the production of anomie, Marx's unrelenting rolling out of capitalism's contradictions or Freud's focus on psychosexual rivalries and the deep imprint of conflict – had little but scepticism for friendship. If they thought about it at all, social observers' anxious prescriptions for an atomizing century assumed the loss of true friendship, along with community, neighbourhood and everything else that was corroded by change.

In hindsight, their anxiety indicated a lack of confidence in people's capacity to manage the new and challenging environments of modernity. But they also ignored the extent to which twentieth-century people were following an already laid-out path. Rather than any fundamental break with the nineteenth-century aspirations traced in the preceding chapter, the twentieth century was characterized by their greater realization. Over time, and with different inflections in different societies, friendship played a more important role in the lives of more people. The friendship of the avant-garde – intimate, reciprocal, open and time-consuming, where the self was formed and realized and in which anything could be shared – became more achievable by the *hoi polloi.* In this sense, friendship is the defining relationship – and aspiration – of modern people: relatively autonomous and mobile individuals who understand themselves as changeable, and as having the right to pursue choices.

In the writing of history, the twentieth century has been characterized as the century of various things: of total war, the automobile, or mass culture. It was the age of extremes and the American century. In the Western world, it was the century in which more people began to live in cities than small towns and in which hundreds of millions of people participated in more-or-less willing continental migrations. It was the century of a Great Depression and unprecedented prosperity, of rapid industrialization and a just-as-rapid deindustrialization. It was the century of private wealth and the growth and then retraction of the welfare state, of population explosion and fertility control, and of a public health revolution that made early death a rarity and a long life a reasonable expectation. It was the century of struggles for human rights and some of the most terrible denials of shared humanity. It will seem strange to call it a century of increasing friendship. Yet a century in which a greater proportion of people enjoyed mobility, affluence, privacy, autonomy and mass communication – and suffered dislocation, terror and war – was also a century in which friendship could play a very important role in negotiating the opportunities and demands of a more self-conscious life. In tracing the story of its first half, it is this emphasis on the life desired, though perhaps not yet realized, that counts for most.

Befriending

Those observing various societies in the first half of the twentieth century were more likely to see the playful ties of friendship as part of a problem, not its solution. Friendship seemed fleeting, even to its admirers. Among the European social scientists, Georg Simmel was most favourable. In his essay "The Metropolis and Mental Life," he described friendship as "inseparable from the immediacy of interaction" and lived through conversation, which maintained "the liveliness, the mutual understanding, the common consciousness." It lacked any purpose outside itself, and had to be between equals since it was "the purest, most transparent, most engaging kind of interaction." It also needed privacy, and thus emerged in the city rather than the village that allowed no secrets. Friendship, then, was an exercise of skill, judgment and imagination between equals. But it remained a "play form" of sociability and, despite its liveliness, vitality, possibility, was relegated by Simmel to the less important private sphere.[3]

In the United States, Robert Park acknowledged the capacity of Chicago's urban subcultures to generate "congenial company," while in the smaller world of Middletown, Robert and Helen Lynd recognized the attractions and benefits of social relationships outside the family.[4] But few saw much wider benefit in the fickleness of friends. For instance, Middletowners' cars and affluence made their networks more extensive, but the Lynds were more concerned about declining friendliness among neighbours and the increasingly private and passive focus of people's leisure, as well as the rise of clubs dedicated to exclusion rather than inclusion.[5] Middletowners themselves were more ambivalent; "people ain't so friendly as they used to be" was a common refrain about neighbours, but most suggested a growing distinction between neighbours and friends, who were often visited and phoned rather than simply being "dropped in on."[6] Whatever the nuances of real lives, in fictional accounts of this same small-town world, especially the unhappy tales of George Babbitt and his ilk, the scramble for social and financial advantage and the pressures of conformity made real friendships seem even more unlikely.

Social scientists, critics and satirists were less mindful, perhaps, of those relationships in which a language of amity and concord continued to play a part. People on both sides of the Atlantic were still using the language of friendship, though with different inflections, to different ends and in ways that reflected the challenges and opportunities they associated with the accelerating "condition" of modernity. It is important to remember that in the first 50 years of the twentieth century, the destination and durability of rapidly modernizing societies, and capitalism itself, were unclear, in a way that later triumphs have tended to obscure. For the great majority of people in those societies, modernity had not yet become a promise of affluence, mobility and a better life. Whatever the blandishments of a growing economy of consumption and leisure, theirs remained lives of austerity and insecurity. For them, as I argue below, the dislocations and possibilities of change created new reasons for making friends and new ways of making them. For others, however, especially among elites nervous of the modern world's direction, extending the hand of friendship promised to allay some of that world's worst aspects.

It is important to note the continuing expressions of friendly intent in social reform, charity and welfare work, for instance. In the early twentieth century, as in the nineteenth, the practice of "friendly visiting" or "befriending" usually implied the transformation, improvement or assimilation of the immigrant, the colonial subject, the social inferior or the hapless victim. In these relationships, friendliness was presumed to strengthen the moral and cultural authority that stemmed from privilege; indeed, the capacity to befriend and soothe an inferior helped to make that authority seem more benign. As had been true in American abolitionism and other reform movements in the United States and Europe, it also relied upon and in turn bolstered a particular form of female benevolence and empathy. This was a patronizing friendship, between people who would remain unequal; the title of a recent collection of essays written by English charity pioneer Octavia Hill – *The Befriending Leader* – aptly captures the spirit, as does her injunction to volunteers that they be "QUEENS as well as FRIENDS."[7]

The principles of friendly visiting – which its main American theorist Mary Richmond described as "intimate and continuing knowledge of and sympathy with a poor family's joys, sorrows, opinions, feelings, and entire outlook upon life" – were perhaps most fully realized in the charity organization societies of North American cities before and after the start of the twentieth century.[8] While they drew upon the English movement and its developers described in the previous chapter, it was Richmond, who worked in Baltimore, Philadelphia and New York between the 1890s and the 1920s, and advocates such as Robert Treat Paine, Josephine Shaw Lowell and Edward T. Devine, who developed a prescription – "not alms, but a friend" – and carried the practice of personal visiting and investigation into the professional social work of the twentieth century. That emphasis was also carried into arguments for reform, including some of the first great works of African-American advocacy: W. E. B. DuBois reminded the readers of his early work *The Philadelphia Negro*, for example, that "after all, the need of the Negro, as of so many unfortunate classes, is 'not alms but a friend.'"[9]

Of course, the emphasis on friendly relations was intended in part as an antidote to the social tensions that boiled out of the Old and New worlds' boom-and-bust economies, as well as to the social and cultural distance between the befrienders and the increasingly alien befriended. It was never the only reason, and for every insistence that friendship created "character" among the poor were reminders (such as those uttered by American reformer Mary McDowell) that true friendly visiting must stem from "the feeling that down underneath is the common relationship, that the difference between us is only the result of development by God's grace and not by any special virtue of our own."[10] The emphasis on equality was particularly characteristic of women's reform organizations, such as Boston's "Fragment Society," in which the friendly manner of giving charity should "make a poor person recognize that you consider him as of the same flesh and blood with yourself ... [and] one of God's children, one for whom, equally with yourself, Christ died."[11]

Still, as was true for those who had earlier befriended slaves, orphans, servant girls and other victims of nineteenth-century wrongs, there was for most friendly visitors both a concern with the potentially antagonizing consequences of distance and a conviction that personal, friendly contact would help convince the sufferers of deprivation that their problem was personal inadequacy more than structural injustice. In this understanding, friendship built bridges and alleviated antagonisms without implying any substantial changes in economic or social structures. It transformed the weaker and less powerful person and helped them "adjust" to the facts of their position. This was also friendliness as a gift, for which gratitude was expected. But, as historian Eileen Yeo observed of early twentieth-century social work in Britain, "class ways of communicating respect and friendship did not always carry the intended messages"; social workers were often unable to understand that "continual exchange of material necessities was precisely the currency of friendship" among the poor and "as often as not, increased class contact aggravated rather than reduced mutual incomprehension."[12]

In the United States and Europe, the severe depression of the 1890s converted many advocates of friendly visiting to the benefits of more comprehensive welfare and public provision. Yet what remains striking is their belief that friendliness had a role to play in overcoming the corrosions of modernity, even as the instruments and institutions of a more recognizably modern welfare state began to take shape. For Mary Richmond, 20 years of work and experience helped to turn friendly visiting into *Social Diagnosis* by 1917, but she never abandoned her faith in "personal service."[13] For others, organizing the wartime United States meant developing unparalleled interventions, some only dreamed of by prewar Progressive reformers, but the voluntary and befriending impulse remained strong. In its Camp Service and Home Service, for instance, thousands of American Red Cross volunteers offered the "helping hand" and advice of a friend to "practically every soldier, sailor and marine in the service of the United States" and to half a million servicemen's families.[14]

Befriending also characterized relationships between other kinds of unequals. It was used, for instance, as a way of identifying the kind of help and uplift that colonizing powers could offer their dependencies or that the agents of imperial authority might extend to those they subjected. The language of colonialism and imperialism often used the terms of friendship, portraying colonization as benevolent and colonized people as beneficiaries. American advocates of empire clearly understood themselves in this light, partly as a means of distinguishing their empire from those of Britain and especially "backward" Spain. Under the policy of "benevolent assimilation" promised to the Philippines, Americans came "not as invaders or conquerors," President McKinley argued, "but as friends, to protect the natives in their homes, in their employments, and in their personal and religious rights."[15] Puerto Ricans and Cubans received similar gestures. In the United States, and in smaller, self-consciously white nations such as Australia, the idea of "Uncle Sam" as a friendly Pacific ruler gained increasing weight after 1900, especially in the light of Japanese expansion. In one Australian cartoon, Uncle Sam was shown as a large but unthreatening figure, shaking the hand of a boyish new nation. That Uncle Sam backed up amicable gestures with a world-touring Great White Fleet of battleships in 1907 made his friendship even more precious.

In the older empires, the rhetoric of friendship emphasized enduring bonds of duty and affection: in the UK, for instance, elite women formed the Victoria League in 1901 as a "society of Friendship" promoting "the interchange of information and hospitality and co-operation in any practical scheme tending to foster friendly understanding and good fellowship within the Empire."[16] During World War I, and again in World War II, the League was one of several organizations that assisted servicemen. It delivered more than a million food parcels to the UK and helped thousands of war brides settle in Australia and New Zealand. The language of "Empire friendship" heightened throughout the British dominions in the 1920s: in a 1930 article, South African political elder J. C. Smuts expressed the common argument that the British Empire had brought "a fourth of the human race together in perpetual peace and friendship."[17]

From the turn of the century onward, friendship was also invoked in discussions of ideal relations between nations, and as a force that could work against suspicion and traditional hostilities. The Entente Cordiale was the most famous example, but the "hand of friendship" was a common currency in the treaties, international agreements and pacts that helped take the world into war in 1914 and then attempted to rebuild it in 1919 and after. The rhetoric of friendship was nowhere stronger than in Woodrow Wilson's arguments for peace. In late 1918, he reminded the United States Congress that "the nations that have learned the discipline of freedom and that have settled with self-possession to its ordered practice are now about to make conquest of the world by the sheer power of example of friendly helpfulness." Two weeks before the Versailles Conference opened, Wilson told a gathering in Rome that "our task at Paris is to organise the friendship of the world."[18] Whatever the scale of his defeat, at Versailles and in the Senate's refusal to include the United States in the League of Nations, Wilson's idealistic principles were not lost upon the thousands of Europeans and Americans who joined support groups for the League. The language of friendship also persisted in international relations: the Kellogg–Briand Pact, for instance, which renounced war "as an instrument of national policy," took as its working title the Pact of Perpetual Friendship.[19]

Actions departed loudly from words. Between nations, bonds of friendship could not survive territorial ambition and enmity. Within empires, the promises of friendship sounded as empty to Filipino, Puerto Rican and Cuban nationalists as they had to the Sioux and other Indian nations offered "perpetual amity" by the United States in the 1870s and 1880s. The hand of friendship easily became the fist of conquest: in the Philippines, for instance, one American military leader's response to nationalist insurrection was, "without altogether ignoring the dictates of justice ... [to] create a reign of fear and anxiety among the disaffected which will become unbearable."[20] In India, as well as other "non-white" European colonies, the subjects of authority had cause to echo what veteran Indian nationalist Sarojini Naidu, in a lecture on "Ideals of Indian Womanhood" in 1928, dismissed as exploitation "in the guise of friendship": "we do not ask any friend or foe in the guise of a friend, to come merely to exploit us while they pretend to interpret, succour and solace our womanhood."[21] When it was conceived as an act of benevolence from a superior to an inferior, the language of friendship all too easily invited questions about what "friendship" might actually mean in the context of conquest, colonization and exploitation.

Of course, ideal and real friendships could also be turned against imperialism and privilege and towards the goals of social reconstruction. As described in the preceding chapter, Leela Gandhi uses specific relationships – such as the one between Edward Carpenter and M. K. Gandhi – to show how "friendship" stood for and fostered cross-cultural, interracial and anti-imperial collaboration. Choosing affinity with the victims of Europe's relentless expansions over loyalty to nation and empire, various activists created what Gandhi calls "anti-colonial friendship." This both symbolized the possibility of cross-cultural concord and made it real. It made the colonized "other" a partner in a relationship of mutual exchange and affection, and, ideally, it could commit the more privileged friend to the cause of liberating and empowering the less privileged. In fiction, the possibilities for such friendship could be explored in terms of its difficulties and eventual failure – as in E. M. Forster's 1924 novel *A Passage to India*, for instance – but here, too, the barriers to true friendship were more apparent among the colonizers than the colonized.

While Leela Gandhi's work focuses on Britain and anti-imperialism, similar ideas about friendship – including the reshaped forms of "civic friendship" that lay at the heart of the ethics of American reformers such as Jane Addams – flowed into other causes as well. The settlement house movement, for example, and the reform arguments of those women (and a few men) historian Maureen Flanagan described as "seeing with their hearts," certainly took befriending to imply something other than preserving established patterns of privilege.[22] On the one hand, their own friendships, founded in the shared immediacy of settlement work and measured in lifelong conversations and intimacies, provided a model of relationships between people joined together by cause, service and commitment rather than kinship. On the other, friendship could also lead to greater understanding of social problems, because it involved listening to and drawing from the experiences of west-side Chicagoans, South End Bostonians or East End Londoners. Here, friendship was idealized as a means of overcoming the consequences of class distance or even the legacies of racial oppression. Of course, settlements, along with other education, reform and improvement groups, could all too easily see their task as friendly direction and dictation, or as the rather soulless collection of facts for analysis. But this was never their only possibility. For Jane Addams, in particular, the meaning of the settlement was to acquire, test and employ knowledge; it was, at least in part, to follow more than lead. To make friends with the marginalized was to accept, at least in some degree, a responsibility to be their advocate as well as their protector. It was to learn something. It could also signal, for people like Addams, Florence Kelley, Julia Lathrop and Lillian Wald, a willingness to be transformed by their example of endurance or courage and to build a larger political advocacy upon the human possibilities they embodied.

Across a spectrum of campaigns – from anti-capitalism and socialist utopianism through anti-imperialism and anti-racism – the ideal and the practice of friendship made real differences to political aspirations. It was often the cause of the most profound transformations, perhaps because it emphasized more clearly than anything else the fact that contact, conversation and amity could change hearts and minds. In all such movements, friendships among activists, and especially their willingness to make friends across seemingly insurmountable barriers of race and class, enabled them to sustain shared – and often deeply unpopular – political convictions. We are more used to such relationships in the last half of the century. But in its first five decades, friendships also transformed what activists and artists thought, wrote, said and sang, in well-known and less-known ways. Around the turn of the century, anti-lynching activist Ida B. Wells utilized her ties with white writer Albion Tourgée to mobilize opinion against the rising tide of racial violence in the American South, while also benefiting from trans-Atlantic friendship circles that assisted her campaign in the UK.[23] The patronage and friendship of Addams, Kelley and the other women of Hull House proved crucial in producing another interwoven generation of women activists in public health (Alice Hamilton), social research (Edith Abbott and Sophonisba Breckinridge) and children's affairs (Grace Abbott), all of whom achieved intellectual and political prominence in the period between the wars. Friendships with British suffragettes and then American campaigners for the vote gave Rosalie Barrow Edge the political experience and confidence to revitalize and lead the American wildlife preservation movement. Woody Guthrie learned about prejudice in 1930s California but he learned about racism through his friendships, first with white anti-racists such as Will Geer and Mike Quin and then with African-American musicians such as Leadbelly, Sonnie Terry and Brownie McGhee in New York City in the early 1940s.[24] Interwar Australia saw collaboration between indigenous and non-indigenous supporters, allies and those designated, for example, as "friends of" new kinds of inter-racial organizations. Given the stringent state controls exercised over indigenous people in the form of various coercive Acts, as well as ongoing institutional and popular racism, these organizations – including the Aborigines Advancement League, the Australian Aborigines' League, and the Australian Aboriginal Progressive Organization – benefited from non-indigenous support. Such support, however, was at the same time highly problematic, not the least because of its inherent paternalism, or maternalism in the case of feminist groups created to support Aboriginal women's rights.[25]

Friendship did not change the world. For some groups – African-Americans, Australian and American indigenous people, for instance – the period of repression and reaction between the wars, or what American presidential candidate Warren G. Harding called the need for "not nostrums, but normalcy; not revolution, but restoration," brought substantial reversals.[26] In some respects, and amid a backlash against feminism, pacifism, internationalism and sexual radicalism, the interwar period was also an unhappy time for activist and political friendships between women. Yet it is important not to submerge the period before 1920 in the apparently conservative sea that followed it. A range of early twentieth-century people used friendship as a model for social and political relationships and tried very hard to translate that idealism into action. As in the nineteenth century, women were becoming friendship's most important proponents. Female friendships, especially those that embodied a feminist critique and spoke of women's solidarity, mutuality and equality as models for human societies remained important, visible and controversial, from the British suffragettes and the close-knit circles of the settlement movement through to pacifism and international feminism. From them, too, continued to flow models of friendship as a communion of equals who nourished the capacity for self-determination. When writing the biography of one of her dearest comrades, Jane Addams could think of no more admiring title than *My Friend, Julia Lathrop*.

New Worlds

If friendship served one group as a model for a world made over, for others it served as a way of coping with the good and bad prospects of a crowded, commercialized, anonymous and uprooted urban world. Of course, this was not true for everyone. For many ordinary people, the benefits of modern living remained elusive; if new ways of understanding the world – through advertising or popular entertainment, for instance – pulled them towards a new century of change and aspiration, most still lived a more austere and nineteenth-century existence of poverty and blunted progress. They faced the continuing dilemmas of friendship in the midst of material deprivation, or, as Ray Pahl has termed them, "communities of fate," where the privacy and autonomy that could nourish friendships were difficult to achieve, and where privileging some relationships over others carried real risks.[27] Here, as the previous chapter suggested, one was more likely to make a friend of a visitor – or perhaps Jesus – than a neighbour or acquaintance. Relationships were local, contingent and had to be tempered by the vexations of close proximity. Friendships between working men were also disrupted by the highly casualized and competitive nature of many working-class jobs; the conditions of life in the slums of London and Berlin, or the *bidonvilles* of Paris, tended to increase the importance of ties to family, and perhaps especially mothers and siblings, and to focus attention on relations with neighbours. Friendship was a rarer luxury. As the weight of need lessened, particularly in newer housing estates separate from crowded inner cities, or in areas where more stable employment provided a little security and prosperity, some working-class men and women devoted more attention to the cultivation and maintenance of friendships outside the circle of kin or neighbours. As Adrian Franklin observed in his historical study of the Bristol suburb of Bedminster, greater stability, time and money tended to increase the family's connections to friends and to lessen the highly privatized and home-based culture of the early twentieth century. Men, women and children had greater access to and made greater use of specific gender and generational networks, but it was also more and more common for husbands and wives to make friends as couples.[28]

    In the period before 1940, these significant changes in the experience and meaning of friendship were most evident in the cities of the New World and among what historian Gunther Barth described as a new kind of "city people."[29] People dislocated by more-or-less voluntary migration managed to join together, but in a new kind of urban culture based on shared participation in city life rather than kinship. The city, especially the New World city, was in part a place in which you remade yourself: "city life" was more likely to nourish the relationships you chose to have. Of course, few could suddenly abandon the obligations of kin or family, and ethnicity, language, religion and class still mattered very much in terms of who people thought they were and how they related to others. But city people also forged new identities and forms of belonging alongside those allegiances. You might be Italian, Jewish or Polish, a cigar-maker, a tailoress or a streetcar brakeman, but you might also be joined unexpectedly to others as a Brooklyn Dodgers or Boston Red Sox follower, or build friendships at dance halls and soda fountains, or find topics of conversation with other devotees of Irene and Vernon Castle's foxtrot, Scott Joplin's ragtime or Irving Berlin's musicals.

British historian Jeffrey Weeks has argued that friendships "flourish when overarching identities are fragmented in periods of rapid social change, or at turning points in people's lives, or when lives are lived at odds with social norms."[30] They also flourish when there are places, times and opportunities for new kinds of connections to be forged, and when friendship becomes the means of both enduring and eventually enjoying modern life. It was through friendships, in other words, that city people helped each other to become modern, by surviving its dislocations and challenges and by learning how to locate and make use of the new possibilities it offered. Spending time with friends, and developing friendships based on shared interests, enjoyments and intimacies, became hallmarks of a way of life that was, for the first time, available to millions of people.

The accuracy of Weeks' description is borne out by considering three examples of the kinds of people for whom friendship was most important in the first half of the twentieth century: urban migrants, homosexual men, and adolescents and young adults. For all, relationships with unrelated people were an important means of coping with the mix of empowerment and coercion, freedom and denial, that characterized modern lives, and all forged distinctive cultures of support, enjoyment and connection in the period before the Great Depression of the 1930s. They might have used various words – compadre, sister, mensch, girlfriend, pal – and the boundaries between friends and other people may not have been precise or sharp, but the importance of these kinds of relationships is clear from what we know of people's lives.

In telling the stories of the millions of migrants who came to the cities of the New World, for instance, many historians have focused upon the family, kin and community ties that prompted migration, helped newcomers adjust to the perils and possibilities of American urban life and tied members of immigrant communities back to places and families of origin. But friendships were also very important. Around three-quarters of the so-called "new" immigrants from southern and eastern Europe between 1890 and 1920 were men, most of them unmarried. Certain groups – including migrant workers from Mexico, Chinese and Japanese migrants in California and the West, and the substantial proportion of immigrants who were sojourners rather than stayers – had even higher proportions of bachelors. They travelled in groups, sharing resources, aspirations and information as they made what were often amazingly complicated travels from villages to towns, cities, migration ports and finally the United States. In ethnic communities in which gender segregation was very strong, such as the Italians, a good number of men lived in an all-male social world of clubs and gangs. Even after marriage, many men spent large amounts of their leisure time in the company of male friends. Single women also formed a substantial element in some groups, including the Irish (still a large migrant group in the period between 1900 and 1920) and migrants from Canada's maritime provinces. Jewish women, too, were more likely than other ethnic women to have migrated independently.

What these men and women confronted in the United States made their ability to form and use networks a very important part of their survival. In most American states, Chinese and Japanese immigrants faced increasing restrictions and hostility, while the defence of "white" Southern borderlands was directed at growing numbers of Mexicans and Cubans as well as African-Americans. In the first two decades of the twentieth century, New York's Italian and Jewish neighbourhoods were the most crowded places upon the earth. While they offered economic opportunity, America's cities also promised exploitation, low wages and militant anti-unionism: the carelessness of early-century American capitalism was nowhere more evident than in its terrible rates of accidental death, in which highly publicized outrages such as the Triangle Shirtwaist Factory fire, where more than a hundred women workers died behind locked doors, were merely the tip of a dreadful iceberg. Immigrant activism and protest, progressive reforms and the changing nature of the migrant flow during and after World War I and the *Immigration Restriction Acts* helped soften "the American system" by the 1920s but it remained an industrial economy in which patronage, support and the pooling of resources remained a crucial component of most workers' lives.

If immigrants' families and kin were a vital source of assistance, most immigrants depended at least in part upon other kinds of relationships, including informal networks of friends. As much as family, friends provided material and emotional resilience and helped each other to negotiate, comprehend and explore the new environment. Italian immigrants in both Buenos Aires and New York certainly drew upon the mixture of close family, kin and *paesani* normally featured in histories of their migration, but also relied upon friends they made in the New World.[31] Indeed, friends were more likely than family members to play particular roles in migrants' exploration of new worlds. Families were more crucial in times of crisis, and in securing jobs, housing and resources. Friends were particularly important in other matters, perhaps more private ones. In immigrant narratives, family is often presented as helping to preserve identities, traditions and behaviour. Friends were more able to help to change and to challenge them. Those more experienced in American ways, or more attuned to the possibilities offered by the modern city, helped shepherd new arrivals and novices. For young, unmarried immigrants, as I argue below, friendship networks often proved a crucial refuge from tradition-bound families, helping men and women to develop more autonomous lives. Among older women, the increasing use of fertility control and the shift to hospital births were social changes forged in large part among friends, in "a sort of no-man's land, where women talked with each other – at school, at work, in a hospital or clinic waiting room, at a social club or card party – about private matters."[32]

In many ways, the new ethnic cultures that were built from the social and cultural deposits of migration relied upon friendship. Italians, in other words, helped each other become Italian-Americans, Greeks helped each other become Greek-Americans, and so on. The majority of immigrants joined formal and informal friendship groups, including mutual aid societies, fraternal orders and the wide range of political and social clubs. In the period before entitlement to welfare benefits, those clubs and societies provided an essential means of surviving illness and unemployment, as well as funeral benefits. Along with the churches, they also generated much of the community's formal social life: dances, balls, picnics, theatre parties and excursions. Members often met once a week, with the formal business accompanied and sometimes overshadowed by card-playing, drinking, smoking and political debate. Some clubs and societies officially or effectively barred women from membership but, by the time of World War I, women's auxiliaries and "sister" clubs were a common feature of many immigrant societies. Similar organizations were a feature of immigrant life in all of the societies in which immigrants settled, from Argentina, Brazil and Canada to the sugar-cane fields of northern Australia.

In the decades between 1910 and 1930, the migration of African-Americans into Northern cities generated a similarly rich mix of associations, churches, clubs and lodges, most famously in New York's Harlem and Chicago's South Side. In New York, the mix included a large number of Caribbean migrants, whose clubs and organizations sustained ties to Trinidad, Jamaica and other homelands while also linking them into the larger culture of "Black Harlem."[33] Indeed, the links between friendship, urban survival and the enjoyment of the city's possibilities are nowhere better exemplified than in 1920s and 1930s Harlem. Its nightclubs and cabarets – the Cotton Club, Connie's Inn and Small's Paradise and the other establishments of what one columnist called "a seething cauldron of Nubian mirth and hilarity" – became a playground for adventurous whites escaping Prohibition.[34] But the flowering of African-American writing, art, politics and debate in the Harlem Renaissance was built out of a more generic and sometimes subterranean culture of speakeasies, rent parties and dances, as well as the more formal literary talks and salons run by Harlem's great hostesses, such as A'Leila Walker. As historian Steven Watson argues, the friendships forged there were the "grease" of the Renaissance.[35]

By the 1920s, Harlem, along with Greenwich Village, was home to another urban subculture in which friendship played a particularly important role: the urban homosexual world described most vividly by George Chauncey in *Gay New York*. This is an example of what Mark Vernon, among others, has emphasized as especially important forms of twentieth-century friendship based on subversion and the circumvention of social and moral norms. "Friendship," he says, "becomes a relationship from which individuals find resources to refuse oppressive social conventions."[36] It also became a kind of pedagogic relationship, in which novices learned where to go, what to wear and say, and how to read and then contribute to the densely coded gay style. Friends may or may not have been or become lovers; in any case, it was the gay social circles that helped newcomers "find jobs, apartments, romance, and their closest friendships."[37] Gay men's narratives of arrival and coming out often emphasized the significance of friends in learning how, where and when to "be gay," and the ways in which friendship networks led to the formation of gay apartment buildings and nascent gay neighbourhoods. It was a form of chain migration based on friendship rather than kin. In this gay urban world, more than any other subculture, friends came to replace family, something symbolized in the playful use of "sisters" to describe close associates.

Gay New York, as Chauncey argues, rested in large part on informal social clubs and groups of friends who met in cafeterias, lunchrooms and restaurants, where they shared space with artists and bohemians. Here, too, would come the gay tourists and new arrivals. Rather like the ethnic and religious societies that shared the same neighbourhoods, these informal networks in turn generated the larger celebrations and enactments of togetherness, such as the great drag balls, common before 1930 but increasingly driven underground thereafter. This was an organized, self-conscious and increasingly commercialized social world, in which gay men became themselves in the company of friends. Alongside it rose just as organized and self-conscious lesbian enclaves. Lesbian and gay networks remained largely separate, but speakeasies featuring white and black lesbian performers – Bessie Smith, Ma Rainey and the tuxedoed Gladys Bentley – and lesbians' patronage of drag balls ensured some friendships across the gender divide.

The links between friendship, entertainment and self-expression were also very important for a third group: the young. At this point, the boundaries between childhood, adolescence and young adulthood remained more fluid than they would become after 1950; in the 1920s and 1930s, it is best to think of a "youth culture" that encompassed both older adolescents and young adults before marriage. Various forces helped to elevate the role of friendship in this culture during the 1920s and 1930s. From the outside came a growing identification of adolescence as a distinct period, lived in specialized institutions and settings, with a much more rigorous segregation of ages and a much greater emphasis on the contributions that a "successful" adolescence and young adulthood made to later life. Theories of personality and child development also began to stress peer relationships and the role of friends in the creation of healthy adults: American philosopher John Dewey even held that friendship, cooperation and play prepared children for participation in a democratic society. In the 1930s, Canadian child psychologist Mary Northway insisted that the study of peer relationships would help to free the study of human behaviour from what she saw as the dead hand of psychoanalysis, replacing it with "a view of society as a potentially rich soil out of which the individual derives nutriment for his growth and the sustenance necessary for an enriched life."[38]

If friendships were a more important component of a good – and healthy – life, the institutions in which adolescents were gathered had to play an important role in building good peer relationships and preventing bad ones. In the United States, particularly, as more and more adolescents stayed in education, their schools began to take on a much more explicit focus on peer culture, aiming to achieve a better fit between stages of development and appropriate relationships and to nourish healthy connections. They began to offer greater opportunities for peer friendships – clubs, for example – and to stress the benefits of team sports and "school spirit" in personal adjustment. The friendless adolescent became a much more worrying figure.

This emphasis on child and youth guidance was informed in part by the reliance on healthy friendships and in part by a fear of the "gangs," shared delinquencies and moral breakdown that also became more prominent in the academic and more popular discussions of youth between the wars. Much of that discussion was animated by the question of whether adolescent girls and boys could be trusted to make the right kinds of friends. In the British world, magazines and books based on school life focused more intently on friendships and rivalries, and organizations such as the Boy Scouts and the Girl Guides added an emphasis on friendship and productive cooperation to their focus on individual loyalty and service to the empire.

At the same time, older adolescents and young adults were forging their own connections between friendship, freedom and fun. In a very important sense, the young people of the 1910s and 1920s helped each other to become modern women and men. For a range of groups – college students, factory girls and immigrants – friends became a more and more important means of accessing a world of entertainment and diversion. In that world, they also watched and listened to films, song and serials; these taught them about the pleasures and pitfalls of romantic love, but they also told them of friendship and its rewards. Friends were collaborators in enjoyment, eager listeners to accounts of dates, "pashes" and encounters, and a refuge from the monotonies and even oppressions of work and family obligation. They were increasingly the people who would help you to "enjoy yourself," attract a partner, and become adult. For young women, especially, friends were the confidants who shared and shaped one's coming of age and with whom all matters affecting the transition from girlhood could be discussed.

There were important class, cultural and gender differences in youth culture within the United States. While the flapper and her beau became its enduring icons, its genesis lay among the factory girls, shop and office workers who filled the dance halls and the fun fairs and cultivated a small clique of people they called "lady friends." Its pioneers were also their older and younger brothers, the gangs of juvenile friends in the nickelodeons, the baseball parks and the amusement arcades. They were the urban bachelors, the "saloon crowd" and the "poolroom platoon," the young men who lived in the lodging and furnished room districts of the cities and "ran together" to find fun. They were also those Joanne Meyerowitz called the "women adrift": the tens of thousands of young women, American and immigrant, who worked and lived apart from family before marriage but who often took rooms with work friends. Worried reformers asked these workers how they had managed to exist in a world of low wages and high rents; as one Chicago woman told an investigator, "they used to get friends to help them."[39]

These were also the young adults of whom some urban reformers despaired, precisely because they seemed to prefer the high life and their friends to the responsible life and family. As Bostonian Robert Woods put it, women and men "postpone marriage or remain permanently unmarried, choosing to live in a respectable-appearing street near the excitements of the city"; the best response was "a systematic organization of informal friendly and neighborly acquaintance to make good to these young people the sustaining power of human ties."[40] All the while, these same young people were often developing something akin to that themselves: mutual aid societies and lodges, unofficial storefront churches and especially social clubs, including Philadelphia's Red Rose Social and Chicago's Lonesome Club, which organized dances "to facilitate the social contacts of those who are alone and without friends in the city."[41]

While immigrant and African-American young people were the pioneers and innovators of a culture in which friends, "buddies" and "pals" played a crucial role, middle-class white youth adopted and adapted its language and rituals and were also the most important targets of its growing commercialization.[42] Their experience was somewhat different, however. Because they participated most in the rapid expansion of high school and college education, their friendship culture was supported and endorsed by those institutions' focus on age segregation and peer relationships. As Paula Fass argued in relation to college students, the seeming iconoclasm of drinking, dancing and sexual freedom went hand in hand with an increasingly prescriptive peer culture. Indeed, she says, it was this very prescriptiveness that gave this culture its strength and allowed it to survive the moral purity crusades of the late 1920s and 1930s.[43] In addition, the mixing of genders in American high schools and colleges emphasized the forming of couples as well as friendship groups, creating hetero- as well as homo-social friendship networks. It was in the 1920s that young men and women, and then adolescents, began "dating," sometimes in groups, and the terms "girlfriend" and "boyfriend" came to describe romantic and sexual partners who might – or might not – be intended as later partners in marriage.

These versions of friendship, which were based in the desire to experience and enjoy the attractions – or perhaps distractions – of the modern world, were not only American. The youth culture of the interwar period was heavily stamped by new forms of American big business, from Hollywood studios and Madison Avenue advertising to Coca-Cola, though it relied for much of its vivacity and appeal on the inventiveness of African-American musicians and dancers and Tin Pan Alley composers. But this culture was enacted by young people themselves, and its reproduction and global spread rested as much upon networks of friends and mentors as upon mass selling and persuasion. Australian, British, German and Canadian youth may have chewed gum, sported "jazz haircuts" or a Louise Brooks "bob," played arcade games and the new pinball machines, and even – if they had the energy – danced the Black Bottom and then the Lindy Hop, but they added their own inflections. Nor was the flow all one way. By the middle of the 1920s, Europeans and Americans were learning the tango from Carlos Gardel and Cuban dance from Xavier Cugat.

The fascination with circuses, films, dance and entertainment was noted, and sometimes criticized, in other societies, where it was linked with triviality, decadence, Americanization and even racial decline. Without wanting to deny their shortcomings, recent historians have generally cast a much more positive light on these cultures, in part because they recognize the agency of women, youth racial minorities and homosexuals in their creation. Against the idea that women's lives, for instance, were reshaped solely from the outside, or as a result of World War I, Birgitte Soland shows how young Danish women, borrowing from various cultural sources and from each other, reshaped gender identities and relations in order to lead what they defined as "modern lives."[44] In the UK, increased access to paid work in offices, shops and factories increased young women's leisure and mobility, and in turn their opportunities and needs for friendship, while young working-class men also formed new kinds of age-specific groups and networks around shared leisure pursuits.[45] In "becoming a woman" in 1920s and 1930s Britain, friends had much to teach and to learn about fashion, style, gesture and look. Much the same could be said about Australia, where the dance hall and picture palace both symbolized and helped produce Sydney's "vernacular modernity."[46] In women's diaries, too, while building and maintaining friendships often took second place to domestic details and romance, friends almost always appear at crucial moments in the narrative, as diversions, as collaborators in romantic pursuits or as receivers of confidences.[47] Indeed, one Australian woman complained, "one might think better of marriage if one's married friends would not confide in one so much."[48]

The Friendships of Women and Men

American historian Linda Rosenzweig argues that during the 1920s, a new emotional culture was taking shape, especially in the United States, in which friendship – and especially female friendship – was diminished by a new focus on heterosexual intimacy.[49] She suggests that while a nineteenth-century or "Victorian" model of love and self-disclosure between women persisted until the time of World War I, the growing importance of successful heterosexual relationships – and the increasing stigmatization of homosexuality – broke down homosocial networks. In a way, all of those friends the modern girl made in high school and college came to serve one end: achieving the kind of popularity that would bolster her heterosexual attractiveness. Marriage manuals and popular expertise told men to develop companionate marriages that would satisfy wives emotionally and sexually, and friendship was assumed to play a more important role in making marriage attractive and successful for both partners. During the 1920s the proportion of American women marrying rose, and their age at marriage dropped; for middle-class women, at least, what has been called the first sexual revolution seems in part to have resulted in the diminishing of women's friendships. There was increasing suspicion directed towards close female friendships in the 1920s and 1930s, which stemmed in part from the increasing conviction that spinsters, even as much as lesbians, were endangered by their refusal of marriage and their lack of "healthy" sexual fulfilment.

Of course, the words of marriage manuals and experts do not always translate directly into changes in actual behaviour. As Rosenzweig says, this changing balance between a homo- and a hetero-social world was largely true for younger women; older women continued to both build more supportive friendships and provide the most significant public examples of female friendship's intimacies and pleasures. However companionate the marriage, real women also continued to rely upon and enjoy close friendships, with other wives, female family members and neighbours. One of the most important indications of that was the way in which female consumers completely reshaped the marketing of the telephone in the decades before 1940. Originally presented largely as an instrument for business, the telephone had become a feminized technology by the 1920s, with women's networks, family ties and friendships becoming the dominant theme of its advertising.[50]

Even the idealization of heterosexual romance in popular fiction and Hollywood movies – which included more-or-less humorous portrayals of women's competition over men – was always tempered by the friendships between female characters and their acknowledgement that there were some things men could not do. In *Stagedoor* (1937), for instance, it is with the friendship and support of the other would-be actresses (played by Ginger Rogers, Eve Arden and Lucille Ball, among others) that Katherine Hepburn's "Terry" learns both how to act and to rise above the machinations of men. Comedies also played on women's alliances: the genre that would culminate in *Gentlemen Prefer Blondes* (1953) was also popular in the 1930s. In movies about gold-diggers, actresses and "girls on the town," popular comic stars, such as Winnie Lightner in *The Life of the Party* (1930), usually showed that while a woman desired a man for some things, no man could satisfy a woman's every need. As Jeanine Basinger argued, American popular cinema, especially after the imposition of the Hays Code in 1934, presented a somewhat ambivalent message: women's only legitimate aims might have been limited to men, marriage and motherhood, but the journey to that eventual destination often included fun, glamour and the friendship of other women.[51]

Some women also challenged the anxiety about spinsterhood. In interwar Britain, for example, doctors such as Esther Harding and Laura Hutton began developing a feminist critique of the spinster stereotype, stressing the importance of women's friendships as places for the expression of emotional and sexual drives. Harding's 1933 book, *The Way of All Women*, for instance, argued that the "bond between such friends is one not of convenience but of mutual love and their life together is consequently likely to be very rich, attaining a permanence and stability equalled only in marriage."[52] Winifred Holtby dramatized the arguments in her novels, most notably *The Crowded Street* (1924), in which her heroine, Muriel, rejects marriage after her friend Delia "let me see ... that there were other things in life. I've actually got tastes and inclinations and a personality."[53] Female friendships also had significance far beyond individual fulfilment; "in the last few decades," Harding wrote:

> friendships between women have come ... to hold a place of un-precedented importance in the community ... [and] our whole civilisation ... the outcome promises an increased solidarity among women, resulting in an entirely new development of those values which have to do with feeling and relationship.[54]

It is interesting to note, too, the growing popularity of children's fiction set in girls' schools, with Elsie Oxenham, Elinor Brent-Dyer and Dorita Fairlie-Bruce all developing series that featured close, intimate and lasting friendships between their adolescent characters.[55]

While recognition of their dynamics and intensity have sometimes waited for their late twentieth-century biographers, some of the female friendships of the 1930s, in particular, were highly visible attempts to enact something of Esther Harding's optimism. In the United States, recent studies of Eleanor Roosevelt help us to grasp the significant role that women's networks – often stemming back to settlement house, Children's Bureau, National Consumers' League and suffrage politics – played in the politics of the New Deal. While her long-term relationship with Lorena Hickok is now the most well known, Roosevelt's friendships with Molly Dewson, who became the head of the Women's Division of the Democratic National Committee, with

Frances Perkins, the first female member of any federal Cabinet, and with lifelong companions and reform activists Marion Dickerman and Nancy Cook, were arguably just as important in shaping the New Deal agenda and wider political culture of 1930s America.[56]

For British, American and Australian women, the mobilizations that accompanied war – and especially World War II – may have been even more important in strengthening the significance of friendships in female culture. Nursing and volunteering brought more young women into the collaborative work of the war effort and took them out into the world; those who did factory and munitions work, or replaced men in a variety of other jobs, or worked in the Women's Land Army and its American and Australian counterparts, also experienced the broadening of social contacts that a fully encompassing war created. The same was true for the women who joined the WRNS, the WAAF and the ATF in the UK or the American WAAF, WAC and WAVES, who ferried aircraft, worked as code-breakers and intelligence officers or participated in organized resistance. In the United States, around a quarter of a million women joined women's services, while the number in the UK exceeded half a million.

For most women, the growing focus on heterosexual intimacy and attractiveness did not exclude friendship so much as temporarily turn it to the specific end of successful courtship. This, the continuing public presence of reforming women, and single women's ability to counter the arguments about repressed spinsters, ensured that women's friendships remained important in personal life and in public debate during the 1920s and 1930s on both sides of the Atlantic. In professions and careers, and in emotional and personal life after marriage or outside marriage, female friendships were still living out that 1907 claim that it was women, and not men, who were able to make the best and most enduring sorts of friends. The modern woman's path to fulfilment was one she travelled with her female companions.

Friendships between men were perhaps even more affected by anxieties about the boundary between healthy comradeship and unhealthy desire, especially after Freud's arguments about unconscious sexual drives filtered into popular consciousness. Men continued to talk of friends, mates and buddies, and, like women, they participated energetically in a new culture of leisure and consumption, especially during adolescence and young adulthood, in which the pursuit of pleasure – and women – was conducted collectively. The business of becoming a man, and maintaining male networks, was often conducted in institutions closed to women, such as the fraternity, the lodge, the service club and the "gang," and through pledging, initiation and bonding rituals that explicitly barred women. At the same time, however, the task of becoming and remaining masculine grew increasingly complicated, as masculinity was evermore oriented around an unshakeable division between heterosexuality and homosexuality. By the 1920s, the real man's relationships with other men were a source of concern, and there was an increasing academic focus on establishing broad gender differences in personal relationships, including how men talked with their friends.[57]

This was not just a concern for experts, psychologists and cultural interpreters. In his fascinating study of photographs of American men, for instance, John Ibson identifies a clear shift in male self-presentation during the 1920s. In the late nineteenth century, studio portraits often showed men holding hands and inclining their heads towards one other. In the 1910s, team photographs showed young sportsmen sprawled on top of each other, hugging or arm-in-arm. From the 1920s onwards, there is a new reserve, and men are separated from each other, at least in part by the fear of what homosocial contact might imply.[58] In similar vein, organizations such as the YMCA, which had fostered and practised the idea of close male friendship and mentoring, became increasingly nervous and precise in its definitions of appropriate and inappropriate "brotherly feeling." In 1892 the handbook compiled by the American and Canadian movements' leaders talked of "the intense love for young men, and a readiness to devote one's life" to their welfare as the "special qualification required in this work." By 1927, ideal leaders needed to show "good judgement" in their relationships, be "friendly but not familiar" and choose their "associates carefully." If spinsters were a matter of widespread cultural concern in the interwar period, so were the bachelors who headed men's service, fraternal and fellowship groups; YMCA leaders were counselled against "intense friendships," which the sex-segregated activities of the organisation were increasingly feared to be producing.[59]

In the twentieth century, men's friendships trod a difficult line between the enjoyments and the dangers of same-sex companionships. They became more closely linked to particular stages of life, at least in the middle class: as in the nineteenth century, adolescents and young men could be friends, often very intimate ones, but boyish enthusiasms were not meant to persist beyond the discovery of dating and "going steady" with girls. Thereafter the demands of marriage and the need to compete with others in business and the professions made making and keeping friends more difficult for adult men and in fact became a responsibility of their wives.[60] Of course, there were major class, ethnic and racial differences in this as in all matters of behaviour, ideas and expectations. A less-anxious mixing of male friendship, intimacy, touching and – for some – sexual contact, which had clearly persisted among lower-class and immigrant groups and among adolescents, was picked up by Kinsey's studies of male sexual experience in the 1940s.

Generally, though, close male friendships could only be celebrated and idealized in contexts that provided some way of explaining their intensity while safeguarding the participants' heterosexual masculinity. In the late nineteenth century, exploring, conquering and taming the wilderness provided just such a context. Though sportsmen were mostly less demonstrative in the earlier part of the century than they would be by its end, team sports provided another justifying environment. In Britain and its dominions, single-sex schools were another; school stories were particularly likely to emphasize the mutual interests and adventures of boys, often in temporary defiance of authority. In sport, and even more dramatically in tackling the wilderness, adult men also relied upon each other in ways that emphasized closeness and dependence, and the joys of shared achievements and exhilaration. Fictional accounts were especially popular in the British world, including its Australian periphery, where tales of intrepid adventure in the Outback commonly involved friends rescuing each other from dangerous animals, strangely out-of-place erupting volcanoes and, in one famous story, a lost tribe of Amazon warriors.[61] Male bonding – sometimes across racial barriers – was also a feature of accounts of the more short-lived German colonization.[62]

After 1912, the tale of Captain Scott and his comrades in the Antarctic provided new material for stories of male friendship – and sacrifice. These were emphasized with particular starkness (to the point of didactic overkill) in stories written for boys, but other accounts also used the theme of friendship to ennoble what might otherwise be seen as futile. In his 1921 account, *The Worst Journey in the World*, Apsley Cherry-Garrard writes what he calls "a sequel" to his friendship with Scott, Bowers and the others and takes as his theme that "the mutual conquest of difficulties is the cement of friendship, as it is the only lasting cement of matrimony."[63]

While true and fictional tales sometimes featured loners and men's more-or-less successful struggles to achieve freedom from constraints, they also made the point that the dangers facing real men were often best faced with friends. In the United States, for example, the male adventure of what Jopi Nyman calls "hard-boiled fiction" can be traced back to western adventure and detective stories of the late nineteenth century. Yet in the 1920s, when the genre flourished in both popular and literary forms, writers like Ernest Hemingway turned the individual man's quest for an alternative to feminized domestic life into a collective drama. In his short story collection, *In Our Time*, "The Three-Day Blow" features a main character using a three-day fishing trip with a friend to recuperate from a love affair, while "Cross Country Snow" laments male friendships diminished by the responsibilities of marriage and fatherhood.[64] The genre was not without its satirists; in his short story, "Mantrap," Sinclair Lewis put New York lawyer Ralph Prescott into the wilderness with his golf partner, E. Wesson Woodbury. Deserted by Woodbury, Prescott survives with the help of a woman and an Indian, and retreats back to civilization equally disillusioned with the "wilderness experience" and the supposed strength of the masculine bonds it is meant to generate.

From World War I on, depictions of male friendship in Europe, Australia and, to a lesser extent, North America came to focus largely upon the camaraderie of soldiers. Perhaps even more so in the trenches than in earlier forms of war-making, soldiering was literally as well as figuratively a place in which male bonds could keep you alive. But in the culture produced and affected by the war, as Sarah Cole has argued, male friendship was both valorized and weakened. In her analysis of war literature, she suggests that comradeship was "offered as a replacement for nearly all other forms of human and social organisation" and "the saving grace of a world in crisis."[65] The comradeship of armies was an improvement upon the lives of men at home, and those singing its praises tended to see it as both dissolving peacetime arguments and class conflicts into fellowship and providing a model for postwar societies. While German memoirists wrote of *Männergemeinschaft*, German soldiers wrote in their letters of "the universal comradeship that runs through the whole German army and is shown by our all calling each other 'du' [the familiar, informal form for 'you']."[66] British official military historian Basil Liddell Hart, writing in the 1930s, emphasized the "bands of men who, if the spirit were right, lived in such intimacy that they became part of one another."

This was the "fellowship of the trenches," which he saw as "redeeming the sordidness and stupidity of war."[67]

Yet the agonies of modern war also – and devastatingly – revealed the limits of friendship: "the war's annihilating power in fact made [friendship] the most vulnerable and dislocating of all relations."[68] The war also revealed the differences between corporate comradeship and intimate friendship. In the poetry of Wilfred Owen and Siegfried Sassoon, and in postwar novels, Cole says, we see a declining faith in comradeship, and a focus on the scarred, devastated or absent friend whose disfigurement and death leaves each man isolated and bereaved. As Sassoon put it, "my killed friends are with me where I go," and survivors lived in "cowed subjection to the ghosts of friends who died." [69] Male friendship failed, because friendship could not survive the unceasing destruction of men. War produced comrades, but it killed friends.

At the same time, there is no question that the experience of friendship, companionship and affection at war was more ambivalent for the men who were there. It is clear from diaries, letters and memoirs that many of the men caught up in the churning horrors of the Great War saw themselves as forming intense and even loving friendships, at least with men of similar rank and location. While they experienced camaraderie, even with the enemy, they also had friends. They knew friends died and that friendship did not mitigate the savagery, insecurity and insanity of the war itself. Yet they still felt themselves – or at least remembered themselves – embracing what one French soldier called "the most tender human experience."[70] Perhaps those who survived to write about their experiences (and were prepared to share them) were more likely to emphasize such relationships. Certainly, in C. B. Purdom's collection of British soldiers' stories, *Everyman at War*, published in 1930, the importance of friendships up to and even after death is a common theme. Private George Brame began his account of his time in France with "my friend H."; "our acquaintance soon developed into the richest friendship" and "we were constantly together until he met his death." W. Walker remembered becoming lost on the battlefield: "it was a cursed bad piece of work to be severed so soon from one's pals. It means a lot, that, in warfare. Friendship strengthens the heart."[71]

Modern war certainly created a temporary expansion of the possibilities for friendship; in the Great War and perhaps even more in World War II, great conscript armies produced an unprecedented

degree of social mixing and percolation. One of the things men remembered about war was the great diversity of people with whom
they associated; in armies, men met men they would never have met
in civilian life and, if the bonds they forged survived the war itself,
those friendships were often extended in returned servicemen's organizations or less formal associations. While those bonds did not automatically span entrenched divisions, especially in the racially
segregated American forces, the possibility of association, as well as
the fact of wartime service, began to erode some very strong prejudices. For many of the men who fought in them, the twentieth century's
great wars did change the nature and extent of their friendships. On
the home front, too, mass mobilizations and a new scale of voluntary
participation brought people together in a spirit of shared vulnerability that some, at least, enjoyed: one British Home Guard member
reported that in his platoon he found "a sort of mass friendship I
would never have experienced in peacetime."[72] The wars also provide strong evidence that the literature of friendship mattered. Whether
prescriptive advice or adventure stories, it is clear that many soldiers
expected to find comradeship with many and deeper friendships with
a few. If war service provided new opportunities for male friendship,
in the world wars, as had been true in America's nineteenth-century
Civil War, a good many men were also drawn into service by networks of friends, associates and fellow workmen.

   Joanna Bourke argues that "relationships between servicemen during the war failed to result in any true reconstruction of masculine
intimacy."[73] This was in part because friendships were subverted by
the exigencies of military hierarchy and by the distinctions of class,
religion, ethnicity and region they often mirrored. Men soon realized
that their temporary dependence upon each other did not always
equate with friendship: "companionship under conditions like ours
was not really possible ... Everything seemed to be on a day to day
basis."[74] Combat experience could also sever prewar friendships, as
men found they could no longer talk to or be understood by those
who had not served. Certainly, both wars gave increased political power
to returned soldiers' organizations, which often insisted on the exclusive bonds and entitlements of men home from war. And postwar
societies placed great stock in images and stories emphasizing true
comradeship and friendship, if only as a form of reassurance that men
who died horrible deaths had perhaps not died alone. In Australia,
the great popularity of Will Dyson's drawings of comrades united in

death during the 1920s and 1930s is testament to the continuing significance of idealized soldier friendships. At the same time, many
soldiers avoided or repudiated the ex-servicemen's organizations and
rejected what they saw as the romanticizing of the soldiers' sufferings.

Those observing the American infantrymen of World War II also
emphasized the importance of something they called "companionship" or "friendship" rather than comradeship. Popular war correspondent Ernie Pyle wrote of the GIs that their "companionship finally
becomes a part of one's soul, and it cannot be obliterated," while a
front-line soldier wrote that "the only permanency [lay in] the human
relationships and bonds of friendship welding us together."[75] Their
most comprehensive historian, Gerald Linderman, argues that "they
felt their friendship profoundly": it stood between them and an awful
isolation, kept them sane, and coarsened and moulded them into effective soldiers.[76] Yet soldiers' friendships had their costs. In severely
affected units, the loss of so many friends could cause almost intoler-
able emotional strains. The exclusions of friendship – especially in
the midst of so much danger – could also make men more indifferent
to and less protective of strangers and loners. There was little time for
dead or even wounded friends. The war's end "revealed how central
survival was to comradeship; with the disappearance of necessity, bonds
loosened rapidly."[77]

For the millions of men who fought in and survived these wars, we
can perhaps characterize the most typical outcomes as the temporary
strengthening of their bonds to their immediate comrades, and a few
more intense friendships, only some of which continued after the war.
Perhaps even more significant was the way in which the soldiers' return from wars, especially in the 1940s, was marked by a strong desire
for "normalcy" and domesticity. Rather than the companionship of
comrades, most men sought a return to wives, sweethearts and mothers and to the intimacies of home and hearth. In that sense, the emphasis on soldiers' bonds – whether mateship, brotherhood or
camaraderie – was a product of stories and memories that helped give
these experiences meaning in war's immediate and more lasting
aftermath.

At least in terms of idealizations and prescriptions, the first half of
the century was characterized by an attempt to ensure that male friendships had a purpose and nature that sharply distinguished them from
homosexuality. The mateship of workers, the temporary intimacies
of school chums, college friends and fellow team members and

especially the camaraderie of soldiers provided ideal and often real men with a way of being intimate that did not call their masculinity into question. It was here that men and women were most different. Among heterosexual men, friendships were much more tied to specific ages and contexts, and could easily wither when the stages or structures that made them safe – adolescence, sport or soldiering, for instance – were relinquished. Among women, individual autonomy could more easily coexist with intimacy, revelation and sharing. For middle-class men, in particular, autonomy and self-mastery were more likely to include some degree of competition with other men. Female friendships were increasingly linked with the exploration and enjoyment of relatively new personal freedoms and with becoming a modern woman. Whatever their origin, they were also more likely to be imagined and sometimes realized as lifelong bonds. Male friendships, on the other hand, tended to be tied to specific moments and contexts, characterized by the absence of women. In a way, some men might occasionally be friends but all men are in some sense rivals.

These differences between women and men were nowhere more starkly demonstrated than in one of the twentieth century's most successful guides to self-creation, Dale Carnegie's *How to Win Friends and Influence People*, first published in 1936. It is apt that a way of reconciling male friendship and competitiveness emerged in the United States and then spread around the world. In a way, of course, *How to Win Friends* was a paean to empathy, and to the power of praise, encouragement and taking an interest in others. To Depression-era Americans, Carnegie provided a way of being successful that depended largely upon personality and things that were free and over which even people with limited education and means had some control. Nor is the book, or the broader philosophy it represents, quite so manipulative as the coupling of objectives in its title implies. Carnegie's point, in a way, was that you could not positively influence people you had not first liked and respected.

How to Win Friends and Influence People is most interesting in terms of the kind of personality and personal relationships it recommended to an audience it assumed to be male (it would take another 20 years for second wife Dorothy Carnegie, in *Don't Grow Old, Grow Up!*, to add women to the lexicon). Carnegie offered a way of rescuing friendship by installing it at the centre of "normal" men's competitive drives. He gave the pursuit of friendship a satisfyingly instrumental flavour, making it a central component of the desire for influence, success and professional recognition. The arts of friendship, in Carnegie's terms, were means to larger individual ends: to make people like you, to win people to your way of thinking and to change people "without giving offence or arousing resentment." Rather than a meeting of equals, the revelation of self to other, and the enjoyment of the other's differences, this was a struggle for mastery, a way of making the other person feel important, getting them to "want to do what you want them to by arousing their desires" and making them "happy about doing what you suggest."

Carnegie's arguments were tellingly popular: his book was a bestseller for more than a decade in the United States and was translated into most European languages, despite often negative reviews: one American literary critic bemoaned "the vogue of a monstrosity like *How to Make Friends and Influence People*, written by an author without the slightest conception of the meaning of disinterested friendship or permanent influence," while psychologist Joseph Jastrow fumed "it has shaken my faith in the potential intelligence of my fellow beings that 750,000 ... have purchased this abyss of advice."[78] It remains a kind of Book of Genesis for the exploding genre of self-improvement literature. In arguing that making friends helped you improve yourself, and that each man had within him the means to having an influence, Carnegie clearly struck a chord with ordinary Americans and Europeans alike. In the end, of course, he explored but did not resolve the essential tensions that affected friendships between men. But in emphasizing the importance of friends and friendliness, and in his belief that the most fulfilling lives could not be imagined without the support and engagement of friends, Carnegie also tells us something very important about the even stronger focus on friendship that would characterize the second half of the century.

Notes

1. Stacey J. Oliker, "The Modernisation of Friendship: Individualism, Intimacy and Gender in the Nineteenth Century," in Rebecca G. Adams and Graham Allan (eds), *Placing Friendship in Context* (Cambridge: Cambridge University Press, 1998), pp. 23–27.

2. Arthur C. Benson, "Essentials of Friendship," *Putnam's Monthly* 2 (1907), cited in Linda W. Rosenzweig, *Another Self: Middle-class American Women and their Friends in the Twentieth Century* (New York: New York University Press, 1999), p. 41.

3. Georg Simmel, "The Metropolis and Mental Life," in David Frisby and Mike Featherstone (eds), *Simmel on Culture: Selected Writings* (London: Sage Publications, 1997 [1902]), pp. 174–87.

4. Robert Park, *Human Communities: The City and Human Ecology* (Free Press, New York, 1952), p. 86.

5. Robert and Helen Lynd, *Middletown: A Study in American Culture* (New York: Harcourt Brace Jovanovich, 1956) [1929]), pp. 272–312.

6. Lynd, *Middletown*, pp. 274–75.

7. Octavia Hill, "Letter to My Fellow Workers' [1874], cited in Jane Lewis, "Social Facts, Social Theory and Social Change: The Ideas of Booth in Relation to Those of Beatrice Webb, Octavia Hill and Helen Bosanquet," in David Englander and Rosemary O'Day (eds), *Retrieved Riches: Social Investigation in Britain, 1840–1914* (Aldershot: Scholar Press, 1995), p. 51.

8. Mary Richmond, *Friendly Visiting among the Poor: A Handbook for Charity Workers* (Montclair NJ: Patterson Smith, 1969 [1899]), p. 180.

9. W. E. B. DuBois, *The Philadelphia Negro* (Philadelphia: University of Philadelphia Press, 1899), p. 358.

10. Mary E. McDowell, "Friendly Visiting," in Isabel C. Barrows (ed.), *National Conference of Charities and Corrections Proceedings* (Boston and London: Geo. H. Ellis, P. S. King & Son, 1896), pp. 253–56 at p. 255.

11. Cited in Sarah Deutsch, "Learning to Talk More Like a Man: Boston Women's Class-Bridging Organizations, 1870–1940," *American Historical Review* 97 (1992), pp. 379–404 at p. 386.

12. Eileen Yeo, *The Contest for Social Science: Relations and Representations of Gender and Class* (London: Rivers Oram Press, 1996), pp. 276–77.

13. Mary Richmond, *The Long View* (New York: Russell Sage Foundation, 1930), p. 190.

14. "The Work of the American Red Cross during the War," American Red Cross, Washington 1919, at http://www.vlib.us/medical/Arc/ARC3.htm, accessed 20 May 2007.

15. Cited in Maria Serena I. Diokno, "'Benevolent Assimilation' and Filipino Responses," in Hazel M. McFerson (ed.), *Mixed Blessing: The Impact of the American Colonial Experience on Politics and Society in the Philippines* (Westport: Greenwood, 2002), pp. 75–87 at p. 75.

16. The Victoria League for Commonwealth Friendship, "History of the Victoria League," at http://www.victorialeague.co.uk/pages/09history.html, accessed 20 May 2007.

17. J. C. Smuts, "The British Empire and World Peace," *Journal of the Royal Institute of International Affairs* 9 (March 1930), pp. 141–53 at p. 144.

18. Woodrow Wilson, "Announcement to the Armistice to Congress' [11 November 1918] in Michael Duffy (ed.), *First World War.com*, http://www.firstworldwar.com/source/armistice_wilson1.htm, accessed 20 May 2007; Albert

Shaw (ed.), *The Messages and Papers of Woodrow Wilson* (New York: The Review of Reviews Corporation, 1924), I, p. 597.

19. Kellog–Briand Pact 1928, at http://www.yale.edu/lawweb/avalon/imt/kbpact.htm, accessed 20 May 2007.

20. Cited in Diokno, "Benevolent Assimilation," p. 77.

21. Cited in Miralini Sinha, "Gender in the Critiques of Colonialism and Nationalism: Locating the 'Indian Woman,'" in Joan Scott (ed.), *Feminism and History* (Oxford: Oxford University Press, 1996), pp. 477–504 at p. 490.

22. Maureen Flanagan, *Seeing with their Hearts: Chicago Women and the Vision of the Good City, 1871–1933* (Princeton, NJ: Princeton University Press, 2002).

23. Mark Elliott, "Race, Color Blindness, and the Democratic Public: Albion W. Tourgee's Radical Principles in *Plessy v. Ferguson*," *Journal of Southern History* 67 (2001), pp. 287–330; Sandra Holton, "Segregation, Racism and White Women Reformers: A Transnational Analysis, 1840–1912," *Women's History Review* 10 (2001), pp. 5–25.

24. Mark Allan Jackson, "Dark Memory: A Look at Lynching in America through the Life, Times, and Songs of Woody Guthrie," *Popular Music and Society* 28 (2005), pp. 663–75.

25. I am grateful to Liz Reed for this information; see also Fiona Paisley, *Loving Protection? Australian Feminism and Aboriginal Women's Rights 1919–1939* (Melbourne: Melbourne University Press, 2000).

26. Warren G. Harding, "Return to Normalcy," Boston, Massachusetss [May 14 1920], at http://www.etsu.edu/cas/history/docs/normalcy.htm, accessed 20 May 2007.

27. R. E. Pahl, *On Friendship* (Cambridge: Polity Press, 2000), p. 5.

28. A. Franklin, "Working-class Privatism: An Historical Case Study of Bedminster, Bristol," *Environment and Planning D: Society and Space* 7.1 (1989), pp. 93–113.

29. Gunther Barth, *City People: The Rise of Modern City Culture in Nineteenth-century America* (New York: Oxford University Press, 1980).

30. Jeffrey Weeks, Brian Heaphy and Catherine Donovan, *Same-Sex Intimacies: Families of Choice and Other Life Experiments* (New York: Routledge, 2001), p. 51.

31. Samuel L. Baily, *Immigrants in the Lands of Promise: Italians in Buenos Aires and New York City, 1870–1914* (Ithaca, New York: Cornell University Press, 1999).

32. Susan Cotts Watkins and Angela D. Danzi, "Women's Gossip and Social Change: Childbirth and Fertility Control among Italian and Jewish Women in the United States, 1920–1940," *Gender and Society* 9 (1995), pp. 469–90.

33. Irma Watkins-Owens, *Blood Relations: Caribbean Immigrants and the Harlem Community, 1900–1930* (Bloomington: Indiana University Press, 1996).

34. *Daily News*, 1 November 1929, cited in Lynn Yeager, "Flapper Fever" at http://www.villagevoice.com/bestof/2006/essays/yaeger, accessed 22 July 2007.

35. Steven Watson, *The Harlem Renaissance: Hub of African-American Culture, 1920-1930* (New York: Pantheon Books, 1995).

36. Mark Vernon, *The Philosophy of Friendship* (London: Palgrave Macmillan, 2005), p. 120.

37. George Chauncey, *Gay New York: Gender, Urban Culture, and the Makings of the Gay Male World, 1890-1940* (New York: Basic Books, 1994), p. 3.

38. Mary L. Northway, *A Primer of Sociometry* (Toronto: University of Toronto Press, 1952), p. 49.

39. Joanne Meyerowitz, *Women Adrift: Independent Wage Earners in Chicago, 1880-1930* (Chicago: Chicago University Press, 1988), p. 93. See also Kathy Lee Peiss, *Cheap Amusements: Working Women and Leisure in Turn-of-the-Century New York* (Philadelphia: Temple University Press, 1986).

40. Robert A. Woods, "The Recovery of the Parish," [1912] in *The Neighborhood and Nation-Building: The Running Comment of Thirty Years at South End House* (Boston: Houghton Mifflin Company, 1923), p. 141.

41. Meyerowitz, *Women Adrift*, p. 99.

42. Randy D. McBee, *Dance Hall Days: Intimacy and Leisure among Working-class Immigrants in the United States* (New York: New York University Press, 2000).

43. Paula S. Fass, *The Damned and the Beautiful: American Youth in the 1920s* (Oxford: Oxford University Press, 1979).

44. Birgitte Soland, *Becoming Modern: Young Women and the Reconstruction of Womanhood in the 1920s* (Princeton, NJ: Princeton University Press, 2000).

45. Selina Todd, *Young Women, Work and Family in England, 1918-1950* (Oxford: Oxford University Press, 2005); David Fowler, *The First Teenagers: The Life-Style of Young Wage-Earners in Interwar Britain* (Woburn: London, 1995); Sally Alexander, "Becoming a Woman in the 1920s and 1930s," *Becoming a Woman and Other Essays in 19th and 20th Century Feminist History* (London: Virago, 1994), pp. 202-24.

46. Jill Julius Matthews, *Dance Hall and Picture Palace: Sydney's Romance with Modernity* (Sydney: Currency Press, 2005).

47. Katie Holmes, *Spaces in her Day: Australian Women's Diaries in the 1920s and 1930* (Sydney: Allen & Unwin, 1995).

48. *Dawn*, 1 May 1904, cited in Katie Holmes, "'This Diary Writing Does Not Really Count as Writing': Women's Writing and the Writing of History" (1995), at http://www.nla.gov.au/events/holmes.html, accessed 20 May 2007.

49. Rosenzwig, *Another Self*, pp. 66-96.

50. Claude S. Fischer, "Gender and the Residential Telephone, 1890-1940: Technologies of Sociability," *Sociological Forum* 3.2 (1988), pp. 11-33.

51. Jeanine Basinger, *A Woman's View: How Hollywood Spoke to Women, 1930-1960* (Middletown, CT: Wesleyan University Press, 1995).

52. M. Esther Harding, *The Way of All Women: A Psychological Interpretation* (London: Longman, 1933), p. 92. See also Alison Oram, "Repressed and Thwarted,

or Bearer of the New World? The Spinster in Interwar Feminist Discourse," *Women's History Review* 1.3 (1992), pp. 413–33 at p. 421.

53. Winifred Holtby, *The Crowded Street* (London: Virago, 1981 [1924]), pp. 269–70.

54. Harding, *The Way of All Women*, pp. 89–90.

55. Rosemary Auchmuty, *A World of Girls* (London: The Women's Press, 1992).

56. Frances M. Seeber, "Eleanor Roosevelt and Women in the New Deal: A Network of Friends," *Presidential Studies Quarterly* 20.4 (Fall 1990), pp. 707–17.

57. Henry T. Moore, "Further Data Concerning Sex Differences," *Journal of Abnormal Psychology* 17 (1922), pp. 210–14.

58. John Ibson, *Picturing Men: A Century of Male Relationships in Everyday American Photography* (Washington, DC: Smithsonian Institution, 2002).

59. John Donald Gustav-Wrathall, *Take the Young Stranger by the Hand: Same-Sex Relations and the YMCA* (Chicago: University of Chicago Press, 2000), pp. 64, 89.

60. Anthony E. Rotundo, *American Manhood: Transformations in Masculinity from the Revolution to the Modern Era* (New York: Basic Books, 1993).

61. Robert Dixon, *Writing the Colonial Adventure: Race, Gender and Nation in Anglo-Australian Popular Fiction, 1875–1914* (Cambridge: Cambridge University Press, 1995); see also Richard Phillips, *Mapping Men and Empire: A Geography of Adventure* (London: Routledge, 1996), pp. 68–88.

62. Suzanne Zantop, *Colonial Fantasies: Conquest, Family and Nation in Pre-Colonial Germany, 1770–1870* (Durham, NC: Duke University Press, 1997), pp. 108–20.

63. Aspley Cherry-Gerrard, "Preface," *The Worst Journey in the World: Antarctic 1910–13* (Harmondsworth, UK: Penguin, 1948 [1923]), pp. 5, 6.

64. Jopi Nyman, *Men Alone: Masculinity, Individualism, and Hard-Boiled Fiction* (Amsterdam: Rodopi, 1997).

65. Sarah Cole, *Modernism, Male Friendship and the First World War* (Cambridge: Cambridge University Press, 2003), p. 18.

66. Kurt Schlenner, cited in Philipp Witkop (ed.), *German Student's War Letters* (trans. A. F. Wedd; Philadelphia: University of Pennsylvania Press, 2002), p. 26.

67. Basil H. Liddell Hart, "Foreword" to Sidney Rogerson, *Twelve Days* (London: Barker, 1933), p. viii.

68. Cole, *Modernism*, p. 18.

69. Siegfried Sassoon, "The Poet as Hero" and "Survivors" in *The War Poems*, arranged and introduced by Rupert Hart-Davis (London: Faber & Faber, 1983), pp. 61, 97.

70. Unknown solidier cited in J. Calvitt Clarke III, "The Great War" at http://users.ju.edu/jclarke/hy150irrationality.htm, accessed 30 September 2007.

71. C. B. Purdom, *Everyman at War* (London: J. M. Dent, 1930); Brame and Walker on *Firstworldwar.com*, http://www.firstworldwar.com/diaries/onthe belgiancoast.htm and http://firstworldwar.com/diaries/battleofloos.htm, both accessed 22 July 2007.

72. Richard Brown, cited in Robert Mackay, *Half the Battle: Civilian Morale in Britain during the Second World War* (Manchester, Manchester University Press, 2002), p. 260.

73. Joanna Bourke, *Dismembering the Male: Men's Bodies, Britain and the Great War* (London: Reaktion Books, 1996), p. 128.

74. Cited in Bourke, *Dismembering the Male*, p. 151.

75. Gerald Linderman, *The World within War: America's Combat Experience in World War II* (New York: Free Press, 1997), pp. 263–64.

76. Linderman, *The World within War*, p. 279.

77. Linderman, *The World within War*, p. 295.

78. Ernest Sutherland Bates, "The Meaning of Recent Trends in Nonfiction," *The English Journal* 27 (1938), p. 713; Joseph Jastrow, *The Betrayal of Intelligence* (Greenberg: New York, 1938), p. 83.

Chapter 9

THE IMPORTANCE OF FRIENDS: THE MOST RECENT PAST

Mark Peel, with Liz Reed and James Walter

The second half of the twentieth century saw the triumph of the particular form of intimate and reciprocal friendship traced in the preceding chapter. In Western societies, and especially in the individualized urban and suburban worlds in which most people made their home, it became more and more common to rely on friends for the kinds of advice, resources and recreation that might once have involved family, kin and neighbours. This form of friendship – both as an experience and as something prescribed in a range of written and visual texts – also came to be characterized by an even greater emphasis on emotional and private rather than practical and public obligations. Now, in the new twenty-first century, friendship may still have practical effects – and even influence people – but gaining advantage or fulfilling obligations are not its chief intentions and in fact could be seen as undermining it. And because friendship is freely chosen, it has become more and more different from other kinds of relationships, in which instrumental benefits or assumed obligations play a larger role, such as those with family, kin, co-workers or neighbours. Indeed, only some of those people will be our friends, and our "real" friends will often help us sort through the difficulties that can arise in those relationships that are chosen for rather than by us. As British sociologist Ray Pahl put it, "friendship is reaching new levels of depth and complexity in the modern world ... [and] is suffusing kin and family relationships as never before."[1]

At the same time, the link between friendship and love is seen as more and more important. In the popular advice of magazine, film and television, love without friendship is an ever-more brittle bond; by century's end, as the Spice Girls sang, "you gotta get with my friends" because "friendship never ends."[2] It became possible for partners, parents, siblings and wider kin to be one's "best friends." In all kinds of ways, it became difficult to conceive of lasting and intimate relationships that lacked friendliness and the kinds of emotional support associated with friends. All of your sisters and brothers would always be your sisters and brothers, but one of them might also be and remain one of your closest friends. In popular culture, advice literature, academic writing and everyday conversation, much of the discussion about life, especially by the 1970s and 1980s, assumed the crucial importance of friendship to happiness and self-worth. As American writer Lillian Rubin put it, "the people we call 'friend' are those who seem to us to call up the best parts of ourselves."[3]

Learning how to make friends was also changed by the expanding scope of vision. Twentieth-century people could see and hear much more of the world, and new or cheaper technologies of recording and sharing information – photographs, cassettes and videos at first, and then the virtual worlds of the computer age – provided a platform for everyday intimacy over long distances. This was the crowning moment for the millions of penpals, penfriends and would-be travellers who could, as affluence increased and the costs went down, begin to visit as well as write to people separated by great distances. There was an increasing capacity to replay and relive the key moments of a life spent with friends, and friends were more and more likely to dominate the supporting cast in each person's photo- or video-documentary of their lives. At the same time, popular culture realized more of its descriptive potential (or its prescriptive threat, according to some). If radio and film had ushered in the twentieth century's first revolutions in the scope of popular experience and aspiration, television was even more influential. With its dramatized guides to selfhood, relationships, emotions and romance, and with its growing focus on talk, "lifestyle," "reality" and everyday living, television became the single most important place in which twentieth-century people could see how they might live, whether that meant changing or staying the same. At first mostly American, television's accessibility increasingly fostered a mix of local and global expression, which belied fears of a world stamped and flattened into one culture.

In a period when friendship loomed ever larger in the popular imagination, however, it was just as likely to evoke pessimism from a new group of elite interpreters: the social scientists and social commentators. If they had cheered up a little by the middle of the century, in part because community, family and sociability seemed more robust than first feared, the lonely crowds and grey flannel suits of the 1950s and 1960s seemed to spell another set of problems. Feminist writers revived friendship in the 1970s and 1980s, but most sociologists, along with the growing band of critics who wrote worried books about sweeping change, wondered whether there was enough friendship and common feeling in the world, or whether mere friendliness was a sufficiently solid bond to withstand the modern or the postmodern condition. Against that stood a new wave of hugely successful performances of friendship's pleasures, from *Friends* to *Sex in the City* and *Will & Grace*. If friendship's revitalizing properties seemed less certain to sociologists, philosophers and social temperature-takers, popular celebrations of enduring, intimate friends made a life without them one of the bleakest prospects that most people could imagine. These celebrations – and earlier ones such as *The Golden Girls* or *The Mary Tyler Moore Show* – also made clear the ways in which female friendships became even more central to popular as well as academic versions of ideal bonds. In movies and television shows, at least, the strongest friendships were between women and, from about the 1980s, between women and gay men. Male friendships did not completely disappear but, by century's end, anxieties over friendlessness and the incapacity to make and keep friends seemed almost to assume that such problems mostly involved heterosexual men.

In a very important way, and as has been true throughout this history, to talk about friendship is to talk about some of the key changes and challenges of a particular time and place. In the second half of the twentieth century, the changes included increased mobility and affluence. Yet it is just as important to trace the dilemmas that friendship helps us understand: between individual choice and collective obligation, for instance, and between inclusion and exclusion. Most of all, the ability to choose friendship with selected people also rested on an increasing ability to suspend, limit and even deny obligations to others, such as kin and neighbours, in the knowledge that they would in some sense be protected by the more distant agencies of the city, state or nation. The ability of a far-greater number of people to

prioritize chosen over obligatory personal relationships and to idealize friendship as an emotional rather than instrumental bond relied
upon robust, universal and public entitlements. Friendship is always
in some part a selective and exclusive relationship. For much of the
twentieth century, the implications of that were tempered by most
people's ability to access forms of entitlement predicated upon less
personal bonds, such as citizenship. As that century ended and a new
one began, the strength of those bonds would once again come into
question.

Affluent Friendship

In the 20 or 30 years after World War II, more and more people in
Europe, North America and Australasia had the means to make the
selective connections of friendship more important than relationships
based on proximity, need or birth. It is easier to prioritize friendships
when you are less likely to need financial or material help from your
neighbours and kin, or others who are close at hand more by happen-
stance than design, and when you are less likely to be called upon for
assistance in turn. As British sociologist Graham Allen pointed out,
patterns of sociability are always best understood as deriving from the
practical circumstances of people's lives.[4] By the 1960s and 1970s,
those circumstances were changing, and among a wider spectrum of
people than ever before. With affluence, people could afford more
privacy and space. They could entertain friends at home, and cook-
books, etiquette guides and manuals for modern living focused much
less on family affairs and much more on dinner and cocktail parties
and buffets "for a crowd." With a bit of money for luxuries and diversions, people could go out more often and to different kinds of places.
While some friendships remained highly local, and formed around
shared pubs, diners or coffee shops, others brought together a wider
range of people who shared an interest or an enjoyment. For adults
and teenagers, cars made friends more mobile and more reachable.
The continuing spread of technologies for mass communication made
it easier to befriend and communicate with far-flung others, including
people you had not met and might not ever meet. Cheaper airmail
made the 1950s and 1960s the great era for penfriends and penpals,
and the dramatic spread of the telephone generated a new culture of
conversation and connection, especially for women and the young. It
was also easier to maintain friendships across greater distances, and to

expect that they could be preserved across time and despite life's changes. For most people, increased privacy, personal mobility and affluence made it possible to draw some people out of more public or obligatory relationships – workmates, fellow students, neighbours and family – and into a closer and more intimate world of friendship.

If the triumph of friendship was one of the twentieth century's most important social changes, it rested in turn upon a range of other profound transformations in the experiences and expectations of ordinary people. It is important to be clear about the ambivalent and variable nature of these changes. Affluence, mobility and privacy could also make people very lonely and, in many ways, the 1950s was the golden age of domestic isolation. The demographic and social changes that would eventually earn the name "baby boom" rested on a relatively novel combination of falling divorce rates, young marriages and high birth-rates, along with increased gender segregation as more women became full-time wives and mothers and left paid work. Suburbanization could mean severing connections; Americans certainly noticed a decline in the social clubs, fraternal orders, workingmen's associations and local organizations that had been so prevalent in urban neighbourhoods before 1940. Australian cities had never been quite as thickly dotted with sites of friendly association, but there too some of the dance halls and picture palaces of an earlier age dwindled and disappeared.

One of the most influential works at mid-century was David Reisman's *The Lonely Crowd* (1950), a title that carries an immediate message concerning friendship. His research was based on interviews rather than statistics but Reisman claimed to find a changing American character manifest in these conversations. The change was driven by the economic demands of the corporate economy. Older forms of character formation – "tradition-directed" (values directed by customs, typical of a static pre-industrial society) and "inner-directed" (strong personal values developed within stable families and communities) – were being displaced by the "other-directed" personality (dependent on external cues from peers, and willing to adjust values in conformity with social change). The "other-directed" personality was malleable and could adapt to the new economy, but had sacrificed the solidarity available to the "tradition-directed" and the strength of the "inner-directed" types. The outcome was conformity, fragile relationships and (as Reisman's title implied) alienation. Friendships did little to remedy the deficiencies of character.

In the hands of more optimistic sociologists like Talcott Parsons, all of this meant that the heroically self-sufficient nuclear family was rising above older and "traditional" entanglements. But as Stephanie Coontz and others have pointed out, the nuclear family forms and values of the 1950s and 1960s were not "the expression of some longstanding tradition" but occurred during a period of "experimentation with the possibilities of a new kind of family."[5] Less commonly asserted is the idea that this was also a time for exploring new kinds of friendships. At the time, or 20 years later, there were all kinds of good reasons for portraying the new suburbs as places that produced loneliness and frustration, where women asked, "Is that all?", while their suit-and-tied husbands glumly travelled the commuter trains or the new freeways. Domestic and conjugal responsibilities were very important, but rather like the pursuit of romance in the 1920s and 1930s, they were neither separated from nor inimical to connections with friends. There is ample evidence of male neighbouring, shared domestic work and befriending in the new communities of suburban America and Australia, while Peter Willmott, David Lockwood and John Goldthorpe seem to have hastened too quickly to the conclusion that the UK's "new" working class had rapidly become privatized and withdrawn.[6]

In fact, some studies in the 1950s suggested a more complex and variable situation. In the UK, J. M. Mogey's 1956 study of Oxford suggested that working-class couples who moved to new housing estates often felt liberated from the claustrophobia of traditional family and neighbourhood life, and tended to seek more expansive associations less fixed to one street or block.[7] Margaret Stacey's study of Banbury also found that new council housing areas had a more selective culture of acquaintance.[8] Peter Willmott and Michael Young, who famously argued for the tenacity and warmth of traditional kin and neighbourhood ties in *Family and Kinship in East London* (1957), published another book in 1960, *Family and Class in a London Suburb*, which suggested that working-class suburbanites regularly visited friends and family and were establishing a wide range of friendship networks in their new environment. That their second book is much less well known than their first tells us something, perhaps, of the power of a suspicious approach to suburban life. Indeed, as Mark Clapson suggested, the evidence of most UK studies was that mobility and affluence usually widened people's social horizons at the same time as they diminished the intensity of everyday interactions.[9]

American sociologists spent much of the 1950s scolding suburban-ites, but here too some research suggested a more nuanced reality. William H. Whyte's *Organization Man*, for instance, while showing that the friendship of suburban block parties and barbecues "stops very clearly at the color line," also lauded the picnics, bake sales and wel-come wagons, and the exchange of lawnmowers, records and sugar, as a "communal sharing" worthy of "pilgrims."[10] Herbert Gans' Levittowners were also given their due: for them, the move to the suburbs meant that "morale goes up, boredom and loneliness are reduced" and "social and organizational activities multiply."[11] The women of Levittown and other postwar American suburbs, in particu-lar, might not have experienced the same density of contacts that char-acterized inner cities, and some of them felt terribly isolated. But others may have felt that their new lives involved a greater degree of choice. Betty Friedan's searing critique of women's experiences in 1950s America is well known, yet Friedan acknowledged her debt to women's networks too: according to *The Feminine Mystique*, she first realized the nature of "the problem that has no name" while "having coffee with four other mothers in a suburban development fifteen miles from New York."[12]

For many people in the 1950s and 1960s, mobility and affluence brought a new combination of greater privacy and wider horizons. Those wider horizons meant that it also became more possible to make friends of people an older generation might never have met. Greater social as well as geographical mobility reinforced the mixing and disruption of social hierarchies that had been such a feature of the war. The expansion of high school, higher education and profes-sional careers, and a greater emphasis on merit, aspiration and inter-est rather than birth, faith or social standing in choices of work and education, widened and diversified the circles from which most people could draw their friends, a process that would be repeated as women and then ethnic minorities began to challenge the greater barriers facing them from the 1960s onwards. Most of World War II's victori-ous nations, for instance, substantially increased social mobility by rewarding their male veterans; the most spectacular example was America's GI Bill, which doubled the proportion of men entering college. Commitments to higher minimum wages – and the industrial strength of unions in times of general labour shortages – also increased the money people had to invest in their children's prospects and mo-bility. It was less and less possible to imagine that a person would or should spend their life associating with the same people with whom they grew up and went to school, or with a small and exclusive group. Mixing eroded and sometimes brought down barriers that earlier generations might have imagined were insurmountable, not least between Catholics and Protestants. It weakened the walls of class, though only for some people and in some ways. The dynamics of mixing were mirrored in popular culture, where the new genre of television comedies and dramas, as well as later films such as *Midnight Cowboy*, featured friendships between those who were out of place or showed the capacity for friendships to stem from unlikely encounters.

The importance of friendship was further reinforced in the 1950s and 1960s by the growing emphasis on age segregation and on friend-making as part of normal child and adolescent socialization. Margaret Kinnell has described a continuing tradition in children's and adolescent fiction of warning against the consequences of bad friends (especially the consequences of misplaced trust) while welcoming the influence of good friends.[13] British fiction, in particular, was more and more likely to feature children and adolescents in groups – the Famous Five, the Secret Seven, Swallows and Amazons – that mixed friends, siblings and cousins and allowed them at least temporary authority and independence over their actions. Interpersonal relationships also became a more and more important subject of psychological and psychiatric study, especially in the work of Karen Horney, Erik Erikson and Erich Fromm. Rather than the harsh conflict of real relations emphasized by Freud, this later generation – which also included Margaret Mahler, Heinz Kohut, D. W. Winnicott, and Wilfred Bion – observed the patterns of feedback, communication, self-expression and self-invention that allowed young children to experiment with identity and independence.[14] Research on older children by Harry Stack Sullivan and others further emphasized the great significance of friendships. In the posthumous 1953 collection of essays, *Interpersonal Theory of Psychiatry*, Sullivan described children's friendships as crucial for the development of self-worth and self-validation. They provided opportunities for intimate self-disclosure and, significantly, they allowed children to develop the interpersonal skills and sensitivities that would see them develop healthy romantic, marital and parental relationships. In these terms, healthy friendships had become a precondition for a fulfilling adult life.

As people focused more on how old they were, and as generation became a more common means of understanding human differences, friendships across age boundaries became less frequent and, in some cases, more problematic. Peer relationships among adolescents also caused anxiety, with as many experts warning of the dangers of peer-induced delinquency as welcoming the positive influences of adolescent friendship. The postwar period saw a renewed focus on the importance of positive peer integration and a revitalized campaign against the wrong kinds of friendships. James Dean may have made the teenage rebel romantic, but American adolescents were also subjected to a series of more-or-less subtle interventions to ensure that peer groups did not become sites of real rebellion: high school fraternities, sororities and secret societies were targeted, while movies and training films made for the classroom provided didactic lessons in "how to be popular" and "how to make friends." For girls, popularity was something of an end in itself, while boys were still expected to use their networks as a means of developing skills in leadership and defeating potential rivals. But for both sexes, the dramatized lives shown in training films made clear that adolescence without "healthy" and normal friendships was almost too horrible to contemplate.

For young and old, what mattered most was a stronger association between friendship and a special kind of emotional intensity and pleasure. Whatever the idealizations of didactic advice, friendship was becoming more significant in real people's lives. Research into how people actually made and felt about their friends during the 1970s suggested that adults grew more selective about friends over time: a shrinking range of acquaintances was often connected with greater intimacies with "real" friends, and older people tended to enjoy the unique qualities of particular friends more than the commonalities of a large friendship group.[15] From this period on, the attention paid to friendship and age began to include a focus on the elderly; as a growing proportion of Britons, Americans and Europeans lived into their 70s and 80s, a number of studies showed the importance of friends for older people's wellbeing and self-esteem, and emphasized that, while families might meet instrumental needs, friends were very important for emotional needs and enjoyment, especially among older women.[16]

With more time to focus on the interior world of feelings, and with growing encouragement from experts and popular culture to regard their personal relationships as important to self-fulfilment, it is reasonable to argue that people's friends became more important to them. Certainly, they played a larger role in leisure and entertainment, but friends also became more and more crucial to people's inner lives, especially at times of change. Your friends were those who saw your "true self" and often participated in its shaping or reshaping. They were the witnesses and often the midwives to your personal formation. They affirmed your choices or helped you to make better ones. Their advice replaced – though it might not entirely supplant – the words of parents and kin, and it was with them that the worries of becoming adult, of romance, love, marriage and parenting, of retiring and ageing were most easily shared.

Indeed, as dependence on others became less material and practical, the ties of friendship could be more easily preferred to the bonds of kinship. Friendship became more differentiated from other relationships, whether with family or neighbours or mere acquaintances, and took on a more distinctive emotional timbre, based on intimacy, shared pleasures and recreations, reciprocity, equality and negotiated (rather than necessary) interdependence. The forces that drew like-minded strangers together as friends also diminished people's reliance on obligatory relationships and made it possible for them to be much more selective about the people with whom they shared their time, thoughts and feelings. Based on choice and the capacity to privilege some relationships over others, friendship fitted well with the aspiration for and growing achievement of privacy and autonomy. Indeed, friendship became the model for other kinds of relationships, which were improved if imbued with it: everyone had neighbours, or siblings, or work colleagues, but only the best of them were also friends.

The relationship between friendship and love is a particularly important feature of later twentieth-century lives. On the one hand, friendship was increasingly seen to sustain and deepen romantic love; it was the mature reflection that followed the rush of attraction. On the other, the success of a romantic relationship also came to depend, at least to some extent, on the lover's compatibility with friends who would predate and probably outlast the romance. In the film comedies and dramas of the 1950s and 1960s, in the shorter bursts of television shows, and especially in the songs that formed an increasingly common backdrop to lived experience, the best lovers and partners were those with whom you enjoyed what you also shared with friends: common interests and passions, in particular. Passion waned but friendship grew. It was even possible to ask, as in Todd Rundgren's song about a failed relationship, "can we still be friends?" To become friends and to remain friends was an ever-more important part of successful romantic and sexual relationships, while paeans to friendship – "You've Got a

Friend," "With a Little Help from My Friends" and "Lean on Me," for instance – made it increasingly clear that friends were perhaps just as or even more important than lovers when you are "down and troubled," "not strong" and when it came to "getting by" (and, perhaps, getting high). In one of the most lush celebrations, Simon and Garfunkel's "Bridge Over Troubled Water," both friend and befriended could be anyone, and it is a friend, not a lover, who makes the commitment to give comfort, dry tears and "take your part," whatever the circumstances.

The capacity – and the desire – to emulate new models of ideal friendship was shaped by gender, generation and class but there is no doubt that the mobile and relatively affluent societies of the century's middle decades made the quantity and quality of people's friendships more important to them than ever before. Of course, this was neither sudden nor universal. In the USA, as Claude Fischer found, clear class differences persisted: longer education and greater affluence tended to mean less reliance on kin and a greater focus on co-workers and especially friends as sources of support and pleasure.[17] In African-American and Hispanic culture, Carole Stack and other observers described the continuing importance of family and kin, especially in the urban ghettos, while also emphasizing the ways in which the boundaries between family, neighbours and friends were blurred by informal adoptions, fictive kinships of "aunties" and "cousins" and shared mothering.[18] In the UK, one sociological survey in 1979 found significant differences between middle- and working-class friendships, with the latter more likely to be gender-segregated and overridden by family and kin obligations.[19] Yet, as Anthony Heath argued in *Social Mobility* (1981), upward social mobility clearly changed the patterns and scope of friendship, while Peter Willmott's studies of "the new kind of sociability" also showed that class differences were diminishing, through a mix of factors including physical and social mobility, rising affluence, diminished material reliance on family and further education.[20] Here, again, these wider horizons were shared with friends rather than kin.

The growing importance of a particular kind of exclusive friendship emphasized another very important point about the third quarter of the twentieth century: the significance of public as well as private affluence. It was possible to be selective and exclusive about the people to whom one felt obliged because it was more and more possible to trust a wider, collective helpfulness. You did not need to befriend your neighbour, because it was possible to live apart and not need each other; conversely, you could befriend one particularly amenable neighbour with whom you shared a particular interest without worrying too much about the impact this would have on others. As Janet Finch showed in particular detail, one of the great gains for many ordinary people in societies such as the UK was the capacity to rely upon universal entitlements – such as pensions or subsidized housing – rather than the more fraught and sometimes difficult obligations that were attached to kinship. As she argued, far from eroding or threatening the family – a common claim among the more aggressive conservatives who increasingly shaped social policy debates from the 1970s onwards – state services and public expenditure actually allowed people to focus on their real ties with particular kin and to invest more time in those relationships they actually enjoyed.[21]

In a very significant way, the ability of a far greater number of people to prioritize chosen over obligatory relationships, to enjoy friendship as an emotional more than instrumental bond and to strive to realize the kinds of ideal friendships portrayed in popular culture, rested upon robust, universal and public entitlements. For most people, a smaller number of intimate friends might or might not include family members, co-workers or neighbours. But we were able to do this, at least in part, because we knew that people towards whom we felt some obligation, or to whom proximity created some kind of bond, would not be harmed. We could rely, in other words, upon a more broadly based structure of entitlement to take care of family or neighbours to whom we were not particularly close. As we have argued in earlier chapters, friendship is always in some part a selective and exclusive relationship. For much of the twentieth century, however, the implications of that were tempered by most people's ability to access forms of entitlement predicated upon less selective bonds, such as citizenship, and based on the hard-won lessons about social security and public welfare learned from the Depression and World War II. The richness of individual friendships could increase, in large part, because of the stronger commitment to collective protection those lessons had forged.

Friendships of Conviction

The late 1960s song "Friendship Train," written by Barrett Strong and Norman Whitfield and covered by both Gladys Knight and the Pips and The Temptations, captured something very important about the anticipated role of friendship in social change: if the world needed "love and understanding," the answer for was for everybody to "shake a hand, make a friend" and "get aboard the friendship train."[22]

By the late 1960s, it was more and more common to suggest that friendships – and especially the kinds of solidarities forged between activists and across the barriers of "race, creed or color" – were both a model of a new kind of world and a way of bringing it about. What distinguished the expectations expressed here from those evident in earlier friendships was the confidence that friendship could bring about major social change and the emphasis on self-transformation; in the last half of the twentieth century, befriending no longer implied improving the "inferior" or "unfortunate." At the very least, it meant trying to join and help them as relatively equal partners in a struggle for reform, liberation or rights. More than that, it sometimes meant being changed and improved by them, learning from them and changing yourself. Even an organization such as the American Peace Corps, which aimed in part to promote a better understanding of the USA across a frustratingly anti-American "Third World," took "world peace and friendship" and a better understanding of the world among young Americans as equally worthy goals.[23] On the other side of the Cold War, friendship leagues and conventions, youth festivals and international solidarity groups sometimes confirmed and sometimes crossed the Iron and Bamboo curtains. By the 1960s and 1970s, there was a renewed focus too on inter-faith conferences and other forms of friendship between believers of different creeds, and on a version of Christian practice that particularly emphasized Jesus as a "friend" in whom one could rejoice without accepting the doctrines of established churches.

In various forms of activism, friendship was both the outcome and the generator of solidarities across racial, national, religious and class divisions: activism built upon friendships, and it built friendships. It was perhaps especially important in the great struggles against racial oppression that characterized the United States and other societies from the 1950s onwards and from which other liberation struggles drew inspiration, resources and styles. Friendships between the leaders of the civil rights movement were important, and the relationships between Martin Luther King Jr, Ralph Abernathy, Bayard Rustin, Andrew Young and others have played an increasingly large role in the way that movement's story is remembered.[24] One of the most important support organizations founded in the North, for example, was In Friendship. Organized by Rustin, veteran activists Ella Baker and A. Philip Randolph, and Jewish lawyer Stanley Levinson, In Friendship gathered funds and support for the Montgomery bus boycott and other civil rights work.[25] The language of friendship was also invoked in gestures towards those who were opposed to change or for whom change came too quickly; one of King's most famous arguments, the "Letter from Birmingham Jail," addressed "fellow clergymen" as "friends" to reinforce the point that those friendly to the cause of racial justice had no place lecturing those who actually knew "the stinging dark of segregation." And King insisted that non-violence "does not seek to defeat or humiliate the opponent, but to win his friendship and understanding."[26]

Just as significant, though, were the myriad relationships built in the Student Non-Violent Coordinating Committee and in the civil rights work – such as 1964's Freedom Summer – that mixed together black and white, older and younger, southern and northern activists. The practical work of civil rights relied heavily on friendship networks growing out of churches and communities; Fannie Lou Hamer's remarkable crusade for voting and civil rights in Mississippi, for instance, would have been impossible without the network of mostly African-American women friends who supported her while she lived away from her home and husband, including Rosemary Freeney-Harding, who took her in after her savage beating by police in Winona. Ella Baker, who was active in civil rights from the 1920s through the 1970s, was sustained in her work by her lifelong bonds with fellow activist Pauli Murray and her friends in the Harlem church and civic organizations she had helped pioneer. As Murray put it, these women "shared a sisterhood that foreshadowed the revival of the feminist movement in the 1960s."[27]

While pre-existing friendships sometimes drew activists into civil rights organizations, the relationships built within the civil rights movement provided white activists, in particular, with a model for a new kind of interracial collaboration that emphasized the transformation of white Americans and saw white racism – implicit as well as explicit – as the primary barrier to change.[28] Of course, the struggle for racial justice could break as well as make friendships, not least in the very difficult question of black and white cooperation, but it seems that bonds between women were stronger than those between men. Anne Moody, born in the Mississippi backwoods, formed her first-ever interracial friendship with Joan Trumpauer, a white SNCC volunteer.[29] The friendship had as strong an impact upon Trumpauer, who continued to participate in sit-ins and other activities in Jackson and enrolled – and eventually joined a sorority – at a formerly all-black college, Tougaloo, in Mississippi.[30] Links between black and white women were also crucial in generating another kind of solidarity, in reaction to the sexism of many male activists. Friendships between white women such as Constance Curry, Casey Cason and Dorothy Dawson and black women such as Hamer not only challenged southern racism, but they also confronted broader gender stereotypes, not least within the activist movement itself.[31]

Other struggles were also shaped by friendship, as part of the ideal aims, as a source of support and as a practical outcome of shared experiences, common visions and ideological solidarity. Some involved public figures and leaders, such as the friendship between Cesar Chavez and Dolores Huerta of the United Farm Workers and Robert Kennedy, which clearly shaped Kennedy's ideas about the inadequacies of 1960s social programs.[32] In Europe, studies of environmental activism during the 1970s and 1980s emphasized the importance of friendship in generating memberships and momentum for the growing green movements.[33] Recent studies of the peace movement also emphasize the importance of friendship bonds in generating and especially sustaining activism: friendship matters, in this context, because it serves as a basis for persistent, creative and adaptive collective action.[34]

Friendships played just as important a role in the struggle against apartheid in South Africa: the bonds between Walter Sisulu, Oliver Tambo and Nelson Mandela, which sustained them all through their long years of imprisonment and separation from family, are among the most famous examples, and there are many instances too of friendships sustaining imprisoned women.[35] As in the American civil rights struggle, equal and intimate friendships across racial barriers were in and of themselves a radical statement against racial privilege and assumptions of superiority and inferiority. While the friendship between Donald Wood and Steven Biko is perhaps most famous, others, white and black, played just as significant a role in undermining racial segregation. These friendships were not established or maintained without difficulty, and novelists such as Nadine Gordimer and Doris Lessing explored those issues in the 1950s and more recently. None the less, the autobiographies of both black and white activists, including

Mandela, Joe Slovo, Bram Fisher and Helen Joseph, stress the importance of these friendships in their capacity to withstand the barriers that the apartheid system imposed upon them. Here too, friendship served as a powerful statement about common humanity, emphasized the absurdity of the logic that justified apartheid's racial taxonomy, and elevated a moral commitment to universal equality above the claims of nation, race and social convention.

A less well-known example, even within the country in which it occurred, is the campaign for the rights of Australian Aboriginal people. Here, the difficulties of friendship that characterized anti-racism campaigns in the USA and South Africa were even more apparent. During the 1950s and 1960s, such collaborative relationships increasingly tested the non-Aboriginal supporters' ability to "be friendly" with Aboriginal people, by de-emphasizing their own importance and respecting the emerging leadership roles and demands of indigenous activists. This meant learning the difficult lesson of giving up power, listening to Aboriginal campaigners, and – perhaps most difficult of all – not speaking for them. Such support, however, was often highly problematic, not the least because of its inherent paternalism.[36]

Such entangled and increasingly contested relationships were represented in what was arguably the most significant campaign of the twentieth century, the 1967 referendum to alter two sections of the 1901 federal Constitution and, in turn, to empower the federal government to legislate directly for Aboriginal people. The political organization that drove this decade-long campaign, initially called the Federal Council for Aboriginal Advancement, later becoming the Federal Council for the Advancement of Aborigines and Torres Strait Islanders (FCAATSI), provides a fascinating example of the ways in which cross-cultural collaboration increasingly became untenable as Aboriginal men and women asserted their right to control it and speak for themselves. As Doug Nicholls patiently explained to non-Aboriginal people present at the organisation's 1970 meeting: "we want you to walk with us but let us take the lead."[37] Similarly, Faith Bandler's personal history of FCAATSI noted the "paternalistic and domineering attitudes" of white supporters, but also recognized the importance of white people's organizational expertise, which made it necessary for both to "work together in a friendly way."[38] Cross-cultural alliances and collaborations would continue, and became a little less difficult, especially as more non-Aboriginal people learned to follow rather than lead.

The Friendships of Women and Men

These great movements for rights, social change and justice all ideal-ized, to some extent, the transforming power of friendship and claimed that this most equal, voluntary and levelling of relationships served as a practical demonstration of people's capacity to resist oppressive struc-tures of conflict and aggression. Friends helped you to transform your-self so that you in turn might help to transform the world. Friends could also help to sustain your self-liberation, help you to become something and someone else. Earlier in the twentieth century, as was argued in the previous chapter, friends had also played a role in per-sonal transformation. What was most different about this later period, however, was its much greater emphasis on the broader political out-comes of personal choices.

If that was true in campaigns against racial oppression, it was even more the case in the struggle against sexual oppression. In a century when it was more and more likely to be seen as a female art, friendship's political possibilities were most clearly realized by women and, to a lesser extent, gay men. Feminism most clearly explored the funda-mental implications of the idea that "the personal is political." Other movements – such as civil rights, anti-war protest and the counter-culture – proved inhospitable to and uninterested in women's rights, so a new generation of activist women discovered afresh the reality of their inequality and oppression. As they turned to their own libera-tion, they also explored forms of political organization and action that emphasized sisterhood, mutual empowerment and the political significance of personal experience. The tools of this particular trans-forming solidarity were in many ways the tools of friendship: listen-ing, sharing, endorsing, witnessing. As Sara Evans argued:

> the small "consciousness-raising" group was the central organising tool ... [and] its brilliance lay in the fact that it repoliticised informal female networks – office friendships, neighbourhood kaffeeklatsches – creating thousands of free social spaces in which women could explore new modes of understanding their lives and new visions for the future.[39]

In a very important way, women's friendships lay near the heart of the political movement called women's liberation and the broader philosophy of feminism. One of the first things that came to the fore in these groups was the way in which long-standing friendships between women, which were fundamental to their lives, were undervalued by husbands and family, as well as the wider society. Indeed, those friendships were often expected to take second place to what might be much more transient, difficult and unfulfilling heterosexual relationships. Feminism took women's now-established capacity for a friendship of disclosure, intimacy and shared exploration and turned it into a tool for personal empowerment and social change.

It is not surprising that one of the most important aspects of feminist writing and scholarship in the 1970s and 1980s – and beyond – was the rediscovery of female friendships that nourished women in the past and the present. In turn, these helped generate a distinctive scholarship about friendships, women's emancipation and the kind of revolution that feminism implied in all kinds of human relationships. Carroll Smith-Rosenberg's "The Female World of Love and Ritual" (1975), Lillian Faderman's *Surpassing the Love of Men* (1981), Martha Vicinus' *Independent Women* (1985) and Philippa Levine's *Feminist Lives in Victorian England* (1990) were particularly important works of history. Sociological studies included Helen Gouldner and Mary Symons Strong's *Speaking of Friendship* (1987), based largely on interviews with middle-class American women, and Pat O'Connor's *Friendships between Women* (1992), while Janice Raymond's *A Passion for Friends* (1986) offered a "philosophy of female affection" and Mary E. Hunt's *Fierce Tenderness* (1991) a "feminist theology of friendship." In biography too women's friendships became a popular and important focus: Eleanor Roosevelt and Lorena Kickok, or Margaret Mead and Ruth Benedict, for example, or the study of *The Life and Death of Emily Wilding Davison* (2001).

There was always a good deal of discussion about the precise nature and meaning of these friendships, particularly in regard to the potential differences between friendship, "romantic friendship," love and sex in the present and the past. The erotic aspects of women's friendships became an important issue, as did the capacity for friendships to merge into lesbian relationships. Although controversial both when it was published and since, Adrienne Rich's insistence on the ways in which women's affection for and dependence upon each other tended to be silenced, and her suggestion that many different kinds of female relationships could be situated on a "lesbian continuum," had a powerful impact on how women understood their relationships with each other in the 1980s. Books such as *Lesbianism: Affirming Non-Traditional Roles* or *Living Boldly: Issues Facing Lesbians* took up the issue of "gyn-affection" and emphasized both the importance of friendship networks for lesbians and the ways in which lesbian "connectedness" could include sexual and non-sexual intimacies. As one of the most important studies of American lesbian culture demonstrated, at least urban women always tended to balance sexual relationships with participation in a wider community.[40] And as one of the lesbians involved in a later study argued, "I don't have friendships on the level that I think heterosexuals have friendships. I think my friendships are more intense."[41]

The other liberation in which friendship played a crucial role involved gay men. While much of the focus of liberation initially concerned sexual behaviour, sensibility and even the idea of a separate "gay spirit," the circumstances of gay men's lives emphasized again and again the importance of friendship networks and a language of friendship – both sisters and brothers – that playfully inverted family bonds. In the transition from the more secret homosexual world of the 1950s to the public gay lives of the 1980s, each process of coming out involved something more than a search for sexual partners. Again and again in gay autobiography and memory, men stress how crucial it was to find friends: as one of Peter Nardi's interviewees put it, "it's a huge thrill the first time you're in a gay crowd ... Because we are oppressed, it's important to have networks of friends."[42] Among gay men, for whom the journey of self-discovery is an extremely important part of a shared identity, it is even more powerfully true that friends bear witness to and help you celebrate achieving your "real" self. They are "there," for your explorations of who you are and who you might want to become. Another intensive study of gay male and lesbian relationships argued that "the non-heterosexual world ... is sustained by the intricately woven but durable strands of a 'friendship ethic.'"[43] Friends, this study's respondents said, "made life liveable" and, among people who are often estranged from all or part of their families, friends are particularly important at what the researchers term "fateful moments" when support is most crucial.[44]

In that regard, one of the most powerful forces shaping gay friendships in the 1980s and 1990s was the onslaught of HIV-AIDS. Mainstream stories – such as the movie *Philadelphia* (1993) – focused on a couple and discrimination, but almost every major representation made by gay men stressed the impact of the death of friends and, equally, the importance of friends in individual and collective survival. Films such as *Longtime Companion* (1990), which aimed for mainstream cinema, certainly made friendship the crucial element, while the

made-for-television movie *A Death in the Family* (1987) posed a stark
contrast between the friends who nurse the dying Andy Boyd and the
family who remain uncomfortably and clumsily distant. It is reasonable to claim that one of the fundamental legacies of AIDS, at least in
the gay community, is the focus it placed on friendship.

Among lesbians and gay men, and also among some heterosexual
feminists, the 1970s and 1980s also saw a revitalized claim that friends
could come to serve as an alternative to family, or indeed *as* family.
Karen Lindsey's 1981 book, *Friends as Family*, helped popularize the
idea, especially her celebration of those who have "consciously
recognised the inauthenticity of the dichotomy between friends and
family, or have simply never acknowledged it, and have deliberately
set out to create a family out of friends."[45] Indeed, some went even
further to suggest that those living outside socially sanctioned relationships could embark on a major challenge to the ways in which
everyone lived, with friendship as their banner. As French theorist
Michel Foucault argued, the most threatening feature of male homosexuality was not that two men might have sex, but that two men
might have love for each other. Accordingly:

> the development toward which the problem of homosexuality
> tends is the one of friendship ... [as] two men ... face each other
> without terms or convenient words ... They have to invent, from A
> to Z, a relationship that is still formless, which is friendship.[46]

A similar sense of possibility was also becoming attached to another
form of friendship, between gay men and heterosexual women
(discussed in the next section).

It is immediately obvious, of course, that the group largely left out
of this new focus on liberating, intense, intimate and reciprocal friendships was heterosexual men. Indeed, much of the focus on women's
friendships or gay friendships took for granted a kind of instrumental-
ism and awkwardness in relationships between straight men. While
the friendships of conviction described above certainly included some
men, the emotional intensity of close friendship continued to be complicated by the fear that one might seem homosexual or, even worse,
be homosexual. The tremendous inhibitions that this introduced in
cultural displays of male friendship may not have always been replicated in real men's lives: most men would have counted on several
mates, buddies, pals, amigos or compadres, and versions of masculinity and even machismo in non-Anglo culture complicated the idea of

male bonding to some extent. During the 1980s too there was talk of a New Man, who could make conversation, experience emotions, reject sexism, dress in colours that matched and have some idea of what to do with a snow pea. The New Man offered some hope for an increased capacity for mature friendship with other men, with his romantic partners and with other women; in a way, of course, he was simply the Old Homosexual stripped of perverse desire. Yet the need for men to display and defend the link between masculinity and heterosexuality, through conspicuous displays of the absence of desire, could also undermine the intimacies and pleasures of "best" friendship. Emotionally charged contexts of masculine performance – sport, especially – or drunkenness could sanction displays of affection that might otherwise appear homoerotic, but even the New Man was otherwise left with backslapping and shoulder-punching.

In various conversations, friendships between men were implicitly or explicitly rendered problematic. Studies of friendship, or studies of community and sociability that also examined friendship, tended to confirm that for men, barriers to friendship were the main issues. Most men had a range of friends in adolescence but the demands of adult life, coupled with the difficulties of intimacy and emotion, meant that they shed friends thereafter. Many were dependent on wives for whatever social networks they enjoyed, and were accordingly very vulnerable to loneliness if marital relationships broke down later in life. Everyone who listened to men reported similar findings. Lillian Rubin, for instance, perhaps the most assiduous of all those collecting testimonies, used a number of 1960s and 1970s sociological studies and her own interviews, all of which showed that men tend to do things with each other, while women become things with each other. Men bond with each other for the moment, and in the absence of women, they do not become intimate.[47] Psychologists and others also pointed to the perils of male solidarity when it was expressed in violent, risky or aggressive behaviour (noted sociologist R. W. Connell's later article, "Live Fast and Die Young," as well as films such as *Idiot Box* and *Trainspotting*, captured something of the same sentiment). Men's friendships, it seemed, could be destructive of themselves and others. Whether or not they were conscious of gender, other sociologists questioned the relationships of "urban man": "people who live in cities may think they have lots of friends; but the word friend has changed its meaning. Compared with friendships of the past, most of these new friendships are trivial," claimed Christopher Alexander, for instance.[48] Joel Block, meanwhile, concluded in his 1980 book, *Friendship*, that "an atmosphere of ambivalence is the most generous characterisation that can be ascribed to the state of male relationships."[49]

The friendless lonely male was just as common in fiction. Consider the characters of postwar novels: Saul Bellow's Herzog, J. D. Salinger's Holden Caulfield or the ineffectual "heroes" of bleak British fiction such as *Saturday Night and Sunday Morning*, *This Sporting Life* or *Billy Liar*. There were later examples too. Australian novelist David Malouf's *Johnno*, in showing how heterosexual reticence hobbles the capacity for male friendship, demolishes the myth of mateship. A different sort of desperation is evident in British black comedies such as Martin Amis' *The Information* or Ian McEwen's *Amsterdam*. Here, the protagonists are mired in macabre and destructive rivalry with their closest "friends," consumed by envy and resentment and, in the case of *Amsterdam*, at least, literally unable to live with the success of their friends. If the possibilities of expressive intimacy are more fully realized in Saul Bellow's *Ravelstein*, it is telling that the central figure, the focus of a friendship network, is a gay man. A comparable exercise in the fictional recovery of a reputation, but this one fiercely attentive to the heterosexual domain, is Phillip Roth's *The Human Stain*. A striking difference, however, is in the central dilemma it posits: the friend's reputation is founded on a lie, and the story becomes a detective hunt for the truth and an implicit questioning of the possibility of candour. It seemed that the late twentieth-century man could be sure of very little, even among and between friends.

Popular Culture and Everyday Lives

Of course, not everyone modelled themselves on novels or read academic sociology. In a century of mass communications and mass popular culture, it is perhaps best to consider how most people saw friendship. After all, it was in film and television, as well as in popular song, that people increasingly found important raw materials for imagining and designing their relationships. While few people believe life is as uncomplicated as it appears on film, most still incorporate "screen talk" and screen thought into the making of their own lives. The case was particularly well put by David Thorburn: television and, to a lesser extent, film, are a form of "consensus narrative," in which beliefs, values and characters are rehearsed, tested, challenged, confirmed and revised.[50] People expect to see versions of themselves and of their own dilemmas, and the producers, writers and designers of popular culture have to try to fathom relevance, popularity and engagement. So, in Australia's most popular "light drama" serial, *Neighbours*, which also became very successful in the UK, the title song promised a show about "good neighbours" who could "become good friends"; the focus on friendship assured audiences that this was a show about the most important relationships they had.

What might people have made of friendship, if they used popular culture as a kind of rehearsal stage? Well, after 1970, any observer would have quickly gained the impression that women made friends with each other, and that sometime in the 1980s, they also began to make friends with gay men. There were warm and supportive male friendships, such as that between Paul Newman and Robert Redford in *Butch Cassidy and the Sundance Kid* (1969) or, on television, the friendships between the key male characters in *MASH* (1972–1983), along with the friendships between male outsiders such as Wyatt and Billy in *Easy Rider* and Joe Buck and Rizzo in *Midnight Cowboy* (both 1969). There were also some friendships between heterosexual men and women though, tellingly, in two of the most popular, the British television series *Man About the House* and the American series *Three's Company*, the man pretends to be gay so that the living arrangement is acceptable to outsiders. The American film *St Elmo's Fire* (1985) focused on a mixed-sex group of friends who rescued each other from past mistakes and helped each other find a path into the future, while *The Breakfast Club* (1985) had young men and women finding commonalities that did not have to lead to romance. In most cases, though, close friendships always seemed to be the prelude for something else, as in *When Harry Met Sally* (1989); popular culture seemed unable just yet to imagine a male–female relationship that would not start or end in sex.

But the period was dominated by shows and movies featuring strong female friendships, and often in which that friendship was the most important theme. There had been friendships before: in the 1950s, television women Gale Storm, Ann Sothern and Donna Reed all relied on friends, and the wives in *I Love Lucy* and *The Honeymooners* formed alliances against their husbands, but these relationships were backdrops to marriages or searches for marriage. And the 1980s also saw some intense female antagonisms, with Joan Collins' "Alexis" to Linda Evans' "Krystle" in *Dynasty* the most delicious of them all. But as television comedies and dramas took on social issues, so they explored at least some of those issues through women's friendships. This was particularly true of American television, beginning with *The Mary Tyler Moore Show*'s Mary and Rhoda, *Laverne and Shirley* (and even *Charlie's Angels*) and *Maude* in the 1970s, and flourishing in the 1980s with *The Golden Girls* (with its theme song, "Thank You For Being A Friend"), *Kate & Allie* – which flirted a little with lesbianism – and *Cagney & Lacey*. In film, the focus on past friendships could be seen in *Julia* (1977), while *Beaches* (1988), *Steel Magnolias* (1989) and *The Turning Point* (1977) emphasized the importance of friendship to women's survival. *Nine to Five* (1980) was an early version of what Karen Hollinger called the "political" female friendship film, a genre capped in the 1990s by *Thelma & Louise* (1991).[51] Other films took slightly riskier directions: *Fried Green Tomatoes* (1991) and *Desert Hearts* (1985) into the spaces between friendship and sexual desire, and *The Color Purple* (1985) into the complex dynamics of American gender and race. European and British cinema was less focused on friendships between women, but there were some important examples, particularly Diane Kurys' *Entre Nous* (1983).

From the late 1980s, television and film also explored relationships between heterosexual women and gay men. David Wyatt's list of gay, lesbian and bisexual television characters in every English-speaking market lists just 58 in the decade of the 1970s (14 of them in the Australian soap-serial *Number 96*), and 89 in the 1980s, when serials like *Eastenders* and American soaps like *As the World Turns* began to include some gay characters. In the decade leading up to 2000, however, Wyatt found 336 characters, and comedies and dramas routinely featured gay, lesbian and bisexual people as part of the social background.[52] At the end of the 1990s, of course, shows like *Will & Grace* and *Sex in the City* made friendships between straight women and gay men an indispensable part of "urban cool." The gay male friend was part confidant, part ally and part unconditional supporter: Rupert Everett for Julia Roberts in *My Best Friend's Wedding* (1997) and Paul Rudd for Jennifer Aniston in *The Object of My Affection* (1998). And if anyone needed written guidance, they could select from what soon became a minor cottage industry: *Straight Women, Gay Men: Absolutely Fabulous Friendships*, *A Couple of Friends: The Remarkable Friendship between Straight Women and Gay Men*, *Why Gay Guys are a Girl's Best Friend* and even *Behind Every Great Woman There's a Fabulous Gay Man*.

Film and television friendships between men and women continued to be problematic; characters are often caught before or after
sexual relationships, or, like the *X-Files'* Mulder and Scully and
Moonlighting's Maddie and David, exist in a state of waxing and wan-
ing sexual tension (unresolved in the former, but resolved in the latter). Sitcom marriages certainly depended more and more on
friendship, with Paul and Jamie in *Mad About You* one of the best
examples. *Seinfeld* played with the bonds between people and made
the point that the solidarities of friendship could be turned against
others. Mark Vernon refers to the very interesting example of *Lost in
Translation* (2003) for a male–female friendship that never becomes
an affair; another example is the friendship between Valentine and
Joseph in Kieslowski's *Three Colours: Red* (1994). While these are interesting, it is surely significant that in both cases the man is much older
than the woman, which apparently offers some explanation for
friendship's triumph over sexual desire. In an earlier film, *Harold and
Maude* (1971), friendship did turn into love, but friendship seemed
more important in the end. *Driving Miss Daisy* (1989) presented an
older woman and a somewhat younger man, for whom friendship –
after much hesitation – can cross the racial divide of the American
South. Yet the variety, complexity and richness of women's relationships continued to play a larger role, from *The Joy Luck Club* (1993) to
The Divine Secrets of the YaYa Sisterhood (2001) and *The Sisterhood of the
Travelling Pants* (2005), while *Sex in the City* took the celebration of
female friendship to perhaps its highest possible point. Beyond that
point, and over the top, women's dysfunctional friendships became
the stuff of comedy with the co-dependent Patsy and Edina from *Absolutely Fabulous*.

And then, of course, there was *Friends*. There was the title, and the
theme song – "I'll Be There for You" – seemed to capture something
very important about the unconditional, constant and reciprocal
nature of twentieth-century friendship. In its first few seasons, *Friends*
broke new ground in its explorations of the friendships that could
form outside traditional family and romantic attachments. In a way,
though, it then became a show about other things: all of the main
characters bar Lisa Kudrow's Phoebe had sexual relationships with
each other, and a good deal of time was spent in relatively conventional stories about romantic entanglement. Rachel and Monica had
a typically strong female bond; the show's most novel relationships,
in one way, were those between Joey and Chandler, which played

very lightly with homosexual overtones, and between Joey and Phoebe, which was never sexualized. What is perhaps most interesting about *Friends* is that it became so emblematic of a particular kind of life, and so successfully played out what various commentators have described as its central, comforting idea: that whatever happens, you can get what you want without having to compromise or leave behind friendship. It's not true, of course, but in presenting friendship as a kind of haven from hard decisions and all the other complications of real adult lives, *Friends* apparently struck a very powerful chord, and not just with Americans.[53]

At the very same time, Americans were also reading books about their inability to form bonds, written by a group of late twentieth-century Cassandras every bit as pessimistic as their forbears. Robert Putnam's *Bowling Alone* (1995) claimed to show a disturbing decline in civic engagement, and with it a decline in social trust; Richard Sennett worried over the "fugitive quality of friendship and local community" in which "no one becomes a long-term witness to another person's life" and people have "no deep reason to care about one another."[54] Robert Lane was even more focused on what he terms "companionship." In place of friendship comes "a relatively enduring, cross-situational pattern of behaviour marked by many acquaintances who are frequently visited, but relatively few, close, affectionate confidants."[55] And a surfeit of individualism, to which we are directed by very strong forces, "is a source of deep unhappiness because it crowds out companionship."[56] Indeed, his central point was that economically developed societies can only achieve sustained wellbeing by shifting their goal from income to companionship.

There is clearly a contrast between these observations and the easy optimism of *Friends*. Does television show us how friendship is lived, or how people expect their futures to be? Or, as these more pessimistic versions might argue, is it a fantasy, detached from how people live now and are likely to live in future? It is interesting in that regard to consider other studies that relied less on sweeping reviews of national data and drew instead on interviews and life histories. Australian political scientist Graham Little confirmed that, for many people, friends provided a "potential space" essential to self-development: "friends are the great agents of self-discovery: they show us who we are when we are not at home."[57] Sociologists Liz Spencer and Raymond Pahl focused on "personal communities" and the idea of a "friendship convoy" – the process by which we acquire new friends (and old ones drop away) as we move through life – and emphasized the importance of friends in most people's lives.[58] Indeed, they argue that rather than being in decline, as some more pessimistic observers have argued, friendship is becoming a more important social glue.

Measurements of real people's friendships in the recent past must of course be speculative, but one thing *Friends* does capture is a further intensification of the importance of intimate friendship in people's lives. If friends are the people with whom one can be – and indeed invent – one's true self, they merit increasing time and energy. It is almost certain that the amount of time spent on friendship has increased, especially for younger people. This measures not just time spent being with friends, but time spent talking with them, thinking about them and planning to see them; with mobile phones and web-based social networking sites, it can seem that some young people are with their friends almost all the time. And perhaps friendship has become a more all-consuming activity: what Lillian Rubin found in her 1980s interviews with hundreds of American men and women – "that it was often harder for [people] to sort out their friendships, and to speak openly and directly about them, than to discuss the highly personal issues of family life ... including even such intimate matters as sexual relations" – is probably even more true today.[59] As having friends becomes more important, it is possible that friendship becomes even more ringed around with concerns about being a good or even a good enough friend. How to make friends, keep friends and nourish friends is a source of constant concern in what are now the most common sources of advice, including magazines such as *Girlfriend* and *Seventeen*. Of course, the perils and pleasure of romance – among celebrities and among the ordinary – remain a major focus of such magazines, as well as talk shows and on-line gossip sites, but the importance of friends is usually not far behind.

In other ways, *Friends* is a less certain guide. Friendship remains a major focus for women and gay men, but it is not yet clear that heterosexual men have moved quite as far in placing friendly intimacies – with each other or with women and gay men – at the centre of a successful and happy life. Among women, and in the context of rising rates of divorce and single parenthood, close, personal relationships outside marriage are ever more important, according to some recent surveys and studies.[60] Indeed, one account of middle-class women's friendship suggests that the women of the last quarter of the twentieth century have recaptured an older focus on female friendship that was dented between 1920 and 1960 by a consuming desire to find and keep a husband.[61] Stacey Oliker showed that women's friendships are often crucial to the success of their other relationships, including marriages.[62] The 1990s and the first part of the twenty-first century have seen a range of other story- and life-based studies confirming the central role that friends play as women plot out, negotiate and reflect on their lives. Some insisted that women could find emotional intimacy without men, while Terri Apter's *Best Friends* (1998) argued that we have if anything underestimated the formative impact of friendships among adolescents and young women.[63] The plethora of self-help books both tracked and generated a concern about adequate self-disclosure, ensuring "true" friendships and even surviving "the friendship crisis": Maria Paul's book, following on from her column in the *Chicago Tribune*, was based on the conviction that "without friends, problems weigh more and pleasures yield less joy ... Nobody expects to come up empty of friends. Men, yes; friends, no."[64]

Of late, there have been studies of – and arguments for – the "queering" of friendship, alongside renewed interest in "intentional families" and lesbian friendship. As one recent writer suggested, the emphasis on friendship among lesbians is part of a wider focus linking community with "self-development"; as she notes, "no one can accuse the modern lesbian of complacency about her own development," but this is firmly linked to a broader politics about women's solidarity as a transforming force.[65] One of the most interesting recent treatments of the entire issue of contemporary friendship is Mark Vernon's *The Philosophy of Friendship*. He follows Andrew Sullivan's argument in *Love Undetectable* that intimate gay friendships might serve as a kind of model for heterosexual men.[66] While Peter Nardi suggests that the iconic friendships between gay men and straight women do not always play out so neatly in real lives, a good many observers still see these as the kind of "unambiguous" friendships that women might want but will rarely enjoy with straight men.[67]

Among heterosexual men, two very recent developments suggest signs of change, at least in terms of what can be imagined. Both involve new words. The first, the "man date," is defined in a recent *New York Times* as "two heterosexual men socializing without the crutch of business or sport" (it refers to the film *Sideways* (2004) as an example). The rules are very difficult: dinners are "normal," but not brunch, which perhaps seems too "gay," the only form of home-cooking allowed is barbecuing, men must keep one empty seat between them at the cinema, and "if a woman enters the picture, a man can drop his buddies, last minute, no questions asked." It is a scenario replete with perils.[68] The second new word is "bromance," and it refers to the friendship between a gay man and a straight man. Nirpal Dhaliwal defined "a true bromance" as something that "happens between men who know themselves, who are over their issues and just want to hang out with other intelligent and open men." He continues, "hanging out with gay men, I talk about my relationships and feelings in a complex way," before revealing one of the most important advantages:

> Whatever else straight men talk about – cars, football, politics – is just a substitute to avoid the envy and dissatisfaction that arises should they honestly discuss their sex lives. I talk about women much more with gay men than I ever have with straight ones. And given that women speak far more openly with gay men – and that gay men actually listen to them – my gay pals provide many useful insights into the female mind.[69]

Of course, what plays in London may take some time to catch on elsewhere. In the United States, bromance quickly lost its homosexual complications, and has become the love and affection shared by two straight males.[70] It is a playful possibility for self-consciously modern characters, such as the lawyers played by James Spader and William Shatner in *Boston Legal*. But it may still attract some resistance: as a contributor to modernredneck.com concluded: "sounds queer to me."[71] If it is possible for heterosexual men to be sociable, it still seems very difficult for them to be intimate. Again, it is always important to be aware of the differences between what is said about all men – often on reasonably strong empirical grounds – and what some men actually do. Sociologist Karen Walker, for instance, found that men and women tended to talk about friendship in ways that agreed with stereotypes: women share feelings, men share activities. In other words, they "emphasize the behavior that corresponds to their cultural notions of what men and women are like." But studying specific friendships reveals that some men – especially working-class men – "report regularly sharing feelings and discussing personal problems."[72] The study pointed out the significance of class and especially occupational and geographical mobility in how people talk about and actually experience friendship in 1990s America.

The Ends of Friendship: The Twenty-first Century

One crucial question for the century that is now beginning concerns how the patterns and opportunities of friendship, especially among the young, are being shaped by new technologies. It is particularly interesting to consider how these technologies create virtual spaces for the kinds of activities in which friends engage, such as playing games, mapping out life's possibilities and discussing shared enjoyment. It would be impossible to live in a contemporary Western city and not understand the significance of mobile phones in the organizing, planning and debriefing of friendship activities. Friends can be gathered together more quickly and easily, and over longer distances, than was true before.[73] It may be possible for some people, and especially younger men, to make and keep friends in new ways.

More people also now have opportunities to make friends at great distances, through travel, study exchanges at schools and universities, overseas job placements in global corporations and institutions, and so on. It is also possible to try out and to invent friendship in a variety of new ways; in virtual worlds such as *Second Life* or games such as *The Sims*, for instance, making friends is an important way of negotiating the challenges of everyday life. In *The Sims*, all relationships begin as friendships and social isolation leads to a kind of self-annihilation. For young people too there are new kinds of written as well as on-line resources. *The Complete Idiot's Guide to Friendship for Teens*, for instance, covers "five steps to making friends," "friendship's skills," "guys and gals as friends" and even "friendship's end," and devotes eight pages to "long-distance and virtual friendships," including email, chatrooms, messaging and other "wonders of technology."[74]

Is there intimacy in email, SMS, blogging, or texting? Does this tend to lead to a greater quantity or quality of contacts, or both? Can we make friends among the virtual "people" we meet on-line? If that seems a very post-modern question, it is important to remember that millions of people in the twentieth century had penpals and penfriends, and some certainly developed the kind of disclosure and reciprocal intimacy we would call friendship. There are predictable predictions: some argue that cyberspace is the death of intimacy and real connection, while others suggest that "the public arena of cyberspace allows us to break our public silence" and that while we "might be alone at our computers as we type, we are participating in some form of public life." Still, as the same author acknowledges, this is "the form of public life that comes about after the mistrust of our neighbours and our intense desires for privacy force us to re-examine our atomized lives."[75] So, in one way, a virtual world emphasizes and confirms the highly selective and exclusive nature of a twenty-first-century friendship divorced from proximity and obligation. Virtual space has all of the barriers – cyber-communities and cyber-gates – of real space. It allows for an intensification of privacy. But in another way, it allows for new kinds of accidental and long-range discoveries of shared ground and broadens the pool of potential friends.[76] It allows easier access to groups who are often silenced or excluded in the "real" public sphere. It might also mean that people inhibited by shyness or awkwardness can be bolder and more adventurous in their friendly encounters.

There are as yet no clear answers to these questions, nor any uncontestable directions that twenty-first-century friendship might take. One possibility, especially among younger urban people, is for "sparsely-knit, loosely-bounded, frequently-changing networks" that require very active maintenance in speaking, texting, writing and meeting.[77] Another is for friendships to become increasingly exclusive; smaller families, greater job mobility and more frequent life changes, alongside an ever stronger focus on privacy and self-realization, might mean that people tend to "'discover' each other in the specialized settings that compose their daily life," while those same conditions "may foster a tendency to remain self-contained, if not self-absorbed, and to avoid intimacy."[78] It is interesting in this regard, of course, that the most popular books for and among children in the first few years of the twenty-first century are about very real relationships, conducted in person in the rather old-fashioned communal setting of a boarding school: the bonds between Harry Potter, Hermione Granger and Ron Weasley suggest a continuing popular attraction to the idea of intense friendships.

One of the most important changes – and perhaps challenges – to the way friendships are built is that people may experience a greater number of real and virtual encounters but across a somewhat narrower social range. In some ways, the scope of potential friendships is increasing, as a result of travel, a more-and-more globalized culture, the spread of English (in various forms, of course) as an international language, and changing ideas about possible relationships between men and women or across other potential barriers. In other ways, though, the range of encounters might be narrowed, as the great mixing institutions of the twentieth century – schools and colleges, the army, mass workplaces and the large, bustling arenas of public leisure and consumption – either shrink in size, fragment into smaller and more exclusive experiences or are reshaped to confirm and maintain rather than overcome social divisions. To put this in more practical terms, it's harder to make friends with a range of others, or to make the kinds of accidental friendships that can be very important in self-discovery, when you're sitting in business class. It's also hard to make friends when you have no public life at all, as can be true for unemployed people and especially jobless men or for people who are sealed behind whatever high walls they can afford.

This is particularly important at those points in life – such as adolescence – when the making of friendships tends to be most intense. Here, again, institutions such as schools and universities are heading simultaneously towards a wider cultural diversity and a narrower social diversity, in terms of class or wealth. A recent survey of Americans' "discussion networks" found that while racial heterogeneity had increased, educational heterogeneity – a fairly good equivalent for class – had decreased since the 1980s.[79] In addition, if friendship formation becomes increasingly virtual, on-line and freed from the constraints of distance, then it is important to remember the still very unequal patterns of access to those communication technologies. In a way, then, what we might be witnessing is an increasing inequality – which may or may not be temporary – in people's access to new ways of making and being friends. In the distinctions she draws between "can-do" girls and "at-risk" girls, for instance, sociologist Anita Harris shows the importance of very different capacities to develop the on-line relationships that help individuals and groups create "virtual freedoms."[80] If you cannot afford a mobile phone or an Internet connection, can you still have friends?

Of course, this will matter less if those who are disadvantaged by these changes are able to continue nourishing more "inclusive" intimacies and solidarities that bind together and mix up neighbours, kin, family and friends. To an extent, this seems to be true, at least among women in some kinds of working-class and ethnic communities, where local solidarities, often formed around shared grievances and activism, continue to foster intense friendships.[81] The consequences for the friendless, however, are potentially dire. Their numbers may be increasing: one study indicates that Americans have smaller networks now than 20 years ago, that nearly a quarter of people have no close confidants and that almost half of the American population reports having no one with whom to discuss personal matters, though it also suggests that what might be happening is a shift from face-to-face to electronic or phone discussion, alongside a greater concentration on a few close friends.[82] In every industrialized country, more and more people are living alone. But the issue is not really whether more people lack friends but what the consequences of friendlessness are and might be. Social isolation may have a cost in and of itself, but the social, political and economic changes of recent times have arguably increased that cost. To be without friends may spell disaster in an early twenty-first-century world, which is likely to be characterized by fewer, meaner and more rigorously policed entitlements. There is little prospect that other relationships – such as neighbouring or employing – will regain the sense of obligation and duty they once had. If people care less for the good of the whole, and more for the people to whom they choose to feel a sense of connection and obligation, who will care for the friendless? In the twenty-first century, the exclusiveness of a particular kind of friendship may come home to roost, and not just in the rare but already highly publicized cases of solitary "shut-ins" lying dead – and unfound – for weeks and even months.

In response to this, it is important to consider whether there is any hope of restoring to ideals of friendship some of the concerns for public and indeed civic obligations that older forms had, or whether indeed this is even a desirable outcome. Mark Vernon's warnings about the limits of civic friendship are very important, and echo similar observations about a communitarian emphasis on "solidarity" that often ignores the potential for exclusion, and the privileging of specific rather than universal bonds.[83] After all, solidarity is mostly enacted against others, and all friendships are to some extent exclusive.

This is a dilemma and, like all dilemmas, it is difficult because it is to pose a choice between two good things: rich, intimate relationships based on choice, on the one hand, and a supportive, nourishing care for others – based on the fact of shared humanity – on the other. In diverse societies, the dilemma might seem even more difficult: how do we find a balance between what we hold in common and what we choose not to share? Of course, this also takes us back to a question that has been central to this entire history: why and how do we value friendship as a relationship that has significance beyond individuals? In other words, what does friendship offer in terms of models for a good life? As we enter the twenty-first century, there have been some interesting responses. Against what he regards as Aristotle's emphasis on shared understandings and qualities, for instance, Canadian philosopher David Kahane argues that both personal and civic friendships can be based upon a valuing of a shared history of contact and interaction. It is a relationship in which you have shaped others and they have shaped you, and in which the quality of your concern for other citizens matters. But it is not a relationship that demands those other citizens agree with you on everything or that they become like you; just as personal friends can help us see ourselves through gentle criticism as well as praise, and just as we enjoy our friends because of their differences from us, so we can enjoy the differences and debates that come from social diversity.[84]

In the view of the writers of this book, there are two other crucial ingredients. The first is the continuing significance of idealizing friendship as one means – though not of course the only means – of undermining structures of oppression. Here, as in some of the famous and less-famous activist friendships of the past, befriending is a model of connection, of listening to others and seeing the world through their eyes and, having listened and seen, being committed to helping them become what they want to be. The second is the emphasis in much recent feminist scholarship, and in the daily lives of women, on friendship as a caring concern for the welfare of others, which can and should be generalized from particular to universal people.[85] This form of friendship, which has also featured in recent queer theory, recognizes and indeed celebrates common needs, takes care of deficiencies and is alive to differences; it also takes note of the possibility to be private and individual without refusing the bonds that stem from shared vulnerabilities.[86] In a way, of course, we have returned to Aristotle, or at least to those questions about the broader qualities and benefits of friendship that have informed this entire history.

The best antidotes to friendlessness do not lie in an emphasis on association and community, which too often end up eroding the privacy and autonomy that wider affluence has helped more people enjoy. There is little evidence that most people want to return to the village, where enemies were as close as friends and everyone knew everyone's business. There is more evidence that people do worry about living in and contributing to a "friendly" society and that most people – if not their political and economic masters – understand that freedom of choice cannot mean freedom from obligation, responsibility and care. It cannot, in other words, mean the freedom to treat friends well and strangers badly. In the end, it might be particularly important to valorize different meanings of friendship, in which deep, intimate and enjoyable bonds function alongside and not instead of more generalized obligations and commitments. People want to live in a friendly world, but they do not expect everyone to be their best friend. The task is not then to make all strangers into friends, but to make sure that we do not treat every stranger as an enemy.

Notes

1. Ray Pahl, *On Friendship* (Cambridge: Polity Press, 2000), p. 69.

2. Richard Stannard, Matt Rowe and the Spice Girls, "Wannabe" (Windswept Pacific Musics/PolyGram Music Publishing Ltd, 1996).

3. Lillian Rubin, *Just Friends: The Role of Friendship in our Lives* (New York: Harper & Row, 1985), p. 41.

4. Graham Allan, "Friendship and the Private Sphere," in Rebecca Adams and Graham Allen (eds), *Placing Friendship in Context* (Cambridge: Cambridge University Press, 1998), pp. 71–91.

5. Stephanie Coontz, "What We Really Miss about the 1950s," in Judith E. Smith, Lois Palken Rudnick and Rachel Rubin (eds), *American Identities* (New York: Blackwell, 2006), pp. 17–28 at p. 19; Mark Peel, "'A New Kind of Manhood': Remembering the 1950s," in John Murphy and Judith Smart (eds), *The Forgotten Fifties* (Melbourne: Melbourne University Press, 1997), pp. 147–57.

6. Ian Procter, "The Privatisation of Working-Class Life: A Dissenting View," *British Journal of Sociology* 41 (1990), pp. 157–80.

7. J. M. Mogey, *Family and Neighbourhood: Two Studies in Oxford* (Oxford: Oxford University Press, 1956).

8. Margaret Stacey, *Tradition and Change: A Study of Banbury* (Oxford: Oxford University Press, 1960).

9. Mark Clapson, "Urban dispersal and its social consequences: town planning, sociology and the English working classes, 1945 – 1980," at http://www.le.ac.uk/urbanhist/uhg/pdf/clapson.pdf, accessed 4 October 2007.

10. William H. Whyte, *The Organization Man* (Philadelphia: University of Pennsylvania Press, 2002 [1956]), p. 311.

11. Herbert Gans, *The Levittowners: Ways of Life and Politics in a New Suburban Community* (New York: Pantheon, 1967), p. 409.

12. Betty Friedan, *The Feminine Mystique* (New York: W. W. Norton, 1963), p. 21.

13. Margaret Kinnell, "Friendship in Children's Fiction," in Roy Porter and Sylvana Tomaselli (eds), *The Dialectics of Friendship* (London: Routledge, 1989), pp. 76–91.

14. Graham Little, *Friendship: Being Ourselves with Others* (Melbourne: Text, 1993), pp. 46–69.

15. L. Weiss and M. F. Lowenthal, "Life Course Perspectives on Friendship," in M. F. Lowenthal *et al.* (eds), *Four Stages of Life* (San Francisco: Jossey-Bass, 1975), pp. 48–61.

16. B. J. Felton and C. A. Ferry, "Do the Sources of the Urban Elderly's Social Support Determine its Psychological Consequences?" *Psychology and Aging* 7 (1992), pp. 89–97, and J. F. Nussbaum, "Perceptions of Communication Content and Life Satisfaction among the Elderly," *Communication Quarterly* 31 (1983), pp. 313–19.

17. Claude S. Fischer, *To Dwell among Friends: Personal Networks in Town and City* (Chicago: University of Chicago Press, 1982), pp. 40–41.

18. Carol Stack, *All our Kin: Strategies for Survival in a Black Community* (New York: Harper & Row, 1974); Karen Lindsey, *Friends as Family* (Boston: Beacon Press, 1981).

19. Graham A. Allan, *The Sociology of Friendship and Kinship* (London: Allen & Unwin, 1979).

20. Anthony Heath, *Social Mobility* (London: Fontana, 1981); Peter Willmott, *Friendship Networks and Social Support* (London: Policy Studies Institute, 1987), p. 100.

21. Janet Finch, *Family Obligations and Social Change* (Oxford: Polity Press, 1989).

22. Barrett Strong and Norman Whitfield, "The Friendship Train" (EMI Music Publishing).

23. *Peace Corps Act*, United States Congress Public Law 87–293, 22 September 1961.

24. Taylor Branch, *Parting the Waters: America in the King Years, 1954–63* (New York: Simon & Schuster, 1988).

25. Belinda Robnett, *How Long? How Long? African-American Women in the Struggle for Civil Rights* (New York: Oxford University Press, 1997), pp. 65–66.

26. "Letter from Birmingham Jail," at http://almaz.com/nobel/peace/MLK-jail.html, accessed 4 October 2007; "Non-Violence and Racial Justice," *The Christian Century* (6 February 1957), p. 167.

27. Cited in Vincent P. Franklin and Bettye Collier-Thomas, *Sisters in the Struggle: African-American Women in the Civil Rights and Black Power Movements* (New York: New York University Press, 2001), p. 47.

28. Doug McAdam, *Freedom Summer* (New York: Oxford University Press, 1990).

29. Anne Moody, *Coming of Age in Mississippi* (New York: Dell, 1968).

30. http://www.outreach.olemiss.edu/Freedom_Riders/Resources/Mulholland_Joan_Trumpower.doc, accessed 4 October 2007.

31. Constance Curry (ed.), *Deep in our Hearts: Nine White Women in the Freedom Movement* (Athens, GA: University of Georgia Press, 2000).

32. Peter B. Edelman, *Searching for America's Heart: RFK and the Renewal of Hope* (New York: Houghton Mifflin, 2001), pp. 43–46.

33 Marco Diani, *Green Networks* (Edinburgh: Edinburgh University Press, 1995).

34. Janes Downton Jr and Paul Wehr, "Persistent Pacifism: How Activist Commitment Is Developed and Sustained," *Journal of Peace Research* 35 (1998), pp. 531–50.

35. Barbara Caine, "Prisons as Spaces of Friendships in Apartheid South Africa," *History Australia* 3 (2006), pp. 42.1–42.13.

36. Ann Curthoys, *Freedom Ride: A Freedom Rider Remembers* (Sydney: Allen & Unwin, 2002); Bain Attwood and Andrew Markus, *The Struggle for Aboriginal Rights: A Documentary History* (Sydney: Allen & Unwin, 1995).

37. Sue Taffe, *Black and White Together: The Federal Council for the Advancement of Aborigines and Torres Strait Islanders* (Brisbane: University of Queensland Press, 2005), p. 263.

38. Faith Bandler, *Turning the Tide: A Personal History of the Federal Council for the Advancement of Aborigines and Torres Strait Islanders* (Canberra: Aboriginal Studies Press, 1989), p. 147.

39. Sara Evans and Harry Boyte, *Free Spaces: The Sources of Democratic Change in America* (Chicago: University of Chicago Press, 1992), p. 105.

40. Elizabeth Kennedy and Madeline Davis, *Boots of Leather, Slippers of Gold: History of a Lesbian Community* (New York: Routledge, 1993).

41. Cited in Jeffrey Weeks, Brian Heaphy and Catherine Donovan, *Same-Sex Intimacies: Families of Choice and Other Life Experiments* (London: Routledge, 2001), p. 52.

42. Cited in Peter M. Nardi, *Gay Men's Friendships: Invincible Communities* (Chicago: University of Chicago Press, 1999), p. 16.

43. Weeks, Heaphy and Donovan, *Same-Sex Intimacies*, p. 51.

44. Weeks, Heaphy and Donovan, *Same-Sex Intimacies*, pp. 58–59.

45. Lindsey, *Friends as Family*, p. 179.

46. Michel Foucault, "Friendship as a Way of Life" [1981], cited in Nardi, *Gay Men's Friendships*, p. 13.

47. Rubin, *Just Friends*, pp. 60–70.

48. Christopher Alexander, "The City as a Mechanism for Sustaining Human Contact," in W. Ewald (ed.), *Environment for Man* (Bloomington: Indiana University Press, 1967), p. 241.

49. Joel Block, *Friendship* (Gretna, LA: Wellness Institute, 1980), p. 84.

50. David Thorburn, "Television as an Aesthetic Medium," *Critical Studies in Mass Communication* 4 (1987), pp. 161–73.

51. Karen Hollinger, *In the Company of Women: Contemporary Female Friendship Films* (Minneapolis: University of Minnesota Press, 1998).

52. David A. Wyatt, "Gay/Lesbian/Bisexual Television Characters," http://home.cc.umanitoba.ca/~wyatt/tv-characters.html, accessed 4 October 2007.

53. Michael Skovmand, "The Culture of Post-Narcissism," http://www.nordicom.gu.se/common/publ_pdf/42_205-214.pdf, accessed 4 October 2007.

54. Richard Sennett, *The Corrosion of Character: The Personal Consequences of Work in the New Capitalism* (New York: Norton, 1998), p. 148.

55. Robert Lane, *The Loss of Happiness in Market Democracies* (New Haven, CT: Yale University Press, 2001), pp. 112–13.

56. Lane, *The Loss of Happiness*, p. 137.

57. Little, *Friendship*, p. 245.

58. Raymond Pahl and Liz Spencer, *Rethinking Friendship: Hidden Solidarities for Today* (Princeton, NJ: Princeton University Press, 2004), p. 95.

59. Rubin, *Just Friends*, p. 14.

60. Kaeren Harrison, "Rich Friendships, Affluent Friends: Middle-class Practices of Friendship," in Adams and Allan (eds), *Placing Friendship in Context*, pp. 92–116.

61. Linda Rosenzweig, *Another Self: Middle-class Women and their Friends in the Twentieth Century* (New York: New York University Press, 1999).

62. Stacey Oliker, *Best Friends and Marriage: Exchange among Women* (Berkeley, CA: University of California Press, 1989).

63. Ellen Trimberger, *The New Single Woman* (Boston: Beacon Press, 2005).

64. Maria Paul, *The Friendship Crisis: Finding, Making and Keeping Friends When You're Not a Kid Anymore* (Chicago: Rodale, 2004), p. 5.

65. Robin Podolsky, "The Ever Changing Lesbian Social Scene," in Betty Berzon (ed.), *Positively Gay* (Berkeley, CA: Celestial Arts, 3rd edn, 2001), p. 44.

66. Mark Vernon, *The Philosophy of Friendship* (Basingstoke: Palgrave MacMillan, 2005), pp. 132–33.

67. Jennifer Coates, *Women Talk: Conversation between Women Friends* (New York: Blackwell, 1995), pp. 36–39.

68. Jennifer Lee, "The Man Date," *New York Times* (10 April 2005).

69. Nirpal Dhaliwal, "A Fine Bromance," *Guardian* (11 June 2007).

70. http://www.associatedcontent.com/article/247320/bromance_finding_your_buddies_mates.html, accessed 4 October 2007.

71. http://www.modernredneck.com/?p=159, accessed 4 October 2007.

72. Karen Walker, "Men, Women, and Friendship: What They Say, What They Do," *Gender and Society* 8 (1994), pp. 246–65 at pp. 246–47.

73. On these and broader issues, see especially James Everett Katz (ed.), *Machines Become Us: The Social Context of Personal Communication Technology* (New York: Transaction Publishers, 2003).

74. Ericka Lutz, *The Complete Idiot's Guide to Friendship for Teens* (New York: Alpha Books, 2001).

75. Jan Fernback, "The Individual within the Collective: Virtual Ideology and the Realization of Collective Principles," in Steven G. Jones (ed.), *Virtual Culture: Identity and Communication in Cybersociety* (London: Sage, 1997), pp. 36–54 at pp. 37–38.

76. Rebecca G. Adams, "The Demise of Territorial Determinism: Online Friendships," in Adams and Allan (eds), *Placing Friendship in Context*, pp. 153–82.

77. Barry Wellman, "I Was a Teenage Network Analyst: The Route from the Bronx to the Information Highway," *Connections* 17 (1994), pp. 28–45 at p. 32.

78. Stephen R. Marks, "The Gendered Contexts of Inclusive Intimacy," in Adams and Allan (eds), *Placing Friendship in Context*, pp. 43–70 at p. 67.

79. Miller McPherson, Lynn Smith-Lovin and Matthew E. Brashears, "Social Isolation in America: Changes in Core Discussion Networks over Two Decades," *American Sociological Review* 71 (2006), pp. 353–75.

80. Anita Harris, *Future Girl: Young Women in the Twenty-first Century* (New York: Routledge, 2004), p. 156.

81. Nancy Naples, *Grassroots Warriors: Activist Mothering, Community Work and the War on Poverty* (New York: Routledge, 1998); Mark Peel, *The Lowest Rung: Voices of Australian Poverty* (Cambridge: Cambridge University Press, 2003), pp. 145–64.

82. McPherson, Smith-Lovin and Brashears, "Social Isolation in America."

83. Vernon, *Philosophy of Friendship*, pp. 142–44.

84. David Kahane, "Diversity, Solidarity and Civic Friendship," *Journal of Political Philosophy* 7 (1999), pp. 267–86.

85. Sybil A. Schwarzenbach, "On Civic Friendship," *Ethics* 107 (1996), pp. 97–128.

86. Sasha Roseneil, "Why We Should Care about Friends: An Argument for Queering the Care Imaginary in Social Policy," *Social Policy and Society* 3 (2004), pp. 409–19.

BIBLIOGRAPHY

Abbey, Ruth. "Back to the Future: Marriage as Friendship in the Thought of Mary Wollstonecraft." *Hypatia* 14.3 (Summer 1999), pp. 78–95.

Aberth, J., (ed.). *The Black Death: The Great Mortality of 1348–1350.* New York: Palgrave Macmillan, 2005.

Aboud, F. E., M. J. Mendelson and K. T. Purdy. "Cross-Race Peer Relations and Friendship Quality." *International Journal of Behavioral Development* 27 (2003), pp. 165–73.

Adams, Glenn, and Victoria C. Plaut. "The Cultural Grounding of Personal Relationship: Friendship in North American and West African Worlds." *Personal Relationships* 10.3 (2003), pp. 333–47.

Adams, Rebecca G. "The Demise of Territorial Determinism: Online Friendships." In Rebecca G. Adams and Graham Allan (eds), *Placing Friendship in Context*, pp. 153–82. Cambridge; New York: Cambridge University Press, 1998.

Adams, Rebecca G., and Graham Allan (eds). *Placing Friendship in Context.* Cambridge; New York: Cambridge University Press, 1998.

Aelred, of Rievaulx, Saint. *De spiritali amicitia.* Ed. A. Hoste; Corpus Christianorum Continuatio Mediaeualis, 1; Turnhout: Brepols, 1971.

—— *Aelred of Rievaulx's Spiritual Friendship: A New Translation.* Trans. Mark F. Williams; Scranton: University of Scranton Press; London; Cranbury, NJ: Associated University Presses, 1994.

Agamben, Giorgio. *Contremps* 5, 2004.

Ailes, M. J. "The Medieval Male Couple and the Language of Homosociality." In D. M. Hadley (ed.), *Masculinity in Medieval Europe*, pp. 214–37. London: Longman, 1999.

Alberoni, Francesco. *L'amicizia.* Milano: Garzanti, 1984.

Alberti, L. B. *The Family in Renaissance Florence.* Trans. R. N. Watkins; Columbia, South Carolina: University of South Carolina, 1969.

—— *De vera amicitia: I testi del primo Certame coronario.* Ed. L. Bertolini; Modena: Panini, 1993.

Alborn, T. "Senses of Belonging: The Politics of Working-Class Insurance in Britain, 1880–1914." *Journal of Modern History* 73.3 (September 2001), pp. 561–602.

Alessio, Gian Carlo, (ed.). *Bene Florentini Candelabrum.* Thesaurus Mundi: Bibliotheca scriptorum latinorum mediae et recentioris aetatis, 23; Padua: Antenore, 1983.

Alexander, Christopher. "The City as a Mechanism for Sustaining Human Contact." In W. Ewald (ed.), *Environment for Man.* Bloomington: Indiana University Press, 1967.

Alexander, Sally. "Becoming a Woman in the 1920s and 1930s." In *Becoming a Woman and Other Essays in 19th and 20th Century Feminist History*, pp. 202–24. London: Virago, 1994.

Allan, Graham A. "Friendship and the Private Sphere." In Rebecca G. Adams and Graham Allen (eds), *Placing Friendship in Context*, pp. 71–91. Cambridge: Cambridge University Press, 1998.

—— *Kinship and Friendship in Modern Britain.* Oxford; New York: Oxford University Press, 1996.

—— *Friendship: Developing a Sociological Perspective.* Hemel Hempstead: Harvester Wheatsheaf, 1989.

—— *The Sociology of Friendship and Kinship.* London; Boston: Allen & Unwin, 1979.

—— "Class Variation in Friendship Patterns." *British Journal of Sociology* 28 (September 1977), pp. 389–93.

Allison, John Murray. *Adams and Jefferson: The Story of a Friendship.* Norman: University of Oklahoma Press, 1966.

Allison, June W. "'Axiosis,' the New 'Arete': A Periclean Metaphor for Friendship." *The Classical Quarterly* 51.1 (Jan–June 2001), pp. 53–64.

Alpern, Kenneth David. *The Nature of Friendship [microform]: Aristotelian and Kantian Themes.* Published on demand: Ann Arbor, MI: University Microfilms International, PhD thesis, University of Pittsburgh, 1980.

Althoff, Gerd. "*Amicitiae* as Relationships between States and People." In Lester K. Little and Barbara H. Rosenwein (eds), *Debating the Middle Ages: Issues and Readings*, pp. 191–210. Oxford: Blackwell, 1998.

—— "Friendship and Political Order." In Haseldine (ed.), *Friendship in Medieval Europe*, pp. 91–105. Stroud: Sutton, 1999.

—— *Family, Friends and Followers: Political and Social Bonds in Early Medieval Europe.* Trans. Christopher Carroll; Cambridge: Cambridge University Press, 2004.

A. M. *Moral Essays, Chiefly Collected from Different Authors.* 2 vols; Liverpool, 1796.

Anderson, J. "Bittersweet Love: Giorgione's Portraits of Masculine Friendship." In D. R. Marshall (ed.), *The Italians in Australia: Studies in Renaissance and Baroque Art*, pp. 87–94. Florence and Melbourne: Centro Di and the Ian Potter Museum of Art, University of Melbourne, 2004.

Andrews, Keith. "Dürer and Pirckheimer: A Renaissance Friendship." *Bulletin of the Society for Renaissance Studies* 4.2 (1986–1987), pp. 7–15.

Annas, J. "Plato and Aristotle on Friendship and Altruism." *Mind: A Quarterly Review of Philosophy* 86 (1977), pp. 532–54.

Annis, D. B. "The Meaning, Value, and Duties of Friendship." *American Philosophical Quarterly* 24 (1987), pp. 349–56.

Archibald, Elizabeth. "Malory's Ideal of Fellowship." *Review of English Studies* 43.171 (1992), pp. 311–28.

Argyle, Michael, and Monika Henderson. *Anatomy of Friendship.* London: Heinemann, 1984.

—— "The Rules of Friendship." *Journal of Social and Personal Relationships* 1 (June 1984), pp. 211–37.

Aries, Elizabeth, and Fern Johnson. "Close Friendship in Adulthood: Conversational Content between Same-Sex Friends." *Sex Roles* 9 (1983), pp. 1183–96.

Aristotle. *Nicomachean Ethics.* Trans. with an introduction, notes and glossary T. Irwin; Indianapolis: Hackett, 2nd edn, 1999.

—— *Eudemian Ethics* and *Politics.* In J. Barnes (ed.), *The Complete Works of Aristotle.* 2 vols; Princeton: Princeton University Press, 1984.

Arneil, Barbara. *John Locke and America: The Defence of English Colonialism.* Oxford: Clarendon Press, 1996.

Arni, Caroline. "Das kultivierte Gefühl: Liebe als Freundschaft in der Ehe um 1900." *WerkstattGeschichte* 28 (2001), pp. 43–60.

Arnim, H. von, (ed.). *Stoicorum Veterum Fragmenta.* 4 vols; Stuttgart: Teubner, 1903–1924.

Ascham, Roger. *The Scholemaster.* Ed. J. E. B. Mayor; London: 1863; reprinted New York: AMS Press, 1967.

Ascher, Carol. Louise DeSalvo and Sara Ruddick (eds), *Between Women: Biographers, Novelists, Critics, Teachers and Artists Write about their Work on Women.* Boston: Beacon Press, 1984.

Attwood, Bain, and Andrew Markus. *The Struggle for Aboriginal Rights: A Documentary History.* Sydney: Allen & Unwin, 1995.

Auchincloss, Louis. *Love without Wings: Some Friendships in Literature and Politics.* Boston: Houghton Mifflin, 1991.

Auchmuty, Rosemary. *A World of Girls.* London: The Women's Press, 1992.

Audley, Matthew. *A Sermon Preach'd at St Paul's, Deptford, Kent, on June 23d, 1739.* London: John Carter, 1739.

Augustine. *City of God.* Trans. H. Bettenson; London: Penguin, 1972.

Ausland, Hayden. "The Mathematics of Justice." In H. Tarrant and D. Baltzly (eds), *Reading Plato in Antiquity*, pp. 107–23. London: Duckworth, 2006.

Austen, Jane. *Pride and Prejudice.* Harmondsworth, UK: Penguin Books, 2001 (1813).

—— *Persuasion.* Oxford: Oxford University Press, 1971 (1817).

Austin, M. M. "Economy and Society." In D. M. Lewis, J. Boardman, S. Hornblower and M. Ostwald (eds), *The Cambridge Ancient History. Vol. VI, The Fourth Century*, pp. 527–64. Cambridge: Cambridge University Press, 2nd edn, 1994.

Bacon, Sir Francis. "Of Friendship" (1625). In Josephine Miles (ed.), *Classic Essays in English*, pp.15–21. Boston: Little, Brown, 1965.

—— "Of Followers and Friends." *Essays Civil and Moral.* London: Cassell & Company, 1895.

—— "Of Followers and Friends" (1625). In *Essayes, Religious Meditations, Places of Perswasion and Disswasion, Seene and Allowed.* London: H. Hooper, 1597.

—— "Of Followers and Friends." In *The Essays.* Harmondsworth, UK: Penguin, 1985.

Badhwar, Neera Kapur, (ed.). *Friendship: A Philosophical Reader*. Ithaca. NY: Cornell University Press, 1993.

Bailey, Shakleton, (ed.). *Cicero: Selected Letters*. Harmondsworth, UK: Penguin, 1982.

Baily, Samuel L. *Immigrants in the Lands of Promise: Italians in Buenos Aires and New York City. 1870–1914*. Ithaca, New York: Cornell University Press, 1999.

Balch, David L. "Political Friendship in the Historian Dionysius of Halicarnassus. *Roman Antiquities*." In John T. Fitzgerald (ed.), *Greco-Roman Perspectives on Friendship*, pp. 123–44. Atlanta, GA: Scholars Press, 1997.

Bald, R. C. *Literary Friendship in the Age of Wordsworth*. New York: Octagon, 1968.

Baldwin, Suzy. *Best of Friends: Australian Women Talk about Friendship*. Ringwood, Victoria: Penguin, 2001.

Baldwin, S., and P. Barrette (eds). *Li Livres dou Tresor*. Tempe, AZ: Arizona Center for Medieval and Renaissance Studies, 2003.

Baltzly, D. "Stoic Pantheism." *Sophia* 34 (2003), pp. 3–33.

Bandler, Faith. *Turning the Tide: A Personal History of the Federal Council for the Advancement of Aborigines and Torres Strait Islanders*. Canberra: Aboriginal Studies Press, 1989.

Barlow, J. "The Moral and Political Philosophy of the Middle Stoa in its Historical Context." MA thesis, Monash University, 2001.

Barrette, Paul, and Spurgeon Baldwin (trans.). *Brunetto Latini, the Book of the Treasure*. Garland Library of Medieval Literature, 90; New York: Garland, 1993.

Barrow, Julia. "Friends and Friendship in Anglo-Saxon Charters." In Julian Haseldine (ed.), *Friendship in Medieval Europe*, pp. 106–23. Stroud, UK: Sutton, 1999.

Barth, Gunther. *City People: The Rise of Modern City Culture in Nineteenth-century America*. New York: Oxford University Press, 1980.

Bartolommeo, Fra, da San Concordio. *Ammaestramenti degli Antichi*. Ed. V. Nannucci; Florence: Ricordi e Compagno, 1840.

Barton, Julie Sian. *An Alternative Approach to the French Enlightenment: Friendship Groups and Private Correspondence*. Clayton, Victoria: Monash Publications in History, Monash University, 1995.

Bashor, Philip S. "Plato and Aristotle on Friendship." *Journal of Value Inquiry* 2 (Winter 1968), pp. 269–80.

Basinger, Jeanine. *A Woman's View: How Hollywood Spoke to Women, 1930–1960*. Middletown, CT: Wesleyan University Press, 1995.

Bates, Ernest Sutherland. "The Meaning of Recent Trends in Nonfiction." *The English Journal* 27 (1938).

Bean, J. M. W. *From Lord to Patron: Lordship in Late Medieval England*. Manchester: Manchester University Press. 1989.

Bec, C. *Les livres des Florentins (1413–1608)*. Florence: Olschki, 1984.

Becker-Cantarino, Barbara. "Friendship." In *Encyclopedia of the Enlightenment*, II, 91–96. Ed. Alan Charles Kors; 4 vols; Oxford: Oxford University Press, 2003.

Belcari, Feo. *Lettere*. Ed. D. Moreni; Florence: Magheri, 1825.

Belfiore, Elizabeth. "Family Friendship in Aristotle's Ethics." *Ancient Philosophy* 21.1 (2001), pp. 113–32.

—— *Murder among Friends: Violation of Philia in Greek Tragedy.* Oxford: Oxford University Press, 2000.

Bell, Quentin. *Bloomsbury.* London: Weidenfeld & Nicolson, 1968.

Bell, Robert R. *Worlds of Friendship.* Beverly Hills: Sage Publications, 1981.

Bell, Sandra, and Simon Coleman (eds). *The Anthropology of Friendship.* Oxford: Berg, 1999.

Bellamy, J. S. *Bastard Feudalism and the Law.* London: Routledge, 1989.

Beltran, E. *Humanistes francais du milieu de xvᵉ siècle.* Geneva: Droz, 1989.

Bennett, Don. "The Cultural Variable in Friendship and Group Formation." *Economic and Social Review* 10.2 (1979), pp. 123–45.

Bennett, Judith M. "Conviviality and Charity in Medieval and Early Modern England." *Past and Present* 134 (Feb 1992), pp. 19–41.

Betensky, C. "Philanthropy, Desire and the Politics of Friendship in *The Princess Casamassima.*" *Henry James Review* 22.2 (2001).

Black, A. *Guilds and Civil Society in European Political Thought from the Twelfth Century to the Present.* London and New York: Methuen, 1984.

Black, C. F. *Italian Confraternities in the Sixteenth Century.* Cambridge: Cambridge University Press, 1989.

Black, J. D. *Friendship.* New York: 1980.

Blickle, P., (ed.). *Resistance, Representation, and Community.* Oxford: Oxford University Press, 1997.

Blieszner, Rosemary, and Rebecca G. Adams. *Adult Friendship.* Newbury Park, CA: Sage Publications, 1992.

Bloch, Marc. *Feudal Society.* Trans. L. A. Manyon; London: Routledge & Kegan Paul, 1961.

Block, Joel D. *Friendship.* New York: Macmillan, 1980.

Block, Joel D., and Diane Greenberg. *Women and Friendship.* New York: F. Watts, 1985.

Bloom, Allan David. *Love and Friendship.* New York: Simon & Schuster, 1993.

Blum, Alan F., and Peter McHugh (eds). *Friends, Enemies and Strangers: Theorizing in Art, Science, and Everyday Life.* Norwood, NJ: Ablex, 1979.

Blum, Lawrence A. *Friendship, Altruism, and Morality.* London; Boston: Routledge & Kegan Paul, 1980.

Blundell, Mary Whitlock. *Helping Friends and Harming Enemies: A Study in Sophocles and Greek Ethics.* Cambridge; New York: Cambridge University Press, 1989.

Boissevain, Jeremy. *Friends of Friends: Networks, Manipulators and Coalitions.* Oxford: Blackwell, 1974.

Bolgar, R. R. *The Classical Heritage and its Beneficiaries.* Cambridge: Cambridge University Press, 1958.

Bolotin, David. *Plato's Dialogue on Friendship: An Interpretation of the Lysis, with a New Translation.* Ithaca: Cornell University Press, 1979.

Bond, Gerald. "'Iocus amoris': The Poetry of Baudri of Bourgueil, and the Formation of the Ovidian Subculture." *Traditio* 42 (1986), pp. 143–93.

Booth, A., and E. Hess. "Cross-Sexual Friendships." *Journal of Marriage and the Family* 36 (1974), pp. 38–47.

Bosch, Mineke, with Annemarie Kloosterman. *Politics and Friendship: Letters from the International Woman Suffrage Alliance, 1902–1942.* Columbus: Ohio State University Press, 1990.

Bossy, J. "Blood and Baptism: Kinship, Community and Christianity in Western Europe from the Fourteenth to the Seventeenth Centuries." In *Studies in Church History*, X, pp. 129–43. Oxford: Oxford University Press, 1973.

—— *Christianity in the West, 1400–1700.* Oxford: Oxford University Press, 1985.

Boswell. D. "Kinship, Friendship and the Concept of Social Network." *Proceedings of the East African Institute of Social Research* 379 (1966).

Boswell, James. *Life of Johnson.* Ed. R. W. Chapman; Oxford: Oxford University Press, rev. edn, 1970.

Boswell, John. *Same-Sex Unions in Premodern Europe.* New York: Villiard Books, 1994.

Bourke, Joanna. *Dismembering the Male: Men's Bodies, Britain and the Great War.* London: Reaktion Books, 1996.

Bouwsma, W. J. *A Usable Past: Essays in European Cultural History.* Berkeley: University of California Press, 1990.

Bowditch, P. Lowell. *Horace and the Gift Economy of Patronage.* Berkeley: University of California Press, 2001.

Bracke, W. *"Fare La Epistola" nella Roma del Quattrocento.* (Rome: Associazione Roma nel Rinascimento, 1992.

Bradley, Marshell Carl, and Philip Blosser (eds). *Of Friendship: Philosophic Selections on a Perennial Concern.* Wolfeboro, NH: Longwood Academic, 1989.

Brady, Bernard V. *Christian Love.* Washington, DC: Georgetown University Press, 2003.

Brain, Robert. *Friends and Lovers.* London: Hart-Davis MacGibbon, 1976.

Branch, Taylor. *Parting the Waters: America in the King Years, 1954–63.* New York: Simon & Schuster, 1988.

Bravo, Anna. "Solidarity and Loneliness: Piedmontese Peasant Women at the Turn of the Century." *International Journal of Oral History* 3.2 (1982), pp. 76–91.

Bray, Alan. *Homosexuality in Renaissance England.* London: Gay Men's Press, 1982.

—— "Homosexuality and the Signs of Male Friendship in Elizabethan England." *History Workshop Journal* 29 (1990), pp. 1–19.

—— "A Traditional Rite for Blessing Friendship." In Katherine O'Donnell and Michael O'Rourke (eds), *Love, Sex, Intimacy, and Friendship between Men, 1550–1800*, pp. 87–98. Houndmills: Palgrave Macmillan, 2003.

—— *The Friend.* Chicago: University of Chicago Press, 2003.

Bray, Alan, and Michel Rey. "The Body of the Friend: Continuity and Change in Masculine Friendship in the Seventeenth Century." In Tim Hitchcock and Michèle Cohen (eds), *English Masculinities, 1660–1800*, pp. 65–84. London: Longman, 1999.

Brenton, Myron. *Friendship.* New York: Stein and Day, 1975.

Brockliss, Lawrence. *French Higher Education in the Seventeenth and Eighteenth Centuries: A Cultural History.* Oxford and New York: Oxford University Press, 1987.

Broughton, H. "The Social Aspect of the Manchester Unity." *Quarterly Magazine of the Independent Order of Odd-Fellows, Manchester Unity* new series 25 (1894).

Brown, Irene Q. "Domesticity, Feminism, and Friendship: Female Aristocratic Culture and Marriage in England, 1660–1760." *Journal of Family History* 7.4 (1982), pp. 406–24.

Bruccoli, Matthew J. *Fitzgerald and Hemingway: A Dangerous Friendship.* New York: Carroll & Graf, 1994.

Brunt, P. A. "Amicitia in the Late Roman Republic." *Proceedings of the Cambridge Philological Society* 191 (1965), pp. 1–20.

—— *The Fall of the Roman Republic and Related Essays.* Oxford: Oxford University Press, 1988.

Burke, Carolyn. "Gertrude Stein, the Cone Sisters, and the Puzzle of Female Friendship." *Critical Inquiry* 8.3 (1982), pp. 543–64.

Burke, Janet M. "Freemasonry, Friendship and Noblewomen: The Role of the Secret Society in Bringing Enlightenment Thought to Pre-Revolutionary Women Elites." *History of European Ideas* 10.3 (1989), pp. 283–93.

Burke, J. *Changing Patrons: Social Identity and the Visual Arts in Renaissance Florence.* University Park, PA: Pennsylvania State University Press, 2004.

Burke, Peter. "Humanism and Friendship in Sixteenth-Century Europe." In Julian Haseldine (ed.), *Friendship in Medieval Europe*, pp. 262–74. Stroud, UK: Sutton, 1999.

Burrell, David B. *Friendship and Ways to Truth.* Notre-Dame, IN: Notre Dame Press, 2000.

Burnett, J. *Destiny Obscure: Autobiographies of Childhood, Education and the Family from the 1820s to the 1920s.* Harmondsworth, UK: Penguin, 1984.

Burstein, Stanley M., (ed. and trans.). *The Hellenistic Age from the Battle of Ipsos to the Death of Kleopatra VII.* Cambridge: Cambridge University Press, 1985.

Burton, Antoinette. *At the Heart of the Empire: Indians and the Colonial Encounter in Late-Victorian Britain.* Berkeley: University of California Press, 1997.

Burton, Paul J. "*Amicitia* in Plautus: A Study of Roman Friendship Processes." *American Journal of Philology* 125 (2004), pp. 209–43.

Buxton, John. *Byron and Shelley: The History of a Friendship.* London. Melbourne: Macmillan, 1968.

Caine, Barbara. *Victorian Feminists.* Oxford: Oxford University Press, 1992.

—— "Prisons as Spaces of Friendships in Apartheid South Africa." *History Australia* 3 (2006), pp. 42.1–42.13.

Calhoun, George Miller. *Athenian Clubs in Politics and Litigation.* New York: Burt Franklin, 1970.

Calitti, F., (ed.). *L'Arte della conversazione nelle corti del Rinascimento.* Rome: Istituto Poligrafico e Zecca dello Stato, 2003.

Callahan, W. "Confraternities and Brotherhoods in Spain, 1500–1800." *Confraternitas* 12 (2001), pp. 17–25.

Campbell, Colin. "Understanding Traditional and Modern Patterns of Consumption in Eighteenth-century England: A Character-Action Approach." In John Brewer and Roy Porter (eds), *Consumption and the World of Goods,* pp. 40–57. London and New York: Routledge, 1993.

Capelle, W. "Griechische Ethik und römischer Imperialismus." *Klio* 25 (1932), pp. S 86–113.

Carnell, Rachel. "It's Not Easy Being Green: Gender and Friendship in Eliza Haywood's *Political Periodicals.*" *Eighteenth-Century Studies* 32.2 (Winter 1998–1999), pp. 199–214.

Carpenter, C. "The Beauchamp Affinity: A Study of Bastard Feudalism at Work." *English Historical Review* 95 (1980), pp. 514–32.

Carpenter, Edward. *Homogenic Love, and its Place in a Free Society*. Manchester: The Labour Press Society, 1894.

—— *Iolaus: An Anthology of Friendship*. Boston: Godspeed, 1902.

Carter, Philip. *Men and the Emergence of Polite Society, Britain 1660–1800*. London: Longman, 2001.

Casey, Michael. "The Virtue of Friendship in the Monastic Tradition – An Introduction." *Tjurunga* (1983), pp. 21–35.

Cassidy, Eoin G. "'He Who Has Friends Can Have No Friend': Classical and Christian Perspectives on the Limits to Friendship." In Julian Haseldine (ed.), *Friendship in Medieval Europe*, pp. 45–67. Stroud, UK: Sutton, 1999.

—— "Friendship and Beauty in Augustine." In Fran O'Rourke (ed.), *At the Heart of the Real: Philosophical Essays in Honour of the Most Reverend Desmond Connell, Archbishop of Dublin*, pp. 51–66. Dublin: Irish Academic Press, 1992.

Cereta, Laura. *Collected Letters of a Renaissance Feminist*. Ed. and trans. D. Robin; Chicago: Chicago University Press, 1997.

Chalus, Elaine. "Elite Women, Social Politics, and the Political World of Late 18th-Century England." *Historical Journal* 43.3 (2000).

Chambliss, W. J. "The Selection of Friends." *Social Forces* 43 (1965), pp. 370–80.

Chapone, Hester. *Letters on the Improvement of the Mind, Addressed to a Young Lady*. 2 vols; London: J. Walter, 1773.

Chartier, R., (ed.). *A History of Private Life: Passions of the Renaissance*. Cambridge, MA: Harvard University Press, 1989.

Chatterjee, Margaret. *Hinterlands and Horizons: Excursions in Search of Amity*. Lanham, MD: Lexington Books, 2002.

Chauncey, George. *Gay New York: Gender, Urban Culture, and the Makings of the Gay Male World, 1890–1940*. New York: Basic Books, 1994.

Chemello, A., (ed.). *Il Merito delle Donne*. Mirano and Venice: Eidos, 1988.

Cherry-Gerrard, Aspley. *The Worst Journey in the World: Antarctic 1910–13*. Harmondsworth, UK: Penguin, 1948 (1923).

Chinn, Carl. *They Worked All their Lives: Women of the Urban Poor in England, 1880–1939*. Manchester: Manchester University Press, 1988.

Cholakian, P. F., and R. C. Cholakian. *Marguerite de Navarre*. New York: Columbia University Press, 2005.

Chong, K.C. "Egoism, Desires, and Friendship." *American Philosophical Quarterly* 21 (1984), pp. 349–57.

Christianson, Aileen. "Jane Welsh Carlyle and her Friendships with Women in the 1840s." *Prose Studies* 10.3 (1987), pp. 283–95.

Cicero. *De Officiis*. Trans. W. Miller; Loeb Classical Library; Cambridge. MA: Harvard University Press, 1913.

—— *De Finibus*. Trans. H. Rackham; Loeb Classical Library; Cambridge. MA: Harvard University Press, 1914.

—— *Tusculan Disputations*. Trans. J. E. King; Loeb Classical Library; Cambridge, MA: Harvard University Press, 1927.

—— *De Re Publica* and *De Legibus*. Trans. C. W. Keyes; Loeb Classical Library; Cambridge, MA: Harvard University Press, 1928.

—— *De Natura Deorum (On the Nature of Gods)*. Trans. H. Rackham; Loeb Classical Library; Cambridge. MA: Harvard University Press, 1931.

—— *Laelius: De amicitia*. Trans. W. A. Falconer; Loeb Classical Library; Cambridge, MA: Harvard University Press, 1948.

—— *Epistulae ad familiars*. Ed. D. R. Shackleton Bailey; 2 vols; Cambridge: Cambridge University Press, 1977. Updated as *Letters to Friends*. 3 vols; Cambridge, MA: Harvard University Press, 2001.

—— *Laelius: De Amicitia*. Trans. Karl Simbeck; Leipzig: Teubner, 1917; repr. Stuttgart: Teubner, 1971.

—— *Letters to Atticus*. Ed. and trans. D. R. Shackleton Bailey; 7 vols; Cambridge: Cambridge University Press, 1965-70.

—— *Of Old Age, of Friendship*. Norwood, NJ: W. W. Johnson, 1977.

—— *Cicero: Selected Letters*. Trans. D. R. Shackleton Bailey; Harmondsworth, UK: Penguin, 1982.

—— *Laelius, on Friendship and the Dream of Scipio*. Ed. and trans. J. G. F. Powell; Warminster: Aris & Phillips, 1990.

—— *Other Selves: Philosophers on Friendship*. Ed. Michael Pakaluk; trans. Frank Copley; Indianapolis: Hackett, 1991.

—— *De re publica; De legibus; Cato maior de senectute; Laelius de amicitia*. Trans J. G. F. Powell; Oxford: Oxford University Press, 2006.

Clark, M. L., and M. Ayers. "Friendship Similarity during Early Adolescence: Gender and Racial Patterns." *Journal of Psychology* 126 (1992), pp. 393–405.

Clarke, Norma. *The Rise and Fall of the Woman of Letters*. London: Pimlico, 2004.

Coates, Jennifer. *Women Talk: Conversation between Women Friends*. New York: Blackwell, 1995.

Cobbe, Frances Power. "Celibacy v. Marriage: Old Maids, their Sorrows and Pleasures." *Fraser's Magazine* 65 (1865), pp. 228–35.

Cocking, Dean, and Jeanette Kennett. "Friendship and the Self." *Ethics* 108.3 (April 1998), pp. 502–27.

Cocking, Dean, and Justin Oakley. "Indirect Consequentialism, Friendship, and the Problem of Alienation." *Ethics* 106 (1995), pp. 86–111.

Cohen, A. I. "Examining the Bond and Bounds of Friendship." *Dialogue-Canadian Philosophical Review* 42.2 (Spring 2003), pp. 321–44.

Cohen, T. "Men's Families, Men's Friendships: A Structural Analysis of Constraints on Men's Social Ties." In P. Nardi (ed.), *Men's Friendships*. Newbury Park: Sage Publishing, 1992.

Cohen, Yehudi. "Patterns of Friendship." In Yehudi Cohen (ed.), *Social Structure and Personality*. New York: Holt, Reinhart and Winston, 1961.

Cohn, S. K. "The Black Death: End of a Paradigm." *American Historical Review* 107 (2002), pp. 703–38.

Cole, Sarah. *Modernism, Male Friendship and the First World War*. Cambridge: Cambridge University Press, 2003.

Collett, B. *Italian Benedictine Scholars and the Reformation.* Oxford: Clarendon Press, 1985.

Colwill, Elizabeth. "Epistolary Passions: Friendship and the Literary Public of Constance De Salm, 1767–1845." *Journal of Women's History* 12.3 (2000), pp. 39–68.

Conley, John. "The Doctrine of Friendship in Everyman." *Speculum* 44.3 (July 1969), pp. 374–82.

Conley, Tom. "Friendship in a Local Vein: Montaigne's Servitude to La Boétie." *South Atlantic Quarterly* 97.1 (1998), pp. 65–90.

Conner, Paul M. *Friendships between Consecrated Men and Women and the Growth of Charity.* Rome: Pontificia Facultas Theologica Institutum Spiritualitatis Teresianum, 1972.

—— "Catherine of Siena and Raymond of Capua: Enduring Friends." *Studia Mystica* 12.1 (1989), pp. 22–29.

Connor, W. Robert. *The New Politicians of Fifth-Century Athens.* Princeton: Princeton University Press, 1971.

Constable, Giles. *Letters and Letter-Collections.* Typologie des sources du moyen âge; Turnhout: Brepols, 1976.

Constant, Jean-Marie. "L'amitié: Le moteur de la mobilisation politique dans la noblesse de la première moitié du xviie siècle." *Dix-Septième Siècle* 51.4 (1999), pp. 593–608.

Coontz, Stephanie. "What We Really Miss about the 1950s." In Judith E. Smith, Lois Palken Rudnick and Rachel Rubin (eds), *American Identities,* pp. 17–28. New York: Blackwell, 2006.

Cooper, John M. "Friendship and the Good in Aristotle." *Philosophical Review* 86.3 (July 1977), pp. 290–315.

—— "Aristotle on Friendship." In Amélie Rorty (ed.), *Essays on Aristotle's Ethics,* pp. 301–40. Berkeley: University of California Press, 1980.

Cormier, R. J. "The Mystic Bond of Ideal Friendship: Virgil's Nisus-Euralus Story Rewritten in the 12th Century Affective Style." *Collegium Medievale* 4 (1991), pp. 49–56.

Coslett, Tess. *Woman to Woman: Female Friendship in Victorian Fiction.* Brighton: Harvester, 1988.

Crain, Caleb. *American Sympathy: Men, Friendship, and Literature in the New Nation.* New Haven, CT: Yale University Press, 2001.

Crèvecoeur, Hector St John de. *Letters from an American Farmer.* London: J. M. Dent, 1912.

Croix, G. E. M., de Ste. *Class Struggle in the Ancient World.* Ithaca: Cornell University Press, 1981.

Cropper, Elizabeth, and Charles Dempsey. *Nicolas Poussin: Friendship and the Love of Painting.* Princeton: Princeton University Press, 1996.

Cunnally, John. "Ancient Coins as Gifts and Tokens of Friendship during the Renaissance." *Journal of the History of Collections* 6.2 (1994), pp. 129–43.

Curry, Constance, (ed.). *Deep in our Hearts: Nine White Women in the Freedom Movement.* Athens, GA: University of Georgia Press, 2000.

Curthoys, Ann. *Freedom Ride: A Freedom Rider Remembers.* Sydney: Allen & Unwin, 2002.

Dahl, Gunnar. *Trade, Trust and Networks: Commercial Culture in Late Medieval Italy.* Lund: Nordic Academic Press, 1998.

Daniel, Walter. *The Life of Ailred of Rievaulx.* Trans. F. M. Powicke; London: Thomas Nelson, 1950.

Davis, Natalie Z. *The Gift in Sixteenth-Century France.* Madison: University of Wisconsin Press, 2000.

Davis, N., (ed.). *Paston Letters and Papers of the Fifteenth Century.* 2 vols.; Oxford: Oxford University Press, 2004.

del Col, Andrea. *Domenico Scandella Known as Menocchio: His Trials before the Inquisition (1583-1599).* Trans. John and Ann Tedeschi; Tempe, AZ: Medieval and Renaissance Texts and Studies, 1997.

Deleyto, C. "Between Friends: Love and Friendship in Contemporary Hollywood Romantic Comedy." *Screen* 44.2 (Summer 2003), pp. 167–82.

Dellamora, Richard. *Friendship's Bonds: Democracy and the Novel in Victorian England.* Philadelphia: University of Pennsylvania Press, 2004.

de Marguenat de Courcelles, Anne Thérèse, Marquise de Lambert. *Essays on Friendship and Old-age, by the Marchioness de Lambert.* London: J. Dodsley, 1780.

—— *Avis à son fils.* London: A. Dulau, 1799 (1726).

—— *Avis d'une mère à sa fille.* London: A. Dulau, 1799 (1728).

Demaria, Jr, Robert (ed.). *British Literature 1640-1789: An Anthology.* Oxford: Blackwell, 1996.

Demosthenes. *Demosthenes.* Trans. J. H. Vince *et al.*; 7 vols; Loeb Classical Library; Cambridge, MA: Harvard University Press, 1926–1949.

Derlega, Valerian J., and Barbara A. Winstead (eds). *Friendship and Social Interaction.* New York: Springer-Verlag, 1986.

Derrida, Jacques. "The Politics of Friendship." *Journal of Philosophy* 85 (1998), pp. 632–44.

—— *Politics of Friendship.* Trans. George Collins; London; New York: Verso, 1997.

Deutsch, Sarah. "Learning to Talk More Like a Man: Boston Women's Class-Bridging Organizations, 1870–1940." *American Historical Review* 97 (1992), pp. 379–404.

Dewey, Clive. *Anglo-Indian Attitudes: The Mind of the Indian Civil Service.* London: Hambledon Press, 1993.

Dhaliwal, Nirpal. "A Fine Bromance." *Guardian* (11 June 2007).

Diani, Marco. *Green Networks.* Edinburgh: Edinburgh University Press, 1995.

Dick, Kay. *Friends and Friendship: Conversations and Reflections.* London: Sidgwick & Jackson, 1974.

Di Leonardo. "Micaela: The Female World of Cards and Holidays: Women, Families, and the Work of Kinship." *Signs* 12 (1987), pp. 440–53.

Dillon, John. *The Heirs of Plato.* Oxford: Oxford University Press, 2003.

Diogenes Laertius. *Lives of Eminent Philosophers.* Trans. R. Hicks; 2 vols; Loeb Classical Library; Cambridge, MA: Harvard University Press, 1925.

Diokno, Maria Serena I. "'Benevolent Assimilation' and Filipino Responses." In Hazel M. McFerson (ed.), *Mixed Blessing: The Impact of the American Colonial Experience on Politics and Society in the Phillipines,* pp. 75–87. Westport: Greenwood, 2002.

Dixon, Robert. *Writing the Colonial Adventure: Race, Gender and Nation in Anglo-Australian Popular Fiction, 1875-1914.* Cambridge: Cambridge University Press, 1995.

Donald, David. *"We Are Lincoln Men": Abraham Lincoln and his Friends.* New York: Simon & Schuster, 2003.

Doreski, William. *The Years of our Friendship: Robert Lowell and Allen Tate.* Jackson: University Press of Mississippi, 1990.

Dover, K. *Greek Popular Morality in the Time of Plato and Aristotle.* Oxford: Oxford University Press, 1974.

Downton, Jr, Janes, and Paul Wehr. "Persistent Pacifism: How Activist Commitment Is Developed and Sustained." *Journal of Peace Research* 35 (1998), pp. 531–50.

Dronke, Peter. *Medieval Latin and the Rise of the European Love Lyric.* 2 vols; Oxford: Oxford University Press, 1968.

Drum, P. "What is the Value of Friendship as a Motivation for Morality for Aristotle?" *Value Inquiry* 37.1 (2003), pp. 97–99.

DuBois, W. E. B. *The Philadelphia Negro.* Philadelphia: University of Pennsylvania, 1899.

Duby, G., (ed.). *A History of Private Life: Revelations of the Medieval World.* Cambridge, MA: Harvard University Press, 1988.

Duck, Steve. *Friends for Life: The Psychology of Close Relationships.* Brighton, Sussex: Harvester Press, 1983.

Duclos, Charles. *Considérations sur les moeurs de ce siècle.* Amsterdam, 1751.

Dugas, Ludovic. *L'amitié antique d'après les mœurs populaires et les théories des philosophes.* New York: Arno Press, 1976.

Dumas, Alexandre. *The Three Musketeers.* Trans. William Barrow; London: Pan, 1968.

Dunne, Michael. "Good Friends or Bad Friends? The Amicitia of Boncompagno da Signa." In Thomas A. F. Kelly and Philipp W. Rosemann (eds), *Amor amicitiae: On the Love That Is Friendship: Essays in Medieval Thought and beyond in Honor of the Rev. Professor James McEvoy,* pp. 147–66. Leuven: Peeters, 2004.

Dupuy, de la Chapelle. *Réflections sur l'amitié.* Paris: Langlois, 1729.

Durham, W. H. *Lord Hastings' Indentured Retainers 1461–1483.* New Haven, CT: Conneticut Academy of Arts and Sciences, 1955.

Earle, T. F., and K. J. P. Lowe (eds). *Black Africans in Renaissance Europe.* Cambridge: Cambridge University Press, 2005.

Edelman, Peter B. *Searching for America's Heart: RFK and the Renewal of Hope.* New York: Houghton Mifflin, 2001.

Eden, Kathy. "'Between Friends All Is Common': The Erasmian Adage and Tradition." *Journal of the History of Ideas* 59.3 (July 1998), pp. 405–19.

—— *Friends Hold All Things in Common.* New Haven, CT, and London: Yale University Press, 2001.

—— "From the Cradle: Erasmus on Intimacy in Renaissance Letters." *Erasmus of Rotterdam Society Yearbook* 21 (2001), pp. 30–43.

Edwards, Elizabeth. "Homoerotic Friendship and College Principals, 1880–1960." *Women's History Review* 4.2 (1995), pp. 149–63.

Edwards, Robert R., and Stephen Spector (eds). *The Olde Daunce: Love, Friendship, Sex, and Marriage in the Medieval World.* Albany: State University of New York Press, 1991.

Eisenstadt, S. N., and L. Roniger (eds). *Patrons, Clients and Friends: Interpersonal Relations and the Structure of Trust in Society.* Cambridge; New York: Cambridge University Press, 1984.

Elliott, Mark. "Race, Color Blindness, and the Democratic Public: Albion W. Tourgee's Radical Principles in *Plessy v. Ferguson.*" *Journal of Southern History* 67 (2001), pp. 287–330.

Ely, John. "Intellectual Friendship and the Elective Affinities of Critical Theory." *The South Atlantic Quarterly* 97.1 (Winter 1998), pp. 187–224.

Emerson, Ralph Waldo. *Friendship.* Melbourne: Lothian Publishing, 1944.

Engel, Barbara Alpern. *Mothers and Daughters: Omen of the Intelligentsia in Nineteenth-Century Russia.* Cambridge: Cambridge University Press, 1983.

Epictetus. *Manual.* Trans. W. A. Oldfather; Loeb Classical Library; Cambridge, MA: Harvard University Press, 1925–1928.

Epistolae Senecae ad Paulum et Pauli ad Senecam. Ed. C. W. Barlow; Horn: American Academy in Rome, 1938.

Equicola, Mario. *De mulieribus.* Ed. G. Lucchesini and P. Totaro; Pisa and Rome: Istituti Editoriali e Poligrafici Internazionali, 2004.

Erasmus. *De conscribendis epistolis.* In *Collected Works,* vol. 25. Ed. J. K. Sowards; trans. C. Fantazzi; Toronto, Buffalo and London: University of Toronto Press, 1985.

Erskine, Andrew. *The Hellenistic Stoa: Political Thought and Action.* Ithaca: Cornell University Press, 1990.

Evans, Katherine. "Friendship in Greek Documentary Papyri and Inscriptions: A Survey." In John T. Fitzgerald (ed.), *Greco-Roman Perspectives on Friendship,* pp. 181–202. Atlanta, GA: Scholars Press, 1997.

Evans, Sara, and Harry Boyte. *Free Spaces: The Sources of Democratic Change in America.* Chicago: University of Chicago Press, 1992.

Faderman, Lillian. *Surpassing the Love of Men: Romantic Friendship and Love between Women from the Renaissance to the Present.* New York: Morrow, 1981.

Farrell, Michael P. *Collaborative Circles: Friendship Dynamics & Creative Work.* Chicago: University of Chicago Press, 2001.

Fass, Paula S. *The Damned and the Beautiful: American Youth in the 1920s.* Oxford: Oxford University Press, 1979.

Faure, Alain. "Local Life in Working-Class Paris at the End of the Nineteenth Century." *Journal of Urban History* 32.5 (July 2006), pp. 761–72.

Fava, Guido. *Exordia.* Giuseppe Vecchi (ed.), "Il proverbio nella pratica letteraria dei dettatori della scuola di Bologna," *Studi mediolatini e volgari* II (1954), pp. 283–302.
—— *Summa Dictaminis,* XXVI. Ed. Augusto Gaudenzi. *Il Propugnatore,* III (1890), 1, pp. 287–338.

Fehr, Beverley. *Friendship Processes.* Thousand Oaks, CA: Sage Publications, 1996.

Felton, B. J., and C. A. Ferry. "Do the Sources of the Urban Elderly's Social Support Determine its Psychological Consequences?" *Psychology and Aging* 7 (1992), pp. 89–97.

Fenves, Peter D. "Politics of Friendship – Once Again." *Eighteenth-Century Studies* 32.2 (Winter 1998–1999), pp. 133–55.

Ferguson, John. *Moral Values in the Ancient World.* London: Methuen, 1958.

Fernback, Jan. "The Individual within the Collective: Virtual Ideology and the Realization of Collective Principles." In Steven G. Jones (ed.), *Virtual Culture: Identity and Communication in Cybersociety,* pp. 36–54. London: Sage, 1997.

Ferrary, Jean-Louis. *Philhellénisme et impérialisme: aspects idéologiques de la conquête romaine du monde hellénistique, de la seconde guerre de Macédoine à la guerre contre Mithridate.* Rome: École française, 1988.

Fersin, N. (trans.). *The Florentine Fio di Virtu of 1491.* Washington, DC: Library of Congress, 1953).

Fiasse, Gaelle. "La problematique de l'amour-eros dans le stoicisme: Confrontation de fragments. paradoxes et interpretations." *Revue Philosophique de Louvain* 97.3–4 (1999), pp. 459–82.

Field, A. *The Origins of the Platonic Academy of Florence.* Princeton, NJ: Princeton University Press, 1988.

Fields, Lanny Bruce. "The Importance of Friendships and Quasi-Kinship Relations in Tso Tsung-T'ang's Career." *Journal of Asian History* 10.2 (1976), pp. 172–86.

Finch, Anne Kingsmill. "Friendship between Ephelia and Ardelia." In *Miscellany Poems on Several Occasions.* London: J[ohn]. B[arber]. and B. Tooke, 1713.

Finch, Janet. *Family Obligations and Social Change.* Oxford: Polity Press, 1989.

Finkelstein, Richard. "Ben Jonson's Ciceronian Rhetoric of Friendship." *Journal of Medieval and Renaissance Studies* 16.1 (1986), pp. 103–24.

Fischer, Claude S. "Gender and the Residential Telephone, 1890–1940: Technologies of Sociability." *Sociological Forum* 3.2 (1988), pp. 11–33.

—— *To Dwell among Friends: Personal Networks in Town and City.* Chicago: University of Chicago Press, 1982.

—— *What Do We Mean by "Friend": An Inductive Study.* Berkeley: Institute of Urban & Regional Development, 1981.

Fischer, Claude S., and Stacey Oliker. "A Research Note on Friendship, Gender and the Life Cycle." *Social Forces* 62 (1983), pp. 124–33.

Fiske, Adele M. *Friends and Friendship in the Monastic Tradition.* Cuernavaca, Mexico: Centro Intercultural de Documentacion, 1970.

—— *The Survival and Development of the Ancient Concept of Friendship in the Early Middle Ages.* Cuernavaca, Mexico: Centro Intercultural de Documentacion, 1970.

Fitzgerald, John T., (ed.). *Greco-Roman Perspectives on Friendship.* Atlanta, GA: Scholars Press, 1997.

—— *Friendship, Flattery, and Frankness of Speech: Studies in Friendship in the New Testament World.* Leiden: E. J. Brill, 1996.

Flanagan, Maureen. *Seeing with their Hearts: Chicago Women and the Vision of the Good City, 1871–1933.* Princeton, NJ: Princeton University Press, 2002.

Fleischner, Jennifer. *Mrs. Lincoln and Mrs. Keckly: The Remarkable Story of the Friendship between a First Lady and a Former Slave.* New York: Broadway Books, 2003.

Flint, K. *The Woman Reader 1837–1914.* Oxford: Oxford University Press, 1993.

Flores, Stephan P. "Orrery's *The Generall* and *Henry the Fifth*: Sexual Politics and the Desire for Friendship." *Eighteenth Century: Theory and Interpretation* 37.1 (1996), pp. 56–74.

Flynn, M. "Rituals of Solidarity in Castilian Confraternities." *Renaissance and Reformation, Renaissance et Réforme* 25 (1989), pp. 53–68.

Foeman, A. K., and T. Nance. "From Miscegenation to Multiculturalism: Perceptions and Stages of Interracial Relationship Development." *Journal of Black Studies* 29 (1999), pp. 540–57.

Fogel, M. *Marie de Gournay.* Paris: Fayard, 2004.

Fonte, Moderata. *The Worth of Women.* Ed. and trans. V. Cox; Chicago: Chicago University Press, 1997.

Forster, E. M. "What I Believe." In *Two Cheers for Democracy.* London: Edward Arnold, 1972.

Fortenbaugh, W. W. "Aristotle's Analysis of Friendship." *Phronesis: A Journal of Ancient Philosophy* 20 (1975), pp. 51–62.

Fortunet, Françoise. "L'amitié et le droit selon Saint Just." *Annales Historiques de la Révolution Française* 54.2 (1982), pp. 181–95.

Fowler, David. *The First Teenagers: The Life-Style of Young Wage-Earners in Interwar Britain.* Woburn: London, 1995.

Foxhall, Lin. "The Politics of Affection: Emotional Attachments in Athenian Society." In Paul Cartledge, Paul Millett and Sitta von Reden (eds), *Kosmos: Essays in Order, Conflict and Community in Classical Athens*, pp. 52–67. Cambridge: Cambridge University Press, 1998.

Fraisse, Jean-Claude. *Philia: la notion d'amitié dans la philosophie antique: essai sur un problème perdu et retrouvé.* Paris: J. Vrin, 1974.

François, duc de la Rochefoucauld. *Maximes, suivies des Réflections diverses.* Paris: Garnier, 1967.

Franklin, A. "Working-Class Privatism: An Historical Case Study of Bedminster. Bristol." *Environment and Planning D: Society and Space* 7.1 (1989), pp. 93–113.

Franklin, Vincent P., and Bettye Collier-Thomas. *Sisters in the Struggle: African-American Women in the Civil Rights and Black Power Movements.* New York: New York University Press, 2001.

Freedman, Marc. *The Kindness of Strangers: Adult Mentors, Urban Youth, and the New Voluntarism.* San Francisco: Josey-Bass, 1993.

Friedan, Betty. *The Feminine Mystique.* New York: W. W. Norton, 1963.

Friedman, Marilyn. *What Are Friends For? Feminist Perspectives on Personal Relationships and Moral Theory.* Ithaca, NY: Cornell University Press, 1993.

Friedman, Rebecca. "Romantic Friendship in the Nicholaevyan University." *Russian Review* 62 (April 2003), pp. 262–80.

Frischer, Bernard. *The Sculpted Word.* Berkeley: University of California Press, 1982.

Froide, Amy M. "Female Relationships in Early Modern England." *Journal of British Studies* 40.2 (2001), pp. 279–89.

Frye, Susan, and Karen Robertson (eds). *Maids and Mistresses, Cousins and Queens: Women's Alliances in Early Modern England.* New York: Oxford University Press, 1999.

Funaro, Liana Elda. "'Colla Lente D'amicizia': Tabarrini, Galeotti, Gli Scritti Sul Capponi E Gli Ultimi Moderati Toscani." *Archivio Storico Italiano* 149.3 (1991), pp. 613–62.

Funk, F., and F. Diekamp (eds). *Epistulae inerpolatae et epistulae suppositiciae.* Laup: Tubingen, 1913.

Furey, Constance. "The Communication of Friendship: Gasparo Contarini's Letters to Hermits at Camaldoli." *Church History* 72.1 (March 2003), pp. 71–101.

Gaden, Tim. "Looking to God for Healing: A Rereading of the *Second Letter of Clement* in the Light of Hellenistic Psychagogy." *Pacifica* 15 (2002), pp. 154–73.

Gaines, Jr, S. O., and W. Ickes. "Perspectives on Interracial Relationships." In S. Duck (ed.), *Handbook of Personal Relationships: Theory, Research and Interventions*, pp. 197–220. Oxford, England: John Wiley & Sons, 2nd edn, 1997.

Gaines, Jr, S. O., and J. Leaver. "Interracial Relationships." In R. Goodwin and D. Cramer (eds), *Inappropriate Relationships: The Unconventional, the Disapproved, and the Forbidden*, pp. 65–78. Mahwah, NJ: Lawrence Erlbaum Associates, 2002.

Gandhi, Leela. *Affective Communities: Anticolonial Thought, Fin-de-Siècle Radicalism and the Politics of Friendship*. Durham: Duke University Press, 2006.

Gans, Herbert. *The Levittowners: Ways of Life and Politics in a New Suburban Community*. New York: Pantheon, 1967.

Ganz, Margery A. "A Florentine Friendship: Donato Acciaiuoli and Vespasiano Da Bisticci." *Renaissance Quarterly* 43.2 (1990), pp. 372–83.

Gareis, Elisabeth. *Intercultural Friendship: A Qualitative Study*. Lanham, MD: University Press of America, 1995.

Garnier, Claudia. *Amicus Amicis, Inimicus Inimicis: Political Friendship and Aristocratic Networking in the Thirteenth-Century*. Stuttgart: Hiersemann, 2000.

Garrioch, David, "Making a Better World. Enlightenment and Philanthropy." In Martin Fitzpatrick, Peter Jones, Christa Knellwolf and Iain McCalman (eds), *The Enlightenment World*, pp. 486–501. London: Routledge, 2004.

Garrison, Mary. "'Send More Socks': On Mentality and the Preservation Context of Medieval Letters." In *New Approaches to Medieval Communication*, pp. 66–99. Ed. Marco Mostert; Turnhout: Brepols, 1999.

Giannantoni, G. *Socratis et Socraticorum Reliquiae*. 4 vols; Naples: Bibliopolis, 1990.

Gigante, Marcello. *Philodemus in Italy: The Books from Herculaneum*. Trans. Dirk Obbink; Ann Arbor, MI: University of Michigan Press, 1995.

Gill, M. J. *Augustine in the Italian Renaissance*. Cambridge: Cambridge University Press, 2005.

Girard, Abbé. *Synonymes françois, leurs différentes significations, et le choix qu'il en faut faire pour parler avec justesse*. Paris: d'Houry, new edn, 1780.

Gleckner, Robert F. *Gray Agonistes: Thomas Gray and Masculine Friendship*. Baltimore, MD: Johns Hopkins University Press, 1997.

Goetz, Hans-Werner. "'Beatus homo qui invenit amicum': The Concept of Friendship in Early Medieval Letters of the Anglo-Saxon Tradition on the Continent (Boniface, Alcuin)." In Julian Haseldine (ed.), *Friendship in Medieval Europe*. Stroud: Sutton, 1999.

Goldberg, J. *Sodometries: Renaissance Texts, Modern Sexualities*. Stanford: Stanford University Press, 1992.

Gonzales, Francisco. "Socrates on Loving One's Own: A Traditional Conception of FILIA Radically Transformed." *Classical Philology* 95 (2000), pp. 379–98.

Gooch, Paul W. "A Mind to Love: Friends and Lovers in Ancient Greek Philosophy." In David Goicoechea (ed.), *The Nature and Pursuit of Love*. Buffalo, NY: Prometheus, 1995.

Gordon, P. "Remembering the Garden: The Trouble with Women in the School of Epicurus." In J. Fitzgerald, D. Obbink, and G. Holland (eds), *Philodemus and the New Testament World*. Leiden: E. J. Brill, 2004.

Gorham, Deborah. "'The Friendships of Women': Friendship, Feminism and Achievement in Vera Brittain's Life and Work in the Interwar Decades." *Journal of Women's History* 3.3 (1992), pp. 44–69.

Gouldner, Helen, and Mary Symons Strong. *Speaking of Friendship: Middle-Class Women and their Friends*. New York: Greenwood Press, 1987.

Gournay, Marie de. "The Promenade of Monsieur de Montaigne." In R. Hillman and C. Quesnel (ed. and trans.), *Apology for the Woman Writing*. Chicago: Chicago University Press, 2002.

Gowing, Laura. "The Politics of Women's Friendship in Early Modern England." In Laura Gowing, Michael Hunter and Miri Rubin (eds), *Love, Friendship and Faith in Europe, 1300–1800*, pp. 131–49. Houndmills: Palgrave Macmillan, 2005.

Grafton, A. *Leon Battista Alberti: Master Builder of the Italian Renaissance*. London: Allen Lane, 2000.

Grant, Michael. *Cicero: The Good Life*. Harmondsworth, UK: Penguin, 1971.

Gray, D. "Some Pre-Elizabethan Examples of an Elizabethan Art." In E. Chaney and P. Mack (eds), *England and the Continental Renaissance: Essays in Honour of J. B. Trapp*, pp. 23–36. Woodbridge, Suffolk: Boydell Press, 1990.

Greiner, Donald J. *Women without Men: Female Bonding and the American Novel of the 1980s*. Columbia, SC: University of South Carolina Press, 1993.

—— *Women Enter the Wilderness: Male Bonding and the American Novel of the 1980s*, Columbia, SC: University of South Carolina Press, 1991.

Grindal, Bruce, and Frank Salamone (eds). *Bridges to Humanity: Narratives on Anthropology and Friendship*. Prospect Heights, IL: Waveland Press, 1995.

Grunebaum, James O. *Friendship: Liberty, Equality, and Utility*. Albany: State University of New York Press, 2003.

Guazzo, Stefano. *La civil conversazione*. Ed. A. Quondam; 2 vols; Modena: Panini, 1993.

Guerlac, Henry. "Amicus Plato and Other Friends." *Journal of the History of Ideas* 39.4 (1978), pp. 627–33.

Gueulette, J. M. "Friendship within the Community: The Theological Issues of a Complex History (Exploring the Anthropological Foundations of Communal Affection)." *Revue Des Sciences Philosophiques et Theologiques* 87.2 (April–June 2003), pp. 261–91.

Guibert of Gembloux. "A Letter of Passionate Friendship." In John Benton and Brian McGuire (eds), *Cahiers de l'Institute du Moyen-Age grec et latin*. pp. 3–14. 53; Copenhagen, 1986.

Guicciardini, Francesco. *Ricordi*. Ed. V. De Caprio; Rome: Salerno Editrice, 1990.

Guillén, C. "Notes toward the Study of the Renaissance Letter." In B. Kiefer Lewalski (ed.), *Renaissance Genres: Essays in Theory, History, and Interpretation*, pp. 70–101. Cambridge, MA: Harvard University Press, 1986.

Gulliver, P. H. *Neighbours and Networks: The Idiom of Kinship in Social Action among the Ndendeuli of Tanzania*. Berkeley: University of California Press, 1971.

Gustav-Wrathall, John Donald. *Take the Young Stranger by the Hand: Same-Sex Relations and the YMCA*. Chicago: University of Chicago Press, 2000.

Haine, W. Scott. *The World of the Paris Café: Sociability among the French Working Class, 1789–1914.* Baltimore, MD: The John Hopkins University Press, 1996.

Hall, Catherine. *Civilising Subjects: Metropole and Colony in the English Imagination 1830–1868.* Cambridge: Polity Press. 2002.

Hallinan, M. T., and S. S. Smith. "The Effects of Classroom Racial Composition on Students' Interracial Friendliness." *Social Psychology Quarterly* 48 (1985), pp. 3–16.

Hallinan, M. T., and R. A. Teixeira. "Opportunities and Constraints: Black-White Differences in the Formation of Interracial Friendships." *Child Development* 58 (1987), pp. 1358–71.

Hallinan, M. T., and R. A. Williams. "The Stability of Students' Interracial Friendships." *American Sociological Review* 52 (1987), pp. 653–64.

Hampsher-Monk, Iain. "Civic Humanism and Parliamentary Reform: The Case of the Society of the Friends of the People." *Journal of British Studies* 18.2 (1978), pp. 70–89.

Handwerker, W. Penn. "Kinship, Friendship, and Business Failure among Market Sellers in Monrovia, Liberia, 1970." *Africa* 43.4 (1973), pp. 288–301.

Harding, M. Esther. *The Way of All Women: A Psychological Interpretation.* London: Longman, 1933.

Harris, Anita. *Future Girl: Young Women in the Twenty-First Century.* New York: Routledge, 2004.

Harrison, Kaeren. "Rich Friendships, Affluent Friends: Middle-Class Practices of Friendship." In R. G. Adams and G. Allan (eds), *Placing Friendship in Context*, pp. 92–116. Cambridge: Cambridge University Press, 1998.

Haseldine, Julian, (ed.). *Friendship in Medieval Europe.* Stroud, UK: Sutton, 1999.

Hatlie, Peter. "Friendship and the Byzantine Iconoclast Age." In Julian Haseldine (ed.), *Friendship in Medieval Europe.* Stroud: Sutton, 1999.

Haywood, Eliza. *History of Miss Betsy Thoughtless.* London and New York: Pandora, 1986.

Heald, Tim. *Networks: Who We Know and How We Use Them.* London: Hodder & Stoughton, 1983.

Heath, Anthony. *Social Mobility.* London: Fontana, 1981.

Heineman, Helen. *Restless Angels: The Friendship of Six Victorian Women: Frances Wright, Camilla Wright, Harriet Garnett, Frances Garnett, Julia Garnett Pertz, and Frances Trollope.* Athens: Ohio University Press, 1983.

Helvétius. *De l'esprit.* Paris: Durand, 1758.

Henderson, J. *Piety and Charity in Late Medieval Florence.* Oxford: Clarendon Press, 1994.

Herman, Gabriel. "The 'Friends' of Early Hellenistic Rulers: Servants or Officials?" *Talanta* 12/13 (1980–81), pp. 103–49.

—— *Ritualised Friendship and the Greek City.* Cambridge; New York: Cambridge University Press, 1987.

Herzen, Alexander. *My Past and Thoughts: The Memoirs of Alexander Herzen.* London: Chatto & Windus, 1968.

Herodotus. *Histories.* Trans. A. D. Godley; 4 vols; Loeb Classical Library; Cambridge, MA: Harvard University Press, 1921–25.

Hesiod. *Works and Days.* Trans. H. G. Evelyn-White; Loeb Classical Library; Cambridge, MA: Harvard University Press, 1936.

Hess. B. "Sex Roles, Friendship and the Life Course." *Research on Aging* 1 (1979), pp. 494–515.

Hickson, S. "Female Patronage and the Language of Art in the Circle of Isabella d'Este in Mantua (c.1470–1560)." PhD thesis, Queens University, 2003.

Hinds, Leonard. "Female Friendship as the Foundation of Love in Madeleine de Scudery's 'Historie de Sapho.'" *Journal of Homosexuality* 41.3–4 (May–June 2001), pp. 23–35.

Hirata, Yoko. "John of Salisbury, Gerard Pucelle and *Amicitia*." In Julian Haseldine (ed.), *Friendship in Medieval Europe*, pp. 153–65. Stroud: Sutton, 1999.

Hobson, G. D. "'Et Amicorum.'" *The Library*, 5th series, 4 (1949), pp. 87–99.

Hoffman, Stefan-Ludwig. "Civility, Male Friendship, and Masonic Sociability in Nineteenth-Century Germany." *Gender & History* 13.2 (2001), pp. 224–48.

—— "Democracy and Associations in the Long Nineteenth Century: Toward a Transnational Perspective." *Journal of Modern History* 75 (2003), pp. 269–99.

Hollinger, Karen. *In the Company of Women: Contemporary Female Friendship Films.* Minneapolis; London: University of Minnesota Press, 1998.

Hollis, Stephanie, (ed.). *Writing the Wilton Women: Goscelin's Legend of Edith and Liber confortatorius.* Turnhout: Brepols, 2004.

Holloway, J. Bolton. *Brunetto Latini: An Analytic Bibliography.* London: Grant & Cutler, 1986.

Holmes, G. *The Estates of the Higher Nobility in Fourteenth-Century England.* Cambridge: Cambridge University Press, 1957.

Holmes, Katie. *Spaces in her Day: Australian Women's Diaries in the 1920s and 1930.* Sydney: Allen & Unwin, 1995.

Holroyd, Michael. *Lytton Strachey.* London: Vintage, 1995.

Holtby, Winifred. *The Crowded Street.* London: Virago, 1981 (1924).

Holton, Sandra Stanley. *Suffrage Days: Stories from the Women's Suffrage Movement.* London: Routledge, 1996.

—— "Segregation. Racism and White Women Reformers: A Transnational Analysis. 1840–1912." *Women"s History Review* 10 (2001), pp. 5–25.

Horsfall, N. *Poets and Patrons: Maecenas, Horace and the "Georgics," Once More.* Sydney: School of History, Philosophy and Politics, Macquarie University, 1981.

Howe, Irving. *A Handbook of Socialist Thought.* London: Victor Gollancz, 1972.

Hughes, Thomas. *Tom Brown's School Days.* London: Macmillan, 1979.

Hume, David. *A Treatise of Human Nature.* Ed. L. A. Selby-Bigge; Oxford: Clarendon Press, 1888.

—— "Of Polygamy and Divorce" (1742). In *Essays and Treatises on Several Subjects.* 2 vols; London: J. Jones, new edn, 1822.

Hunt, A. S., and C. C. Edgar (eds). *Select Papyri* 1. Loeb Classical Library; London: Heinemann, 1949.

Hunt, Mary E. *Fierce Tenderness: A Feminist Theology of Friendship.* New York: Crossroad, 1991.

Hunter, L., and M. J. Elias. "Interracial Friendships, Multicultural Sensitivity, and Social Competence: How Are They Related?" *Journal of Applied Developmental Psychology* 20 (1999), pp. 551–73.

Hutcheon, Linda. "'Sublime Noise' for Three Friends: E. M. Forster, Roger Fry, and Charles Mauron." *Modernist Studies* 3.1–3 (1979), pp. 141–50.

Hutcheson, Francis. *System of Moral Philosophy.* 2 vols; London: A. Millar & T. Longman, 1755.

Hutson, Lorna. *The Usurer's Daughter: Male Friendship and Fictions of Women in Sixteenth-Century England.* London; New York: Routledge, 1994.

Hutter, Horst. *Politics as Friendship: The Origins of Classical Notions of Politics in the Theory and Practice of Friendship.* Waterloo. ON: Wilfrid Laurier University Press, 1978.

Hyatte, Reginald. "Complementary Humanistic Models of Marriage and Male *Amicitia* in Fifteenth-Century Literature." In Julian Haseldine (ed.), *Friendship in Medieval Europe*, pp. 251–61. Stroud: Sutton, 1999.

—— *The Arts of Friendship: The Idealization of Friendship in Medieval and Early Renaissance Literature.* Leiden; New York: E. J. Brill, 1994.

Hyland, Drew A. "Eros Epithymia and Philia in Plato." *Phronesis: A Journal of Ancient Philosophy* 13 (1968), pp. 32–46.

Iamblichus. *Commentary on Nicomachus of Gerasa's Introduction to Arithmethic.* Ed. H. Pistelli; Leipzig: Teubner, 1894.

—— *On the Pythagorean Way of Life.* Trans. John Dillon and Jackson Hershbell; Atlanta, GA: Scholars Press, 1991.

Ibson, John. *Picturing Men: A Century of Male Relationships in Everyday American Photography.* Washington, DC: Smithsonian Institution, 2002.

Isocrates. *Orations*; *Gorgias.* Trans. with notes by Terence Irwin; Oxford: Oxford University Press, 1979.

—— *Orations.* Trans. George Norlin; 3 vols; Loeb Classical Library; Cambridge, MA: Harvard University Press, 1928–45.

Jabour, Anya. "Male Friendship and Masculinity in the Early National South: William Wirt and his Friends." *Journal of the Early Republic* 20.1 (Spring 2000), pp. 83–84.

—— "Albums of Affection: Female Friendship and Coming of Age in Antebellum Virginia." *The Virginia Magazine of History and Biography* 107.2 (Spring 1999), pp. 125–58.

Jackson, Mark Allan. "Dark Memory: A Look at Lynching in America through the Life, Times, and Songs of Woody Guthrie." *Popular Music and Society* 28 (2005), pp. 663–75.

Jackson, Susan Klem. "Disengaging Isabelle: Professional Rhetoric and Female Friendship in the Correspondence of Mme De Charriere and Mlle De Gelieu." *Eighteenth-Century Life* 13.1 (1989), pp. 26–41.

Jacob, Margaret C. "Polite Worlds of Enlightenment." In Martin Fitzpatrick, Peter Jones, Christa Knellwolf and Iain McCalman (eds), *The Enlightenment World*, pp. 272–87. London and New York: Routledge, 2004.

Jaeger, Stephen. *Ennobling Love.* Philadelphia: University of Pennsylvania Press, 1999.

James, Carolyn. "A Woman's Path to Literacy: The Letters of Margherita Datini (1384–1410)." In M. Cassidy Welch and P. Sherlock (eds), *Practices of Gender in Late Medieval and Early Modern Europe*, pp. 43–56. Turnhout: Brepols, 2008.

—— "Friendship and Dynastic Marriage in Renaissance Italy." *Literature and History* 17.1 (2008), pp. 4–18.

James, C., and F. W. Kent. "Margherita Cantelmo and Agostino Strozzi: Friendship's Gifts and a Portrait Medal by Costantino da Ferrara." *I Tatti Studies: Essays in the Renaissance* 12 (2008), forthcoming.

James, L. *Fiction for the Working Man 1830–1850.* Oxford: Oxford University Press, 1963.

James, Muriel, and Louis M. Savary. *The Heart of Friendship.* New York: Harper & Row, 1976.

Jastrow, Joseph. *The Betrayal of Intelligence.* Greenberg: New York, 1938.

Jay, Peter, (ed.). *The Greek Anthology.* Harmondsworth: Penguin Classics, 1982.

Jerome, D. "The Significance of Friendship for Women in Later Life." *Ageing and Society* 1 (1981), pp. 175–97.

Jollimore, Troy Allen. *Friendship and Agent-Relative Morality.* New York; London: Garland, 2001.

Jones, John Garrett. *Alfred and Arthur: An Historic Friendship.* Hertford: Authors OnLine, 2001.

Jones, J. R. "The Social Aspect of Oddfellowship." *Quarterly Magazine of the Independent Order of Odd-Fellows. Manchester Unity,* new series 25 (1894).

Jones, P. D. "Jesus Christ and the Transformation of English Society: The 'Subversive Conservatism' of Frederick Denison Maurice." *Harvard Theological Review* 96.2 (2003).

Kadushin, Charles. "Friendship among the French Financial Elite." *American Sociological Review* 60.2 (1995), pp. 202–21.

Kaeuper, R. W., and E. Kennedy. *The Book of Chivalry of Geoffroi de Charny.* Philadelphia: University of Pennsylvania Press, 1996.

Kahane, David. "Diversity, Solidarity and Civic Friendship." *Journal of Political Philosophy* 7 (1999), pp. 267–86.

Kant, Immanuel. "Friendship." In *Lecture on Ethics.* Trans. Louis Infield; New York: Harper Torchbooks, 1963.

Katz, James Everett, (ed.). *Machines Become Us: The Social Context of Personal Communication Technology.* New York: Transaction Publishers, 2003.

Keen, M. "Brotherhood in Arms." *History* 47 (1962), pp. 1–17.

Kelly, Patrick H. "Locke and Molyneux: The Anatomy of a Friendship." *Hermathena* 126 (1979), pp. 38–54.

Kennedy, Elizabeth, and Madeline Davis. *Boots of Leather, Slippers of Gold: History of a Lesbian Community.* New York: Routledge, 1993.

Kennedy, Robinette. "Women's Friendships on Crete: A Psychological Perspective." In Jill Dubisch (ed.), *Gender and Power in Rural Greece,* pp. 121–38. Princeton, NJ: Princeton University Press, 1986

Kent, D. *The Rise of the Medici.* Oxford: Clarendon Press, 1978.

Kent, F. W. "'Un paradiso habitato da diavoli': Ties of Loyalty and Patronage in the Society of Medicean Florence." In A. Benvenuti, *et al.* (eds), *Le Radici Cristiani di Firenze,* pp. 183–210. Florence: Alinea, 1994.

—— "'Lorenzo ... amico degli uomini da bene.'" In G. C. Garfagnini (ed.), *Lorenzo il Magnifico e il suo Mondo,* pp. 43–60. Florence: Olschki, 1994.

—— "Patronage." In P. F. Grendler (ed.), *Encyclopedia of the Renaissance,* IV, pp. 422–24. New York: Charles Scribner's Sons, 1999.

——— "'Be Rather Loved than Feared': Class Relations in Quattrocento Florence." In W. J. Connell (ed.), *Society and Individual in Renaissance Florence*, pp. 13–50. Berkeley: University of California Press, 2002.

Kent, F. W., and G. Corti. *Bartolommeo Cederni and his Friends*. Florence: Olschski, 1991.

Kete, Kathleen. *The Beast in the Boudoir: Petkeeping in Nineteenth-Century Paris*. Berkeley: University of California Press. 1994.

Kettering, Sharon. "Friendship and Clientage in Early Modern France." *French History* 6.2 (1992), pp. 139–58.

Kilpatrick, R. S. *The Poetry of Friendship: Horace, Epistles I*. Edmonton, Alberta: University of Alberta Press, 1986.

Kinnell, Margaret. "Friendship in Children's Fiction." In Roy Porter and Sylvana Tomaselli (eds), *The Dialectics of Friendship*, pp. 76–91. London: Routledge, 1989.

Kirkham, V. "The Classic Bond of Friendship in Bocaccio's Tito and Gisippo (*Decameron* 10.8)." In A. S. Bernardo and S. Levin (eds), *The Classics in the Middle Ages: Papers of the Twentieth Annual Conference of the Centre for Medieval and Early Renaissance Studies*, pp. 223–35. Medieval and Renaissance Texts and Studies, 69; New York: Binghamton, 1990.

Klapisch-Zuber, C. *La maison et le nom*. Paris: Éditions de l'École des Hautes Études en Sciences Sociales, 1990.

Klonoski, Richard J. "'Homonoia,' in Aristotle's Ethics and Politics." *History of Political Thought* 17.3 (1996), pp. 313–25.

Knight, Gillian R. "Uses and Abuses of *Amicitia*: The Correspondence between Peter the Venerable and Hato of Troyes." *Reading Medieval Studies* 23 (1997), pp. 35–67.

Kolsky, S. *The Ghost of Boccaccio, Writings on Famous Women in Renaissance Italy*. Turnhout: Brepols, 2005.

Konstan, David. *Friendship in the Classical World*. Cambridge: Cambridge University Press, 1997.

——— "Philoctetes' Pity: Commentary on Moravcsik." *Proceedings of the Boston Area Colloquium in Ancient Philosophy* 13 (1997), pp. 276–82.

——— "Problems in the History of Christian Friendship." *Journal of Early Christian Studies* 4 (1996), pp. 87–113.

——— "Friendship and the State: The Context of Cicero's *De Amicitia*." *Hyperboreus* 2 (1994/1995), pp. 1–16.

——— "Friends and Lovers in Ancient Greece." *Syllecta Classica* 4 (1993), pp. 1–12.

——— "Greek Friendship." *American Journal of Philology* 117 (1980), pp. 71–94.

Kord, Susanne T. "Eternal Love or Sentimental Discourse? Gender Dissonance and Women's Passionate 'Friendships.'" In Alice A. Kuzniar (ed.), *Outing Goethe and his Age,* pp. 228–49. Stanford: Stanford University Press, 1996.

Korgen, Kathleen Odell. *Crossing the Racial Divide: Close Friendships between Black and White Americans*. Westport, CT: Praeger, 2002.

Körntgen, Ludger. "The Emperor and his Friends: The Ottonian Realm in the Year 1000." In *Europe around the Year 1000*, pp. 465–88. Urbanczyk: Warschau, 2001.

Koven, S. *Slumming: Sexual and Social Politics in Victorian London*. Princeton, NJ: Princeton University Press, 2004.

Kraemer, R. *Her Share of the Blessings*. Oxford: Oxford University Press, 1992.

Krahmer, S. M. "Interpreting the Letters of Bernard of Clairvaux to Ermengarde. Countess of Brittany: The Twelfth-Century Context and the Language of Friendship." *Cistercian Studies Quarterly* 27 (1992), pp. 217–50.

Kraut, Richard. "The Importance of Love in Aristotle's Ethics." *Philosophy Research Archives* 1.1060 (1975).

Kraye, J., (ed.). *Cambridge Translations of Renaissance Philosophical Texts*. Vol. I, *Moral Philosophy*. Cambridge: Cambridge University Press, 1997.

Kreilkamp, Ivan. "Petted Things: *Wuthering Heights* and the Animal." *Yale Journal of Criticism* 18.1 (2005).

Kristeller, P. O. *Studies in Renaissance Thought and Letters*. Rome: Edizioni di Storia e Letteratura, 1985.

Kupperman, Karen Ordahl. *Indians and English: Facing Off in Early America*. Ithaca and London: Cornell University Press, 2000.

Kurth, S. "Friendships and Friendly Relations." In G. McCall, *Social Relationships*, pp. 136–69. Chicago: Aldine, 1970.

Kutcher, Norman. "The Fifth Relationship: Dangerous Friendships in the Confucian Context." *American Historical Review* 105.5 (2000), pp. 1615–29.

Kuzniar, Alice A., (ed.). *Outing Goethe and his Age*. Stanford: Stanford University Press, 1996.

Lafleur, Claude. *Pétrarque et l'amitié*. Paris: Vrin, 2001.

Lambert, Frank. "Subscribing for Profits and Piety: The Friendship of Benjamin Franklin and George Whitefield." *The William and Mary Quarterly*, 3rd Series, 50.3 (July 1993), pp. 529–54.

Lander, J. R. "'Family,' 'Friends,' and Politics in Fifteenth-Century England." In Ralph A. Griffiths and James Sherborne (eds), *Kings and Nobles in the Later Middle Ages: A Tribute to Charles Ross*, pp. 27–40. New York: St. Martin's Press, 1986.

Landino, Cristoforo. *Scritti Critici e Teorici*. Ed. R. Cardini; 2 vols; Rome: Bulzoni, 1974.

Lane, Christopher. *Burdens of Intimacy: Psychoanalysis and Victorian Masculinity*. Chicago: University of Chicago Press, 1999.

Lane, Robert. *The Loss of Happiness in Market Democracies*. New Haven, CT: Yale University Press, 2001.

Langer, Otto. "*Teleia philia* und *amicitia spiritalis*: zwei Formen rationaler Personenbeziehungen im Abendland." In Georg Wieland (ed.), *Aufbruch – Wandel – Erneuerung: Beiträge zur "Renaissance" des 12. Jahrhunderts. 9. Blaubeurer Symposion vom 9. bis 11 Oktober 1992*, pp. 45–64. Stuttgart: Frommann-Holzboog, 1995.

Langer, Ullrich. "Friendship and the Adversarial Rhetoric of Humanism." *Common Knowledge* 3.1 (1994), pp. 40–53.

—— *Perfect Friendship: Studies in Literature and Moral Philosophy from Bocaccio to Corneille*. Geneva: Droz, 1994.

Lanham, Carol Dana. "Freshman Composition in the Early Middle Ages: Epistolography and Rhetoric before the Ars Dictaminis." *Viator* 23 (1992), pp. 115–34.

—— *Salutatio Formulas in Latin Letters to 1200: Syntax, Style, and Theory*. Eugene, OR: Wipf & Stock, 2004 (1974).

Lanser, Susan S. "Befriending the Body: Female Intimacies as Class Acts." *Eighteenth-Century Studies* 32.2 (Winter 1998), pp. 179–98.

Lapsley, Hilary. *Margaret Mead and Ruth Benedict: The Kinship of Women.* Amherst. MA: University of Massachusetts Press, 1999.

Laskin, David. *A Common Life: Four Generations of American Literary Friendship and Influence.* New York: Simon & Schuster, 1994.

Lasser, Carol. "'Let Us Be Sisters Forever': The Sororal Model of Nineteenth-Century Female Friendship." *Signs* 14.1 (1988), pp. 158–81.

Latini, Brunetto. *Il Tesoretto: Il Favoletto.* Ed. F. Mazzoni; Alpignano: A. Tallone, 1967.

—— *Llibre del Tresor.* Ed. C. J. Wittlin; Barcelona: Editorial Barcino, 1971.

—— *The Book of the Treasure.* Trans. Paul Barrette and Spurgeon Baldwin; Garland Library of Medieval Literature, 90; New York: Garland, 1993.

—— *Li Livres dou Tresor.* S. Baldwin and P. Barrette (eds.); Tempe, AZ: Arizona Center for Medieval and Renaissance Studies, 2003.

Le Faye, Deirdre, (collected and ed.). *Jane Austen's Letters.* Oxford: Oxford University Press, 1985.

Leaman, Oliver, (ed.). *Friendship East and West: Philosophical Perspectives.* Richmond, Surrey: Curzon, 1996.

Leclercq, Jean. "L'amitié dans les letters au moyen âge." *Revue du moyen âge latin* 1 (1945), pp. 391–410.

Lee, Jennifer. "The Man Date." *New York Times* (10 April 2005).

Leefeldt, Christine, and Ernest Callenbach. *The Art of Friendship.* New York: Pantheon Books, 1979.

Lehmann, John. *Three Literary Friendships: Byron & Shelley, Rimbaud & Valaire, Robert Frost & Edward Thomas.* London: Quartet, 1983.

Lepp, Ignance. *The Ways of Friendship.* Trans. Bernard Murchland; Toronto: Collier-Macmillan Canada, 1969.

Lesses, Glenn. "Socratic Friendship and Euthydemean Goods." In Thomas M. Robinson (ed.), *Plato: Euthydemus, Lysis Charmides: Proceedings of the V "Symposium Platonicum" Selected Papers.* Sankt Augustin: Academia, 2000.

—— "Austere Friends: The Stoics and Friendship." *Apeiron* 26.1 (1993), pp. 57–75.

The Letters of Marsilio Ficino. No ed.; 4 vols; London: Shepheard-Walwyn, 1975–1988.

Levaillant, Maurice. *The Passionate Exiles.* New York: Freeport, 1958.

Levine, Philippa. *Victorian Feminism.* London: Hutchinson Education, 1971.

—— "Love, Friendship, and Feminism in Later 19th-Century England." *Women's Studies International Forum* 13.1–2 (1990), pp. 63–78.

Levy, H. L. "Does Aristotle Exclude Women from Politics?" *Review of Politics* 52 (1990), pp. 397–416.

Levy, Paul. *G. E. Moore and the Cambridge Apostles.* London: Weidenfeld & Nicolson, 1979.

Levy, Shawn. "The Buddy System." *American Film* 16.5 (May 1991), pp.11–12.

Levy, William Turner, and Victor Scherle. *Affectionately, T.S. Eliot: The Story of a Friendship. 1947–1965.* London: Dent, 1968.

Lewis, Jane. "Social Facts, Social Theory and Social Change: The Ideas of Booth in Relation to Those of Beatrice Webb, Octavia Hill and Helen Bosanquet." In David Englander and Rosemary O'Day (eds), *Retrieved Riches: Social Investigation in Britain, 1840–1914.* Aldershot: Scholar Press, 1995.

Lewis, Michael, and Leonard A. Rosenblum (eds). *Friendship and Peer Relations.* New York: Wiley, 1975.

Lewis, P. S. *Essays in Later Medieval French History.* London and Ronceverte: Macmillan, 1985.

Leyton, Elliot, (ed.). *The Compact: Selected Dimensions of Friendship.* Newfoundland Social and Economic Papers No. 3; Institute of Social and Economic Research, Memorial University of Newfoundland; Toronto: University of Toronto Press, 1974).

Libanius. *Autobiography and Selected Letters.* Ed. and trans. A. F. Norman; 2 vols; Cambridge, MA: Harvard University Press, 1992.

Licitra, Vincenzo. "La *Summa de arte dictandi* di Maestro Goffredo." *Studi medievali,* 3rd series, 1966 (VII), pp. 865–913.

Licitra, Vincenzo, (ed.). *Il* Pomerium Rethorice *di Bichilino da Spello.* Spello: Centro Italiano di Studi sull'Alto Medioevo, 1992.

Linderman, Gerald. *The World within War: America's Combat Experience in World War II.* New York: Free Press, 1997.

Lindsey, Karen. *Friends as Family.* Boston: Beacon Press, 1981.

Linton, Marisa. "Fatal Friendships: The Politics of Jacobin Friendship, 1793–1794." *French Historical Studies* 31.1 (2008), pp. 51–76.

Lis, C. *Social Change and the Labouring Poor: Antwerp, 1770–1860.* New Haven, CT: Yale University Press, 1986.

Little, Graham. *Friendship: Being Ourselves with Others.* Melbourne: Text Publishing, 1993.

—— "Freud, Friendship and Politics." In Roy Porter and Sylvana Tomaselli (eds), *The Dialectics of Friendship.* London; New York: Routledge, 1989.

Loane, M. *Neighbours and Friends.* London: Edward Arnold, 1910.

Lochrie, Karma. "Between Women." In *The Cambridge Companion to Medieval Women's Writing,* pp. 70–88. Cambridge: Cambridge University Press, 2003.

Loiselle, Kenneth. "'Nouveaux mais vrais amis': La franc-maçonnerie et les rites de l'amitié au dix-huitième siècle." *Dix-huitième siècle* 39 (2007), pp. 303–18.

Longo, N. "De Epistola condenda: L'arte di 'componer lettere' nel Cinquecento." In A. Quondam (ed.), "Le *Carte Messaggiere,*" pp. 177–201. Rome: Bulzoni, 1981.

Lopata, Helena Znaniecka. "Friendship: Historical and Theoretical Introduction." In Helena Z. Lopata and David Maines (eds), *Research in the Interweave of Social Roles: Friendship, a Research Annual,* pp. 1–19. Greenwich. CT: JAI Press. 1981.

Lowe, Kate J. P. "Towards an Understanding of Goro Gheri's Views on *Amicizia* in Early Sixteenth-Century Medicean Florence." In Peter Denley and Caroline Elam (eds), *Florence and Italy: Renaissance Studies in Honour of Nicolai Rubinstein,* pp. 91–105. London: Westfield College, 1988.

Lubenow, W. C. *The Cambridge Apostles, 1820–1914 Liberalism, Imagination, and Friendship in British Intellectual and Professional Life.* Cambridge: Cambridge University Press, 1998.

Luftig, Victor. *Seeing Together: Friendship between the Sexes in English Writing from Mill to Woolf.* Stanford. CA: Stanford University Press, 1993.

Lutz, Ericka. *The Complete Idiot's Guide to Friendship for Teens.* New York: Alpha Books, 2001.

Lynch, J. *The School of Aristotle.* Berkeley: University of California Press, 1972.

Lynd, Robert and Helen. *Middletown: A Study in American Culture*. New York: Harcourt Brace Jovanovich, 1956 (1929).

Lysias. *Orations*. Trans. W. R. M. Lamb; Loeb Classical Library; Cambridge, MA: Harvard University Press, 1930.

Lytle, Guy Fitch. "Friendship and Patronage in Renaissance Europe." In F. W. Kent and Patricia Simons with J.C. Eade (eds), *Patronage, Art, and Society in Renaissance Italy*, pp. 47–61. Canberra: Humanities Research Centre Australia, 1987.

MacFarlane, A. *The Family Life of Ralph Josselin*. Cambridge: Cambridge University Press, 1970.

Machiavelli, Niccolò. *Tutte le Opere*. Ed. M. Martelli; Florence: Sansoni, 1971.

Mackay, Robert. *Half the Battle: Civilian Morale in Britain during the Second World War*. Manchester: Manchester University Press, 2002.

Macken, R. "Human Friendship in the Philosophy of Henry of Ghent." *Franziskanische Studien* 70 (1988), pp. 176–84.

Maddern, Philippa. "'Best Trusted Friends': Concepts and Practices of Friendship among Fifteenth-Century Norfolk Gentry." In Nicholas Rogers (ed.), *England in the Fifteenth Century: Proceedings of the 1992 Harlaxton Symposium*, pp. 100–17. Harlaxton Medieval Studies, 4; Stamford: Paul Watkins, 1994.

Maggini, F., (ed.). *La Rettorica*. Florence: Galletti e Cocci, 1915.

Mayhew, Henry. *London Labour and the London Poor*. London: Griffin, Bohn & Company, 1851.

Mahoney, Timothy R. "'A Common Band of Brotherhood': Male Subcultures, the Booster Ethos, and the Origins of Urban Social Order in the Midwest in the 1840s." *Journal of Urban History* 25.5 (July 1999).

Maignon, L. "Friendship and Salvation in the Testament de Bernat Serradell de Vic." *Forum for Modern Language Studies* 19 (1983), pp. 375–83.

Malebranche, Nicolas. *Treatise on Ethics*. Trans. Craig Walton; Dordrecht, Kluwer, 1993 (1684).

Manton, K. "The Fellowship of the New Life: English Ethical Socialism Reconsidered." *History of Political Thought* 24.2 (Summer 2003).

Marchalonis, Shirley, (ed.). *Patrons and Protégées: Gender, Friendship, and Writing in Nineteenth-Century America*. New Brunswick: Rutgers University Press, 1988.

Marks, Stephen R. "The Gendered Contexts of Inclusive Intimacy." In R. G. Adams and G. Allan (eds), *Placing Friendship in Context*, pp. 43–70. Cambridge: Cambridge University Press, 1998.

Marshall, J. *John Locke: Resistance, Religion and Responsibility*. Cambridge: Cambridge University Press, 1994.

Martin, Sylvia. "Rethinking Passionate Friendships: The Writing of Mary Fullerton." *Women's History Review* 2.3 (1993), pp. 395–406.

Matthews, Jill Julius. *Dance Hall and Picture Palace: Sydney's Romance with Modernity*. Sydney: Currency Press, 2005.

Matthews, Sarah H. *Friendships through the Life Course: Oral Biographies in Old Age*. Beverly Hills: Sage Publications, 1986.

Maximus of Tyre. *The Philosophical Orations*. Trans. M. B. Trapp; Oxford: Clarendon Press, 1997.

McAdam, Doug. *Freedom Summer.* New York: Oxford University Press, 1990.

McBee, Randy D. *Dance Hall Days: Intimacy and Leisure among Working-Class Immigrants in the United States.* New York: New York University Press, 2000.

McDowell, Mary E. "Friendly Visiting." In Isabel C. Barrows (ed.), *National Conference of Charities and Corrections Proceedings,* pp. 253–56. Boston and London: Geo. H. Ellis, P. S. King & Son, 1896.

McEvoy, James. *"Philia* and *Amicitia:* The Philosophy of Friendship from Plato to Aquinas." *Sewanee Mediaeval Colloquium Occasional Papers* 2 (1985), pp. 1–23.

——— "Anima Una et Cor Unum: Friendship and Spiritual Unity in Augustine." *Recherches de Théologie ancienne et médiévale* 53 (1986), pp. 80–91.

——— "Zur Rezeption des Aristotelischen Freundschaftsbegriffs in der Scholastik." *Freiburger Zeitschrift für Philosophie und Theologie* 43.3 (1996), pp. 287–303.

——— "The Theory of Friendship in the Latin Middle Ages: Hermeneutics. Contextualization and the Transmission and Reception of Ancient Texts and Ideas, from c. AD 350 to c.1500." In Julian Haseldine (ed.), *Friendship in Medieval Europe,* pp. 3–36. Stroud, UK: Sutton, 1999.

McGoldrick, Terence A. *The Sweet and Gentle Struggle: Francis De Sales on the Necessity of Spiritual Friendship.* Lanham. MD: University Press of America, 1996.

McGuire, Brian Patrick. "Love. Friendship and Sex in the Eleventh Century: The Experience of Anselm." *Studia Theologica* 28 (1974), pp. 111–52.

——— "The Collapse of Monastic Friendship: The Case of Jocelin and Samson of Bury." *Journal of Medieval History* 4 (1978), pp. 369–97.

——— "The Cistercians and the Transformation of Monastic Friendships." *Anal. Cist.* 37 (1981), pp. 1–63.

——— "Monastic Friendship and Toleration in Twelfth-Century Cistercian Life." In W. J. Sheils (ed.), *Monks, Hermits and the Ascetic Tradition,* pp. 147–60. Studies in Church History, 22; Oxford: Blackwells, 1985.

——— "Looking Back on Friendship: Medieval Experience and Modern Context." *Cistercian Studies* (1986), pp. 123–42.

——— *Friendship and Community: The Monastic Experience, 350–1250.* Kalamazoo, MI: Cistercian Publications, 1988.

——— *Brother and Lover: Aelred of Rievaulx.* New York: Crossroad, 1994.

——— *Friendship and Faith: Cistercian Men, Women, and their Stories, 1100–1250.* Aldershot: Ashgate, 2002.

McKibbin, R. *Class and Cultures: England 1918–1951.* Oxford: Oxford University Press, 1998.

McLaughlin, John. *"Amicitia* in Practice: John of Salisbury (c. 1120–1180) and his Circle." In Daniel Williams (ed.), *England in the Twelfth Century: Proceedings of the 1988 Harlaxton Symposium,* 99, pp. 165–80. Woodbridge, Suffolk: Boydell & Brewer, 1990.

McNamara, Marie Aquinas. *Friendship in St. Augustine.* Fribourg: The University Press, 1958.

McPherson, Miller, Lynn Smith-Lovin and Matthew E. Brashears. "Social Isolation in America: Changes in Core Discussion Networks over Two Decades." *American Sociological Review* 71 (2006), pp. 353–75.

Meilaender, Gilbert C. *Friendship: A Study in Theological Ethics.* Notre Dame. IN: University of Notre Dame Press, 1981.

Merlin, Hélène. "L'amitié entre le même et l'autre: Ou quand l'héterogène devient principe constitutif de société." *Dix-Septième Siècle* 51.4 (1999), pp. 657–78.

Merrick, Jeffrey. "Male Friendship in Prerevolutionary France." *GLQ: A Journal of Lesbian and Gay Studies* 10.3 (2004), pp. 407–32.

Mervaud, Michel. "Amitié et polémique: Herzen critique de Quinet." *Cahiers du Monde Russe et Soviétique* 17.1 (1976), pp. 53–79.

Mews, Constant J. *The Lost Love Letters of Heloise and Abelard: Perceptions of Dialogue in Twelfth-Century France.* New York: Palgrave, 1999.

Meyerowitz, Joanne. *Women Adrift: Independent Wage Earners in Chicago, 1880–1930.* Chicago: Chicago University Press, 1988.

Michaelis, David. *The Best of Friends: Profiles of Extraordinary Friendships.* New York: Morrow, 1983.

Migne, Abbé. *Nouvelle encyclopédie théologique.* Vol. 50, *Dictionnaire des confréries et corporations d'arts et métiers.* Paris: J-P. Migne, 1854.

Miller, Peter N. "Friendship and Conversation in Seventeenth-Century Venice." *The Journal of Modern History* 73.1 (March 2001).

Mills, J. K., J. Daly, A. Longmore, and G. Kilbride. "A Note on Family Acceptance Involving Interracial Friendships and Romantic Relationships." *Journal of Psychology* 129 (1995), pp. 349–51.

Mills, Laurens Joseph. *One Soul in Bodies Twain: Friendship in Tudor Literature and Stuart Drams.* Bloomington, IN: Principia Press, 1937.

Minnich, Elizabeth Kamarck. "Friendship between Women: The Act of Feminist Biography." *Feminist Studies* 11.2 (1985), pp. 287–305.

Mitchell, Lynette G. *Greeks Bearing Gifts: The Public Use of Private Relationships in the Greek World. 435–323 B.C.* Cambridge; New York: Cambridge University Press, 1997.

—— "New For Old: Friendship Networks In Athenian Politics." *Greece & Rome* 43.1 (April 1996), pp. 10–21.

Mitchell, R. J. *John Tiptoft (1427–1470).* London: Longmans Green, 1938.

Mitchell, S. "The Forgotten Women of the Period: Penny Weekly Family Magazines of the 1840's and 1850's." In M. Vicinus (ed.), *A Widening Sphere: Changing Roles of Victorian Women.* Bloomington, IN: Indiana University Press, 1977.

Mogey, J. M. *Family and Neighbourhood: Two Studies in Oxford.* Oxford: Oxford University Press, 1956.

Molho, A. "Cosimo de' Medici: Pater Patriae or Padrino?" *Stanford Italian Review* I (1979), pp. 5–33.

Moltmann, J. "Open Friendship: Aristotelan and Christian Concepts of Friendship." In Leroy S. Rouner (ed.), *The Changing Face of Friendship.* Notre Dame, IN: University of Notre Dame, 1994.

Monsour, Michael. *Women and Men as Friends: Relationships across the Life Span in the 21st Century.* Mahwah, NJ; London: L. Erlbaum, 2002.

Montaigne. "Of Friendship." In Donald M. Frame (ed. and trans.), *The Complete Works of Montaigne,* pp. 135–44. Stanford: Stanford University Press, 1958.

Moody, Anne. *Coming of Age in Mississippi.* New York: Dell, 1968.

Moore, G. E. *Principia Ethica.* Cambridge: Cambridge University Press, 1966.

Moore, Henry T. "Further Data Concerning Sex Differences." *Journal of Abnormal Psychology* 17 (1922), pp. 210–14.

Moore, Lisa. "'Something More Tender Still Than Friendship': Romantic Friendship in Early-Nineteenth-Century England." *Feminist Studies* 18.3 (1992), pp. 499–520.

Moravcsik, Julius M. "Development of Friendship and Values in the 'Philoctetes.'" *Proceedings of the Boston Area Colloquium in Ancient Philosophy* 13 (1997), pp. 255–75.

—— "The Perils of Friendship and Conceptions of the Self." In J. Dancy, J. Moravcsik, and C. W. W. Taylor (eds), *Human Agency: Language, Duty, and Value,* pp. 132–51. Stanford: Stanford University Press, 1988.

Morlet-Chantalat, Chantal. *La Clélie de Mademoiselle de Scudéry.* Paris: Champion, 1994.

Moser, Patrick. "Montaigne's Literary Patrons: The Case of La Boetie." *Sixteenth Century Journal* 31.2 (2000), pp. 381–97.

Mosse, George L. "Friendship and Nationhood: About the Promise and Failure of German Nationalism." *Journal of Contemporary History* 17 (1982), pp. 351–67.

Mulgan, Richard. "Aristotle and the Political Role of Women." *History of Political Thought* 15 (1994), pp. 179–202.

Mullet, Margaret. "Friendship in Byzantium: Genre, Topos and Network." In Julian Haseldine (ed.), *Friendship in Medieval Europe.* Stroud: Sutton, 1999.

—— "Byzantium: A Friendly Society?" *Past and Present* 118 (1988), pp. 3–24.

Munzel, G. Felicitas. "Menschenfreundschaft: Friendship and Pedagogy in Kant." *Eighteenth-Century Studies* 32.2 (Winter 1998–1999), pp. 247–59.

Murray, Jacqueline. "Kinship and Friendship: The Perception of Family by Clergy and Laity in Late Medieval London." *Albion* 20.3 (1988), pp. 369–85.

Myers, Sylvia Harcstark. *The Bluestocking Circle: Women, Friendship, and the Life of the Mind in Eighteenth-Century England.* Oxford: Clarendon Press; New York: Oxford University Press, 1990.

Naegale, K. "Friendship and Acquaintances: An Exploration of Some Social Distinctions." *Harvard Educational Review* 28 (1958), pp. 232–52.

Najemy, John M. *Between Friends: Discourses of Power and Desire in the Machiavelli-Vettori Letters of 1513–1515.* Princeton: Princeton University Press, 1993.

Naples, Nancy. *Grassroots Warriors: Activist Mothering, Community Work and the War on Poverty.* New York: Routledge, 1998.

Naples, Nancy, (ed.). *Community Activism and Feminist Politics: Organizing across Race, Class, and Gender.* New York: Routledge, 1998.

Naples, Nancy, and Marnie Dobson. *"Gay Men's Friendships: Invincible Communities.* Chicago: University of Chicago Press, 1999.

Nardi, Peter M. *Men's Friendships.* Newbury Park: Sage Publications, 1992.

—— *Gay Men's Friendships: Invincible Communities.* Chicago: University of Chicago Press, 1999.

Nathan, Sarina, (ed.). *Amicitia di Maestro Boncompagno da Signa.* Miscellanea di Letteratura del Medio Evo, III; Rome: Società Filologica Romana, 1909.

Navarre, Marguerite de. *The Heptameron.* Trans. P. A. Chilton; Harmondsworth, UK: Penguin, 1984.

Nederman, Cary J. *John of Salisbury*. Tempe, AZ: Arizona Center for Medieval and Renaissance Studies, 2005.

Nestor, Pauline. *Female Friendships and Communities: Charlotte Brontë, George Eliot, Elizabeth Gaskell.* Oxford: Clarendon Press; New York: Oxford University Press, 1985.

Newbiggin, N. *Feste D'Oltrarno: Plays in Churches in Fifteenth Century Florence.* 2 vols; Florence: Olschki, 1997.

Nicole, Pierre. *Essais de morale contenus en divers traittez sur plusieurs devoirs importants.* 3 vols; Paris: G. Desprez, 1701.

Nicotera, Anne Maydan. *Interpersonal Communication in Friend and Mate Relationships.* Albany: State University of New York Press, 1993.

Northway, Mary L. *A Primer of Sociometry.* Toronto: University of Toronto Press, 1952.

Nussbaum, J. F. "Perceptions of Communication Content and Life Satisfaction among the Elderly." *Communication Quarterly* 31 (1983), pp. 313–19.

Nussbaum, Martha. *The Therapy of Desire.* Princeton, NJ: Princeton University Press, 1994.

—— *The Fragility of Goodness: Luck and Ethics in Greek Tragedy and Philosophy.* Cambridge, UK; New York: Cambridge University Press, 2000.

—— *Love's Knowledge: Essays on Philosophy and Literature.* New York: Oxford University Press, 1990.

Nye, Robert A. "Kinship, Male Bonds, and Masculinity in Comparative Perspective." *American Historical Review* 105.5 (2000), pp. 1656–66.

Nyman, Jopi. *Men Alone: Masculinity, Individualism, and Hard-Boiled Fiction.* Amsterdam: Rodopi, 1997.

O'Brien, M. "Patterns of Kinship and Friendship among Lone Fathers." In C. Lewis and M. O'Brien (eds), *Reassessing Fatherhood: New Observations on Fathers and the Modern Family.* London: Sage, 1987.

O'Connor, David K. "Two Ideals of Friendship." *History of Philosophy Quarterly* 7.2 (April 1990), pp. 109–22.

O'Connor, Pat. *Friendships between Women: A Critical Review.* Hemel Hempstead, UK: Harvester Wheatsheaf, 1992.

—— "The Adult Mother-Daughter Relationship: A Uniquely and Universally Close Relationship." *Sociological Review* 38 (1990), pp. 293–323.

O'Donnell, Katherine, and Michael O'Rouke (eds). *Love, Sex, Intimacy, and Friendship between Men, 1550–1800.* New York: Palgrave Macmillan, 2002.

Oliker, Stacey J. "The Modernisation of Friendship: Individualism, Intimacy, and Gender in the Nineteenth Century." In R. G Adams and G. Allan (eds), *Placing Friendship in Context.* Cambridge, pp. 23–27. Cambridge: Cambridge University Press, 1998.

—— *Best Friends and Marriage: Exchange among Women.* Berkeley: University of California Press, 1989.

Olive, K. "Creation, Imitation, Fabrication: Renaissance Self-Fashioning in the Codex Rustici." 3 vols; PhD thesis, University of Sydney, 2004.

O'Meara, D. J. *Pythagoras Revived: Mathematics and Philosophy in Late Antiquity.* Oxford: Oxford University Press, 1989.

Oram, Alison. "Repressed and Thwarted, or Bearer of the New World? The Spinster in Interwar Feminist Discourse." *Women's History Review* 1.3 (1992), pp. 413–33.

Orbach, Susiem, and Luise Eichenbaum. *Between Women: Facing Up to Feelings of Love, Envy and Competition in Women's Friendships.* London: Arrow, 1994 (1987).

Origo, I. "The Domestic Enemy: The Eastern Slaves in Tuscany in the Fourteenth and Fifteenth Centuries." *Speculum* 30 (1955), pp. 321–66.

—— *The Merchant of Prato.* New York: J. Cape, 1957.

Pahl, R. E. *On Friendship.* Cambridge: Polity Press, 2000.

—— "A Sociological Portrait: Friends and Associates." *New Society* 18 (1971), pp. 980–82.

Pahl, Raymond, and Liz Spencer. *Rethinking Friendship: Hidden Solidarities for Today.* Princeton, NJ: Princeton University Press, 2004.

Paine, Robert. "In Search of Friendship: An Exploratory Analysis in 'Middle-Class' Culture." In *Colloquium on the Comparative Sociology of Friendship*, pp. 505–24. Memorial University of Newfoundland, 1969.

Paisley, Fiona. *Loving Protection? Australian Feminism and Aboriginal Women's Rights 1919–1939.* Melbourne: Melbourne University Press, 2000.

Pakaluk, Michael. *Aristotle "Nicomachean Ethics": Books VIII and IX.* New York: Clarendon Oxford Press, 1998.

—— "Political Friendship." In Leroy S. Rouner (ed.), *The Changing Face of Friendship.* Notre Dame, IN: University of Notre Dame, 1994.

Pakaluk, Michael, (ed.). *Other Selves: Philosophers on Friendship.* Indianapolis: Hackett, 1991.

Palmieri, M. *Vita Civile.* Ed. G. Belloni; Florence: Sansoni, 1982.

Pardon, G. F. "Odd-Fellowship: Its Principles and Practice, Part V." *Quarterly Magazine of the Independent Order of Odd-Fellows, Manchester Unity* new series II (1859–1860).

Park, Robert. *Human Communities: The City and Human Ecology.* New York: Free Press, 1952.

Passerini, G. "Dora Guidalotti del Bene: Le Lettere (1381–1392)." *Letteratura Italiana Antica* 4 (2003), pp. 101–59.

Paton, H. J. "Kant on Friendship." In Neera Kapur Badhwar (ed.), *Friendship: A Philosophical Reader*, pp. 133–54. Ithaca, NY: Cornell University Press, 1993.

Patrick, Simon. *Advice to a Friend.* London: printed for R. Royston, 4th edn, 1681.

Patt, William D. "The Early 'ars dictaminis' as Response to a Changing Society." *Viator* 9 (1978), pp. 133–55.

Paul, Maria. *The Friendship Crisis: Finding, Making and Keeping Friends When You're Not a Kid Anymore.* Chicago: Rodale, 2004.

Payne, Andrew. "Character and the Forms of Friendship in Aristotle." *Apeiron* 33.1 (2000), pp. 53–74.

Peachin, Michael, (ed.). *Aspects of Friendship in the Graeco-Roman World: Proceedings of a Conference Held at the Seminar Für Alte Geschichte, Heidelberg, on 10–11 June, 2000.* Portsmouth, RI: Journal of Roman Archaeology LLC, 2001.

Pearson, Lionell C. *Popular Ethics in Ancient Greece.* Stanford: Stanford University Press, 1962.

Peel, Mark. "'A New Kind of Manhood': Remembering the 1950s." In John Murphy and Judith Smart (eds), *The Forgotten Fifties*, pp. 147–57. Melbourne: Melbourne University Press, 1997.

—— *The Lowest Rung: The Voice of Australian Poverty.* Cambridge: Cambridge University Press, 2003.

Peiss, Kathy Lee. *Cheap Amusements: Working Women and Leisure in Turn-of-the-century New York.* Philadelphia: Temple University Press, 1986.

Peretti, P. O. "Elderly–Animal Friendship Bonds." *Social Behavior and Personality* 18 (1990), pp. 151–56.

Perkin, Harold. *The Origins of Modern English Society, 1780–1880.* London: Routledge and Kegan Paul, 1969.

Perosa, A. *Giovanni Rucellai ed il suo Zibaldone, I, "Il Zibaldone Quaresimale."* London: Warburg Institute, University of London, 1960.

Perry, Ruth. "Interrupted friendships in Jane Austen's Emma." *Tulsa Studies in Literature* 5.2 (1986), pp. 185–202.

Peter of Blois. *De amicitia Christiana.* Ed. M.-M. Davy; Paris: De Boccard, 1932.

—— Pierre de Blois. *Un traité de l'amour du XIIe siècle.* Ed. M.-M. Davy; Paris: De Boccard, 1932.

Peter of Celle. *L'Ecole du Cloître.* Ed. Gérard de Martel; Sources chrétiennes, 47; Paris, 1977.

—— *The Letters of Peter of Celle.* Ed. Julian Haseldine; Oxford: Clarendon Press, 2001.

Petrucci, A. *Writers and Readers in Medieval Italy.* Trans. C. M. Radding; New Haven, CT, and London: Yale University Press, 1995.

Phillips, Richard. *Mapping Men and Empire: A Geography of Adventure.* London: Routledge, 1996.

Philostratus. *Lives of the Sophists.* Trans. W. C. Wright; Loeb Classical Library; Cambridge, MA: Harvard University Press, 1921.

Pike, Jon. "Aristotle and Marx: Egalitarianism. Civic Friendship and Rights." *Skepsis* 12 (2001), pp. 142–56.

Pindar. *Odes.* Trans. J. Sandys; Loeb Classical Library; Cambridge, MA: Harvard University Press, 1937.

Pizzolato, L. *L'idea d'amicizia nel mondo antico classico e cristiano.* Turin: Einaudi, 1993.

Platina, Bartolomeo. *De optima cive.* Ed. F. Battaglia; Bologna: N. Zanichelli, 1944.

Plato. *Complete Works.* Trans. H. N. Fowler; Loeb Classical Library; Cambridge, MA: Harvard University Press, 1914.

—— *Laws.* Trans. with notes and an interpretative essay Thomas Pangle; Chicago: University of Chicago Press, 1979.

—— *Complete Works.* Ed. J. Cooper; Indianapolis: Hackett, 1997.

Plutarch of Chaeronia. *Moralia.* Trans. F. C. Babbit *et al.*; 16 vols; Loeb Classical Library; Cambridge, MA: Harvard University Press, 1927–1976.

Podolsky, Robin. "The Ever Changing Lesbian Social Scene." In Betty Berzon (ed.), *Positively Gay.* Berkeley: Celestial Arts, 3rd edn, 2001.

Polybius. *The Histories.* Trans. W. R. Paton; 6 vols; Loeb Classical Library; Cambridge, MA: Harvard University Press, 1922–27.

Porter, Roy, and Sylvana Tomaselli (eds). *The Dialectics of Friendship.* London; New York: Routledge, 1989.

Potkay, Adam, and Sandra Burr (eds). *Black Atlantic Writers of the Eighteenth Century.* London: Macmillan, 1995.

Poulet, Robert. "Histoire D'une Amitié." *Ecrits de Paris* 372 (1977), pp. 28–36.

Powis, J. *Aristocracy.* Oxford: B. Blackwell, 1984.

Price, A. W. *Love and Friendship in Plato and Aristotle.* Oxford: Clarendon Press; New York: Oxford University Press, 1989.

Procter, Ian. "The Privatisation of Working-Class Life: A Dissenting View." *British Journal of Sociology* 41 (1990), pp. 157–80.

Purdom, C. B. *Everyman at War.* London: J. M. Dent, 1930.

Quillet, Jeannine. "Nicole Oresme glossateur de la doctrine aristotélicienne de la philia." In Burkhard Mojsisch and Olaf Pluta (eds), *Historia Philosophiae Medii Aevi: Studien zur Geschichte der Philosophie des Mittelalters,* II, pp. 887–97. Amsterdam: B.R. Grüner, 1991.

Quondam, A. "Dal 'Formulario' al 'Formulario': Cento anni di 'Libri di Lettere.'" In A. Quondam (ed.), "Le *Carte Messaggiere,*" pp. 13–156. Rome: Bulzoni, 1981.

Radice, B., (trans.). *The Letters of Abelard and Heloise.* London: Penguin, 1974.

Rawson, Beryl. *The Politics of Friendship: Pompey and Cicero.* Sydney: Sydney University Press, 1978.

Raymond, Janice G. *A Passion for Friends: Toward a Philosophy of Female Affection.* London: Women's Press, 1986.

Reason, W., (ed.). *University and Social Settlements.* London: Methuen, 1898.

Redford, Bruce. *The Converse of the Pen: Acts of Intimacy in the Eighteenth-Century Familiar Letter.* Chicago: University of Chicago Press, 1986.

Reid, D. "Measuring the Impact of Brotherhood." *Confraternitas* 14 (2003), pp. 3–12.

—— "Moderate Devotion, Mediocre Poetry and Magnificent Food: The Confraternity of the Immaculate Conception of Rouen." *Confraternitas* 7 (1996), pp. 3–10.

Reid, H., and G. Fine. "Self-Disclosure in Men's Friendships: Variations Associated with Intimate Relations." In Peter M. Nardi (ed.), *Men's Friendships.* Newbury Park: Sage Publications, 1992.

Reina, Ruben E. "Two Patterns of Friendship in a Guatamalan Community." *American Anthropologist* 61 (1959), pp. 44–50.

Reisman, John M. *Anatomy of Friendship.* New York: Irvington, 1979.

Rendall, Jane. "Friendship and Politics: Barbara Leigh Bodichon (1827–1891) and Bessie Raynor Parkes (1829–1925)." In Susan Mendus and Jane Rendall (eds), *Sexuality and Subordination: Interdisciplinary Studies of Gender in the Nineteenth Century.* London and New York: Routledge, 1989.

Reohr, Janet. *Friendship: An Explanation of Structure and Process.* New York: Garland Publications, 1991.

Rey, Michel. "Communaute et individu: L'amitie comme lien social a la Renaissance." *Revue d'Histoire Moderne et Contemporaine* 38 (Oct–Dec 1991), pp. 617–25.

Reynolds, K. D. *Aristocratic Women and Political Society in Victorian Britain.* Oxford: Clarendon Press, 1998.

Riccoboni. *Histoire de Miss Jenny.* 4 vols; Paris: Brocas & Humblot, 1764.

Richards, Cynthia. "'The Pleasures Of Complicity': Sympathetic Identification and the Female Reader in Early Eighteenth-Century Women's Amatory Fiction." *Eighteenth Century: Theory and Interpretation* 36.3 (1995), pp. 220–33.

Richardson, Samuel. *Clarissa, or the History of a Young Lady.* Ed. Angus Ross; Harmondsworth, UK: Penguin, 1985 (1747–1748).

Richmond, Mary. *The Long View.* New York: Russell Sage Foundation, 1930.

—— *Friendly Visiting among the Poor: A Handbook for Charity Workers.* Montclair, NJ: Patterson Smith, 1969 (1899).

Ritter, Harry. "The Remarkable Partnership: Three Recent Interpretations of the Marx-Engels Friendship." *Studies in History and Society* 1.2 (1976), pp. 51–57.

Rizzo, Betty. *Companions without Vows: Relationships among Eighteenth-Century British Women.* Athens: University of Georgia Press, 1994.

Roberts, E. *A Woman's Place: An Oral History of Working-Class Women 1890–1940.* Oxford: Basil Blackwell, 1984.

Roberts, R. *The Classic Slum: Salford Life in the First Quarter of the Century.* Harmondsworth, UK: Penguin, 1973.

Robertson, I. *Tyranny under the Mantle of St. Peter: Pope Paul II and Bologna.* Turnhout: Brepols, 2002.

Robin, Léon. *Greek Thought and the Origins of the Scientific Spirit (La pensée greque et les origines de l'esprit scientifique).* Trans. M. R. Dobie; New York: Russell & Russell, 1967.

Robinson, David. "Unravelling the 'Cord which Ties Good Men to Good Men': Male Friendship in Richardson's Novels." In Margaret Anne Doody and Peter Sabor (eds), *Samuel Richardson. Tercentenary Essays,* pp. 167–87. Cambridge: Cambridge University Press, 1989.

Robinson, I. S. "The Friendship Circle of Bernold of Constance and the Dissemination of Gregorian Ideas in Late Eleventh-Century Germany." In Julian Haseldine (ed.), *Friendship in Medieval Europe.* Stroud: Sutton, 1999.

—— "The Friendship Network of Gregory VII." *History* 63 (1978), pp. 1–22.

Robnett, Belinda. *How Long? How Long? African-American Women in the Struggle for Civil Rights.* New York: Oxford University Press, 1997.

Rocke, Michael. *Forbidden Friendships: Homosexuality and Male Culture in Renaissance Florence.* Oxford: Oxford University Press, 1996.

Rogerson, Sidney. *Twelve Days.* London: Barker, 1933.

Rolland, Patrice. "La signification politique de l'amitié chez Saint Just." *Annales Historiques de la Révolution Française* 55.3 (1984), pp. 324–38.

Romano, D. *Patricians and Popolani: The Social Foundations of the Venetian Renaissance State.* Baltimore, MD: Johns Hopkins University Press, 1987.

Rondeau, J. Fisk. "Homosociability and Civic (Dis)order in Late Medieval Italian Confraternities." In N. Terpstra (ed.), *The Politics of Ritual Kinship: Confraternities and Social Order in Early Modern Italy,* pp. 30–47. Cambridge: Cambridge University Press, 2000.

Roosevelt, Franklin D. *Roosevelt and Daniels, a Friendship in Politics.* Ed. with an introduction Carroll Kilpatrick; Chapel Hill, University of North Carolina Press, 1952.

Rose, S., and L. Roades. "Feminism and Women's Friendships." *Psychology of Women Quarterly* 11 (1987), pp. 243–54.

Rosen, Frederick. "Obligation and Friendship in Plato's 'Crito.'" *Political Theory* 1 (1973), pp. 307–16.

Roseneil, Sasha. "Why We Should Care about Friends: An Argument for Queering the Care Imaginary in Social Policy." *Social Policy and Society* 3 (2004), pp. 409–19.

Rosenmeyer, Patricia A. "The Epistolary Novel." In J. R. Morgan and Richard Stoneman (eds), *Greek Fiction: The Greek Novel in Context*, pp. 146–65.London and New York: Routledge, 1994.

Rosenzweig, Linda W. *Another Self: Middle-Class American Women and their Friends in the Twentieth Century*. New York; London: New York University Press, 1999.

Ross, Ellen. "Survival Networks: Women's Neighbourhood Sharing in London before World War One." *History Workshop* 15 (Spring 1983).

Ross, James B. "Gaspare Contarini and his Friends." *Studies in the Renaissance* 17 (1970), pp. 192–232.

Rosser, G. *Medieval Westminster, 1200–1540*. Oxford: Clarendon Press, 1989.

Rotundo, E. Anthony. "Romantic Friendship: Male Intimacy and Middle-Class Youth in the Northern United States, 1800–1900." *Journal of Social History* 23.1 (Fall 1989), pp. 1–25.

—— *American Manhood: Transformations in Masculinity from the Revolution to the Modern Era*. New York: Basic Books, 1993.

Roulston, Christine. "Separating the Inseparables: Female Friendship and its Discontents in Eighteenth-century France." *Eighteenth Century Studies* 32.2 (1998–1999), pp. 215–31.

Rouner, Leroy S., (ed.). *The Changing Face of Friendship*. Notre Dame, IN: University of Notre Dame, 1994.

Rousseau, Jean-Jacques. *La nouvelle Héloïse, ou Lettres de deux amans, habitans d'une petite ville au pied des Alpes*. London (Paris: Cazin), 1781.

Rubin, Lillian B. *Just Friends: The Role of Friendship in our Lives*. New York: Harper & Row, 1985.

Russell, C. *Giulia Gonzaga and the Religious Controversies of Sixteenth-Century Italy*. Turnhout: Brepols, 2006.

Russell, Daniel C. "Epicurus on Friends and Goals." In Dane R. Gordon (ed.), *Epicurus: His Continuing Influence and Contemporary Relevance*. Rochester: RIT Cary Graphic Arts Press, 2003, pp. 167–81.

Ryan, Mary P. "The Power of Women's Networks." In Judith L. Newton, Mary P. Ryan and Judith R. Walkowitz (eds), *Sex and Class in Women's History*. London: Routledge & Kegan Paul, 1983.

Sabbadini, R. *Guariniana*. Ed. M. Sancipriano; Turin: Bottega d'Erasmo, 1964.

Sacy, Louis-Silvestre, de. *A Discourse of Friendship*. London, 1707.

Sadler, Jr, W. A. "The Experience of Friendship." *Humanitas* 6 (1970), pp. 177–209.

Saint-Just, Louis de. *Oeuvres choisies*. Paris: Gallimard, 1968.

Sales, François de. *Introduction to the Devout Life*. Trans. Allan Ross; London: Burns Oates & Washbourne, 1950 (1608).

Saller, Richard. "Patronage and Friendship in Early Imperial Rome: Drawing the Distinction." In Andrew Wallace-Hadrill (ed.), *Patronage in Ancient Society*, pp. 49–62. London: Routledge, 1989.

Santas, Gerasimos. *Plato and Freud: Two Theories of Love*. New York: Blackwell, 1988.

Sapori, A. "Cosimo Medici e un 'patto giurato' a Firenze nel 1449." In *Eventail de l'histoire vivante –Hommage à Lucien Febvre*, II, pp. 115–32. 2 vols; Paris: A. Colin, 1953.

Sassoon, Siegfried. "The Poet as Hero" and "Survivors." In *The War Poems*, arranged and introduced by Rupert Hart-Davis. London: Faber & Faber, 1983.

Savage, M. *The Dynamics of Working Class Politics: The Labour Movement in Preston, 1880– 1940.* Cambridge: Cambridge University Press, 1987.

Schestag, Thomas. "Friend ... Brockes: Heinrich Von Kleist in Letters." *Eighteenth-Century Studies* 32.2 (1998–1999), pp. 261–77.

Schmekel, A. *Die Philosophie der mittleren Stoa in ihrem geschichtlichen Zusammenhänge.* Hildesheim: Weidmann, 1892.

Schmidt, M. "An Example of Spiritual Friendship: The Correspondence between Heinrich of Nördlingen and Margaretha Ebner." In U. Wiethaus (ed.), *Maps in Flesh and Light: The Religious Experience of Medieval Women Mystics.* Syracuse, NY: 1993.

Schmidt, S. W., J. C. Scott, C. Landé and L. Guasti (eds). *Friends, Followers and Factions: A Reader in Political Clientelism.* Berkeley: University of California Press, 1977.

Schnegg, Brigitte. "Gleichgestimmte Seelen: Empfindsame Inszenierung und intellektueller Wettstreit von Männern und Frauen in der Freundschaftskultur der Aufklärung." *Werkstatt Geschichte* 28 (2001), pp. 23–42.

Schoeck, R. J. *Erasmus of Europe: The Making of a Humanist, 1467–1500.* Edinburgh: Edinburgh University Press, 1990.

Schollmeier, Paul. *Other Selves: Aristotle on Personal and Political Friendship.* Albany: State University of New York Press, 1994.

Schulte-Sasse, J. "Toward a 'Culture' for the Masses: The Socio-Psychological Function of Popular Literature in Germany and the U.S., 1880–1920.'" *New German Critique* 29 (Spring–Summer 1983).

Schulz, Janice. "Love of Friendship and the Perfection of Finite Persons." In R. E. Houser (ed.), *Medieval Masters: Essays in Memory of Msgr. E. A. Synan*, pp. 209–32. Houston: University of St Thomas, 1999.

Schwarzenbach, Sibyl A. "On Civic Friendship." *Ethics* 107.1 (1996), pp. 97–128.

Scott, Jeremy. *Friends & Friendship; Conversations and Reflections.* London: Sidgwick & Jackson, 1974.

Seeber, Frances M. "Eleanor Roosevelt and Women in the New Deal: A Network of Friends." *Presidential Studies Quarterly* 20.4 (Fall 1990), pp. 707–17.

Sellner, E. C. "A Common Dwelling: Soul Friendship in Early Celtic Monasticism." *Cistercian Studies Quarterly* 29 (1994), pp. 1–21.

Senault, Jean-François. *De l'usage des passions.* Paris: Fayard, 1987 (1641).

Seneca. *Ad Lucilium epistulae morales.* Ed. and trans. Richard M. Gummere; London: Heinemann, 1917–1925.

—— *Letters from a Stoic: Epistulae morales ad Lucilium.* Trans. Robin Campbell; Harmondsworth: Penguin, 1969.

—— *Seventeen Letters.* Ed. and trans. C. D. N. Costa; Warminster, Wiltshire: Aris & Phillips, 1988.

Sennett, Richard. *The Corrosion of Character: The Personal Consequences of Work in the New Capitalism.* New York: Norton, 1998.

Shannon, Laurie. *Sovereign Amity: Figures of Friendship in Shakepearean Contexts.* Chicago: University of Chicago Press, 2001.

—— "Monarchs, Minions, and 'Soveraigne' Friendship." *The South Atlantic Quarterly* 97.1 (Winter 1998), pp. 91–112.

Sharp, Ronald A. *Friendship and Literature: Spirit and Form.* Durham: Duke University Press, 1986.

Shaw, Albert, (ed.). *The Messages and Papers of Woodrow Wilson.* New York: The Review of Reviews Corporation, 1924.

Sherk, Robert K., (ed. and trans.). *Rome and the Greek East to the Death of Augustus.* Cambridge: Cambridge University Press, 1984.

Sherman, Nancy. "Aristotle on Friendship and the Shared Life." *Philosophy and Phenomenological Research* 47 (1987), pp. 589–613.

Shlapentokh, Vladimir. *Love, Marriage, and Friendship in the Soviet Union: Ideals and Practices.* New York: Praeger, 1984.

Sigelman, L., and S. Welch. "The Contact Hypothesis Revisited: Black-White Interaction and Positive Racial Attitudes." *Social Forces* 71 (1993), pp. 781–95.

Sigurdsson, J. V. "Friendship in the Icelandic Commonwealth." In G. Palsson (ed.), *From Sagas to Society: Comparative Approaches to Early Iceland*, pp. 205–15. Middlesex: Enfield Lock, 1992.

Silver, Allan. "Friendship in Commercial Society: Eighteenth-Century Social Theory and Modern Sociology." *American Journal of Sociology* 95.6 (1990), pp. 1474–504.

Simmel, Georg. "The Metropolis and Mental Life." In David Frisby and Mike Featherstone (eds), *Simmel on Culture: Selected Writings*, pp. 174–87. London: Sage Publications, 1997 (1902).

Simons, P. "Lesbian (In)Visibility in Italian Renaissance Culture: Diana and Other Cases of *donna con donna*." *Journal of Homosexuality* 27 (1994), pp. 81–122.

Sinha, Miralini. "Gender in the Critiques of Colonialism and Nationalism: Locating the 'Indian Woman.'" In Joan Scott (ed.), *Feminism and History,* pp. 477–504. Oxford: Oxford University Press, 1996.

Smith, Adam. *The Theory of Moral Sentiments.* Ed. Raphael and Macfie; Oxford: Clarendon Press, 1976 (1759).

Smith, Charles George. *Spenser's Theory of Friendship.* New York: AMS Press, 1972.

Smith-Pangle, Lorraine. *Aristotle and the Philosophy of Friendship.* Cambridge: Cambridge University Press, 2003.

—— "Friendship and Human Neediness in Plato's Lysis." *Ancient Philosophy* 21.2 (Fall 2001), pp. 305–23.

Smith-Rosenberg, Carroll. "The Female World of Love and Ritual: Relations between Women in Nineteenth-Century America." *Signs* 1.1 (1975), pp. 1–29.

Smuts, J. C. "The British Empire and World Peace." *Journal of the Royal Institute of International Affairs* 9 (March 1930), pp. 141–53.

Snaith, Guy. "All For Friendship: La Calprenede's Phalante and Other Friends." *Seventeenth-Century French Studies* 17 (1995), pp. 147–55.

Snyder, Jane McIntosh. *The Woman and the Lyre: Women Writers in Classical Greece and Rome.* Carbondale: Southern Illinois University Press, 1989.

Soble, Alan. *Eros, Agape and Philia: Readings in the Philosophy of Love*. New York: Paragon House, 1989.

Soland, Birgitte. *Becoming Modern: Young Women and the Reconstruction of Womanhood in the 1920s*. Princeton, NJ: Princeton University Press, 2000.

Sorabji, Richard. *Emotion and Peace of Mind*. Oxford: Oxford University Press, 2000.

Southern, R. W. *Medieval Humanism and Other Studies*. Oxford: Basil Blackwell, 1970.

Spencer, Jane. *The Rise of the Woman Novelist: From Aphra Behn to Jane Austen*. Oxford: Blackwell, 1986.

Speroni, Sperone. "Dialogo della Amicizia." In *Opere*, II, pp. 368–74. Ed. M. Pozzi; 5 vols; Rome: Vecchiarelli, 1988.

St Clare Byrne, M., (ed.). *The Lisle Letters: An Abridgement*. London: Folio Press, 1983.

Stacey, Margaret. *Tradition and Change: A Study of Banbury*. Oxford: Oxford University Press, 1960.

Stack, Carol. *All our Kin: Strategies for Survival in a Black Community*. New York: Harper & Row, 1974.

Staël, Germaine de. *Corinne, ou l'Italie*. 3 vols; Paris: INALF, 1961.

Stanley, Liz. "Feminism and Friendship – Pt. III. On Feminist Auto/Biography." In *The Auto/Biographical I: The Theory and Practice of Feminist Auto/Biography*. Manchester; New York: Manchester University Press, 1992.

—— *Feminism and Friendship: Two Essays on Olive Schreiner*. Studies in Sexual Politics, 8; Manchester: University of Manchester, 1985.

Stansell, Christine. *American Moderns: Bohemian New York and the Creation of a New Century*. New York: Henry Holt, 2000.

Stansky, Peter. *On or about December 1910*. Cambridge, MA: Harvard University Press, 1996.

Starn, R., (ed.). *Donato Gianotti and his Epistolae*. Geneva: Droz, 1968.

Stephanson, Raymond. "'Epicoene Friendship': Understanding Male Friendship in the Early Eighteenth Century with Some Speculations about Pope." *The Eighteenth Century* 38 (1997), pp. 151–70.

Stephens, William O. "If Friendship Hurts, and Epicurean Deserts: A Reply to Andrew Mitchell." *Essays in Philosophy* 3.1 (2002), pp. 1–3.

Stern, Fritz. "Gold and Iron: The Collaboration and Friendship of Gerson Bleichroder and Otto von Bismarck." *The American Historical Review* 75.1 (October 1969), pp. 37–46.

Stern-Gillet, Suzanne. *Aristotle's Philosophy of Friendship*. Albany: State University of New York Press, 1995.

—— "Epicurus and Friendship." *Dialogue* 28.2 (1989), pp. 275–88.

Stocker, Michael. "Values and Purposes: The Purposes of Teleology and the Ends of Friendship." *Journal of Philosophy* 78 (1981), pp. 747–65.

Stoler, Ann Laura. *Carnal Knowledge and Imperial Power: Race and the Intimate in Colonial Rule*. Berkeley: University of California Press, 2002.

Stowers, Stanley K. *Letter Writing in Greco-Roman Antiquity* .Philadelphia: The Westminster Press, 1986.

Straaten, M. van. *Panétius, sa vie ses écrits et sa doctrine avec une édition des fragments*. Amsterdam: H. J. Paris, 1946.

Strabo. *Geography.* Trans. H. L. Jones; 8 vols; Loeb Classical Library; Cambridge, MA: Harvard University Press, 1930–1937.

Strehlke, C. B., (ed.). *Pontormo, Bronzino, and the Medici.* Philadelphia: Philadelphia Museum of Art, 2004.

Strong, Barrett, and Norman Whitfield . "The Friendship Train" (EMI Music Publishing).

Strozzi, Agostino. *De amicitia.* Venice: Biblioteca Marciana Codici italiani, Classe II, 106.

Suitor, J. "Friendship Networks in Transition: Married Mothers' Return to School." *Journal of Social and Personal Relationships* 4 (1987), pp. 445–61.

The Surprize. London: J. Roberts, 1724.

Sutcliffe, J. P., and B. D. Crabbe. "Incidence and Degrees of Friendship in Urban and Rural Areas." *Social Forces* 42 (1963), pp. 60–67.

Sutherland, Alistair, and Patrick Anderson (eds). *Eros, an Anthology of Friendship.* London: Blond, 1961.

Suttles, G. D. "Friendship as a Social Institution." In G. J. McCall, M. M. McCall, N. K. Denzin, G. D. Suttles and S. B. Kurth (eds), *Social Relationships,* pp. 95–135. Chicago: Aldine, 1970.

Swett, Katharine W. "'The Account between Us': Honor, Reciprocity and Companionship in Male Friendship in the Later Seventeenth Century." *Albion* 31.1 (1999), pp. 1–30.

Symmachus. *Lettres.* Ed. and trans. Jean Pierre Callu; Paris: Belles lettres, 1972–1982.

Tadmor, Naomi. *Family and Friends in Eighteenth-Century England: Household, Kinship, and Patronage.* Cambridge: Cambridge University Press, 2001.

—— "'Family' and 'Friend,' in *Pamela*: A Case-Study in the History of the Family in Eighteenth-Century England." *Social History* 14 (1989), pp. 289–306.

Talbot, Hugh. *Christian Friendship, by Saint Ailred of Rievaulx.* London: Catholic Book Club, 1942.

Taffe, Sue. *Black and White Together: The Federal Council for the Advancement of Aborigines and Torres Strait Islanders.* Brisbane: University of Queensland Press, 2005.

Tarabochia, A. Canavero. "L'amicizia nell'epistolario di Marsilo Ficino." *Rivista di Filosofia Neo-Scolastica* 67 (1975), pp. 422–31.

Tasso, Torquato. "Il Manso overo de l'amicizia." In G. Baffetti (ed.), *Dialoghi,* II, pp. 900–55. 2 vols; Milan: Rizzoli, 1998.

Taylor, Jeremy. 1613–1667. *A Discourse of the Nature, Offices, and Measures of Friendship: With Rules of Conducting It / Written in Answer to a Letter from the Most Ingenious and Vertuous M.K.P. by J.T.* London: Printed for R. Royston, 1657.

Taylor, J. "Letters and Letter Collections in England. 1300–1420." *Nottingham Medieval Studies* 24 (1980), pp. 57–70.

Tebbutt, M. *Women's Talk: A Social History of "Gossip," in Working-Class Neighbourhoods, 1880–1960.* Aldershot: Scolar Press, 1995.

Telle, E. "Érasme et les Mariages Dynastiques." *Bibliothèque d'Humanisme et Renaissance* 12 (1950), pp. 7–13.

Telfer, Elizabeth. "Friendship." *Proceedings of the Aristotelian Society* 71 (1970–1971), pp. 223–41.

Tepas, K. M. "*Amor, Amicitia,* and *Misericordia*: A Critique of Aelred's Analysis of Spiritual Friendship." *Downside Review* 112 (1994), pp. 249–63.

—— "Spiritual Friendship in Aelred of Rievaulx and Mutual Sanctification in Marriage." *Cistercian Studies Quarterly* 27 (1992), pp. 63–76.

Themistius. *The Private Orations of Themistius*. Trans. Robert J. Penella; Berkeley: University of California Press, 2000.

Thiroux d'Arronville, Marie-Charlotte. *De l'amitié* (1761). Published as *Les Oeuvres morales de Monsieur Diderot*. Franckfort, 1770.

Thomas, Antoine Léonard. *Essai sur le caractère, les moeurs et l'esprit des femmes dans les différents siècles*. Paris: Moutard, 1772.

Thompson, P., and T. Lummis. *Family Life and Work Experience before 1918, 1870–1973*. Computer file; Colchester. Essex: UK Data Archive (distributor), 5th edn, April 2005.

Thorburn, David. "Television as an Aesthetic Medium." *Critical Studies in Mass Communication* 4 (1987), pp. 161–73.

Thucydides. *History of the Peloponnesian War*. Trans. Rex Warner; Harmondsworth and New York: Penguin, 1954.

—— *Thucydides on Justice, Power and Human Nature – Selections from the History of Peloponnesian War*. Trans. Paul Woodruff; Indianopolis: Hackett, 1993.

Tilney, Edmund, (ed.). *The Flower of Friendship: A Renaissance Dialogue Contesting Marriage*. Ithaca, NY: Cornell University Press, 1992.

Tobin, Robert D. "In and against Nature: Goethe on Homosexuality and Heterotextuality." In Alice A. Kuzniar (ed.), *Outing Goethe and his Age*, pp. 94–110. Stanford: Stanford University Press, 1996.

Todd, Janet M. *Women's Friendship in Literature*. New York: Columbia University Press, 1980.

Todd, Selina. *Young Women, Work and Family in England, 1918–1950*. Oxford: Oxford University Press, 2005.

Tortaire, Raoul. *Ami and Amile*. Trans. Samuel Danon and Samuel N. Rosenberg; York, South Carolina: French Literature Publications Company, 1981.

Trapp, J. B. *Erasmus, Colet and More: The Early Tudor Humanists and their Books*. London: British Library, 1991.

Trexler, R. C. *Public Life in Renaissance Florence*. New York: Academic Press, 1980.

Trimberger, Ellen. *The New Single Woman*. Boston: Beacon Press, 2005.

Trumbach, Randolph. *The Rise of the Egalitarian Family*. New York: Academic Press, 1978.

Utz, K. "Friendship and Friendliness in Aristotle." *Zeitschrift Fur Philosophische Forschung* 57.4 (Oct–Dec 2003), pp. 543–70.

Uyl, Douglas J. Den. "Friendship and Transcendence." *International Journal for Philosophy of Religion* 41.2 (April 1997), pp. 105–22.

van Duzee, Mabel. *A Medieval Romance of Friendship: Eger and Grime*. New York: B. Franklin, 1963.

Velásquez, Eduardo A., (ed.). *Love and Friendship: Rethinking Politics and Affection in Modern Times*. Lanham, MD: Rowman & Littlefield, 2003.

Verity, William. "Haldane and Asquith." *History Today* 18.7 (July 1968).

Vernon, Mark. *The Philosophy of Friendship*. London: Palgrave Macmillan, 2005.

Veyne, Paul. *Roman Erotic Elegy: Love, Poetry and the West*. Trans. David Pellauer; Chicago: University of Chicago Press, 1988.

Vicinus, Martha. *Intimate Friends: Women Who Loved Women, 1778–1928.* Chicago: University of Chicago Press, 2004.

Vincent-Buffault, A. *De l'exercice de l'amitié: Pour une histoire des pratiques amicales aux XVIIIe et XIXe siècles.* Paris: Seuil, 1995.

Wadell, Paul J. *Friendship and the Moral Life.* Notre Dame, IN: University of Notre Dame Press, 1989.

Wahl, Elizabeth Susan. *Invisible Relations: Representations of Female Intimacy in the Age of Enlightenment.* Stanford, CA: Stanford University Press, 1999.

Walbank, Frank. "Monarchies and Monarchic Ideals." In F. W. Walbank, A. E. Astin, M. W. Fredriksen and R. M. Ogilvie (eds), *The Cambridge Ancient History*, VII (Part 1), pp. 62–100. Cambridge: Cambridge University Press, 2nd edn, 1984.

Walker, Karen. "Men, Women, and Friendship: What They Say, What They Do." *Gender and Society* 8 (1994), pp. 246–65.

Walker, S. *The Lancastrian Affinity, 1361–1399.* Oxford: Clarendon Press, 1990.

Ward, Janet Doubler, and JoAnna Stephens Mink (eds). *Communication and Women's Friendships: Parallels and Intersections in Literature and Life.* Bowling Green, OH: Bowling Green State University Popular Press, 1993.

Watkins, Susan Cotts, and Angela D. Danzi. "Women's Gossip and Social Change: Child-birth and Fertility Control among Italian and Jewish Women in the United States, 1920–1940." *Gender and Society* 9 (1995), pp. 469–90.

Watkins-Owens, Irma. *Blood Relations: Caribbean Immigrants and the Harlem Community, 1900–1930.* Bloomington: Indiana University Press, 1996.

Watson, Steven. *The Harlem Renaissance: Hub of African-American Culture, 1920–1930.* New York: Pantheon Books, 1995.

Weaver, William N. "'A School-Boy's Story': Writing the Victorian Public Schoolboy Subject." *Victorian Studies* 46.3 (2004), pp. 455–87.

Webb, D. "On Friendship: Derrida. Foucault, and the Practice of Becoming." *Research in Phenomenology* 33 (2003), pp. 119–40.

Weeks, Jeffrey, Brian Heaphy and Catherine Donovan. *Same-Sex Intimacies: Families of Choice and Other Life Experiments.* London: Routledge, 2001.

Weisbrod, Andrea. "Geliebte Freundin: Madame De Pompadour Oder: Von der Freundschaft als Strategie des Machterhalts." *WerkstattGeschichte* 28 (2001), pp. 61–70.

Weiss, L., and M. F. Lowenthal. "Life Course Perspectives on Friendship." In M. F. Lowenthal *et al.* (eds), *Four Stages of Life*, pp. 48–61. San Francisco: Jossey-Bass, 1975.

Weissman, Ronald F. E. *Ritual Brotherhood in Renaissance Florence.* New York: Academic Press, 1981.

Weller, Barry. "The Rhetoric of Friendship in Montaigne's *Essais.*" *New Literary History* 9.3 (1978), pp. 503–23.

Wellman, Barry. "Men in Networks: Private Communities, Domestic Friendships." In Peter M. Nardi (ed.), *Men's Friendships.* Newbury Park: Sage Publications, 1992.

—— "I Was a Teenage Network Analyst: The Route from the Bronx to the Information Highway." *Connections* 17 (1994), pp. 28–45.

West, M. L. *The Orphic Poems.* Oxford: Oxford University Press, 1983.

West, William C. "Hellenic Homonoia and the New Decree from Plataea." *Greek, Roman, and Byzantine Studies* 18 (1977), pp. 307–19.

Westhauser, Karl E. "Friendship and Family in Early Modern England: The Sociability of Adam Eyre and Samuel Pepys." *Journal of Social History* 27.3 (Spring 1994), pp. 517–36.

Wheeler, Mark R. "Epicurus on Friendship: The Emergence of Blessedness." In Dane R. Gordon (ed.), *Epicurus: His Continuing Influence and Contemporary Relevance.* Rochester: RIT Cary Graphic Arts Press, 2003, pp. 183–94.

White, Carolinne. "Friendship in Absence – Some Patristic Views." In Julian Haseldine (ed.), *Friendship in Medieval Europe.* Stroud: Sutton, 1999.

—— *Christian Friendship in the Fourth Century.* Cambridge, UK; New York: Cambridge University Press, 1992.

White, John L. *Light from Ancient Letters.* Philadelphia: Fortress Press, 1986.

Whiting, Jennifer E. "Impersonal Friends." *Monist* 74 (1991), pp. 3–29.

Whyte, William H. *The Organization Man.* Philadelphia: University of Pennsylvania Press, 2002 (1956).

Wicksteed, P. H., (ed.). *Villani's Chronicle.* Trans. R. E. Selfe; London: Constable, 1906.

Wiethaus, Ulrike. "In Search of Medieval Women's Friendships: Hildegard of Bingen's Letters to her Female Contemporaries." In Ulrike Wiethaus (ed.), *Maps of Flesh and Light: The Religious Experience of Medieval Women Mystics.* Syracuse, NY: Syracuse University Press, 1993.

Wilkerson, Jerome F. *The Concept of Friendship in the "Nicomachean Ethics" of Aristotle.* Microform; Ann Arbor, MI: University Microfilms, n.d.

Williams, R. H. "Friendship and Social Values in a Suburban Community: An Exploratory Study." *Pacific Sociological Review* 2 (1959), pp. 3–10.

Willmott, Peter. *Friendship Networks and Social Support.* London: Policy Studies Institute, 1987.

Wilson, B. V. "A Florentine Chronicler of the Fifteenth Century: Francesco di Tommaso Giovanni and his Ricordanze." MA thesis, Monash University, 1980.

Wilson, Jean. "'Two Names of Friendship, but One Starre': Memorials to Single-Sex Couples in the Early Modern Period." *Church Monuments* 10 (1995), pp. 70–83.

Wilson, John. "Towards a Society of Friends: Some Reflections on the Meaning of Democratic Socialism." *Canadian Journal of Political Science* 3.4 (December 1970).

Winston-Allen, A. *Convent Chronicles.* University Park, PA: Pennsylvania State University Press, 2005.

Wiseman, J. P. "Friendship: Bonds and Binds in a Voluntary Relationship." *Journal of Social and Personal Relationships* 3 (1986), pp. 191–211.

Witkop, Philipp, (ed.). *German Student's War Letters.* Trans. A. F. Wedd; Philadelphia: University of Pennsylvania Press, 2002.

Witt, R. G. *Italian Humanism and Medieval Rhetoric.* Aldershot: Ashgate, 2001.

Wolf, Eric R. "Kinship, Friendship, and Patron-Client Relations in Complex Societies." In M. Banton (ed.), *The Social Anthropology of Complex Societies.* London: Tavistock, 1966.

Wolff, Larry. "The Enlightened Anthropology of Friendship in Venetian Dalmatia: Primitive Ferocity and Ritual Fraternity among the Morlacchi." *Eighteenth-Century Studies* 32.2 (Winter 1998), pp. 157–78.

Wollstonecraft, M. *A Vindication of the Rights of Woman* (1792). Ed. Miriam Brody Kramnick; Harmondsworth, UK: Penguin, 1975.

Woods, Ralph L., (ed.). *A Treasury of Friendship.* New York: McKay, 1957.

Woods, Robert A. "The Recovery of the Parish." In *The Neighborhood and Nation-Building: The Running Comment of Thirty Years at South End House.* Boston: Houghton Mifflin, 1923 (1912).

Woolf, Leonard. *Sowing, an Autobiography of the Years 1880–1904.* London: Hogarth Press, 1960.

Woolf, Virginia. *A Room of One's Own.* Harmondsworth, UK: Penguin, 1945 (1928).

Wootton, David. "Friendship Portrayed: A New Account of *Utopia.*" *History Workshop Journal* 45 (1998), pp. 29–47.

—— "Francis Bacon: Your Flexible Friend." In J. H. Elliott and L. W. R. Brockliss (eds), *The World of the Favourite.* New Haven, CT, and London: Yale University Press, 1999, pp. 184–204.

Wright, P. H. "Men's Friendships, Women's Friendships and the Alleged Inferiority of the Latter." *Sex Roles* 8 (1982), pp. 1–20.

Wright, T. *Some Habits and Customs of the Working Classes.* London: Tinsley Brothers, 1867.

Xenophon. *Memorabilia.* Trans. E. C. Marchant; Loeb Classical Library; Cambridge, MA: Harvard University Press, 1923.

Yeo, Eileen. *The Contest for Social Science: Relations and Representations of Gender and Class.* London: Rivers Oram Press, 1996.

Yohe, Katherine M. "Did Ælred of Rievaulx Think Friends Are Necessary?" *Cistercian Studies Quarterly: An International Review of the Monastic and Contemplative Spiritual Tradition* 35.1 (2000), pp. 29–46.

Zantop, Suzanne. *Colonial Fantasies: Conquest, Family and Nation in Pre-Colonial Germany, 1770–1870.* Durham, NC: Duke University Press, 1997.

Zeller, Eduard. *Outlines of the History of Greek Philosophy.* Trans. Palmer; London: Thoemmes Press, 1955.

INDEX

A

Abelard, Peter, 84–86, 102, 104, 174

Abernathy, Ralph, 329

Achilles, 2

Adalberto, 96

Addison, Joseph, 248

adolescence, 14, 234, 244–45, 252, 296–99, 302, 304–305, 320, 324–25, 348

Aelred of Rievaulx, 76, 87–89, 91, 93, 97–98, 102–104

African-Americans and friendship, 284, 289–90, 293, 295, 299

agape, 78–79

Ainsworth, W. H., 239–40

Albert of Morra, 94

Albertano of Brescia, 76, 89–90, 102

Alberti, Leon Battista, 117, 127, 136–38, 144, 150, 152

Alborn, Timothy, 260

Alcott, Louisa M., 221, 236

Alexander, Christopher, 337–38

Alexander the Great, 26, 35

Alfassa, Mirra, 265

Allan, Graham, 261, 320

Alphonso X, 102

Althoff, Gerd, 82

Alvarez, Alfonso, 144

America, 166, 186, 188, 204, 224, 229, 242–43, 271, 281

American Revolution, 167, 197

amicitia, 65–66, 69–70, 76–79, 82–83, 87, 89, 96, 101, 104, 120–22, 138, 140, 152

Amis, Martin, 338

Amsterdam, 166

Andronicus of Rhodes, 13, 14

animals

dogs, 241

horses, 240–41

pets, 241

Anniceris, 38

Anselm, St, 84, 87

Anthony, Susan B., 243

Apter, Terri, 344

Aquinas, Thomas, 100–101

Archelochos, 28

Argentina, 295

Aristophanes, 8, 28

Aristippus the Elder, 37–38

Aristippus the Younger, 38

Aristotle, x, 1–3, 5–7, 11–15, 22–26, 31–32, 41, 46–48, 65–66, 100–102, 111–12, 118–19, 123, 126, 131, 137–38, 150–51, 153, 168, 170, 183, 202, 228, 249, 265, 349–50

ars dictaminis, dictatores, 75, 94, 123

Armstrong, Nancy, 230

Arnold, Thomas, 234

Arnolfi, Filippo, 127